Chaucer's *Squire's Tale, Franklin's Tale,* and *Physician's Tale*

AN ANNOTATED BIBLIOGRAPHY 1900 TO 2005

Kenneth Bleeth

The latest volume in the Chaucer Bibliography Series, meticulously assembled by Kenneth Bleeth, is the most comprehensive record of scholarship on Chaucer's *Squire's Tale, Franklin's Tale,* and *Physician's Tale*. The bibliography treats each tale as a unit, enables the reader to track the many connections between *The Squire's* and *The Franklin's Tales,* and records the recent resurgence of interest in *The Physician's Tale*. Each bibliographical entry includes an annotation summarizing the content or key argument of the publication. Each of the three chapters includes a section on the work's sources, analogues, and later influence, and is prefaced by an essay that surveys the critical reception of the work. Containing more than two thousand entries, this volume covers publications both major and minor from 1900 to 2005.

KENNETH BLEETH is a professor emeritus in the Department of English as well as the former director of the Medieval Studies Program at Connecticut College.

The Chaucer Bibliographies

Chaucer's *Squire's Tale, Franklin's Tale,* and *Physician's Tale*

AN ANNOTATED BIBLIOGRAPHY 1900 TO 2005

edited by Kenneth Bleeth

Published in association with the University of Rochester by

UNIVERSITY OF TORONTO PRESS

Toronto Buffalo London

Toronto Buffalo London
www.utorontopress.com
Printed in the U.S.A.

ISBN 978-1-4426-4722-0 (cloth)

♾ Printed on acid-free, 100% post-consumer recycled paper.

Library and Archives Canada Cataloguing in Publication

Chaucer's Squire's tale, Franklin's tale, and Physician's tale : an annotated bibliography, 1900 to 2005 / edited by Kenneth Bleeth.

(Chaucer bibliographies ; [9])
Includes bibliographical references and index.
ISBN 978-1-4426-4722-0 (cloth)

1. Chaucer, Geoffrey, –1400. Squire's tale – Bibliography.
2. Chaucer, Geoffrey, –1400. Franklin's tale – Bibliography. 3. Chaucer, Geoffrey, –1400. Physician's tale – Bibliography. I. Bleeth, Kenneth, 1942–, editor II. Series: The Chaucer bibliographies ; [9]

Z8164.C428 2016 016.821'1 C2016-904570-6

University of Toronto Press acknowledges the financial assistance to its publishing program of the Canada Council for the Arts and the Ontario Arts Council, an agency of the Government of Ontario.

Canada Council for the Arts
Conseil des Arts du Canada

Funded by the Government of Canada
Financé par le gouvernement du Canada
Canada

For Willard Spiegelman

Contents

ꟹ General Editor's Preface

The Chaucer Bibliographies will encompass, in a series of some eighteen volumes, a complete listing and assessment of scholarship and criticism on the writings of Geoffrey Chaucer (d. 1400), and on his life, times, and historical context. Eight volumes – on Chaucer's short poems and *Anelida and Arcite*, on the translations, scientific works, and apocrypha, on the *General Prologue* to the *Canterbury Tales*, on the *Knight's Tale*, on the *Tales* of the Miller, Reeve, and Cook, on the *Wife of Bath's Prologue and Tale*, on the *Pardoner's Prologue and Tale*, and on the *Tales* of the Monk and Nun's Priest – have already appeared. The present volume, on the *Tales* of the Squire, Franklin, and Physician, extends the coverage of the *Canterbury Tales* in taking up the two tales that constitute one complete fragment (Group F, Fragment V), and the first tale in the following fragment (Group C, Fragment VI); the latter section complements Marilyn Sutton's volume on *Chaucer's 'Pardoner's Prologue' and 'Tale'* (2000). Additional volumes addressing other groupings of tales (the *Tales* of the Friar and the Summoner; the *Tales* of the Clerk and of the Merchant; the *Tale of Melibee*; and the *Tales* of the Second Nun, Canon's Yeoman, Manciple, and Parson, with the Retraction) are in preparation, and should follow the present volume in a timely fashion. Each volume in the series will continue to center on a particular work, or a connected group of works; most contain material on backgrounds or related writings, and several will be wholly topical in their coverage (taking up music, the visual arts, rhetoric, the life of Chaucer, and other relevant subjects). Although the series perforce places unswerving emphasis on accuracy and comprehensiveness, the distinctive feature of the Chaucer Bibliographies is the fullness and particularity of the annotations provided for each entry. (The present volume offers an especially striking instance of the detail and comprehensiveness of the series.) Annotations have averaged more than one-third of a page in the first seven volumes; these thick descriptions of intellectual and critical activity (as opposed to simple itemizations or arbitrarily telegraphic summaries) have thus constituted more than four-fifths of each volume's content.

The individual volumes in the Chaucer Bibliographies series do not therefore constitute a reference tool in the ordinary sense of that term. While they will take in virtually every Chaucerian publication worthy of notice, and give complete coverage to materials through the twentieth and into the twenty-first centuries, they go far beyond the usual bibliographic compilation, companion, or guide to research. Though the Bibliographies necessarily begin from a database, each volume makes extensive use of the intellectual engagement, learning, and insight of scholars actively at work on Chaucer. The series therefore offers not simply a listing of all relevant titles on a subject, but serves as both an introduction and an advanced guide to the reading and study of Chaucer's poetry. In this, the Chaucer Bibliographies provides innovative and penetrating access to what Chaucer means, and has meant, to his readers in the present, and for the last century and more. The project unfolds the full richness and detail of Chaucer's thought and world for a much wider audience than they have, even after more than one hundred years of energetic scholarship, ever before reached.

Before all else, then, the series provides a means of making practical headway in the study of earlier literature in English and in the appreciation of its broadest cultural contexts. These volumes help make the writing of Chaucer – the earliest figure in the canon of great writers in the English language – more immediate and more directly accessible to readers, whatever their background or level of interest. Although Chaucer has elicited praise for six centuries as a moving, superb, complex writer, even teachers of his writing sometimes feel at a loss when faced with the linguistic, historical, and critical complexities packed into every line. Consequently, despite his canonical stature, Chaucer has often remained unread, or read only in translation or paraphrase. The goal of this project, at its first level, is to increase the numbers of those who read him with genuine understanding and pleasure by increasing the kinds of things that can be readily known about Chaucer. In offering such broad access to specialized knowledge, the Chaucer Bibliographies aspires to expand and enhance how Chaucer gets read, at what levels, and by whom.

As tools for both students and teachers, the Chaucer Bibliographies seeks to intensify the comprehension and enjoyment of beginning readers in university, college, and high school classrooms. The series will move undergraduates more quickly from the generalizations and observations of textbooks and instructors to a direct access to the richness and variety of Chaucer's writing, and to its connections with medieval realities and modern understandings. For graduate students, the books will constitute a crucial resource for course work, exam preparation, and research. For non-specialist teachers of Chaucer in survey, masterpiece, and special topic courses, the series provides the means to a broader base of knowledge and to a more intense and shapely preparation than instructors, given the constraints of their work time, are sometimes able to manage. By clarifying and connecting both recent and long-available materials, and by making them readily accessible, the Chaucer Bibliographies refreshes the teaching and reading of Chaucer, and enables the development of alternative approaches to understanding his writing.

The series holds yet additional resources for specialist readers. The fullness and detail of the annotations in each volume serve, in the first instance, as a check against duplication and redundancy in academic publication; individual scholars, and editors or readers at presses and journals, will be able to chart the place of new or proposed work quickly. Likewise, Chaucerians engaged with a topic or set of issues will be able to advance or situate their work more readily by reference to the materials in the appropriate volumes within the series. In consolidating the massive work that has been done in the last century and more in medieval studies, and particularly on Chaucer, the Bibliographies provide the ground on which new appreciations of Chaucer can build. Their presence in the field will encourage more efficient research on restricted as well as expansive topics, and will likewise facilitate work on the ways in which institutions have fostered and used the reading and study of his writing.

In addition to Chaucerians, the series potentially benefits other specialists in medieval literature in offering ready access to publications on Chaucer that touch on a variety of materials relevant to other fields. Whatever use the materials gathered in these volumes may have for particular queries or problems, they also address interests of a range of scholars whose expertise extends to Chaucer, but whose intellectual concerns may seem stymied by the daunting mass of Chaucer scholarship. The Chaucer Bibliographies places interdisciplinary research before scholars in History, Art History, Philosophy, French and Italian, Cultural Studies, and other related areas, and so makes multidisciplinary, collaborative work more possible and even more likely. In short, the project's collective effort to bring knowledge about Chaucer together strives to open up, rather than to close off, further innovative work on pre-modern culture.

The present volume, on the *Tales* of the Squire, Franklin, and Physician, generously extends the sweeping and meticulous coverage that marks earlier volumes in the series, marshalling some two thousand entries and annotations. Their purview takes in editions of Chaucer's writing, studies of language, manuscripts, and audiences, his sources and their contexts and intellectual connections, directly relevant background materials (e.g., gendered identities, estates satire, medieval science and medicine, generic constraints and innovations, philosophical traditions) and all traceable publications (in whatever language) bearing directly on Chaucer's poetry. The earlier volumes have succeeded in sorting out and making accessible materials that are confused or obscure, including early philological publications in German and Scandinavian languages, privately printed or scarce volumes, and recent work in Australia, Europe, Japan, and South Korea. But even more strikingly, in bringing together all the materials on specific poems and subjects, these volumes have given new definition to the boundaries of Chaucer studies. Rather than working as a mopping-up operation, telling scholars what they already knew, or students what they might well forget, these volumes attempt to contribute to a new flourishing of Chaucer research and criticism, assisting the creation of fresh and solidly grounded interrogations of the poetry. They stand not simply as the summation of a great tradition, but as an impetus for more intense and expanded understandings of Chaucer. The sweeping vision of late medieval writing offered in each volume represents a reconfiguration of knowledge that justifies and fosters informed work by an expanded community of scholars, of whom Chaucerians form merely the core.

In producing volumes that record all relevant titles and that specify the content and interconnections of Chaucerian criticism, the Chaucer Bibliographies defines a new space for itself as a reference tool in its own field, and potentially within affiliated fields as well. The volumes, published and projected, differ markedly in purpose and use from other introductory bibliographies and cumulative listings. Standard bibliographies – unmarked or minimally annotated compilations – furnish helpful listings of publications, but offer limited assistance to the specialist, and still less orientation or access to the uninitiated. Volumes in the Chaucer Bibliographies project take these publications as a base of information (and make reference to them), but the aim of each volume is to offer in-depth coverage of the work(s) at hand. Contributors initially review annual and collected listings, but acquired learning, developed instincts, and the concentrated reading demanded for the preparation of each volume turn up leads and titles that supplement and complete the search for all relevant materials. The series through its individual volumes seeks to stand as a definitive companion to the study of Chaucer, a starting point from which present work may be assessed, and future work may proceed. It addresses itself to an audience beyond the community of professional Chaucerians, inviting non-Chaucerian scholars and non-specialist teachers and students to take part in the continuous process of understanding Chaucer. The exhaustiveness of the project offers assurance and, we hope, some surprises to both the expert and the novice.

The series achieves this inclusiveness through its inventory of all known publications, its full and strategic commentary, its attention to backgrounds and corollary issues, and its demarcation of interrelationships and connected themes; annotations, cross-referencing, generous indices, and the report of significant reviews help insure this high level of comprehensiveness. Contributors essay to encounter every relevant published item, in all foreign languages, though these scholars rely on their own expertise and discretion in determining the choice and extent of annotations. Information on a 'ghost' or an inaccessible but pointless item may prove as valuable to users of these volumes as careful assessments of well known books in the field; it is therefore crucial for contributors not to pass over inadvertently or deliberately omit any 'trivial' writings. The specification of items in these volumes should obviate the need for many vain entanglements in the trammels of scholarship as readers of Chaucer pursue their special interests.

The Chaucer Bibliographies is produced through the work of a diverse and distinguished array of experts. Its format – in which the individual efforts of autonomous scholars take their place within a single project's well articulated, coherent framework – accommodates in a peculiarly appropriate way its broad base and intentionally wide appeal. The authors of individual volumes include both distinguished and younger Chaucerians. The comprehensive work for each volume has been carried out over a period of years by an individual scholar or a team in close collaboration, conceiving each volume as a unified intellectual project. Having a collective of more than two dozen Chaucerians actively engaged in the same project has already led to a more thorough cross-checking, a richer array of suggestions and shared information, and a larger number of surprising finds – some obscure, some obvious – than any individual or more limited collaborative effort could have produced.

Since materials for the entire series have been electronically processed and stored, it will be possible for the University of Toronto Press to provide online access to published volumes, to issue supplements and revisions, and eventually to produce a general index to all volumes. Ultimately the complete series and its component parts may be accessible to a wide range of general users and scholars in a variety of formats.

The work of the Chaucer Bibliographies was sustained from 1989 to 1995 by a series of grants from the National Endowment for the Humanities (USA), through its Division of Research Programs; without NEH support, it would have been impossible for the collective efforts of the project to continue, or for the work of individual scholars to issue in published form. Library staff at the University of Rochester – in particular, Interlibrary Loan, and the Rossell Hope Robbins Library and its Curator, Dr. Alan Lupack – have provided invaluable and unstinting bibliographic and research aid. In the final stages of editing, the Department of English and the Office of Undergraduate Research at the University of Rochester provided crucial material support. Pivotal phases of the research and editing that produced our final copy were resourcefully and meticulously carried out at Rochester by Caroline Callahan-Floeser, John Chandler, Samantha Dressel, and Maria Kane. Kyle Huskin has with painstaking intensity overseen the entire operation of bringing the manuscript to print, showcasing her own acute intelligence, her ingenuity and foresight, and her technical savvy at every phase of the process.

ꝏ Preface

The aim of this bibliography is to annotate all books, chapters of books, articles, and notes devoted exclusively or primarily to *The Squire's, Franklin's,* and *Physician's Tales,* and all significant discussions of the tales in studies not primarily devoted to these works. Substantive discussions in editions of Chaucer's works are also annotated, as are reviews that comment on the author's treatment of the tales, although I cannot claim to have examined every published review of every book cited in this volume. I have annotated commentaries on the Squire's, Franklin's, and Physician's portraits in *The General Prologue* only when these items have a direct bearing on the interpretation of the tales or on the relation of the narrator to the tales. Scholarship on textual matters has been included on a similar basis; omitted, for example, are discussions of the position of Fragment VI that make no reference to the content of *The Physician's Tale* or its relation to other tales. I have attempted to annotate all doctoral dissertations devoted exclusively to any of the volume's three tales. Other dissertations have been included when their comments on the tales seemed of particular significance, although doubtless some worthy items have slipped through my net. (With one exception, MA theses and their equivalents have been excluded.) Editions and modernizations are included selectively. I record all editions of any textual significance (including several published before 1900) and editions in which the introductions, notes, or glossaries are noteworthy. Modernizations are included when the text or illustrations throw light on a tale's reception. (Translations of *The Canterbury Tales* into foreign languages have been excluded.) In the sections on Sources, Analogues, and Later Influence, I attempt to annotate all significant treatments of these topics, and I list as well selected editions of the tales' certain and conjectural sources. The final sections in each chapter are devoted primarily to interpretive commentaries, but also include selected reference works, manuscript and textual studies, and discussions of the tales' language and dates of composition. Non-specialized encyclopedia entries and study guides, both print and electronic, have been excluded, as have digital files, films, recordings, and student essays and projects posted on Internet sites. In accordance with the guidelines for this series, my chronological point of departure is 1900. I have, however, included a few important earlier articles, as well as book reviews, references to essay collections, and book chapters incorporating previously published material, and for *The Squire's Tale,* fourteen items (**747–57**) exemplifying an important recent critical turn, that fall after the 2005 cut-off date. (Post-1900 revisions of pre-1900 publications have been excluded.) I am aware that my coverage of material published in Japan and South Korea is incomplete. I have read and summarized most English-language items, but I have been unable either to examine, or to obtain translations of, others and hence I list only titles and bibliographical information.

A note on the format of this bibliography: entries are arranged chronologically, and alphabetically by author, and by title for editions, within a given year. Page numbers are given for quotations and for summarized material that may be difficult to locate in the source text (e.g., in book-length studies or long articles). Quotations from Chaucer's works are given according to *The Riverside Chaucer* (**108**), except when they occur in citations from a critic who uses another version of the text. (Line references are to *The Riverside Chaucer* throughout. Unless otherwise identified, line numbers refer to Fragment V in the *Squire's Tale* and *Franklin's Tale* chapters and to Fragment VI in the *Physician's Tale* chapter.) I have also preserved in quotations the author's spelling (e.g., 'Appius'/'Apius') and treatment of terms and titles (e.g., whether italicized or placed in quotation marks). The standard abbreviations of Chaucer's works used in this series have been substituted for the full form in quotations, but not in the titles of books and articles. I have occasionally made minor adjustments in punctuation and capitalization to fit quotations into my own sentences; a few obvious errors have also been silently corrected. Revised editions with unchanged titles are indicated by the dates of the original and the revised editions, separated by a forward slash (e.g., '1968/1987' or '1958/1960, 1990, 1996'). When a revision has been published under a new title, both the original and the new title are given. I cite information about reprints where it seems useful (e.g., when a book has been reprinted by a different publisher or in a paperback edition), but I make no attempt to record the entire publication history of each volume. When an item has been reprinted or published in a revised edition, page references are to the original edition unless otherwise noted. If the entire annotation for an item consists of a reference to another item (e.g., 'See **100**'), the relevant material in the former appears in the latter in substantially the same form. Rebuttals, corrections, and direct responses to a publication are cited either in the body of the annotation or in cross-references at the end of an entry.

My primary indebtedness in the making of this volume is to those scholars who compiled the bibliographies, reference guides, and annotated editions on which my initial research was based. (In the past few years, I have relied heavily on electronic databases, especially Google Scholar and the New Chaucer Society's Chaucer Bibliography Online.) More than once when I was at work on this book, I benefited from a piece of advice that B.J. Whiting, my first Chaucer teacher, claimed to have received from *his* first Chaucer teacher, George Lyman Kittredge: 'When found, make note of.' The staff of Connecticut College's Shain Library has been unfailingly helpful. Several grants from the College's Faculty Development Fund enabled me to visit the British Library, the Harvard University Libraries, the Library of Congress, and the New York Public Library. Two month-long residencies at the Bogliasco Foundation's Centro Studi Ligure provided me with uninterrupted time to work. Uwe Böker, Marianne Børch, C.R. Conradie, Keiko Hamaguchi, Tadao Kobuchi, An Sonjae (Brother Anthony), and the National Library of Ireland, Maynooth, supplied publications unavailable in the United States. Tom Couser and Stephen Orgel helped with library chores closer to home. My students Scott Borchert, Benjamin Courchesne, and Brian Sendrowski checked references. Gregory Foran reformatted a lengthy text, which was improved at a later stage by the copyediting, formatting, and indexing skills of Caroline Callahan-Floeser, John Chandler, Samantha Dressel, Maria Kane, Alexander Zawacki, and (especially) Kyle Huskin. My Power User friend Jeff Strabone solved some word-processing problems, and Andrew Lopez shared his indexing expertise. For help with scholarship in Chinese, German, Italian, Japanese, Polish, and Spanish, my thanks to Anna Adams, Tim Albrecht, Geoffrey Atherton, Enrique Cucurella, Denis Ferhatović, Lee Fontanella, Marc Forster, Juan-Miguel Godoy, Tek-Wah King, Hisae Kobayashi, Jens Kreinath, Michael Molasky, Fulvio Orsitto, Tad Pioro, and Paola Sica. Lee Patterson encouraged me to take on this project and promised to read the introductions. Had Lee lived longer, this book would have been better for his deep learning and sharp wit. Early on, Monica McAlpine gave good advice, as did Christopher Cannon in a later conversation. Thomas Hahn, general editor of the series, has been warmly supportive throughout – no small feat, considering all the deadlines I missed. Willard Spiegelman has lived with this volume from its inception. It would not have been completed without his daily encouragement.

Abbreviations and Works Cited

GENERAL ABBREVIATIONS

ca	*circa*, 'about'
cf.	compare
ch., chs	chapter, chapters
col., cols	column, columns
d.	died
dir	directed by, director
diss.	dissertation
ed.	edited by, edition, editor
eds	editors
El	Ellesmere [manuscript]
et al.	and others
fol., fols	folio, folios
gen. ed.	general editor
Hg	Hengwrt [manuscript]
ME	Middle English
ModE	Modern English
MS, MSS	manuscript, manuscripts
n.	note
n.d.	no date [of publication]
no.	number
n.p.	no page number, no place [of publication], no publisher
n.s.	new series
OFr.	Old French
pbk	paperback
r	recto
repr.	reprint, reprinted
reprs	reprints
rev.	revised, revised by
ser.	series
trans.	translated by, translator
UP, U … P	University Press

v	verso
vol., vols	volume, volumes

LITERARY WORKS CITED

Anel	*Anelida and Arcite*
Astr	*A Treatise on the Astrolabe*
BD	*The Book of the Duchess*
Bo	*Boece*
CA	*Confessio Amantis* (Gower)
CkP	*The Cook's Prologue*
CkT	*The Cook's Tale*
Cleo	*Cleomadés* (Adenet le Roi)
ClT	*The Clerk's Tale*
Consol	*The Consolation of Philosophy* (Boethius)
CT	*The Canterbury Tales*
CYT	*The Canon's Yeoman's Tale*
Dec	*The Decameron* (Boccaccio)
DV	*De Virginibus* (St Ambrose)
Equat	*The Equatorie of the Planetis*
Fil	*Il Filocolo* (Boccaccio)
FQ	*The Faerie Queene* (Spenser)
FrT	*The Friar's Tale*
FranP	*The Franklin's Prologue*
FranT	*The Franklin's Tale*
Gent	*Gentilesse*
GP	*The General Prologue*
HF	*The House of Fame*
HRB	*Historia Regum Brittaniae* (Geoffrey of Monmouth)
Jov	*Epistola adversus Jovinianum* (St Jerome)
KnT	*The Knight's Tale*
LGW	*The Legend of Good Women*
ManT	*The Manciple's Tale*
Mars	*The Complaint of Mars*
Mel	*The Tale of Melibee*
MerE	*Merchant Epilogue*
MerT	*The Merchant's Tale*
MilT	*The Miller's Tale*
MkT	*The Monk's Tale*
MLE	*Man of Law Endlink*
MLT	*The Man of Law's Tale*
NPT	*The Nun's Priest's Tale*
PardT	*The Pardoner's Tale*

ParsP	*The Parson's Prologue*
ParsT	*The Parson's Tale*
PF	*The Parliament of Fowls*
PhyT	*The Physician's Tale*
Phy–PardL	*Physician–Pardoner Link*
PrT	*The Prioress's Tale*
Ret	*Chaucer's Retraction*
Rom	*The Romaunt of the Rose*
RR	*Le Roman de la Rose* (G. de Lorris and J. de Meun)
RvT	*The Reeve's Tale*
SGGK	*Sir Gawain and the Green Knight* (anonymous)
ShT	*The Shipman's Tale*
SNT	*The Second Nun's Tale*
Sq–FranL	*Squire–Franklin Link*
SqH	*Squire Headlink*
SqT	*The Squire's Tale*
Sted	*Lak of Stedfastnesse*
SumT	*The Summoner's Tale*
TC	*Troilus and Criseyde*
Tes	*Il Teseida* (Boccaccio)
Thop	*The Tale of Sir Thopas*
Truth	*Truth: Balade de Bon Conseyl*
WBP	*The Wife of Bath's Prologue*
WBT	*The Wife of Bath's Tale*

JOURNALS, SERIES, AND REFERENCE WORKS CITED

AB	*Anglia Beiblatt*
ABELL	*Annual Bibliography of English Language and Literature* (Modern Humanities Research Association)
ABR	*American Benedictine Review*
Acad	*Academy* (London, England)
Allegorica	*Allegorica: A Journal of Medieval and Renaissance Literature*
ALM	*Anuario de letras modernas* (Facultad de Filosofía y Letras Universidad Nacional Autónoma de México)
Al-Māsaq	*Al-Māsaq: Journal of the Medieval Mediterranean*
Anglia	*Anglia: Zeitschrift für Englische Philologie*
AnM	*Annuale Mediaevale*
ANQ	*American Notes and Queries: A Quarterly Journal of Short Articles, Notes, and Reviews*
Archiv	*Archiv für das Studium der neueren Sprachen und Literaturen*
AS	*American Scientist*
Assays	*Assays: Critical Approaches to Medieval and Renaissance Texts*

Atlantic	*The Atlantic Monthly*
Atlantis	*Atlantis. Journal of the Spanish Association for Anglo-American Studies*
AUMLA	*AUMLA: Journal of the Australasian Universities Language and Literature Association*
BBSANZ	*Bulletin for the Bibliographical Society of Australia and New Zealand*
BFL	*Bulletin of the Faculty of Literature* (Aoyama Gakuin University)
Bonnes Feuilles	*Les Bonnes Feuilles*
BPMELLJ	*A Bibliography of Publications on Medieval English Language and Literature in Japan* (Centre for Medieval English Studies, Tokyo)
BSUF	*Ball State University Forum*
BYWJC	*Bulletin of Yamamura Women's Junior College*
C&L	*Christianity and Literature*
CahiersE	*Cahiers Elisabéthains*
Caligrama	*Caligrama: Revista Insular de Filologia*
CarmP	*Carmina Philosophiae: Journal of the International Boethius Society*
CCM	*Cahiers de civilisation mediévale*
CE	*College English*
CEA	*CEA Critic: An Official Journal of the College English Association*
ChauN	*Chaucer Newsletter*
ChauR	*Chaucer Review*
CIF	*Cuadernos de Investigacion Filologica*
Cithara	*Cithara: Essays in the Judeo-Christian Tradition*
CL	*Comparative Literature* (Eugene, OR)
Comitatus	*Comitatus: A Journal of Medieval and Renaissance Studies*
Communiqué	*Communiqué* (University of the North, Pietersburg, South Africa)
Comparatist	*The Comparatist: Journal of the Southern Comparative Literature Association*
Conradian	*The Conradian: The Journal of the Joseph Conrad Society*
ContempR	*Contemporary Review* (London, England)
CR	*The Critical Review*
Criticism	*Criticism: A Quarterly for Literature and the Arts*
CSR	*Christian Scholar's Review*
CY	*Chaucer Yearbook: A Journal of Late Medieval Studies*
DA	*Dissertation Abstracts*
DAI	*Dissertation Abstracts International*

DelNotes	*Delaware Notes*
DL	*Doshisha Literature. A Journal of English Literature and Philology*
DR	*Dalhousie Review*
E&S	*Essays and Studies* (London, England)
EBSN	*Early Book Society Newsletter*
Edebiyât	*Edebiyât: Journal of Middle Eastern Literatures*
EETS	*Early English Text Society*
EIC	*Essays in Criticism: A Quarterly Journal of Literary Criticism* (Oxford, England)
EJ	*English Journal*
ELH	*ELH* (formerly *ELH: A Journal of English Literary History*)
ELL	*English Language and Literature* (Korean Society of English Language and Literature)
ELN	*English Language Notes*
ELR	*English Literary Renaissance*
ELWIU	*Essays in Literature* (Macomb, IL)
EM	*English Miscellany*
EMSt	*Essays in Medieval Studies* http://www.illinoismedieval.org/ems/
English	*English: The Journal of the English Association* (London, England)
Envoi	*Envoi: A Review Journal of Medieval Literature*
EQ	*English Quarterly*
ER	*English Review*
ES	*English Studies: A Journal of English Language and Literature*
ESA	*English Studies in Africa: A Journal of the Humanities*
ESC	*English Studies in Canada*
ESK	*English Studies* (Seoul, South Korea)
ESt	*Englische Studien*
Exemplaria	*Exemplaria: A Journal of Theory in Medieval and Renaissance Studies*
Expl	*Explicator*
Florilegium	*Florilegium: Carleton University Annual Papers on Classical Antiquity and the Middle Ages*
FolkloreC	*Folklore* (Calcutta, India)
FS	*French Studies*
Genre	*Genre: Forms of Discourse and Culture*
GRM	*Germanisch–Romanische Monatsschrift*
HLB	*Harvard Library Bulletin*
HLQ	*Huntington Library Quarterly: Studies in English and American History and Literature*

HSELL	*Hiroshima Studies in English Language and Literature*
IJES	*Indian Journal of English Studies*
ILCT	*International Journal of the Classical Tradition*
InG	*In Geardagum: Essays in Old and Middle English Language and Literature*
InParen	*In Parentheses: Papers in Medieval Studies* http://www.yorku.ca/inpar
JAF	*Journal of American Folklore*
JCERL	*Journal of Classic and English Renaissance Literatures* (Seoul, South Korea)
JEGP	*Journal of English and Germanic Philology*
JELL	*Journal of English Language and Literature* (Seoul, South Korea)
JMRS	*Journal of Medieval and Renaissance Studies*
JPC	*Journal of Popular Culture*
JPsy	*Journal of Psychohistory*
JRMMRA	*Journal of the Rocky Mountain Medieval and Renaissance Association*
JWCI	*Journal of the Warburg and Courtauld Institutes*
JWSL	*Journal of Women's Studies in Literature*
KPAB	*Kentucky Philological Association Bulletin*
KWSC	*Key-Word Studies in Chaucer* (Centre for Medieval Studies, Tokyo)
L&H	*Literature and History*
L&P	*Literature and Psychology*
Lang&S	*Language and Style: An International Journal*
LeedsSE	*Leeds Studies in English*
Lore&L	*Lore and Language*
LT	*Levende Talen*
M&H	*Medievalia et Humanistica: Studies in Medieval and Renaissance Culture*
MÂ	*Le Moyen Âge: Revue d'Histoire et de Philologie*
MÆ	*Medium Ævum*
MayR	*Maynooth Review*
MC	*The Monthly Criterion*
Mediaevalia	*Mediaevalia: An Interdisciplinary Journal of Medieval Studies Worldwide*
MedPers	*Medieval Perspectives* (Southeastern Medieval Association)
Meridian	*Meridian: The La Trobe University English Review*
MESt	*Medieval English Studies: The Journal of the Medieval and Early Modern English Studies Association of Korea*
MichA	*Michigan Academician: Papers of the Michigan Academy of*

	Science, Arts, and Letters
MLN	*Modern Language Notes*
MLQ	*Modern Language Quarterly: A Journal of Literary History*
MLR	*The Modern Language Review*
Mosaic	*Mosaic: A Journal for the Interdisciplinary Study of Literature*
MP	*Modern Philology: A Journal Devoted to Research in Medieval and Modern Literature*
MQ	*Mississippi Quarterly*
MRDE	*Medieval and Renaissance Drama in England*
MS	*Mediaeval Studies* (Toronto, Canada)
MSE	*Massachusetts Studies in English*
N&Q	*Notes and Queries*
Names	*Names: Journal of the American Name Society*
Nation	*The Nation*
Neophil	*Neophilologus*
NLH	*New Literary History: A Journal of Theory and Interpretation*
NM	*Neuphilologische Mitteilungen: Bulletin of the Modern Language Society*
NMS	*Nottingham Medieval Studies*
NYT	*The New York Times*
OL	*Orbis Litterarum*
ParAns	*Partial Answers: Journal of Literature and the History of Ideas*
Parergon	*Parergon: Journal of the Australian and New Zealand Association for Medieval and Early Modern* [formerly *Renaissance*] *Studies*
PBA	*Proceedings of the British Academy*
PhilosLit	*Philosophy and Literature*
PLL	*Papers on Language and Literature: A Journal for Scholars and Critics of Language and Literature*
PMAM	*Publications of the Medieval Association of the Midwest*
PMASAL	*Papers of the Michigan Academy of Sciences, Arts, and Letters*
PMLA	*Publications of the Modern Language Association of America*
PMR	*Proceedings of the PMR Conference: annual publication of the Patristic, Medieval, and Renaissance Conference*
PoeticaT	*Poetica: An International Journal of Linguistic–Literary Studies* (Tokyo, Japan)
PQ	*Philological Quarterly*
PVR	*Platte Valley Review*
Quidditas	*Quidditas: Journal of the Rocky Mountain Medieval and Renaissance Association* (formerly *Journal of the Rocky Mountain Medieval and Renaissance Association*)
QPar	*Qui Parle: A Journal of Literary and Critical Studies*
RCEI	*Revista Canaria de Estudios Ingleses*

REALB	*REAL: The Yearbook of Research in English and American Literature*
REL	*Review of English Literature*
RenD	*Renaissance Drama*
RenP	*Renaissance Papers*
RenQ	*Renaissance Quarterly*
RES	*Review of English Studies*
Rev	*Review* (Charlottesville, VA)
RLMC	*Rivista di Letterature Moderne e Comparate*
RLV	*Revue des Langues Vivantes*
Romania	*Romania: Revue consacreé à l'étude des langues et des littératures modernes*
RomR	*Romanic Review*
RPhil	*Romance Philology*
RSTC	*Revised Short Title Catalogue*
RUO	*Revue de l'Université d'Ottawa*
S&T	*Sky and Telescope*
SAB	*South Atlantic Bulletin*
SAC	*Studies in the Age of Chaucer*
SAJMRS	*Southern African Journal of Medieval and Renaissance Studies*
SAQ	*South Atlantic Quarterly*
SatR	*Saturday Review of Literature*
SB	*Studies in Bibliography: Papers of the Bibliographical Society of the University of Virginia*
SCB	*South Central Bulletin*
SE	*Studies in English*
SEL	*Studies in English Literature, 1500–1900*
SELIM	*SELIM: Journal of the Spanish Society for English Medieval Language and Literature*
SELit	*Studies in English Literature* (Tokyo, Japan)
SFLL	*Studies in Foreign Languages and Literature* (Aichi University of Education, Japan)
Shaw	*Shaw: The Annual of Bernard Shaw Studies*
SMART	*Studies in Medieval and Renaissance Teaching*
SMC	*Studies in Medieval Culture*
SMy	*Studia Mystica*
SN	*Studia Neophilologica: A Journal of German and Romance Languages and Literatures*
SoAR	*South Atlantic Review*
SoRA	*Southern Review: Literary and Interdisciplinary Essays* (Adelaide, Australia)
SP	*Studies in Philology*

SPCT	*Studi e Problemi di Critica Testuale*
Speculum	*Speculum: A Journal of Medieval Studies*
SQ	*Shakespeare Quarterly*
SRAZ	*Studia Romanica et Anglica Zagrabiensia*
SS	*Shakespeare Studies*
SSEng	*Sydney Studies in English*
SSF	*Studies in Short Fiction*
Style	*Style* (DeKalb, IL)
T&L	*Translation and Literature*
TCAAS	*Transactions of the Connecticut Academy of Arts and Sciences*
Theoria	*Theoria: A Journal of Studies in the Arts, Humanities and Social Sciences* (Natal, South Africa)
TkR	*Tamkang Review: A Quarterly Journal of Comparative Studies between Chinese and Foreign Literatures*
TLS	*Times Literary Supplement* (London, England)
TMR	*The Medieval Review* https://scholarworks.iu.edu/dspace/handle/2022/3631
Traditio	*Traditio: Studies in Ancient and Medieval History, Thought, and Religion*
TSL	*Tennessee Studies in Literature*
TSLL	*Texas Studies in Literature and Language*
UCC	*University of California Chronicle*
UoE	*Use of English*
UTQ	*University of Toronto Quarterly: A Canadian Journal of the Humanities*
Viator	*Viator: Medieval and Renaissance Studies*
VLang	*Visible Language*
WS	*Women's Studies: An Interdisciplinary Journal*
WSL	*Wisconsin Studies in Literature*
WUS	*Washington University Studies*
YES	*Yearbook of English Studies*
YFS	*Yale French Studies*
YWES	*Year's Work in English Studies*
ZRP	*Zeitschrift für Romanische Philologie*

Chaucer's *Squire's, Franklin's,* and *Physician's Tales*

ꝏ *The Squire's Tale*: Introduction

> [*The Squire's Tale*] shows ... how the historical study of criticism itself ... is a thoroughly worthwhile critical discipline. It raises all the questions that need asking.
> —David Lawton, 'The Literary History of the Squire's Tale' (1985)

> The very incompleteness of the tale makes literary criticism somewhat superfluous.
> —Morton Bloomfield, 'Chaucer's *Squire's Tale* and the Renaissance' (1981)

In contrast to those parts of *The Canterbury Tales* that have been perennially valued – *The General Prologue*, the tales of the Knight, the Pardoner, and the Nun's Priest, among others – *The Squire's Tale* has undergone striking shifts in its ranking among the narratives in Chaucer's collection. Admired by Spenser, Milton, and Thomas Warton (who awards it 'the next place' after *The Knight's Tale*), the tale was until the middle of the twentieth century viewed as a largely successful attempt on Chaucer's part to introduce the wonders of romance into the tale-telling competition. Over the next few decades, this untroubled interpretation was called into question by resisting readers: judgments like 'a complete misfire' (**505**) and 'a sophisticated hoax' (**577**) appear with some frequency in critical discussions of the tale through the early 1980s. Commenting on this reversal of fortune in the introduction to the 1990 Variorum edition, Donald Baker observes that 'given the constant flux in literary fashion, it would be no great surprise to find *SqT* ... rather soon restored to the rank of those tales of considerable interest in their own right' (**112**). And so it has proved. In her Biennial New Chaucer Society lecture for 2006, Susan Crane stated that 'in scholarly circles, it's a good moment for *The Squire's Tale*'; emerging from 'a few decades of disrepute as no more than the clumsy utterance of its youthful teller,' the tale is now 'looking much more substantial' (**747**). The ups and downs of the tale's reputation over the past century are documented in the editorial activity and critical commentary summarized in four of this volume's nine annotation chapters. As is the case with the other contributions to the Toronto Chaucer

Bibliographies, the annotations, in addition to recording the fortunes of an individual work or group of works, will allow readers to track the conventions of interpretation by which Chaucer's writings have been understood over time – that is, the history of Chaucer reception itself, a subject that in recent years has become central to our understanding of the Chaucerian literary text.

The Squire's Tale's critical afterlife has been examined twice before – by David Lawton in 'The Literary History of the Squire's Tale' (**598**) and in the Variorum edition's Survey of Criticism. Lawton's study was published in 1985, the same year that Baker gives as the *terminus ad quem* for his survey. For a student who seeks a comprehensive history of *The Squire's Tale*'s reception, Baker's and Lawton's commentaries are essential reading. The observations that follow build on the work of these two scholars, but focus on items that appeared after 1985. I have, however, attempted to provide sufficient context for my survey of recent scholarship to make visible both continuities with and departures from earlier investigations. Sometimes characterized as an outlier in the Canterbury collection, *The Squire's Tale* resists easy generalizations about the nature of Chaucerian narrative. Lawton is right to say that the tale 'would make an ideal set text for a modern introduction to Chaucer studies.'

Source Study and *The Squire's Tale*

The 'desire for origins' (I'm borrowing the title of Allen Frantzen's polemical history of Anglo-Saxon studies) characteristic of nineteenth- and early twentieth-century medieval literary scholarship encountered a substantial challenge in *The Squire's Tale*. Students of Chaucer conditioned by the bulk of the poet's writings to expect that individual works will be traceable to documented antecedent sources responded to the absence of a definitive point of origin for *The Squire's Tale* with mixture of puzzlement and frustration. In the 1874 edition of four tales that preceded the publication of the Oxford Chaucer, Skeat begins his introduction to *The Squire's Tale* by describing an agon between the text and its annotators – it is this tale 'which *has most resisted* all attempts to discover an immediate original for it' (**2**; my italics). Writing twenty-four years after Skeat, Pollard employs the language of the whodunit to characterize the tale's silence about its origins: the tale's genesis has 'defied detection' (**6**), 'baffled investigation' more than any other of the poet's works (**9**). Even as he concedes the possibility that 'we are here in the presence of one of Chaucer's rare attempts at a more or less original plot' (**9**), Pollard qualifies his suggestion by linking the tale's unfinishedness – the absence at its end – to a parallel absence at its beginning: unable to draw on an existent narrative, Chaucer 'broke down for lack of a plot ready furnished to him' (**6**). The reticence that Pollard displays in presenting *The Squire's Tale* as an original creation is a milder version of the overt skepticism expressed by others. In his 1775 edition of the *Tales,* Thomas Tyrwhitt observed that he 'would be very hardly brought to believe that the whole, or even any considerable part of it, was of Chaucer's invention' (**2**). Writing in 1896, Manly asserts that he 'can hardly resist the conviction that Chaucer found all his characters named and his scene laid in the source – written or oral – from which he derived his plot' (**131**; see also **55, 147r, 440**). In his 1907 *Notes on Chaucer,* Hinckley proposes a more specific model: 'The immediate original for this *Tale* is likely to have been a French version of a Tartar romance,' perhaps a 'romance of metallurgy' that formed part of a now-vanished cycle devoted to Genghis Khan (**380**). Although Hinckley's speculation strikes us as particularly farfetched, it nevertheless exemplifies the impulse among scholars at the turn of the century to call into being earlier sources – now lost – that will fill out a work's incomplete backstory. And once orality is admitted into the picture (**131, 147**), it is an easy (indeed, inevitable) step to positing multiple and fragmentary origins, including what Root calls (with a touch of dismissiveness), 'such scraps of knowledge about Tartary and the Far East as [Chaucer] had picked up in reading or conversation' (**378**; see also **147, 377**). H.S.V. Jones, the most assiduous student of the tale's 'narrative neighborhood' (**139**), gave his imprimatur to this position in the 1941 *Sources and Analogues of Chaucer's Canterbury Tales*: 'The best critical opinion favors the theory that Chaucer derived the material for his *Squire's Tale* from many quarters and worked inventively with a free hand' (**174**). In abandoning the search for an 'unquestioned source of any portion of the tale' and devoting his chapter to parallels and analogues to some of the tale's features, Jones established the agenda for subsequent commentary, which accepts almost without dissent the conclusion that the tale is a composite, multi-sourced production (**108, 582, 598, 601, 602, 631, 635, 698, 743**). This consensus governs Vincent DiMarco's chapter on *The Squire's Tale* in the first volume of the revised edition of *Sources and Analogues,* published in 2002 (**242**). In addition to literary analogues (two passages from Girart d'Amiens' *Meliacin* replace Jones's excerpts from the related romance of *Cleomadés*), DiMarco prints material that contextualizes the treatment of magic in Part 1 of the tale, summarizes historical events involving relations between 'Middle India' and the Mongols of Russia in the fourteenth century, and argues for 'the strong likelihood of Chaucer's dependence on oral reports and reminiscences of travelers and merchants.' By including ethnographic and intellectual frameworks in addition to written texts, DiMarco's presentation extends our sense of what might constitute a source and reminds us as well that Chaucer's relation to his materials was not monolithic; as Stephen Knight remarks in a review of the revised *Sources and Analogues*, 'Chaucer rarely did the same thing twice: a clear source, much modified, in The Clerk's Tale, stands against a range of minor stimuli in The Squire's Tale' (**242r**). Among these stimuli are other Chaucerian works – *The Knight's Tale*, *The Parliament of Fowls*, and *Anelida and Arcite*. For Elizabeth Scala, these recycled texts reflect the tale's quest for its own origins, origins that are nevertheless 'illusory ... demand[ing] construction over and over again' (**731**). Scala's claim sits comfortably alongside the work of theorists like Judith Butler, Edward Said, and Michel Serres, all of whom, from different perspectives, question the notion of a privileged, stable 'original' text. To read *The Squire's Tale* as (in Knight's words) 'one of Chaucer's most up-to-date efforts, then and now' is to view its 'missing' source not as a puzzle requiring a solution, but rather as part of a pattern of absences that has come to seem a constitutive feature of the poem.

Genre

In a review of the Variorum *Squire's Tale*, Joseph Dane reminds us that, owing to the tale's relation to the genre of romance, 'its reception changes as definitions of the genre change' (**112r**). The poem's eighteenth-century and early nineteenth-century admirers noted both its Gothic elements and its vein of Eastern fancy. For these readers, the poem's hybridity constituted a virtue rather than a problem; in Warton's succinct formulation, the story's 'imagination ... consists in Arabian fiction grafted on Gothic chivalry,' while George Nott (who thought *The Squire's Tale* superior to *The Knight's Tale*) remarks approvingly that the tale's subject, figures, ideas, and machinery 'are all purely Gothic, with a mixture of eastern imagery which gave, at the time of the Crusades, a peculiar colouring to our northern romances' (**112**).

When Kittredge turned his attention to *The Squire's Tale* a century later, the mixed heritage observed by Warton, Nott, and others had disappeared from view. The tale is for Kittredge 'pure romance, in the medieval sense,' its genre defined by what it excludes – the 'moral or social or matrimonial theorizing' of the neighboring tales that comprise Kittredge's Marriage Group (**380**; see also **373**). Over the next three decades, and occasionally after, critical comments on the tale's genre mostly reiterated Kittredge's judgment (**398, 407, 408, 412, 450, 601**). The first fully developed alternative to the view of the poem as 'a sustained performance in the romantic vein' (**407**) appeared in 1948, with the publication of Gardiner Stillwell's 'Chaucer in Tartary' (**446**). Representing the tale's relation to romance as problematic rather than straightforward, Stillwell focused on the poem's mercurial tone, singling out passages in which we hear the poet 'importing humanity into his story, somewhat to its detriment as a typical romance.' Stillwell's experiment in reading the tale 'closely and realistically' without 'romantic preconception[s] of its solemnity' was succeeded by other interpretations that also made room for moments of comic incongruity and imagined Chaucer as temperamentally at odds with romance forms and themes (**456**, **457**, **468**, **471**, **502**, **516**). Some critics took the discovery of 'parodic tone' (**598**) in isolated episodes several steps further, declaring the entire poem a parody or burlesque of romance (**502**, **504r**, **514**, **538a**, **549**, **625**, **633r**, **640**). This claim in turn generated correctives and rebuttals (**479**, **690**, **735**, **736**), and, in one important instance, historical contextualization. The latter is Joseph Dane's examination of the tale's eighteenth-century reception, in which Dane shows that the poem, although it was acknowledged to contain burlesque passages, 'was never referred to as *a* parody or *a* burlesque' by eighteenth-century readers (**218**). This interpretive position, which admits parodic or incongruous elements into romance without positing a wholesale transformation of the story type, reappears in the work of twentieth- and twenty-first century critics and is where, at least for the moment, the discourse seems to have settled: neither 'pure romance' nor a dedicated send-up of romance, *The Squire's Tale,* especially in its mixture of tones and styles, displays both 'the pleasures and the limits' of the genre (**602**; see also **598**, **602**, **611r**, **635r**, **693**, **743**, **744**).

Among those parts of the tale that fall into both the 'pleasure' and 'limits' categories is the synopsis of coming events that concludes Part 2 (lines 651-70), a passage that, on the one hand, has been used to construct possible scenarios for the poem's unwritten or 'lost' episodes (**112**) and, on the other, has been read as a joke about the prolixity of romances or about the youthful Squire's unrealistic literary ambitions (**394**, **471**, **515**, **601**, **634**, **693**). In a 1942 article entitled 'The Genre of Chaucer's *Squire's Tale,*' Haldeen Braddy cites the Squire's précis as evidence that the poet was modeling his narrative on the oriental framing tale (**440**). A more widely-accepted hypothesis proposes that the lines contain a plan for an interlaced narrative of the sort usually associated with the French prose romances (**112**, **528**, **581**, **629**, **635**, **736**), although Helen Cooper observes that the breathless piling up of events in the Squire's prospectus evokes an 'unsophisticated interlace romance' rather than the 'elegant *entrelacement*' of the best French examples (**581**; see also **715**). While agreeing that the interlaced romance is the tale's primary model, Carol Heffernan revives Braddy's long-dormant theory in her suggestion that the Squire, in choosing the most complex western genre he knows, may be attempting to imitate the equally complicated structure of an Eastern frame story (**736**; see also **204**, **653**, **671**, **769**).

The Squire's Tale's relation to interlaced romance received additional fine-tuning in Jennifer Goodman's claim that Chaucer's poem shares elements of content and structure with late fourteenth- and fifteenth-century

English 'composites of courtly romance,' narratives that attempted to 'rival in verse the complexity of the early prose romances' (**582**). Building on Goodman's suggestion about the poem's genre, W.A. Davenport extended the notion of 'compositeness' to include the tale's rhetoric, its handling of point-of-view, its inclusion of both human and animal characters, and its attempt (unsuccessful, in Davenport's opinion) to reconcile romance narrative with lyrical *dit* (**631**). Alert to what Susan Crane calls the 'provisional and protean' nature of medieval romance (**670**) and to the 'excess of generic markers' present in any literary text (**237**, p 183), Davenport is less convinced than Goodman that comparisons with extant composite romances will endow *The Squire's Tale* with 'a recognizable genre and a coherent form' and will therefore put to rest misgivings about the poem's imperfect fusion of its disparate elements (see also **551**, **637**, **666**). Implicit in a commentary such as Davenport's is a recognition that (*pace* Kittredge) none of the tales in Chaucer's collection is a 'pure' example of its genre and that a tale can manifest the features of a genre and pass judgment on the genre at the same time.

Teller and Tale

Near the beginning of the chapter entitled 'Some Portraits' in his critical study of *The Canterbury Tales* (**601**), Derek Pearsall distinguishes between the three tales – those of the Wife of Bath, the Pardoner, and the Canon's Yeoman – that are prefaced by extended autobiographical monologues and therefore ask to be read as developments of or commentaries on the pilgrims' self-revelations, and the rest of the series, in which the perception of a relation between the character of teller and tale is 'a suggestion, a temptation, a provocative juxtaposition or a delusion.' Most readings of *The Squire's Tale* fall into Pearsall's first three categories, with the exception of a flurry of articles and book chapters in the 1960s, 1970s, and early 1980s that propose close connections between tale and teller. In the section on 'The Suitability of *The Squire's Tale* to the Squire' in the Variorum edition (**112**), Baker examines critical treatments of the tale-teller question from the eighteenth century through the mid-1980s. In what follows, I take a fresh look at the material covered in Baker's survey, adjusting some of his emphases and supplying additional evidence (especially from work published after 1985), and conclude by speculating briefly on future possibilities for thinking about the Squire's presence in his tale.

Until the middle of the twentieth century, critics were almost unanimous in finding an unproblematic relation between the Squire and the tale he tells; extrapolating from the Squire's portrait in *The General Prologue,* they point to the romantic character of the story, its high-minded sentiments, its fascination with the marvelous, and its Eastern setting as aspects of the tale that make it 'perfectly suited' (**378**) to the temperament of its youthful teller (**112**, pp 39–45; see also **398**, **412**, **416**). That said, none of these critics pursue Kittredge's 'dramatic principle' – that 'it was Chaucer's artistic duty ... to make the method of delivery correspond to the character of the teller' (**1622**) – much beyond noting an overlap between the Squire's presumed interests and the themes of his tale. A representative opinion is that of Lumiansky (**462**), who cites the Squire's contribution as an example of 'the simple suiting of tale and teller ... there are no dramatic complications ... or axes ground' for the performances in this category.

A decade after Lumiansky's book was published, arguments for a less simple relation between the Squire and his tale began to appear, all of which expand the claims for the tale as a uniformly impersonated utterance that represents the distinct subjectivity of the text's fictional speaker ('no other tale is so immediately revealing ... of the mentality assumed for the teller'; **612**; see also **596**), and almost all of which explain its supposed defects by invoking corresponding flaws in the pilgrim narrator's character: his youth and inexperience (**483**, **492**, **502**, **546**, **549**, **562**, **654**), his faulty grasp of rhetoric and logical argument (**487**, **492**, **496**, **497**, **502**, **508**, **555**, **557**, **574**, **621**, **640**, **715**), his literary and social pretensions (**483**, **497**, **506**, **545**, **556**, **557**, **729a**), his superficiality (**545**, **557**, **612**), and his 'profane' nature (**506**). The best commentary on this extended episode of Squire-bashing is Lawton's (**598**). Using the readings of Pearsall (**483**), Haller (**487**), McCall (**492**), and Peterson (**506**) as his main evidence, Lawton explains how, in a 'progressive crudification of Stillwell's insights' into the poem's unstable tone, 'all the Tale's perceived faults are ... laid at the Squire's door, and all the good things ... are brushed aside, if they are considered at all, as involuntary flashes of Chaucer's genius from behind the mask.' As Pearsall (who revises his earlier 'dramatic' reading of the tale in his 1985 book) points out, the notion that Chaucer deliberately wrote bad poetry to demonstrate a narrator's shortcomings is 'methodologically suspect' – *Sir Thopas* being the exception that proves the rule (**601**; see also **500**, **528**, **617**, **631**, **735**). The indiscriminate application of the dramatic principle, moreover, produces a paradoxical effect: even as teller and tale are diminished through irony, the teller's interiorated selfhood, shouldering aside the tale's ostensible topics, *becomes* its subject, the tale's 'artistic infelicities [serving as] Chaucer's means of representing dramatically the as-yet-unstructured mind of the narrator' (**612**; see also **549**).

In a claim like the one I have just cited, the dramatic approach would seem to have run its course (or overstayed its welcome). Dane (**112r**) is doubtless correct that a topic like 'The Suitability of *The Squire's Tale* to the Squire' no longer represents a fruitful line of inquiry. But questions that seem dated can always be reframed. With recent work on medieval first-person narrative – particularly A.C. Spearing's *Textual Subjectivity* (2005) and its companion volume *Medieval Autographies: The "I" of the Text* (2012) – opening up new ways of conceiving subjectivity as a textual phenomenon, it seems likely that Chaucer studies will have more to tell us about narratorial discourse in 'the story of Cambuscan bold.'

Orientalism and the Exotic

Reviewing scholarship on *The Squire's Tale*'s genesis in a 1995 *Speculum* article, Kathryn Lynch points out that 'what all these theories of origin share … is the centrality of the Oriental motif to the Squire's Tale; the tale wraps itself in an aura of exotic alterity, an insistent Orientalism in much the sense that Edward Said has defined that term' (**679**). In an essay published five years after Lynch's article and following her lead (**727**), I examine representative responses to the poem from the eighteenth century to the 1970s and suggest that orientalist discourse – the ways of imagining and describing the East set out in Said's *Orientalism* (1978) – have left their mark on the study of virtually all aspects of the tale: its genre, its sources and analogues, its narrative structure, its 'Squire-specific' features, its incompleteness, and its place in the Canterbury collection. Among the topics I consider (paired here with references to texts that exemplify specific attitudes and critical approaches) are:

- The opposed impulses of wonder before the marvels of the East and the skeptical or rationalist need to demystify the marvelous (Warton; see **112**, pp 59–60).
- The essentializing of the East, the conflation of aesthetic and moral judgments, and the association of the East with waywardness and sensuality (Jephson; see **112**, pp 61–2).
- The construction of the East as the 'other,' located 'beyond the central realm of sober experience' and thus the West's binary opposite (**32**, **381**, **421**).
- The disengagement required of the European spectator of oriental difference and Chaucer's inability in *The Squire's Tale* to maintain this disinterested stance (**446**).
- A penchant for the exotic as characteristic of late-medieval aristocratic fads and fashions and as a symptom of the waning Middle Ages (**520**, **545**).
- A taste for exotic stories as a sign of an immature imagination, and hence suited to the young and callow Squire (**447**, **471**, **612**).
- The outline of coming events at the end of Part 2, which presages a 'monstrous oriental saga' apparently modeled on the Eastern framing

tale, as evidence that the Squire has lost control of his story (**440**, **483**, **490**).

- The motif of the East as insidiously dangerous, reflected in Braddy's hypothesis that Chaucer may have discovered an incest narrative in his oriental source, and hence terminated his tale prematurely (**440**).

The scholarship and criticism I have just summarized (and which I treat at greater length in my essay) incorporates a set of mostly tacit assumptions about the Orient and its relation to European culture. In recent decades, critics have taken a fresh look at the tale's cultural geography, with a more nuanced sense of what's at stake in Chaucer's refashioning of Eastern romance, a self-awareness prompted in part by Said's essential study and the published responses to it.

Although John Fyler's 'Domesticating the Exotic in the *Squire's Tale*' (**632**) makes no direct reference to Said's work, Fyler's reading demonstrates that some of the impulses Said locates in modern orientalist discourse – the wish to control or assimilate the 'other' and the corresponding resistance of the exotic to demystification, the vacillation between the alien and the familiar – are present as well in Chaucer's tale, reflecting both the paradoxes of romance as a genre and the mixed motives of the Squire as storyteller. Fyler's examples – a Christian European imagining a heathen Tartar, a human being imagining a bird, and a man imagining a woman – establish continuities between the two parts of the tale (a feature often thought to be absent from the poem) and locate the Squire within his narrative while avoiding the reductiveness that compromises many 'dramatic' readings of the tale.

Building on Fyler's observations in her study of Chaucerian romance, Susan Crane (**670**) introduces gender into the tale's program for managing the exotic: although Cambyuskan's daughter Canacee 'is an instance of the exotic for the narrator,' her own relation to the marvelous is contrasted with the masculine desire for appropriation and control. Gender is also one of the subjects of the essay by Kathryn Lynch cited at the beginning of this section; examining the ways in which Chaucer consciously 'out-Easts the East' in *The Squire's Tale*, Lynch sees the Squire as 'setting up an argument about women, pleasure, and the East that the Franklin will dismantle' (**679**). Like Lynch, Suzanne Akbari reads the two Fragment V tales 'geographically' in her interrogation of Said's paradigm of East and West as mirroring binaries (**707**). The dominant medieval world division, Akbari maintains, was tripartite (Asia, Europe, and Africa), and uneven; Chaucer's pairing of *The Squire's Tale* and *The Franklin's Tale* forms part of her evidence for the gradual emergence, in the late fourteenth century, of the soon-to-be standard dichotomy – a 'cold, dispassionate, northerly Occident' that is the mirror image of an Orient associated with heat and the sun. In her 2006 New Chaucer Society lecture (**747**; see also **757**), Crane returns to and develops her earlier thoughts about orientalism and romance, examining how, and with what results, 'the orientalized "other" shifts from the Eastern to the animal realm' in the tale's second part. Crane's observations about language (Canacee's magic ring, 'a perfect manifestation of animal orientalizing,' turns out not to be entirely necessary for her communication with the tercel) complement Alan Ambrisco's characterization of the Canacee-falcon episode as 'a fantasy of linguistic competence' that serves as a contrast to the ambivalent orientalism of the tale's first part (**740**).

In their engagement, implicit and explicit, with the issues raised by Said's work, these commentaries on *The Squire's Tale* form part of a larger conversation about the usefulness of postcolonial methodologies for the study of the Middle Ages. Unlike criticism of other Chaucerian texts, which has only in the past few decades taken up the topic of Chaucer's orientalism, interpretations of *The Squire's Tale* have traditionally given space to Chaucer's refashioning of the culturally alien Eastern romance. This record of attention offers an unusually full picture of the premises that have shaped attitudes toward the *Squire's Tale*'s oriental subject over time, and provides a historical perspective from which we can judge the impact, both realized and potential, of recent work in cultural studies on the reception of Chaucer's text.

Magic, Science, Technology

In the introduction to his compendium of analogues to *The Squire's Tale*'s magical features, W.A. Clouston announces that 'the magical elements in the *Squire's Tale* constitute its great attraction' (**129**, p 276). Clouston's mildly self-promoting assertion requires some correction, but not much: magic is in fact a recurrent topic in discussions of the poem from the eighteenth century onward. Commenting on *The Squire's Tale* in his *History of English Poetry* (**112**, **727**), Warton traces the magical elements in Western romance to accounts of Arabian astrology and magic and devotes a dozen pages to 'the wonderful discoveries and mysterious inventions' of Eastern learning that parallel the stranger knight's gifts. But Warton's admiration of the tale's glamorous surface is qualified by his ambivalence about the objects brought to Cambyuskan's court. On the one hand, the horse, ring, mirror, and sword are instances of natural magic, 'a favorite pursuit of the Arabians, by which they imposed false appearances on the spectator.' On the other hand, he remarks of the horse of brass that 'by such inventions we are willing to be deceived' (**112**). Three decades later, Charles Lamb registers a similarly divided response to the tale's representation of magic in a letter to Thomas Manning: ''tis the reading of Chaucer has misled you; his foolish stories about Cambyuskan and the ring, and the horse of brass. Believe me there's no such things, 'tis all the poet's *invention*; but if there were such *darling* things as old Chaucer sings, I would up behind you on the Horse of Brass and frisk off for Prester John's country' (**112**). At the beginning of the next century, Root connects the magical objects with the 'limitless fields of pleasing conjecture' that the tale opens up to the reader's imagination: 'the very name of magic has its fascination for our poor race of mortals ... Let the magic horse, the ring, the sword, and mirror be put to practical use ... and they are immediately vulgarized' (**378**). One practical use to which Root presumably would not have objected is the quest for sources; in studies contemporary with Root's volume, Jones (**133**) and Lowes (**147**) cite the flying horse, the mirror, and the ring as evidence of the tale's possible connections with the French romance *Cleomadés* and the *Epistola Presbyteri Johannis,* while, later in the century, Jennifer Goodman (**582**) notes that these objects also appear in the composite romances that she believes to be examples of *The Squire's Tale*'s 'recognizable genre.'

As is the case with other aspects of *The Squire's Tale* examined in this introduction, the poem's treatment of magic receives its first demystifying scrutiny in Stillwell's 'Chaucer in Tartary' (**446**); alternately 'learned' and 'commonsense,' the courtiers' speculations about the magical objects work against the romance '*naïveté*' that, in Stillwell's opinion, is required to sustain our belief in (or to suspend our disbelief about) the announced powers of the stranger knight's gifts. In his first published interpretation of the tale (**483**), Pearsall reads the tonal incongruities assumed by Stillwell to be Chaucer's (or the tale's) effects as manifestations of the Squire's anti-intellectualism, his 'indignant contempt for what is not understood.' Revisiting the Squire's contribution in his full-length study of the *Tales* (**601**), Pearsall modifies his earlier position somewhat; he now presents the poem's 'inclination to scepticism and rationalisation' in its treatment of the supernatural as a reflection of 'Chaucer's own individual reception of the genre' rather than as a character trait of the Squire-as-narrator.

The most vigorous argument for the tale's rationalization of magic is that of Vincent DiMarco (**684**; see also **207**, **208**, **242**, **513**, **690**), who maintains that there is in fact '*no* magic in the SqT'; the gifts are interpreted as magical by '*lewed* observers who fail to understand their scientific or technological basis ... In the accounts of each of the gifts, myth and legend are rationalized scientifically.' Other readers, while acknowledging the episode's striking depiction of scientific curiosity (**570**; see also **725**), stop short of eliminating magic from the tale, arguing instead for a complex interplay of the marvelous and the rational or scientific. Corinne Saunders (**743**, **744**) observes that our belief in the marvelous, initially qualified by the presence of natural science, technology, and astrology, is revived when, in part two of the tale, the ring's power enables Canacee to understand the speech of birds (see also **637, 686, 750a**). For Aranye Fradenburg (**742**), it is precisely by locating the stranger's gifts at the 'edge of the known and the unknown and on the border between technology and magic' that Chaucer provokes the sense of wonder that is a hallmark of romance narrative. Examining the *Squire's* and *Franklin's Tale*'s magical features in her study of gender and Chaucerian romance (**670**), Susan Crane also designates wonder (rather than 'attempted explanation') as the right response to clerical magic in romance, even as she notes the 'double movement' that strives to protect wonder from demystification and disengages from it at the same time.

In some ways comparable to Crane's exploration of magic as a means of expressing gender difference are readings that invoke courtly ritual and social hierarchy as contexts for interpreting the gift-giving episode. If, as Anne Middleton argues (**600**), the magical gifts are 'rhetorical devices in material form,' the ability to deploy and respond to these representations becomes a criterion of *gentil* behavior. In his study of courtly *mirabilia* (**722**), Scott Lightsey also denotes wonder at the objects' marvelous features as 'the aristocratic view,' but observes that the scene also includes 'a more skeptical mechanistic view,' presented from perspective of the sciences and the crafts-classes. For Andrew James Johnston (**700**), the juxtaposition of wonder and disenchanted curiosity functions as social commentary: the former is an aristocratic virtue, the latter risks the charge of academic pedantry, a deadly trait in the Squire's elegant courtly world.

Described in greater detail than the other gifts, the horse of brass has elicited responses from readers of the tale almost as varied as those proffered by the members of Cambyuskan's court. In his monograph on the tale's magical elements (**129**), Clouston devotes twenty-two pages to instances of flying horses in folklore and literary texts. Comparing the opening scene of *The Squire's Tale* to the corresponding episode in *Sir Gawain and the Green Knight*, a poem more to his taste, John Speirs (**454**) dismisses the horse as 'nothing more than a curious mechanical contrivance, a flying machine.' In a memorable aside, E.T. Donaldson (**471**) connects the horse's narrative fate with the tale's leisurely plot; having introduced and developed at length the story of Canacee and the falcon, the teller 'will not quickly be able to get the brass horse and the rest out of storage and into action' (see also **543**). For Joyce Lionarons (**669**), the hidden knowledge required to fashion and operate the horse, which blurs the line between magic and technology, foregrounds the device's capacity for deceiving the ignorant. Jane Chance (**675**) also connects the brass steed with deceit by way of the reference to the Trojan horse, an association redeemed somewhat by the allusion to Pegasus in the same passage. Linked by Ovid and other classical authors with literary origins, Pegasus receives due attention in an article by Craig Berry (**238**), who interprets the brass steed as 'a figure for the poem' and its creator as equivalent to 'a poetic *makere*' (see also **552**, **675**). Other metatextual readings argue for parallels between the description of the horse and the structure of the *Tales* as a whole (**651**) and for the steed's ability to transport its riders to the place of their hearts' desire (V.119–20) as a form of *translatio* similar to the ring's power to transpose bird language into human language (**702**).

The sixty lines devoted to the brass horse and the courtiers' speculations about it continue to invite new discoveries and fresh critical insights. In *Time and the Astrolabe in The Canterbury Tales* (**730**), Marijane Osborn advances an argument for the horse as a 'metaphor' for the astrolabe, and proposes a further connection with the constellation Pegasus; 'more than it appears,' the horse-as-astrolabe may have been intended by Chaucer as entertainment for 'the astronomically skilled members of his audience' or as a tribute to Muslim science. Like Osborn, but with different interpretive goals in mind, Crane also takes her argument about the steed of brass beyond the immediate confines of the poem. Alert to the ways in which literary representations encode cultural processes, Crane shows in her chapter on 'knight and horse' in *Animal Encounters* (**757**) that the apparently 'fully technologized horse' presented to Cambyuskan's court also manifests 'living physicality,' and thus reflects the double function of a knight's warhorse as a 'dream weapon' and as an 'object of chivalric devotion.'

The Squire's Tale, Part 2

Early commentators found more to admire in Part 1 than in Part 2 of *The Squire's Tale*. Speaking for 'every reader of taste and imagination,' Warton expressed regret that, in place of adventures that might have been performed with the assistance of the horse of brass, Chaucer settled for the 'tedious detail' of Canacee's encounter with the falcon (**112**). Writing in 1874 and 1892, respectively, Skeat and Lounsbury detected in Part 2 lapses in structure and grammar that they attributed to hasty composition (**112**). Until the middle of the twentieth century, commentary on Part 2 consisted almost entirely of source studies and questionable attempts at historical allegory (**112, 166, 174, 373, 403, 404, 432, 440**). When it was drawn into the orbit of 'dramatic' readings of the tale, the Canacee-falcon episode joined Part 1 in supplying evidence for the Squire's ostensible failures of artistic control and moral insight (**483, 487, 492, 497, 506, 612, 640, 642**). And for some critics, it is the poet, not the narrator, who nods; one learned (and outspoken) scholar ranks the 'sentimental avian romance' that comprises most of the tale's *pars secunda* as 'among the worst narrative sequences [Chaucer] ever wrote' (**608**).

Amid this record of dismissal and neglect, several critics offer more favorable assessments of Part 2. Of particular note are Jill Mann's nuanced explications of *pitee* and *newefangelnesse* in the falcon's monologue, a passage that for Mann includes Chaucer's most moving representation of his 'ideal of harmonious unity in love' (**729**; see also **545r, 565, 745, 750**). Douglas Gray (**561, 620**), Charles Owen (**657**), and – modifying his earlier view (**483**) of the humanized birds as inadvertently comic at the Squire's expense – Derek Pearsall (**601**) also read Canacee's dialogue with the falcon as an unironic treatment of essential Chaucerian themes and techniques. One should observe as well that the Canacee-falcon episode appears frequently in illustrated editions and modernizations of *The Canterbury Tales*, where its visual possibilities (especially Canacee holding out her *lappe* to catch the bleeding bird) are treated by the books' artists with imagination and sympathy (**5, 11, 20, 37, 39, 43, 52, 53, 63**).

The argument for Part 2 of *The Squire's Tale* as worthy of serious critical attention has been strengthened by insights drawn from gender studies and, more recently, animal studies. In monographs on gender and Chaucerian romance that appeared in the mid-1990s, Susan Crane (**670**; see also **747, 757**) and Angela Weisl (**681**) employ the Canacee-falcon scene to explore, among other significant topics, the association between femininity and the body, the relation of female characters to the romance plot, and the instability of gender categories. In some respects analogous to these gender-focused readings are studies that revisit the tale's representation of animal-human relations. In his notes to the Oxford edition, Skeat maintained that the falcon was probably a princess in animal shape who, if the tale had been completed, would have been restored to her original form by the magic ring (**4, 374**; see also **378**, p 268). A number of subsequent commentaries on Canacee's encounter with the lovelorn falcon, although they do not (as does Skeat) erase the falcon-as-bird from the tale, nevertheless diminish or foreclose possible sympathy for the formel's plight by invoking 'the comic disparity between the avian world and the human world' (**599**; see also **471, 483, 500, 516, 608, 693**). In the past two decades, scholars from a variety of disciplines have questioned such absolute assertions of human/animal difference and put forward alternative paradigms for interpreting the representation of animals in a range of cultural productions, literature included. This shift in perspective can be seen in commentaries on *The Squire's Tale* published between 2004 and 2013 (**740, 745–57**). Making use of recent thinking about such topics as cross-species contact and cross-species translation, animal agency, female autonomy, female homosocial bonding and 'natural' bonds between human and animal, avian hybridity, and anthropomorphism (enabling, unstable, and 'reversed'), this body of work shows how well the Canacee-falcon scene responds to fresh approaches, and lays a solid foundation for further informed attention to a long-undervalued part of *The Canterbury Tales*.

The Tale as Fragment

No feature of *The Squire's Tale* has received more scrutiny than its lack of an ending. Baker's and Lawton's surveys record the main patterns of response to the tale's incompleteness through the mid-1980s:

- Early admiration for the tale and regret for its incompleteness, as exemplified in Spenser's continuation of the tale in Book 4 of *The Faerie Queene*; in Milton's reference to Chaucer as 'him that left half told / The story of *Cambuscan* bold' ('Il Penseroso,' lines 109–10); and in Thomas Warton's lament that the most interesting part of the story, 'the notable achievements ... performed by the assistance of the horse of brass,' was either lost or never written (**112**).
- Romantic fascination with 'the power of the incomplete' that construes the tale's unfinishedness (whether by accident or by design) as a spur to the readers' 'vague imaginings' (**378**; see also **650**).
- Chaucer deliberately abandoned the tale; he had moved too far in Part 2 from his initial premise (**411, 601**), lost interest in his subject or recognized that it didn't suit his talents (**112, 446, 448, 471, 505, 538a, 586**), realized that his original plan was unworkable (**112, 436, 483, 582**), intended the unwritten portion for the return journey, which itself remained unwritten (**129**), or discovered in his oriental source an incest motif that brought him to a sudden halt (**440**).
- The tale is cut off by the Franklin, who attempts diplomatically to end a story that threatens to go on indefinitely, or to let the Squire off the hook when the younger man becomes lost in the labyrinth of his plot (**442, 447, 483, 502, 505, 577, 581, 594r, 764, 767, 768, 775, 784a**), or to register 'frustrated expectations' as do the Host and the Knight in their more forthright interruptions of *Sir Thopas* and *The Monk's Tale* (**506**).
- The tale's incompleteness comically mirrors the delayed conclusions of romance narratives (**490**) or (if read as produced by the Franklin's interruption) satirizes 'the long-windedness and absurdities of the romance-writers' (**394**).
- *The Squire's Tale* was neither aborted by Chaucer nor intended to be read as interrupted by the Franklin (**500, 579, 581r, 765, 781a**). Arguing on codicological grounds, Norman Blake maintains that Chaucer probably planned to finish the tale and that it may have been in progress when he died (**102, 452, 558, 569, 593, 594**).

In the two decades following Baker's survey of criticism, these positions were variously called into question, examined from fresh perspectives, and supplemented with new information. Three interpretive stances dominated the discussion:

- Critics unpersuaded by arguments that Chaucer gave up on the tale or that attribute its incompleteness to contingent events proposed that the poem is unfinished by design, in accordance with the open-ended nature of frame stories (**653**); as a way of including a composite romance in the tale-telling competition without actually producing a complete narrative (**582**); as an analogue to the Squire's own 'unfinishedness' (**582**, **714**); as a feature of the 'roundabout inconclusion' that characterizes the tale as a whole and that contrasts it with the *Franklin's Tale*'s conclusiveness (**663**); as a means of sharpening the reader's curiosity in the manner of oriental tales (**671**); and as dictated by a 'poetics of Chaucerian fragments' manifested in the intentional unfinishedness of *The Canterbury Tales* itself (**694**).

- Interpretations of the Franklin's words to the Squire as a deliberate stinting of the latter's tale continued to make an appearance (**621**, **625**, **653**, **715**, **736**, **768**, **786**, **789**, **791**), but they are now put forward more cautiously – compare, for example, Pearsall's advocacy of a 'dramatic' reading in 1964 (**483**; see also **505**) with his modified observations twenty years later, which invoke the poet's immediate compositional needs rather than assuming a pre-existent dramatic frame (**601**). Also absent, for the most part, are the detailed stage directions that characterize some earlier glosses on the episode (e.g., **442**).
- Taking issue with the views summarized in the preceding two paragraphs, a number of critics adduced additional evidence that the tale is actually – rather than 'dramatically' or designedly – unfinished. Lawton makes a detailed case for this view, noting, inter alia, that the Franklin's words do not sound like an interruption (**598**; see also **452**, **650**, **765**, **781a**, **783**); that the Squire's prospectus of coming attractions 'read[s] like the poet's own notes, jotted down at the time when he laid the work aside'; and that several scribes seem to have expected further copy. In 'Poems Without Endings' (**650**), John Burrow (who believes Lawton's chapter to be 'the best modern discussion of the tale') juxtaposes the earliest responses by scribes, printers, and poets, all of whom take it for granted that the poem is incomplete, with interpretations by twentieth-century critics that reflect a post-romantic taste for the fragmentary, a modern wariness of definitive closure, and a reluctance to entertain the possibility that 'disinclination or distraction or death' rather than artistic purpose explain the tale's lack of a conclusive ending. Burrow's account finds further support in Joseph Dane's demonstration that early printed books presented the tale not as interrupted but as unfinished or incomplete (**710**). Published in the same year as Dane's essay, Stephen Partridge's wittily titled 'Minding the Gaps' draws on manuscript evidence rather than printed texts to argue that the blank spaces following *The Cook's Tale* and *The Squire's Tale* and the

notes on the tales' incompleteness may be authorial rather than scribal; the incompleteness of these two tales is thus essentially different from that of *Sir Thopas* and *The Monk's Tale,* the two clearly interrupted tales (**713**). Completing a trio of commentaries on *The Squire's Tale*'s unfinishedness that appeared in the year 2000 is Elizabeth Scala's 'The Deconstructure of the *Canterbury Tales*' (**714a**). Building on Partridge's evidence for the authorial nature of the manuscript gaps that follow *The Cook's* and *The Squire's Tales,* Scala maintains that these absences should be presented 'as part of the text (rather than as a lack of text).' The tales may thus be considered not simply poems without conclusions, but rather 'poems with blank, and therefore, potential lines written into the page.' Despite its frequently-noted singularity among the Canterbury stories, *The Squire's Tale* is for Scala a paradigm of the entire *Tales,* itself a work fueled by gaps and absences 'that are not only necessary but structurally central.'

ꕥ *The Franklin's Tale*: Introduction

With the exception of *The General Prologue, The Knight's Tale, The Pardoner's Tale*, and *The Wife of Bath's Prologue and Tale, The Franklin's Tale* has generated as substantial a body of commentary as any other segment of *The Canterbury Tales*. In these introductory remarks, I attempt to provide an overview of this mass of criticism that will highlight some of its key concerns and suggest something of its richness, variety, and occasional quirkiness. As others have noted, the history of the poem's reception involves a paradox: the seemingly benign figure we meet in *The General Prologue* – sanguine in temperament, an accomplished host, an honored public servant – contributes to the Canterbury competition a tale that has polarized its readers to a striking degree. (A distinguished Chaucerian once remarked in conversation that 'no one likes anyone else's interpretation of *The Franklin's Tale*.') The observations that follow will allow users of this volume to track some of these controversies and to see how they arise not only from the critical allegiances of its interpreters, but also (and perhaps more importantly) from the kind of story that Chaucer assigns to the Franklin. The first section of the introduction surveys scholarship on the tale's sources and analogues. In the second section, I examine five topics and a selection of key passages that have produced some of the most significant critical writing on the tale since 1900. I intend these comments as a kind of tasting menu, a sampling of the thematic emphases and interpretive approaches set out at greater length in the individual entries.

Sources and Analogues of *The Franklin's Tale*

At least since Clouston (**129**), scholars have recognized that *The Franklin's Tale* is a version of the folktale most commonly designated as 'The Damsel's Rash Promise,' but identified more accurately by Utley as 'Which Was the Noblest Act?' (**944**). Clouston's investigations were expanded by Aman (**258**) and Schick (**275**) and several commentators subsequently examined the tale in the light of its eastern or folk analogues (**283, 307, 362, 368, 1275, 1507**).

The largest body of work on *The Franklin's Tale*'s sources, however, responds to the narrator's claim that he is retelling a Breton lay. Taking the Franklin at his word, Schofield (**246**) argued for the tale's Celtic origins, pointing to similarities of plot and phraseology between *The Franklin's Tale* and the *lais* of Marie de France that, in his view, confirm the claim for a Breton source. In 1903, Rajna (**249**) rejected Schofield's analogies as unpersuasive, making a detailed case for the fourth *questione d'amore* in Boccaccio's *Il Filocolo* (and, to a lesser extent, *Decameron* 10.5) as the only texts that offer substantial parallels to Chaucer's poem. Rajna's identification of *Il Filocolo* as Chaucer's primary source has been almost universally accepted. Some critics, however, point out that the poet shapes Boccaccio's narrative to capture the spirit of a Breton lay (**252, 267, 338, 862, 1329, 1363a, 1422**); the editors of *The Franklin's Tale* chapter in the first edition of *Sources and Analogues of Chaucer's Canterbury Tales* (**281**) gave authority to this view by supplementing Boccaccio's *questione d'amore* with excerpts from four French and three English lays. Numerous scholars argue that Chaucer's knowledge of the genre was derived solely from English texts – perhaps exclusively from the lays in the Auchinleck MS (**252, 282, 301a, 308, 311, 313, 337, 955, 972**). The shift in opinion about the tale's indebtedness to Celtic and French sources is reflected in the second edition of *Sources and Analogues* (**367**), in which the lays are represented only by the opening lines of the Auchinleck *Lay le Freine*.

The Franklin's identification of his tale as a Breton lay has prompted speculation both about his character and about the kind of story he presents to the pilgrim audience. If, as some critics claim, the Breton lay had lost its vogue in England by the late fourteenth century, the Franklin's choice of genre may mark him as old fashioned and nostalgic for the tales of his youth (**311, 909, 955, 958, 1016, 1067, 1069**; for a dissenting opinion, see Pearsall [**1179**], p 146); it may also underline his interest in (or alternatively, his misunderstanding of) *gentilesse* (**1003, 1061, 1231, 1349**). The tale's announced genre has been invoked in connection with its treatment of astrology and magic (**812, 1003, 1248, 1422**); its portrayal of human feelings (**1426**); its pre-Christian setting (**1003, 1179**); its echoes of ancient chronicle (**1230**); its investment in fantasy and wish fulfillment (**1252**); and with Chaucer's desire to give the black rocks a correspondingly full Breton setting (**955, 1339**), to achieve generic variety in the *Tales* (**296**), and to introduce contradictory elements into his story (**1385**). In contrast to those critics who establish links between the Breton lays and Chaucer's handling of his narrative, a smaller number see the poet as working against the grain of known examples of the genre, either by undercutting generic expectations in his treatment of relations between men and women (**1409**) and its handling of magic (**1130**), or by deflating the tale's romantic atmosphere (**1022, 1259**).

Until the middle of the twentieth century, the interest of Chaucerians in the tale's relation to Boccaccio rarely went beyond confirming – or, in one instance, arguing against (**264**) – Rajna's identification of *Il Filocolo* as the poem's primary source. When source scholarship began to join forces with interpretive analysis, comparative approaches to *The Franklin's Tale* and its Italian models enabled critics to speak with greater precision about the poem's structure and themes. Among the subjects that have been illuminated by intertextual commentaries are Chaucer's innovations in plot (**296, 345**); his treatment of character, especially that of Dorigen (**335, 345, 834, 838, 880, 890, 1159, 1179, 1189, 1230, 1390**); the nature of promises (**926, 1179**); the tale's moral argument, its ethical complexity, and its open-endedness (**1189, 1200, 1230, 1366, 1372**); the significance of the garden (**830, 852, 994, 1312**); and the representation of social, class, and gender issues in the Italian and English versions of the tale (**355, 363, 365, 1493**).

The substantial body of scholarship on the tale's relation to the Breton lays and to Boccaccio has been supplemented by commentaries on its minor sources. Among these studies, the investigations of Chaucer's use of St Jerome's *Epistola adversus Jovinianum* in Dorigen's Complaint are notable, offering a close look at the poet's compositional habits as he adapts an earlier authority to the needs of characterization and the dramatic purposes of his narrative (**298, 304, 358, 367, 847, 850, 863, 912, 921, 943, 1281, 1310, 1459**).

The Twentieth- and Twenty-First-Century Critical Tradition

THE FRANKLIN'S TALE AND THE MARRIAGE DEBATE

In 1912, George Lyman Kittredge proposed that *The Franklin's Tale* provides a solution to a debate on marriage begun by the Wife of Bath and continued by the Clerk and the Merchant (**805, 815**). Kittredge's remarks established the terms that dominated critical discussion of the tale for the next five decades. The staying power of Kittredge's comments stemmed in part from the satisfying economy of his assertion that the Franklin reconciles the seemingly incompatible claims of courtly love and marriage, but also from his breezily authoritative tone ('The thing is possible. The problem need puzzle us no longer'), and from his belief that, in depicting the requirements for a happy marriage, the Franklin speaks for Chaucer the man. Approximately one-third of the commentaries summarized in the *Franklin's Tale*'s chapters of this bibliography engage with the subject of marriage. Not all of these items refer to Kittredge by name. But his observations may be said to have produced – even if indirectly – the ubiquitous focus on marriage in a half-century's worth of writing on the tale.

Some critics are content to cast their vote with Kittredge (**315, 829, 861, 865,**

867, 889, 896, 939, 1004, 1038, 1132, 1243, 1408). Others begin from his basic premises, but extend his formulations in a variety of directions, particularly toward the claim that the marriage of Dorigen and Arveragus is meant to serve as a model for human relations more generally (**854, 942, 1173, 1190, 1248, 1305, 1389**). As with any strong interpretation, Kittredge's thesis – that the union of Dorigen and Arveragus provides a model of domestic equality that brings to a satisfying conclusion the preceding conversation on marriage – has generated equally strong resistance, both at the level of detail and in its larger thematic and structural implications. Some scholars chip away at the bedrock of Kittredge's argument by questioning the concept of a coherent Marriage Group of tales (**818, 845, 1196**). Others take issue with the central tenets of his thesis, claiming that the tale fails to establish a harmonious balance between marriage and courtly love (**937, 1165, 1175, 1286, 1355, 1485**) or that the poem's penultimate scene, in which Arveragus orders Dorigen to fulfill her promise to the squire, undercuts Arveragus's earlier forswearing of *maistrye*, and thus disqualifies Kittredge's humanistic reading of the marriage contract (**852, 1029, 1057, 1097, 1149, 1186, 1196, 1198, 1244, 1288r, 1337, 1339, 1358, 1382, 1495**). In one of his first published articles, Donald Howard argued that the Franklin's worldly compromise between *amour courtois* and husbandly authority is unlikely to represent Chaucer's view of marriage, especially in light of the poet's attention to virginity and chaste marriage in *The Physician's Tale* and *The Second Nun's Tale* (each of which follows *The Franklin's Tale* in some manuscripts) respectively (**910**; see also **977, 1050**). Two years after Howard's essay appeared, D.W. Robertson, Jr. advanced a more uncompromising critique of the Franklin's representation of marriage from a Christian perspective in *A Preface to Chaucer* (**918**; see also **1030**). According to Robertson, the Franklin's endorsement of marital equality runs counter to the Pauline doctrine of the husband's sovereignty in wedlock. To commend the Franklin for being ahead of his time in his treatment of the relations between the sexes is, in Robertson's opinion, to indulge in wishful thinking that neglects the historical constraints implied in the subtitle of his book – *A Study in Medieval Perspectives*. The influence of Robertson's argument may be seen in commentaries that propose what their authors believe to be properly historical readings of the Franklin's portrait of marriage (**926, 929, 948, 965, 1027, 1109, 1201, 1286, 1293, 1484**). Common to all of these exegeses is the severity with which the Franklin is judged for his supposed blindness to the true nature of virtuous Christian unions.

Beginning at mid-century and continuing with increasing frequency to the end of the period covered by this volume, various subjects – noble behavior (**865**); *trouthe, pitee, fredom,* and *gentilesse* (**900, 880, 955, 969, 1122, 1136, 1339, 1441**); honor (**928**); the sanctity of the pledged word (**973**); *maistrye* (**1029**); male bonding (**1366**); illusion and indeterminacy (**1388**); human vulnerability (**1414**) – have been proposed as supplements or alternatives to marriage as the tale's center of meaning. Although Chaucerians will doubtless have more to say about the Franklin's treatment of marriage, this topic is no longer an inevitable feature of commentaries on the poem. An essay like V.A. Kolve's iconographic study of magic and poetic fiction (**1285**), for example, demonstrates that it is possible to write profoundly and at length about *The Franklin's Tale* while avoiding the issue of marriage almost entirely.

THE TELLER AND THE TALE

Another of Kittredge's legacies is his case for the tales as dramatic monologues that reveal the personalities of the tellers. The debates over and revisions of Kittredge's view of the Canterbury narratives as a Human Comedy have produced some of the best writing on the tales, and the subject is by no means a dead one. (For an energetic defense of reading the tales in the light of their tellers, see Lee Patterson's introduction to *Geoffrey Chaucer's Canterbury Tales: A Casebook* [Oxford, New York: Oxford UP, 2007].) Although no one claims for *The Franklin's Tale* the confessional dimension present in the contributions of the Wife of Bath, the Pardoner, or the Canon's Yeoman, the gradual accumulation of characterological detail as we move from the *General Prologue* portrait to the dramatic interplay of *The Squire–Franklin Link* to the Franklin's own Prologue has encouraged readers to seek in the tale additional evidence for constructing the consciousness of its pilgrim narrator.

For many critics, the Franklin's supposed concern with (for some, his anxiety about) his class status forms the bridge connecting teller and tale. It was Kittredge (**758**) who first suggested that the Franklin's praise of the Squire's *gentilesse* reveals his own social ambitions. Subsequent variations on this claim range from mild condescension (e.g., the Franklin as an 'unpolished but quietly enthusiastic admirer of fine behaviour' [**969**]) to outright condemnation (e.g., the Franklin's address to the Squire 'reeks of servile toadying to the aristocracy' [**766**]); for a representative selection of opinions, see **554, 764, 769, 777, 779, 780, 789, 790, 792, 793, 794, 872, 895, 909, 926, 955, 958, 965, 967, 1000r, 1036, 1042, 1142, 1152, 1205, 1222, 1308, 1317, 1339, 1496, 1503**). Such perceived character traits have in turn served as a lens through which the tale is shown to reveal or explain the Franklin's inadequate understanding of *gentilesse* (**918, 926, 929, 958, 1036, 1042, 1049, 1050, 1061, 1152, 1222, 1251, 1395, 1449**); his vacillation between the courtly and the everyday (**872**); his projections of a desired social self onto his dramatis personae (**1030, 1142**); his choice of an old-fashioned literary form (**909, 958, 1016, 1067**); his allusions to *The Squire's Tale* (**769**); and his intrusions into his narrative (**1042**).

In 1981, Henrik Specht, building on the work of G.H. Gerould (**825**), investigated in detail the question of the Franklin's social rank and concluded that the Franklin is a 'worthy and ... unexceptionable' member of the country gentry (**1124**). Although Specht's study did not, as one reviewer hoped it would (**1124r**), put to rest the view of the Franklin as a parvenu, interpretations based on this premise gradually became less thick on the ground in the final decades of the twentieth century. Even before Specht's monograph appeared, in fact, some critics were unpersuaded by the notion of a social-climbing Franklin (**764, 1056r, 1110**). These skeptical voices grew more prominent in the 1980s (**1141, 1156, 1179, 1190, 1203, 1248, 1256**), and in turn cleared the way for readings of the tale's engagement with social issues that moved beyond the old controversies – for example, Paul Strohm's examination of oaths and social structures (**1256**), Susan Crane's yoking of class and gender (**1261, 1330**), and Robert Edwards's intertextual studies of social relations in Boccaccio and *The Franklin's Tale* (**355, 363**).

Until the publication of D.W. Robertson's *A Preface to Chaucer* in 1962 (**918**), critiques of the Franklin had for the most part been limited to his supposed class-related ambitions. For Robertson, the Franklin's social instability signifies a more profound moral disorder – a worldly and self-indulgent Epicureanism that manifests itself in a preoccupation with external appearances and a consequent blindness to virtue and truth. Robertson's portrait of the Franklin (developed more fully in **1030**) introduced a vocabulary that was assimilated by critics sympathetic to his reading. In addition to 'externals,' 'blind(ness),' and 'worldly,' the key terms are 'appearance,' 'illusion,' 'literal(ism),' 'myopia,' 'self-deception,' 'shallow,' 'superficial,' and 'surface' (**918, 929, 948, 949, 958, 965, 967, 970, 1030, 1061, 1076, 1079, 1147, 1149, 1201, 1204, 1205, 1317, 1321, 1371, 1388, 1395**). These words acquired the force of mantras that allowed critics to find the Franklin's putative personal and intellectual shortcomings reflected in almost every aspect of his tale, from the most minute to the largest: its handling of personal names (**1273**), physical setting (**1287**), treatment of astrology (**1061, 1147**), representation of magic (**956**), rhetoric (**557, 958, 1061, 1109, 1251**), genre (**958, 1061, 1349**), themes (**958**), characterization (**958, 965, 1030, 1251**), ethics (**956, 1061, 1109, 1251**), and metaphysics (**958, 965**). For these commentators, the Franklin does not speak for Chaucer, as Kittredge had maintained; rather, the tale encourages its readers to bond with the poet in relishing the ironies directed against the shortsighted pilgrim narrator (**926, 958, 967, 1061, 1205, 1388**).

The flurry of 'Franklin bashing' (**1201r**) that followed in the wake of Robertson's book elicited dissenting responses from a number of Chaucerians. In a notably level-headed essay published in 1974, Gertrude White urged a return to Chaucer's own writings – particularly his treatment of *gentilesse, fredom, honour,* and *curteisie* elsewhere in *The Canterbury Tales* and in his short poems – as a corrective to the 'learned but sometimes misguided and insensitive historical criticism' on display in Robertsonian approaches to the poem (**1033**). Others have pointed to the dangers of invoking the Franklin's supposed uneasiness about his social status or of using what Derek Pearsall (**1179**) calls a 'jaundiced reading' of the *General Prologue* portrait as templates for interpreting the tale (**972, 1056r, 1141, 1156, 1190, 1203, 1248**). In a move that has become increasingly familar in the debate over the Canterbury tale-tellers as subjects, these commentators question the critical habit of understanding *The Franklin's Tale* as an expression of its narrator's psychology or values. While acknowledging that some of the poem's themes are anticipated in the *General Prologue* portrait and the Franklin's own Prologue, they also observe that the voice narrating the poem changes in accordance with the subject at hand and cannot be reduced to a set of stable personality traits that we ascribe to the Franklin (**874, 1014, 1174, 1248, 1291, 1339, 1437**).

CHARACTERIZATION

Although commentators are almost unanimous in their praise of Chaucer's delineation of character in the tale (**835, 871, 954, 1248**), there has been nothing like a consensus about the motives, actions, and moral attributes of the poem's dramatis personae. Within the critical literature, each of the three male characters exists in versions so different as to seem irreconcilable. The clerk, viewed by some readers as an honorable, rational figure, charitable and selfless in the concluding episode (**929, 1122, 1164, 1199, 1246, 1465**), is for others deceptive, superficial, 'theologically suspect,' and sexually manipulative (**956, 1049, 1204, 1238, 1311, 1330, 1347**). The squire Aurelius has been labeled both 'the tale's villain' (**1175**) and 'the Franklin's real favorite' (**1257**). Seen through one set of interpretive lenses, Arveragus is honorable and generous (**942, 954, 1033, 1248**), 'extraordinarily wise and idealistic' (**767**), the embodiment of integrity and *trouthe* (**871, 942, 1033, 1118, 1124, 1199, 1339**). For critics who read the tale as questioning the values it appears to espouse, Arveragus's governing traits are moral blindness (**948, 967, 1036, 1061, 1343**), male egotism and tyranny (**1029, 1097, 1186, 1343, 1465**), reductive binary thinking (**1353**), preoccupation with his public image (**965**), and self-serving hypocrisy (**1205**).

Although she seems, by the end of the tale, to be excluded from its 'homoerotic economy' (**1309**), Dorigen has received more attention than any of the poem's male characters. However different their interpretive approaches, commentators agree that Dorigen is depicted with considerable psychological finesse: she is more complex and believable than her counterpart in *Il Filocolo* (**335, 834, 838, 1159, 1506**) and her conflicting emotions are effectively captured in the stylistic range and subtlety of her speech (**979, 1013, 1248**). Chaucer's skill in characterizing Dorigen has not, however, guaranteed universal approval of her actions and motivations. Although a small number of readers express unreserved admiration for her integrity, her selfless love for her husband, and her nobility of soul (**871**, **1161**, **1199**, **1200**, **1438**), commentators more frequently point to Dorigen's shortcomings – lack of patience, instability, imperfect self-knowledge, childishness, egocentricity – either in relation to her gender (**904**: 'she is only a daughter of Eve'; see also **976**, **1012**, **1014**, **1052**, **1402**, **1457**) or as part of a larger pattern of philosophical or religious meaning that subjects human failings to critical scrutiny (**926**, **949**, **956**, **958**, **965**, **967**, **978**, **1030**, **1036**, **1052**, **1395**). Such stringent judgments of Dorigen's limitations – many of them published in the 1960s and 1970s, the decades that produced the most severe evaluations of the Franklin himself – inevitably generated feminist counter-critiques. Dorigen, it is argued, must be understood as a product of the masculine imagination, a male fantasy that bears little relation to the lived experience of medieval women (**1072**, **1086**). Dorigen's much remarked-on passivity, for example, should be viewed less as a function of character than of situation. A woman in a man's world where homosocial rivalry underlies romantic courtship, Dorigen becomes the locus of male competition (**1107**, **1300**, **1337**, **1355**, **1366**, **1382**, **1386**, **1389**, **1495**) and, in the poem's final episodes, is reduced to an object of exchange (**1309**, **1311**, **1339**, **1355**, **1366**, **1370**, **1395**, **1418**, **1464**). In the introduction to his revised edition of *The Franklin's Tale*, A.C. Spearing observes that an interpretation of the tale as reflecting the patriarchal repression of female desire is unlikely to have been one that Chaucer consciously intended (**1339**, pp 59–61). In fact, most recent discussions focus less on the political implications of Dorigen's role than on the degree to which she exhibits agency within Chaucer's narrative. At one extreme of the interpretive spectrum, Dorigen is in control of her own story and free to contruct her identity (**1306**, **1343**); at the other, she is wholly subordinated to the tale's male characters (**1262**, **1311**, **1355**, **1375**, **1386**). Less polarized accounts of Dorigen's presence in the tale acknowledge the difficulty of arriving at a 'comprehensive judgment' of her behavior (**1339**), and depict her at the intersection of competing, even contradictory, discourses: at once passive in a male-dominated world and able to shape her own selfhood (**1314**, **1377**); 'silenced' yet available for 'counter-tales' generated by the reader (**1354**); both a fully realized subject and a narrative object ineligible for the reader's empathy (**1506**); deprived of physical agency but intellectually mobile (**1390**); and transformed by a shift of tone and genre in the poem's final scenes from a plausibly realistic figure to 'a participant in a story' (**1053**, **1179**).

ASTROLOGY AND MAGIC

Two essays by Tatlock (**810**, **812**) established the terms for much subsequent commentary on these linked subjects. Tatlock unpacks the details of the dense astrological passages and argues for a double perspective on astrology and magic; the Franklin at once provides a fully imagined account of the clerk's magical practices that integrates them into the poem's pre-Christian setting and, as an orthodox contemporary believer, puts space between himself and these pagan rituals. While recognizing that the Franklin is simultaneously drawn to and made uneasy by astrological magic, critics tend to align themselves with one of these two positions. For those who embrace the possibilities of the tale's magic, the clerk is a 'creator-poet' (**942**, **1011**) who embodies aspects of both the Franklin (**1236**, **1444**) and of Chaucer (**372**, **1339**), and who, by means of 'genuine astrological magic' (**1238**) based on calculations that, as reported by the Franklin, are precise and comprehensible (**1131**, **1238**), produces 'saving illusions' that have the capacity to edify (**1113**, **1444**). More numerous are those critics who are either wary of magic's power to entrap both the tale's characters and its audience (**1255**) or who echo outright the Franklin's condemnation of astrological magic as 'swich folye / As in oure dayes is nat worth a flye' (lines 1130–1). For these readers, the clerk's magic is the most palpable manifestation of the dangerous *illusioun* that for a time threatens to obscure the tale's central value of *trouthe* (**911**, **956**, **963**, **1079**, **1114**, **1136**, **1147**, **1189**, **1229**, **1230**, **1312**, **1330**, **1444**, **1489**). Represented as bogus science manipulated by the clerk for deceptive ends (**1147**), it may be no more than a version of the mechanical stage tricks performed by *tregetoures* – the professional conjurers recalled by Aurelius's brother (**901**, **1076**, **1169**, **1320**) – or, in its astrological guise, merely computational hocus-pocus designed to mystify the clerk's prediction of a high tide that will temporarily hide the coastal rocks (**803**, **956**, **1076**, **1147**, **1421**). Less polemical approaches to the tale's treatment of magic point to its association with rhetorical artifice (**957**, **1088**, **1177**, **1213**), to the deflation of its traditional aura of wonder by its representation as a 'scientific commodity' (**1432**, **1433**), and to the juxtaposition of the clerk's illusionistic art with the 'truth-telling potential' of Chaucer's own poetic fiction (**1285**). Particularly compelling, finally, is the claim that the tale is ultimately concerned not with whether the clerk's magic produces its advertised effects but rather with the characters' response to its announced results (**1048**, **1297**, **1482**), and the related insight that the tale's real magic lies in human actions and emotions: patience and pity, the transformative power of Arveragus's assertion of *trouthe*, and the squire Aurelius's change of heart (**1033**, **1133**, **1177**).

THE TALE'S SETTING

Among the most striking features of the tale is its location in Brittany – in particular the chain of black rocks along the coast. Initially enmeshed in debates about the poem's Celtic origins (see above, p 21), the Breton setting received its first extended examination in Tatlock's 1914 monograph (**812**; see also **810**); the tale's geography and its pre-Christian context, Tatlock argued, allowed Chaucer to offer a detailed representation of astrology and magic even as he distanced himself from these pagan practices in time and space. In the decades following Tatlock's essay, interest in the poem's physical scene shifted from its possible relation to real topographic features to its symbolic overtones. The rocks have been said to embody Dorigen's loyalty to Arveragus (**830, 883**); the obstacles that prevent worldly happiness (**876, 911, 1360**); physical materiality (**880, 967, 1170**); the perverseness of Dorigen's and Arveragus's marriage (**929**); the problem of evil (**1204**); masculine fantasies about female sexuality (**911, 1300**); Dorigen's sexual repression (**1019**); a flaw in the divinely ordered course of nature (**1264, 1339, 1463, 1489**); the 'old simple world of nature' (**1471**); and personal obsession and illusion (**957, 1312**). Several critics have entered caveats about symbolic readings of the rocks' possible connotations: Owen (**883, 1064**), Spearing (**955**), and Brunetti (**1228**) observe that the rocks' significance is not static, but rather changes under the pressure of human actions, while Kolve argues that, although the rocks are made to signify something by the despairing Dorigen, 'they must be seen as no more than rocks' (**1285**; see also **929r**). The May garden in which Dorigen makes her promise to Aurelius, on the other hand, carries with it well-established meanings and shows Chaucer shaping conventional tropes – in this case, those of Eden and the courtly paradise of love – to suit his dramatic and thematic needs (**913, 942, 949, 950, 955, 957, 963, 994, 1085, 1102, 1017, 1150, 1188, 1285, 1312, 1375, 1463**).

SIX PASSAGES

A number of passages in *The Franklin's Tale* have regularly attracted commentary; the changing currents of the poem's reception could be succinctly mapped by using these moments as epitomes of the larger issues that have occupied students of the tale. Such a map would include the following passages, among others:

(1) The Franklin's Prologue (lines 709–28). In the first seven lines of his Prologue, the Franklin offers a snapshot of the Breton lay and announces that he will retell one such lay as his contribution to the Canterbury competition. The thirteen remaining lines are his apology in advance for his lack of rhetorical sophistication. Commentary on this passage has focused on the seeming contradiction between the Franklin's disclaimer and the presence in the poem of the very 'colours of rethoryk' he has just disavowed. Some treat the inconsistency as another black mark in the Franklin's book (**958, 1081, 1079**). Most readers, however, see it as a conscious irony that allows

the Franklin at once to deprecate and parade his verbal skill (**825, 844, 860, 919, 933, 946, 955, 1020, 1046, 1339**). The Franklin's remarks have also been viewed as a more mature version of the Squire's apologies for his linguistic ineptness (**946**) and as a reflection on both the dangers and the truth-telling potential of rhetorical figuration (**1046, 1135**).

(2) Dorigen and Arveragus's marriage contract (lines 738–98). The apparent establishment of domestic equality and the forswearing of *maistrye* recorded in this passage was for Kittredge (**805, 815**) a harmonious and definitive conclusion to the debate about wedlock carried on in the preceding Marriage Group tales. Some critics echo Kittredge's view; some build on it, suggesting, for example, that the domestic arrangement provides a model for social relations more generally (see above, p 23). Others, while acknowledging the passage's centrality, supplement or propose alternatives to Kittredge's terms, drawing on medieval doctrines of friendship (**1004, 1160, 1295, 1305, 1491**) or placing patience and *suffraunce* rather than equality at the center of the depiction of power relations (**1133, 1450**). The inclusion of these discourses, it has been argued, complicates and compromises the marriage agreement without entirely invalidating it (**1305, 1344, 1423**). To many commentators, however, the passage has seemed contradictory, evasive, incoherent, or simply irrelevant (**1075, 1097, 1136, 1186, 1286, 1325, 1355, 1423**). Counterarguments to Kittredge's untroubled reading of the marriage contract include its failure to reconcile the claims of Christian wedlock and courtly love (**937, 963, 1065, 1125, 1286, 1355**); the undercutting of the passage's depiction of mutuality by the subsequent events of the tale, in particular Arveragus's command that Dorigen fulfill her promise to Aurelius (**1057, 1068, 1100, 1136, 1160, 1186, 1198, 1245, 1318, 1337, 1339, 1382, 1485**); and (for Robertson and others), the presence of a muddled Epicureanism at odds with the medieval belief in hierarchy (**918, 929, 948, 1030, 1109**). As with several other passages examined here, the differences between critical evaluations of the marriage agreement are stark; what for one reader is a delicately calibrated 'mutual surrender of *maistrye*' (**1450**) is for another no more than 'a fine example of double-talk' (**872**).

(3) Dorigen's two monologues. Dorigen's lament over the coastal rocks (lines 865–93) has been read from a variety of perspectives: as a revelation of character (**900, 904, 949, 957, 1036, 1065, 1161, 1230, 1313, 1322, 1332, 1339, 1353**); as the speech of a shortsighted pagan (**949**); as the speech of an enlightened pagan (**1002, 1199**); as an exploration of fantasy (**957, 1209, 1210, 1312**); as a commentary on the role of providence (**1197, 1339**); as an investigation of questions of moral freedom (**1230**); as an examination of the soliloquy form (**1374**); as an unanswered question (**932, 1128**) or a thematic loose end (**955, 1122**); as a failed consolation (**1138**); and as evidence of the Franklin's superficiality (**1079, 1395**). The longer of the two soliloquies – the

complaint against Fortune (lines 1355–1456), with its extended catalogue of women who preferred death to dishonor – is the tale's most commented-upon interpretive crux. Manly's view of the passage as a failed flight of rhetoric (**826**) has been echoed by later critics, although there is no agreement about whether the misstep is Chaucer's (as Manly believed), the Franklin's, or Dorigen's (**833, 839, 843, 847, 934, 953, 958, 1036, 1065, 1127, 1161, 1228, 1358**). Others have defended the passage as engaged with serious moral issues (**942, 1062, 1110, 1200, 1230**). Its rhetorical excesses have been presented as dramatically and structurally functional, marking a shift in the tale's tonal register from tragic to tragicomic or comic (**863, 986, 1077, 1088, 1179, 1198, 1347**) or from realism to conventionalism (**1053, 1179, 1465**); as a contrast to the Franklin's concern for his audience in the tale's concluding scenes (**957**); as a deliberate suspension of the poem's action (**1230, 1339**); as a dramatic or verbal dead end (**918, 1235, 1350**); and as a marker to elaborate on Dorigen's dilemma (**1023**). Although the speech has been read in the light of the Franklin's character (**872, 955, 1395**), most critics focus on Dorigen's voicing of the monologue and take a variety of positions on her agency as a speaking subject. The lines have been understood as evidence of Dorigen's imperfect understanding of (or of her failure to match) the examples she cites (**1089, 1149, 1339, 1406**); of her struggle among multiple courses of action (**912**); of her isolation (**1106**); of her feminine sensibility (**1012**); of her moral integrity (**1200**); of her ability to make independent decisions (**1306**); of her witty (or evasive) use of the speech to defer a decision (**1077, 1164, 1183, 1330, 1339, 1368, 1371**); and of her double role as passive subject and self-shaper (**1314, 1330**). Finally, the lengthy list of virtuous women that constitutes the bulk of Dorigen's speech – a favorite topic for students of Chaucer's use of his sources (see above, p 22) – has also received a number of gender-inflected readings, several of which find in Dorigen's seemingly rote recital a dramatically rendered critique of patristic standards of female virtue (**994, 1149, 1281, 1310, 1343, 1347**).

(4) The much-admired seasonal vignette (lines 1244–55), proof of Chaucer's familiarity with calendar iconography (**841, 880, 902**), has seemed to many readers a microcosm of the poem's central concerns: as a foreshadowing of the movement from romance (or illusion) to reality (**876, 1017, 1136**); as an emblem of the fulfillment of Old Testament *trouthe* by New Testament *fredom* (**900, 1339, 1416**) or of the primacy of civilized values over natural forces (**1179**); as the center of 'the seasonal cycle of romance' (**1248**); as a contrast to the lack of purpose in the protagonists' lives (**1258**); as an image of the Franklin's balanced sense of life's rhythms (**957, 969**) or, conversely, of his Epicureanism (**1140**).

(5) 'Trouthe is the hyeste thyng that man may kepe' (line 1479). A student seeking a single line that could serve as a litmus test for a critic's in-

terpretation of *The Franklin's Tale* might well choose Arveragus's invocation of *trouthe,* embedded in his response to his wife's confession of her promise to Aurelius. Few of *The Canterbury Tales* turn as completely as does the Franklin's on a set of key words and concepts; among these (the list includes *fredom, gentilesse, pacience,* and *pitee*), *trouthe* has received the most attention – as a thematic element, as a plot device, and as a lexical item. All three of these categories are relevant to our interpretation of Arveragus's assertion: partly because of its epigrammatic concision, his proposition serves as the culminating instance of the numerous occurrences in the tale of *trouthe, trewe,* and *trewely;* it juxtaposes the *trouthe* of Dorigen's pledge to Aurelius (line 998) with her earlier vow of *trouthe* to Arveragus (lines 758–9) and underlies Arveragus's command that Dorigen must fulfill her promise to the squire; and it asks us to sort out the several meanings that have attached themselves to the word in the course of the tale.

For one group of critics, Arveragus's statement demonstrates his mature wisdom and expresses his 'moral solidarity' (**1200**) with Dorigen; invoking a knightly standard of loyalty to one's pledged word, he honors her integrity and free will (**1033, 1118, 1124, 1156, 1221, 1234, 1318, 1359, 1450**). In addition, Arveragus's declaration marks the moment at which the tale begins to right itself, signaling a shift away from the dominance of *illusioun* (*trouthe*'s opposite) toward the restoration of *fredom* and genuine *gentilesse* (**900, 911, 983, 989, 994, 1136, 1229, 1339, 1359, 1451a**). As used here, *trouthe* refers to fidelity to a promise, to integrity more broadly, and to the reality of things as they are – the last sense present at the edges of Arveragus's maxim in the line's short form, 'trouthe is the hyeste thing' (**880, 942, 983, 994, 1005, 1018, 1103, 1118, 1156, 1200, 1278, 1290, 1318, 1364, 1372**).

Other scholars take a more disenchanted view of Arveragus's pronouncement, registering from a variety of perspectives and with varying degrees of force their doubts about an idealized reading. On the mild end of the spectrum, some critics observe that the multiple versions of *trouthe* present in the key phrase are contradictory and remain unresolved (**1212, 1289, 1291, 1475, 1483**), with the result, according to Spearing, that we are left with 'uncertainty' (not a bad thing, in Spearing's opinion) rather than 'unequivocal doctrine' (**1339**, p 31). Arveragus's assertion has also been understood as expressing a limited concept of *trouthe* that privileges chivalric values that are of little use to the tale's sole female protagonist at this moment of intense personal distress (**899, 1149, 1155, 1160, 1161, 1309, 1314, 1337, 1366, 1375, 1455**). Other readings of Arveragus's response to Dorigen's plight interpret his words as a way of salvaging his public reputation (**1079**) or as a reflection of the Franklin's own social ambitions (**1042**) and (in the suggestion that Arveragus treats Dorigen's promise as a kind of business contract) his mercantile values (**1149, 1228, 1301**). Those commentators least inclined to endorse Arveragus's declaration and actions in this scene argue that his application of an 'inhuman, abstract principle' (**1100**) tied to 'the letter of the law' (**1060, 1233**), one that requires Dorigen to uphold a 'meaningless' *trouthe* (**1061, 1311**), is tyrannical, deceitful, immoral, and stupid (**1086, 1100, 1315**). Such extreme judgments arise in part from a belief that *trouthe* in the poem is absolute and unchanging, a product of unreflexive aristocratic thinking imposed on Dorigen (**1155, 1160, 1488**). An alternative view, which most readers will find more congenial, is the one put forward by Paul Strohm (**1256**), Lee Patterson (**1290**), and (with qualifications) by A.C. Spearing (**1339**, pp 39–42): that the tale enacts a transformation of *trouthe* from a public, chivalric, 'quasi-feudal' virtue to one grounded in personal integrity and in qualities available to both sexes and to all levels of society.

(6) 'Which was the mooste fre, as thynketh yow?' (line 1622). The Franklin's concluding *demande* has amply fulfilled its implicit purpose of stimulating debate. Critics have cast votes for a particular character (**929, 1124, 1164, 1257, 1305, 1306, 1345; 1500**); argued that no one is truly *fre* (**948, 963, 1027, 1111, 1350, 1456**); that the question is a kind of joke (**878, 899, 963, 1024, 1111, 1418**); that it is not meant to produce a definitive answer (**950, 1136, 1144, 1291, 1292, 1304, 1437**); that it is intended to resolve questions about marriage and *gentilesse* (**1164**); that it pointedly omits Dorigen (**1262, 1344, 1354, 1375, 1400, 1448**); that it suggests Dorigen as the 'mooste fre' (**1305, 1306**); that *fre* contains its modern sense as well as implying generosity (**355, 367**); that it sends a mixed message about material possession (**1479**); that it echoes the literary debates of clerks and knights (**1028**); that Chaucer envisioned a discussion of the Franklin's question in an unwritten endlink (**816**); and that it is a social act, moving the poem's focus from private to public, from its characters to its listeners and readers (**957, 1272**). If we agree with Anne Middleton that, for the Franklin, 'stories … are social parables whose power lies in the quality of talk they create' (**1108**), the multiple and often conflicting responses to his final question may stand as a paradigm for the century's worth of 'talk' about the tale summarized in the pages that follow.

ꙮ *The Squire's Tale* and *The Franklin's Tale*: Editions and Modernizations

Nine nineteenth-century editions are followed by a selective listing of twentieth- and twenty-first-century editions and modernizations. Earlier editions, beginning with that of Caxton (ca 1478), are described by Hammond (**382**), pp 114–49, 202–19. Hammond also lists selections from and modernizations and translations of *SqT* and *FranT* published before 1900 (pp 311–12, 314). (Page numbers for *SqT* include *Sq–FranL*.)

1 *A Six-Text Print of Chaucer's Canterbury Tales. Group F. Fragment VII. The Squire's Head-Link and Tale. The Squire–Franklin Link. The Franklin's Tale.* Ed. Frederick J. Furnivall. Chaucer Society, First Series, 31. London: Trübner, 1868. Repr. New York: Johnson, 1967. [*Six-Text Edition.*] *SqT*: pp 478–99; *FranT*: pp 500–25.
The text is printed in parallel columns as it appears in the following MSS: El, Hg, Cambridge Gg.4.27, Corpus, Petworth, and Lansdowne. The tales are given in the following order: I (A) II VII (B^1+ B^2) VI (C) III (D) IV (E) V (F) VIII (G) IX (H) X (I). See also **4**, **6**, **9**, **10**, **16**, **47**, **55**, **65**, **99**, **102**, **113**, **160**.

2 *Chaucer: The Prioresses Tale, Sire Thopas, The Monkes Tale, The Clerkes Tale, The Squieres Tale from The Canterbury Tales.* Ed. Walter W. Skeat. Oxford: Clarendon, 1874. Nine rev. eds through 1906. *SqT*: pp 103–27.
The text, explanatory notes, and introductory remarks form the basis for Skeat's treatment of *SqT* in the *Oxford Chaucer* (**4**). This edition also includes an extended metrical analysis of *SqT* and a full glossary with line numbers.

3 *Squieres Tale.* London: Chambers, 1882. Repr. New York: Maynard, Merrill, [1885].
A school edition. Introductory material on Chaucer's life, grammar, and versification. The text of *SqT* is based on El, with explanatory notes and a glossary.

4 *The Complete Works of Geoffrey Chaucer, Edited from Numerous Manuscripts.* Ed. Walter W. Skeat. 6 vols with a supplement, *Chaucerian and Other Pieces* (vol. 7). London: Oxford UP, 1894–7. 2nd ed. 1899–1900. [*The Oxford Chaucer.*] *SqT*: text, 4:461–81; explanatory notes, 5:370–87; *FranT*: text, 4:482–508; explanatory notes, 5:387–400.

Skeat's text of the *CT* is based on El, collated with Harley 7334 and the five MSS that, along with El, had been published by the Chaucer Society as the *Six-Text* print of the *CT* (**1**). Selected variants are recorded below the text. The copious explanatory notes have influenced many later editors; for Skeat's comments on individual passages, see **374**, **795**. In the section on *SqT* in his general discussion of *CT*'s sources (3:462–79), Skeat quotes from Thomas Warton on the analogues of the magic gifts, argues that the portrait of Cambyuskan is modeled in part on Marco Polo's account of Kublai Khan and his court, suggests that the completed tale would have shown the falcon (evidently a human being in animal shape) restored to her original form by the magic ring, notes Spenser's and John Lane's continuations (the latter is 'bad almost beyond belief,' p 478), and summarizes parts of Clouston's study of the tale's magical elements (**129**). *FranT* is adapted from a Breton lay, not from the Italian. The tale's ultimate source is Eastern. Skeat reproduces the 'Story of Madanasena' from the *Vetala Panchavinsati*, summarizes Clouston on the story's analogues, and summarizes *Dec* 10.5 (3:480–5). Vol. 6 contains essays on Chaucer's pronunciation, grammar, and versification, a glossary of over three hundred pages, an index of proper names, and a list of authors and biblical passages cited by Chaucer. For Skeat's earlier edition of *SqT*, see **2**. For references to or editions based on Skeat, see **5**, **7**, **8**, **16**, **19**, **22**, **23**, **28**, **30**, **32**, **32r**, **37**, **39**, **50**, **51**, **52**, **54**, **58**, **59**, **65**, **69**, **73**, **77**, **79**, **85**, **111**, **131**, **144**, **160**, **341**, **378**, **387**, **464**, **885**, **888**. For a detailed commentary on Skeat's edition, see **590**.

5 *The Works of Geoffrey Chaucer*. Ed. F.S. Ellis. Illustrations by Edward Burne-Jones. Printed by William Morris. Engraved by W.H. Hooper. Hammersmith, UK: Kelmscott, 1896. [*The Kelmscott Chaucer*.] *SqT*: pp 151–9; *FranT*: pp 160–70.

Ellis's text is based on Skeat (**4**), with additional corrections approved by Skeat. The eighty-seven illustrations by Burne-Jones include two for *SqT* (the steed of brass appears at Cambyuskan's feast; Canacee and the falcon) and six for *FranT* (Dorigen views the black rocks; Dorigen and her companions; the clerk produces magical illusions for Aurelius; Aurelius tells Dorigen that the rocks have disappeared; Dorigen on her knees before Arveragus; the clerk forgives Aurelius his debt). For facsimile editions, see **73**, **95**.

6 *The Works of Geoffrey Chaucer*. Ed. Alfred W. Pollard, H. Frank Heath, Mark H. Liddell, and William S. McCormick. London: Macmillan, 1898; repr. with corrections 1899/1928. Numerous reprs, including Freeport, NY: Books for Libraries, 1972. [*The Globe Chaucer*.] *SqT*: pp 219–27; *FranT*: pp 228–39.

The text of the *CT* (prepared by Pollard) is based on El, emended by collation with the other *Six-Text* MSS (**1**) and the Chaucer Society's edition of Harley 7334. Explanatory and textual notes appear at the bottom of the page. Pollard notes that the sources of *SqT*, while clearly Eastern, have eluded detection; attempts to prove direct indebtedness to Marco Polo's *Travels* (see **4**) are not convincing. Chaucer's failure to complete the tale may be due to 'the lack of a plot ready furnished to him' (xxxi). For Pollard's separate edition of *SqT*, see **9**. See also **14, 15, 32r, 48, 75, 888.**

7 *The Squieres Tale.* Ed. E. Winckler. Madras: Madras Central Book Depot, 1899. A school edition. An introduction treats Chaucer's life, works, language, *SqT*'s Oriental analogues, and its relation to Marco Polo's *Travels*. The text, based on Skeat (**4**), includes a modern English translation at the bottom of the page and is followed by explanatory notes and appendices on Chaucer's grammar, meter, and spelling, questions for students, and a glossary.

8 *The Squires Tale.* Ed. W.J. Goodrich. Madras: Srinivasa, Varadachari, 1899.
The text of this school edition is based on Skeat (**4**), with explanatory notes at the bottom of the page. Introductory discussions of Chaucer's life, writings, and language, *SqT* as a fragment, its Oriental analogues, Marco Polo on Kublai Khan, and Spenser's continuation; appendices on Chaucer's language and versification, and a glossary.

9 *The Squire's Tale.* Ed. Alfred W. Pollard. London: Macmillan, 1899. Repr. New York: St Martin's, 1959.
The text is based on El, emended by collation with the other MSS in the *Six-Text* edition (**1**) and the Chaucer Society's edition of Harley 7334; departures from El are somewhat more frequent than in the *Globe Chaucer* (**6**). The introduction treats *SqT*'s historical setting, the question of its indebtedness to Marco Polo's *Travels* (unlikely, in Pollard's view), analogues to the magic gifts, and Spenser's and John Lane's continuations, and speculates on how Chaucer might have developed the plot. The edition includes a discussion of Chaucer's astrology, detailed explanatory notes, illustrations of Chaucer's grammar, and a full glossary.

10 *The Complete Works of Geoffrey Chaucer.* With an Introduction by Thomas R. Lounsbury. New York: Crowell, 1900. *SqT*: pp 683–92; *FranT*: pp 692–705.
Comments on Chaucer's life, work, and language introduce the text (the basis of which is not stated), printed in double columns without notes; a full glossary with line references concludes the volume. The text of *CT* follows the Chaucer Society order (**1**). Crowell also published this edition in two volumes (not seen). See **17**.

11 *The Story of the Canterbury Pilgrims. Retold from Chaucer and Others.* Trans. F.J. Harvey Darton. Illustrations by M.L. Kirk. Philadelphia: Lippincott, 1900. Repr. New York: Stokes, 1914. *SqT*: pp 164–88; *FranT*: 188–200.
A free prose modernization. 'The Story of Cambuscan Bold' is divided into Part 1 ('The Magic Gifts and the False Tercelet'), which translates *SqT*; Part 2 ('The Brethren Three'), adapted from Spenser's continuation; and Part 3 ('Fierce Wars and Faithful Loves'), 'taken from an inferior writer of the eighteenth century named Stirling ... to provide some sort of end for the tale, which both Chaucer and Spenser left unfinished' (p 179). In addition

to a full-page portrait of the Squire (on horseback, playing a flute), three episodes are illustrated in the 1900 edition: the stranger knight with sword, mirror, and horse; crowds pressing forward to see the horse of brass; Canacee holding out the lap of her skirt to catch the bleeding falcon. The 1914 edition exists both without illustrations and with a color plate of Canacee and the falcon. 'Epicurus' own Son,' a conflation of *FranP* and the *GP* portrait of the Franklin, is followed by 'The Rocks Removed,' which condenses the Franklin's disquisition on *maistrye* and patience, Aurelius's prayer to Apollo, the clerk's astrology, and Dorigen's Complaint.

12 *Chaucer's Canterbury Tales*. The Bibelots. Ed. J. Potter Briscoe. London: Gay and Bird, 1901. *SqT*: pp 67–91; *FranT*: pp 92–105.
Includes 'The Squire's Tale, or, The Adventures of the Tartar King and His Family, A Fragment, Modernised by Leigh Hunt' and a verse modernization by R.H. Horne of selections from *FranT*.

13 *The Cambridge MS. Dd.4.24 of Chaucer's Canterbury Tales. Completed by the Egerton MS. 2726 (The Haistwell MS)*. Parts I and II. Ed. Frederick J. Furnivall. 2 vols. Chaucer Society, First Series, 95, 96. London: Kegan Paul, Trench, Trübner, 1902. Repr. New York: Johnson, 1967. *SqT*: 1:311–32; *FranT*: 1:333–58.
The Cambridge MS has lost the leaves containing lines 673–753 and 1455–73; the missing lines are supplied from Egerton. Vol. 2 reproduces woodcuts of the pilgrims based on the Ellesmere miniatures and on the six pilgrim portraits in Cambridge Gg.4.27, 'being all that were not cut out of the MS. by some scoundrel' (2: Appendix 3, n.p.).

14 *Chaucer's Canterbury Tales. Reprinted from the Globe Edition*. Ed. Alfred W. Pollard. London: Macmillan, 1902. *SqT*: pp 219–28; *FranT*: pp 228–39.
The *Globe* text of *CT* (**6**), reprinted without introduction or glossary.

15 *English Tales in Verse*. Ed. C.H. Herford. Warwick Library. London: Blackie, 1902. *SqT*: pp 1–21.
SqT, PrT, PardT, and *NPT* are reprinted from the *Globe Chaucer* (**6**) 'with slight occasional divergences' (v). *SqT* is 'in romantic beauty the finest of all' (xviii).

16 *The Select Chaucer*. Ed. J. Logie Robertson. Edinburgh: Blackwood, 1902. *SqT*: pp 191–200; *FranT*: pp 201–2.
Comments on Chaucer's life and times, language, and meter introduce selections from *CT*; the text is based on El and Harley 7334, collated with the *Six-Text* (**1**) and Skeat (**4**). *SqT* is represented by approximately two-thirds of Part 1. *FranT* is represented by the description of winter (lines 1245–55). The volume includes brief explanatory notes and a glossary.

17 *The Canterbury Tales by Geoffrey Chaucer*. Introduction by Thomas R. Lounsbury. New York: Crowell, [1903]. *SqT*: pp 219–28; *FranT*: pp 228–41.
This school edition reprints the introduction, text, and glossary of **10**.

18 *Chaucer: The Canterbury Tales, The Prologue and the Squire's Tale*. Ed. A.J. Wyatt. University Tutorial Series. London: Clive, 1903/1960. *SqT*: pp 113–33.
A school edition. An introduction treats Chaucer's life, works, language and meter, *CT*, *GP*, and *SqT* (Oriental and French analogues, the possible influence of Marco Polo's *Travels*, the unrevised state of Part 2, and later continuations of the tale). The text (based on El) is followed by explanatory notes and a glossary.

19 *The Poetical Works of Geoffrey Chaucer, from the Text of Professor Skeat*. 3 vols. The World's Classics, 42, 56, and 76. London: Richards (vols 1 and 2); London: Oxford UP (vol. 3), 1903. Vol. 3: *SqT*: pp 418–36; *FranT*: pp 437–60.
The text of the *Oxford Chaucer* (**4**) is followed by a note on language and meter and a glossary.

20 *Stories from Chaucer: The Canterbury Tales*. Trans. William T. Stead. Illustrations by Edith Ewen. London: Books for the Bairns, [1903]; Philadelphia: Penn, 1908; London: Benn, 1910; Boston: Palmer, 1911. *SqT*, pp 30–5; *FranT*, pp 36–43.
A prose modernization for children. Most of the descriptive passages, narrative interpolations, and rhetorical periphrases are omitted. Four woodcuts for *SqT*: the stranger knight on horseback, holding a mirror; Canacee beneath the falcon's tree; the falcon and the tercelet; Canacee holding the falcon. Four woodcuts for *FranT*: Aurelius declaring his love to Dorigen; Dorigen with her friends at the seaside; the magician and his wand; Dorigen weeping.

21 *The Canterbury Tales of Geoffrey Chaucer*. Trans. Percy MacKaye. Illustrations by Walter Appleton Clark. New York: Fox, Duffield, 1904. Repr. as *The Canterbury Tales of Geoffrey Chaucer: A Modern Rendering into Prose of the Prologue and Nine Tales*. New York: Avenel, 1987. *SqT*: 173–87; *FranT*: pp 188–209.
This edition of **22** omits *PrT*.

22 *The Canterbury Tales of Geoffrey Chaucer. A Modern Rendering into Prose of the Prologue and Ten Tales*. Trans. Percy MacKaye. Illustrations by Walter Appleton Clark. New York: Fox, Duffield, 1904. Repr. London: Richards, 1907; [Whitefish, MT]: Kessinger, 2005. *SqT*: pp 173–87; *FranT*: pp 188–209.
A prose translation of *GP*, *KnT*, *PrT*, *NPT*, *PhyT*, *PardT*, *WBT*, *ClT*, *SqT*, *FranT*, and *CYT*, based on Skeat (**4**). 'The method followed has been to present, so far as possible, Chaucer's *ipsissima verba*' (viii). A color plate for *SqT* depicts the knight's arrival on the steed of brass. See **21**.

23 *The Man of Law's Tale, The Nun's Priest's Tale, The Squire's Tale, by Geoffrey Chaucer, done into modern English*. Trans. Walter W. Skeat. The King's Classics. London: De la More, 1904. *SqT*: pp 79–110.
A modernization, in rhymed couplets; omits the 2 lines of *pars tercia*. Introductory remarks on *SqT* as a fragment, its magical elements, and its relation to Marco Polo's *Travels*, adapted from Skeat (**4**), and brief explanatory notes.

24 *Pilgrims' Tales from "Tales of the Canterbury Pilgrims."* Trans. F.J. Harvey Darton. Illustrations by Hugh Thomson. London: Wells Gardner, Darton, [1904]. Repr. New York: Dodge, [1908]. *FranT*: pp 79–96.
See **11**. Includes a color plate of squires and ladies dancing in a garden.

25 *Tales of the Canterbury Pilgrims. Retold from Chaucer and Others*. Trans. F.J. Harvey Darton. Introduction by Frederick J. Furnivall. Illustrations by Hugh Thomson. London: Wells Gardner, Darton; New York: Stokes, 1904. *SqT*: pp 200–30; *FranT*: pp 230–43.
Reprints **11**, including its illustrations. Includes an image of the Franklin as 'Epicurus' own Son,' seated at a table awaiting his meal, and a black-and-white version of the color plate in **24**.

26 *The Works of Geoffrey Chaucer and Others, Being a Reproduction in Facsimile of the First Collected Edition 1532, From the Copy in the British Museum*. Introduction by Walter W. Skeat. London: Oxford UP, 1904. *SqT*: pp 76–84; *FranT*: pp 139–49.
The introduction to this facsimile of William Thynne's black-letter edition surveys earlier editions of Chaucer's works, the contents and foliation of 1532 and the contents of the 1542, ca 1550, and 1561 editions, Sir Brian Tuke's preface, Thynne's text, the arrangement of *CT*, the woodcuts (all but those of the Squire and the Knight are from Caxton's second edition), and other Chaucerian and spurious works in the volume. For a later facsimile, see **91**.

27 *The Squieres Tale*. Ed. Arthur D. Innes. London: Blackie, 1905.
A school edition. A brief introduction treats Chaucer's life and language, *SqT* as a fragment, its Oriental background, and Spenser's continuation. The text (the basis of which is not stated) is followed by explanatory notes.

27a *Stories from Chaucer told to the Children*. Trans. Janet Harvey Kelman. Illustrations by W. Heath Robinson. New York: Dutton; London: Nelson, [1905]. *FranT*: pp 1–25.
Free prose retellings of *FranT*, *KnT*, and *MLT*, renamed after their central female characters (e.g., 'Dorigen: The Story by a Man of Land'). Dorigen's vow to love Aurelius becomes a promise to give him a jewel that Arveragus had given her on their wedding day. Two color plates: a pre-Raphaelite Dorigen, in a wimple and long cape, gazing out to sea; the magician, surrounded by mists, commanding the rocks to disappear.

28 *English Poetry, 1170–1892*. Ed. John Matthews Manly. Boston: Ginn, 1907. *SqT*: pp 38–45.
GP and *SqT* are Manly's selections from *CT*. The text, apparently based on Skeat (**4**), is printed with glosses at the foot of the page.

29 *Stories from Chaucer. Retold from the Canterbury Tales*. Trans. J. Walker McSpadden. Illustrations by Victor Prout. London: Harrap, 1907/1932; New York: Crowell, 1907. *FranT*: pp 179–96/pp 185–200.
A free prose retelling of *FranT* for children (Dorigen's Complaint and the as-

trological material are omitted) with interpolated passages in verse. A 1908 reprint includes two illustrations: Aurelius and his brother; Dorigen (indoors, seated on a bench) contemplating suicide. The revised edition omits the verse passages and includes only the first of the illustrations that appear in the 1908 reprint.

30 *Chaucer's Canterbury Tales for the Modern Reader*. Ed. Arthur Burrell. Everyman's Library. London: Dent; New York: Dutton, 1908. *SqT*: pp 366–82; *FranT*: pp 383–405.
Prints all of the *CT* except the *CkPT*. *GP, SqT, FranT*, and fourteen other tales are presented in spelling 'modernised just enough to leave its quaintness and take away some of its difficulty' (viii). Seven others (*MilT, RvT, ShT, Thop, FrT, SumT, MerT*), 'so broad, so plain-spoken, that no amount of editing or alteration will make them suitable for the twentieth century' (vii–viii), are printed in ME. The basis of the text is not stated, but Skeat's edition (**4**) is mentioned. For the later Everyman's Library edition, see **72**.

31 *The Chaucer Story Book*. Trans. Eva March Tappan. Boston: Houghton Mifflin, 1908. *SqT*: pp 161–81; *FranT*: pp 183–200.
A free prose rendering. *SqT* ('Cambuscan and the Brazen Horse') condenses the falcon's tale of betrayal into a single sentence and appends Spenser's conclusion. *FranT* ('The Promise of Dorigen') omits or condenses the Franklin's remarks on *maistrye* and patience, Dorigen's meditation on the rocks and her Complaint, and the astrological passages.

32 *The Clerkes Tale and The Squieres Tale*. Ed. Lilian Winstanley. Cambridge: Cambridge UP, 1908. *SqT*: pp 42–65.
The text (the source of which is not stated, but apparently based on Skeat [**4**]) is preceded by a general introduction to Chaucer's life, works, place in English literature, language, and meter, and more detailed introductions to *ClT* and *SqT*. The latter treats connections with *The Arabian Nights, Cleo* (Chaucer did not have the poem before him, but may have known it in outline form), Marco Polo (not a direct model, but perhaps recalled from memory), *Mandeville's Travels*, and *Anel* (Chaucer's use of this unfinished story in the Canacee–falcon episode suggests that he was combining elements according to an original plan rather than following a specific source); analogues to the magic gifts; and Spenser's continuation. The edition concludes with explanatory notes and a glossary.
• Review by J. Koch, *AB* 20 (1909), 166–9: Winstanley's introduction is useful, but her text – often arbitrary in its choice of manuscript readings – makes no advance over those of Skeat (**4**) or the *Globe* edition (**6**).

33 *The Story of the Canterbury Pilgrims Retold for Children*. Ed. Katherine Lee Bates. Chicago: Rand, McNally, 1909. *SqT*: pp 259–81.
Reprints Leigh Hunt's modernization, with a black-and-white reproduction of the Ellesmere portrait of the Squire.

34 *The Ellesmere Chaucer, Reproduced in Facsimile*. Preface by Alix Egerton. 2 vols. Manchester: Manchester UP, 1911. Repr. as *The Ellesmere Manuscript of Chaucer's Canterbury Tales: A Working Facsimile*. Introduction by Ralph Hanna III. Cambridge: Brewer, 1989.

The Ellesmere MS (El), owned by the Huntington Library, San Marino, California, has been used as the basis for many editions. The most elaborately decorated of the extant *CT* MSS, it contains celebrated miniatures of the individual pilgrims. In the 1911 facsimile, *SqT, FranT,* and the portrait of the Squire and Franklin appear in vol. 1 (folios unnumbered in the reproduction). For a later facsimile, see **118**.

35 *Stories from Chaucer*. Trans. Ada Hales. London: Methuen, 1911. *SqT*: pp 119–31.

A prose modernization for children. Omits several allusive or sententious passages and the two lines of *pars tercia*.

36 *Stories from Chaucer Re-told from The Canterbury Tales*. Trans. Margaret C. Macaulay. Cambridge: Cambridge UP, 1911/1926. *SqT*: pp 169–72.

A prose retelling for children. Most of the dialogue, the narrator's comments, and the descriptive passages are omitted or paraphrased.

37 *The Complete Poetical Works of Geoffrey Chaucer*. Trans. John Strong Perry Tatlock and Percy MacKaye. Illustrations by Warwick Goble. New York: Macmillan, 1912/1936. Repr. New York: Free Press, 1966. Repr. as *The Modern Reader's Chaucer: The Complete Poetical Works of Geoffrey Chaucer*, 1914. *SqT*: pp 238–51; *FranT*: pp 251–66.

A prose modernization, based on Skeat (**4**). *SqT* includes a color plate of Canacee and the falcon. *FranT* includes a color plate of 'Dorigen pledging Aurelius'; the garden is on a cliff, overlooking the rocks.

38 Underdown, Emily. *The Gateway to Chaucer. Stories told by Emily Underdown, from the "Canterbury Tales" of Geoffrey Chaucer*. Illustrations by Anne Anderson. London: Nelson, 1912. *FranT*: pp 225–52.

A free prose rendering of *FranT* that condenses or eliminates the tale's set speeches and the astrological passages. Two color plates depict Dorigen contemplating the rocks and Aurelius approaching Dorigen in the street.

39 *The Canterbury Tales of Geoffrey Chaucer. Illustrated after Drawings by W. Russell Flint*. 3 vols. London: Philip Warner for the Medici Society, 1913. Repr. in 1 vol., 1928. *SqT*: 3:1–20; *FranT*: 3:21–38.

The text of this artistic edition is based on Skeat (**4**). *SqT* includes a color plate of Canacee, accompanied by three female attendants, holding out her skirt to the falcon, perched on a bare tree. *FranT* includes three color plates: Dorigen, seated on a cliff, gazing down at the black rocks; Aurelius dancing in a walled garden; the magician at home, conjuring up Dorigen for the rapt Aurelius.

40 *The College Chaucer*. Ed. Henry Noble MacCracken. New Haven, CT: Yale

UP; London: Humphrey Milford, 1913. *SqT*: pp 318–38; *FranT*: pp 339–67.
A school edition. The text of *CT* is based on El, with textual notes at the foot of the page. *MilT, RvT, CkT, ShT, FrT, SumT, MerT, CYT, Mel,* and *ParsT* are omitted. An appendix includes notes on Chaucer's language and meter, life, writings, dates, sources, a discussion of the *CT* as a human comedy, and a full glossary.

41 Item cancelled.

42 *Geoffrey Chaucer's Canterbury Tales. Nach dem Ellesmere Manuscript mit Lesarten, Anmerkungen, und einem Glossar.* Ed. John Koch. Englische Textbibliothek 16. Heidelberg: Winter, 1915. *SqT*: pp 198–211; *FranT*: pp 211–18.
A school edition, based on El. A general introduction treats the MSS, development, sources, and previous editions of the *CT*. Textual and explanatory notes, Latin marginal glosses from selected MSS, and a full glossary.

43 *The Canterbury Pilgrims. Retold from Chaucer.* Trans. J. Walker McSpadden. Illustrations by M.L. Kirk. London: Harrap, [1917]. *SqT*: pp 163–70; *FranT*: pp 171–90.
This edition uses the same images as those in **11**, including the color plate of Canacee holding out the lap of her dress to the bleeding falcon. Includes a condensed prose modernization of *SqT* ('Cambuscan and the Brazen Horse'). For *FranT,* see **29**.

44 Bailey, Carolyn Sherwin. *Stories of the Great Adventures (Adapted from the Classics).* Illustrations by Clara M. Burd. Springfield, MA: Bradley, 1919. *FranT*: pp 154–63.
In this free prose adaptation for children ('The Rocks Removed'), Dorigen's vow to love Aurelius becomes a promise to give him a precious jewel that she had received on the day of her birth.

45 *The Canterbury Pilgrims; Being Chaucer's Canterbury Tales Retold for Children.* Trans. Mary Sturt and Ellen C. Oakden. New York: Dutton; London: Dent, 1923; [Whitefish, MT]: Kessinger, 2010. *SqT*: pp 121–9; *FranT*: pp 129–38.
Free prose modernizations of *SqT* and *FranT* as two of the Tales of the Fourth Day. Technical, allusive, and discursive passages are condensed or omitted. Reproduces the Ellesmere portraits of the Squire and the Franklin.

46 *The Approach to Chaucer.* Trans. Emily Underdown, R.H. Horne, Leigh Hunt, and Thomas Powell. London: Nelson, 1925. *SqT*: pp 74–90; *FranT*: pp 136–51.
Reprints Leigh Hunt's verse modernization of *SqT* and Underdown's translation of *FranT* (**38**).

47 *Canterbury Tales by Geoffrey Chaucer.* Ed. John Matthews Manly. New York: Holt; London: Harrap, 1928. *SqT*: text pp 361–79, notes pp 597–605; *FranT*: text pp 379–403, notes pp 605–11.
This incomplete and bowdlerized edition (*PhyT, MerT,* and *ManT* are omitted; *MilT, RvT, CkT, SumT, Mel, MkT,* and *ParsT* are represented by excerpts) is based on El, with minimal corrections from other MSS; 'it is in no sense

an attempt at a critical text' (vi). (For Manly's critical edition, see **61**.) Manly prints *CT* in the Ellesmere order in preference to the Chaucer Society order (**1**). The extensive introductory matter treats Chaucer's life and times, the general plan of *CT*, the pilgrims, earlier frame stories, the order of the tales (with useful information on the MSS), Chaucer's language and versification, and his astronomy and astrology. The text is supplemented by detailed explanatory and textual notes, a full glossary, and a general index. See **59**, **888**.

48 *The Works of Geoffrey Chaucer*. 8 vols. Shakespeare Head Press. Oxford: Blackwell, 1928–9. *SqT*: 3:85–108; *FranT*: 3:109–38.
The text of this artistic edition is that of the corrected *Globe* edition (**6**). Portraits of the pilgrims, modeled on the Ellesmere miniatures, appear with the *GP* descriptions and again at the heads of the individual tales. Edition limited to 375 copies, and eleven on vellum.

49 *A First Book About Chaucer*. Trans. Dorothy Martin. London: Routledge, 1929; New York: Dutton, 1930. *SqT*: pp 105–14.
A modernization for children, mostly in prose but with some passages in 'updated' ME verse. The narrator's interpolations and rhetorical excurses are condensed or omitted. Reproduces the Ellesmere miniature of the Squire.

50 *Geoffrey Chaucer: The Canterbury Tales*. Ed. Walter W. Skeat. Introduction by Louis Untermeyer. New York: Modern Library, 1929. *SqT*: pp 439–57; *FranT*: pp 458–82.
Skeat's text (**4**) is presented with a brief introduction, notes on Chaucer's language and meter, and a glossary.

51 *The Canterbury Tales by Geoffrey Chaucer. With Wood Engravings by Eric Gill*. 4 vols. Waltham Saint Lawrence, UK: Golden Cockerel Press, 1929–31. *SqT*: 4:1–24; *FranT*: 4:25–56.
The text of this artistic edition is based on Skeat (**4**). Includes elegantly stylized engravings of the stranger knight riding the magic horse, sword at his belt, mirror in his hand (*SqT*); Aurelius importuning Dorigen; and the magician, in a pointed cap, holding a quill pen and a book depicting the black rocks (*FranT*).

52 *The Canterbury Tales of Geoffrey Chaucer, Together with a Version in Modern English Verse by William van Wyck*. Illustrations by Rockwell Kent. 2 vols. New York: Covici, Friede, 1930. *SqT*: 2:373–88; *FranT*: 2:389–410.
This artistic edition prints Skeat's text (**4**) and van Wyck's translation in parallel columns. Includes a black-and-white engraving of a falcon on a branch and of the Franklin's 'table dormant' (I.353) and full-length portraits of the Squire and the Franklin.

53 *Tales from Chaucer: The Canterbury Tales Done into Prose*. Trans. Eleanor Farjeon. Illustrations by W. Russell Flint. New York: Jonathan Cape and Harrison Smith; London: Medici Society, 1930. Repr. Boston: Branford, 1959. *SqT*: pp 135–42; *FranT*: pp 143–53. Rev. ed., London: Oxford UP, 1959, with illustrations by Marjorie Walters. *SqT*: pp 135–42/pp 131–8; *FranT*: pp 143–53/pp 139–49.

Descriptive and allusive passages, astronomical periphrases, and the narrator's commentaries are mostly condensed or omitted from *SqT*. *FranT* omits the description of the *tregetoures'* illusions, the astrological passages, and Dorigen's Complaint. The 1930 edition includes a color plate showing Aurelius dancing in the garden. The revised edition includes color plates of Canacee, holding a mirror, with a falcon, and of Dorigen and Aurelius in the garden, with rocks in the background.

54 *The Frankeleyns Tale, by Geoffrey Chaucer*. Pittsburgh, PA: Bentley, 1931.

The text of this hand-press edition (234 copies of which were printed) is that of Skeat (**4**). (The '2nd ed., rev. and enlarged' listed by D.D. Griffith, *Bibliography of Chaucer, 1908–1953* [Seattle: U of Washington P, 1955] p 41, could not be located.)

55 *The Complete Works of Geoffrey Chaucer*. Ed. F.N. Robinson. Boston: Houghton Mifflin; London: Oxford UP, 1933. [In American printings after 1945, the title is changed to *The Poetical Works of Chaucer*.] 2nd ed. published as *The Works of Geoffrey Chaucer*. Boston: Houghton Mifflin, 1957; pbk ed., London: Oxford UP, 1974. [*The New Cambridge Chaucer*.] *SqT*: text pp 154–62/pp 128–35, explanatory notes pp 821–6/pp 715–21, textual notes p 1010/p 894; *FranT*: text pp 163–74/pp 135–44, explanatory notes pp 827–31/pp 721–6, textual notes pp 1010–11/p 894.

The text of *CT*, 'corrected for grammatical accuracy and for the adjustment of rimes' (xxxv/xxix), is based on El, collated with the Chaucer Society prints of Hg, Cambridge Dd.4.24, Cambridge Gg.4.27, Corpus, Petworth, Lansdowne, and Harley 7334, with Thynne's 1532 edition, and with the unpublished Cardigan and Morgan MSS. The general introduction to *CT* (pp 9–10) and the introduction to the explanatory notes (*SqT*: pp 821–2/p 717; *FranT*: pp 826–7/pp 721–2) treat themes, sources and analogues, and possible dates of composition. In the second edition, in response to Manly and Rickert (**61**), Robinson introduced twelve new readings into his text of *SqT* and eight new readings into his text of *FranT* (p 884). The explanatory notes have been slightly expanded; the introductory material and the textual notes are unchanged. The *Riverside Chaucer* (**108**) is based on Robinson's second edition. For responses to, comments on, and editions based on Robinson's text and notes, see **58, 59, 65, 72, 76, 77, 79, 80, 86, 88, 89, 99, 103, 106, 115, 341, 438, 587, 590, 888, 1865**.

56 *The Canterbury Tales*. Trans. Frank E. Hill. 2 vols. London: Limited Editions Club, 1934. Rev. ed., 1 vol. Miniatures by Arthur Szyk. New York: Heritage, 1946. *SqT*: 2:476–96/pp 394–411; *FranT*: 2:497–525/pp 412–36.

A modernization in rhymed couplets. The 1946 edition includes color plates of the Squire and the Franklin.

57 *Geoffrey Chaucer: Canterbury Tales.* Trans. J.U. Nicolson. Illustrations by Rockwell Kent. Garden City, NY: Garden City, 1934; London: Harrap, 1935. *SqT*: pp 443–60; *FranT*: pp 461–86.

A modernization in rhymed couplets. Includes full-length portraits of the Squire and the Franklin.

58 *The Prologue and Four Canterbury Tales [by] Geoffrey Chaucer.* Ed. Gordon Hall Gerould. New York: Nelson; Ronald, 1935. *FranT*: pp 268–97.

A school edition of *GP, FranT, PardT, NPT,* and *SNT,* with a brief introductory essay on Chaucer's life and works, glosses at the foot of the page, explanatory notes, and a glossary. The basis of the text is not stated; the editions of Skeat (**4**) and Robinson (**55**) are mentioned.

59 *The Canterbury Tales of Chaucer.* Ed. Edwin Johnston Howard and Gordon Donley Wilson. Ann Arbor, MI: Edwards, 1937; Oxford, OH: Anchor, 1938. Rev. as *The Canterbury Tales by Geoffrey Chaucer*. Oxford, OH: Anchor, 1942. Rev. as *The Canterbury Tales of Geoffrey Chaucer*. New York: Prentice-Hall, 1947. *FranT*: pp 48–58 [1937]/pp 138–59 [1938]/pp 104–23 [1942]/pp 266–92 [1947].

A discussion of Chaucer's times, life, works, language, and versification introduces the text of this school edition, which is followed by explanatory notes and a glossary. No basis is indicated for the text, although Skeat (**4**), Manly (**47**), and Robinson (**55**) are cited in the notes.

60 *Canterbury Tales: Prologue; Nun's Priest's Tale; Squire's Tale.* [No editor listed.] London: Nelson, 1938. *SqT*: pp 73–96.

A school edition. A brief introduction is followed by the texts listed in the title, accompanied by explanatory notes. The basis of the text is not indicated.

61 *The Text of The Canterbury Tales, Studied on the Basis of All Known Manuscripts.* Ed. John Matthews Manly and Edith Rickert. 8 vols. Chicago: U of Chicago P, 1940. Classification of manuscripts: *SqT*: 2:288–97; *FranT*: 2:300–15; *SqT* and textual notes: 4:1–32; *FranT* and textual notes: 4:33–63; critical notes: *SqT*: 4:479–85; *FranT* 4:485–8; glosses: *SqT*: 3:511–12; *FranT*: 3:512–15; corpus of variants: *SqT*: 6:505–72; *FranT*: 6:573–671.

Manly and Rickert sought to establish the archetype of the extant *CT* texts by collating all existing manuscripts against Skeat's 'Student's Edition' (2:5). Manly and Rickert print their text without punctuation, in a spelling based on that of Hg and El (1:x). The tales are arranged in the Ellesmere order (I [A] II [B[1]] III [D] IV–V [E–F] VI [C] VII [B[2]] VIII [G] IX [H] X [I]). In their Classification of Manuscripts, the editors propose four lines of descent for *SqT*. Most MSS (the 'Large Group') were derived from the same ultimate ancestor; MSS outside this group include Hg and El. In his comments on Rickert's theory that the Fitzwilliam MS [Fi] contains traces of Chaucer's early drafts, Manly cites Fi's version of lines 261–96 as evidence that the scribe may have memorized some of his texts and tried to reproduce them from memory

(2:512–13). The editors propose twelve lines of descent for *FranT*, including a number of single MSS and close pairs that appear to be of independent descent. The editors comment on misplaced passages, on the possibility that the archetype of the MSS was 'an unpolished working draft,' and on the provenance of the glosses from *Jov* in El and Additional 35286 (2:314–15). The Critical Notes treat sources of error in the archetype. The Corpus of Variants records all the variants of all the MSS with the exception of spelling variants of nonclassificatory value. See also **436**. For editions based on Manly and Rickert, see **68**, **69**, **88**, **103**, **128**. On Manly and Rickert, see **590**.

62 *Tales from Chaucer: The Canterbury Tales*. Trans. Charles Cowden Clarke. Illustrations by Arthur Szyk. New York: Heritage, 1947. *SqT*: pp 106–24.
A prose modernization for children. The falcon's story is omitted, with the explanation that it would prove uninteresting to young readers. The tale is completed with a detailed paraphrase of Spenser's continuation.

63 *The Canterbury Tales of Geoffrey Chaucer*. Trans. R.M. Lumiansky. Illustrations by H. Lawrence Hoffman. New York: Simon and Schuster, 1948; pbk ed., New York: Washington Square, 1971; New York: Pocket Books, 2001. *SqT*: pp 191–203; *FranT*: pp 204–19.
A prose modernization. A color plate shows Canacee under a stylized magenta tree, with a blue falcon in the tree's branches.

64 *The Portable Chaucer*. Trans. Theodore Morrison. New York: Viking, 1949/1975. Repr. Harmondsworth, UK: Penguin, 1977. *FranT*: pp 308–30.
A verse modernization. Selections from *CT* include *GP*, twelve tales, and *Ret*. An introduction discusses Chaucer's life and times, later reception, learning, obscenity, religion, and 'on modernizing Chaucer.'

65 *The Canterbury Tales. Translated into Modern English*. Trans. Nevill Coghill. Harmondsworth, UK: Penguin, 1951/1958. Numerous reprs (1960, 1975, and 1977 with revisions) through 2003. Illustrated ed., woodcuts by Edna Whyte. 2 vols. London: Folio Society, 1956. 2nd ed., 1 vol., 1974. *SqT*: pp 413–32 [1951]/2:182–201 [1956]; *FranT*: pp 443–57 [1951]/2:202–29 [1956].
This widely used verse modernization (with synopses of *Mel* and *ParsT*) is based on Skeat (**4**) and Robinson (**55**) and follows the Chaucer Society order (**1**). See **97**.

66 *Chaucer: The Squire's Tale and the Tale of Sir Thopas*. Trans. E.J. Frank Davies and Myfanwy G. Davies. London: Brodie, [1951]. *SqT*: pp 5–19.
A prose translation for secondary school students.

67 *The Canterbury Tales, Selections, Together with Selections from the Shorter Poems, by Geoffrey Chaucer*. Ed. Robert Archibald Jelliffe. New York: Scribner's, 1952. *FranT*: pp 270–97.
A school text, based on El. Includes a brief introduction on Chaucer's life, times, and language, and a glossary.

68 *A Chaucer Reader: Selections from the Canterbury Tales*. Ed. Charles W. Dunn.

New York: Harcourt, Brace and World, 1952. *FranT*: pp 127–51.
A school edition. Text based on Manly and Rickert (**61**), with difficult words glossed in the margin. The introduction treats Chaucer's life, literary development, and language.

69 *The Squire's Tale and Sir Thopas*. Ed. F.W. Robinson. London: Brodie, [1956]. *SqT*: pp 2–61.
A school edition. Introductory discussions of Chaucer's life and language are followed by the text, a note on versification, explanatory notes, a list of difficult words in *SqT*, and a glossary. The basis of the text is not stated, but the editions of Skeat (**4**) and Manly and Rickert (**61**) are mentioned.

70 Item cancelled.

71 *Chaucer's Poetry: An Anthology for the Modern Reader*. Ed. E. Talbot Donaldson. New York: Ronald, 1958/1975. Repr. New York: Scott, Foresman, 1984. *SqT*: 1975, pp 343–66; *FranT*: pp 275–30/pp 366–96.
Donaldson omits *SqT* from the first edition of his anthology. It is reinstated in the 1975 edition. Donaldson follows the Ellesmere tale order, but uses Hg as the basis for his text, which is presented in regularized spelling with glosses and brief explanatory notes at the foot of the page. *FranT*, lines 1455–6, 1493–8 (747–8, 785–90 in Donaldson's numbering), present in El but not in Hg, are silently restored. The text is followed by discussions of Chaucer's life and language, extensive commentaries on individual works, and a glossary. For Donaldson's commentaries on *SqT* and *FranT*, see **471**, **900**. See **79**.

72 *Geoffrey Chaucer: Canterbury Tales*. Ed. A.C. Cawley. Everyman's Library. London: Dent; New York: Dutton, 1958/1960, 1990, 1996; pbk ed. with revisions, 1975. *SqT*: pp 290–309; *FranT*: pp 310–34.
The text is that of Robinson's second edition (**55**), with glosses in the margins and at the foot of the page. An introduction treats Chaucer's life, and the text, language, and themes of *CT*. An appendix includes brief notes on Chaucer's pronunciation, grammar, and versification. The 1990 and 1996 revisions incorporate readings from *The Riverside Chaucer* (**108**). For the earlier Everyman's Library edition, see **30**. See also **125**.

73 *The Works of Geoffrey Chaucer. A Facsimile of the William Morris Kelmscott Chaucer, with the Original 87 Illustrations by Edward Burne-Jones*. Introduction by John T. Winterich. Cleveland, OH: World, 1958. *SqT*: pp 152–9; *FranT*: pp 159–71.
A brief discussion of Chaucer's life, works, language, Morris's career and the printing of the *Kelmscott Chaucer* (**5**) introduces this reduced-type facsimile. A glossary based on the *Oxford Chaucer* (**4**) concludes the volume. For a later facsimile, see **95**.

74 *The Franklin's Tale*. Ed. Phyllis Hodgson. London: Athlone, 1960. 7th impression, with new bibliography, 1973.
The text, based on El, is preceded by discussions of the Franklin's character,

social status, and literary interests and of the tale's possible sources (with special attention to *Fil* and *Dec*). It is followed by detailed explanatory notes, four appendices (The Poet and His Works; Chaucer's English; Versification; Astronomy, Astrology, and Magic), a bibliography, and a full glossary. See **296**, **909**.

• Review by R.T. Davies, *N&Q* n.s. 7 (1960), 478–9: A study of *FranT* in this edition would make an excellent introduction to medieval literature. In her account of the tale's sources, Hodgson might have made more of the pagan setting, Chaucer's way of rendering the magic plausible.

75 *Selections from Chaucer: The Prologue; the Nun's Priest's Tale; the Pardoner's Tale; the Squire's Tale*. Ed. Marjorie M. Barber. London: Macmillan; New York: St Martin's, 1961. *SqT*: pp 134–53.
The text of this school edition, based on the *Globe Chaucer* (**6**), is followed by a glossary and explanatory notes. The introduction includes commentaries on Chaucer's life, the literary background, structure, and modes of characterization in *CT* and brief appreciations of *GP* and the three tales. 'Unused to inventing or organising a plot, Chaucer put [*SqT*] aside, wrote the Franklin's comment on it, and waited to finish it for a moment that never came' (xxix).

76 *The Franklin's Tale. Rendered into Modern English Prose*. Trans. John Hobday. London: Brodie, 1962.
A prose modernization, based on Robinson's second edition (**55**).

77 *Chaucer*. Ed. Louis O. Coxe. New York: Dell, 1963. *FranT*: pp 176–99.
An introduction, brief bibliography, chronology of Chaucer's life, and a note on Chaucer's language are followed by selections from *CT* and *TC*. The text, based on Skeat (**4**) and Robinson's second edition (**55**), is not annotated, but the edition includes a glossary.

78 *Chaucer's Major Poetry*. Ed. Albert C. Baugh. New York: Appleton-Century-Crofts; London: Routledge and Kegan Paul, 1963. *SqT*: pp 459–70; *FranT*: pp 471–84.
After an introduction to Chaucer's life, language, versification, a short bibliography, and an introduction to *CT*, the text of *CT* (based on El and complete except for *Mel* and *ParsT*) is presented. Explanatory notes and glosses are printed at the foot of the page, along with brief discussions of sources, analogues, and possible dates of composition. A full glossary with line references and a list of common words concludes the volume.

79 *The Canterbury Tales of Geoffrey Chaucer*. Ed. A. Kent Hieatt and Constance Hieatt. New York: Bantam, 1964. *FranT*: pp 439–98.
A selection with facing-page translations, based on Skeat (**4**) with some variants supplied from Robinson's second edition (**55**) and Donaldson (**71**). There is an introduction and a brief glossary.

80 *Geoffrey Chaucer: The Canterbury Tales*. Trans. David Wright. London: Barrie and Rockliff, 1964; New York: Random House, 1965. *SqT*: pp 266–77; *FranT*: pp 278–95.

A prose modernization based on Robinson's second edition (**55**). The tales are printed in the Chaucer Society order (**1**).

81 *A Taste of Chaucer. Selections from The Canterbury Tales*. Trans. Anne Malcolmson. Illustrations by Enrico Arno. New York: Harcourt, Brace and World, 1964. *FranT*: pp 103–19.

A verse modernization for children. 'The Rocks of Brittany' condenses or eliminates the Franklin's remarks on *maistrye* and patience, Dorigen's lament over the rocks and her Complaint, Aurelius's prayer to Apollo, and the astrological passages. A woodcut shows a tearful Dorigen kneeling before Aurelius.

82 *The Breton Lays in Middle English*. Ed. Thomas C. Rumble. Detroit, MI: Wayne State UP, 1965. *FranT*: pp 229–59.

Texts of *Sir Launfal, Sir Degaré, Lay le Freine, Emaré, The Erle of Tolous, Sir Gowther, Kyng Orfew*, and *FranT*, the last said to be 'edited anew' (viii), but with no indication of its textual basis. Difficult words and phrases are glossed at the foot of the page. An introduction treats the origins of the Breton lay, its relation to French court culture in the twelfth and thirteenth centuries, and its fourteenth-century English adaptations. Also included are facsimiles of initial manuscript pages for each of the poems (*FranT* from El) and a bibliography.

83 *The Squire's Tale*. Ed. Dorothy Bethurum. Oxford: Clarendon, 1965.

The text of this student's edition is based on El, with textual notes printed at the foot of the page. The introduction surveys in detail the sources and nature of medieval Europe's knowledge of the Tartar empire (Chaucer may have seen a copy of *Mandeville's Travels* and perhaps knew as well Odoric of Pordenone's account of his journey to Cathay). More briefly discussed are the analogues to the magical gifts, the Canacee episode, and the framing tale structure; Chaucer's earlier treatments of talking birds, his interest in unfaithful lovers and the possible reasons for the story's incompleteness; the continuations of Spenser and John Lane; the place of *SqT* in the Canterbury sequence; Chaucer's astronomy and astrology; and the poet's life and literary connections. The extensive explanatory notes, which digest much previous scholarship, examine points of language, identify allusions, and supply literary and historical contexts. The volume includes an introduction to Chaucer's language and versification, a glossary, and six plates: the miniature of the Squire from El; the Month of May from *Queen Mary's Psalter*; depictions of the Suitor's Gifts and the Flying Horse from a MS of *Cleo*; and representations of the Great Khan's feast and a banquet with minstrels from fourteenth-century MSS. See **485**.

84 *The Canterbury Tales*. Trans. Dulan Barber. Illustrations by Geoffrey Fraser.

London: Blackie, 1966. *FranT*: pp 104–28.
A condensed prose retelling for children.

85 *Chaucer: The Franklin's Tale*. Ed. F.W. Robinson. Bath: Brodie, [1966].
A school edition. Introductory discussions of Chaucer's life, language, and versification are followed by the text, explanatory notes, a glossary, and a list of difficult words in *FranT*. The basis of the text is not stated, but the editions of Skeat (**4**) and Manly and Rickert (**61**) are mentioned.

86 *The Franklin's Prologue and Tale from the Canterbury Tales by Geoffrey Chaucer*. Ed. A.C. Spearing. Cambridge: Cambridge UP, 1966/1994. Repr. with corrections 1972.
The text, based on Robinson's second edition (**55**), is followed by explanatory notes and a glossary. An extensive introduction treats the *GP* portrait of the Franklin, *Sq–FranL*, Breton lays and the sources of *FranT*, rhetoric, the Tale's subjects (*trouthe*, marriage, *gentilesse*), and aspects of convention and realism. The 1994 introduction, completely rewritten, treats the tale's themes, characters, and teller (see **1339**). See also **352**, **493**, **789**, **955**.

87 *Geoffrey Chaucer: A Selection of His Works*. Ed. Kenneth Kee. New York: Odyssey, 1966. *FranT*: pp 147–77.
GP, WBP, WBT, MerT, FranT, NPT, PardT, and *Ret* are printed in a text based on El and Hg as published by the Chaucer Society (**1**). The edition also includes six of Chaucer's short poems, a brief biography of Chaucer, a general introduction, a discussion of Chaucer's language, and a short bibliography. For Kee's comments on *FranT*, see **950**.

88 *Selections from The Tales of Canterbury and Short Poems*. Ed. Robert Armstrong Pratt. Boston: Houghton Mifflin, 1966. *SqT*: pp 309–28; *FranT*: pp 328–50.
Discussions of Chaucer's life, works, learning, language, the tale order and literary art of *CT* introduce the text, based on Robinson's second edition (**55**), with frequent recourse to Manly and Rickert (**61**), in an attempt 'to recreate the text as Chaucer wrote it' (xxxviii). Lexical and explanatory glosses on the page are supplemented by a basic glossary. See **94a**.

89 Item cancelled.

90 *Geoffrey Chaucer, The Canterbury Tales. A Selection*. Ed. Donald R. Howard, with the assistance of James Dean. New York: New American Library, 1969. *FranT*: pp 340–69.
An introductory commentary on Chaucer's artistry in *CT*, notes on the text and Chaucer's pronunciation, a chronology, and a selected bibliography introduce an 'eclectic' text in normalized spelling (xxxix). Lexical and explanatory notes on the page are supplemented by a glossary of basic words.

91 *Geoffrey Chaucer, The Works, 1532, with supplementary material from the Editions of 1542, 1561, 1598, and 1602*. Ed. Derek S. Brewer. Ilkeley, UK: Scolar, 1969.
A description of the sixteenth-century editions of Chaucer's works introduces a facsimile of William Thynne's black-letter edition of 1532, supplement-

ed by material from the 1542 reprint of Thynne, Stow's 1561 edition, and Speght's editions of 1598 and 1602. *SqT*, illustrated with the woodcut of the Squire from Caxton's second edition, appears on fols xxviii^{v}–xxxii^{v} (following *MLT*). *FranT*, illustrated with the woodcut of the Franklin, appears on fols lx^{r}–lxv^{r}. For an earlier facsimile, see **26**.

92 *Knights, Beasts, and Wonders: Tales and Legends from Medieval Britain*. Trans. Margaret J. Miller. New York: David White, 1969.
Includes a free abbreviated prose rendering of *FranT* (pp 99–105). Omits, inter alia, Aurelius's prayer to Apollo, the astrological passages, and Dorigen's Complaint. Miller also adds material not in Chaucer (e.g., Arveragus's 'Do you not love this man [Aurelius]?' and Dorigen's reply 'No! No! And I never will').

93 *The Canterbury Tales. A Facsimile Edition of Caxton's Second Edition*. Introduction by J.A.W. Bennett. Cambridge: Cornmarket, 1972.
A reprint of Pepys's copy of Caxton's second (1484) edition of *CT*. Woodcuts of the pilgrims introduce their respective tales. *SqT* appears on fols N8r–P1v. *FranT* appears on fols P1v–Q6r.

94 *The Franklin's Tale*. Trans. Ian Serraillier. Illustrations by Philip Gough. London: Kaye and Ward; New York: Warne, 1972.
A free prose rendering; Dorigen's Complaint and the astrological passages are omitted. The color illustrations are loosely based on Chaucer's text: Dorigen plays with a unicorn in a garden; the clerk, in a pointed hat and cape, carries a magic wand that he uses to cover the rocks with mist. See **101**.

94a *The Tales of Canterbury, Complete*. Ed. Robert Armstrong Pratt. Boston: Houghton Mifflin, 1974. *SqT*: pp 372–89; *FranT*: pp 389–412.
A revised and expanded version of **88**. The thirty-four readings in *SqT* and eight readings in *FranT* that differ from those in Robinson's second edition (**55**) are listed on p 573. Includes a reproduction of the magical ebony horse from a MS of Girart d'Amiens' *Méliacin* (Bibliothèque Nationale fr. 1589).

95 *The Kelmscott Chaucer*, a facsimile edition, with *A Companion Volume to the Kelmscott Chaucer* by Duncan Robinson. London: Basilisk, 1975.
A full-size facsimile of the 1896 edition (**5**). The *Companion Volume* reproduces Burne-Jones's pencil drawings (Fitzwilliam Museum, Cambridge) for the *Kelmscott* illustrations, including two for *SqT* (plates 20–1), as well as an early study for the steed of brass, based on the Parthenon frieze, and six for *FranT* (plates 22–7). The facsimile edition and the *Companion* were produced in 515 copies on paper. For an earlier facsimile, see **73**.

96 *The Complete Poetry and Prose of Geoffrey Chaucer*. Ed. John H. Fisher. New York: Holt, Rinehart, and Winston, 1977. Glossary added in 3rd printing (1979); bibliography revised in 7th printing (1982); however, reprints carry unchanged copyright date of 1977. 2nd ed., 1989. *SqT*: pp 188–98; *FranT*: pp

199–212. 3rd ed. Rev. Mark Allen. Boston: Thomson Wadsworth, 2006. *SqT*: pp 189–200; *FranT*: pp 201–14. See **1080**.

Fisher's text of *CT* is based on El, occasionally corrected with Hg and/or other MSS. The textual notes, printed with glosses and explanatory notes on the page, list substantive variants from Hg and the 'more interesting' variants from other MSS (p 967). End matter includes discussions of Chaucer's literary place, time, language, and versification and (from the 3rd printing onwards) a short glossary. A notable feature of Fisher's edition is the substantial bibliography (revised in the 2nd and 3rd editions) of recent and important older studies; for *SqT*, see p 1003/p 1000/p 431; for *FranT*, see pp 1003–4/pp 1000–1/pp 431–2. For Fisher's critical commentary on *SqT*, see **548**; for *FranT*, see **1058**.

• Review by Roy Vance Ramsey, *SAC* 1 (1979), 163–7: Although there might have been warrant for Fisher's choice of El for *FranT* (which contains passages not in Hg that may be authorial additions to the text) and *GP*, there is none for doing so elsewhere.

97 *Geoffrey Chaucer, The Canterbury Tales: An Illustrated Selection Rendered into Modern English by Nevill Coghill*. 32 plates. London: Lane; Harmondsworth, UK: Penguin, 1977. *FranT*: pp 336–59.

A selection from Coghill's complete translation (**65**). Includes woodcuts of the Squire and the Franklin from Pynson's print of *CT* (ca 1490).

98 *The Canterbury Tales, Geoffrey Chaucer: A Facsimile and Transcription of the Hengwrt Manuscript, with Variants from the Ellesmere Manuscript*. Ed. Paul G. Ruggiers. Introduction by Donald C. Baker, A.I. Doyle, and M.B. Parkes. *A Variorum Edition of the Works of Geoffrey Chaucer*, Vol. 1. Gen. eds Paul G. Ruggiers and Donald C. Baker. Norman: U of Oklahoma P; Folkestone, UK: Dawson, 1979.

The Hengwrt MS, reproduced here with a paleographical introduction, is the base text for the Variorum edition of the *CT* (in progress). *SqT* (fols 129r–137r) appears on pp 510–45, *FranT* (fols 153v–165r) on pp 609–54, both with facing-page plates and transcription.

99 *Chaucer's Canterbury Tales Complete in Present-Day English*. Trans. James J. Donohue. Dubuque, IA: Loras, 1979. *SqT*: pp 440–59; *FranT*: pp 460–83.

A modernization, in rhymed couplets. Based on Robinson (**55**); the tales are given in the Chaucer Society order (**1**).

100 *The Poetical Works of Geoffrey Chaucer. A Facsimile of Cambridge University Library MS GG.4.27*. With introductions by M.B. Parkes and Richard Beadle. 3 vols. Cambridge: Brewer; Norman, OK: Pilgrim, 1979.

A facsimile edition of 'the only surviving example of a fifteenth-century attempt to collect Chaucer's poetical works in one volume' (3:1). The text of *SqT* (2: fols 277–84) is imperfect; lines 1–33 and 47–74 are mutilated and the tale ends at line 614. The text of *FranT* (2: fols 287–97) is incomplete, ending at line 1574.

101 *The Road to Canterbury. Tales from Chaucer*. Retold by Ian Serraillier. Illustrated with woodcuts by John Lawrence. Harmondsworth, UK: Kestrel, 1979; London: Heinemann, 1981. *FranT:* pp 97–106.
Reprints **94** as 'The Black Rocks of Brittany.'

102 *The Canterbury Tales by Geoffrey Chaucer, Edited from the Hengwrt Manuscript*. Ed. N.F. Blake. York Medieval Texts, Second Series. London: Arnold, 1980. *SqT*: pp 289–309; *FranT*: pp 344–69.
Alone among editors of *CT*, Blake follows the tale order as well as the text of Hg, which is printed with textual and explanatory notes at the foot of the page. Hg's text 'makes good sense with a minimum of emendation' (p 12); in *SqT*, it is emended only at lines 127, 516, and 568, in *FranT*, only in line 188. Hg's spellings are retained as well. As an alternative to the Chaucer Society division of the *CT* into nine fragments (**1**), Blake proposes a scheme of twelve sections. *SqT* is section 4; it occurs in Hg after *MLT* (section 3) and before *MerT* (section 5). Blake believes that *SqT* may have been in progress when Chaucer died and that the assignment of it to the Squire is almost certainly editorial. But the attribution is a felicitous one and may reflect what Chaucer would have done if he had finished *CT*. Blake also rejects lines 1–8 and 673–708 (in Hg, the conclusion of the Merchant–Franklin Link and the Squire–Merchant Link) as spurious and prints the passages in an Appendix (pp 667–8; see p 8). In his Introduction (pp 3–13), Blake reconstructs the history of Hg's compilation and explains his editorial decisions (e.g., the omission of *CYT*) in the light of that history. See **598, 1219**.
• Review by T.A. Shippey, *TLS*, 16 January 1981: The Ellesmere tale order has the advantage of placing the Squire and the Franklin together in 'one of the best bits of by-play in the sequence ... a fine example of social observation in which the Franklin's age and solid respectability compensate for his being not quite out of the top drawer.' Hg chooses the 'desperate expedient' of giving this interchange to the Merchant; in relegating the passage to an appendix as spurious, Blake acknowledges that Hg is 'obviously botching' here.

103 *The Franklin's Tale from The Canterbury Tales*. Ed. Gerald Morgan. London: Hodder and Stoughton; New York: Holmes and Meier, 1980. Repr. Blackrock, Co. Dublin: Irish Academic Press, 1992.
The text, based on Robinson's second edition (**55**), with occasional emendations from Manly and Rickert (**61**), includes lexical glosses at the foot of the page and is followed by detailed explanatory notes (pp 84–114) and a brief bibliography. It is preceded by an extensive introduction (pp 1–47) that treats 'the challenge of Chaucerian poetry,' Chaucerian narrative voice, the tale's central themes (love and marriage), and its meaning. See **1110**.
• Review by J.D. Burnley, *Lore&L* 3 (1980), 140–1: Morgan's text marks this as a school edition, but his erudite introduction and notes are more suited to

a scholarly audience than to undergraduate readers.

• Review by Nicholas Jacobs, *MÆ* 52 (1983), 126–31: The substantial introduction is the most notable part of Morgan's edition, but much of the material presented will be over the heads of an undergraduate audience.

104 *The Canterbury Tales*. Trans. Geraldine McCaughrean. Illustrations by Victor G. Ambrus. Oxford: Oxford UP, 1984; pbk ed., 1988. *FranT*: pp 84–91.

A free prose adaptation for children ('The Franklin's Romance, entitled Love on the Rocks'). The Franklin's final question includes Dorigen and is debated by the Plowman, the Wife of Bath, and the Knight. Illustrations include Dorigen on a high cliff overlooking the rocky coastline; Aurelius on his knees before Dorigen; the clerk conjuring a vision of Dorigen for Aurelius and his brother; Dorigen confessing her misadventures to Arveragus.

105 *Geoffrey Chaucer: The Canterbury Tales*. Trans. David Wright. Oxford: Oxford UP, 1985. *SqT*: pp 344–61; *FranT*: pp 361–85.

A modernization in rhymed couplets of all the tales except *Mel* and *ParsT*, which are summarized, with a brief introduction, select bibliography, and notes. See **106**.

• Review by Derek Pearsall, *SAC* 9 (1987), 199–203: Typical of the losses incurred in Wright's translation is the rendering of Dorigen's 'I wol be his to whom that I am knyt' (line 986) as 'I shall be his to whom I have been knit,' which implies an agency other than Dorigen's choice and implies as well an act completed in the past 'of which the present is a mere consequence, rather than the everlasting present of Dorigen's vow of constancy' (p 202).

106 *Geoffrey Chaucer: The Canterbury Tales.* Original text ed. F.N. Robinson. Trans. David Wright. 3 vols. London: Folio Society, 1986. *SqT*: 2:286–325; *FranT*: 2:327–79.

The text of Robinson's second edition (**55**) and Wright's modernization (**105**) are printed on facing pages. (An appendix prints *Mel* and *ParsT* in ME only.) Reprints Wright's introduction and Robinson's introductions to *CT* and to the individual fragments. Illustrations by twelve artists. A wood engraving by Peter Reddick shows Dorigen gazing out over the rocks.

107 *The Canterbury Tales: Geoffrey Chaucer.* Simplified by Michael West. Illustrations by Victor Ambrus. Harlow, UK: Addison Wesley-Longman, 1987. *FranT*: pp 46–54.

A prose retelling for children. One illustration: 'Aurelius tells Dorigen that he loves her.'

108 *The Riverside Chaucer*. Gen. ed. Larry D. Benson. Boston: Houghton Mifflin; Oxford: Oxford UP, 1987. *SqT*: text pp 169–77, explanatory notes pp 890–5, textual notes pp 1128–9; *FranT*: text pp 178–89, explanatory notes pp 895–901, textual notes p 1129.

Based on Robinson's second edition (**55**). Departs from Robinson's text at lines 94, 105, 171, 201, 211, 266, 529, 657 for *SqT*, lines 1408 and 1430 for

FranT, and in minor matters of punctuation. Glosses appear at the foot of the page. The explanatory notes (by Vincent J. DiMarco for *SqT* and Joanne Rice for *FranT*) have been thoroughly revised, as have the selective textual notes (by Ralph Hanna III). The latter indicate all changes from Robinson and 'attempt to provide some notice of all those major readings about which editors in the past century have offered conflicting opinions' (p 1121). The volume also includes introductory essays on Chaucer's life, the canon and chronology of his works, his language and versification, and the treatment of his texts in this edition, a detailed bibliography, and a full glossary with line references. See **112**, **124**, **127**.

109 *The Canterbury Tales by Geoffrey Chaucer*. Trans. Selina Hastings. Illustrations by Reg Cartwright. New York: Holt, 1988. *FranT*: pp 70–5.
A free prose modernization. Color plates of the clerk conjuring up a hawk pursuing a heron (see line 1199) and Aurelius greeting Dorigen.

110 *Geoffrey Chaucer: Canterbury Tales*. Trans. Barbara Cohen. Illustrations by Trina Schart Hyman. New York: Lothrop, Lee and Shepard, 1988. *FranT*: pp 64–84.
A free modernization for children. Color plates of the Franklin and of Dorigen and Arveragus (in vaguely Roman dress) embracing, observed by Aurelius.

111 *The Canterbury Tales: Nine Tales and the General Prologue*. Ed. V.A. Kolve and Glending Olson. Norton Critical Edition. New York: Norton, 1989. *FranT*: pp 169–91. Rev. ed., *The Canterbury Tales: Fifteen Tales and the General Prologue*. 2005. *FranT*: pp 212–33.
The text, based on Skeat (**4**) but with readings from facsimiles and modern editions, is glossed in the margins and at the foot of the page; it is preceded by a preface and a discussion of Chaucer's language. The edition also includes sources and analogues (for *FranT*, excerpts from *Fil* [omitted in revised edition] and *Dec*, and Bartholomæus Anglicus on love and marriage), a selection of critical essays (including Kittredge [**815**] on the Marriage Group), a chronology of Chaucer's life, and a bibliography.

112 *The Squire's Tale*. Ed. Donald C. Baker. *A Variorum Edition of the Works of Geoffrey Chaucer*, Vol. 2, Part 12. Gen. eds Paul G. Ruggiers, Donald C. Baker, and Daniel J. Ransom. Norman: U of Oklahoma P, 1990.
In addition to the text, this edition contains a Critical Commentary, a Textual Commentary, bibliographical and general indexes, and reproductions (one in color) of Hg, fols 133r (lines 325–58) and 129r (lines 9–44). The Critical Commentary treats Sources and Analogues, Date, the Question of Allegory, the Fragment and Its Continuations, Relation to *CT*, Suitability to the Squire, Relation of *SqT* and *KnT*, Relation of *SqT* and *MerT* and *FranT*, and Genre. It concludes with a survey of criticism through 1985. The Textual Commentary examines the Textual Tradition, the Evidence of the Glosses, Spurious Lines, and *SqT* and the Order of *CT*. It includes as well a description of ten

MSS collated for the Variorum Chaucer, a description of the printed editions from Caxton to *The Riverside Chaucer* (**108**), and a Table of Correspondences (a comparative tabulation of three categories of variants for the ten collated MSS and Caxton's 1478 edition). In accordance with the principles of the Variorum, the text is based on Hg; it is emended at line 135 and (from El) at 283, 454, 524, 576, and 602. In Hg, *MerE–SqH* are adapted to link *MerT* to *FranT;* Baker emends Hg to accommodate the order of link and tale as they appear in El. Collations from the base ten MSS and the printed editions are given below the text, followed by textual and explanatory notes.
• Review by Karl Heinz Göller and Richard J. Utz, *SAC* 13 (1991), 162–5: Although Baker urges caution in assuming that Chaucer drew directly on *SGGK* in *SqT,* the parallels between the poems are thematically functional: 'Chaucer counted on his audience's knowledge of *SGGK*' (p 163).
• Review by N.F. Blake, *ES* 73 (1992), 189–91: Of the six places in Hg emended in this edition, three (in lines 283, 454, 602) may be defended as Chaucerian. Like the other Variorum editors, Baker records variations in punctuation irregularly; this matter needs to be given more consideration. Baker's Critical Commentary is 'wide-ranging, fair-minded, and level-headed' (p 189); the volume as a whole 'could well serve as a model for later editors' (p 191).
• Review by Joseph A. Dane, *Envoi* 3 (1992), 321–6: The chapter headings adopted by Baker do not accurately represent the history of criticism; they suggest a naïve view of critical history, privileging the biases of the mid-twentieth century. The edition 'reads like a nostalgic monument to the form of Chaucerianism that was ending when the Variorum committee first began to meet' (p 326).
• Review by E.G. Stanley, *N&Q* n.s. 39 (1992), 210–11: 'The "Textual Commentary" is far too short to be clear ... Though I would not wish to part with the survey of criticism up to 1900, I would gladly give a wilderness of critical monkeys, such as is let loose in the introduction and notes, for one golden ring of interconnected textual problems fully explained' (p 210).
• Review by Julian N. Wasserman, *JEGP* 91 (1992), 427–9: *SqT* 'has a unique way of frustrating efforts to place it in context – whether date, source, or relation to other tales' (p 428). Baker presents the diversity of opinion about *SqT* deftly and openhandedly, 'facilitating rather than controlling future criticism of the tale' (p 429).
• Review by Kenneth Bleeth, *Speculum* 68 (1993), 731–3: Baker's volume reflects a confusion built into the Variorum project as a whole. Although its stated claims for the text are modest, its confidence in Hg as witness to 'what Chaucer must have written' invests the text with unusual authority. As a record of the critical reception of *SqT,* this edition is 'built to last. As a presentation of the poem's text, however, it shares with the other *CT* volumes in this series a degree of uncertainty about what sort of edition it wishes to

be' (p 733).

113 *Geoffrey Chaucer: The Canterbury Tales. The General Prologue and Twelve Major Tales in Modern Spelling*. Ed. Michael Murphy. Lanham, MD: University Press of America, 1991. *FranT*: pp 276–302.
The text of this 'modspell edition' (xv) is based on Hg as given in the *Six-Text* print of *CT* (**1**); grammar, syntax, and vocabulary are essentially unchanged from the language of the original. The text, glossed in the margins and at the foot of the page, is preceded by a general introduction to *CT*, a brief life of Chaucer, and a description of the language of this edition.

114 Partridge, Stephen Bradford. *Glosses in the Manuscripts of Chaucer's Canterbury Tales: An Edition and Commentary*. PhD diss., Harvard University, 1992. Dir. Larry D. Benson. Ann Arbor, MI: University Microfilms International, 1992. See also *DAI*–A 53/05 (1992): 1529.
An edition of the manuscript glosses to all of *CT* except *Mel* and *MkT*. Variant readings are recorded and the sources of the glosses, where known, are identified. For *SqT*, eighteen glosses are listed. Rejects Persius as a source for either text or gloss at line 207. For *FranT*, seventy-two glosses are listed.

115 *The Canterbury Tales of Geoffrey Chaucer*. Trans. Ronald L. Ecker and Eugene Crook. Palatka, FL: Hodge and Braddock, 1993. *SqT*: pp 284–301; *FranT*: pp 302–26.
A modernization of the verse tales (by Ecker) and the tales in prose (by Crook), based on Robinson's second edition (**55**).

116 *Stories from Chaucer*. Trans. Barbara Baddoo. Accra, Ghana: Ammasbooks, 1993. *FranT*: pp 46–53.
A free condensed prose modernization, for students.

117 *Geoffrey Chaucer: The Canterbury Tales*. Trans. Fiona Simpson. Paramus, NJ: Globe Fearon, 1995. *FranT*: pp 67–71.
A radically condensed prose modernization, for children.

118 *The New Ellesmere Chaucer Facsimile (of Huntington Library MS EL26 C9)*. Ed. Daniel Woodward and Martin Stevens. Tokyo and San Marino, CA: Yushudo and Huntington Library Press, 1995 (color), 1997 (monochrome). *SqH*: fols 115r–v; *SqT*: fols 115r–22v; *Sq–FranL*: fol. 123r; *FranP*: fol. 123v; *FranT*: fols 123v–33r.
Limited to 250 copies in color and one thousand copies in monochrome. For an account of the production of the facsimile, see Daniel Woodward, 'The New Ellesmere Chaucer Facsimile,' in *The Ellesmere Chaucer: Essays in Interpretation* (San Marino, CA and Tokyo: Huntington Library and Yushudo, 1995), pp 1–13.

119 Best, Suky. *Dorigen's Promise*. Totnes, UK: Festerman, 1997.
An illustrated adaptation of *FranT* with 'moral tags' (e.g., 'Why not postpone important plans for a bit?'; 'You're a complex person but that's what being an Aries is all about').

120 *The New Ellesmere Chaucer monochromatic facsimile (of Huntington Library MS EL26 C9)*. 1997. See **118**.
A full-size monochromatic facsimile of **118**, made using the transparencies of the color facsimile. Limited to one thousand copies.

121 *Chaucer to Spenser: An Anthology of Writings in English, 1375–1575*. Ed. Derek Pearsall. Oxford: Blackwell, 1999. *FranT*: pp 143–63.
The text, based on Hg, is provided with marginal glosses and explanatory notes at the foot of the page. The volume includes a list of textual variants and a glossary of common hard words.

122 *Canterbury Marriage Tales: Geoffrey Chaucer*. Ed. Michael Murphy. Brooklyn, NY: Conal and Gavin, 2000. *FranT*: pp 195–234.
GP, WBT, ClT, MerT, and *FranT* are presented in modernized spelling, with marginal glosses and explanatory footnotes. The volume includes essays on Chaucer's life and language, brief introductions to each tale, and a select glossary.

123 *The Franklin's Prologue and Tale*. Ed. Valerie Allen and David Kirkham. Cambridge: Cambridge UP, 2000.
The text of this school edition, with glosses, explanatory notes, and study questions on facing pages, is preceded by general introductions to *CT* and Chaucer's language, and followed by brief essays on symbolism, literary devices, *gentilesse*, astrology and astronomy and a glossary of frequently used words.

124 *Geoffrey Chaucer: The Canterbury Tales, Complete*. Ed. Larry D. Benson. Boston: Houghton Mifflin, 2000. *SqT*: text pp 151–9; explanatory notes pp 416–21; *FranT*: text pp 160–71; explanatory notes pp 421–7.
The text is that of *The Riverside Chaucer* (**108**), as are the glosses at the foot of the page. The *Riverside* textual notes have been omitted. The explanatory notes have been extensively revised and provided with an index to the principal matters treated in the notes.

125 *Geoffrey Chaucer: Three Tales of Love and Chivalry*. Ed. Malcolm Andrew and A.C. Cawley. London: Dent, 2000. *SqT*: pp 61–80; *FranT*: pp 81–105.
The text of *KnT, SqT*, and *FranT* is reproduced from Cawley's Everyman edition (**72**) with a critical introduction by Andrew (see **708**).

126 Item cancelled.

127 *The Canterbury Tales in Modern Verse*. Trans. Joseph Glaser. Indianapolis, IN: Hackett, 2005. *SqT*: pp 220–4; *FranT*: pp 225–40.
Short excerpts from Part 2 of *SqT* and about three-quarters of *FranT*, translated into couplets. (The omitted material is summarized.) An introduction surveys Chaucer's life, times, and works, 'The Religious Establishment in the *Canterbury Tales*,' and contains notes on the text (based on **108**) and translation. There is a select bibliography.

128 *Geoffrey Chaucer: The Canterbury Tales*. Ed. Jill Mann. London: Penguin, 2005.

SqT: text pp 382–407, explanatory notes pp 940–9; *FranT*: text pp 407–38, explanatory notes pp 949–65.

A chronology, critical introduction, discussion of Chaucer's language, and a note on the text are followed by the text of *CT*, which is 'squarely based on' both El and Hg, with occasional emendations from other MSS and on metrical grounds (lxii–lxiii). The spelling follows that of Manly and Rickert (**61**). Lexical glosses appear at the foot of each page; the text is followed by detailed interpretive notes (pp 795–1111) and a glossary. See **745**, **794**.

℘ Sources, Analogues, and the Posterity of *The Squire's Tale*

See also **4, 6, 7, 8, 9, 18, 32, 78, 83, 112, 112r, 378, 379, 380, 391, 408, 409, 440, 454, 464, 497, 500, 513, 530, 538a, 541, 591, 597, 617, 635, 642, 651, 665, 670, 692, 698, 700, 716, 718, 729, 732, 736, 741, 743, 750**.

In the absence of any close literary model for *SqT*, scholarship has focused on analogues of the motif of the flying horse in Part 1, on the falcon's narrative in Part 2, and on materials that contextualize the tale's treatment of the Mongol court and its presentation of the emissary's magic gifts. This chapter also annotates commentary on Spenser's continuation of *SqT* in Book 4 of *FQ* that throws retrospective light on Chaucer's tale.

For a guide to the literature on the sources and analogues of Chaucer's writings, see **218a**.

129 Clouston, W.A. *On the Magical Elements in Chaucer's Squire's Tale, with Analogues*. Part 2.2 of *John Lane's Continuation of Chaucer's 'Squire's Tale.'* Ed. Frederick J. Furnivall. Chaucer Society Publications, Second Series, 23, 26. London: Trübner, 1887–90.
Prints ancient, medieval, and modern analogues of 'Chaucer's finest tale' (p 266), mostly from folk sources. Includes instances of knights riding into banqueting halls; magic horses, flying chariots, 'shoes of swiftness,' and self-moving ships; magic mirrors and images; magic rings and gems; the language of animals, especially of birds; and magic swords and spears. Also included are abstracts of the prose *Cléomadès et Claremond*, *Valentine and Orson*, the tale of the Ebony Horse from *The Arabian Nights* with a Turkish variant, and various folktales involving flying objects and human flight. See **4, 147r**.

130 Furnivall, Frederick J., ed. *John Lane's Continuation of Chaucer's 'Squire's Tale.' (Part I). Glossary and Index (Part II)*. Chaucer Society Publications, Second Series, 23, 26. London: Trübner, 1887–90.
Lane's five thousand-line continuation of *SqT* is printed in its 1616 version, with variants from the revision of 1630. The reprint 'is due to no merit in Lane's poem, for it has none ... The completion of *SqT* would have taxt Chaucer's utmost power, even when he was at his best. The subject is one

into which he could have imported little humanity ... The work wouldn't have repaid the effort, and so the Poet turnd it up ... Who of us, in his own line, has not done the like? Man is mortal; and when a fellow man doesn't see his way thro' a bit of work, it bores him, and he drops it' (xi–xii). See **132**, **137**, **164**, **214**.

131 Manly, John Matthews. 'Marco Polo and the Squire's Tale.' *PMLA* 11 (1896), 349–62.
Reviews the parallel passages cited by Skeat (**4**) as evidence of Chaucer's indebtedness to Marco Polo's *Travels*, concluding that 'if Chaucer used Marco Polo's narrative, he either carelessly or intentionally confused all the features of the setting that could possibly be confused, and retained not a single really characteristic trait of any person, place, or event. It is only by twisting everything that any part of Chaucer's story can be brought into relation with any part of Polo's' (p 360). Chaucer might have obtained his information about Tartary from a number of sources, or from a lost original, either written or oral, which contained the names of *SqT*'s characters and the details of its setting. See **378**.

132 Tobler, Alfred. *Geoffrey Chaucer's Influence on English Literature*. Berne: Haller, 1903. Repr. New York: AMS, 1973.
Summarizes Spenser's working out of *SqT*'s plot in *FQ* 4.2–3; prints extended excerpts from Furnivall's introduction to his edition of John Lane's continuation (**130**); provides information on the eighteenth-century modernizations of *SqT* and of Spenser's continuation by Boyse and Ogle and a summary of Sterling's continuation, appended to Boyse and Ogle's version (1785); and summarizes Richard Wharton's 1805 modernization (*Cambuscan, An Heroic Poem*), with excerpts from his prefatory advertisement (pp 23–37).

133 Jones, H.S.V. 'Some Observations upon the Squire's Tale.' *PMLA* 20 (1905), 346–59.
Among the analogues that have been proposed for *SqT*, Chaucer probably knew *Cleo* and may have known Girard of Amiens' *Méliacin*. Similarities between *Cleo* and *SqT* include the occasion of a birthday feast with the giving of gifts, a magic horse operated by pins, and a gift that has the power to discover treason. Two allusions help to explain the gift of a mirror to Canacee: the description in *Cleo* of Virgil's treason-revealing mirror and the connection, in Froissart's *L'Espinette Amoureuse*, of *Cleo* with a magic mirror. Froissart's poem provides as well a parallel to Canacee's mirror-inspired vision when its hero places a mirror under his pillow and sees his beloved in a dream. See **380**, **598**.

134 Lowes, John Livingston. 'The Prologue to the *Legend of Good Women* Considered in its Chronological Relations.' *PMLA* 20 (1905), 749–864.
Notes a parallel between lines 399–400 and Sir John Clanvowe's *Book of Cupid*, in a similar situation involving knowledge of the language of birds (p

754n2).

135 Jones, H.S.V. 'Chaucer's *Squire's Tale*: An Investigation of the English Fragment, the Old French *Cléomadès*, and Analogous Folk-Tales.' PhD diss., Harvard University, 1906. Dir. G.L. Kittredge and F.N. Robinson.
See **133**, **136**, **139**.

136 ———. 'The Cléomadès, the Méliacin, and the Arabian Tale of the "Enchanted Horse."' *JEGP* 6 (1906), 221–43.
Examines the relations among the several versions of the *cheval de fust* story, concluding that *Cleo* and the *Méliacin* probably derive from a common source, in all likelihood a lost Spanish poem that itself goes back to a version of the Arabian story of the Enchanted Horse. Includes a detailed summary of *Cleo*.

137 Hertwig, Doris. *Der Einfluss von Chaucers "Canterbury Tales" auf die englische Literatur*. Marburg: Noske, 1908.
Brief comments on Spenser's and John Lane's continuations of *SqT* (**130**) and on Leigh Hunt's modernization of Part 1 (pp 35–7).

138 Hinckley, Henry Barrett. 'The Brazen Horse of Troy.' *MLN* 23 (1908), 157–8.
The brass horse in *SqT* is likened to the Trojan horse, which in Virgil is made of wood. In the *Historia destructionis Troiae*, Guido delle Colonne describes the horse as brass. Passages in Pausanias and Aristophanes suggest that a tradition of a brazen horse already existed in antiquity.

139 Jones, H.S.V. 'The *Cléomadès* and Related Folk-Tales.' *PMLA* 23 (1908), 557–98.
A survey of the 'narrative neighborhood' of *SqT* and 'its nearest analogue' (p 557), examining the motifs of the enchanted horse and the aerial journey in German, Slavic, Sanskrit, Celtic, Persian, and Mongolian folktales, and in the *Gesta Romanorum*. Perhaps Chaucer was following no one source, but 'working freely, with a knowledge of *Cleo* and related folktales' (p 598n). See **140**.

140 Hinckley, Henry Barrett. 'Chaucer and the *Cléomadès*.' *MLN* 24 (1909), 95.
Jones's proposal (**139**) that *Cleo* was one of the models for *SqT* is weakened by the absence of verbal echoes of the French text in Chaucer's poem. See **141**.

141 Jones, H.S.V. 'Chaucer and the *Cléomadès*.' *MLN* 24 (1909), 158.
A response to Hinckley (**140**). 'The tired parallel passage argument fails to prove anything in particular, – except, perhaps, that parallel passages meet at infinity' (p 158).

142 Skeat, Walter W. 'Chaucer's Two Allusions to Persius.' *N&Q*, 10th ser., 12 (1909), 6.
According to a side note in El, line 721 was suggested by the Prologue to Persius's *Satires*, line 2. Chaucer was indebted to the same Prologue for the form *Pegasee* (for Latin 'Pegaseus') in line 207. A side note in Cambridge MS Dd.4.24 refers to Persius, line 14: *Cantare credas Pegaseium nectar*.

143 Kittredge, George Lyman. 'Chauceriana.' *MP* 7 (1909–10), 465–83.

The account of the stranger knight's rhetorical skill may be indebted to Geoffrey of Vinsauf's *Poetria Nova*, which urges a speaker to consider tongue, countenance, and bearing (p 481).

144 Bushnell, A.J. de Havilland. 'The Names and Sources of Chaucer's "Squieres Tale."' *Blackwood's Magazine* 187 (1910), 654–7.
Disputes the suggestion of Sir Henry Yule (*The Book of Ser Marco Polo* [London: Murray, 1871]) and Skeat (4) that Chaucer drew on Marco Polo's account of the court of Kublai Khan in *SqT*. Chaucer is describing the Tartars of the Golden Horde, whom he might have learned about from Genoese merchants. Proposes Mongol derivations for the names Cambynskan [*sic*], Canacee, and Cambalo, and suggests Arabic etymologies for Elpheta and Algarsyf.

145 Rosenthal, Bruno. *Spensers Verhältnis zu Chaucer*. Berlin: Buschhardt, 1911.
Brief comments on Spenser's treatment of Cambalo and Canacee in his continuation of *SqT* in *FQ* 4.2–3. Spenser apparently assumed that the Cambalo who is Canacee's brother is also the Cambalo who fights for her (pp 39–41).

146 Saintsbury, George. 'Chaucer.' In *The Cambridge History of English Literature*. Ed. A.W. Ward and A.R. Waller. 15 vols. Cambridge: Cambridge UP, 1912–29. 2:156–96.
Spenser did not so much continue as branch off from *SqT*, 'much as the minor romances of adventure branch off from the Arthurian centre' (p 184).

147 Lowes, John Livingston. 'The Squire's Tale and the Land of Prester John.' *WUS* 1 (1913), 3–18.
Chaucer may have drawn some of the details of *SqT* from the legends of Prester John, in particular from the *Epistola Presbyteri Johannis*. Prester John, king of India (also represented in Chaucer's day as king of Arabia; cf. line 110), sends to the emperor at Rome three gifts, one of which is a magic ring that protects its wearer from enemies; most versions of the *Epistola* describe a mirror that is kept at the summit of a great tower (cf. lines 174–6); it is guarded by officers and reveals its owner's friends and enemies (cf. lines 132–6); the birthday feast of Prester John plays an important part in the *Epistola*, and takes place in a 'birthday chapel' (cf. lines 295–7); musicians go before Prester John, as they do before Cambyuskan; members of both courts eat strange foods; like *SqT*, the *Epistola* describes a Dry Tree; the first appearance of Prester John is in connection with a fight between two brothers, recalling Cambalus's promised battle with 'bretheren two' (line 668). 'For the *setting* of *SqT*, and in part for the *gifts*, we have in the Prester John material, if not a direct source, very probably an element which may have entered into such a source' (p 15). Several motifs in *SqT* not present in the Prester John legends can be paralleled in other sources (e.g., the flying horse in *Cleo*). It seems likely that Chaucer combined these details himself, attempting seriously 'what in *Thop* he had thrown off as a *jeu d'esprit*, a romance of his own,

into which [were] woven motives from various sources' (p 17). See **598**.
• Review by J. Koch, 'Neuere beiträge zur Chaucerliteratur aus Amerika.' *AB* 25 (1914), 327–42: Many of the parallels cited as evidence of Chaucer's possible use of the *Epistola* are also present in the analogues printed by Clouston (**129**). Lowes believes that *SqT* was woven together from many sources. But Chaucer did not usually work in this way; it seems more likely that the *Epistola, Cleo,* and *SqT* derive from a common original (pp 332–5).

148 Fansler, Dean Spruill. *Chaucer and the Roman de la Rose*. New York: Columbia UP, 1914. Repr. Gloucester, MA: Peter Smith, 1965.
Finds possible echoes of *RR* in lines 52–5, 57, 164–6, 202–3, 228–33, and 483 (see index, p 260).

149 Spurgeon, Caroline F.E. *Five Hundred Years of Chaucer Criticism and Allusion (1357–1900)*. Chaucer Society Publications, Second Series, 48 (1914), 49–50 (1918), 52 (1921), 53 (1922), 55 (1924), 56 (1924). London: Kegan Paul, Trench, Trübner and Oxford UP, 1914–24. Repr. (in 3 vols) Cambridge: Cambridge UP, 1925, and New York: Russell and Russell, 1961. See also *Supplement Containing Additional Entries, 1868–1900* (London: n.p., 1920).
Not all of the references to *SqT* are listed under that heading in the Index. Other items include: in Part 1, B. Twyne (p 181), B. Jonson (p 217), B. Jones (p 237), T.P. Blount (p 267), J. Aubrey (p 267), T. Hearne (p 306), J. Upton (p 403), R. Hurd (pp 421–2), T. Warton (pp 482, 487); in Part 2, C. Lamb (p 9), J. Ruskin (p 13), D. Wordsworth (p 130), L. Hunt (pp 144, 254), J.H. Hippisley (p 215), R. Horne (p 238); in Part 4, G. Harvey (pp 49, 51).

150 Cook, Albert Stanburrough. 'Skelton's "Garland of Laurel" and Chaucer's "House of Fame."' *MLR* 11 (1916), 9–14.
Garland of Laurel, line 1471, echoes *SqT*, line 671 (p 14).

151 Jefferson, Bernard L. *Chaucer and the Consolation of Philosophy of Boethius*. Princeton, NJ: Princeton UP, 1917. Repr. New York: Haskell, 1965; Gordian Press, 1968.
Lists one certain (lines 608–17) and one doubtful (line 258) allusion to *Consol*. The Franklin's remarks to the Squire on *gentilesse* (lines 684–94) also echo Boethius (p 147).

152 Cook, Albert Stanburrough. 'Chaucerian Papers (I): VII. Chaucer's "Swerd of Winter."' *TCAAS* 23 (1919), 32.
Compares 'swerd of wynter' (line 57) with *LGW* F125–7 and with similar expressions in *RR*, Lucretius, Virgil, and Martial.

153 Tatlock, John Strong Perry. 'The Source of the Legend, and Other Chauceriana.' *SP* 18 (1921), 419–28.
Lines 479–82 may recall *Inferno* 20.20–3 (p 420n).

154 ———. 'Chaucer's Whelp and Lion.' *MLN* 38 (1923), 506–7.
Cites parallels to the falcon's 'as by the whelp chasted is the leon' (line 491) in Vincent of Beauvais, Thomas of Cantimpré, Bartholomaeus Anglicus,

Pliny, and St Ambrose.

155 Landrum, Grace W. 'Chaucer's Use of the Vulgate.' *PMLA* 39 (1924), 75–100.
In lines 518–20 (the falcon's tomb simile), Chaucer supplements a reminiscence of *RR* with a passage in Matthew 23:27 (pp 90–1).

156 Item cancelled.

157 Magoun, Francis P., Jr. 'Chaucer and the Roman de la Rose, vv. 16096–105.' *RomR* 17 (1926), 69–70.
A response to Hinckley (**380**). The description of the manufacture of glass from fern ashes (lines 253–60) is not merely 'the same illustration' as that used in *RR*, but is an actual borrowing from the French poem.

158 Bethel, John Perceval. 'The Influence of Dante on Chaucer's Thought and Expression.' PhD diss., Harvard University, 1927. Dir. C.H. Grandgent and F.N. Robinson.
SqT is permeated with Dante's spirit, although Chaucer's touch is lighter than that of his predecessor (p 151). Dante's influence is felt generally in the numerous references to *gentilesse* in Part 2, and specifically in lines 236–42 (cf. *Inferno* 31, lines 1–6), line 479 (cf. *Inferno* 5, line 100 and *Convivio* 4.3.105f), and line 568 (cf. *Purgatorio* 33, lines 130–1) (pp 154–5, 324–6). See **215**.

159 Hinckley, Henry Barrett. 'Chauceriana.' *PQ* 6 (1927), 313–14.
Line 203 parallels Terence, *Phormio*, line 454: *Quod* [*sic*] *homines tot sententiae.*

160 Magoun, Francis P., Jr. 'The Chaucer of Spenser and Milton.' *MP* 25 (1927), 129–36.
Milton's use of Speght's 1602 edition of Chaucer's works is reflected in the form 'Cambuscan' and perhaps in his reference to *SqT* as 'half told' in "Il Penseroso"; the 'argument' to *SqT* in Speght's edition emphasizes the unfinished character of the poem, and may have caught Milton's eye. Skeat (**4**) and the *Six-Text* (**1**) print the name of the Tartar king as 'Cambinskan,' but the testimony of the manuscripts supports 'Cambiuskan,' which is etymologically a more likely derivation of Genghis Khan.

161 Bush, Douglas. 'Chaucer's "Corinne."' *Speculum* 4 (1929), 106–7.
A gloss on *Anel,* line 21 ('First folowe I Stace, and after him Corynne'). A list of authors in Lydgate's *Troy Book* includes Statius and Corynne, the latter possibly a reference to the Corinna to whom Ovid (*Amores* 2.6) gives a lament for a dead parrot. Given the connections between *Anel* and Part 2 of *SqT,* it is perhaps significant that Ovid's poem states that the parrot and a turtledove lived together and that the faithful mate lives to mourn the parrot.

162 Shannon, Edgar Finley. *Chaucer and the Roman Poets.* Harvard Studies in Comparative Literature 7. Cambridge, MA: Harvard UP, 1929. Repr. New York: Russell and Russell, 1957.
Cites Ovidian parallels for lines 220–3, 238–40, and 479 (p 321).

163 Bond, Richmond, John W. Bowyer, C.B. Millican, and G. Hubert Smith. 'A

Collection of Chaucer Allusions.' *SP* 28 (1931), 481–512.
Records an allusion to *SqT* by Richard Hole (1789) (p 505).

164 Emerson, Francis Willard. 'The Spenser in John Lane's Chaucer.' *SP* 29 (1932), 406–8.
Despite his reservations about Spenser's handling of *SqT* in Book 4 of *FQ*, Lane's own continuation of *SqT* (**130**) is as much indebted to Spenser as it is to Chaucer. Spenserian elements include the division of the poem into canto-length sections, elements of plot, allegorical trappings, and symbolic names.

165 ———. 'Why Milton Uses "Cambuscan" and "Camball."' *MLN* 47 (1932), 153–4.
The forms 'Cambuscan' (for 'Cambyuskan') and 'Camball' (for 'Camballo') used by Milton in "Il Penseroso" probably derive from his reading of John Lane's continuation of *SqT* (**130**). Lane himself seems to have borrowed the form 'Camball' from Spenser.

166 Braddy, Haldeen. 'The Oriental Origin of Chaucer's Canacee–Falcon Episode.' *MLR* 31 (1936), 11–19. Repr. in Braddy, *Geoffrey Chaucer: Literary and Historical Studies*. Port Washington, NY: Kennikat, 1971. Pp 43–53.
The main points of Chaucer's falcon episode are paralleled in the tale of Tāj al-Mulūk and Princess Dunyā in *The Arabian Nights*: the princess has a dream in which a male pigeon deserts his trapped mate; awake, the princess concludes that all men resemble the faithless bird; walking in a garden with her attendants, she sees pictures of birds which confirm her aversion to men. Although *The Arabian Nights* was too late a compilation to have served as Chaucer's model for *SqT*, the poet might have encountered some earlier version of the tale as it migrated to Western Europe. The connection in the Oriental tales between avian and human suggests that, had he completed *SqT*, Chaucer would have extended the falcon's lesson of male unfaithfulness to Canacee's relations with men. Canacee's magic mirror possesses the power to reveal to a woman the treason of her beloved, and Spenser's continuation of *SqT* tells us that Canacee, 'wondrous chast of life,' refused all suitors (*FQ* 4.2.35–7). See **204**, **242**.

167 Loomis, Roger Sherman. 'Gawain in the *Squire's Tale*.' *MLN* 52 (1937), 413–16.
Graindor de Brie's *Bataille Loquifer* (ca 1180) and the *Miroir des Histoires* of Jean d'Outremeuse (ca 1380), which describe Gawain as residing in Avalon, are cited as analogues to the Squire's implication that Gawain is still living in *Fairye* (lines 95–7).

168 Boys, Richard C. 'Some Chaucer Allusions 1705–1799.' *PQ* 17 (1938), 263–70.
Records an allusion to *SqT* by William Massey (1759) (p 265).

169 Braddy, Haldeen. 'Cambyuskan's Flying Horse and Charles VI's "Cerf Volant."' *MLR* 33 (1938), 41–4. Repr. in *Geoffrey Chaucer* (see **166**). Pp 71–5.
In Froissart's account of the dream of Charles VI of France, the king, out

hunting, is in danger of losing his favorite falcon; a winged stag appears; Charles mounts it, retrieves the falcon, and adopts the *cerf-volant* as his personal emblem. If, as seems likely, Chaucer knew the story (his friend Deschamps wrote a ballad about Charles and the flying stag), the conjunction of a flying animal, a dream, and 'un faucon pelerin' is highly suggestive for the genesis of *SqT*.

170 Harris, Brice. 'Some Seventeenth-Century Chaucer Allusions.' *PQ* 18 (1939), 395–405.
Records allusions to *SqT* by John Lane (1648) and Anon., *The Arraignment of CoOrdinate Power* (1683) (pp 397, 403).

171 Ueno, Naozo. 'Spenser's Attitude in the Continuation of Chaucer's "The Squire's Tale."' *DL* (March 1939), 3–16.
Not seen. Listed in *BPMELLJ* (1983), p 154.

172 Brown, Calvin S., Jr., and Robert H. West. '"As by the Whelp Chastised Is the Leon."' *MLN* 55 (1940), 209–10.
In addition to its proverbial origins, the falcon's analogy (line 491) may refer to actual medieval practice. The sketchbook of Villard de Honnecourt (ca 1240) contains a drawing, with accompanying text, of a trainer beating two dogs in front of a lion tied to a stake. See **173**.

173 Frank, Grace. 'Correspondence, "As by the Whelp Chastised Is the Leon." Squire's Tale, 491.' *MLN* 55 (1940), 481.
A response to Brown and West's characterization (**172**) of the falcon's phrase as 'a learned proverb of obscure origin,' documenting the saying's popularity. Given the early and widespread diffusion of the expression, it seems unlikely that Chaucer was referring to the actual art of the lion tamer.

174 Jones, H.S.V. 'The Squire's Tale.' In *Sources and Analogues of Chaucer's Canterbury Tales*. Ed. W.F. Bryan and Germaine Dempster. Chicago: U of Chicago P, 1941. Repr. New York: Humanities Press, 1958. Pp 357–76.
No unquestioned source exists for *SqT*; Chaucer employed a variety of materials, working 'inventively with a free hand' (p 357). Parallels to Part 1 are supplied from the Latin *Epistola Presbyteri Johannis*, the mid-fourteenth-century German verse rendering of the letter by Osswalt der Schribar, the Arabic tale of the ebony horse, and *Cleo*. Includes two Oriental analogues to the Canacee–falcon episode, both involving birds: the first from the Hindu *Kadambari* and, from *The Arabian Nights*, the story of Tāj al-Mulūk and Princess Dunyā. See **598**.

175 Braddy, Haldeen. 'Chaucerian Minutiae.' *MLN* 58 (1943), 18–23. Repr. in *Geoffrey Chaucer* (see **166**). Pp 96–101.
Elphita (cf. line 29) appears as a woman's name in a fifteenth-century Catalan *chanson*. The name may have been current at an earlier period and hence possibly known to Chaucer, whose access to Spanish culture included his friendship with Oton de Graunson, who was imprisoned in Catalonia.

176 Mounts, C.E. 'The Place of Chaucer and Spenser in the Genesis of *Peter Bell.*' *PQ* 23 (1944), 108–15.
The references to 'a flying horse' and 'a magic ring' in the Prologue to Wordsworth's *Peter Bell* recall *SqT.*

177 Whiting, B.J. 'A Fifteenth-Century Chaucerian: the Translator of *Partonope of Blois.*' *MS* 7 (1945), 40–54.
Partonope contains one 'fairly clear borrowing' (p 41) from *SqT* (line 505) and one close echo of its idiom (line 458).

178 ———. 'Froissart as Poet.' *MS* 8 (1946), 189–216.
The references in Froissart's *L'Espinette Amoureuse* to *Cleo* and its magic horse may have introduced Chaucer to this material, which remained in the poet's memory until he found a place for it in *SqT* (p 195n).

179 Braddy, Haldeen. *Chaucer and the French Poet Graunson.* Baton Rouge: Louisiana State UP, 1947. Repr. Port Washington, NY: Kennikat, 1968. Pp 51–3. See **175**, **180**.

180 ———. 'Two Chaucer Notes: 1. Chaucer on Murder: *De Petro Rege de Cipro;* 2. Chaucer's "Bretheren Two" and "Thilke Wikke Ensample of Canacee."' *MLN* 62 (1947), 173–9. Repr. in *Geoffrey Chaucer* (see **166**). Pp 116–21.
The Squire says he will tell how Cambalo 'faught in lystes with the bretheren two / For Canacee er that he myghte hire wynne' (lines 668–9), a situation similar to the battle between a single man and 'deux freres iermayns et twynlynges de Inde' recounted in the *Anonimalle Chronicle* for 1337; two men pitted against one is said to be an Eastern custom, and is thus appropriate to the setting of *SqT.* In the Arabian tale closest to the Canacee–falcon episode, the character analogous to Cambalo unwittingly weds his sister, providing a parallel to the hint of incest in lines 667–9.

181 Whiting, B.J. 'Gawain: His Reputation, His Courtesy and His Appearance in Chaucer's *Squire's Tale.*' *MS* 9 (1947), 189–234. Repr. in *Twentieth Century Interpretations of Sir Gawain and the Green Knight. A Collection of Critical Essays.* Ed. Denton Fox. Englewood Cliffs, NJ: Prentice-Hall, 1968, pp 73–8, and in *Gawain: A Casebook.* Ed. Raymond H. Thompson and Keith Busby. New York: Routledge, 2006, pp 45–94.
The reference to 'Gawayn, with his olde curteisye' (line 95) may reflect Chaucer's familiarity with *SGGK.* The alliterative poem strongly emphasizes Gawain's courtesy, and the opening scenes of both poems share two elements: a king's feast and an unexpected guest. See **182**.

182 Magoun, Francis P., Jr. 'Chaucer's Sir Gawain and the OFr. *Roman de la Rose.*' *MLN* 67 (1952), 183–5.
Responding to Whiting (**181**), Magoun notes that the Squire's reference to Gawain's 'olde curteisye' (line 95) is more likely to reflect Chaucer's memory of *RR* 2209–10 ('Gauvains … Par sa cortosie ot li pris') than his reading of *SGGK.* It is doubtful that *SGGK* circulated widely outside of the area in

which it was written. Chaucer would have found the alliterative poem difficult going, and, in any event, cared little for Arthurian romance.

183 Bennett, Josephine Waters. 'Chaucer and *Mandeville's Travels.*' *MLN* 68 (1953), 531–4.
The Squire's comment on the strange food at Cambyuskan's court may recall the description of the diet of the Khan's Tartar subjects in *Mandeville's Travels*. Although the *Travels* is apparently echoing Vincent of Beauvais, Chaucer's 'as tellen knyghtes olde' (line 69) suggests that he had the English author in mind; 'Ther nys no man that may reporten al' (line 72) recalls the disclaimer at the end of the *Travels*.

184 Chapman, Coolidge Otis. 'Chaucer and the *Gawain*-Poet: A Conjecture.' *MLN* 68 (1953), 521–4.
Argues that Chaucer used the first part of *SGGK* as a model for *SqT*. Similarities include two kings holding state banquets upon festival days in their capital cities, the entrance of a stranger knight at a specified point in the banquet, the wonder of the courtiers when the knight appears, the mention of Gawain by name and the reference to his courtesy in *SqT*, the sudden departure of both knights, the courtiers' association of the Green Knight and the flying horse with *fairye*, the resumption of the banquets after the interruptions and the connection of marvelous events and the siege of Troy. 'It seems beyond the possibility of coincidence that Chaucer and the author of *Gawain* could have worked in complete independence of each other' (pp 521–2).

185 Allen, Don Cameron. *The Harmonious Vision: Studies in Milton's Poetry*. Baltimore, MD: Johns Hopkins UP, 1954/1970.
Spenser was charmed by *SqT*'s courtliness; Milton's interest lay in the poem's magical objects (the ring, the glass, the horse) as symbols of intellectual power (pp 12–13).

186 Bennett, Josephine Waters. *The Rediscovery of Sir John Mandeville*. New York: Modern Language Association, 1954.
See **183**.

187 Emerson, Francis Willard. 'The Bible in Spenser's Chaucer.' *N&Q* n.s. 5 (1958), 422–3.
Spenser is indebted to 2 Kings for certain elements of his treatment of magic and human actions in his continuation of *SqT* in *FQ*, Book 4.

188 ———. 'The Spenser-Followers in Leigh Hunt's Chaucer.' *N&Q* n.s. 5 (1958), 284–6.
Character and place names, the description of the stranger knight's gifts, and the actions of characters in Hunt's modernization of *SqT*, Part 1 reveal his indebtedness to seventeenth- and eighteenth-century modernizations and continuations of the tale by John Lane, Samuel Boyse, George Ogle, and Joseph Sterling.

189 Nelson, William. *The Poetry of Edmund Spenser: A Study*. New York: Columbia UP, 1963.

The influence of *SqT* and *KnT* is felt throughout Book 4 of *FQ*, both in specific allusions and in the overarching themes of father and children, brothers fighting against a lover, the difficult winning of a lady, and close friendship turning to enmity and then reestablished (pp 237–8).

190 Fowler, Alastair. *Spenser and the Numbers of Time*. London: Routledge and Kegan Paul, 1964.

Cambina's caduceus (*FQ* 4.3.46) is linked, by way of an allusion to the ring of Gyges, with Canacee's ring in *SqT* (pp 189–90).

191 Heuston, Edward F. 'The Chaucer Sprig in Wordsworth's "Liberty."' *N&Q* n.s. 11 (1964), 20–1.

The source of the Chaucer passage in Wordsworth's 'Liberty' has been wrongly identified as *SqT* (lines 610–20). The correct source is *ManT* (IX.163–74).

192 Hoffman, Richard L. *Ovid and the Canterbury Tales*. Philadelphia: U of Pennsylvania P, 1966.

Notes Ovidian parallels to lines 238–40 (the spear used by Achilles, first to wound and then to heal King Telephus), line 207 ('the Pegasee'), and lines 220–4 (the idle speculations of the ignorant crowd) (pp 161–4).

193 Maxwell, J.C. '"The Ancient Mariner"' and "The Squire's Tale."' *N&Q* n.s. 13 (1966), 224.

Cites lines 393–4 as a possible source for Coleridge's 'broad bright Sun' (*Rime of the Ancient Mariner*, line 174).

194 Bawcutt, Priscilla. 'Gavin Douglas and Chaucer.' *RES* n.s. 21 (1970), 401–21.

Lines 30–2 of the Prologue to Book 12 of Douglas's *Eneados* echo *SqT* (line 671).

195 Friend, Albert C. 'The Tale of the Captive Bird and the Traveler: Nequam, Berechiah, and Chaucer's *Squire's Tale*.' *M&H* n.s. 1 (1970), 57–65.

Near the end of Part 2, the Squire promises that he will explain how the caged falcon will find its mate again by mediation of Prince Cambalus. In Alexander Nequam's *De naturis rerum*, in a late twelfth-century compilation of fables by Rabbi Berechiah, and in two medieval Persian poems, a caged bird, aided by a traveler or friendly knight, feigns death in order to gain its freedom and search for its mate. Had he finished *SqT*, Chaucer might have used a plot similar to this one.

196 Wimsatt, James I. '*Anelida and Arcite*: A Narrative of Complaint and Comfort.' *ChauR* 5 (1970), 1–8.

Given the parallels between *Anel* and *SqT*, the predicted happy ending of the incomplete love story in the latter (lines 654–5) suggests that *Anel*, if completed, would tell of the happy reunion of the lovers (p 7).

197 Arthurs, Judith Gott. *Edmund Spenser and Dan Chaucer: A Study of the Influence of The Canterbury Tales on The Faerie Queene*. PhD diss., University of

Arkansas, 1973. Dir. Lawrence E. Guinn and David W. Hart. Ann Arbor, MI: University Microfilms International, 1971. See also *DAI*–A 34/06 (1973): 3334.

In his continuation of *SqT* in *FQ* 4, Spenser's main interest was in the suggestion of a battle for Canacee's hand; love and friendship were intimately connected in Spenser's mind (p 94). In the Renaissance, the heroic was one of the arenas of allegorical action. Spenser's characterization of Chaucer as the poet of 'warlike numbers and Heroicke sound' helps explain the insistently allegorical mode of *FQ* 4.2–3, in which the magical properties and astrological allusions of *SqT* are provided with a new layer of moral significance, as in Spenser's handling of the final lines the Squire's narrative: 'Chaucer promises battles, then Apollo moves into the house of Mercury. Spenser provides the battles, then Cambina – Mercury's representative – brings a new day of peace' (p 120).

198 Halaby, Raouf Jamil. *Arabic Influences on Chaucer: Speculative Essays on a Study of a Literary Relationship.* PhD diss., East Texas State University, 1973. Dir. Laurence F. McNamee. Ann Arbor, MI: University Microfilms International, 1973. See also *DAI*–A 34/09 (1974): 5911–12.

Notes similarities between the Canacee–falcon episode and the 'Exemplum of the Two Pigeons' in Ibn al-Muqaffa's *Kaleela wa Dumna* (pp 69–70).

199 Wimsatt, J.I. 'Chaucer and French Poetry.' In *Geoffrey Chaucer*. Writers and their Work. London: Bell, 1974; Athens: Ohio State UP, 1974; pbk ed., 1974. Pp 109–36.

Had Chaucer completed *Anel* and *SqT*, the formal complaints of Anelida and the falcon might have resulted in comfort being provided, perhaps in a separate speech by the loved one, as in Machaut's *Fonteinne amoureuse*.

200 Hieatt, A. Kent. *Chaucer, Spenser, Milton: Mythopoeic Continuities and Transformations*. Montreal: McGill-Queens UP, 1975.

In his continuation of *SqT* in *FQ* 4.2–3, Spenser reworks the themes and narrative materials of *KnT*; he would have been encouraged to do so by the position of *SqT* in his text of *CT* (one of the Thynne family of editions), where it follows the sequence *KnT–MilT–RvT–CkT–MLT*. In the Thynne editions, *SqT* immediately precedes the Marriage Group tales. In his continuation, Spenser introduces the motif of discord and ensuing concord, thus creating a version of *SqT* that anticipates the resolution of the marriage debate in *FranT* (pp 75–8).

• Review by John Buxton, *RES* n.s. 28 (1977), 345–6: Hieatt's consideration of tale order in the Chaucerian texts available to Spenser produces a 'new and convincing' (p 345) discussion of the latter's indebtedness to the former.

201 Miskimin, Alice S. *The Renaissance Chaucer*. New Haven, CT: Yale UP, 1975.

Spenser's continuation of *SqT* is his answer to Chaucer's anxiety, as expressed in *TC* 5.1793–9, about the vulnerability of his text. By carrying Chaucer's unfinished tale to its conclusion, Spenser preserves the older poet's 'sweete spirit' even though his words decay (pp 280–1).

202 Hieatt, A. Kent. '*The Canterbury Tales* in *The Faerie Queene*.' In *Spenser in the Middle Ages*. Ed. David A. Richardson. Proceedings from a Special Session at the Eleventh Conference on Medieval Studies in Kalamazoo, Michigan, 2–5 May 1976. Cleveland: Cleveland State UP, 1976. Pp 217–29.
See **200**. See also **203**.

203 Holahan, Michael. 'A Commentary on "*The Canterbury Tales* in *The Faerie Queene*," by A. Kent Hieatt.' In *Spenser and the Middle Ages*. 1976. See **202**. Pp 230–6.
A response to **202**. 'Discontinuity and change' (p 230) are the central elements in Spenser's reinterpretation of Chaucer in *FQ* 4.2–3. Spenser believed *SqT* to be 'unfinished by Time rather than abandoned by its author' (p 231); he attempts to redeem this loss by working variations on Chaucerian themes within a new context. By means of specific allusions to *KnT* and *FranT*, whose narrators are the Squire's literal and figurative fathers, respectively, Spenser foregrounds the issue of authority; the younger poet makes us aware that, in attempting to overcome distance and difference, he is himself the author of those continuities that extend from Chaucer's work to his own.

204 Metlitzki, Dorothee. *The Matter of Araby in Medieval England*. New Haven, CT: Yale UP, 1977.
Chaucer 'clearly intended to develop [*SqT*] on an Arabian model' (p 141). One such model can be found in the tale of King Omar Bin al-Nu'uman in *The Arabian Nights*, which contains among its episodes an already recognized analogue to the Canacee–falcon episode (see **166**); like *SqT*, this group of interlinked stories is a family romance set in a royal household that includes two sons and a daughter. Further parallels to *SqT* can be found in the Byzantine epic *Digenes Akritas* (e.g., a noble household consisting of a famous father and a sister and two brothers, an elopement on a famous horse, and a fight against two brothers for a captured maiden). The episode of Canacee and the falcon bears a general similarity to a scene in which Digenes overhears the lament of a lady betrayed by her lover, whom Digenes seeks out and reconciles with the girl he had abandoned (pp 140–52). See **242**, **504**.

205 Fox, Alistair. 'Thomas More's *Dialogue* and the *Book of the Tales of Canterbury*: "Good Mother Wit" and Creative Imagination.' In *Familiar Colloquy: Essays Presented to Arthur Edward Barker*. Ed. Patricia Carr Brückmann. Ontario: Oberon, 1978. Pp 15–24.
Finds an echo of *SqT* (lines 258–60) in More's *Dialogue Concerning Heresies* (pp 17–18).

206 Donaldson, E. Talbot. 'Chaucer and the Twentieth Century.' *SAC* 2 (1980), 7–13.
'The seventeenth century took [Chaucer's] poems seriously enough … to

regret the incompleteness of one of them, as Milton did, or to rectify its incompleteness, as John Lane did (one would have to say that while the seventeenth century had grown up to *TC*, it failed to outgrow *SqT*)' (p 7).

207 DiMarco, Vincent. 'A Note on Canacee's Magic Ring.' *Anglia* 99 (1981), 399–405.

Chaucer's immediate source for the allusion to Moses's magic ring (lines 247–51) may be a passage in Roger Bacon's *Opus maius*, which, unlike other analogues, associates Moses with Solomon and links magic with astrology, as does *SqT*. The function of the ring in the promised continuation of the tale might have developed its 'Mosaic' aspects, its power to affect memory and confer forgetfulness.

208 ———. 'Richard Hole and the *Merchant's* and *Squire's Tales*: An Unrecognized Eighteenth-Century (1797) Contribution to Source and Analogue Study.' *ChauR* 16 (1981), 171–80.

Richard Hole, in his *Remarks on the Arabian Nights Entertainments* (1797), was the first to point out the connection between *SqT* and the Oriental tale of the Enchanted Horse. Hole also suggests that the 'magic' of the sword brought by the stranger knight should be understood in a scientific context. (An appendix cites Pliny on the healing properties of certain metals.) Editions of *Cleo* and the *Méliacin* published since Jones's studies (**133**, **135**) call into question his assertion that both French poems derive from a common source. DiMarco also refers to work in progress in which he will argue that 'the *Méliacin* is at all points closer to *SqT* than is *Cleo*' (p 179n10).

209 Goldberg, Jonathan. *Endlesse Worke: Spenser and the Structures of Discourse*. Baltimore, MD: Johns Hopkins UP, 1981.

The attempt to end *SqT* in Book 4 of *FQ* exemplifies the problematic nature of Spenserian narration. Spenser's task is to restore the lost ending of *SqT* by entering into the voice of another – an act of surrogacy that characterizes narration in *SqT* itself (see **572**). The ending to *SqT* supplied in *FQ* is not conclusive; the text continues beyond it, proceeding by 'further acts of annihilation and repudiation' (p 43). Book 4 'so fully absorbs the voice of its source that it cannot end itself except by undoing itself. This, as *SqT* implies, is the nature of narrative ... Rather than supplying the loss in *SqT*, finishing it and making it whole, book IV imitates the lacuna that the Chaucerian tale defines as the space of narration' (p 44).

• Review by Eric Sacks, *MLN* 97 (1982), 1298–1303: Goldberg idealizes the loss of the ending of *SqT* as absolute. 'But Chaucer was never really as lost in canto 2, where *SqT* is first mentioned, as Spenser, and Goldberg following him, would have liked'; canto 12 discovers 'that this place belongs to Chaucer' (p 1302).

210 Marrani, Najiyah Ghafil. *Athar 'Arabiyah fi Hikayat Kantirburi: Dirasah Muqaranah*. [The impact of the Arab in the Canterbury Tales: a comprehensive study.] [Baghdad]: al-Jumhuriyah al-'Iraqiyah, Wizarat al-Thaqafah wa-al-I'lam, Dar al-Rashid lil-Nashr: al-Dar al-Wataniyah lil-Tawzi' wa-al-I'lan, 1981.

Surveys the presence of Arabic culture in *CT,* focusing on the plots and sources of *SqT* and *PardT,* the frame-tale structure of *CT,* allusions to Arabic personages, and uses of words that derive from Arabic. In Arabic. (Not seen. Summary from http://newchaucersociety.org/pages/entry/chaucer-bibliography.)

211 O'Neill, William. '"L'Allegro", "Il Penseroso", and Some Daybreak Scenes from *The Canterbury Tales.*' *N&Q* n.s. 29 (1982), 494–5.

Lines 131–2 of Milton's "Il Penseroso" echo *SqT,* lines 391–4.

212 Richardson, J.M. 'More Symbolic Numbers in Spenser's "Aprill."' *N&Q* n.s. 29 (1982), 411–12.

If the lay to Elisa in 'Aprill' is divided according to the ratio of the Golden Section, the division falls on line 72 ('That it a heaven is to heare'). The line contains Chaucerian echoes (cf. *TC* 2.826 and 3.1742; *SqT,* line 271); Chaucer is 'one of the Tityri Spenser wishes to rival' (p 412).

213 Best, Thomas W. *Reynard the Fox.* Boston: Twayne, 1983.

The late fourteenth-century Dutch *Reinaerts Historie,* which contains a description of a magical ring and mirror and alludes to the ebony horse in *Cleo,* should perhaps be counted as one of the sources of *SqT* (p 123).

214 Baldi, Sergio. 'Di un poema non scritto.' *RLMC* 37 (1984), 285–305.

Milton's allusion to *SqT* in "Il Penseroso" may be read as a tribute to his father's friend John Lane, who wrote a continuation of Chaucer's poem, or perhaps as evidence that Milton found gnostic symbolism in the horse, mirror, and magic ring.

215 Schless, Howard H. *Chaucer and Dante: A Revaluation.* Norman, OK: Pilgrim, 1984.

Questions Bethel's assertion (**158**) that Dante's influence is discernible in *SqT*'s frequent references to *gentilesse.* The verbal parallels are not striking, and the Squire's type of *gentilesse,* focused on courtly love, is significantly different from Dante's conception of this virtue (pp 198–203).

216 Cheney, Patrick. 'Spenser's completion of *The Squire's Tale*: love, magic, and heroic action in the Legend of Cambell and Triamond.' *JMRS* 15 (1985), 135–55.

In imitating and completing *SqT,* Spenser at once retains and alters Chaucer's treatment of love, magic, and heroism. The Squire wishes to depict the magical power of romantic love, but the three elements of the traditional *mythos* exist in a fragmented state, without a visionary or active quest that might link them. In *FQ* 4.2–3, Spenser reintegrates these fragments in a metaphysical allegory that reveals love 'as the true magical form of heroism' (p 145). Spenser's imitation of Chaucer – the poetic process of 'infusion sweete' (*FQ* 4.2.34) whereby the spirit of the dead poet survives in the living one – is paralleled in the heroic process of 'traduction,' in which the souls of Priamond and Diamond, the first and second sons of Agape slain in battle with Cambell, survive in their brother Triamond.

217 Conner, Edwin Lee. '*The Squire's Tale* and Its Teller: Medieval Tradition and Chaucer's Artistry of Allusion.' PhD diss., Vanderbilt University, 1985. Dir. Emerson Brown, Jr. See also *DAI*–A 47/02 (1986): 534–5.
As part of his gently satiric treatment of romantic love, Chaucer embeds in the falcon episode a sustained pattern of allusions to *Inferno* 5, together with an imitation of some of its rhetorical and structural conventions (pp 223–9). Appendix B (pp 301–2) prints parallel passages.

218 Dane, Joseph A. 'Genre and Authority: The Eighteenth-Century Creation of Chaucerian Burlesque.' *HLQ* 48 (1985), 345–62. Repr. in Dane, *Parody: Critical Concepts Versus Literary Practices, Aristophanes to Sterne*. Norman: U of Oklahoma P, 1988. Pp 185–203.
In contrast to *Thop*, labeled a burlesque by eighteenth-century commentators, *SqT* was viewed as a serious poem containing burlesque or parodic elements. The difference in the two poems' reception is based on the different criteria used to evaluate them. The availability of the literary categories of burlesque and parody, newly imported into England from France, provided authority for reading *Thop* as a 'meta-poem' (p 355), a critical commentary on the genre of which it is an example. The authority of Spenser's and Milton's praise, on the other hand, dictated interpretations of *SqT* as a noble and heroic narrative. 'When the evidence [e.g., the passages of 'tedious detail' noted by Thomas Warton] and the authorities came into conflict, the authorities were slow to give way, and did so only with the creation of newer, less assailable authorities, such as unwritten and imaginary portions of Chaucer's text' (p 357–8) – as in Warton's regret that the most interesting parts of the poem were either lost or had never been composed.

218a Morris, Lynn King. *Chaucer Sources and Analogue Criticism: A Cross-Referenced Guide*. New York: Garland, 1985.
A guide to the literature (through 1981) on the sources and analogues of Chaucer's writings, indexed by title of Chaucerian work, author of source or analogue, genre or origin of source, and title of source or analogue. The entry for *SqT*, pp 177–9, lists 104 sources, analogues, and allusions, with accompanying bibliographical references. Single works are sometimes listed under separate titles (e.g., Epistle of Prester John; Epistola Presbyteri Johannes).

219 Cheney, Donald. 'Envy in the Middest of the 1596 *Faerie Queene*.' In *Edmund Spenser*. Ed. Harold Bloom. New York: Chelsea House, 1986. Pp 267–83.
The 'infusion' of Chaucer's spirit into the living Spenser (*FQ* 4.2.34) parallels the passage of life from brother to brother in *FQ* 4.3. Spenser's relation to Chaucer is based on the possibilities and limitations of fantasy. Chaucer's

Squire is a figure of the youthful poet, and is also subordinate to the will of another (his father). His tale breaks off just after we learn that Cambalo will marry his own sister. Spenser's revision of *SqT* avoids this difficulty by having brothers and sisters intermarry rather than marry, and by producing a supernatural drug that makes closure possible.

220 Bowden, Betsy. *Chaucer Aloud: Varieties of Textual Interpretation*. Philadelphia: U of Pennsylvania P, 1987.
Brief comments on George Ogle's 1741 modernization of Spenser's *SqT* continuation (pp 168–9).

221 Martin, Ellen E. 'Spenser, Chaucer, and the rhetoric of elegy.' *JMRS* 17 (1987), 83–109.
In his continuation of *SqT* in *FQ* 4.2–3, Spenser transmutes loss into invention. Although *SqT* has been eroded by time, Spenser restores it by assuming Chaucer's authority, imagining him as 'a kind of holy ghost breathing upon later poets' (p 106). Spenser's idea of a literary metempsychosis is figured in the narrative of Priamond, Diamond, and Triamond; 'the event and the telling of it are both infusions of spirits into other spirits' (p 106).

221a Besserman, Lawrence. *Chaucer and the Bible: A Critical Review of Research, Indexes, and Bibliography*. New York: Garland, 1988.
Lists eight certain or possible biblical allusions in *SqT* (lines 249–51, 499, 512–13, 518–20, 550–1, 552, 555, 596), with references to scholarly discussions (p 121).

222 Hollander, John. *Melodious Guile: Fictive Pattern in Poetic Language*. New Haven, CT: Yale UP, 1988.
Milton's allusion to *SqT* in 'Il Penseroso,' lines 109–115, contains a suppressed reference to Spenser, who completed Chaucer's 'half told' tale, and who tells us that 'Triamond had Canacee to wife' (cf. 'And who had Canace to wife,' 'Il Penseroso,' line 112) in *FQ* 4.3.52 (p 167).

223 Anderson, Judith. '"Myn auctour": Spenser's Enabling Fiction and Eumnestes' "immortal scrine."' In *Unfolded Tales: Essays on Renaissance Romance*. Ed. George M. Logan and Gordon Teskey. Ithaca, NY: Cornell UP, 1989. Pp 16–31.
Spenser's blending of *KnT* with *SqT* in his extension of the latter in *FQ* 4.2–3 – a fusion of the father's work with the son's – is a paradigm of his own relation to Chaucer's text. Spenser hopes not to complete *SqT* but to 'meete' with Chaucer's 'meaning,' to participate in rather than appropriate the sources of Chaucer's ideas, and thus to permit the 'infusion' of the older poet's 'spirit' into his own (p 30).

224 Tonkin, Humphrey. *The Faerie Queene*. London: Unwin Hyman, 1989.
Spenser does not attempt to complete *SqT*, but rather to capture its combination of the 'fantastic and the chivalric' (p 138). Spenser distributes elements of *SqT* through Books 3 and 4, the magic mirror in the former, Cambalo and

Canacee in the latter. In the final fragment of *SqT*, Apollo enters into 'the god Mercurius hous.' Mercury is the God of Concord whose main symbol is the caduceus. It is just such a caduceus that Cambina carries when she intervenes to establish harmony between Cambell and Triamond (*FQ* 4.3.42–3) (pp 138–9).

225 Burrow, John A. 'Chaucer, Geoffrey.' In *The Spenser Encyclopedia*. Gen. ed. A.C. Hamilton. Toronto: U of Toronto P, 1990. Pp 145–8.
In the prologue to his continuation of *SqT* (*FQ* 4.2), Spenser imitates the opening of *Anel*, in which Chaucer had lamented the near loss of an old story rescued from a Latin source. Spenser stands in the same relation to Chaucer as Chaucer stood to his Latin forebears. In speaking of Chaucer's 'warlike numbers,' Spenser clearly had *KnT* as well as *SqT* in mind. Spenser makes what he can of Chaucer's puzzling hints for future action, but his claim to having discovered Chaucer's lost meaning (*FQ* 4.2.34) cannot be taken seriously. Spenser's regard for *SqT* as one of Chaucer's major achievements appears not only in his development of the Cambell–Canacee plot, but also in his treatment of magic in Book 4 and elsewhere in *FQ*.

226 Higgins, Anne. 'Spenser Reading Chaucer: Another Look at the *Faerie Queene* Allusions.' *JEGP* 89 (1990), 17–36.
In announcing that he will complete *SqT*, Spenser 'lays down a false trail' (p 23): his continuation in *FQ* 4.2–3 relies less on *SqT* than on the structure and themes of *KnT*. By seeming to finish the fragmentary *SqT* while actually reworking the monumental *KnT*, Spenser deflects the charge that he insufficiently venerates one of the older poet's most revered narratives. Declaring his intention to renew the tale of the son while in reality rewriting the work of the father, Spenser signals his own ambivalent attitude toward Chaucer, a mixture of filial respect and brash confidence in his own poetic powers.

227 Windeatt, Barry. 'Chaucer and fifteenth-century romance: *Partonope of Blois*.' In *Chaucer Traditions: Studies in Honour of Derek Brewer*. Ed. Ruth Morse and Barry Windeatt. Cambridge: Cambridge UP, 1990. Pp 62–80.
The values Melior hopes to find in Partonope ('Loo yender goþ the welle of gentylnes,' line 1857) echo the gentle falcon's expression of trust in her lover ('That semed welle of alle gentillesse,' line 505) (p 76).

228 Bowden, Betsy, ed. *Eighteenth-Century Modernizations from The Canterbury Tales*. Rochester, NY: Brewer, 1991.
Reprints modernizations of *SqT* by Samuel Boyse (1741), John Penn (1794), and an anonymous version from *The Monthly Magazine, and British Register* for 1796. The three translators' renderings of lines 373–83 are briefly compared in the introduction.

229 Sanders, Arnold A. 'Ruddymane and Canace, Lost and Found: Spenser's Reception of Gower's *Confessio Amantis* 3 and Chaucer's *Squire's Tale*.' In *The Work of Dissimilitude: Essays from the Sixth Citadel Conference on Medieval and*

Renaissance Literature. Ed. David G. Allen and Robert A. White. Newark: U of Delaware P; London: Associated University Presses, 1992. Pp 196–215.
Spenser's account of the dying Amavia (*FQ* 2.1.35–56) may owe something to the scene of Canacee's death (itself based on Ovid's *Heroides*) in *CA* 3.312–15. Gower's Canacee, who has innocently committed incest with her brother, is made the victim of her father Eolus's wrath. Spenser's reception of Gower's poem may reflect his reading of *SqT*. Motivated by his desire to evade the bourgeois pilgrims' threats to his social status and by his wish to display his capacities as a courtly poet, the Squire allows his heroine to escape the fate to which she has been condemned by Ovid and Gower, using the falcon's tale as a warning against the fickleness of princely lovers and defending her from 'the perils of uninstructed sensuality' (p 208). In *FQ* 4, Spenser completes the task begun by Chaucer, presenting Canacee as an embodiment of chastity.

230 Lerer, Seth. *Chaucer and His Readers: Imagining the Author in Late-Medieval England.* Princeton, NJ: Princeton UP, 1993.
In Ch. 2, 'Reading Like the Squire: Lydgate, Clanvowe, and the Fifteenth-Century Anthology' (pp 57–84), Lerer argues that 'the drama of [the Squire's] predicament – being trapped between the desire to emulate the fatherly *auctoritas* of the Knight and to live up to the paternalistic critical expectations of the Franklin – offered Chaucer's imitators a model for articulating their relationship to their master' (p 58). In his *Book of Cupid,* John Clanvowe situates himself in relation to 'father' Chaucer by playfully adopting the Squire's voice. The Squire's performance may also be read as encapsulating the literary tastes of the readers who commissioned the collections that transmitted Clanvowe's poem, many of Chaucer's minor works, and the courtly imitations of Lydgate and Hoccleve. Like the Squire, these readers are 'members of the rising gentry who … share a taste for courtly making in the service of the god of love' (p 59).
• Review by Derek Pearsall, *YES* 25 (1995), 247–9: Lerer's argument that 'the early Chaucerians were prompted to read and construct Chaucer according to models of relations between speakers and audiences in the writings of Chaucer himself' is 'an unfortunate conceit that the book would have been better without' (p 248).

231 Ryan, Francis X., 'Sir Thomas More's Use of Chaucer.' *SEL* 35 (1995), 1–17.
More's *Dialogue Concerning Heresies* contains echoes of *SqT* lines 253–5 and 258–60 (p 6).

232 Berry, Craig A. '"Sundrie Doubts": Vulnerable Understanding and Dubious Origins in Spenser's Continuation of the Squire's Tale.' In *Refiguring Chaucer in the Renaissance.* Ed. Theresa M. Krier. Gainesville: UP of Florida, 1998. Pp 106–27.
Spenser's proposal to continue the unfinished *SqT* in *FQ* 4.2 illuminates his

attempt to overcome his doubts about his place in the English poetic tradition. Part 1 of *SqT* shares with *FQ* 4 a preoccupation with doubts that lead to conflicting or multiple interpretations; 'both poets show us what good readers should be like by showing us what bad readers are like' (p 111). Whereas Chaucer's parable of readerly interpretation revels in the multiplication of doubt, Spenser attempts to resolve doubts about the interpretation of his poem. By 'quiting' *SqT* with a poem of his own that dilates on the meaning of its predecessor, Spenser simultaneously renders homage to and distances himself from the older poet, balancing his evocation of an authoritative continuity of poetic endeavor with a staking out of new territory that escapes the limits of tradition.

233 Hieatt, A. Kent. 'Room of One's Own for Decisions: Chaucer and *The Faerie Queene*.' In *Refiguring Chaucer in the Renaissance*. 1998. See **232**. Pp 147–64.
The Franklin's words on the incompatibility of love and *maistrye* (lines 761–70), paraphrased once in Book 3 (1.12) and twice in Book 4 (1.42, 9.37) of *FQ*, provide a key to Spenser's treatment of the relation between friendship and amatory choice. The uniting of love and friendship in Spenser's completion of the unfinished *SqT* in Book 4 of *FQ* turns Chaucer's tale into the first member of a Marriage Group that ends with the moral of *FranT*. The model of the consolatory love–friendship pattern of *KnT* also helped Spenser complete the Knight's son's tale.
• Review by Carol V. Kaske, *JEGP* 99 (2000), 448–51: Hieatt's case for the centrality of the Franklin's echoed words to the central books of *FQ* is 'unified, far-reaching, and convincing' (p 450).

234 Stubblefield, Jay. 'A Note on Spenser's *Faerie Queene* IV and Chaucer's *Squire's Tale*.' *ELN* 36 (1998), 9–10.
Near the end of the *pars secunda* of *SqT*, Chaucer promises that he will speak of Cambalo's battle in the lists with 'the bretheren two' (lines 667–9); the story is never told because Part 3 is broken off. In his continuation of *SqT* in *FQ* 4, Spenser introduces Cambel in canto 2, but defers the story of his battle with Triamond until canto 3, thus following closely the 'footing' of Chaucer's 'feete' as he had promised to do in his invocation of the older poet at the end of canto 2.

235 Kennedy, William J. 'Spenser's Squire's Literary History.' In *Worldmaking Spenser: Explorations in the Early Modern Age*. Ed. Patrick Cheney and Lauren Silberman. Lexington: UP of Kentucky, 2000. Pp 45–62.
In attempting to complete *SqT* in Book 4 of *FQ*, Spenser foregrounds a complex interaction between Chaucer's Squire and his own Squire of Dames and between Chaucer's self-representation and his own narrator. The interruption of *SqT* (by the Merchant in the edition of Chaucer that Spenser most likely used) calls attention to the tale's patrimonial focus and its link with Spenser's continuation. In *FQ* 4.3, Spenser supplements the authority of

Chaucer with that of Ariosto, thus deepening the question of who owns the tale. 'The tale's continuation functions as a magic talisman enabling Spenser to overcome the tyranny of Chaucer by annexing foreign resources from Ariosto' (p 52).

236 Mehl, Dieter. '"A Lover's Complaint": Shakespeare and Chaucer.' *Archiv* 237 (2000), 133–8.
Part 2 of *SqT* is a possible source for Shakespeare's 'A Lover's Complaint.' In both cases, the pathos of the betrayed lover is undercut by the manner of presentation, in particular the 'self-consciously literary character' of the forsaken lady's complaint (p 136), and by the absence of any perspective other than the speaker's that would provide a unbiased impression of the male wooer.

237 Westrem, Scott D. 'Geography and Travel.' In *A Companion to Chaucer*. Ed. Peter Brown. Oxford: Blackwell, 2000. Pp 195–217.
Finds echoes of *The Book of John Mandeville* in *SqT* lines 59–61 and 69–72.

238 Berry, Craig A. 'Flying Sources: Classical Authority in Chaucer's *Squire's Tale*.' *ELH* 68 (2001), 287–313.
In *SqT*, Chaucer employs classical authorities as models for the poem's rhetorical operations. The steed of brass is 'a figure for the poem' (p 292). Its creator is analogous to a poetic *makere*, and the narrator's dismissive comments on the court's reception of the horse – something 'made, not begotten' (p 294) – seems to suggest that the poem owes its authority to its teller rather than to its predecessors. Yet Chaucer employs classical sources that are themselves about fiction making. The comparison of the horse to 'the Pegasee' (lines 207–8) – linked in Ovid with poetic origins – engages the tension between originality and dependence on tradition. The allusion to Sinon (line 209), whose deceptive words persuaded the Trojans to bring the horse into their city, foregrounds questions of linguistic truth and falsehood in the tale. Sinon's rhetorical excess suggests parallels with the Squire-as-narrator, while his status both as an outsider and an insider clarifies the Squire's stance in relation to his audience. A trickster and courtly performer, the narrator is linked with the tale's *jogelours* (line 519), a role not inconsistent with his status as heir to classical tradition, since the medieval Virgil was often represented as magician and is said in *Cleo* to have created a metal horse. Mercury, the winged trickster god, is a better model than the authoritative Apollo (see lines 671–2) for Chaucer's poetic activity in a poem that never permits us to hear the unmediated voice of authority.

239 Boffey, Julia, and A.S.G. Edwards. 'An Unpublished Middle English Lyric and a Chaucer Allusion.' *Archiv* 238 (2001), 327–30.
Bodleian Library MS Bodley 120 contains an unpublished ME lyric that contains the phrase 'norice of deiestion' (line 15), an echo of *SqT* line 347.

240 Krier, Theresa M. *Birth Passages: Maternity and Nostalgia, Antiquity to Shake-*

speare. Ithaca, NY: Cornell UP, 2001.
Spenser's revivification of Chaucer in *FQ* 4 includes his reimagining of Canacee as a woman whose understanding of animal languages derives not (as in Chaucer) from magic but from her erudition (*FQ* 4.2.35), which is made possible by her resistance to the courtly world and its available forms of erotic love (p 218).

241 Lightsey, Scott. 'Lydgate's "Stede of Bras," A Chaucerian Analogue in *Troy Book* IV.' *ELN* 38 (2001), 33–40.
In the Trojan horse episode of his *Troy Book*, Lydgate's amplifications of his primary source (Guido delle Colonne's *Historia destructionis Troiae*) suggest that he had in mind Chaucer's account of the 'steede of bras' (line 81) in *SqT*. Developing the moral implications of deception present in Chaucer, Lydgate folds the image of deception into his own account of the Trojan horse.

242 DiMarco, Vincent. 'The Squire's Tale.' In *Sources and Analogues of The Canterbury Tales*. Vol. 1. Ed. Robert M. Correale and Mary Hamel. Woodbridge, UK: Brewer, 2002. Pp 169–209.
This work incorporates scholarship on the sources and analogues of *CT* produced since Bryan and Dempster's compilation (**174**). With the exception of Nature's confession in *RR*, no close literary source for *SqT* has come to light. Part 1 bears some similarities to the oriental 'Tale of the Enchanted Horse,' which was retold in two OFr. romances, *Cleo* and the *Meliacin* of Girart d'Amiens. Chaucer may have known one or both of these romances, but the absence of verbal parallels suggests a general familiarity rather than a close acquaintance. The historical setting is Chaucer's fictionalizing of the relationship between the court of Sarai (the fourteenth-century capital of the Golden Horde) and the kingdom of Middle India, centered in Cairo (see **636**). Chaucer's rationalistic treatment of the marvelous in Part 1 links *SqT* with the late-medieval tradition of speculation and experiment regarding magical phenomena. Part 2 may be a reworking of earlier material that appears in *Anel*. DiMarco cites but expresses reservations about the suggestions of Braddy (**440**) and Metlitzki (**204**) regarding possible parallels to Part 2. The analogue in the tenth-century *Katha Sarit Sagara* of Somadeva seems closer to Chaucer's treatment than the analogues proposed by these scholars. The texts printed by DiMarco include excerpts from Girart's *Meliacin*; analogues to material in Part 2 from *Consol*, *RR*, and Alexander Nequam (see **195**); and a range of passages illustrative of the steed of brass, the magic mirror, ring, and sword, meteorological science (cf. lines 258–60), 'marvels and causes,' and Mongol customs.
• Review by Robert Hanning, *TMR* (November 2002), n.p.: DiMarco's chapter reconceptualizes the positivist model that shaped Bryan and Dempster's work by including ethnographic and intellectual contexts unconsidered in the earlier volume.

• Review by Stephen Knight, *Speculum* 79 (2004), 1057–9: DiMarco's 'vigorous contextualization' shows *SqT* as 'one of Chaucer's most up-to-date efforts, then and now' (p 1058).

• Review by Jill Mann, *JEGP* 104 (2005), 103–28: 'The snippets of Grosseteste, Roger Bacon, and Adelard of Bath ... do not really convince ... either as sources or analogues, particularly as the passages of the Squire's Tale to which they are compared very evidently have their source in the *Roman de la Rose*' (p 106).

243 Walker, Lewis. '"Il Penseroso" and *The Squire's Tale*: Milton and the Attractions of Incompleteness.' In *Reassembling Truth: Twenty-first-Century Milton.* Ed. Charles W. Durham and Kristin A. Pruitt. Selinsgrove, PA: Susquehanna UP; London: Associated University Presses, 2003. Pp 49–62.
Milton's account of the 'half-told' *SqT* in "Il Penseroso" (lines 109–15) shows him to be attracted less by the allegorical possibilities of the romance genre than by romance's openness and indeterminacy. The Squire recognizes that careful progress toward a definitive conclusion would be 'the death of the story and ... the annihilation of the genre in which he is working.' Milton acknowledges this quality in *SqT* by making his summary of that tale 'resemble in little the inconclusive disposition of events in the original' (p 57).

244 Carlson, David R. 'The Chronology of Lydgate's Chaucer References.' *ChauR* 38 (2004), 246–54.
Lydgate's *Debate of the Horse, Goose, and Sheep* (ca 1436–7) contains an allusion to *SqT*: 'Chaunser [*sic*] remembrith the swerd, the ryng, the glas, / Presentid wern vpon a stede of bras' (p 248).

244a Heffernan, Carol F. 'Heliodorus's Æthiopica and Sidney's *Arcadia*: A Reconsideration.' *ELN* 42 (2004), 12–20.
SqT may have been among Sidney's models for his *New Arcadia*, especially for its interlocking structure.

❧ *The Franklin's Tale*: Sources, Analogues, and Later Influence

See also **4**, **200**, **233**, **779**, **801**, **812**, **819**, **830**, **834**, **838**, **847**, **848**, **852**, **855**, **862**, **868**, **880**, **890**, **894**, **900**, **909**, **912**, **921**, **926**, **943**, **955**, **958**, **970**, **972**, **981**, **994**, **1003**, **1020**, **1022**, **1028**, **1048**, **1056r**, **1061**, **1069**, **1106**, **1109**, **1143**, **1179**, **1189**, **1199**, **1200**, **1208**, **1230**, **1230r**, **1231**, **1248**, **1257**, **1275**, **1281**, **1286**, **1294**, **1295**, **1310**, **1314**, **1329**, **1344**, **1348**, **1349**, **1350**, **1354**, **1356**, **1363a**, **1366**, **1372**, **1378**, **1385**, **1390**, **1401**, **1405**, **1409**, **1422**, **1425**, **1426**, **1459**, **1468**, **1481**, **1489a**, **1493**, **1497**, **1499**, **1502**, **1504**, **1506**, **1507**.

Although scholars agree that the likeliest source for *FranT* is Menedon's tale in Boccaccio's *Il Filocolo*, the Franklin's identification of his story with the 'layes' of the 'olde gentil Britouns' (lines 709–10) has prompted speculation about the possible relation of the tale to extant and lost Breton lays, both the French originals and their ME redactions. In addition to work on the indebtedness of *FranT* to Boccaccio and the lays, folk analogues and minor sources (notably St Jerome's *Epistola adversus Jovinianum*) have been identified, as have instances of the tale's later influence. This section lists several editions and translations of *Fil* and *Jov*, but otherwise annotates only items that comment directly on *FranT*. For additional scholarship on *Fil*, see Vittore Branca, *Linee di una storia della critica al "Decameron" con bibliografia Boccaccesca* (Milan: Società Anonima Editrice Dante Alighieri, 1939); Enzo Esposito and Christopher Kleinhenz, *Boccacciana: Bibliografia delle edizioni e degli scritti critici (1939–1974)* (Ravenna: Longo, [1976]); Joseph P. Consoli, *Giovanni Boccaccio: An Annotated Bibliography* (New York: Garland, 1992); F.S. Stych, *Boccaccio in English: A Bibliography of Editions, Adaptations, and Criticism* (Westport, CT: Greenwood, 1995); Victoria Kirkham, *Fabulous Vernacular: Boccaccio's Filocolo and the Art of Medieval Fiction* (Ann Arbor: U of Michigan P, 2000); Victoria Kirkham, Michael Sherberg, and Janet Levarie Smarr, eds., *Boccaccio: A Critical Guide to the Complete Works* (Chicago: U of Chicago P, 2013); the annual bibliographies in *Studi sul Boccaccio* (Firenze: Sansoni, 1963–); and *Heliotropia* (www.heliotropia.org). For bibliography on the Breton lay, see **299**; Jean Charles Payen, *Le Lai narratif* (Turnhout: Brepols, 1975); Glyn S. Burgess, *Marie de France: An Analytical Bibliography* (London: Grant and Cutler, 1977) and Supplements (1986, 1997); Glyn S. Burgess and

Giovanna Angeli, *Marie de France: An Analytical Bibliography. Supplement no. 3* (Woodbridge, UK: Tamesis, 2007); and Glyn S. Burgess, *The Old French Narrative Lay: An Analytical Bibliography* (Cambridge: Brewer, 1995).

For a guide to the literature on the sources and analogues of Chaucer's writings, see **337a**.

245 Clouston, W.A. 'The Damsel's Rash Promise: Indian Original and Some Asiatic and European Variants of the Chaucer's *Franklin's Tale*.' In *Originals and Analogues of Some of Chaucer's Canterbury Tales*. Ed. Frederick J. Furnivall, Edmund Brock, and W.A. Clouston. Chaucer Society Publications, Second Series, 7, 10, 15, 20, 22. London: Trübner, 1872–88. Repr. London: Oxford UP, 1937.

The oldest known form of *FranT* story – the Indian version in the *Vetala Panchavinsati* – is printed together with Burmese, Persian, Indo-Persian, Hebrew, 'Germano-Jewish,' Siberian, Turkish, and Gaelic analogues. The versions of the story in *Dec* 10.5 and Boiardo's *Orlando Innamorato* are also included (20:291–340).

246 Schofield, William Henry. 'Chaucer's Franklin's Tale.' *PMLA* 16 (1901), 405–49. The account of the marriage of the British chieftain Arviragus in *HRB* was probably based on an early Celtic story, a form of which Chaucer may have employed in composing *FranT*. Numerous parallels exist between Chaucer's tale and Celtic tradition as reflected in Geoffrey, in the Breton lays, in proper names and place names, and in Arthurian narratives (e.g., a task imposed upon a lover, rock removal, the likeness of the clerk's magic and that of Merlin, the name Aurelius and the place names Penmark and Kayrrud). Parallels of plot and phraseology between *FranT* and the *lais* of Marie de France – e.g., the love of a Breton lord for a married woman (*Equitan*), an avowal of love in a garden (*Lanval*), loyalty in marriage shattered by guilty love (*Eliduc*) – confirm Chaucer's claim for a Breton source for *FranT*. Breton lays frequently incorporated themes and details not of Celtic origin, hence the presence of Oriental motifs in *FranT*. The discussion of comparative generosity that ends Chaucer's tale is a feature of the Oriental stories, and was probably connected for the first time with the Arviragus story in the French lay that served as Chaucer's immediate source. The idea of faithfulness in keeping a promise, essential to *FranT* and prominent in early Celtic stories, Breton lays, and romances based on the Matter of Britain, may also have been central to the 'Lay of Arviragus.' But Chaucer added material not in his source – astrological lore, courtly sentiment, narrative asides – that is 'out of harmony with spirit of a Breton lay' (p 447); in reading *FranT*, 'we do not really breathe the pure atmosphere of Breton romance' (p 446). See **249, 258, 264, 267, 812, 812r**.
• Anonymous review, *Nation* 73 (1901), 284–5: 'Schofield writes with complete mastery of the subject, and makes out as strong a case as the nature of

the question allows' (p 285).

• Review by F. Lot, *MÂ* 15 (1902), 108–12: There is no evidence linking Geoffrey of Monmouth's use of the name *Arviragus* with a Celtic tradition of a love affair between Arveragus and Dorigen and hence no reason to suppose that the Franklin's identification of his tale as a Breton lay is anything more than a literary device. Chaucer may have recalled the names Arveragus and Aurelius from his reading of Geoffrey; the name Dorigen was probably his own invention. Unlike the Celtic sources proposed by Schofield, *FranT* is a finished work of art that proposes a moral about fidelity to one's plighted word. See **258**, **264**.

• Review by Gustav Binz, *AB* 14 (1903), 368–70: Schofield's parallels between Celtic tradition and *FranT* confirm the poet's assertion that his poem's source is a Breton lay. Schofield is particularly sure-handed in distinguishing between inherited material and Chaucer's original contributions to the tale.

• Review by J. Koch, *Literaturblatt für germanische und romanische Philologie* 24 (1903), 153–61: Schofield's case for the presence of Oriental motifs in *FranT* is unconvincing. Only one version of the story, of Celtic origin, accounts for all the themes shared by Boccaccio, Boiardo, and Chaucer. Nor is it necessary to assume a single point of origin for *FranT*; Chaucer may have drawn eclectically on a variety of sources in composing his narrative.

247 Ballmann, Otto. 'Chaucers Einfluss auf das englische drama im zeitalter der königen Elisabeth und der beiden ersten Stuart-könige.' *Anglia* 25 (1902), 1–85.

Beaumont and Fletcher's *The Triumph of Honour* (1612) is based on *FranT* and not, as has been suggested, on *Dec* 10.5. Although the setting and aspects of the plot have been altered, several details clearly link the play with Chaucer's tale (pp 30–1). Also noted is an extended quotation from *FranT* in Dekker's 1613 prose pamphlet *A Strange Horse-Race* (pp 73–4).

248 Rajna, Pio. 'L'Episodio delle questioni d'amore nel *Filocolo* del Boccaccio.' *Romania* 31 (1902), 28–81.

Chaucer claims to have based *FranT* on a Breton lay, but his real source is the tale that appears first in the *questioni d'amore* episode in *Fil* and later in *Dec*. Although some scholars take Chaucer at his word, the poet fails to provide sufficient evidence to support his assertion. The setting in Armorica exists only to authenticate the supposed Breton provenance of the tale, while the names Arveragus and Dorigen are of Celtic and Greek origin, respectively. The similarities between Chaucer and Boccaccio are many; the only substantial difference between *FranT* and Boccaccio's version of the story is the alteration of the nature of impossible task (pp 41–2).

249 ———. 'Le origini della novella narrata del "Frankeleyn" nei *Canterbury Tales* del Chaucer.' *Romania* 32 (1903), 204–67.

In arguing that *FranT* is based on an early Celtic story incorporated in a lost French lay, Schofield (**246**) overlooks evidence that the Celtic material in *FranT* is derived directly from *HRB*. Focusing almost exclusively on the tale's supposed Celtic origins, Schofield neglects Boccaccio's role in the genesis of the poem. Boccaccio's adaptation of Menedon's *questione d'amore* in *Fil* to its new place in *Dec* 10.5 makes plausible Chaucer's subsequent reworking of the episode in *FranT*; in both cases, the same narrative skeleton is reclothed in a different body ('rivestito d'altre carni,' p 217). Schofield's argument for the presence of Oriental motifs in *FranT* is weak; the figure of the magician, for example, is generally absent from the Oriental analogues, nor do they involve the lady's setting of an impossible task. With the exception of analogies between the opening lines of Marie de France's *Equitan* and *FranP*, most of Schofield's proposed correspondences between *FranT* and the Breton lays are unpersuasive. Only *Fil* and, to a lesser extent, *Dec* 10.5 offer substantial parallels to Chaucer's poem: the introductory words of the stories, the wooing of Aurelius and Tarolfo, the December setting for the two miracles, the question posed at the end of *Fil* ('dubitasi ora quale di costoro fosse maggiore liberalità') and the Franklin's concluding *demande*. One need not assume that Chaucer had Boccaccio's works before him as he composed *FranT* and other tales that recall *Dec*; the echoes may well reflect the poet's memories of his earlier reading of the Italian texts, perhaps during his visits to Italy in the 1370s. Given the large number of anonymous manuscripts of Boccaccio's works, Chaucer may have read *Fil* without identifying its author. And if he was in fact aware that Boccaccio was his model, he was unlikely to have acknowledged this indebtedness outright, hence his claim that *FranT* was derived from a Breton lay. See **252**, **258**, **264**, **267**, **812**.

250 Reinmold, Franz. *Beaumont und Fletcher's "The Triumph of Honour" und Seine Quelle*. Halle: Kaemmerer, 1903.
A detailed comparison of *The Triumph of Honour* with *Dec* 10.5 and *FranT*, concluding that Chaucer, not Boccaccio, is the play's primary source.

251 Tuckwell, Rev. William. *Chaucer*. London: Bell, 1904.
Dorigen's 'horror of the rocks and breakers which she fears may wreck her returning husband's ship is finely turned by Gay in his exquisite ballad "'Twas when the seas were roaring"' (p 74).

252 Foulet, Lucien. 'Le Prologue du *Franklin's Tale* et les Lais bretons.' *ZRP* 30 (1906), 698–711.
The Franklin's remarks on the Breton lay, which according to Rajna (**249**) may reflect Chaucer's familiarity with Marie de France's *Equitan*, are more likely to derive from English tradition. Marie's influence is nowhere else evident in Chaucer's works. Chaucer could, however, have read the ME translations of Marie's *Lanval* and *Le Fraisne*, as well as *Sir Orfeo*; the prologue to the latter may have supplied him with his characterization of the Breton lay. The example of *Sir Orfeo* may also have encouraged Chaucer to adapt

Boccaccio to a Breton setting; he recognized that, by adding a prologue and exercising a little cleverness, any story could be transformed into a Breton lay. The Franklin's observation that the ancient Bretons either sang or read their lays reflects the term's double history. Chaucer normally employs *lay* as a synonym for 'song' or 'complaint,' echoing the standard French usage; only in *FranT* does the word signify a narrative poem on a Breton subject, a neologism introduced by Marie and reproduced by her fourteenth-century English translators.

253 Schofield, William Henry. *English Literature from the Norman Conquest to Chaucer*. London: Macmillan, 1906. Repr. New York: Haskell, 1968; Phaeton, 1969.
The illusion created by the clerk that the rocks along the coast of Brittany have disappeared resembles the achievement ascribed by Geoffrey of Monmouth to Merlin, that of transporting the Giant's Dance from Ireland to the Salisbury Plain (p 89). We should accept the Franklin's assertion that the source is a Breton lay; he almost certainly had a French *lai* before him when he wrote *FranT*, which he followed in all the essentials of his narrative (p 194).

254 Hertwig, Doris. *Der Einfluss von Chaucers "Canterbury Tales" auf die englische Literatur*. 1908. See **137**.
Brief comments on *FranT* as a source for Beaumont and Fletcher's *The Triumph of Honour* (1612) and on allusions to the tale in *The Two Merry Milkmaids, or the Best Words Wear the Garland* (1620) and Dekker's 1613 pamphlet *A Strange Horse-Race* (pp 38–9).

255 Young, Karl. *The Origin and Development of the Story of Troilus and Criseyde*. Chaucer Society Publications, Second Series, 40. London: Kegan Paul, Trench, Trübner, 1908.
Although Chaucer probably used some form of the Breton lay in composing *FranT*, he may also have been influenced by *Fil* (p 181n).

256 Lowes, John Livingston. 'Chaucer and the *Miroir de Mariage*.' *MP* 8 (1910–11), 305–34.
Line 1412 echoes a phrase that appears in Deschamps's *Miroir de Mariage* in a similar context (pp 324–5).

257 ———. 'Illustrations of Chaucer. Drawn Chiefly from Deschamps.' *RomR* 2 (1911), 113–28.
A *balade* and a passage from the *Miroir de Mariage* are cited as contexts for the Franklin's depiction of student life in Orléans.

258 Aman, Anselm. *Die Filiation der Frankeleynes Tale in Chaucers Canterbury Tales*. Erlangen: Junge & Sohn, 1912.
The story told by the Franklin exists in multiple versions that probably derive from a common source. The Eastern and Western versions of the tale are distinguished by the presence in the latter of a magician, who is absent from

all the Eastern versions. The Eastern group includes Indian, Burmese, Persian-Turkish, and Hebrew versions. The Western group includes versions in Spanish (Don Juan Manuel's *El Conde Lucanor*), French (Jean de Condé's *Le Chevalier a le Mance* and a nouvelle by Nicolas de Troyes), Italian (Boccaccio's *Fil* and *Dec*, Boiardo's *Orlando Innamorato*), German (an abbreviated version of *Fil* by Johann Valentin Andraes), and English (*FranT*, Beaumont and Fletcher's *Triumph of Honour*, *The Two Merry Milkmaids*). The stories are either summarized or translated, and the relations among them described. Boccaccio borrowed from Don Juan Manuel; both versions show the influence of the Eastern stories, although the precise route of transmission is uncertain (pp 103–12). Rajna (**249**) and Lot (**246r**) have convincingly refuted Schofield's theory (**246**) that *FranT* is derived from an OFr. lay. Chaucer's primary source was *Fil*; he may also have known the version of the story in *Dec* (pp 128–9). See **275**.

259 Hammond, Eleanor Prescott. 'Chaucer and Lydgate Notes.' *MLN* 27 (1912), 91–2.
A passage from Fulgentius, *Liber Mitologiarum*, is cited as a gloss on lines 1017–18.

260 Legouis, Émile. *Geoffrey Chaucer*. Trans. L. Lailavoix. London: Dent; New York: Dutton, 1913. Repr. New York: Russell and Russell, 1961. Originally published as *Geoffroy Chaucer* (Paris: Bloud, 1910).
The winter description at lines 1243–55 suggests that the poet did not know *Dec* 10.5, in which the lady asks her suitor for a spring garden in January. Had Chaucer known Boccaccio's story, he would not have introduced the winter scene gratuitously; 'he could not possibly read Boccaccio and remain indifferent' (p 118n).

261 Tatlock, John Strong Perry. 'Boccaccio and the Plan of Chaucer's *Canterbury Tales*.' *Anglia* 37 (1913), 69–117.
The Love Questions in *Fil* (summarized on pp 70–4) may have served as the model for *CT*. The fourth question is undoubtedly the source of *FranT*.

262 Fansler, Dean Spruill. *Chaucer and the "Roman de la Rose."* 1914. See **148**.
Finds possible echoes of *RR* in lines 764–90, 792–6 (see index, p 260).

263 Spurgeon, Caroline F.E. *Five Hundred Years of Chaucer Criticism and Allusion (1357–1900)*. 1914–24. See **149**.
Not all of the references to *FranT* are listed under that heading in the Index. Other items include: in Part 1, G. Harvey (p 127), J. Aubrey (pp 268–9), R. Henry (p 463), P. Neve (p 489); in Part 2, J.C. Dunlop (p 62), I. D'Israeli (p 191); in Part 3, J. Ruskin (p 34); in Part 4, G. Harvey (pp 50–1), T. Dekker (p 62), Z. Grey (p 91).

264 Cummings, Hubertis M. *The Indebtedness of Chaucer's Works to the Italian Works of Boccaccio (A Review and Summary)*. Menasha, WI: Banta, 1916. Repr. New York: Haskell, 1965; Phaeton, 1967.

The parallel passages cited by Rajna (**249**) do not provide convincing evidence for Chaucer's use of *Fil* in *FranT*; it seems more likely that both Chaucer's and Boccaccio's tales independently echo a primitive version of the story. As Schofield (**246**) and Tatlock (**812**) maintain, *FranT* probably is based upon Chaucer's knowledge of Breton material (pp 180–97). See **267**.

265 Jefferson, Bernard L. *Chaucer and the Consolation of Philosophy of Boethius.* 1917. See **151**.
Lists seven passages or lines in *FranT* that directly echo *Consol* or show Boethian influence (p 148).

266 Lowes, John Livingston. 'Chaucer and Dante.' *MP* 14 (1917), 705–35.
The description of Aurelius's torment (lines 949–50, 1101) may echo Dante's account of the Furies (*Inferno* 9.37–51) (p 145).

267 ———. 'The *Franklin's Tale*, the *Teseide*, and the *Filocolo*.' *MP* 15 (1918), 689–728.
Lines 901–1037 – barring the conversation in lines 960–1010 – are a free reworking of material drawn from the third and fourth books of *Tes*, notably the account of Arcita's unspoken passion for Emilia. (Borrowings elsewhere from *Tes* are noted, as are echoes of Machaut's *Dit dou Lyon*.) Details attributed by Schofield (**246**) to the Breton lay and by Rajna (**249**) to *Fil* are directly explicable by *Tes*. Yet Chaucer regularly combined sources, and here he seems to be drawing on both Boccaccian texts. Lowes adduces evidence outside of *FranT* for Chaucer's knowledge of *Fil*. Cummings's critique of Rajna (**264**) is fundamentally flawed. Rajna's parallels between *Fil* and *FranT* remain valid and are supported by additional echoes that he failed to consider; the parallels between the two texts are 'greater than has been hitherto recognized' (p 722), although Chaucer deals freely with *Fil*, as he did with *Il Filostrato* in *TC*. In claiming that *FranT* is a Breton lay, it seems likely that Chaucer is either combining an actual Breton lay with *Fil* or imitating the type of the Breton lays while drawing the story itself from Boccaccio.

268 Korten, Hertha. *Chaucers literarische Beziehungen zu Boccaccio: Die künstlerische Konzeption der Canterbury Tales und das Lolliusproblem.* Rostock: Hinstorff, 1920.
FranT resembles *Dec* 10.5 in that the concluding *questione d'amore* is posed to the tale's listeners as a group. In *Fil*, Fiametta alone gives the answer to Menedon's *questione* (p 23).

269 Schirmer, W.F. 'Boccaccio's Werke als Quelle G. Chaucers.' *GRM* 12 (1924), 288–305.
A common source rather than direct borrowing accounts for the similarities between *FranT* and *Dec* 10.5. Genre and setting point to an intermediary French source for *FranT*.

269a Koch, J. 'Der gegenwärtige Stand der Chaucerforschung.' *Anglia* 49 (1925), 193–243.
Although he may have been familiar with *Fil*, Chaucer connected it with a

Breton legend that contained material analogous to the magic that appears in *FranT* (p 231).

270 Wrenn, C.L. 'Chaucer's Knowledge of Horace.' *MLR* 18 (1925), 286–92.
Chaucer's clear echo of Persius (line 721) without naming him supports the argument for the poet's similarly unacknowledged familiarity with Horace.

271 Bethel, John Perceval. 'The Influence of Dante on Chaucer's Thought and Expression.' 1927. See **158**.
FranT illustrates Dante's idea that true nobility does not depend on rank or birth. 'The general attitude toward "gentillesse" which finds expression in [*SqT* and *FranT*] ... point[s] much more strongly to the influence of Dante than of any other author' (p 328). See **779**.

272 French, Robert Dudley. *A Chaucer Handbook*. New York: Crofts: 1927/1947; London: Bell, 1947. Repr. New York, AMS, 2006.
The Franklin's assertion that his tale is based upon a Breton lay must be regarded skeptically. The story, Oriental in origin, appears in *Dec* and *Fil*. The latter is the probable direct model for *FranT*; one need not posit a common lost source for Boccaccio's and Chaucer's tales (pp 319–24).

273 Shannon, Edgar Finley. *Chaucer and the Roman Poets*. 1929. See **162**.
Cites Ovidian sources for lines 951–2 (Echo and Narcissus) and 1077 (Delphos) (pp 321–2).

274 Looten, Camille. *Chaucer, ses modèles, ses sources, sa religion*. Lille: l'Économat des Facultés Catholiques, 1931.
Chaucer's transformation of Boccaccio in *FranT* is typical of his use of sources; he keeps to the general outline of his model, but introduces new elements with a free hand (e.g., the astrological material, perhaps drawn from a treatise on occult sciences), and delves more deeply into the inner lives of his characters (p 96). See **285**.

275 Schick, J. 'Die ältesten Versionen von Chaucers Frankeleynes Tale.' In *Studia Indo-Iranica. Ehrengabe für Wilhelm Geiger zur Vollendung des 75. Lebensjahres*. Ed. Walther Wüst. Leipzig: Harrassowitz, 1931. Pp 89–107.
Supplements and brings up to date the work of Aman (**258**) on the earliest analogues of *FranT*. The Indian version of the story of competition among noble men, found in the twenty-five stories by Somadeva in the *Vetālapañcavimshati* and striking in its similarities to *FranT*, is related to the *Brihatkatha* by Gunadhya (ca fifth century A.D.), which in turn was translated into verse in the eleventh-century *Brhatkathamañjari* by Ksemendra. The parallels between the latter and the version by Somadeva may be attributed to their use of a common source rather than to direct borrowing. Other related Indian versions include those of Sivadasa and Jambhaldatta; the presence of a demonic figure (*rākasasa*) in the latter allows us to establish its connection with earlier versions. Antedating the Indian texts is a version found in the third-century Chinese *Tripitaka* (*Dazang Jing*), and itself translated from a

lost Indian source – which reappears as a subplot in an archaic Jain version. In later Jain versions of the story, the nobility test becomes a test of shrewdness or sagacity.

276 Dempster, Germaine. *Dramatic Irony in Chaucer*. Stanford University Publications; University Series, Language and Literature, vol. 4, no. 3. Stanford, CA: Stanford UP; London: Humphrey Milford, 1932. Repr. New York: Humanities Press, 1959. Doubly paginated as 3–102 and 247–346.
Notes parallels between *FranT* and Geoffrey of Monmouth's account of Merlin's transformation of King Uther, in order that he may gain access to Igerna (*HRB*, Book 8, Ch. 9). In both texts, the scene is a seashore castle, and magic is used for the fulfillment of a lover's desire. In addition, the names 'Dorigen' and 'Igerna' are similar (pp 65–6/pp 309–10).

277 Hankins, John E. 'Chaucer and the *Pervigilium Veneris*.' *MLN* 49 (1934), 80–3.
Lines 907–8 recall *Pervigilium Veneris*, line 22.

278 Raith, Josef. *Boccaccio in der englischen Literatur von Chaucer bis Painters Palace of Pleasure*. Leipzig: Noske, 1936.
The fourth *questione d'amore* in *Fil* and *Dec* 10.5 are the closest analogues to *FranT* (p 70).

279 Boccaccio, Giovanni. *Il Filocolo*. Ed. Salvatore Battaglia. Bari: Gius, Laterza, 1938.
Menedon's *questione* is on pp 311–25. See **281**.

280 Lange, Hugo. 'Chaucer und Mandeville's Travels.' *Archiv* 174 (1938), 79–81.
Cites parallels between *Mandeville's Travels* and *FranT* (lines 942–3, 1031ff, 1148, 1151, 1200–1, and 1228ff).

281 Dempster, Germaine, and John Strong Perry Tatlock. 'The Franklin's Tale.' In *Sources and Analogues of Chaucer's Canterbury Tales*. 1941. See **174**.
The probable source of *FranT* – Menedon's tale in *Fil* – is reprinted from Battaglia's edition (**279**). Included as well are excerpts from *HRB* which provide parallels to the names Arveragus and Aurelius, and to the use of magic to remove the coastal rocks; passages from seven English and French Breton lays similar in theme and spirit to *FranT*; and, from *Jov*, the catalogue of virtuous pagan virgins and widows employed in Dorigen's Complaint. See **288**, **367**.

282 Loomis, Laura Hibbard. 'Chaucer and the Breton Lays of the Auchinleck MS.' *SP* 38 (1941), 14–33. Repr. in Loomis, *Adventures in the Middle Ages: A Memorial Collection of Essays and Studies*. New York: Franklin, 1962. Pp 111–30.
Chaucer's ideas about the Breton lay as set forth in *FranP* appear to be based on the prologue to *Lay le Freine* in the Auchinleck MS (the same prologue, although missing in the MS, almost certainly prefaced the Auchinleck *Sir Orfeo* as well). The Auchinleck *Sir Orfeo* may have suggested to Chaucer the association of the Breton lay type with the theme of married love; it also exhibits thematic parallels with Chaucer's poem (e.g., Orfeo's insistence that the Fairy King keep his word and Arveragus's exaltation of *trouthe*-keeping).

The Breton elements in *FranT* are better explained by Chaucer's use of the Auchinleck MS (from which he borrowed other material, notably in *Thop*) than by any of the collections of French lays. See **300**, **308**, **351**.

283 Bøgholm, N. 'A Rash Promise.' *SN* 15 (1942), 41–2.
The denouement of the Sanskrit version of the Damsel's Rash Promise folktale depends on an exercise of Solomonic wisdom in discovering a thief among the three admirers of a young woman. In *Fil*, sorcery and a courtly love problem take the place of the wisdom element. In *FranT*, the central issue is not magic or competition in love, but human sympathy.

284 Whiting, B.J. 'A Fifteenth-Century Chaucerian: the Translator of *Partonope of Blois*.' *MS* 7 (1945), 40–54.
Partonope contains one fairly clear borrowing from *FranT* (lines 1091–2) and two close echoes of its idiom (lines 804, 1088).

285 Delcourt, Joseph, ed. *Chaucer: Contes de Cantorbéry*. Paris: Aubier, 1946.
The immediate source of *FranT* is not a Breton lay, but *Fil* and perhaps *Dec*; Boccaccio's source may have been a Spanish version of an Oriental tale. Although Looten (**274**) believes that Chaucer examined alchemical treatises while writing *CYT*, it is not necessary to suppose that the poet actually read a book of astrological magic of the sort mentioned in *FranT*. In borrowing from *Jov* for Dorigen's Complaint, Chaucer viewed Jerome's treatise as a source of rhetorical exempla rather than a statement of Christian doctrine. Dorigen's list of virtuous heroines is the least successful part of *FranT*; it seems mere filler (pp 257–61).

286 Pratt, Robert Armstrong. 'Chaucer's Use of the *Teseida*.' *PMLA* 62 (1947), 598–621.
In *FranT*, Chaucer's debt to *Tes* is not in borrowed lines or words, but in time descriptions and the general shaping of scenes involving the experience of lovers.

287 Loomis, Roger Sherman. 'A Parallel to the Franklin's Discussion of Marriage.' In *Philologica: The Malone Anniversary Studies*. Ed. Thomas A. Kirby and Henry Bosley Woolf. Baltimore, MD: Johns Hopkins UP, 1949. Pp 191–4.
A passage in the thirteenth-century *Enfances Gauvain* describing the harmonious marriage of Artus and Guinemars parallels Dorigen and Arveragus's 'humble, wys accord' (line 791).

288 Archer, Jerome W. 'On Chaucer's Source for "Arveragus" in the *Franklin's Tale*.' *PMLA* 65 (1950), 318–22.
Arveragus, the name of a British king in *HRB* also appears in Layamon's *Brut*, where the ruler is said to be loved by his wife and is associated with a story involving the importance of the plighted word. The latter details, not present in Geoffrey, suggest that Chaucer took the name *Arveragus* from some source similar to Layamon rather than from *HRB* (cf. **281**). In addition, Geoffrey's *Aurelius* is a Christian hero-king who fights against pagans and

hence is an unlikely model for Chaucer's pagan squire.

289 Makarewicz, Sister Mary Raynelda. *The Patristic Influence on Chaucer*. Washington, DC: Catholic U of America P, 1953.
Prints Dorigen's Complaint and its sources in *Jov* in parallel columns, and summarizes Dempster's analysis (**847**) of Chaucer's working methods (pp 81–7). Contrasted with Aurelius's courtly desire for a wedded lady, the married love of Dorigen and Arveragus represents the triumph of charity over cupidity (pp 106–7).

290 Blenner-Hassett, Roland. 'Yeats' Use of Chaucer.' *Anglia* 72 (1954), 455–62.
Yeats's treatment of the moon's phases in *A Vision* and 'The Phases of the Moon' may reflect his reading of *FranT* (cf. lines 1123–34).

291 Parks, Edd Winfield. 'Hayne's Adaptation of Chaucer's Franklin's Tale.' In *Essays in Honor of Walter Clyde Curry*. [No ed. listed.] Nashville, TN: Vanderbilt UP, 1954. Pp 103–15.
Paul Hamilton Hayne's 'The Wife of Brittany' (1870), a verse adaptation of *FranT*, is summarized, and its deviations from and additions to Chaucer's poem are described.

292 Sells, A. Lytton. *The Italian Influence in English Poetry from Chaucer to Southwell*. Bloomington: Indiana UP, 1955.
Reviews scholarly opinion on the sources of *FranT*, concluding that the Breton atmosphere of the tale makes it unlikely that *Fil* was Chaucer's immediate model (pp 52–4).

293 Zanco, Aurelio. *Chaucer e il suo mondo*. Turin: Petrini, 1955/1965.
Brief comments on *FranT* as a Breton lay (Chaucer may have known the prologue to Marie de France's lays; *FranT* also contains parallels to the first part of Marie's *Equitan*), on the relation of *FranT* to *Fil* and *Dec* 10.5, on the folk analogues of the poem's plot, and on the mixture of conventional and individual traits in the characterization of Dorigen (pp 242–7).

294 Donovan, Mortimer J. 'The *Anticlaudian* and Three Passages in the *Franklin's Tale*.' *JEGP* 56 (1957), 52–9.
Parallels to Alanus de Insulis's *Anticlaudian* clarify three passages in *FranT*: lines 721–5 (*colours* designates 'rhetorical modes or figures'); 829–34 (*scalprum rationis* – Nature's sculpturing of her own reason – is analogous to the imprinting of Dorigen's mind with comfort 'by resoun'); and lines 1613–15 ('as thou right now were cropen out of the ground' links Aurelius with Alanus's personified Youth, who is prodded by the Tartarean Furies to attack Virtue).

295 Hazelton, Richard. 'Chaucer and Cato.' *Speculum* 35 (1960), 357–80.
The Franklin's remarks on patience (lines 773–7) echo medieval glosses on Cato.

296 Hodgson, Phyllis, ed. *The Franklin's Tale*. 1960. See **74**.
A small number of significant details in *FranT* are paralleled in Menedon's tale in *Fil* and *Dec* 10.5; Chaucer may have known both of these narratives.

The differences from Boccaccio, however, are more striking than the similarities. Arveragus, Aurelius, and Dorigen are more fully developed than their Boccaccian counterparts; the clerk, the most subtly portrayed character in *FranT*, owes almost nothing to the magician in *Fil*. Although Boccaccio, like Chaucer, treats the infectious influence of generosity, Chaucer expands Boccaccio's love problem to include a consideration of the nature of marriage and the significance of promises. Chaucer also transforms the situational irony of Boccaccio's tale into a dramatization of the irony of fate. Although it is possible that *FranT* may be based on a lost Breton lay, it is more likely that Chaucer, wishing to achieve generic variety in *CT*, clothed Boccaccio's plot in Breton dress. Echoes of and implied responses to previous tales indicate that the Franklin's story was intended for a particular stage in the pilgrimage drama; the chief inspiration for *FranT* lies in what preceded it in *CT*.

297 Burgess, C.F. 'Gay's "'Twas When the Seas Were Roaring" and Chaucer's "Franklin's Tale": A Borrowing.' *N&Q* n.s. 9 (1962), 454–5.
The fourth stanza of the ballad ''Twas when the seas were roaring,' sung by a maiden awaiting the return of her lover, absent at sea, in Gay's *The What D'ye Call It* (1715), is modeled on the opening of Dorigen's soliloquy.

298 Silvia, Daniel S., Jr. *Chaucer's Use of Jerome's Adversus Jovinianum, with an Edition of Book I, Chapters 40–49, Based on Medieval Manuscripts*. PhD diss., University of Illinois, 1962. Dir. G. Blakemore Evans. Ann Arbor, MI: Xerox University Microfilms, 1975. See also *DAI*–A 23/11 (1963): 4345–6.
Records MS glosses to *FranT* from *Jov* (pp 16–19) and lists parallels between Dorigen's Complaint and *Jov* (pp 109–21). *Jov*, Book I, Chapters 40–9 (the source of Dorigen's Complaint) is edited from Pembroke College, Cambridge, MS 234, collated with twenty-four other MSS (Appendix A). Silvia surveys scholarly commentary on the Complaint (pp 157–65), disputing Baker's view of the passage as a carefully constructed artistic unit and his speculations about Dorigen's familiarity with *Jov* (**912**) and supporting Dempster's reconstruction of the genesis of the Complaint (**847**). In the Marriage Group tales, *Jov* provides 'background color' (p 173) rather than thematic material; the rejection of sovereignty for *gentilesse*, evident in *FranT*, was foreign to Jerome's conception of marriage. *FranT* and the G Prologue to *LGW* (in which Jerome is mentioned among those who praised women) were probably the last pieces Chaucer wrote using *Jov*. After writing the G Prologue, Chaucer may have returned to Dorigen's Complaint, adding the 'inappropriate' examples from *Jov*, and thus giving the Complaint a comic slant in which a woman hater is used as the source of instances of womanly virtue (pp 187–9).

299 Baader, Horst. *Die Lais. Zur Geschichte einer Gattung der altfranzösischen Kurzerzälungen*. Analecta Romanica 16. Frankfurt: Klostermann, 1966.
FranP is cited as a possible example of the influence of Marie de France on

English literature (pp 185–6).

300 Heydon, Peter N. 'Chaucer and the *Sir Orfeo* Prologue of the Auchinleck MS.' *PMASAL* 51 (1966), 529–45.
In some details of theme and diction, *FranP* is closer to the *Sir Orfeo* prologue (missing from the Auchinleck *Sir Orfeo*, but preserved in two fifteenth-century redactions of the romance) than to the prologue to the Auchinleck *Lay le Freine* cited by Loomis (**282**) as the probable source of *FranP*. In addition, the opening lines of *Sir Orfeo* and *FranP* both function as characterization: the Franklin's deprecation of his rhetorical abilities may be seen as an 'ironic refraction' (p 542) of the hyperbolic account of Orfeo's prowess as a harper.

301 Hoffman, Richard L. *Ovid and the Canterbury Tales*. 1966. See **192**.
Ovidian sources or allusions are cited for lines 771–8, 829–36, 1031–7, 1077, 1252–5, 1442–7 (pp 165–78). Like Ovid, the Franklin comments on patience in love (lines 771–8); the patience of the foolish lover in *Ars amatoria* and *Amores* parallels Arveragus's misdirected patience in courting Dorigen. The Franklin's analogy between stone carving and the assuaging of Dorigen's grief (lines 829–36) probably derives from *Ars amatoria* I.476; the context in Ovid – that persistent entreaty will overcome the resistance even of a Penelope – establishes a contrast between Penelope's steadfastness and Dorigen's flightiness. In praying to Apollo (lines 1031–7), Aurelius appropriately invokes a physician (*Metamorphoses* I.521–4) who could not cure himself. In *Tristia* V and *Ex Ponto* III, Ovid alludes to Alcestis, Penelope, and Laodamia to assure his wife that, unlike these women, she need not sacrifice her life to demonstrate her conjugal love. The appearance of the same three examples in Dorigen's Complaint ironically contrasts their fidelity with her promise to Aurelius to commit adultery under certain circumstances.

301a Spearing, A.C., ed. *The Franklin's Prologue and Tale from the Canterbury Tales by Geoffrey Chaucer*. 1966/1994. See **86**.
Fil supplies the version of the Damsel's Rash Promise folktale that is closest to *FranT*. Chaucer adapted *Fil* freely, and was probably retelling it from memory. As in *TC* and *KnT*, Chaucer adds to his Boccaccian source philosophical questioning from *Consol*. Although Chaucer identifies *FranT* as a Breton lay, there is no evidence that he would have read any of the Breton lays in French. Possible reasons for the poet's claim of a Breton lay as his source include the Franklin's old-fashioned notion of *gentilesse*, appropriate to a genre that had, by the late fourteenth century, lost its vogue; the crucial role of magic; the emphasis given to human feelings, in particular those of Dorigen, a character who would have appealed to Marie de France; and the 'remarkably full and coherent' Breton background – paradoxically unlike the fairyland milieux of most genuine Breton lays, and unlike them as well in its thoroughly classicized and paganized setting (1994, p 14).

302 Witke, Charles. '*Franklin's Tale*, F 1139–1151.' *ChauR* 1 (1966), 33–6.

Cites the OFr. *Floire et Blancheflor,* Version I, as a possible source for the description of the *tregetours.*

303 Boccaccio, Giovanni. *Filocolo.* Ed. Antonio Enzo Quaglio. In *Tutte Le Opere di Giovanni Boccaccio.* Gen. ed. Vittore Branca. Vol. 1. Milan: Mondadori, 1967. Text: pp 47–675; notes: pp 708–970.
The standard modern edition. Menedon's *questione* is on pp 396–410. See **327**.

304 Brennan, John Patrick, Jr. *The Chaucerian Text of Jerome Adversus Jovinianum: An Edition Based on Pembroke College, Cambridge, MS 234.* PhD diss., University of California, Davis. 1967. Dir. Daniel S. Silvia. Ann Arbor, MI: University Microfilms International, 1984. See also *DAI*–A 28/11 (1968): 4622–3.
Ch. 1 provides a brief history of *Jov,* discusses Chaucer's use of Jerome's tract, and surveys previous editions of *Jov.* Ch. 2 supplies information about the forty-three MSS collated for this edition. Ch. 3 lays out the textual principles of the edition, concluding that, of the MSS examined, Pembroke College 234 (Pc) is closest to the point in the MS tradition at which Chaucer encountered *Jov.* (Glosses on lines 1456 and 1462 are adduced for their bearing on chapter numeration as evidence for the choice of a base MS.) Ch. 4 presents the text of *Jov,* with all substantive variants recorded at the foot of the page. In Pc, the material used in Dorigen's Complaint appears in Book I, chs 36–7.

305 Garbáty, Thomas Jay. '*Pamphilus, De Amore*: An Introduction and Translation.' *ChauR* 2 (1967), 108–34.
Lines 1109–15 echo the image of the arrow hidden in the breast from the opening of *Pamphilus, De Amore* (ca 1200).

306 Baum, Richard. *Recherches sur les œuvres attribuées à Marie de France.* Heidelberg: Winter, 1968.
Cites and comments on Thomas Tyrwhitt's remarks on the Breton lay in the notes to *FranP* in his 1775 edition of *CT* (pp 69–73).

307 Mukerji, N. 'Chaucer's Franklin's [Tale] and the Tale of Madanasena of Vetalapachisi.' *FolkloreC* 9 (1968), 75–85.
FranT shares plot elements with the tenth tale of the Sanskrit *Vetalapachisi* (*The Twenty-five Tales of a Vetala*): a lady makes a rash vow in a garden to an unwelcome suitor; her husband asks her to keep her bargain; moved by her promise to return to a thief who has seized the lady on her way to the suitor's house, the latter releases her from her vow; a question about generosity is posed at the conclusion. The tale of Madanasena subordinates characterization to plot, in the usual manner of folk narratives.

308 Donovan, Mortimer J. *The Breton Lay: A Guide to Varieties.* Notre Dame, IN: U of Notre Dame P, 1969.
FranT's length, its prologue, and its setting are cited as evidence of Chaucer's knowledge of the Breton lay. Chaucer departs from earlier Breton lays, however, in using pentameter couplets rather than octosyllables, and in the prominence he gives to rhetorical devices. The Breton lay was not, as Loomis

(**282**) assumes, an old-fashioned form in Chaucer's day: 'the popularity dating from 1330–40 [the date of the Auchinleck MS] must have been continuous, although perhaps thin at any one point' (p 174). *FranP* 'contains a body of ideas, common enough in the introductory and concluding lines of the *French* Breton lays, but found in no single example' (p 180). All *FranP*'s ideas, however, are present in the prologue of the Auchinleck *Lay le Freine*, suggesting that Chaucer knew about the Breton lay chiefly from this source. *FranT* is almost certainly based on Menedon's story in *Fil*; the Italian narrative is summarized and Chaucer's additions noted. A comparison of the treatment of courtly idealism in *FranT* and other Breton lays, notably *Lai le Fraisne* and *Eliduc*, reveals that Chaucer used the form as a vehicle for his own reflections on marriage; *FranT* is 'more expressive of the author's personality, and more individualized' (p 186) than most Breton lays.

• Review by G.C. Britton, *N&Q* n.s. 17 (1970), 317–19: Although Donovan regards as unnecessary Loomis's view that the lay was out of vogue by Chaucer's time (**282**), a poem like *Degaré* may merely be evidence of a revival of interest sparked by *FranT*.

• Review by Basil Cottle, *JEGP* 69 (1970), 304–6: Some of Donovan's criticism is perceptive, but the book is 'a record of wasted opportunities' (p 306), marred throughout by egregious misquotation and mistranslation and by sloppy proofreading.

• Review by W.H.W. Field, *MLQ* 31 (1970), 372–3: The decision to devote three chapters to the ME lay and only two to the OFr. lay creates a damaging disproportion in the book's argument. The self-imposed limitations of Donovan's study reduce much of his discussion to generalization; when he attempts more extended treatment, his account is marred by misleading emphases and errors of fact.

• Review by Derek Pearsall, *MÆ* 39 (1970), 207–8: The discussion of *FranT* is 'the merest gesture,' and reverts to an earlier stratum of criticism to accommodate the poem to its limited terms of reference (p 207).

• Review by Derek S. Brewer, *MLR* 67 (1972), 164–5: Donovan's ideas of form are questionable; *FranT* is said to imitate the form of a twelfth-century lay, of which Marie de France's quite dissimilar poems are the only true examples.

• Review by Jeanne Lods, *CCM* 15 (1972), 236–7: Donovan presents an overview of a complex subject that underlines the continuity of Anglo-French tradition too often studied in a fragmentary fashion. But the book's overly schematic categories fail to do justice to the richness and idiosyncrasies of individual lays and Donovan's arbitrary working definition of the Breton lay, based on its fidelity to a courtly ideal, distorts and oversimplifies the range of subjects present in the works of Marie and their progeny.

• Review by D.D.R. Owen, *FS* 26 (1972), 59: Donovan oversimplifies critical problems (e.g., the etymology of the word *lai*), and is less than rigorous in defining and using key terms (e.g., courtly love).

309 Lord, Mary Louise. 'Dido as an Example of Chastity: The Influence of Example Literature.' *HLB* 17 (1969), 22–44, 216–32.
Chaucer includes almost all of Jerome's examples of virtuous women in Dorigen's Complaint, including Hasdrubal's wife and her leap into the fire. One can assume that Chaucer knew her companion example in Jerome, the chaste Dido. By omitting her from the list, he demonstrates his preference for the Vergilian and Ovidian forms of the Dido story (p 225).

310 Bawcutt, Priscilla. 'Gavin Douglas and Chaucer.' 1970. See **194**.
Lines 1–13 of the Prologue to Book 7 of Douglas's *Eneados* echo the Franklin's description of winter (lines 1243–55) (p 70).

311 Johnston, Grahame. 'Chaucer and the Breton Lays.' In *Proceedings and Papers of the Fourteenth Congress of the Australian Universities Language and Literature Association Held 19–26 January 1972 at the University of Otago, Dunedin, New Zealand*. Ed. K.I.D. Maslen. Dunedin: AULLA, 1972. Pp 230–41.
Of the ME poems usually categorized as Breton lays, *Sir Orfeo, Lay lẹ Freine, Sir Degaré,* and the two versions of the Lanval story have the strongest claim to this generic classification, given their probable early date of composition, their Celticity, and/or their relation to Marie de France. Three of these poems also appear in the Auchinleck MS (copied ca 1330–40). The accurate description of the genre of the lay in *FranP* suggests Chaucer's familiarity with this MS. In assigning a Breton lay – 'not a romance … but a tale in an associated genre of more modest dimensions' (p 238) – to the Franklin, Chaucer matches social with literary status; drawing on his memory, the elderly narrator tells a tale in a form that would have been popular in his youth, around 1330–50, just when the four early lays were in circulation. The remaining ME lays (*Emaré, The Erle of Tolous, Sir Gowther*) are of a later date, and reflect the prestige conferred on the form by Chaucer's use of it.

312 Tedeschi, Svetko. 'Some Recent Opinions about the Possible Influence of Boccaccio's "Decameron" on Chaucer's "Canterbury Tales."' *SRAZ* 33–36 (1972–3), 849–72.
Agrees with Praz (**862**) that Chaucer did not use *Dec* 10.5 in composing *FranT*.

313 Frappier, Jean. Review of **308**. *RPhil* 27 (1973–4), 244–50.
Chaucer's knowledge of the Breton lay was probably based on the ME translations of French originals. *FranT* takes playful liberties with the genre it presumes to imitate. In the idealism and generosity that dictate the conduct of its characters, *FranT* remains most faithful to the essence of the lay.

314 Johnston, Grahame. 'The Breton Lays in Middle English.' In *Iceland and the Mediaeval World: Studies in Honour of Ian Maxwell*. Ed. Gabriel Turville-Petre and John Stanley Martin. Victoria, Australia: Wilkes, 1974. Pp 151–61.
See **311**.

315 Hieatt, A. Kent. *Chaucer, Spenser, Milton: Mythopoeic Continuities and Trans-*

formations. 1975. See **200**.

Spenser used the Thynne family of editions of Chaucer, which places *FranT* after *MerT, WBT,* and *ClT,* and hence exposes as deficient the contests of male and female mastery in the earlier tales when set against the more harmonious and collaborative union of Dorigen and Arveragus, based on a formula similar to the Boethian one of friendship found in *KnT*. Spenser's continuation of *SqT* (which appears in Thynne directly before the Marriage Group tales) looks ahead to the final, enlightened version of married love in *FranT*. See **202**.

• Review by John Buxton, *RES* n.s. 28 (1977), 345–6: see **200r**.

316 Kehler, Joel R. 'A Note on the Epigraph to Conrad's *The Rescue*.' *ELN* 12 (1975), 184–7.

Conrad's Chaucerian epigraph (lines 1342–4) alerts us to parallels of plot, character, and theme in the novel and *FranT*.

317 Thompson, Ann. '"Our revels now are ended": an allusion to *The Franklin's Tale*?' *Archiv* 212 (1975), 317.

The verbal parallel between lines 1202–4 and *The Tempest* 4.1.148 is reinforced by a similarity of context: the magician dismisses his *apparences*, Prospero dissolves his masque.

318 Noakes, David. 'Pope's Chaucer.' *RES* n.s. 27 (1976), 180–2.

In his copy of Speght's Chaucer, Pope marked the Franklin's seasonal description (lines 1243–55) 'Winter.' He may have noted the passage as a possible source for his fourth Pastoral, but when he came to write the poem, he decided instead to rely on more traditional classical pastoral motifs.

319 Miller, Robert P., ed. *Chaucer: Sources and Backgrounds*. New York: Oxford UP, 1977.

Includes a translation of Menedon's *questione, Fil* 4 (pp 121–35).

320 McGrady, Donald. 'Chaucer and the *Decameron* Reconsidered.' *ChauR* 12 (1977–8), 1–26.

FranT resembles *Dec* 10.5 as much as *Fil,* which is commonly cited as Chaucer's principal source.

321 Hanning, Robert, and Joan Ferrante, trans. *The Lais of Marie de France*. New York: Dutton, 1978.

Although the Franklin's tale of the difficulties created for a faithful wife by her husband's departure in pursuit of chivalric honor recalls the situation in *Milun,* there is no evidence that Chaucer had direct knowledge of Marie's *lais* (p 24).

322 Peck, Russell A. *Kingship and Common Profit in Gower's Confessio Amantis*. Carbondale: Southern Illinois UP, 1978.

Contrasts Gower's 'Tale of Mundus and Paulina' (*CA*, Book 1) with *FranT*. Unlike Dorigen, who, upon the threat of infidelity, weeps and wails and contemplates suicide, Paulina immediately seeks her husband's advice.

Where Arveragus attempts to hide the situation, Paulina's husband first reassures his wife; they confront the problem rationally together, an action that reconfirms and strengthens their marriage (p 44).

323 Ross, Gordon M. '"The Franklin's Tale" and "The Tempest."' *N&Q* n.s. 25 (1978), 156.
Notes the similarity between 'And farewel! Al oure revel was ago' (line 1204) and 'Our revels now are ended' (*Tempest*, 4.1.148).

324 Thompson, Ann. *Shakespeare's Chaucer: A Study in Literary Origins*. Liverpool: Liverpool UP; New York: Barnes and Noble, 1978.
Beaumont and Fletcher drew on *FranT* for the plot of *The Triumph of Honour* (1612). Chaucer is more successful than the dramatists in his handling of character and in his presentation of a moral conflict; Beaumont and Fletcher reduce Chaucer's 'delicate balancing of different kinds of honor' to 'a dull and predictable opposition between lust and chastity' (p 51). See **317**.

325 Field, P.J.C. 'Malory's Minor Sources.' *N&Q* n.s. 26 (1979), 107–10.
Lancelot's explanation that he could not make himself love Elayne of Astolat ('for love must only aryse of the hart selff and nat by non constreynte') may echo *FranT* lines 764–6 and recall as well Aurelius's attempt to constrain Dorigen to love.

326 Reisner, Thomas A., and Mary Ellen Reisner. 'A British Analogue for the Rock-Motif in the *Franklin's Tale*.' *SP* 76 (1979), 1–12.
St Balred's removal of a dangerous rock from a shipping channel near the Firth of Forth is proposed as a possible source for the rock removal in *FranT*. Balred's remains were enshrined at Durham Cathedral, and men known to Chaucer (e.g., Lewis Clifford) traveled near the site of Balred's feat. Since the introduction of a miraculous agency would have been incongruous with the magical plot of *FranT*, Chaucer may have chosen the Breton setting as a means of disguising the hagiographic overtones of his source – although the topography of the East Lothian coast offers a more plausible geographical parallel to the landscape described in *FranT* than the nominal locale of the poem's action.

327 Havely, N.R., ed. and trans. *Chaucer's Boccaccio: Sources of Troilus and the Knight's and Franklin's Tales*. Cambridge: Brewer; Totowa, NJ: Rowman and Littlefield, 1980; pbk ed., 1992.
A translation of excerpts from Menedon's *questione* in *Fil* (pp 153–61). Based on **303**.

328 Rosenberg, Bruce. 'The Bari Widow and the *Franklin's Tale*.' *ChauR* 14 (1980), 344–52.
The story of 'The Widow of Bari,' included in the St Nicholas legend cycle, assembles folklore motifs (e.g., 'The Blind Promise,' 'The Impossible Task,' 'The Task Performed Through Cleverness,' 'Which Was the Noblest Act?') in an order identical to that in the fourth *questione* in *Fil* and in *FranT*, and thus

clarifies the structure of the antecedent versions of Boccaccio's and Chaucer's tales. Although the Bari Widow story is not a direct source of *FranT*, a comparison of the two illuminates Chaucer's treatment of moral issues, his emphasis on 'life's ambiguity' (p 351) and on the effect of time's passage on his actors, and his transformation of the Blind Promise motif from a mere narrative crux into an emblem of his heroine's character.

329 Bleeth, Kenneth A. 'The Rocks in the *Franklin's Tale* and Ovid's Medea.' *ANQ* 20 (1982), 130–1.
The Medea episode in *Metamorphoses* 7 includes among the sorceress's feats the power to remove rocks from their natural place. The episode served as the model for Tebano's creation of his garden in *Fil*. Chaucer's familiarity with Boccaccio's source may have contributed to his substitution of the removal of the Breton rocks for the assigned task in *Fil* – the production of a spring garden in winter.

330 Miller, Lucien. 'Marital Love in Two Early Chinese Narrative Ballads – with Analogues from Chaucer's *Canterbury Tales*.' *TkR* 13 (1982), 37–53.
Both *FranT* and the early Chinese ballad 'The Peacock Flies South' treat conflicts between love and authority, but in the latter, the conflict can be resolved only through the heroine's suicide. 'The Mulberry' is closer to *FranT* in that the wife proclaims her husband's authority and submits herself to it.

331 Bregoli-Russo, Mauda. 'Boccaccio tra le fonti dell'*Orlando Innamorato*?' *SPCT* 26:8 (1983), 21–7.
Surveys relations of plot among *Dec* 10.5, the fourth *questione d'amore* in *Fil*, *FranT*, and the novella of Tisbina, Iroldo, and Prasildo in canto 12 of Boiardo's *Orlando Innamorato*. Both *FranT* and Boiardo's novella cite Breton material as among their sources.

332 Hillman, Richard. 'Chaucer's Franklin's Magician and *The Tempest*: An Influence Beyond Appearances?' *SQ* 34 (1983), 426–32.
The echo of 'And farewel! Al oure revel was ago' (line 1204) in 'Our revels now are ended' (*Tempest*, 4.1.148) points up larger resemblances between the magician in *FranT* and Prospero. Both are experts at scheduling and managing events, both practice natural rather than diabolical magic, the magician's covering of the rocks – an illusion of protection from shipwreck – 'is merely a mirror image' (p 428) of Prospero's tempest. The pattern of reunion after trial in *FranT* looks toward Shakespeare's romance, as does the clerk's relationship with Aurelius: 'the final presentation of Chaucer's magician as an agent of release and forgiveness, as he surrenders his hold over the penitent Aurelius, is the most vital point of contact between the two works' (p 431). Although Shakespeare drew on a number of sources in writing *The Tempest*, 'only in *FranT* do we find a precedent for his use of the magician's powers to effect a spiritual reformation' (p 431).

333 Kollmann, Judith J. 'Ther is noon oother incubus but he: *The Canterbury Tales*,

Merry Wives of Windsor and Falstaff.' In *Chaucerian Shakespeare: Adaptation and Transformation*. Ed. E. Talbot Donaldson and Judith J. Kollmann. Detroit: Published for the Michigan Consortium for Medieval and Early Modern Studies, 1983. Pp 43–68.

The central issue of Shakespeare's play – 'the achievement of emotional and spiritual equality and the "gentilesse" that consists of treating each partner with respect' (p 49) – may reflect the influence of *FranT*.

334 McWilliams, G.H. Review of **327**. *MLR* 78 (1983), 133–5.

It is unlikely that Chaucer read *Dec*. The narrative technique of *FranT* has more in common with *Fil* than with the 'astringent' style of the comparable episode in *Dec* (p 133).

335 Wallace, David. 'Chaucer and Boccaccio's Early Writings.' In *Chaucer and the Italian Trecento*. Ed. Piero Boitani. Cambridge: Cambridge UP, 1983. Pp 141–62.

The world of the Love Questions in *Fil* is suspended, like *FranT*, between Christian and pagan terms of reference. The episode gives rise to a debate between the merits of 'honest love' and 'love for pleasure' that is absorbed into the dramatic action of Chaucer's poem. The two stories share thematic elements – Ovidian exempla, scenes of magical transformation – but Dorigen's dramatic prominence and psychological complexity are a striking departure from Boccaccio's undeveloped treatment of his heroine.

336 Boccaccio, Giovanni. *Il Filocolo*. Trans. Donald Cheney with the collaboration of Thomas G. Bergin. Garland Library of Medieval Literature. Vol. 43, Series B. New York: Garland, 1985.

A translation of *Fil*, complete. The fourth *questione d'amore* is on pp 254–66.

337 Finlayson, John. 'The Form of the Middle English *Lay*.' *ChauR* 19 (1985), 352–68.

Chaucer's acquaintance with the genre of the lay may have been limited to the poems in the Auchinleck MS. *Sir Orfeo* may have provided the motifs and a concept of the genre for *FranT*, which, because it forms part of the Marriage Group and is adapted to the character and social position of its teller, cannot be used as direct evidence of the concept of the lay in late fourteenth-century England.

337a Morris, Lynn King. *Chaucer Sources and Analogue Criticism: A Cross-Referenced Guide*. 1985. See **218a**.

A guide to the literature (through 1981) on the sources and analogues of Chaucer's writings, indexed by title of Chaucerian work, author of source or analogue, genre or origin of source, and title of source or analogue. The entry for *FranT* lists 144 sources, analogues, and allusions, with accompanying bibliographical references. Single works are sometimes listed under separate titles (e.g., Breton Lay: Eliduc; Marie de France: Eliduc) and occasionally misattributed (e.g., Gottfried von Eshenbach [*sic*]: Tristan; Chrétien de Troyes: Lancelot du Lak).

338 Nicholson, R.H. '*Sir Orfeo*: A "Kinges Noote."' *RES* n.s. 36 (1985), 161–79.
Describing himself as a *burel* man (line 716), not interested in rhetoric but willing to recount one of the old *aventures* told for *plesaunce* (lines 710–13), the Franklin leads us to expect a Breton lay. Breton 'in performance, not by provenance' (p 174), the ME lay is distinguished less by its subject matter or verse form than by the kind of story it tells – the joyous recovery of prosperity after a period of loss or distress – and by the presence of two linked plots.

339 Simons, John. 'Chaucer's *Franklin's Tale* and *The Tempest*.' *N&Q* n.s. 32 (1985), 56.
Similarities of action (hand clapping), language (line 1204 and *Tempest* 4.1.148), and context (actors as 'spirits') suggest that Prospero's dissolving of his masque embodies Shakespeare's memories of *FranT*.

340 Wallace, David. *Chaucer and the Early Writings of Boccaccio*. Cambridge: Brewer, 1985.
See **335**.

341 Wilson, Edmund. 'An Aristotelian Commonplace in Chaucer's *Franklin's Tale*.' *N&Q* n.s. 32 (1985), 303–5.
Compares Dorigen's address to God ('in ydel, as men seyn, ye no thyng make,' line 867) with Aristotle's *De caelo et mundo* (trans. William of Moerbeke): *Deus autem et natura nichil frustra faciunt*. The Aristotelian maxim is closer to Chaucer's phrase than the analogues in Boethius and Boccaccio cited by Skeat (**4**) and Robinson (**55**).

342 Anderson, Earl R. 'Malory's "Fair Maid of Ascolat."' *NM* 87 (1986), 237–54.
FranT, line 1390, is cited in connection with the unnamed Diana figure who injures Lancelot in a hunting accident just before the Candlemas tournament.

343 Martin, W.R., and Warren U. Ober. 'The Provenience of Henry James's First Tale.' *SSF* 24 (1987), 57–8.
Echoes of *FranT* in "A Tragedy of Error" (e.g., 'in Armorik' [line 729] / 'a vessel, the *Armorique*') encourage us to read James's first piece of fiction as a deliberate subversion of the values of honor and *gentilesse* present in Chaucer's tale. See **364**.

344 Besserman, Lawrence. *Chaucer and the Bible: A Critical Review of Research, Indexes, and Bibliography*. 1988. See **221a**.
Lists eleven certain or possible biblical allusions in *FranT* (lines 777, 779–80, 879–80, 885–6, 888, 911–12, 983, 989, 1321, 1487–92, 1558), with references to scholarly discussions (pp 122–3).

345 Cooper, Helen. *The Canterbury Tales*. Oxford Guides to Chaucer. Oxford: Clarendon, 1989; pbk ed., 1991. 2nd ed., 1996.
The closest analogues to *FranT* are *Fil* and *Dec* 10.5. The former is generally thought to be Chaucer's immediate source, but the case for *Dec* is stronger than is usually supposed. The differences between *FranT* and Boccaccio's

tales are extensive, and include the nature of the impossible task, the parallel between the love triangle and that in *MerT,* and Arveragus's concern for his wife's *trouthe.* Chaucer's plotting is tighter, more focused on the wife's love for her husband, and more concerned with emotional responses and morality. Three passages have clearly established sources: the discourse on marriage is influenced by Ami's speech in *RR,* Dorigen's questioning of God's providence is based on *Consol,* and her Complaint draws extensively on *Jov.*

346 Kolve, V.A., and Glending Olson, eds. *The Canterbury Tales: Nine Tales and the General Prologue.* 1989. See **111**.
Includes translations of Menedon's story (*Fil*), *Dec* 10.5, and a discussion of love and marriage from Bartholomaeus Anglicus's *De proprietatibus rerum.*

347 Axton, Richard. 'Spenser's "faire hermaphrodite": Rewriting *The Faerie Queene.*' In *A Day Estivall: Essays on the Music, Poetry, and History of Scotland and Poems Previously Unpublished in Honour of Helena Mennie Shire.* Ed. Alisoun Gardner-Medwin and Janet Hadley Williams. Aberdeen: Aberdeen UP, 1990. Pp 35–47.
The motto for the story of Scudamour and Amoret (*FQ,* Books 3 and 4) is present in Britomart's speech in Book 3.1.25, a quotation from *FranT* (lines 765–6) on the incompatibility of love and *maistrye.*

348 Windeatt, Barry. 'Chaucer and fifteenth-century romance: *Partonope of Blois.*' In *Chaucer Traditions: Studies in Honour of Derek Brewer.* 1990. See **227**. Pp 62–80.
Partonope's delight in his new love – 'Fresshe and lusty ys Partonope; / For in hys armes hys loue haþe he' (lines 5274–5) – echoes *FranT* lines 1090–2.

349 Flahiff, F.T. 'Mysteriously Come Together: Dickens, Chaucer, and *Little Dorrit.*' *UTQ* 61 (1991–2), 250–68.
Aurelius's courtship of Dorigen and the disappearance of the black rocks in *FranT* supply a subtext for aspects of *Little Dorrit* – the relationship of Amy Dorrit and John Chivery, and Dickens's account of the metamorphosis of the Marshalsea Prison in his Preface.

350 White, Patrick. '*Candida*: Bernard Shaw's Chaucerian Drama.' *Shaw* 12 (1992), 213–28.
Shaw admired Chaucer's poetry. It is possible that he had *FranT* in mind when writing *Candida.* Parallels exist between characters (Morell and Arveragus, Marchbanks and Aurelius, Candida and Dorigen), plot (both works turn on a reckless declaration by the wife), theme (magnanimity resolves the crisis in both works), and tone.

351 Cook, Robert. 'Chaucer's Franklin's Tale and *Sir Orfeo.*' *NM* 95 (1994), 333–6.
Loomis's argument (**282**) for Chaucer's use of *Sir Orfeo* in *FranP* can be supplemented by another instance of possible indebtedness: the things that Orfeo sees during his period of exile, leading up to his vision of Heurodis – a hunting scene with hounds, armed knights, ladies with falcons on a hawking expedition – may have provided some of the details for the illusions

shown by the magician to Aurelius.

352 Item cancelled.

353 Bawcutt, Priscilla. '*Pamphilus de amore* "in Inglish toung."' *MÆ* 64 (1995), 264–72.
Chaucer may not have associated the *Pamphilles* cited in *Mel* as a source for proverbs about the usefulness of money with the 'Pamphilus' to whom he compared the lovesick Aurelius in lines 1109–10 (p 265).

354 Stevenson, Barbara. 'West Meets East: Geoffrey Chaucer's "Franklin's Tale" and the Japanese "Captain of Naruto."' *PoeticaT* 44 (1995), 41–52.
Four traits – fragmentation, retrospection, profundity, and subtlety – attributed to medieval literature by Jin'ichi Konishi (*A History of Japanese Literature*, ed. Earl Miner, vols 2 and 3 [Princeton, NJ: Princeton UP, 1986, 1991]) establish the 'inherent medieval nature' of *FranT* and a Japanese analogue (p 45). Chaucer depicts the emergence of 'individual rights' from the 'decaying feudalism' of fourteenth-century England, while 'The Captain of Naruto' reflects the complex social obligations arising from the new phenomenon of feudalism in thirteenth-century Japan (p 45). While Chaucer advocates an equality at odds with feudal Christian Europe, the Japanese author insists on maintaining a peaceful status quo among social classes.

355 Edwards, Robert R. 'Source, Context, and Cultural Translation in the *Franklin's Tale*.' *MP* 94 (1996), 141–62.
The evidence for *Fil* as a source for *TC* is inconclusive; the only clear link between Chaucer's poetry and Boccaccio's prose romance is the use in *FranT* of Menedon's story, which Chaucer may have read in a MS that contained only the thirteen Love Questions. The four MSS that present the Love Questions as a separate entity display variants that produce both textual differences and differences in poetic nuance. Among the items of interest for a reading of *FranT* is the replacement of *liberalità* (generosity) by *libertà* (freedom) at several crucial junctures, a variant that underscores the possible range of meanings of *fre* in the Franklin's closing question. The Love Questions depict a closed, aristocratic world in which love casuistry promises pleasure rather than disruption. In *FranT*, social relations are more mobile – 'at once inherited and constructed' (p 157) – and display a complex interpenetration of courtly and mercantile values. In contrast to Menedon's story, *FranT* marks 'levels of social differentiation' (p 158) and grants its characters private, interiorized feelings. Boccaccio's untroubled distinctions among kinds of *liberalità* become blurred in Chaucer's tale, which offers no differential for separating social rank from noble behavior. *Trouthe* therefore serves more as a social mechanism than as a value; Arveragus insists, with 'reductive literalism,' that Dorigen keep her promise because in *FranT* 'the domain of social relations ... is indeed at risk' (p 162). Although the tale is marked by the Franklin's nostalgia for the world of Boccaccio's aristocratic speakers,

the mixed courtly and mercantile language of Chaucer's characters voices a broader range and more complex variety of registers.

356 Serrano Reyes, Jésus L. *Didacticismo y Moralismo en Geoffrey Chaucer y Don Juan Manuel: Un Estudio Comparativo Textual*. Córdoba: Universidad de Córdoba, 1996.

A comparative analysis of four tales – *FranT,* Exemplum 50 ('De lo contesçió a Saladín con una dueña, muger de su vasallo') in Don Juan Manuel's *El Conde Lucanor, Dec* 10.5, and tale 1 ('Leo') from the thirteenth-century *Cuentos de Sendebar* – reveals several structural and thematic parallels. An examination of *FranT* and 'De lo contesçió' using Vladimir Propp's analysis of folk-tale structure uncovers additional parallels in the shape of the two narratives. Like *CT, El Conde Lucanor* contains a debate about marriage. Exemplum 50 concludes with an answer to the initial proposition in the debate – 'la vergüença es la mejor cosa que omne puede aver in sí' (shame is the best thing a man can have in him) – that corresponds to Arveragus's 'trouthe is the hyeste thyng that man may kepe' (line 1479). In addition to the word-for-word parallelism of the two sentences, *vergüença* and *trouthe* both signify 'moral awareness,' the human quality that allows us to distinguish good from evil. A semiotic analysis reveals that both authors organize their tales according to the same moral–didactic structure: framing of story, introductory moralizing passage, application of introductory passage to the story, transcendence and universality. The evidence provided by these different methods of analysis suggests that the Spanish work is not simply an analogue to *FranT,* but that it served as a source for Chaucer's poem.

357 Thompson, N.S. *Chaucer, Boccaccio, and the Debate of Love: A Comparative Study of The Decameron and The Canterbury Tales*. Oxford: Clarendon, 1996.

Menedon's narrative in *Fil* is concerned with distinguishing true virtue from deceptive appearances. In the debate that follows the story, Menedon accepts Fiammetta's judgment that the husband showed the greatest *liberalità* in giving up his honor; 'personal integrity within marriage' overrides considerations of class and wealth (p 256). In Boccaccio's second version of the story (*Dec* 10.5), the center of interest lies in the courtly lover's change of heart, his curbing of illicit desire in response to the husband's magnanimous gesture. Boccaccio's transformation of the 'abstract dilemma' (p 263) of Menedon's *questione* into an exemplary story about the magnanimous behavior of a group of noble characters anticipates two narrative modes that will reappear in Chaucer's version of the tale.

358 Hanna, Ralph, III, and Traugott Lawler, eds. *Jankyn's Book of Wikked Wyves.* Vol. 1: *The Primary Texts. Walter Map's "Dissuasio," Theophrastus' "De Nuptiis," Jerome's Adversus Jovinianum.* The Chaucer Library. Athens: U of Georgia P, 1997.

Lines 1364–1454 of Dorigen's Complaint comprise 'brief and summary excerpts' from the catalogue of noble wives and maidens in *Jov* (p 75). In lines 1364–1404, Dorigen follows Jerome fairly closely; from lines 1405 to 1441, she tends to reduce Jerome's detail and occasionally to add material of her own devising; at line 1442, she returns to something like direct translation. The source material for the lines in Dorigen's Complaint appears on pp 163–75 of this edition, with facing English translation. For the editing of the excerpts from *Jov*, see pp 113–18.

359 Pireddu, Nicoletta. 'Ca*R*terbury Tales: Romances of Disenchantment in Geoffrey Chaucer and Angela Carter.' *Comparatist* 21 (1997), 117–48.
A comparative reading of *Thop*, *FranT*, *WBP*, *WBT*, and four stories from *The Bloody Chamber* and *Saints and Sinners*. Chaucer and Carter 'stage the textual nature of romance and make it inseparable from a critical examination of the ideology it transmits' (p 120). *FranT* and Carter's 'The Kiss' initially situate themselves in relation to idealized literary worlds, but ultimately adopt illusion-breaking strategies that dissipate any nostalgia for the romance world and call into question the values on which it is founded.

360 Cooper, Helen. 'Jacobean Chaucer: *The Two Noble Kinsmen* and Other Chaucerian Plays.' In *Refiguring Chaucer in the Renaissance*. 1998. See **232**. Pp 192–209.
Honor in Beaumont and Fletcher's *The Triumph of Honor* means less chivalric reputation (as it does in *FranT*) than female chastity. Dorigen, its strong-minded female protagonist, has more in common with the Volumnia of Shakespeare's *Coriolanus* than with Chaucer's gentle heroine. By the end of the play, the men 'have all disgraced themselves to some degree, and only Dorigen has set an unambiguous moral standard' (p 195).

361 Battles, Dominique. 'Chaucer's *Franklin's Tale* and Boccaccio's *Filocolo* Reconsidered.' *ChauR* 34 (1999), 38–59.
FranT reflects the influence not only of Menedon's tale in Part 4 of *Fil*, but also of the larger frame narrative of Florio and Biancofiore. Features of *FranT* that are absent from Menedon's tale but central to the frame narrative include the prominence of the sea; the dichotomy of sea and garden; the separation of the couple and the heightened pathos that results therefrom; the preoccupation with marriage; Dorigen's lengthy rhetorical laments, paralleled in *Fil* by Florio's laments, which include the speaker's comparison of herself or himself to classical heroines or heroes; and the narrator's assurance that fears raised in the laments are groundless. Although the frame narrative does not account for all of the changes Chaucer made in Menedon's tale, we should read *FranT* as an 'on-going dialogue' (p 54) with both the *questione d'amore* and its larger narrative context in *Fil*.

362 Walker, Warren S. 'Extant Analogues of the *Franklin's Tale* in the Turkish Oral Tradition.' *ChauR* 33 (1999), 432–7.
Summarizes four Turkish oral analogues to Aarne–Thompson type 976

('Which Was the Noblest Act?') in which the final question becomes 'Which of the evaluators of husband, admirer, and thief [in place of the magician] is the most ignoble?'

363 Edwards, Robert R. 'Rewriting Menedon's Story: *Decameron* 10.5 and the *Franklin's Tale*.' In *The Decameron and the Canterbury Tales: New Essays on an Old Question*. Ed. Leonard Michael Koff and Brenda Deen Schildgen. Madison, NJ: Fairleigh Dickinson UP; London: Associated University Presses, 2000. Pp 226–46. Repr. with revisions in Edwards, *Chaucer and Boccaccio: Antiquity and Modernity*. Houndmills, UK: Palgrave, 2002. Pp 153–72.

Dec 10.5 and *FranT* reconceive Menedon's story from the *questioni d'amore* of *Fil* in different social visions and historical contexts. Boccaccio's revision moves the tale from a feudal, aristocratic milieu to an urban locale, and shows how new bonds of solidarity can replace traditional class identity. Chaucer looks back nostalgically to the feudal world of the *questioni*, while the social relations in his tale belong to an emergent mercantile culture. The circular narrative structure underlying Menedon's story – beginning with the social world in equilibrium and reestablishing that equilibrium at the end – supplies the framework for analyzing the two revisions. Both *Dec* and *FranT* reimagine the nature of the marriage in *Fil*. In *FranT*, Dorigen and Arveragus are bound by *accord* (line 791), 'the freedom of the interiorized, mercantile subject to negotiate and act in his best interests' (p 233). It is this private agreement that is threatened by Aurelius's solicitations. In a world constructed on the strength of a promise, every pledge must be taken at face value. Dorigen's failure to separate reality from play in her vow to Aurelius is a move toward the literal that is also present in the Franklin's replacement of the supernatural magic of *Fil* by 'a natural world whose laws are finally literal and reductive' (p 237). In both *Fil* and *Dec*, the husband separates his wife's intent from the literalism of her promise, distinguishing the personal from the social. In *FranT*, Arveragus wishes that Dorigen's dishonor remain a private matter between them. In *Dec*, Boccaccio reimagines the conclusion of the tale in ethical rather than social terms, as a conversion of desire to charity. Chaucer's revision of the ending keeps class issues to the fore, even while encoding the ethical in the social. In both *Dec* and *FranT*, 'the solidarity of class values gives way in some measure to other claims on allegiance, such as charity and character' (p 243).

• Review of *Chaucer and Boccaccio* by Nick Havely, *MLR* 99 (2004), 456–7: The final chapter on *FranT* 'lacks an overview of the whole subject in conclusion, nor is enough of a case made for allotting the tale this position within the structure of *CT* or within Chaucer's rewriting of Boccaccio' (p 457).

364 Ellis, Steve. *Chaucer at Large: The Poet in the Modern Imagination*. Minneapolis: U of Minnesota P, 2000.

The parallels between *FranT* and Henry James's 'A Tragedy of Error' suggested by Martin and Ober (**343**) surface again in James's *The Spoils of Poynton* (1897), in which the protagonists find themselves trapped in 'an exacting and self-punishing system of honor' (p 89).

365 Taylor, Karla. 'Chaucer's Uncommon Voice: Some Contexts for Influence.' In *The Decameron and The Canterbury Tales: New Essays on an Old Question*. 2000. See **363**. Pp 47–82.
Read as a response to *Dec* 10.5, *FranT* signals Chaucer's 'critical distance from Boccaccio's optimistic social agenda' (p 71). A possible echo of Boccaccio's *saramento* (sworn oath) in Aurelius's *serement* (line 1534) marks a shift from feudal to contractual values, and shows Aurelius adapting aristocratic forms to his opportunistic motives, while the squire's mercantile prudence is evident in his reluctance to pay the clerk for his services. In contrast to the real magic of Boccaccio's tale, magic in *FranT* is rationalized, with the result that Aurelius's conversion and 'sudden access of fellow feeling' (p 73) are made to seem sentimental, 'the favorite magic of a particular social group' (p 74). Chaucer's departures from *Dec* 10.5 show him as skeptical of Boccaccio's ideal of the 'classless inward nobility of the "cuor gentili"' (p 75) and of the possibility of generalizing aristocratic ideals and behavior into a new and broader community.

366 Walker, Lewis. 'Chaucer's Contribution to *The Tempest*: A Reappraisal.' *RenP* 47 (2000), 119–35.
Shakespeare's indebtedness to *FranT* in *The Tempest* extends beyond the resemblances noted by previous scholars. The clerk's dispelling of his visions with a handclap is paralleled not only in Prospero's similar action, but also when Ariel '*claps his wings upon the table*' (stage direction 3.3.52). Other parallels between the works include their special interest in the act of eating, their fascination with the technical aspects of magic, analogies between Prospero's betrothal masque and the continuously changing scenes produced by Chaucer's magician, the two characters' obsession with timing, and the importance of books and the place where books are kept. Both works are structured around various configurations of three characters (Prospero combines aspects of Arveragus, Aurelius, and the clerk), both blend narrative and dramatic modes, and both contain significant interruptions. Prospero's interruption of the betrothal masque may be read in the light of the interruption of *SqT* as Chaucer's 'self-acknowledged failure ... to finish a work of romance that he had started' (p 133).

367 Edwards, Robert R. 'The Franklin's Tale.' In *Sources and Analogues of The Canterbury Tales*. Vol. 1. 2002. See **242**. Pp 211–65.
This work incorporates scholarship on the sources and analogues of *CT* produced since Bryan and Dempster's compilation (**174**, **281**). Edwards reviews the scholarship on the possible indebtedness of *FranT* to the Breton lays; on the relation of the tale to its primary source – Menedon's story in *Fil*, which

Chaucer may have read in a collection of the *questioni d'amore* excerpted from the longer work; on the relation of Menedon's tale to *Dec* 10.5; and on sources that provided new details for Chaucer's retelling of the basic story (e.g., *HRB,* which gives the names of the two principal male characters and perhaps suggested the miraculous removal of the rocks from the Breton coast, and Layamon's *Brut,* which includes an episode focused on the subject of fidelity). Chaucer significantly modified the marriage theme in his reimagining of the *Fil* tale; the Franklin's speech on marriage echoes passages in *RR*. The Breton lays, extensively excerpted in Bryan and Dempster, are represented by a single passage from the ME *Lay le Freine*. Menedon's tale and *Dec* 10.5 are included complete; notes to the text of the former record manuscript variants that suggest how Boccaccio's concluding question about generosity (*liberalità*) might have produced the Franklin's question about freedom (*libertà*). Edwards prints two passages from *HRB,* three passages from Wace's Anglo-Norman imitation of *HRB,* an excerpt from Layamon's *Brut* in which Genuis reminds Arviragus about faith and promises, three excerpts from *RR* (Ami on equity in marriage, Ami's reproof of the jealous husband, and Nature's claim that women are born free and desire liberty), and the material from *Jov* (reprinted from **358**) that Chaucer employed in composing Dorigen's Complaint. The excerpt from *Lay le Freine* is glossed; ModE translations are provided for all other sources and analogues.

• Review by Daniel Wakelin, *RES* 54 (2003), 516–17: Although *FranT* vaguely resembles the sorts of tales found in *Dec,* its primary connections are with *Fil.* One can question whether Chaucer would have needed to read *Dec* closely to add 'compassion' to his story.

• Review by Stephen Knight, *Speculum* 79 (2004), 1057–9: The chapter on *FranT* creates a 'new gap' when the Breton lay is omitted as a possible source or analogue; Edwards is uninterested in 'Celtic depths' or in a Franco–Breton conflict that may 'lurk unseen beneath the text.' Orality could be explored further as a way of explaining Chaucer's relation to his sources – 'including the nearly forgotten Breton lays' (p 1059).

• Review by Jill Mann, *JEGP* 104 (2005), 107–28: The passage from Layamon cited in connection with the theme of *trouthe* stretches the notion of a source rather far, especially since the theme is found in works much closer to Chaucer's own time (e.g., *Sir Orfeo, SGGK)* (p 107).

368 Walker, Warren S. 'Redemption from Hazardous Vows in Turkish Folklore.' *JAF* 116 (2003), 206–11.
Summarizes two Turkish oral analogues to Dorigen's vow in *FranT,* in which those who utter hasty oaths or make hazardous vows find themselves trapped by their own words.

369 Baxter, Katherine Isobel. 'The Strange Spaces of *The Rescue.*' *Conradian* 29 (2004), 64–83.

The geography of *The Rescue* recalls that of *FranT* in the parallel between the rocky coast of Brittany and Conrad's 'Shallows,' a dangerous, invisible mingling of land and sea. The Orléans magician's visual and spatial illusions reappear in the novel's trope of disrupted perspective. The magician's conjuring of scenes of romance and their subsequent disappearance may underlie Conrad's view of *The Rescue* as 'the swan song of Romance as a form of literary art' (p 83).

370 Cooper, Helen. *The English Romance in Time: Transforming Motifs from Geoffrey of Monmouth to the Death of Shakespeare*. New York: Oxford UP, 2004.
Spenser's quotation of the Franklin on the subject of mutual respect within marriage (*FQ* 3.1.25; cf. *FranT* lines 764–6) is precise enough to bring its original context with it (p 253).

371 Fumo, Jamie. 'Aurelius' Prayer, *Franklin's Tale*, 1031–79: Sources and Analogues.' *Neophil* 88 (2004), 623–35.
Aurelius's prayer to Apollo contains echoes and latent allusions that characterize the speaker and help us to understand the methods of Chaucer's mature style. Arcita's prayer to Apollo in *Tes* 4 (a prayer granted by the gods) serves as a negative source, embodying 'a tradition that will ... *not* be fulfilled in its new incarnation' (p 635). Echoes of *Consol* 1.m5, ironically invert Boethius's celebration of natural order. Allusions to the prayer of the magician Tebano in *Fil* 1.4 suggest parallels between Aurelius and the clerk, the Tebano-figure in Chaucer's poem. The story of Apollo and Daphne in Ovid's *Metamorphoses* 1 supplies a starting point for Chaucer's 'creative mythography' (p 630), in which Dorigen – a Diana/Daphne figure – is ensnared by *not* outrunning Apollo. Aurelius's request for Apollo's aid builds on the form of prayers to the Virgin Mary for intervention with Christ. But the theological design 'cannot support the prayer's comic weight: Apollo seems less like the mediatrix of Christianity ... than like a go-between, a Pandarus' (p 632).

372 Knopp, Sherron. 'Poetry as Conjuring Act: The *Franklin's Tale* and *The Tempest*.' *ChauR* 38 (2004), 337–54.
The verbal echoes of *FranT* in *The Tempest* point to 'a shared engagement on the part of both poets with the status of poetry as illusion and conjuring act' (p 338). In *FranT*, the art of the Orléans magician is identified with that of the poet himself. In *The Tempest*, Ariel's transformations at Prospero's command at once celebrate the mimetic power of the poetic imagination and echo Plato's condemnation of art as imitation. In both cases, the illusionist's real power 'has nothing to do with morality. His goal is simply to compel belief' (p 347). Just as Prospero's activities suggest that 'morality may itself be a fictional construct' (p 346), so Chaucer's art in *CT* strives not to lead an audience to virtue, but to persuade them that they hear actual pilgrim narrators speaking.

ಖ *The Squire's Tale*, 1889–2005

See also **75**, **158**, **166**, **204**, **207**, **215**, **216**, **217**, **229**, **236**, **238**, **271**, **555**, **761**, **769**, **828**, **875**, **1042**, **1079**, **1141**, **1242**, **1248**, **1276**, **1303**, **1320**, **1350**, **1361**, **1433**, **1441**, **1488**.

The Squire's Tale, 1889–1949

373 Kittredge, George Lyman. 'Supposed Historical Allusions in the Squire's Tale.' *ESt* 13 (1889), 1–24.
Brandl's reading (*ESt* 12 [1889], 161–86) of *SqT* as an allegory of events at the court of Edward III misrepresents Chaucer's language, is internally inconsistent, and rests on errors of fact. *SqT* is a romance, free from any hidden meaning; we cannot believe that the tale's 'splendid vigor ... merely subserves the purposes of a frigid, half-allegorical occasional poem' (p 4).

374 Skeat, Walter W., ed. *The Complete Works of Geoffrey Chaucer, Edited from Numerous Manuscripts*. 1894–7. See **4**.
Among Skeat's notes to *SqT*, the following have attracted comment. The description of *Sarray* (line 9) better suits Cambaluc (Beijing), the seat of Kublai Khan's court; Chaucer has confused accounts of Genghis and Kublai Khan (5:370–1). The second part of the tale seems to have been hastily composed and never revised (5:382). The falcon is probably a princess who has been changed into a bird; her *roche* (line 500) may signify a palace, the tercelet a prince (5:384). *Cambalo* (line 667) is not the same person as *Cambalus* (line 656; also called *Cambalo*, line 31). The former is Canacee's lover, the latter her brother (5:386).

375 ———. *The Chaucer Canon*. Oxford: Clarendon, 1900.
The chief features of Chaucer's grammar and versification, intended to enable readers to distinguish the genuine poems from spurious attributions. Ch. 3 (pp 30–44) analyzes the inflectional system of Chaucer's ME, drawing its examples from *SqT*.

376 Snell, F.J. *The Age of Chaucer*. London: Bell, 1901. Repr. New York: AMS, 1970.
Cambyuskan represents Genghis Khan, but the character is that of his grand-

son Kublai. 'Is it not singular, almost a fatality, that the two English poets – Chaucer and Coleridge – who essayed to sing this Tartar ruler should have abandoned their tasks unfinished?' (p 213).

377 Lowes, John Livingston. 'The Dry Sea and the Carrenare.' *MP* 3 (1905–6), 1–46.

In support of his identification of the 'Drye Se' and the 'Carrenar' (*BD* 1028–9) with the Gobi Desert and the 'Black Lake' (Kara-nor) on the east side of the Gobi, Lowes argues that Chaucer could have known a good deal about Tartary and Russia, not only from books and maps, but also from the reports of merchants, missionaries, and foreign visitors to London.

378 Root, Robert Kilburn. *The Poetry of Chaucer: A Guide to Its Study and Appreciation.* Boston: Houghton Mifflin, 1906/1922. Repr. Gloucester, MA: Peter Smith, 1934.

Much of *SqT*'s appeal derives from its unfinishedness; any conclusion Chaucer might have provided 'would be barren and commonplace compared with our vague imaginings' of possible developments (p 268). Chaucer probably recognized the 'power of the incomplete, and deliberately left his tale half told' (p 269). The tale is perfectly suited to the youthful Squire; 'his charm, like that of the tale he tells, is in large measure the charm of incompleteness' (p 270). *SqT* is more likely to be an amalgam of themes from Oriental sources than an imitation of a single narrative. Nor did Chaucer appear to have any connected account of the Tartars before him when he wrote, as Skeat (**4**) and Manly (**131**) assume (p 270). (The revised edition contains additional bibliography, pp 294–300.) See **439**.

379 Schofield, William Henry. *English Literature from the Norman Conquest to Chaucer*. 1906. See **253**.

The tradition that Gawain, like Arthur and Launfal, mysteriously disappeared from this world was probably in Chaucer's mind when he observed that Gawain, if he had come 'ayeyn out of Fairye' (line 96), could not have spoken more courteously than did the stranger knight (p 226). *SqT* is probably based on an Arabian story that the Moors brought to Spain, akin to the source of *Cleo* (p 304). Whatever its relation to Marco Polo's *Travels*, *SqT* is essentially romance. *SqT* and *KnT* are evidence that Chaucer valued romance and enjoyed writing it (p 305).

380 Hinckley, Henry Barrett. *Notes on Chaucer: A Commentary on the Prolog and Six Canterbury Tales.* Northampton, MA: Nonotuck, 1907. Repr. New York: Haskell, 1964.

SqT was probably modeled on 'a French version of a Tartar romance' (p 210) which 'perpetuated features of prehistoric tradition' (p 211), in particular superstitious reverence for the craft of the blacksmith. Magical objects similar to the steed of brass, mirror, ring, and sword appear in Tartar tradition, suggesting that Chaucer's source was a 'romance of metallurgy' (p 213), perhaps part of a lost cycle devoted to Genghis Khan, who may himself have been a smith. Hinckley believes that Chaucer was 'entirely ignorant' (p 212) of *Cleo* (see **133**). *SqT* was probably conceived and written before the *CT* period; the rhetorical preoccupations of the narrator are unsuitable for the Squire, whose *songes* (I.95) would not have included long epics. Hinckley annotates numerous words and lines, including *Elpheta* (line 29; 'a feminine diminutive of *elf*'); *kyng of Arabe and Inde* (line 110; perhaps a King of Delhi in Chaucer's source); *the Pegasee* (line 207; is *Pegasee* a noun, or an adjective to be taken with *hors* understood?); *at a* (line 299; if this reading is correct, *hath* in line 300 is a Gallicism, suggesting that Chaucer's immediate original for *SqT* was written in French); *as wommen be* (line 362; 'women require less sleep than men'), *his similitude* (line 480; animals in Sanskrit fables speak of the virtue of putting oneself in another's place, a possible indication of the Hindu origin of Chaucer's story) (pp 210–36). See **157**.

381 Manly, John Matthews. 'A Knight Ther Was.' *Transactions and Proceedings of the American Philological Association* 38 (1907), 89–107. Repr. in *Chaucer: Modern Essays in Criticism*. Ed. Edward Wagenknecht. New York: Oxford UP, 1959. Pp 46–59.
To us, *SqT* seems a 'curious ... flight of the oriental imagination'; to Chaucer's contemporaries, it was a 'strange but credible transcript of life beyond the Christian pale' (p 91). Chaucer may have heard the story from a knight who had fought in the East; information is provided about such figures in connection with the list of the Knight's battles in *GP*.

382 Hammond, Eleanor Prescott. *Chaucer: A Bibliographical Manual*. New York: Macmillan, 1908. Repr. New York: Peter Smith, 1933.
Discusses *SqT*'s position in the MSS, lists editions, continuations, modernizations, and translations, summarizes previous work on the tale's sources and analogues and date, and prints the spurious conclusion found in the Selden and Lansdowne MSS and in Speght's 1687 edition (pp 310–14).

383 Hinckley, Henry Barrett. 'Elfeta.' *Acad* 74 (1908), 866.
Certain star lists in Skeat's edition of *Astr* give their twenty-ninth star the name 'Elfeta' or 'Alfeta.' This star name is likely to be the source of the name of Cambyuskan's queen, *Elpheta* (line 29).

384 Root, Robert K. 'Chaucer's Legend of Medea.' *PMLA* 24 (1909), 124–53.
In referring to Jason, along with Paris of Troy, as a type of lover who deserts one lady for another (lines 548–551), Chaucer may have had *LGW* in mind. The deserted falcon's story of her faithless lover recalls the language of the early part of the 'Legend of Medea' (pp 133–4).

385 Tatlock, John Strong Perry. *The Harleian Manuscript 7334 and Revision of the Canterbury Tales*. Chaucer Society Publications, Second Series, 41. London: Kegan Paul, Trench, Trübner, 1909.
Nine-syllable lines are frequent in *SqT*, which may be one of Chaucer's last

works (p 13). The Harley reviser 'corrects' such lines at 252, 266, and 330. Other notable Harleian readings cited are lines 95 and 516.

386 Lowes, John Livingston. 'As by the whelp chasted is the leoun.' *Archiv* 124 (1910), 132.
Jacobus de Voragine on the question 'Quare Christus sanguinem suderit' is cited as a gloss on line 491: 'Animalia autem domesticatur tribus modis. Aliquando per flagellationem, quia quando canis flagellatur, leo domesticatur ... Christus igitur, qui est leo, ante nos canes, ut nos domesticaret, flagellari voluit.' 'The point of the proverb ... is only heightened by the vivid reversal of its order in the allegorical application to Christ.'

387 Skeat, Walter W. 'Chaucer: Names of Characters in "The Squire's Tale."' *N&Q*, 11th ser., 1 (1910), 118.
In response to a query (*N&Q*, 11th ser., 1 [1910], 50) about character names in *SqT*, Skeat directs the reader to the notes on *Cambuscan* and *Camballo* in the Oxford edition (**4**) and observes that the origin of *Algarsif* and *Elpheta* must await further study of Chaucer's sources.

388 Brown, Carleton. '*Shul* and *Shal* in the Chaucer Manuscripts.' *PMLA* 26 (1911), 6–30.
The variation between *shul* and *shal* in the manuscripts of Chaucer's poems derives either from the scribes intermediate between Chaucer and the extant copies or from Chaucer himself; the predominance of *shal* forms in *MLT* and *SqT* supports the placement of the latter after the former in many of the *CT* manuscripts, as one would expect if the two tales 'had been copied by an "a" scribe and put into circulation in a single fascicule' (p 28). *SqT*'s unfinished state may be due to a scribe rather than to Chaucer; the only other instance of such an abrupt ending occurs at the end of Fragment I, likewise written by a *shal* scribe – 'perhaps the same person' (p 29). See **761**.

389 Corson, Hiram. *Index of Proper Names and Subjects to Chaucer's Canterbury Tales together with Comparisons and Similes, Metaphors and Proverbs, Maxims, etc., in the Same*. Introduction by Walter W. Skeat. Chaucer Society Publications, First Series, 72. London: Kegan Paul, Trench, Trübner, and Henry Frowde, 1911. Repr. New York: Johnson, [1967].
The index of names and subjects (including scriptural quotations and allusions) is followed by separate listings of comparisons and similes (six in *SqT*); metaphors (one in *SqT*); proverbs, maxims, and sententious expressions (seven in *SqT*); prayers, entreaties, and imprecations (two in *SqT*).

390 Kittredge, George Lyman. 'Chaucer's Discussion of Marriage.' *MP* 9 (1912), 435–67. Repr. in *Chaucer: Modern Essays in Criticism* (see **381**), pp 188–215; in *Chaucer Criticism: The Canterbury Tales*. Ed. Richard J. Schoeck and Jerome Taylor. Notre Dame, IN: U of Notre Dame P, 1960, pp 130–59; in *Chaucer—The Canterbury Tales: A Casebook*. Ed. J.J. Anderson. London: Macmillan, 1974, pp 61–92; in *Chaucer: The Critical Heritage*. Ed. Derek S. Brewer. 2 vols.

London: Routledge and Kegan Paul, 1978, 2:305–28; and in *Critical Essays on Chaucer's Canterbury Tales.* Ed. Malcolm Andrew. Toronto: U of Toronto P, 1991, pp 8–35.

'There is no psychology about *SqT*, – no moral or social or matrimonial theorizing. It is pure romance, in the mediaeval sense. The Host understood the charm of variety. He did not mean to let the discussion drain itself to the dregs' (p 457).

391 Schofield, William Henry. *Chivalry in English Literature: Chaucer, Malory, Spenser and Shakespeare.* Cambridge, MA: Harvard UP, 1912. Repr. Port Washington, NY: Kennikat, 1964.

SqT shares certain moral preoccupations with *Anel;* its central subject is the noble man's love of *newefangelnesse* (p 51). One may compare the address to Tarquin ('Legend of Lucrece,' 1819–24) in *LGW.*

392 Dodd, William George. *Courtly Love in Chaucer and Gower.* Harvard Studies in English 1. Boston: Ginn, 1913. Repr. Gloucester, MA: Peter Smith, 1959.

References to courtly love conventions – service to a deity of love, the gaiety required of a lover, the need for secrecy – are found in Part 1 of *SqT.* The false tercel in Part 2 is a hypocrite who acts to perfection the courtly lover's part, in his apparent humility, earnestness, reverence for his lady, gaiety, and cultivation of *gentilesse* (pp 247–8).

393 Koch, John. 'Textkritische bemerkungen zu Chaucers *Canterbury Tales.*' *ESt* 47 (1913), 338–414.

Textual notes on lines 4, 138, 515, 585, and 608–9 (pp 378–80).

394 Hadow, Grace E. *Chaucer and His Times.* London: Williams and Norgate; New York: Holt, 1914. Repr. New York: Books for Libraries Press, 1970.

Chaucer deliberately left *SqT* unfinished. The Franklin's interruption 'gently satirises the long-windedness and absurdity of the romance-writers.' *SqT* is a 'half-way house' between the serious treatments of romance in *TC* and *KnT* and the 'pure parody' of *Thop* (p 82).

395 Heidrich, Käte. *Das geographische Weltbild des späteren englischen Mittelalters mit besonderer Berücksichtigung der Vorstellungen Chaucer's und seiner Zeitgenossen.* Albert-Ludwigs-Universität diss. (Freiburg). 1915. Dir. Prof. Brie. Published Freiburg: Hammerschlag & Kahle, 1915.

Brief discussions of place names in *SqT*, beginning with *Sarray* (line 9) and ending with *Tartre* (line 266).

396 Cook, Albert Stanburrough. 'The Historical Background of Chaucer's Knight.' *TCAAS* 20 (1916), 161–240.

The 'steede of Lumbardye' (line 193) to which the brass horse is compared may recall the horses given as gifts or present at the festivities accompanying the marriage in 1367 of Prince Lionel of England to Violante, daughter of Galeazzo Visconti of Milan, which Chaucer is likely to have attended. Cook proposes an elaborate allegory in which Cambyuskan stands for Galeazzo,

Canacee for Violante, Algarsyf for her brother Gian Galeazzo, the stranger knight for Lionel, and Cambyuskan's feast for the wedding banquet – but admits that his suggestion is probably 'too fanciful' (pp 184–5).

397 Korsch, Hedwig. *Chaucer als Kritiker*. Friederich-Wilhelms-Universität diss. (Berlin). 1916. Published Berlin: Mayer & Müller, 1916.
Lines 401–7 are cited as an example of Chaucer's insistence that a narrative lead up to a well-defined climax (p 118).

398 Wells, John Edwin. *A Manual of Writings in Middle English, 1050–1400*. New Haven: Connecticut Academy of Arts and Sciences, 1916.
One of Chaucer's most successful adaptations of tale to narrator, *SqT* is an interlude of pure romance that has no connection with the marriage debate. The tale remained unfinished because further development of the magic element would have necessitated its association with the mundane and the commonplace. Surveys scholarship on *SqT*'s models and possible date (p 734) and supplies bibliographical references (p 880). Nine supplements (1919–52) take the survey of scholarship through 1945.

399 Baum, Paull F. 'Notes on Chaucer.' *MLN* 32 (1917), 376–7.
The Squire's 'Have me excused if I speke amys; / My wyl is good ...' (lines 7–8) is not an apology for his lack of eloquence, but a courteous expression – with a slight stress on *my* – of his disapproval of the Merchant's inelegant tale, just ended. His later disclaimer of rhetorical skill (lines 383–41) should also be taken as a rhetorical ploy, a way of saying that Canacee is indescribably beautiful.

400 Jefferson, Bernard L. *Chaucer and the Consolation of Philosophy of Boethius*. 1917. See **151**.
SqT and *FranT* are 'companion tales of gentilesse. *SqT* might well have for a text ... "pitee renneth sone in gentil herte"' (p 101). In multiplying his allusions to *gentilesse*, the Squire wishes to impress his understanding of this courtly virtue on the humbler members of the pilgrim audience.

401 Hinckley, Henry Barrett. 'Chauceriana.' *MP* 16 (1918), 39–48.
Examples of a personal pronoun before a proper name in Middle Welsh are cited as parallels to line 250, 'he Moyses' (p 43).

402 Jack, Adolphus Alfred. *A Commentary on the Poetry of Chaucer and Spenser*. Glasgow: Maclehose, Jackson, 1920. Repr. Folcroft, PA: Folcroft, 1969.
'From the Franklin's words one is precluded from supposing, what otherwise one might have supposed,' that *SqT* was 'purposely left unfinished ... in refined mockery of the never-ending "Tales of Faery"' (p 108). We must accept *SqT* as serious, and assume that Chaucer 'found space in his collection for one of the very stories at which in another humour he had laughed' (p 109).

403 Tupper, Frederick. 'Chaucer's Tale of Ireland.' *PMLA* 36 (1921), 186–222.
Anne Welle, Countess of Ormonde, and the earl of Ormonde are the origi-

nals for Anelida and Arcite (*Anel*) and the falcon and the false tercelet in *SqT*. The earl's fathering of two illegitimate sons in the mid-1380s roused Chaucer's moral indignation; in *Anel*, he blames Ormonde's duplicity in love, and repeats the charge in *SqT*, which he probably wrote with *Anel* before him. The peregrine falcon appears as the crest of the Irish houses of Ormonde and Mountgarrett, and was apparently associated with the rank of earl. Tupper also links *Camb*alus (lines 654–7) with Edmund Langley, earl of *Camb*ridge; he admits, however, that Langley's position as keeper of the royal falcons is probably a coincidence (pp 196–9). See **404**, **438**.

404 Koch, John. 'Ein neues Datum für Chaucers *Quene Anelida and Fals Arcite*.' *ESt* 56 (1922), 28–35.
Dismisses as fanciful the historical allegory proposed by Tupper (**403**) for *Anel* and *SqT*. The suggested link between the Ormonde coat of arms and the falcon is improbable. It would have been tactless of Chaucer to allude to the earl of Ormonde's infidelities in *SqT*; by the time the tale was composed (probably in the 1390s), Ormonde had once again become a good family man.

405 Jones, Richard F. 'A Conjecture on the Wife of Bath's Prologue.' *JEGP* 24 (1925), 512–47.
'The Host, wishing to escape from the bitter thoughts of his own unhappy married life into the fairy land of romance, wisely requests a tale of love from the Squire, the one embodiment of romantic love among the pilgrims' (p 527).

406 Manly, John Matthews. 'Chaucer and the Rhetoricians.' *PBA* 12 (1926), 95–113. Also printed separately, London: Humphrey Milford, 1926. Repr. in *Chaucer Criticism: The Canterbury Tales* (see **390**), pp 268–89, and in *Chaucer: The Critical Heritage* (see **390**), 2:384–402.
Occupatio ('the refusal to describe or narrate') occurs with special frequency in *SqT*; lines 34–5, 67, 73, and 283–7 are cited as examples of the figure (p 106).

407 Patch, Howard Rollin. 'Chaucer and Medieval Romance.' In *Essays in Memory of Barrett Wendell*. [No ed. listed.] Cambridge, MA: Harvard UP, 1926. Pp 95–108. Repr. in *On Rereading Chaucer*. Cambridge, MA: Harvard UP, 1939. Pp 195–212.
SqT shows 'a conscious effort at a sustained performance in the romantic vein, and it seems to have sprung from the poet's ripest years' (1926, p 107).

408 Cowling, George H. *Chaucer*. New York: Dutton; London: Methuen, 1927. Repr. Freeport, NY: Books for Libraries Press, 1971.
The opening scene of *SqT* recalls the arrival of the Green Knight in Arthur's hall in *SGGK*; perhaps *SqT* was Chaucer's attempt to rival the wonders of contemporary romance. If Chaucer had carried out the plan suggested in the final lines of the fragment, *SqT* 'would have been as long as a book of *FQ*, and as coherent' (p 175).

409 French, Robert Dudley. *A Chaucer Handbook*. 1927/1947. See **272**.
Discusses the placement of *SqT* in the MSS and early editions, the lack of

a single source and the use of Oriental motifs, the Tartar background, and the continuations by Spenser (who 'neglects the very features which most excite our curiosity in Chaucer's fragmentary tale,' p 319) and John Lane (pp 316–19).

410 Thompson, Nesta M. 'A New Way with Chaucer.' *UCC* 29 (1927), 366–79.
Out of context, sleep's 'galpyng mouth' (line 350) calls up the image of 'a small boy, tired with play, making the round of the company at bedtime' (p 370).

411 Ker, William Paton. *Form and Style in Poetry*. Ed. R.W. Chambers. London: Macmillan, 1928. Excerpts in *Geoffrey Chaucer: A Critical Anthology*. Ed. J.A. Burrow. Harmondsworth, UK: Penguin, 1969. Pp 104–11.
Chaucer repeats the 'tactical mistake' (pp 76–7) of *Anel* in *SqT*. He begins with the promise of action and adventures, but moves to pathetic subject matter incongruent with his narrative frame. Although the love story is good enough for us to wish more of it, Chaucer was probably wise to stop; he had gotten too far away from his initial premise.

412 Getty, Agnes K. 'Chaucer's Changing Conceptions of the Humble Lover.' *PMLA* 44 (1929), 202–16.
True to his character, the Squire tells a tale of purely romantic love, in which even the false tercelet imitates the ideal conduct of the humble lover. In its tone and intent, *SqT* is closest to the Prologue of *LGW*.

413 Naunin, Traugott. *Der Einfluss der mittelalterlichen Rhetorik auf Chaucers Dichtung*. Friedrich-Wilhelms-Universität diss. (Bonn). 1929. Dir. W.F. Schirmer. Published Grossenhain: Plasnick, 1929.
In this study of Chaucer's use of medieval rhetorical figures, *SqT* is cited to illustrate *praecisio* (lines 283–7, 298–300) and to exemplify the poet's playful allusions to rhetorical precepts (lines 38–40, 99–108).

414 Evans, Joan. 'Chaucer and Decorative Art.' *RES* 6 (1930), 408–12.
The decoration of Canacee's mew for the wounded hawk (lines 646–50) recalls the representations of other birds mobbing the owl in carved church misericords.

415 Vallese, Tarquinio. *Goffredo Chaucer visto da un italiano.* Rome: Albrighi, Segati, 1930.
The account of the crowd's speculations about the three magic gifts is one of Chaucer's most vivid descriptive passages, superior even to the crowd scene in Book 3 of *HF*; the minds of the ignorant are revealed in their spontaneous but childish opinions (p 122).

416 Engel, Hildegard. *Structure and Plot in Chaucer's Canterbury Tales*. Bonn: Neuendorff, 1931.
SqT is skillfully adapted to the character of its teller. Where the Knight gives a real picture of western chivalry, his son, the young Squire, delights in the romantic remoteness of the fairytale world of eastern fiction (p 50).

417 Getty, Agnes K. 'The Mediæval–Modern Conflict in Chaucer's Poetry.' *PMLA* 47 (1932), 385–402.
In *SqT,* Chaucer acknowledges the value of brevity (lines 401–8) and tells his story with 'modern' economy. 'We find neither enumeration, detailed description, nor enumeration of non-enumeration – all of which, if used, would be entirely in keeping with the fanciful, mediæval character of the tale' (p 396).

418 Harrison, Benjamin Samuel. *The Colors of Rhetoric in Chaucer.* PhD diss., Yale University, 1932. Ann Arbor, MI: University Microfilms, 1969. See also *DA* 27 (1966): 1786A.
The Squire's self-deprecating claims of verbal ineptitude are belied by the rhetorical skill of his tale. His knowledge of such figures as *pronunciatio* and *digressio* and his sophisticated use of exempla and *sententiae* make his apologies seem affected (pp 315–22).

419 McCormick, William, with the assistance of Janet Heseltine. *The Manuscripts of Chaucer's Canterbury Tales, a Critical Description of Their Contents.* Oxford: Clarendon, 1933.
Describes the contents of fifty-seven complete or virtually complete copies of *CT* (including Caxton's first and second printed editions) and twenty-eight defective MSS. For *SqT,* the details noted include omitted lines, conflated lines, blank lines, repeated lines, anticipated lines, transposed lines, inserted lines, missing passages, missing headlinks, the presence and omission of special capitals, and scribal rubrics. The rubrics include the following descriptions of the tale: *the Squyers tale* (p 16 et passim), *fabula Armigeri* (p 49 et passim), *the Squyeres tale as meche as Chaucer made* (p 98), *fabula … Armigeri de Equo de Stanno* (p 122), *the Squiers tale of the horse of brasse* (p 225), *Of this Squyers tale Chaucer makith no more* (p 417).

420 Tuve, Rosemond. *Seasons and Months: Studies in a Tradition of Middle English Poetry.* Paris: Librarie Universitaire, 1933. Repr. Folcroft, PA: Folcroft, 1970; Cambridge: Brewer, 1974. Excerpts in *Chaucer: The Critical Heritage* (see **390**), 2:493–8.
Notes the resemblance of lines 40–4 to diagrams and tables that appear in medieval calendar treatises (p 184).

421 Lowes, John Livingston. *Geoffrey Chaucer and the Development of His Genius.* Boston: Houghton Mifflin, 1934. Numerous reprs under the title *Geoffrey Chaucer,* including Bloomington: U of Indiana P, 1958.
'Magic and illusion and enchanted princesses, in that remote and mysterious Orient where anything may happen … forms the background of the half-told tale which so captivated Milton … It is the glamour of that world which Chaucer, turning for a moment from his world of wool and hides and ditches,' sheds on *SqT* (pp 225–6).

422 Tupper, Frederick. 'The Bearings of the Shipman's Prologue.' *JEGP* 33 (1934),

352–72.

Responding to Kase's argument (**761**) that the Squire is the speaker of *MLE*, Tupper observes that the 'well-bred lad' of the Squire's Prologue, the 'perfect exponent of "gentilesse"' who uses the word nine times in his tale and wins the Franklin's praises for his elegant speech, is unlikely to be the source of the rude address to the Parson in *MLE* (p 362). Contrasted with the final line of *MLE* ('Ther is but litel Latyn in my mawe,' II.1190), the Squire's elaborate apology for his inability to describe Canacee's beauty reveals an utterly different personality.

423 Whiting, B.J. *Chaucer's Use of Proverbs*. Harvard Studies in Comparative Literature 11. Cambridge, MA: Harvard UP, 1934. Repr. New York: AMS, 1973.
SqT contains four proverbs (lines 202–3, 536–7, 593, and 602–4) and nine sententious remarks. Three of the former and seven of the latter are spoken by the falcon, an 'obvious effort to use proverbs and sententious remarks as an aid to characterization' (p 109).

424 Tatlock, John Strong Perry. 'The Canterbury Tales in 1400.' *PMLA* 50 (1935), 100–39.
Scribes sometimes concealed gaps in their texts by the excision or mending of ragged edges. Although *SqT* was never completely cut out, the fragmentary *pars tercia* is eliminated in fifteen manuscripts (p 111).

425 ———. 'The Date of the *Troilus*: and Minor Chauceriana.' *MLN* 50 (1935), 277–96.
Real-life examples of horsemen riding into large buildings (e.g., the appearance of the King's Champion at English coronation banquets) are cited as parallels to the stranger knight's entrance into Cambyuskan's hall.

426 Wager, Willis J. 'The So-Called Prologue to the *Knight's Tale*.' *MLN* 50 (1935), 296–307.
As an addendum to his argument that I.875–92 was added by Chaucer when he incorporated the early *Palamon and Arcite* into *CT*, Wager suggests that lines 73–5 of *SqT* may also be a later interpolation, intended to link the tale to the Canterbury framework. Other similarities between *KnT* and *SqT* include the lack of connection between tale and teller, the division into parts, and the relation of subject matter through the intermediary of *Anel*.

427 Crow, Martin Michael. 'Unique Variants in the Paris Manuscript of Chaucer's Canterbury Tales.' *SE* 16 (1936), pp 17–41.
After twenty lines of *SqT* in the Paris manuscript (Ps) of *CT*, the scribe, John Duxworth, writes: 'Ista fabula est valde absurda in terminis et ideo ad presens pretermittatur nec ulterius de ea precedatur' (p 18).

428 Hawkins, Laurence Faulkner. *The Place of Group F in the Canterbury Chronology*. PhD diss., New York University, 1940. Published [New York?]: n.p., 1937.
Chaucer wrote *SqT* in the early 1380s and later adapted it for *CT*. The narrator's apologies for his lack of skill suit the persona of the early dream visions

better than the pilgrim Squire. The falcon episode contains parallels to *PF* and *Anel*; the latter 'seems like a more careful and leisurely development of the preliminary sketch' (p 19) in the falcon's story, and may have been based on the earlier version of the same theme in *SqT*. Additional items that point to an early date of composition include a possible echo of lines 156–65 in *TC* 4.927; the cynical echo in *MerT* (IV.1986) of the Squire's sincere expression of the same sentiment (line 479), suggesting the priority of the latter; and the characterization of Canacee as 'ful mesurable, as wommen be' (line 362), a statement which would have been unlikely during the period when Chaucer was producing his portraits of 'likerous' women like the Wife of Bath, May, and Alison in *MilT*.

• Review by Dorothy Everett, *YWES* 18 (1937), 79: Hawkins demonstrates more clearly than has yet been done the connections between *SqT* and *Anel* and the use in *SqT* and *FranT* of *RR* and *Consol*. But the inferences he draws from these parallels are open to question; it is difficult to accept as certain his far-reaching conclusions about the tales' early dates of composition.

• Review by Dorothy Everett, *MÆ* 7 (1938), 213–16: The conclusions Hawkins draws from his evidence are vitiated by assumptions about the consistency of Chaucer's subject matter and his attitudes towards it in a given period of his career.

• Review by Hermann Heuer, *AB* 50 (1939), 296–8: Hawkins's chronological arguments, based on unprovable assumptions about Chaucer's artistic development, are unlikely to convince many readers.

429 Holmes, Urban T. 'Chaucer's *tydif* "a small bird."' *PQ* 16 (1937), 65–7.
Identifies *tydif* (line 648) with Greek τυτω, the poetic designation of the 'little owl' (*Athene noctua*). See **433**.

430 Mersand, Joseph. *Chaucer's Romance Vocabulary*. Brooklyn, NY: Comet, 1937. Repr. Port Washington, NY: Kennikat, 1968.
A response to George Marsh's conclusion, based on an investigation of rhymes in *SqT* (*Lectures on the English Language*, 1885), that the proportion of French rhymes in his original works (e.g., *SqT*) is about equal to that in works translated or paraphrased from the French. 'Dicta about a poet's practice in over 30,000 lines of poetry cannot be accurately formulated ... from an examination of six-hundred and twenty-two [*sic*] lines' (p 26).

431 Whitmore, Sister Mary E. *Medieval English Domestic Life and Amusements in the Works of Chaucer*. Washington, DC: Catholic University of America, 1937. Repr. New York: Cooper Square, 1972.
Prints a description of a mew (cf. lines 643–5) – a cage or coop for molting birds – from *Le Ménagier de Paris* and an account of the appropriate care for a caged bird from *The Book of St Albans*. 'One may be sure that Canacee, in her tender solicitude for the falcon, would see that the mew was properly tended' (p 43).

432 Galway, Margaret. 'Chaucer's Sovereign Lady: A Study of the Prologue to the *Legend* and Related Poems.' *MLR* 33 (1938), 145–99.
The poet's 'sovereign lady' is Joan, the Fair Maid of Kent, who in her youth was betrothed to and then deserted by Sir Thomas Holland. Galway identifies Joan with Alceste in *LGW* and with Anelida. *SqT* 'deals with the same theme ... the falcon's story is Anelida's story in ampler form, and, combined with Canacee's, also Joan's story' (pp 180–1). The faithless tercelet is Holland, who on his return from his French campaigns successfully sued for the renewal of the marriage contract; hence Joan 'gat hire love ageyn' (line 654). Cambalo represents Edward, the Black Prince (later to be Joan's husband); Cambyuskan is Edward III. The historical dates of Joan and Holland's affair (1346–9) correspond to the period indicated for 'the cohabitation and separation' (p 182) of the falcon and tercelet, arrived at through the internal dating of events in *Anel* and *SqT*. The numerous similarities between the two poems – parallel stories, allegorical overtones, praise of the heroines' fidelity, unfinishedness – corroborate the identification of Anelida and the falcon with Joan.

433 Wilson, F.P. 'The Tidy.' *PQ* 17 (1938), 216–18.
Tidy (cf. line 648) may refer to a number of small, common birds (the wren is one likely possibility), but not, as Holmes (**429**) proposes, to the small brown owl. The name may also be derived from *tiddy*, 'small or tiny.'

434 Héraucourt, Will. *Die Wertwelt Chaucers, die Wertwelt einer Zeitwende*. Heidelberg: Winter, 1939.
Cites some thirty lines from *SqT* in this study of Chaucer's value system, organized around four cardinal virtues: wisdom, justice, valor, and moderation. Chaucer's use of terms in *SqT* (e.g., *just, pitee, stable, benignitee, subtil, craft*) is compared with his use of these terms elsewhere in his writings.

435 Bronson, B.H. 'Chaucer's Art in Relation to His Audience.' In *Five Studies in Literature*. University of California Publications in English, VIII, No. 1. Berkeley: U of California P, 1940. Pp 1–53.
Although *SqT* is generally suited to the personality of its teller, the satirical treatment of the idle populace and the disclaimers of knowledge of courtly behavior seem out of character for the Squire. The preoccupation with the jangling of the 'lewed' folk and the falcon's story – a 'transparent allegory' (p 47) of human double dealing – suggest some special occasion for the composition of *SqT* other than the Canterbury pilgrimage.

436 Manly, John Matthews, and Edith Rickert, eds. *The Text of The Canterbury Tales, Studied on the Basis of All Known Manuscripts*. 1940. See **61**.
Recognizing that the completed *SqT* would have been longer than *KnT*, Chaucer may have aborted it deliberately, although line 672 'is certainly an astonishing place to end, unless the author had a stroke of apoplexy' (2:484). There is no evidence that Chaucer completed *SqT*, but it is possible that there

may have been a single copy that the scribes failed to locate when they assembled their texts of *CT*.

437 Shelly, Percy Van Dyke. *The Living Chaucer*. Philadelphia: U of Pennsylvania P, 1940. Repr. New York: Russell and Russell, 1968.
The Squire presents the long message of the stranger knight 'in the best of all styles – simple, clear, swift, and flexible' (p 288), a style that achieves its explanatory purpose better than could the devices of rhetoric and fine writing.

438 Tupper, Frederick. 'Chaucer and the Cambridge Edition.' *JEGP* 39 (1940), 503–26.
Responding to Robinson's (**55**) skeptical assessment of his reading of *Anel* and Part 2 of *SqT* as historical allegories (**403**), Tupper restates his earlier argument, noting that, unlike those 'twentieth-century scholars sadly insensitive to [Chaucer's] skilful and repeated play on names' (p 511), the poet's original audience would have recognized and appreciated his witty allusions.

439 Vallese, Tarquinio. *La Poesia di Chaucer*. Naples: Lupi, 1941/Naples: Pironti, 1946.
If, as Root (**378**) argues, the fascination of *SqT* is due to its incompleteness, readers would have an equally high regard for *CkT* and *HF*. The tale's appeal lies rather in its treatment of magic themes that appeal to young and old (pp 135–7/pp 145–6).

440 Braddy, Haldeen. 'The Genre of Chaucer's *Squire's Tale*.' *JEGP* 41 (1942), 279–90. Repr. in *Geoffrey Chaucer: Literary and Historical Studies* (see **166**). Pp 85–95.
Insofar as it can be inferred from the unfinished text, the structure of *SqT* resembles that of one major type of Oriental framing tale, exemplified by the Persian *Thousand and One Days*, in which a principal story serves as a frame for a series of intercalated incidents before being resumed and completed. The story of Canacee and the falcon would appear to be the frame narrative, the 'knotte why that' *SqT* 'is toold' (line 401); the events summarized in lines 661–70 represent the subsidiary episodes to be developed before returning to Canacee and her falcon. Like the story of Tāj al-Mulūk and Princess Dunyā in *The Arabian Nights*, Chaucer's frame tale may be intended to apply a moral about infidelity among birds to men and women. Oriental models for the possible development of the intercalated material are proposed, including one group of family adventures, which suggests that Cambalo's winning of Canacee may involve incest. The appearance of the incest motif in his source could explain Chaucer's abrupt termination of *SqT*. See **242**, **500**.

441 Crow, Martin Michael. 'John of Angoulême and His Chaucer Manuscript.' *Speculum* 17 (1942), 86–99. Repr. in *Studies in Medieval, Renaissance, American Literature. A Festschrift Honoring Troy C. Crenshaw, Lorraine Sherley, Ruth Speer Angell*. Ed. Betsy Feagan Colquitt. Fort Worth: Texas Christian UP, 1971. Pp 33–44.

In the manuscript of the *CT* owned by John, count of Angoulême (a royal prisoner in England from 1412 to 1445), *SqT* is terminated after twenty lines with the note (written by the scribe John Duxworth, 'probably at Angoulême's dictation') 'Ista fabula est valde absurda in terminis et ideo ad presens pretermittatur nec ulterius de ea procedatur' (p 97). See **427**, **709**.

442 Sullivan, Frank. 'Finished Fragments in Chaucer.' *SatR* 26 (16 October 1943), 27.

SqT is among those fragments that Chaucer might have considered finished. The Squire, 'speaking for the first time before such a large gathering,' becomes flustered and stops 'with his mind desperately, desolately blank.' The Franklin, 'ever the perfect host,' puts the Squire at ease by bridging the awkward gap in his speech. His words to the Squire are 'consoling ... to one who has failed, but hardly proper for congratulations.'

443 MacDonald, Charlotte. 'Drayton's "Tidy" and Chaucer's "Tydif."' *RES* 21 (1945), 127–33.

The bird referred to by Chaucer (line 648) and Drayton is probably the great tit. The great tit was known to kill smaller birds by splitting the skull, hence its association with 'tercelets and oules.' In regard to its falseness, the great tit 'is not necessarily monogamous in breeding season' (p 133).

444 Castelli, Alberto. *Geoffrey Chaucer*. [Brescia]: Morcelliana, 1946.

The Squire's references to Lancelot and to Gawain's 'olde curteisye' (line 95) recall, with a touch of irony, the irreparable disappearance of the knights of the Round Table. For Chaucer, associated with a company of pilgrims rather than with a group of knights-errant, the figures of romantic chivalry were, like Lancelot, dead (p 74).

445 Chute, Marchette. *Geoffrey Chaucer of England*. New York: Dutton, 1946.

The Squire is not a professional writer; the attack on rhetorical rules is Chaucer speaking through one of his characters. 'Chaucer was usually sure enough of himself to ignore without comment the strict rules on writing that bedeviled his generation, or else to make fun of them. But when he was writing *SqT* something evidently occurred that made Chaucer wish to make his position on the matter of rhetoric unmistakably clear' (p 287).

446 Stillwell, Gardiner. 'Chaucer in Tartary.' *RES* 24 (1948), 177–88.

Chaucer is 'not altogether at home in Tartary' (p 179). His 'realistic and humorous' (p 179) temperament, at odds with the romance elements in *SqT*, manifests itself in his repeated refusals to describe courtly rituals, in his shying away from itemizing the details of Canacee's beauty, in the 'elvish elusiveness' and 'ironic understatement' (p 183) of his account of the strange foods at the Tartar court, and in his (or the Squire's) disclaimer of expertise in matters of *amour courtois*. Conversely, in his treatment of the magic gifts, rather than employing 'nervous *occupatio*' (p 184), he says too much; the courtiers' 'commonsense' (p 185) speculations about the nature of the horse and mirror make them sound like 'the arch-realist Jean de Meung' (p 186). 'Precisely those traits which we most love in Chaucer – sagacious realism, humour, critical intellect, subtlety of mood, and natural human gusto – keep him from maintaining the wide-eyed *naïveté* and quaint curiosity required by his theme, and make him realize that it is better to abandon his attempt to force an entrance into fairyland than to get stuck in a magic casement' (p 188). See **598, 612**.

447 Coghill, Nevill. *The Poet Chaucer*. London: Oxford UP, 1949/1967.
Part 2 of *SqT* reads as if the formel eagle of *PF* had been deserted by the royal tercel she is advised to marry, or as if one of *LGW* had been 'the Legend of a Good Bird' (1967, p 124). The tale reflects 'the tapestry world of Chaucer's own youthful vision. Chaucer had passed beyond it into the common light of day, but it was a world he had never forgotten and could still recapture as if he had never grown old' (p 167). Except for the Knight, the Franklin is the only person present fit to interrupt the Squire's 'endless recital'; he does so by smothering the young man with praise (p 123).

448 Patch, Howard Rollin. 'Geoffrey Chaucer and Youth.' *CE* 11 (1949), 14–22.
The crowd's speculation about the horse of brass exemplifies Chaucer's realism and his modernity. 'The modern American off duty seldom takes the road to Xanadu or Tryermaine; in the same mood, perhaps, the medieval poet left *SqT* unfinished' (p 16).

The Squire's Tale, 1950–1959

449 de Tollenaere, F. '"To maken of fern-asshen glas" (G. Chaucer, *The Squire's Tale* 246 [c. 1386]).' *ES* 31 (1950), 97–9.
Cites examples from French and Dutch eighteenth-century sources of fern ashes being used in the making of glass.

450 Lawrence, William Witherle. *Chaucer and the Canterbury Tales*. New York: Columbia UP; London: Oxford UP, 1950.
SqT is 'pure romance, of the rich Eastern variety' (p 143). Although there is no place in *SqT* for questions of marital sovereignty, its appearance among the tales of the Marriage Group is not accidental. The courtly Squire speaks for a code that exalted women, and the placement of his tale after the bitterly misogynistic *MerT* shows Chaucer 'preserving the dramatic balance by weighting the scales in favor of the gentler sex' (p 143).

451 Malone, Kemp. *Chapters on Chaucer*. Baltimore, MD: Johns Hopkins UP, 1951.
The Squire's statement that he is a dull man, ignorant of love and love's service (lines 278–88), contradicts the characterization of him in *GP* and the Host's comments at lines 1–3. Perhaps Chaucer had himself in mind here, forgetting for the moment that the Squire is supposed to be telling the tale

(pp 230–1).

452 Neville, Marie. 'The Function of the *Squire's Tale* in the Canterbury Scheme.' *JEGP* 50 (1951), 167–79.
SqT was planned not as an interruption of the Marriage Group but as a link among the Marriage Group tales and as an integral part of the Canterbury scheme as a whole. The tale's closest connections are with *KnT*. Wishing at once to compliment and surpass his father, the Squire tells a tale of chivalric romance that contains numerous echoes of the Knight's characteristic locutions and which promises, in the Squire's summary of events to come, a multiplication of incidents similar to those in Palamon and Arcite's contest for Emelye. In its attention to the 'niceties of the chivalric code' (p 177), *SqT* is sharply contrasted with *WBT* and *MerT*. Unlike the Wife, the Squire believes that noble deeds are more likely to be performed by nobles, and his treatment of the falcon story implicitly denies mastery in love. His hesitation in describing 'subtil lookyng and dissymulynges' (line 285) and his account of Cambyuskan's dignified birthday feast may be read as an implicit criticism of the 'bourgeois aping of courtly manners' (p 178) in *MerT*. *FranT*, on the other hand, takes up and develops the Squire's concern with equality in love and his interest in *gentilesse*; it is probably intended as a compliment to the younger man.

453 Pratt, Robert Armstrong. 'The Order of the *Canterbury Tales*.' *PMLA* 66 (1951), 1141–67.
Although widely attested in the MSS, the sequence *MLT–SqT* and the identification of the Squire as the speaker in *MLE* are unlikely to be authorial. *SqT* 'fully meets the Franklin's comment … that the Squire has acquitted himself "gentilly," a comment that can in no sense be applied to the behavior of the [speaker] in *MLE*' (p 1153). In addition, *MLT* begins at 'ten of the clokke' (II.14), while the Squire says 'it is pryme' (line 73), further evidence against the authority of the *MLT–SqT* sequence.

454 Speirs, John. *Chaucer the Maker*. London: Faber and Faber, 1951/1960; pbk ed., 1964.
The entrance of the knight in the midst of Cambyuskan's birthday feast recalls the opening scene of *SGGK*. But the foreign knight lacks 'the rich significance of the anthropological Green Man,' and the horse of brass 'is nothing more than a curious mechanical contrivance, a flying machine' (p 163).

455 Bloomfield, Morton W. 'Chaucer's Sense of History.' *JEGP* 51 (1952), 301–13. Repr. in *Discussions of the Canterbury Tales*. Ed. Charles A. Owen, Jr. Boston: Heath, 1961, pp 98–104, and in Bloomfield, *Essays and Explorations: Studies in Ideas, Language, and Literature*. Cambridge, MA: Harvard UP, 1970, pp 12–26.
Chaucer's enumeration of the virtues of the pagan Cambyuskan may be seen as a 'strong criticism of contemporary "Christian" rulers' (p 310). In surrounding the Khan's geographically distant court with an 'almost Arthu-

rian aura,' Chaucer substitutes space for time (p 310).

456 Preston, Raymond. *Chaucer*. London: Sheed and Ward, 1952. Repr. New York: Greenwood, 1969.
SqT is Chaucer's 'most mispraised' poem (p 271). It will disappoint readers who, encouraged by Spenser and Milton, earnestly look for romance; once amused by classical marvels and Oriental tales, Chaucer is now bored with them, and 'laughing in his sleeve' (p 271). Much of the tale is carelessly composed, although the falcon's condemnation of her faithless lover displays 'a truly dramatic syntax ... something ... not of the best but the second-best' (pp 272) of *LGW*. The Franklin's praise of the Squire is 'a blunderingly tactful interruption ... The young man was not to be expected, after all, to win the Canterbury competition, but has as it were "passed" in English' (p 273).

457 Brewer, Derek S. *Chaucer*. London: Longmans, Green, 1953/1960/1973.
We expect a tale of love from the Squire, but Chaucer's 'mature imagination' (p 168) is unable or unwilling to supply one. The tale is most memorable in its account of Cambyuskan's birthday feast, 'perhaps the nearest we shall ever get to a full description of a great fourteenth-century festival at Court' (p 168). A continuation of the tale might have 'dulled its edge ... what we are promised, of "aventures and of batailles", though doubtless a fair indication of popular interest, seems never to have been greatly to Chaucer's own taste' (p 170). Lines 280–2, which characterize the teller as a dull man ignorant of love, are inappropriate for the Squire, but consonant with Chaucer's self-presentation elsewhere in his poems (1973, p 213).

458 Dempster, Germaine. 'A Period in the Development of the *Canterbury Tales* Marriage Group and of Blocks B^2 and C.' *PMLA* 68 (1953), 1142–59.
Chaucer established a relationship between the Marriage Group and *Mel*, *ClT*, and *NPT* and put Fragments B2 (VII) and C (VI) in their final forms in the 'middle third of the Canterbury period' (p 1154). *SqT* cannot be dated with certainty, but its links were probably not written until well after this period.

459 Francis, W. Nelson. 'Chaucer Shortens a Tale.' *PMLA* 68 (1953), 1126–41.
In employing *occupatio*, the Squire at once pokes gentle fun at the rhetorical device, indulges in a 'mild parody' of his father's fondness for 'self-conscious abbreviation' (p 1140), and parodies his own earlier asides on the dangers of prolixity. 'The tone is no longer one of depreciation, but of complete faith that the audience will follow ... every sudden twist and subtle turn of wit and irony' (p 1141).

460 Kökeritz, Helge. 'Rhetorical Word-Play in Chaucer.' *PMLA* 69 (1954), 937–52.
The *rime riche* of *stile*:*style* (lines 105–6) contains 'an obvious pun' (p 945).

461 Schaar, Claes. *Some Types of Narrative in Chaucer's Poetry*. Lunds Universitets Årsskrift. N.F. Avd. 1. Bd. 50. Nr. 8. Lund Studies in English 25. Lund: Gleerup, 1954.
Chaucer uses 'close chronological narrative' (a detailed account of a chain of

events falling within a brief period) in lines 439–43 and 472–8; the two pieces of narrative frame Canacee's speech to the falcon (p 153). In two linking episodes (lines 168–88 and 263–74) Chaucer uses 'loose chronological narrative,' in which digressions are more frequent, and descriptions more loosely connected with the essential elements of the narrative (pp 232–3).

462 Lumiansky, R.M. *Of Sondry Folk: The Dramatic Principle in the Canterbury Tales*. Austin: U of Texas P, 1955; pbk ed., 1980.
The appropriateness of *SqT* to its teller is evident not only in its theme (love) and genre (romance), but also in the expository comments that flesh out the traits enumerated in *GP* (e.g., the Squire's humility) reflected in his disclaimers of rhetorical skill; his interest in courtesy and horsemanship; his 'zest for nature' (p 179); his familiarity with singing and dancing. The verbal echoes of *KnT* (e.g., I.890 and 73–4, I.761 and 479, I.3042 and 593) also reinforce the suitability of tale to teller (pp 175–80).

463 Schaar, Claes. *The Golden Mirror: Studies in Chaucer's Descriptive Technique and its Literary Background*. Acta Regiae Societatis Humaniorum Litterarum Lundensis 54. Lund: Gleerup, 1955. Repr. with index, 1967.
Descriptions of pure feelings are less common in *SqT* than 'behaviouristic description,' representation of emotion through bodily or facial expression (pp 78–9). Character portraits are a mixture of idealizing traits and more objective, item-by-item description, the former recalling the practice in French courtly poetry, the latter familiar from English romances and alliterative poems (pp 229–30, 349). Representations of nature combine abstract and impressionistic description; the account of the birds' response to spring weather (lines 52–7) evokes the creatures' feelings more vividly than does an analogous passage in *RR* (pp 416–17).

464 Zanco, Aurelio. *Chaucer e il suo mondo*. 1955/1965. See **293**.
Brief comments on *SqT* as an interlude in the Marriage Group, on its Eastern character and setting (*SqT* seems almost to have been imagined by an Oriental writer), on its possible indebtedness to travel narratives and the *Epistola Presbyteri Johannis*, and on Skeat's view (**4**) of Marco Polo's *Travels* as an immediate source (unlikely, in Zanco's opinion) (pp 239–42).

465 Baum, Paull F. 'Chaucer's Puns.' *PMLA* 71 (1956), 225–46.
The pun on *fern* (lines 255–6) draws deliberate attention to the different meanings of the words; the main sense of *furial* (line 448) is 'furious,' but 'fiery' is also suggested; *lighte* (line 396) implies both 'lighter' and 'brighter'; *stile … style* (lines 105–6) is both an echo rhyme and a true pun.

466 Coghill, Nevill. *Geoffrey Chaucer*. London: Longmans, Green, for the British Council and the National Book League, 1956. Repr. Lincoln: U of Nebraska P, 1963. Repr. in *The Collected Papers of Nevill Coghill, Shakespearian and Medievalist*. Ed. Douglas Gray. Brighton: Harvester; New York: St Martins, 1988. Pp 1–53.

Quotes lines 65–72 as an example of Chaucerian *occupatio*. 'But the Squire's use of *Occupatio* is tame compared to that of his father the Knight' (p 18).

467 Kleinstück, Johannes Walter. *Chaucers Stellung in der Mittelalterlichen Literatur*. Hamburg: Cram, de Gruyter, 1956.
Lines 419–22 and 479–82 are cited as evidence for weeping as a sign of spiritual nobility in the late Middle Ages (p 45).

468 Mroczkowski, Przemysław. *Opowieści Kanterberyjskie na tle Epoki*. Lublin: Katolickiego Uniwersytetu Lubelskiego, 1956.
SqT is not purely a tale of courtly love, for it combines romantic and realistic elements, imparting a grotesque character to the fabulous world it represents. Unusual for the convention of *amour courtois* are the depth of emotion in the narrator's language and the skeptical reception of the envoy's gifts by the Tartar court. This shifting or combining of literary conventions may indicate Chaucer's refusal to assume authorial responsibility for adhering to any one convention; since the tale is unfinished, however, we can only speculate about his reasons for doing so (pp 274–80).

469 Schlauch, Margaret. *English Medieval Literature and its Social Foundations*. Warsaw: PNW – Polish Scientific Publishers, 1956.
If finished, *SqT* would probably have told of the exploits of Canacee's suitor, interwoven with the exploits of her brothers Algarsyf and Cambalo. The fragment is remarkable for its success in evoking a sense of exotic opulence, 'the magic of little-known lands beckoning beyond the Eastern horizon' (p 261).

470 Slaughter, Eugene Edward. *Virtue According to Love—in Chaucer*. New York: Bookman, 1957. Repr. New York: AMS, 1972.
Analyzes the medieval ideas of love and virtue, both earthly and spiritual. Love is an axis with charity and cupidity as its two poles; the goodness or badness of a desire depends upon the system of virtues being invoked. The virtues and vices mentioned in *SqT* are listed and classified either as 'heroic' or 'courtly' (p 225).

471 Donaldson, E. Talbot, ed. *Chaucer's Poetry: An Anthology for the Modern Reader*. 1958/1975. See **71**.
An example of the Oriental type of medieval romance, 'full of the strange and the marvelous and remote from the problems of everyday life,' *SqT* breaks off after the second line of the third part, at which point the Franklin congratulates the Squire as if the latter had actually completed his story. 'Probably Chaucer became impatient with the tale, the genre of which is not the sort to give full play to his real interests, and the prospectus of future action makes the ending appear to be thousands of lines away. We do not know whether we are to think of the Franklin as interrupting the Squire or as speaking after the tale has been finished' (p 923). *SqT* may be one of Chaucer's youthful efforts, later assigned to the young Squire; 'it reads at times as if its author had swallowed a rhetorical handbook whole but had

not fully digested it' (1975, p 1086). The magic objects in Part 1 are lovingly catalogued, but it is clear from the episode of Canacee and the magic ring that 'the teller will not quickly be able to get the brass horse and the rest out of storage and into action' (1975, p 1086). In Part 2, pathos always verges on sentimentality or absurdity; 'it is hard to believe that the creator of Chantecleer and Pertelote could with a straight face describe a hawk as a "tigre" who falls on his knees to his love' (1975, p 1086). At some point Chaucer may have begun to parody the romance form, and then given the tale to the Squire. The summary of coming attractions at the end of Part 2 is a joke at the Squire's expense, while the Franklin's words to the young man are probably intended to extricate him and his listeners 'from a narrative in which they might be caught forever' (1975, p 1087).

472 Emerson, Francis Willard. 'Cambalus in The Squire's Tale.' *N&Q* n.s. 5 (1958), 461.
Cambalus (line 656) can be read as a plural (i.e., two brothers, each named 'Cambalu' or 'Cambalo'). Also proposes that *hewe* (line 640) should be *shewe*.

473 Owen, Charles A., Jr. 'The Development of the *Canterbury Tales*.' *JEGP* 57 (1958), 449–78.
Verbal parallels between the caged bird simile in *SqT* and the Manciple's related analogy (IX.163–74) suggest that the latter may have influenced the former. Although there is no firm evidence for dating *SqT*, it shares with *Mel*, *PhyT*, *ClT*, and *MLT* an interest in virtuous women, and was probably composed during the earliest *CT* period, when Chaucer envisioned the poem 'as a more varied *LGW*' (p 467). The characteristic traits of the narrative voice – the professions of poetic inadequacy, the pedestrian treatment of magic – suggest that *SqT* was written with a specific pilgrim in mind.

474 Osgerby, J.R. 'Chaucer's Squire's Tale.' *UoE* 11 (1959), 102–7.
In *SqT*, *gentilesse* is largely a matter of education. The 'lewed peple' (line 221) are suspicious of everything because they are uneducated; the tercelet's 'gentillesse of blood' (line 620) does not prevent his villainy. Compassion and eloquence mark the educated person; Gawain stands as the tale's model of successful education. Chaucer may have intended to portray an educational process, 'to conduct his characters from spring through summer, from youth to maturity, from gentilesse of birth to gentilesse of character' (p 106). The Franklin's response suggests that (in contrast to his own son) the Squire has proved himself educated; 'he has confirmed his own 'gentilesse' through his own probationary period' (p 106).

The Squire's Tale, 1960–1969

475 Magoun, Francis P., Jr. *A Chaucer Gazetteer*. Chicago: U of Chicago P, 1961.

Alphabetized entries on Chaucer's place names include etymologies; variant manuscript spellings; brief discussions of the names' use in Chaucer's works; ancient, medieval, and modern geographical information; and citations of scholarship. The entry on *Tartarye,* for example, observes that the name's correct form, *Tatarye,* was transformed under the influence of Classical *Tartarus,* notes Chaucer's distinct applications of the name in *BD* (line 1025) and *SqT* (line 9), and establishes the geographical boundaries of the latter as corresponding to the Tatar Autonomous Soviet Socialist Republic. The book conflates Magoun's articles on Chaucerian place names in *MS* 15 (1953), 107–36; 16 (1954), 131–56; and 17 (1955), 117–42.

476 Beck, Richard J. 'Educational Expectations and Rhetorical Result in *The Canterbury Tales.*' *ES* 44 (1963), 241–53.
Although Chaucer disclaims the ability to describe Canacee in detail (line 32–41), he phases his disclaimer in such a way to suggest 'that he considers his own straightforward method artistically superior while his use of technical terminology proves he could have written rhetorically had he so wished.' In lines 401–8 Chaucer is more specific; 'plainly he considers that the invasion of poetry by rhetoric has a damaging effect upon the writer's invention and the reader's engagement' (p 243).

477 Payne, Robert O. *The Key of Remembrance: A Study of Chaucer's Poetics.* New Haven, CT: Yale UP for the University of Cincinnati, 1963. Repr. Westport, CT: Greenwood, 1973.
Although Chaucer's romances in *CT* are less episodic than their conventional models, *MLT* and *SqT* 'still show fairly clearly their ancestry of rambling and inconsequent narrative' (p 161 and n).

478 Bowden, Muriel. *A Reader's Guide to Geoffrey Chaucer.* New York: Farrar, Straus and Giroux, 1964. Repr. Syracuse, NY: Syracuse UP, 2001.
The Squire in *GP* is 'in love with love' (p 43), an interest reflected in his tale, which focuses on romance rather than (as in his father's tale) on the more philosophical aspects of knighthood.

479 Corsa, Helen Storm. *Chaucer: Poet of Mirth and Morality.* Notre Dame, IN: U of Notre Dame P, 1964.
SqT seems like a first draft to which Chaucer intended to return. It is not clear why he abandoned it, or how he would have developed it; although a conventional romance would be ill suited to the 'narrative and dramatic framework' (p 167) of *CT,* nothing in the tone of *SqT* suggests that Chaucer conceived it as a parody of romance. The tale does, however, reveal a personality with 'comic potential' (p 168), whose idealistic view of experience contains implicit responses to the treatment of human relationships in *WBT, ClT,* and *MerT,* and prepares the ground for the Franklin's more mature handling of questions of love and *gentilesse.*

480 Howard, Edwin H. *Geoffrey Chaucer.* New York: Twayne, 1964.

The position of *SqT* in the Canterbury sequence may have been dictated by Chaucer's desire to present a love story that would offset the cynical treatment of love in *MerT* (p 155). If Chaucer had intended 'the wordes of the Frankeleyn' as a deliberate attempt to break off *SqT*, he would have made the interruption clearer than he did (p 125).

481 Masui, Michio. *The Structure of Chaucer's Rime-Words: An Exploration into the Poetic Language of Chaucer*. Tokyo: Kenkyusha, 1964. Repr. Folcroft, PA: Folcroft, 1975.

The address of the stranger knight is cited to illustrate Chaucer's use of enjambment in a formal stylistic context (pp 298–9).

482 Murphy, James J. 'A New Look at Chaucer and the Rhetoricians.' *RES* n.s. 15 (1964), 1–20. Excerpts in *Critics on Chaucer*. Ed. Sheila Sullivan. London: Allen and Unwin, 1970. Pp 31–8. Repr. in Murphy, *Latin Rhetoric and Education in the Middle Ages and Renaissance*. Variorum Collected Studies Series. Aldershot, UK: Ashgate, 2005. N.p.

Rethor (line 38) means 'writer or poet,' echoing French vernacular usage. The Squire's 'oblique disapproval' (p 11) of the stranger knight's style (lines 105–6) may reflect his own inability to match this style. We need not take these comments as Chaucer's own opinion of the *stilus elevatus*.

483 Pearsall, Derek. 'The Squire as Story-Teller.' *UTQ* 34 (1964), 82–92. Repr. in *Geoffrey Chaucer*. Ed. Willi Erzgräber. Darmstadt: Wissenschaftliche Buchgesellschaft, 1983. Pp 287–99.

SqT is the performance of 'a very young, young man' (p 82), nervous and apologetic about his speaking ability. The Squire's limitations as a storyteller lend an ironic appropriateness to the large concentration of modesty and brevity formulas in the first part of the tale, 'since he has so much to be modest about' (p 84). His natural curiosity is tinged with anti-intellectualism; like John in *MilT* and the Franklin in his dismissal of astrological magic, the Squire displays a kind of 'indignant contempt for what is not understood' (p 88). Only a 'very sober reader' could accept the falcon's tale 'with an entirely straight face' (pp 88–9); the bird's fondness for learned allusions brings Chauntecleer and Pertelote to mind. The 'monstrous oriental saga' (p 90) promised in the Squire's summary of coming attractions shows that he has lost control of his tale. Rejecting the view that *SqT* is incomplete, Pearsall argues for a dramatic interpretation of the Franklin's words, which can be read either as a public-spirited effort to cut off the Squire's narrative by pretending to believe that he has finished, or as tempered praise – given his youth and inexperience, the Franklin implies, the Squire hasn't managed badly. See **500**.

484 Walter, Gertrud. *Grundtypen der Erzähl- und Darstellungstechnik bei Chaucer*. Ludwig-Maximilians-Universität diss. 1964. Dir. Wolfgang Clemen and F. Wölcken. Published Munich: Schön, 1964.

In presenting the responses of Cambyuskan's court to the stranger knight's gifts primarily through précis rather than direct quotation or description, Chaucer integrates the scene more smoothly into his narrative of the birthday festivities (p 60).

485 Bethurum, Dorothy, ed. *The Squire's Tale*. 1965. See **83**.
Although Chaucer might have finished *SqT* in his youth, it offers scant opportunity for the interior treatment of love that had engaged his imagination in *TC*, while pure adventure was of little interest to him in his maturer years. The poem's strengths are its depiction of magic and wonders, and its realistic treatment of the crowd's speculations about the brass steed (xxiii–xxvi).

486 Greene, Richard Leighton. '"Foules of Ravyne" and "Foules Smale" in Chaucer's "Squire's Tale."' *N&Q* n.s. 12 (1965), 446–8.
In claiming that 'both men and birds are, by nature, given to "newefangelnesse,"' Haller (**487**) misinterprets the falcon's use of the image of the caged bird. The female falcon speaks of the faithless tercel 'as a male human being, not as a representative of both sexes of *genus homo* … Male human beings are then likened to *cage-birds*, not to falcons at all' (p 447). Also misleading is Haller's invocation of Boethius, whose reference in *Consol* 3.m4 is to songbirds, not to birds of prey. The difference between the two kinds of birds should be evident to any reader of *PF*. The *SqT* passage is straightforward, not ironic, and throws no special light on the Squire's character.

487 Haller, Robert S. 'Chaucer's *Squire's Tale* and the Uses of Rhetoric.' *MP* 62 (1965), 285–95.
The Squire would have studied rhetoric as part of his formal education, but his handling of rhetorical tropes reveals his immaturity. The use of *descriptio, diminutio, occupatio,* and *paronomasia* in Part 1 calls attention to his inability to construct a coherent narrative; his allusions to Lancelot and Gawain are self-aggrandizing, hints that he 'acts and speaks in their image' (p 288). The story of Canacee and the hawk is undercut not only by rhetorical blunders, but also by the misapplication of a Boethian analogy; the falcon's exemplum seems to identify *gentilesse* with the false goods of the world, and thus ironically judges both the hawk and the Squire, who is 'as disordered philosophically as he is poetically' (p 293). The tale's satirical thrust is confirmed by its ending – 'a recapitulation of the faults which have already appeared and an indication that the poem would have to continue according to the same principles' (p 293) – and by the praise of the 'self-indulgent' (p 294) Franklin, who 'accepts the Squire's implicit claims for his tale at face value' (p 293). See **486**, **500**.

488 Hodge, James L. 'The Marriage Group: Precarious Equilibrium.' *ES* 46 (1965), 289–300.
SqT replies indirectly to the Merchant's attack on women and chivalry. The Squire depicts a faultless female betrayed by an unscrupulous male; he em-

phasizes the chivalric code and reasserts the high-minded meaning of 'pitee renneth soone in gentil herte' (line 479), used cynically by the Merchant. 'Instead of answering sarcasm with sarcasm, the Squire has demonstrated that youth can still believe in an ideal cast off by disillusioned age' (p 292).

489 Williams, George. *A New View of Chaucer*. Durham, NC: Duke UP, 1965.
The falcon's diatribe against the false tercelet recalls 'Chaucer's long obsession with women betrayed by their lovers' (p 160), and specifically his fear that John of Gaunt would desert Katherine Swynford, leaving Katherine's sister, Philippa Chaucer, and Geoffrey himself without a patron and protector. Gaunt's departure for Spain in 1386 and his possible involvement with Queen Constance is represented by the tercelet's desertion of the falcon for a *kyte*; when Gaunt returned and renewed his former relationship with Katherine, Chaucer decided 'either to abandon this harsh poem altogether, or to destroy its ending' (p 161).

490 Berger, Harry, Jr. 'The F-Fragment of the *Canterbury Tales*, Part I.' *ChauR* 1 (1966), 88–102.
SqT is 'pure fantasy ... the infinite freedom characteristic of such a world is matched by the infinite leisure of the Squire's narration' (p 88). Since delayed conclusions are a stock-in-trade of romance narrative, the tale's incompleteness 'has something of the air of a joke' (p 88). Nevertheless, the Squire's breaking off saves the pilgrims from a continuation 'which would surely have exhausted the combined lung-power of Scheherazade and Ariosto' (p 88). The Squire and the Knight share a concern about 'the proper *ordonnance* of their stories' and betray nostalgia for vanished ideals (p 90). But the Knight controls his relation to his narrative, whereas the Squire is 'at once too little and too much involved in his tale' (p 91). The Squire's inability to distance himself from his act of telling is underlined by his apologies for not getting on with his story, and produces 'violent' attempts to 'reaffirm the primacy of the narrative'; the prospectus of coming attractions is in part a recognition that, in the falcon's lament, 'action has been sacrificed to the pleasures of lyric complaint' (p 92). *SqT* is, nevertheless, a 'fresh, charming and immediate' performance that sets up a reciprocal relation between the Squire's need for his father's 'experience and discipline' and the Knight's presumed dependence in the past on the 'springtime energy' exhibited in his son's tale (p 93). The Franklin's response to the Squire acknowledges the attractions of the 'aristocratic idyll' (p 94) but also contains an implied warning: the Squire must 'cultivate and not merely luxuriate in the May garden of his natural gifts' (p 96).

491 Coghill, Nevill. 'Chaucer's Narrative Art in *The Canterbury Tales*.' In *Chaucer and Chaucerians: Critical Studies in Middle English Literature*. Ed. Derek S. Brewer. University: U of Alabama P, 1966. Pp 114–39.
Passages from *SqT* (lines 401–5), *ParsP* (X.71), and *TC* (2.256–60, 1037–40) are

cited for the 'principles of short-storytelling' (p 119) they contain. Like Pandarus, the Squire urges the need both for a theme and a climax or termination of that theme. He goes on to talk of the importance of economy or pace, recommending a terseness that he himself is not practicing (pp 119–21).

492 McCall, John P. 'The Squire in Wonderland.' *ChauR* 1 (1966), 103–9.
SqT leaves its readers wondering, just as Cambyuskan's courtiers wonder about the magic gifts. Their responses are divided between Fancy and Reality, but the Squire refuses to adjudicate between these two schools of thought, and the debate on the gifts leads nowhere. *SqT* as a whole, in fact, creates 'a series of expectations without fulfillment' (p 105). None of the characters engages in any significant action; the falcon's story is 'nothing more than a shaggy bird tale' (p 108); the summary of things to come at the end of Part 2 promises no resolution; and many of the tale's subsidiary motifs (e.g., the treatment of time) fall into a 'pattern of elaborate inconsequence, incongruity and downright bathos' (p 108). In one sense 'a chaotic and fragmentary failure' attributable to the Squire's immaturity, the tale is also 'one of Chaucer's complete and engaging masterpieces' (p 109), in which the poet shapes the teller's solecisms to his own comic ends.

493 Spearing, A.C., ed. *The Franklin's Prologue and Tale from the Canterbury Tales by Geoffrey Chaucer*. 1966/1994. See **86**.
In its exoticism and multiplication of wonders, *SqT* suits perfectly the character of its teller, who presents his story of marvels with 'naïf enthusiasm' (p 5). The story is broken off with Apollo in midair, 'as if [he] has been shot down by a ground-to-air missile' (1994, p 72). The Franklin's response to *SqT* is at once a brilliantly tactful interruption of a narrative that has gotten out of hand and a way of asserting his own social standing by patronizing the youthful pilgrim.

494 Fifield, Merle. 'Chaucer the Theater-goer.' *PLL* 3 (summer supplement, 1967), 63–70.
Chaucer's familiarity with court theater, evident in *MerT* and *FranT*, is most fully displayed in the masque-like aspects of Cambyuskan's feast: the stranger knight – a 'highly competent actor' (p 62) – fills the role of the gift-giving 'presenter' in the masque; the horse of brass is compared to a piece of stage machinery, and in addition serves as a pageant car for the masque's actor; the dance that follows the meal is the traditional conclusion for a court revel. The press of curious courtiers who examine the horse comes in the position of the antimasque, 'a comic contrast between the opening solemnities and the closing formal dance' (p 70).

495 Gardner, John. 'The Case Against the "Bradshaw Shift"; or, the Mystery of the Manuscript in the Trunk.' *PLL* 3 (summer supplement, 1967), 80–106.
The magic mirror, which can reveal to a lady whether or not her lover is true, was perhaps eventually to be used by Canacee (p 102).

496 Daye, Mary Louise. *The Rhetoric of Narration: A Study of Narrative Intrusion in Chaucer's Tales of the Squire, Manciple, Merchant, and Nun's Priest*. PhD diss., University of Wisconsin, 1968. Dir. Robert K. Presson. Ann Arbor, MI: University Microfilms, 1969. See also *DAI*–A 29/02 (1968): 563–4.
Examines the Squire's intrusions into his story under the headings of narrative tag, *transitio*, sententious poetics, the 'outdoing' topos, rhetorical questions, *superlatio*, appeal to authority, *occupatio*, and the 'affected modesty' topos. The cumulative effect of these intrusions is to characterize the Squire as 'a novice in narration,' fascinated by the formal requirements of chivalric romance, but 'incapable of judging his success or failure with them' (p 42). *SqT* may also embody a mocking critique of the emptiness of the romance tradition itself (pp 40–74).

497 Göller, Karl Heinz. 'Chaucers "Squire's Tale": "The knotte of the tale."' In *Chaucer und seine Zeit: Symposion für Walter F. Schirmer*. Ed. Arno Esch. Tübingen: Max Niemeyer, 1968. Pp 163–88.
Although early readers neglected Part 2 of *SqT*, the episode of the falcon contains the core of the story, named by the Squire (lines 401, 407) as the *knotte* of the tale. By *knotte*, the Squire seems to mean the central point of the narrative, perhaps a misunderstanding of Horace's use of *nodus* to signify a complication requiring a *deus ex machina*. This possible misreading is consistent with the Squire's faulty knowledge of rhetorical figures, exemplified in his commentary on the stranger knight's speech and in his lavish use of *amplificatio* and *digressio*, in which the Squire's attempts to send up his father's rhetorical excesses provoke the reader's laughter at the Squire's own solecisms. The Squire's understanding of courtly literature is equally deficient. His reference to Gawain's 'olde curteisye' (line 95) and his equation of courtesy with elegance of speech and demeanor suggest that he is unaware of the erosion of Gawain's courtesy in late French romance and of the ethical issues surrounding courtesy in *SGGK*. The Squire's allusions to the latter text are tendentious and superficial; in conjunction with the reductive reference to Lancelot, these parallels demonstrate both the Squire's desire to parade his literary knowledge and the limitations of that knowledge. The Squire's promise that Part 2 will contain the *knotte* of the tale also serves a characterizing function; the structural and stylistic weaknesses of the falcon episode reveal a narrator who has lost the thread of his story. But Chaucer did not write *SqT* solely to expose the Squire's failings. Rather, the poet uses the Squire to examine naïve and romantic attitudes toward such topics as knighthood, courtesy, marriage, honor, and the relations between the sexes. We can often distinguish between the Squire's attitude and that of his creator; in the portrait of Canacee, for example, we sense the Squire's identification with his heroine, even as Chaucer exposes the young man's admiration for the lady to good-natured mockery. Comparing the falcon episode with

Anel, we note that, whereas in the latter our sympathies are wholly with the forsaken Anelida, in *SqT* the ethical issues are blurred; the tercelet isn't wholly reprehensible, nor is the self-pitying female bird wholly admirable. The youthful Squire is entirely on the falcon's side, judging men according to the precepts of courtly love. The Boethian birdcage simile, however, invokes the law of kind as a possible critique of courtly convention. The true *knotte* of the tale – quite different for Chaucer than for the Squire – lies in Part 2's subtly ironic perspectives on narrow and idealized views of social codes and human nature.

498 Griffith, Richard R. *A Critical Study Guide to Chaucer's The Canterbury Tales.* Totowa, NJ: Littlefield, Adams, 1968.

In Part 2, the Squire may be responding to the Wife of Bath's democratic treatment of *gentilesse,* hinting that it would be un-*gentil* of him to desert his lady for another (p 119).

498a Rodax, Yvonne. *The Real and the Ideal in the Novella of Italy, France, and England. Four Centuries of Change in the Boccaccian Tale.* University of North Carolina Studies in Comparative Literature, 44. Chapel Hill: U of North Carolina P, 1968.

SqT's composite design from many sources proved too demanding for Chaucer to complete. For all its exotic trappings, *SqT*'s moral elements replicate the conventions of *KnT*'s high chivalry (p 17).

499 Scott, Kathleen L. 'A Mid-Fifteenth-Century English Illuminating Shop and Its Customers.' *JWCI* 31 (1968), 170–96.

The motif of the owl mobbed by flights of little birds, frequently attested in misericords and illuminated MSS, appears as well in Canacee's decoration of the falcon's mew in *SqT,* lines 646–50.

500 Severs, J. Burke. 'The Tales of Romance.' In *A Companion to Chaucer Studies.* Ed. Beryl Rowland. Toronto: Oxford UP, 1968/1979. Pp 229–46/pp 269–95.

This bibliographic essay summarizes scholarship on *SqT*'s analogues; the tale as fragment (it is unlikely that Chaucer broke off the tale because he belatedly discovered incest in his source, as Braddy [**440**] maintains); its relation to other tales; and the character of the narrator (the arguments of Pearsall [**483**] and Haller [**487**] are 'exaggerated and unconvincing' [p 234/p 275]). In the revised edition, Severs observes that 'the poor Squire … continues to be castigated for his ineptitude as a storyteller and his deficiencies of character … These views are usually accompanied by the gratuitous latter-day heresy that the Franklin interrupts the tale to rescue a suffering audience … a heresy which should be effectually silenced by Clark's [**765**] sensible and convincing two-page rebuttal' (1979, p 283).

501 Wagenknecht, Edward C. *The Personality of Chaucer.* Norman: U of Oklahoma P, 1968.

The Man of Law's remark that Chaucer wrote no word of 'thilke wikke ensample of Canacee' (II.78) suggests the poet's attitude toward incest. Perhaps Chaucer decided to break off *SqT* before the point when incest might have entered it (p 68n).

502 Whittock, Trevor. *A Reading of The Canterbury Tales*. Cambridge: Cambridge UP, 1968.
Given the ineptness of the Squire's handling of his narrative, it seems likely that the Franklin's comments are intended as a deliberate interruption of the young man's performance. In contrast to his father's skillful employment of *occupatio*, the Squire's rhetorical disclaimers serve mainly to call attention to himself. His treatment of romance wonders, moreover, robs them of depth and suggestiveness; Chaucer 'seems deliberately bent here on emphasizing the emptiness of the romance' (p 166). The court's reaction to the strange knight's gifts contains touches of realism and comic exaggerations that undercut the scene's potential mystery; in general, the Squire's rhetoric 'parodies itself' (p 167), exposing the youthful pilgrim's 'immature imagination' (p 168).

503 North, J.D. 'Kalenderes Enlumyned Ben They: Some Astronomical Themes in Chaucer (Part II).' *RES* n.s. 20 (1969), 257–83.
North reads Part 1 of *SqT* as an astronomical allegory. European star catalogues give the name Elpheta to α Coronae Borealis; Algari (γ Corvi) and Calbalacet (α Leonis) may correspond to Algarsyf and Cambalo; Cauda Ceti (ι Ceti) may be the source of Canacee's name. Cambyuskan corresponds 'beyond all reasonable doubt' (p 258) to Mars; the king's rising from his table is the allegorical counterpart of the exaltation of Mars on 15 March 1390. The stranger knight, 'a man of great subtlety, skill, and learning' (p 260), is Mercury; his steed of brass represents the Sun, while Canacee's 'ten or twelve' (line 383) attendants correspond to the twelve visible stars between Cauda Ceti and the ecliptic. The two lines of Part 3 show that the action of *SqT* was meant to continue 'at least until 13 May (1390?) and possibly until 14 June (1390?) … One must regret the Franklin's intrusion, not only because Chaucer the astronomer and astrolabist can be seen at work more clearly in *SqT* than anywhere outside *Astr* itself, but because Chaucer the mercurial was in the process of revealing himself' (p 262). (For a revision of some of these conclusions, see **633**, pp 273n, 275–6n.) See **529**, **586**.
• Review in *TLS*, 2 October 1970: North's reading of *SqT* as an astronomical allegory is 'one of his most fascinating and well-sustained propositions … If this is true it is a wonderful Chaucerian joke, that has taken almost 600 years to ripen.'

The Squire's Tale, 1970–1979

504 Finkelstein, Dorothee. 'The Celestial Origin of *Elpheta* and *Algarsyf* in Chau-

cer's Squire's Tale.' *Euroasiatica* 4 (1970), 3–13.
The Arabic version of Ptolemy's *Almagest* 'lists the stars of each constellation as a family' (p 9), an 'arrangement perfect for the structure of *SqT*, a family romance' (p 10). Elpheta, the name of the constellation *corona borealis*, contains eight stars, with the main star near the middle of the crown, and is thus 'a perfect frame' for Cambyuskan's family, comprised of 'a royal couple, two sons and a daughter to be perfected and rounded by the addition of two daughters-in-law and a son-in-law' (p 10). Algarsyf appears to be a transposition of 'Saif al-jabbar, the Sword of the Powerful One ... the name of the three central stars in the constellation Orion' (p 11); as one of Cambyuskan's three children, Algarsyf forms part of 'an astronomical pattern of numbers which Chaucer deliberately wove into the "knotte" of the tale' (p 12). Descriptions of Orion and Pegasus in the Alfonsine manuals may have influenced Chaucer's treatment of the sword and the magic steed. See **204**, pp 74–80.
• Review of Metlitzki (**204**) by Paul Kunitzsch, *Der Islam* 55 (1978), 131–3: Metlitzki's derivation of Algarsyf from 'Saif al-jabbar' is unconvincing; more likely sources include various forms of Arabic names for the phases of the moon, and several star names in the *Liber Alfadol*, which also contains the name *elpheta*.
• Review of Metlitzki (**204**) by M.C. Seymour, *ES* 61 (1980), 556–9: In discussing the origin of *Algarsyf* and *Elpheta* in *SqT*, Metlitzki 'ignores its basic parody ... and postulates ingenious explanations which, by the nature of parody's need for instant recognition, are impossible' (p 557).

505 Pearsall, Derek. '*The Canterbury Tales*.' In *History of Literature in the English Language*. Vol. 1: *The Middle Ages*. Ed. W.F. Bolton. London: Barrie and Jenkins, 1970. Pp 163–94. Rev. ed., *The New History of Literature*. Vol. 1: *The Middle Ages*. Ed. W.F. Bolton. New York: Bedrick, 1986. Pp 237–66.
SqT is 'a complete misfire.' Chaucer probably began it 'with the best will in the world,' but 'found it offered no sustenance to his kind of imagination, and so ... made the best of a bad job by intruding a sense of the Squire's incompetence, not his own, into the narrative, thus preparing for the Franklin's marvellously well-timed interruption' (p 181/p 254).

506 Peterson, Joyce E. 'The Finished Fragment: A Reassessment of the *Squire's Tale*.' *ChauR* 5 (1970), 62–74.
SqT is 'intentionally a fragment in the same way that *Thop* is intentionally a fragment' (p 62). The interruptions of *Thop* and *MkT* are in part generated by the failure of Chaucer and the Monk to tell the sorts of tales expected of them. The Franklin's interruption of *SqT* 'by *pretending* to think him finished' (p 66) is also the result of 'frustrated expectations' (p 65): disappointment at the Squire's refusal to respond in kind to the Merchant's crude attack on amorous squires and the courtly love tradition, and dismay at the

Squire's inadequacies as a storyteller. The Squire's triviality and frivolity are established in *GP*; in his tale, he displays 'his snobbery, his ineptness, and his essential cupidity' (p 68). Although he tries to dissociate himself from 'the Damyans of this world' (p 70), the attempt backfires, revealing him to be cut from the same cloth as the lecherous squire in *MerT*. The 'profanity of the Squire's nature' (p 70) and 'the perniciousness of his kind of gentillesse' (p 74) are especially visible in Part 2 – in the use of Christian imagery and scriptural allusions to exalt courtly love, and in the garbled allusion to Boethius. 'Having done all this, he is finished even if he doesn't know it. The Franklin's interruption merely cuts him off at the point of completion' (p 74). The Franklin's words to the Squire, although ambiguous in their intent, hint at the older man's own material nature. Hence the Host's 'Straw for youre gentillesse' (line 695) may be taken as addressed to both pilgrims.

507 Weidenbrück, Adolf W. *Chaucers Sprichwortpraxis: Eine Form- und Funktionsanalyse*. Rheinischen Friedrich-Wilhelms Universität diss. 1970. Dir. D. Mehl and K. Dietz. Published Bonn: Warburg, 1970.
A particularly dense concentration of proverbs occurs in the falcon's speech, between lines 479 and 611 (p 93).

508 Wood, Chauncey. *Chaucer and the Country of the Stars: Poetic Uses of Astrological Imagery*. Princeton, NJ: Princeton UP, 1970.
The Squire's astronomical digressions mirror the larger rhetorical ineptness of his tale. Lines 47–57 – 'the most astrologically oriented of all the astronomical periphrases in Chaucer' (p 97) – are parodic in their overspecification; patterned after the opening of *GP*, they also function as Chaucerian self-parody, humorously implying that squires – the pilgrim Squire, Chaucer the former squire – 'cannot control rhetoric' (p 99). Lines 263–74 pervert one of the most beautiful astrological images in medieval poetry, the opening of Dante's *Purgatorio*. Dante uses the image for the dawn when he emerges from Hell; the Squire employs it to signal Cambyuskan's rising from the dinner table. The sense of lines 384–7 is 'that Canacee rose up looking like the ruddy, bright March sun and managed to get herself ready the same day' (p 101). Appropriately, the tale is cut short in the middle of one of those astronomical tropes the Squire 'loves so well and uses so badly' (p 102).
• Review by J.D. North, *RES* n.s. 22 (1971), 471–4: In his reading of the astronomical allusions in *SqT* as uniformly parodic, Wood often fails to convince. 'Granted that the Squire was a young and rather *gauche* poet, and not Dante's equal, might we not at least allow him to have included the astronomy for his own purposes?' (p 473).

509 Burrow, J.A. *Ricardian Poetry: Chaucer, Gower, Langland and the 'Gawain' Poet*. London: Routledge and Kegan Paul, 1971.
The tree 'for drye as whit as chalk' (line 409) demonstrates Chaucer's skill in discovering new uses for old similes: '"white as chalk" was proverbial …

but in its application to the strange, dry, white tree it gains extra meaning, because chalk is dry as well as white, and makes a powerful contribution to the extraordinary atmosphere of the whole episode in the Squire's story' (p 138).

510 Robinson, Ian. *Chaucer's Prosody: A Study of the Middle English Verse Tradition.* Cambridge: Cambridge UP, 1971.
In lines 212 and 541–2, the Squire's 'immature haste makes him drop –e's his father would have retained' (p 103).

511 Rowland, Beryl. *Blind Beasts: Chaucer's Animal World.* Kent, OH: Kent State UP, 1971.
In his description of the steed of brass, the Squire 'waxes as enthusiastic about a horse as the young man today would over a model car' (p 123). The brass steed exemplifies the horsely traits of beauty, form, and merit praised by Isidore of Seville and repeated in Trevisa's translation of *De proprietatibus rerum.* The 'steede of Lumbardye' (line 193), noted for its strength and agility, was a favorite of English kings; the Squire appears to be riding such a horse in the Ellesmere illustration (pp 123–4). The sententiousness of 'as by the whelp chasted is the leon' (line 491) is not especially suited either to the falcon or the Squire. Rowland cites illustrations of the practice of beating a dog to discipline a lion in Villard de Honnecourt's sketchbook and *Queen Mary's Psalter* (pp 159–60). The falcon's comparison of her false lover to a 'tigre, ful of doublenesse' (line 543) recalls the conventional deceitfulness of the tiger in attracting and stalking its victims (pp 14–15).

512 Strohm, Paul. 'Jean of Angoulême: A Fifteenth-Century Reader of Chaucer.' *NM* 72 (1971), 69–76.
A manuscript of *CT*, Bibliothèque Nationale MS, fonds anglais 39, was part of the library of Jean d'Orleans, count of Angoulême (d. 1467); it contains a table of contents and numerous corrections in his own hand, and a number of literary judgments which 'presumably embody Jean's opinions' (p 70) in the hand of the scribe, John Duxworth. *SqT* is broken off at line 20 with the following comment: 'Ista fabula est valde absurda in terminis et ideo ad presens pretermittatur nec ulterius de ea procedatur.' A similar gloss on *CYT* (also abbreviated) suggests that Jean must have favored 'a middle style, somewhere between the exoticism of [*SqT*] and the ultra realism' of *CYT* (p 73). See **697a**.

513 DiMarco, Vincent Joseph. *Literary and Historical Researches Respecting Chaucer's Knight and Squire.* PhD diss., University of Pennsylvania, 1972. Dir. Robert Armstrong Pratt. Ann Arbor, MI: University Microfilms, 1974. See also *DAI*–A 33/04 (1972): 1667.
Ch. 3, Part 4 ('The Historical Relevance of Chaucer's *SqT*,' pp 328–58) argues that Chaucer may have associated the kingdom of 'Arabe and of Inde' (line 110) with Middle India, the area in southern Arabia controlled by the Mam-

luks of Egypt from the mid-thirteenth to the late fourteenth centuries. *Sarray* (line 9) was the seat of the Golden Horde, at the height of its fame during the reign of Uzbek Khan (1313–41), the most likely model for Cambyuskan. (Although Chaucer's primary reference is to the New Sarai, his knowledge of the city was probably colored by the extensive references in earlier medieval texts to the first capital, founded by Batu Khan.) The circumstances surrounding the marriage in 1319 of a Tartar princess to Melik-Nasir of Egypt, negotiated to cement the Mongol–Mamluk alliance, offer parallels to *Cleo* and Girard d'Amiens' *Méliacin*; the situation at Uzbek's court may have served 'as a real and historical framework for the romantic situation Chaucer knew from *Cleo*' (p 350). Ch. 3, Part 5 ('Magic, Science, and Romance in Chaucer's *SqT*,' pp 359–91), presents evidence that the stranger knight's magic gifts are rooted in scientific and historical reality; the mirror that reveals friend or foe recalls accounts of a similar device in the Pharos lighthouse at Alexandria, for example. The Squire's satirical treatment of the courtiers who dismiss the gifts as mere *fairye* (line 201), and the implication that, in the unwritten conclusion of the tale, the gifts will resolve problems in human relationships belie the view of the Squire as an empty-headed romantic. Rather, he shows himself to be knowledgeable about contemporary political realities and scientific discoveries and aware of 'the value of a world beyond the confines of Christian Europe' (p 381).

514 Eliason, Norman E. *The Language of Chaucer's Poetry: An Appraisal of the Verse, Style, and Structure*. Anglistica, vol. 17. Copenhagen: Rosenkilde and Bagger, 1972.

The Squire's promises to speed up his story are 'mock-promises,' the transitions 'mock-transitions' (p 146). *SqT* is a parody of the chaotic structure of verse romances – 'their inordinate length, their prolixity, their labyrinthian complexities of plot' (p 146). The Franklin's words to the Squire are not intended to cut him off; it is therefore surprising that no one 'stints' the young man: 'we must suppose that Chaucer either did not get around to it or that the stinting speech somehow got mislaid' (p 194). The likeliest choice for someone to stop the Squire would be the Knight.

515 Kean, P.M. *Chaucer and the Making of English Poetry*. 2 vols. Vol. 2: *The Art of Narrative*. London: Routledge and Kegan Paul, 1972.

Chaucer employs the common structural formula 'now we will leave A and turn to B' to end each part of *SqT*, but with a blatancy that raises questions about his seriousness. The 'table of contents' (p 63) at the end of Part 1 suggests an episodic romance on the scale of *FQ*, and was probably intended to point up the Squire's youthful exuberance rather than to serve as a genuine plan for composition. Nevertheless, the passage is not simply a list of adventures to be related; it reveals Chaucer's awareness of the constructional problems involved in long romance narrative (p 64). The Franklin's romance may be intended as a compliment to the Squire's tastes, but it is also a marked contrast to the structurally complicated tale that the younger man had set out to tell.

516 Muscatine, Charles. *Poetry and Crisis in the Age of Chaucer*. Notre Dame, IN: U of Notre Dame P, 1972. Repr. in *Medieval Literature, Style, and Culture: Essays by Charles Muscatine*. Columbia: U of South Carolina P, 1999. Pp 65–163.
Chaucer seems uncomfortable in the eastern atmosphere of *SqT*. The poem proceeds 'against some resistance,' evident in the Squire's self-conscious remarks about rhetoric, the 'woodenness' of the end-stopped lines, the needless repetitions, the limping plot. The Canacee–falcon story returns us to the 'almost too familiar' romantic pathos of *LGW*. Whether or not the tale's failures and its abrupt termination can be blamed on the Squire, 'the fact remains that the exotic magic leaks out of it early; oriental romance finally succumbs either to irony or boredom' (p 128/pp 150–1).

517 Robinson, Ian. *Chaucer and the English Tradition*. London: Cambridge UP, 1972; pbk ed., 1975. 2nd ed., Harleston, UK: Edgeways, 2004.
At first glance, *SqT* looks unfinished and chaotic; in fact, it is neither. Its subject is 'the Falcon's lament ... courtly-love sadness itself, and nothing need follow it' (pp 181–2). But this love, however beautiful, is also limited, and Chaucer shows its limitations by placing *SqT* next to *FranT*, which dramatically reevaluates the Squire's vision.

518 Ross, Thomas W. *Chaucer's Bawdy*. New York: Dutton, 1972.
Includes entries on *Launcelot* (line 287); *queynte* (lines 234, 239, 369, 433; Canacee's change of color at lines 368–70 may suggest 'repeated orgasms, as she takes joy in her "queynte ryng"' [p 178]); *ryng* (line 369); *lappe* (line 441); *love* (line 529); and 'incest.'

519 Eliason, Norman E. 'Personal Names in the *Canterbury Tales*.' *Names* 21 (1973), 137–52.
The names *Cambyuskan, Elpheta, Canacee, Algarsyf,* and *Cambalo* are purposefully strange, as befits a tale set in the mysterious East. (The variant *Cambalo/ Cambalus* exists for the sake of rhyme.) The confusion over whether *Cambalo* designates both Canacee's brother and her lover is a sign that Chaucer 'deliberately botched the tale' (p 141).

520 Kahrl, Stanley J. 'Chaucer's *Squire's Tale* and the Decline of Chivalry.' *ChauR* 7 (1973), 194–209.
'*SqT* contains in miniature many of the symptoms of the waning of the middle ages' (p 209). These signs of decline include the cultivation of the exotic for its own sake, exemplified in the Squire's choice of setting and in his focus on novel, but nonfunctional, details; the uneasy fit between conventions and their contexts, evident in his handling of figures of rhetoric, particularly *occupatio*; and the forms of aristocratic life without their function, visible in the Squire's inept treatment of *gentilesse* and in his own social and intellectual

snobbishness. Compared to the tale of the Knight, 'one of the last of the *defensores fidei*' (p 208), *SqT* manifests the growing gap between chivalric ideals and social reality in the late fourteenth century, and perhaps reflects as well Chaucer's sense of 'the futility of Richard II's attempts to reassert the full panoply of a feudal court' (p 209).

521 Knight, Stephen. *The Poetry of the Canterbury Tales*. Sydney: Angus and Robertson, 1973.
SqT is similar to *KnT* in its high style and use of rhetorical figures, but adapted to the character and interests of its youthful teller in its subject matter. Knight, who believes that Chaucer meant to finish the tale, briefly analyses some especially effective passages (e.g., lines 89–97 and 189–262) (pp 102–5).

522 Stevens, John. *Medieval Romance: Themes and Approaches*. London: Hutchinson, 1973.
The element of the marvelous in *SqT* first manifests itself as the exotic, in the form of the stranger knight from the eastern kingdoms, and then as the 'marvellous proper' (p 100), in the knight's gifts to Cambyuskan. Marvelous objects or happenings defy the ordinary laws of Nature; within this category, the marvels in *SqT* are 'fairly routine' (p 100).

523 Brewer, Derek S. 'Chaucer and Chrétien and Arthurian Romance.' In *Chaucer and Middle English Studies in Honour of Rossell Hope Robbins*. Ed. Beryl Rowland. London: George Allen and Unwin; Kent, OH: Kent State UP, 1974. Pp 255–9. Repr. in Brewer, *Tradition and Innovation in Chaucer*. London: Macmillan; Atlantic Highlands, NJ: Humanities Press, 1982. Pp 137–41.
In the flippant reference to Lancelot (lines 283–7), we hear the poet speaking in his own voice; the passage is not 'in character' for the Squire, who would surely be an enthusiast for Arthurian legend (p 257).

524 ———. 'Towards a Chaucerian Poetic.' *PBA* 60 (1974), 219–52. Repr. London: Oxford UP, [1974]. Repr. in Brewer, *Chaucer: The Poet as Storyteller*. London: Macmillan; Atlantic Highlands, NJ: Humanities Press, 1984. Pp 54–79.
SqT 'collapses as completely as *HF*.' Although it is not mentioned in the Prologue to *LGW*, *SqT* should probably be dated before the main *CT* period. The teller's characterization of himself as a 'dul man' (line 279) recalls Chaucer's mocking self-presentation, but is hardly appropriate for the Squire (p 225 and n).

525 Dillon, Bert. *A Chaucer Dictionary: Proper Names and Allusions (Excluding Place Names)*. Boston: Hall, 1974.
Entries for the proper names in *SqT*, arranged alphabetically, give variant spellings, identifications, references to other literary works and scholarly studies, and a list of occurrences in Chaucer's works. Also included are authors and texts used by Chaucer, with a list of specific indebtednesses (e.g., the entry for *RR* cites seven passages in *SqT*).

526 Elliott, R.V.W. *Chaucer's English*. London: Deutsch, 1974.

In his disclaimer of rhetorical skill at lines 37–41, the Squire speaks 'with the unmistakable voice of Geoffrey Chaucer' (p 130). Chaucer eschews the technical vocabulary of physics in his work. The magic mirror in *SqT* would lose its mystery if its secret were unraveled; Chaucer refers to a few famous physicists and leaves it at that (p 324).

527 Hatton, Thomas J. 'Thematic Relationships between Chaucer's Squire's Portrait and Tale and the Knight's Portrait and Tale.' *SMC* 4 (1974), 452–8.
SqT is consistent with the *GP* portrait of the Squire, which gently mocks the young man's sensuality and lack of self-discipline. In contrast to *KnT*, which illustrates its teller's wisdom, the account of Cambyuskan and his court celebrates 'temporal magnificence and extravagance rather than moderation and public service' (p 457). The second part of the tale comments ironically on the false values of Part 1; Canacee, the only member of the court who abstains from sensual indulgence, learns in her encounter with the falcon that 'the delights of hot love, the pleasures of the senses, ultimately betray one' (p 457). Chaucer may have intended this lesson to apply as well to the court of Richard II, criticized by contemporary chroniclers for its failure to uphold chivalric ideals of the sort the Knight embodies.

528 Lenaghan, R.T. 'The Clerk of Venus: Chaucer and Medieval Romance.' In *The Learned and the Lewed: Studies in Chaucer and Medieval Literature*. Ed. Larry D. Benson. Harvard English Studies 5. Cambridge, MA: Harvard UP, 1974. Pp 31–43.
The first part of *SqT* presents 'the image of chivalric magnificence,' the second part 'the image of *fin amour*' (p 34). Such interests are proper to romance, but there are awkwardnesses that undermine this clear alignment of genre and theme. Although the tale's lapses can be taken as a negative characterization of its teller – the *CT*'s 'layered narration' (p 34) invites this dramatic ironic reading – 'the problem ... is that the critic's convenience quickly develops such a potency as to become a universal solvent. All is irony and negation' (p 34). A simpler solution would be to treat the tale's weaknesses as reflecting more upon Chaucer than upon the Squire.

529 Manzalaoui, Mahmoud. 'Chaucer and Science.' In *Geoffrey Chaucer*. Ed. Derek S. Brewer. Writers and their Background. London: Bell, 1974; Athens: Ohio State UP, 1975; pbk ed., 1975. Pp 224–61.
North's astronomical allegory (**503**) may reveal some 'private desire ... at the back of Chaucer's mind,' but it is of little use as interpretation, 'for the obvious reason that no clear-minded reader of *SqT* ... is conscious that he is reading an account of astronomical events' (pp 242–3).

530 Moseley, C.W.R.D. 'Chaucer, Sir John Mandeville, and the Alliterative Revival: A Hypothesis Concerning Relationships.' *MP* 72 (1974), 182–4.
Although *Mandeville's Travels* survives in a large number of MSS written in England, it is echoed only in the works of the *Pearl* poet, in the alliterative

Morte Arthure, and in *FranT* and *SqT*. Given the link between *SqT* and *SGGK*, it is possible that the circulation of the English text of the *Travels* may have been restricted to the north of England, and that Chaucer may have been familiar not only with the poets of the alliterative school, but also with their source material.

531 Olson, Clair C. 'The Interludes of the Marriage Group in the *Canterbury Tales*.' In *Chaucer and Middle English Studies in Honour of Rossell Hope Robbins*. 1974. See **523**. Pp 164–72.
Planned as a vehicle for an account of pure and idyllic love, *SqT* is the precise opposite of *MerT*. Chaucer seems to have designed the tales 'to show how one extreme might call forth its counterpart' (p 171).

532 Prins, A.A. 'The Dating in the Canterbury Tales.' In *Chaucer and Middle English Studies in Honour of Rossell Hope Robbins*. 1974. See **523**. Pp 342–7.
In support of his argument that lines 7–8 of *GP* refer not to the zodiacal sign Aries 'but to the constellation of fixed stars, i.e. the stellar zodiac' (p 343), Prins points out that in lines 264–7, Chaucer 'clearly does not indicate the ascendant by the zodiacal sign Leo, in his ninth sphere, but by the stellar constellation in sphere eight' (p 344).

533 Reiss, Edmund. 'Chaucer's Courtly Love.' In *The Learned and the Lewed: Studies in Chaucer and Medieval Literature*. 1974. See **528**. Pp 95–111.
The falcon's lament may be compared to Thopas's love longing for his 'elf-queene' (VII.790). The 'burlesque of romantic clichés' in *Thop* and the 'bombastic treatment of trivia' in *SqT* keep us from taking love or lover seriously in either instance (p 99).

534 Schmidt, A.V.C., ed. *The General Prologue to the Canterbury Tales and the Canon Yeoman's Prologue and Tale*. London: U of London P, 1974; New York: Holmes and Meier, 1976.
'The Squire is not "superficial" in a bad sense, but he clearly *is* concerned with outward appearance … in a way the Knight is not … Appropriately, therefore, his (unfinished) Tale turns out to be a treatment more of the superficies of the chivalric life than the Knight's, which penetrates beneath the trappings to the moral essence of knighthood' (p 128).

535 Scott, A.F. *Who's Who in Chaucer*. London: Hamilton; New York: Taplinger, 1974.
The names of characters and historical and mythological personages in *SqT* are briefly glossed, along with names of other people (and animals) in Chaucer's writings.

536 Brody, Saul N. 'The Comic Rejection of Courtly Love.' In *In Pursuit of Perfection: Courtly Love in Medieval Literature*. Ed. Joan M. Ferrante and George D. Economou. Port Washington, NY: Kennikat, 1975. Pp 221–61.
The tercelet in Part 2 of *SqT* woos the falcon in courtly fashion, but is motivated by his own sexual pleasure; he belongs more to the world of fabliau than to the improbably romantic world described by the Squire (p 252).

537 Economou, George D. 'Chaucer's Use of the Bird in the Cage Image in the *Canterbury Tales.*' *PQ* 54 (1975), 679–84.
Chaucer uses the image of the caged bird (adapted from Boethius and Jean de Meun) in *ManT, MilT,* and *SqT*. In *SqT,* the figure is employed by the heartsick falcon to describe the behavior of her faithless tercelet. The image, generally used to elucidate the character of a human, is here humorously employed to comment on a bird that behaves like a man of the noble class. 'With the happy ending intimating that it is the tercelet's proper nature to be true after all, Chaucer brings the application of the Boethian image full circle by comparing the bird to a bird' (p 682).

538 Elliott, R.V.W. '"Faire subtile wordes": An Approach to Chaucer's Verbal Art.' *Parergon* 13 (1975), 3–20.
The Squire's 'myn Englissh eek is insufficient' (line 37) may be read as a conventional modesty formula, as an indication that the Squire customarily spoke French, or as Chaucer's own diffidence posing behind the pilgrim's words (pp 5–6).

538a Howard, Donald R. "Flying Through Space: Chaucer and Milton." In *Milton and the Line of Vision*. Ed. Joseph Anthony Wittreich. Madison: U of Wisconsin P, 1975. Pp 3–23.
Milton's allusion to *SqT* in 'Il Penseroso' suggests that he viewed Chaucer's poem through the lens of Spenser's continuation in Book 4 of *FQ*. But the lengthy interlaced romance that *SqT*'s early readers assumed Chaucer was writing is the very structure that the tale subjects to ridicule. Although it is not as broad a parody as *Th, SqT* satirizes both a literary form and the aristocratic taste for such meandering tales. Chaucer never meant to finish *SqT* any more than he intended to finish *Th* (pp 9–10).

539 Jordan, Robert M. 'The Question of Genre: Five Chaucerian Romances.' In *Chaucer at Albany*. Ed. Rossell Hope Robbins. New York: Franklin, 1975. Pp 77–103.
'Compositional technique' (p 81) makes a better criterion than subject matter in determining whether *SqT, WBT, KnT, FranT,* and *Thop* qualify as romances. The narrative structure of *SqT* substitutes juxtaposed disquisitions and descriptions for the linear progression of action; the tale 'observes the prescriptions of *amplificatio* to an extreme degree' (p 83). Part 1 is almost entirely descriptive; juxtaposed rather than fused, the elements 'relate to one another somewhat in the manner of a laundry list' (p 84). Part 2 displays on a larger scale the same formal organization as Part 1; there is still no central action, no protagonist. 'It might be claimed that *SqT* is a *conjointure* without a *conte*' (p 86).

540 Miskimin, Alice S. *The Renaissance Chaucer*. 1975. See **201**.
The tone of the Squire's allusion to Lancelot (lines 283–90) is elusive; neither dry nor skeptical, it partakes of the Squire's characteristic 'youthful hyper-

bole' (p 100), and is thus self-satirizing.

541 Moseley, C.W.R.D. 'Some Suggestions about the Writing of *The Squire's Tale*.' *Archiv* 212 (1975), 124–7.
The echoes in *SqT* of *SGGK* and *Mandeville's Travels* – the latter apparently restricted in its early circulation in England to the north and west – suggest that Chaucer may have written it for a northern audience, perhaps at one of the great provincial courts. The tale's incompleteness can be explained if we imagine the poem as having been prepared as a draft for a public performance that never took place.

542 Scheps, Walter. '"Up roos oure Hoost, and was oure aller cok": Harry Bailly's Tale-Telling Competition.' *ChauR* 10 (1975), 113–28.
SqT quits his father's tale by emphasizing courtly rather than military virtues. The central character in *KnT* is the conqueror Theseus; the Squire's ideal figure is the courteous Gawain (pp 121–2).

543 Cooper, Helen. 'Magic That Does Not Work.' *M&H* n.s. 7 (1976), 131–46.
In *SqT,* Chaucer 'assembles a fine collection of magic objects ... and then stops short, as if, having once gathered all these marvels together, he was not really interested in developing a plot from them' (p 131).

544 David, Alfred. *The Strumpet Muse: Art and Morals in Chaucer's Poetry*. Bloomington: Indiana UP, 1976.
However *SqT* might have ended, 'its moral is clearly going to be, "That pitee renneth soone in gentil herte"' (p 184).

545 Howard, Donald R. *The Idea of the Canterbury Tales*. Berkeley: U of California P, 1976.
The subject matter of *SqT* suits its teller, but we sense Chaucer's presence in the incongruities that undercut the narrative. The tale's absurdities reflect less on the Squire than on 'the aristocratic fads and fashions of his day' (p 266). Like the Franklin, we admire the Squire's earnest efforts to tell his tale. But the aristocracy's contribution to the discourse of the Wife, the Clerk, and the Merchant is no more than 'fantasy and convention ... courtly clichés and rhetorical posturing, bromides about love-longing, courtesy, honor, gentilesse ... hearsay tales of distant princes ... it is a moment when Chaucer shows himself out of sympathy with the knightly classes' (p 267). Although we cannot fault the Squire for telling the sort of story required by current fashions, those fashions are 'empty and jejune' (p 267).
• Review by Jill Mann, *MÆ* 47 (1978), 356–60: Howard's insistence on the tale's superficiality cuts us off from any emotional connection with it, as, for example, in the speech of the deserted falcon, which 'contains some of the most moving lines ... that Chaucer ever wrote about the loss of love' (p 357).

546 Tristram, Phillipa. *Figures of Life and Death in Medieval English Literature*. New York: New York UP, 1976.
SqT exists to dramatize its speaker; although the narrative reflects the

Squire's naïveté, the impulses behind it are generous ones. Significantly, the Franklin praises not the tale, but the teller, who fulfills the Franklin's ideal of *gentilesse*, in contrast to the reality of his own wastrel son (pp 27–8).

546a Wenzel, Siegfried. 'Chaucer and the Language of Contemporary Preaching.' *SP* 73 (1976), 138–61.
Knotte (line 401) signifies 'the central or main part' or 'the gist of the story' (p 156), a meaning that agrees with the view common in medieval rhetoric that the climax of an argument should come at the end of the *proces*, or careful development of an argument's subject.

547 Cornelia, Marie. 'Chaucer's Tartarye.' *DR* 57 (1977), 81–9.
Summarizes what a fourteenth-century European would have known about the Tartars. In the early Middle Ages, knowledge of the Orient was based primarily on myth and fable, mingled with some hazy geographical lore; legends of the utopian kingdom of Prester John, culminating in a letter supposedly from the Prester himself, were especially powerful in shaping the European image of the East. By the middle of the thirteenth century, the westward surge of Genghis Khan's Golden Horde and the subsequent open-door policy of the Tartars allowed travelers, merchants, and missionaries to see Tartary and Cathay for themselves, and to report back in accounts which 'fuse strange fable with stranger fact' (p 88). Later centuries have forgotten how familiar 'the land of Tartarye' (line 9) was to fourteenth-century Europe, especially to Italian merchants regularly engaged in the Eastern trade. But Chaucer, who traveled to Italy and spent his days in the customs house, would have been aware of these trade connections.

548 Fisher, John H., ed. *The Complete Poetry and Prose of Geoffrey Chaucer*. 1977. See **96**.
Among the *SqT*'s faults are an excess of undeveloped motifs in Part 1 and the entirely unrelated topic introduced in Part 2. The tale's deficiencies may have been intended to make a dramatic point about the Franklin, whose praise of the Squire's performance exposes his own lack of judgment (pp 186–7).

549 Gardner, John. *The Poetry of Chaucer*. Carbondale: Southern Illinois UP, 1977.
SqT is intentionally bad art, a 'splendid burlesque' (p 289) in which the tale counts less than the teller. As a storyteller, the Squire has none of the Knight's authority because he lacks his father's worldly experience.

550 Larson, Charles. '*The Squire's Tale*: Chaucer's Evolution from the Dream Vision.' *RLV* 43 (1977), 598–607.
Chaucer may have composed *SqT* at the time he was writing his dream visions and later assigned it to the Squire. The tale's modest narrator displays little of the self-confidence we would expect from the *GP*'s 'lusty bacheler' (I.80), but is strikingly similar to the self-deprecating speakers of the dream visions. Moreover, the tale's 'disjunctive' (p 602) narrative technique – the

abrupt shifts from one 'plane of reality' to another, the unexplained gaps in the story – produce 'an almost surreal aura' reminiscent of the dream visions (p 603). *SqT*'s uncertainties suggest a young poet experimenting with genre, theme, and style; he may have abandoned it for some of the same reasons he left *HF* and *Anel* unfinished.

551 Owen, Charles A., Jr. *Pilgrimage and Storytelling in the Canterbury Tales: The Dialectic of "Ernest" and "Game."* Norman: U of Oklahoma P, 1977.
In *SqT*, Chaucer is experimenting with a combination of several genres, but it is questionable whether he could have fused them meaningfully, as he did in *MerT* and *NPT*. The description of the steed of brass throws light on the Squire's imagination. 'People wonder "How that it koude gon," and so may we with a tale so "plotly"' (p 202).

552 Pichaske, David R. *The Movement of the Canterbury Tales: Chaucer's Literary Pilgrimage*. [Norwood, PA]: Norwood, 1977. Repr. Folcroft, PA: Folcroft, 1978.
SqT is concerned with 'will and fruition' (p 96) and comments as well on 'the function and possibilities of art' (p 99). The danger of subjugating one's will to the wrong sort of governor, obliquely touched on in the falcon's tale, is more central to the Squire's submission to the Host, an act which produces 'artistic … disorder' (p 98) in the form of the Squire's inept tale. The marvelous properties of the stranger knight's gifts are analogous to Chaucer's poetic powers. But these powers must be placed in the right hands. The Squire, 'distrustful of art and inexperienced as an artist' (p 99), cannot make the brass steed move.

553 Storm, Melvin. 'The Tercelet as Tiger: Bestiary Hypocrisy in the Squire's Tale.' *ELN* 14 (1977), 172–4.
Cites parallels to the falcon's description of the false tercelet as a 'tigre, ful of doublenesse' (line 543) in commentaries on Job 4:11 ('Tigris periit') by Isidore of Seville, Rabanus Maurus, and Garnerus of Saint Victor that interpret the tiger as a figure of hypocrisy.

554 Mehl, Dieter. 'Chaucer's Audience.' *LeedsSE* n.s. 10 (1978), 58–73.
SqT is the performance of a young man who has acquired the trappings of the chivalric style without the substance. The Franklin's words to the Squire, which imply no criticism of the tale, show him to be interested primarily in the Squire's demonstration of *gentilesse*, and reveal his own social naïveté. His response points up *SqT*'s 'particular class character, its almost elitist preoccupation with a fictional world and an embellished rhetoric' (p 70), and encourages us to make our own assessment of the Squire's narrative.

555 Miller, Robert P. 'Augustinian Wisdom and Eloquence in the F-Fragment of *The Canterbury Tales*.' *Mediaevalia* 4 (1978), 245–75.
Fragment F (V) is centrally concerned with Cicero's ideal of rhetoric, which links Wisdom and Eloquence. The final, interrupted figure in *SqT* describes Apollo, the god of wisdom, entering the astrological house of Mercury, god

of eloquence. But Mercury's epithet, 'the slye' (line 672), undercuts the Ciceronian ideal, and reminds us that *SqT* has been 'a rhetorical disaster ... innocent of wisdom, discipline, or substance' (p 246). From a rhetorical point of view, *SqT* is 'literally the funniest deed' in *CT*, an instance of 'Chaucer's own rhetorical sophistication in writing badly' (p 246).

556 Stark, Marilynn Dianne. *Chaucer as Literary Critic: The Medieval Romance Genre in The Canterbury Tales.* PhD diss., University of Illinois, 1978. Dir. Jackson J. Campbell. Ann Arbor, MI: University Microfilms International, 1981. See also *DAI*–A 39/05 (1978): 2925.

In developing the tale by means of descriptions and displays of rhetoric rather than coherent narrative, Chaucer shows how displays of good manners and social style can replace meaningful action. The Squire's satire of the 'lewed' responses to the magical gifts undercuts the marveling tone that his description of the gifts is intended to convey. In Part 2, the Squire's superficial understanding of *gentilesse* and *amour courtois* ridicules courtly values. *SqT* shows Chaucer 'gently mocking the dilemma of a young narrator, who does not really know how to come to grips with the genre he has chosen, and who hence falls back on the excessive use of convention and pathos, two faults that the romance genre was often prone to' (p 187).

557 Andersen, Wallis May. *Rhetoric and Poetics in the Canterbury Tales: the Knight, the Squire, and the Franklin.* PhD diss., University of Detroit, 1979. Dir. Edward J. Wolff. Ann Arbor, MI: University Microfilms International, 1998. See also *DAI*–A 41/01 (1980): 239.

Chaucer employs figures of rhetoric to characterize the pilgrims in their tales; the relationship among tales suggests that *CT* is a debate on poetics. Ch. 3, 'The Squire as Poet' (pp 93–145), examines the Squire's use of *occupatio, brevitas* and modesty formulae, *digressio,* and *descriptio.* The Squire's 'preoccupation with story-telling as a knightly virtue reveals him as a self-consciously superior young man who is immersed in the superficial and the trivial'; when compared with the Knight's handling of rhetorical figures, the Squire's 'superficial understanding of rhetoric, and, by extension, his own personal superficiality' become evident (p 140). A comparison of the two tales also demonstrates the virtues of the Knight's 'ordered, planned narrative,' in contrast to the 'overall lack of purpose' of *SqT* (p 139). The Squire's treatment of rhetorical techniques contains a measure of social criticism; his 'fatuous regard for knights ... as rhetoricians must be ironic in the eyes of Chaucer-the-poet, the commoner' (p 141).

558 Blake, N.F. 'The Relationship between the Hengwrt and the Ellesmere Manuscripts of the "*Canterbury Tales.*"' *E&S* n.s. 32 (1979), 1–18.

SqT was in progress at Chaucer's death, and hence not yet incorporated into the framework of *CT* (the links at lines 1–8 and 673–708 are probably spurious). Unlike *MkT* or *Thop,* which were meant to be incomplete for dramatic reasons, *SqT* is incomplete because Chaucer had not finished it (p 11). See **625**.

559 Burnley, J.D. *Chaucer's Language and the Philosophers' Tradition*. Cambridge: Brewer; Totowa, NJ: Rowman and Littlefield, 1979.
The interdependence of *gentilesse, pitee,* and love are illustrated in the falcon's address to Canacee (p 157). The falcon's account of the conditions she imposed on the tercelet's wooing exemplifies the courtly attempt to reconcile sexual love and reason and the ultimate futility of such a project (p 132).

560 Gaylord, Alan T. 'Chaucer's Dainty "Dogerel": The "Elvyssh" Prosody of *Sir Thopas*.' *SAC* 1 (1979), 83–105.
The exhaustion of romance is expressed in those works – notably *SqT* – that Chaucer didn't finish. This predicament is reflected in *Thop* (p 102).

561 Gray, Douglas. 'Chaucer and "Pite."' In *J.R.R. Tolkien, Scholar and Storyteller: Essays in Memoriam*. Ed. Mary Salu and Robert T. Farrell. Ithaca, NY: Cornell UP, 1979. Pp 173–203.
The close connection between *pite* and *gentilesse* is given its fullest Chaucerian expression in Canacee's encounter with the falcon. The falcon's speech defines *pite* as a natural affection, a deeply intense emotion virtually synonymous with 'compassion.'

562 Mehl, Dieter. 'Chaucer, Geoffrey.' In *Enzyklopädie des Märchens: Handwörterbüch zur historischen und vergleichenden Erzählforschung*. Ed. Kurt Ranke. 1975– .Vol. 2. Berlin: de Gruyter, 1979. Pp 1255–67.
SqT expresses the mentality of an immature but promising courtier, typical of his class, a characterization achieved by allowing the Squire to pile up exotic clichés drawn from the romance tradition.

563 Satow, Tsutomu. *Sentence and Solaas: Thematic Development and Narrative Technique in the Canterbury Tales*. Tokyo: Kobundo, 1979.
SqT suits its narrator, who had perhaps heard of magical events in his travels to strange lands. The Franklin's praise of the Squire's eloquence prepares us for his tale, in which Aurelius is modeled on the pilgrim Squire (pp 199–200).

The Squire's Tale, 1980–1989

564 Lawler, Traugott. *The One and the Many in the Canterbury Tales*. Hamden, CT: Archon, 1980.
Chaucer's failure to complete *CkT* and *SqT* may be related to a more general pattern of diminishment or increasing selectivity in *CT*. Realizing that the scheme for hearing from 'ech degree' (X.18) was fulfilled even before each pilgrim told one tale, Chaucer deliberately reduced his poem's scope (pp 118–19).

565 Mann, Jill. 'Troilus' Swoon.' *ChauR* 14 (1980), 319–35.

The falcon's speech at lines 562–73 is Chaucer's fullest and most touching expression of love's miraculous power to create mutual *obeisaunce* in a pair of lovers.

566 Wolpers, Theodor. *Bürgerliches bei Chaucer. Mit einer skizze des spätmittelalterlichen London*. Göttingen: Vandenhoeck & Ruprecht, 1980.
Chaucer's lengthy narrative preambles reflect both generic conventions and the poet's pleasure in his craft. But he is also aware of the dangers of excessive deferral of the main point of a story, as in the *SqT*, in which clumsy digressions reflect poorly on the teller's abilities (p 275).

567 Allen, Judson Boyce, and Theresa Anne Moritz. *A Distinction of Stories: The Medieval Unity of Chaucer's Fair Chain of Narratives for Canterbury*. Columbus: Ohio State UP, 1981.
Attention to fifteenth-century orderings of *CT* other than the Ellesmere order reveals new connections among the tales. The common sequence *SqT–MerT–WBT*, for example, links three tales in which magical events surround courtship and marriage. In its fairyland atmosphere and its concern with insight into the true desires of the opposite sex, *SqT* is linked with *WBT*, a relation hidden in the Ellesmere order (p 102). *SqT* is one of the 'tales of magic' (p 137), in which real magic or kindred deceptions create disorder. Chaucer ironically undercuts the notion that magic will bring about social harmony by presenting the stranger knight's magical gifts, with their implicit promise to Cambyuskan that 'nothing should ever go wrong' (p 145), as 'a parallel and parody of the gifts of God personified in Saint Cecilia and her fellowship,' and by subjecting them to a 'lewed' interpretation, 'full of disagreement and comic pretentiousness' (pp 145–6). In Part 2, the portrait of the false tercelet connects him with the hypocritical scribes and Pharisees denounced by Christ, and thus derives from an avian love affair 'a general insight about true and false responsibility in human relationships at large,' with the faithless tercelet 'representing a specific case of general disorder' (p 146). The Squire's exemplum about *gentilesse* and its betrayal anticipates *FranT* in the 'courtly love posturing through which both relationships are established' (p 147) and in the tercelet's and Arveragus's promises of good faith, broken by both males when they desert their ladies for the sake of personal honor.
• Review by Theodore A. Stroud, *MP* 80 (1982), 177–80: Stroud questions the claim that each tale reflects Chaucer's view of reality. Although the parallels between *SqT* and *SNT* are genuine ones, 'it does not seem to follow that, in describing the flying horse or [Cecilia's] golden legend, Chaucer was expressing his own priorities or trying to influence ours' (p 180).

568 Barney, Stephen A. 'Suddenness and Process in Chaucer.' *ChauR* 16 (1981), 18–37.
The suddenness in *SqT* comes early, with the entry of the strange knight.

The remainder of the tale moves slowly; 'the eloquent gestures which soothe and retard the pace of romance finally displace the action altogether' (p 26).

569 Blake, N.F. 'Critics, Criticism, and the Order of *The Canterbury Tales*.' *Archiv* 218 (1981), 47–58.
It is possible to deduce from Hg that *SqT, FranT, MerT,* and *SNT* were tales without links or tellers when Chaucer died. The poet's death also explains the unfinished state of *SqT* (p 54).

570 Bloomfield, Morton W. 'Chaucer's *Squire's Tale* and the Renaissance.' *PoeticaT* 12, for 1979 (1981), 28–35.
Although *SqT* may reflect aspects of the 'waning' Middle Ages, it also embodies the new spirit of the Renaissance in its attitude toward natural law as a common bond among diverse cultures and religions, its interest in the non-European world, and especially in its fascination with the mysteries of nature and technology. The courtiers' speculations about the flying horse may be the first literary description of scientific curiosity.

571 Chamberlain, David. 'Musical Signs and Symbols in Chaucer: Convention and Originality.' In *Signs and Symbols in Chaucer's Poetry*. Ed. John P. Hermann and John J. Burke, Jr. University: U of Alabama P, 1981. Pp 43–80.
The 'social eroticism' of Cambyuskan's birthday feast is presented in part through musical signs. 'The license of this scene may also reflect the highly discordant narrative techniques of the tale' (p 74).

572 Goldberg, Jonathan. *Endlesse Worke: Spenser and the Structures of Discourse*. 1981. See **209**.
'Narration in *SqT* repeatedly occurs in situations of surrogacy that carry their attendant losses.' The squire, who begins his narrative as 'a (mis)recognized communal representative,' steps aside in the second part of his story to allow the falcon to tell the tale. Yet the new narrator agrees to her task only because of Canacee's empathy, her request that she tell her story. At the climax of the tale of loss in love, 'another loss occurs, for her story enters antecedent texts, and their demands overwhelm hers. In both the citation from Boethius and the reversal that occurs when the falcon speaks as a person and not as a bird, text and tale seem to absorb the teller … As boundaries between tellers and tales keep dissolving, a virtually endless chain of surrogacy is generated.' Although the squire promises a variety of possible endings to his tale, he is unable to provide one; 'all he can do is defer to the voice of another' (p 41).

573 Kelly, Henry Ansgar. 'Chaucer's Arts and our Arts.' In *New Perspectives in Chaucer Criticism*. Ed. Donald M. Rose. Norman, OK: Pilgrim, 1981. Pp 107–20.
When Chaucer says that neither Nature nor art could improve on the mechanical brass horse of *SqT* (line 197), the principal art to be applied would no doubt come under what John Gower refers to as 'art mechanique' (*CA*

7.1694) (p 108).

574 Orme, Nicholas. 'Chaucer and Education.' *ChauR* 16 (1981), 38–59. Repr. in Orme, *Education and Society in Medieval and Renaissance England.* London: Hambledon, 1989. Pp 221–42.

The Squire's rhetorical ambitions reflect his training in public speaking, an aspect of late medieval aristocratic education. His extravagant rhetorical flights suggest that he has been well schooled in the techniques of rhetoric, but still lacks the maturity to use them effectively; in commenting on his promise of future eloquence (lines 677–9), the Franklin suggests that the Squire's education needs to be improved upon by age and experience. The presence of Canacee's *maistresse* (line 377) recalls the late-medieval practice of deputing the responsibility for the training of noble girls to governesses.

575 Peck, Russell A. 'St. Paul and the *Canterbury Tales.*' *Mediaevalia* 7 (1981), 91–131.

Chaucer's characters, both in and out of the tales, worry about making a good end. In lines 401–8, the Squire brings Canacee's morning walk to a close, 'but he does not find the knot to his own wandering tale, which, rather than revealing its meaning, becomes lost in loose threads' (p 103).

576 Reiss, Edmund. 'Chaucer's Thematic Particulars.' In *Signs and Symbols in Chaucer's Poetry*. 1981. See **571**. Pp 27–42.

The dry tree and the bird that makes itself bleed (lines 409–18) are familiar mystical symbols: the bird that pricks its own breast is the pelican, a symbol of Christ's self-sacrifice; the dry tree is a type of the Cross. In *SqT*, the 'fullness of meaning' present in these images contrasts with the 'vacuousness' of the tale's other particulars (p 33). The traditional associations of the falcon – the vanity of earthly love, avarice, cruelty to its young – make it diametrically opposed to the pelican. These contrasts 'allow Chaucer's audience to assess the action of the tale and offer a corrective to what is at hand' (p 34).

577 Stroud, Theodore A. 'Chaucer's Structural Balancing of *Troilus* and "Knight's Tale."' *AnM* 21 (1981), 31–45.

SqT is a 'sophisticated hoax,' 'obviously' broken off, but treated by the Franklin as if it has been creditably completed (p 33).

578 Boitani, Piero. *English Medieval Narrative in the Thirteenth and Fourteenth Centuries*. Trans. Joan Krakover Hall. Cambridge: Cambridge UP, 1982; pbk ed., 1986. Originally published as *La Narrativa del Medioevo Inglese.* Biblioteca di Studi Inglesi 36. Bari: Adriatica, 1980.

Formally divided into three parts, *SqT* is a typical example of interlaced narrative, as the Squire makes clear in his preview of coming attractions at the end of the *secunda pars* (p 257). The tale is placed in an ironic light by *Thop,* which serves as an 'anti-model' (p 247) not only for popular romance but also for the type of narrative the Squire sets out to tell.

579 Burrow, J.A. *Medieval Writers and Their Work: Middle English Literature and its*

Background, 1100–1500. Oxford: Oxford UP, 1982.
Spenser and Milton valued *SqT* for qualities we no longer respond to. Although critics have proposed that Chaucer deliberately aborted the poem out of impatience with its 'insipid marvels, a more attentive and unprejudiced reading, such as Milton ['Il Penseroso,' lines 109–15] may prompt, will put that suggestion out of court' (p 129).

580 Burnley, J.D. *A Guide to Chaucer's Language*. Norman: U of Oklahoma P, 1983. Repr. as *The Language of Chaucer*. Basingstoke, UK: Macmillan, 1989.
In line 22 ('Of his corage as any centre stable'), *stable* is used in its technical sense, referring to the still center of a moving circle (p 160). The strange knight's greeting to Cambyuskan from the 'kyng of Arabe and of Inde' (line 110) recalls, in its syntax and diction, the high style of royal epistles (pp 188–9).

581 Cooper, Helen. *The Structure of the Canterbury Tales*. London: Duckworth, 1983; Athens: U of Georgia P, 1984.
'Pitee renneth soone in gentil herte' occurs in *KnT*, *MerT*, and *SqT*. *KnT* uses the line straight; *MerT* uses it ironically. In *SqT*, 'it applies literally to Canacee, but given the context of a lover's unfaithfulness it carries a reminder that its opposite is also true' (p 89). The tale's perceived aesthetic failures may be a function of its genre; an unsophisticated interlaced romance, it proceeds by 'sheer multiplication of incident' (p 145) rather than by elegant *entrelacement*. The tale's genre also throws light on the question of its unfinishedness. The Franklin interrupts it deliberately, the summary of coming events just before the interruption allowing Chaucer to 'indicate the nature of the creature without actually having to write the rest' (p 146). Just as *SqT* passes judgment on its own genre, it also creates its own narrator; the youthful and energetic speaker is implied by the nature of the tale itself. Although *SqT*'s placement in the Marriage Group sequence is something of a pseudo problem, the Squire's performance balances the demeaning portrait of the squire Damian in *MerT* and prepares us for Aurelius's *gentil* actions at the conclusion of *FranT*. The pairing of *SqT* and *FranT* – the only place in *CT* where two romances are juxtaposed – creates both parallels (e.g., *gentilesse* and hospitality) and contrasts. The latter include the Franklin's more accomplished use of rhetorical figures; the formal economy of the Breton lay as opposed to the shapelessness of the interlaced romance; and the Squire's interest in the affairs of birds in contrast to the 'solidly human' (p 151) concerns of *FranT*, including the humanizing or rationalizing of the marvelous. If the Franklin interrupts *SqT*, he also completes it, by redefining its treatment of the role of the supernatural in human affairs, and suggesting that happy endings are brought about not by magic, but by human virtue (pp 144–54). See **714a**.

• Review by J.A. Burrow, *N&Q* n.s. 32 (1985), 94: The trend of some recent criticism to 'treat gaps in the text as deliberate structural markers or else to argue them away altogether' is exemplified in Cooper's endorsement of the proposal that the Franklin interrupts *SqT*. But there is no reason to believe that Chaucer did not intend to complete the tale and so close the gap. 'Dr. Cooper is, for once, less than sympathetic in her account of this Tale and of the genre of interlaced romance to which she assigns it.'

582 Goodman, Jennifer R. 'Chaucer's *Squire's Tale* and the Rise of Chivalry.' *SAC* 5 (1983), 127–36.

SqT 'possesses both a recognizable genre and a coherent form' (p 134). Like *Partonope of Blois, Valentine and Orson, Generides,* and *Huon of Bordeaux, SqT* is a composite of courtly romance, an eclectic amalgam of themes from earlier romances that combines minute realism with a taste for the fantastic. The flying horse, the magic ring, mirror, and sword, and the threat of incest can be paralleled in the composite romances, as can such formal devices as multiple plots and open-ended story lines. Chaucer probably left *SqT* unfinished by design; whereas a full-length composite romance would have competed in length with the entire *CT*, a fragment 'enables Chaucer to expand the generic variety of *CT* without damaging the design of the work as a whole' (p 155). *SqT*'s lack of an ending also serves to characterize its young teller; 'both the Squire and his tale are "to be continued"' (p 136).

583 Meindl, Robert J. '"For Drye as Whit as Chalk": Allegory in Chaucer and Malory.' *SMy* 6:1 (1983), 45–58.

The episode of Canacee and the falcon 'can be read as an allegory … in which a noble peregrine falcon stands for a sinful human pilgrim … who falls from grace due to an improper commitment to "will" … This pilgrim is lured from the church – the rock of marble gray – by the devil or one of his sinful followers, who then abandons her. Suffering already from the pains of hell … the peregrine confesses her sin to Canacee, who protects and heals her and … brings it about that her brother Cambalo … causes the wicked tercelet to repent … Thus seen, the tale is also an allegory of the Virgin Mary and her role as mediatrix to her son on man's behalf' (p 52).

584 Ames, Ruth M. *God's Plenty: Chaucer's Christian Humanism*. Chicago: Loyola UP, 1984.

'An extreme example' of Chaucer's 'rather offhand respect for other religious laws' (p 217) is the praise of Cambyuskan for keeping the law 'of the secte of which that he was born' (line 17).

585 Blake, N.F. 'Geoffrey Chaucer: The Critics and the Canon.' *Archiv* 221 (1984), 65–79.

The placement of *SqT* in Hg suggests that the scribe realized that Chaucer had written no more and that the rest of the tale would not be forthcoming. It seems likely that Chaucer died before he could complete the tale (p 75).

586 Brewer, Derek S. *An Introduction to Chaucer*. London: Longman, 1984. 2nd ed., *A New Introduction to Chaucer*. 1998.

SqT is probably the work of Chaucer's maturity, unfinished because the poet has gone beyond an interest in youthful love. If, as North (**503**) has argued, an astronomical allegory underlies *SqT*, 'Chaucer may have ingeniously dabbled in some of these correspondences, rather in the spirit of composing a crossword puzzle, and then found it got too complicated ... How many people would have appreciated his ingenuity?' (p 227). The differences between the treatment of *SqH* and the placement of the tale in Hg and El (the Host's words to the Squire in El are in Hg addressed to the Franklin and lead into his tale) exemplify the 'slipperiness' of the texts of *CT*; the textual situation represents a work in progress, and is hence 'a weak foundation for modern psychosocial theories about tellers based on the tales they tell' (1998, p 329).

587 Eade, J.C. *The Forgotten Sky: A Guide to Astrology in English Literature*. Oxford: Clarendon, 1984.

To avoid the impossible suggestion that the sun's exaltation coincided with one of the faces of Mars (the sun's exaltation lies at Aries 19, whereas Mars owns the first ten degrees of that sign), Eade repunctuates Robinson's text (**55**) at lines 48–51 as follows: 'Phebus the sonne ful joly was and cleer; / For he was neigh his exaltacioun, / In Martes face, and in his mansioun / In Aries ...' With this repunctuation, 'the sun sits in Aries his mansion, near his exaltation, which lies just past the middle of the sign, and is still in Mars's face' (p 142). The date is 15 March ('the laste Idus of March'); 'this places the sun at Aries 3 – a longitude ... that *is* within Mars's face and the sun's mansion, and *does* place the sun near ... his exaltation in Aries 19' (p 142). At dawn on the following day, Canacee 'up riseth' like 'the yonge sonne / That in the Ram is foure degrees up ronne' (lines 385–6). The variation of the MSS between 'foure' and 'ten' degrees can be explained as a scribal failure to understand that the sun 'could be "up ronne" in the sense of being elevated above the horizon, not in the sense of being advanced in longitude' (p 144). Scribes amended '10' to '4' since they thought that otherwise there would be a weeklong gap in the chronology.

588 Kolve, V.A. *Chaucer and the Imagery of Narrative: The First Five Canterbury Tales*. Stanford, CA: Stanford UP, 1984.

Chaucer 'clearly meant to finish *SqT* ... for he writes as though he had: the Franklin tactfully praises it before beginning his own tale of courtesy' (pp 472–3).

589 Rudat, Wolfgang E.H. '*Gentillesse* and the Marriage Debate in the *Franklin's Tale*: Chaucer's Squires and the Question of Nobility.' *Neophil* 68 (1984), 451–70.

Although the Squire tells a tale of false *gentilesse* in an aristocratic courtly love relationship, he is only apparently criticizing the nobility; his target is young males in general, whether of noble blood or not, and the indictment of male falsehood is ironized by its source – a deserted female.

590 Ruggiers, Paul G., ed. *Editing Chaucer: The Great Tradition*. Norman, OK: Pilgrim, 1984.
A survey of editions of Chaucer's works from Caxton to Robinson. Includes essays on Skeat (**4**) by A.S.G. Edwards (pp 171–89), Manly and Rickert (**61**) by George Kane (pp 207–29), and Robinson (**55**) by George F. Reinecke (pp 231–51).

591 Sklute, Larry. *Virtue of Necessity: Inconclusiveness and Narrative Form in Chaucer's Poetry*. Columbus: Ohio UP, 1984.
The Franklin admires the Squire's *gentil* manner and his own tale is about *gentilesse*. Part 2 of *SqT* implies that *gentilesse* may easily be feigned; the Franklin, on the other hand, understands the term 'as a genuine condition of character, not influenced by birth or limited to class' (p 127). A comparison of *SqT* and *Anel* as fragments suggests that, whereas *SqT* may be intended as an ironic demonstration of 'a young man's inability to organize ... poetic materials' (p 60), *Anel* cannot be viewed so charitably; its narrator is Chaucer and the work does not suggest an ironic intention.

592 Smith, Eric. *A Dictionary of Classical Reference in English Poetry*. Cambridge: Brewer; Totowa, NJ: Barnes and Noble, 1984.
Lists classical references in some eighty English poets, with paragraphs of background material at the beginning of each entry and an index of poems, poets, and references. Eleven classical references are cited from *SqT*.

593 Blake, N.F. 'The Debate on the Order of *The Canterbury Tales*.' *RCEI* 10 (1985), 31–42.
Responding to Larry Benson's assertion that 'unfinished as *CT* obviously is, [Chaucer] was finished with it' ('The Order of the *Canterbury Tales*,' *SAC* 3 [1981], 80), Blake asks whether Chaucer would have allowed *CkT* and *SqT* to be published in an unfinished form. The scribes after the poet's death may have wanted to include everything intended for *CT*, but he might not have taken the same view. What in Hg appear as the Squire–Merchant and Merchant–Franklin links appear in El as the Squire–Franklin and Merchant–Squire links, respectively. In response to Benson's assumption that the Hg links are spurious adaptations of the Ellesmere links, Blake demonstrates how the Ellesmere readings might have derived from Hg.

593a Burnley, J.D. 'Chaucer, Usk, and Geoffrey of Vinsauf.' *Neophil* 69 (1985), 284–93.
The speech of the messenger-knight in *SqT*, lines 89–109, is the best example of the relatively few instances in the poetry of Chaucer and his contemporaries that show a specific acquaintance with the precepts of rhetorical teaching. Of its three main points – the knight's knowledge of courtly custom and diplomacy, his mastery of the necessary style of speech, and the skill of his delivery – the second replicates comments ubiquitous in grammar books

and rhetorical manuals, while the allusion to 'heigh ... style' (line 108) is 'illustrated by a parody of a particular kind of high style common in diplomatic letters of the period' (p 289).

594 Blake, N.F. *The Textual Tradition of the Canterbury Tales*. London: Arnold, 1985. Chaucer may have been working on *SqT* when he died; this was probably the assumption of the Hg scribe, who allowed only a small space after the tale, enough for a link but not for the ending of the poem (p 86). Lines 1–3, which in Hg are the Host's invitation to the Franklin to 'sey vs a tale,' are adapted in Cambridge Dd.4.24 to the Squire, who is asked to 'seye som what of loue,' the subject of the tale he is about to tell (pp 125–6).

• Review by Helen Cooper, *RES* n.s. 38 (1987), 237–8: Although its concluding plot summary suggests that *SqT* may have been deliberately broken off, Blake never considers this possibility (p 238).

• Review by Charles A. Owen, Jr., *SAC* 9 (1987), 183–7: Blake's argument for the scribal nature of the linking in Hg of *SqT, MerT,* and *FranT* shows 'the danger of ignoring aesthetic considerations' (p 186).

595 Collins, Marie. 'Feminine Response to Masculine Attractiveness in Middle English Literature.' *E&S* 38 (1985), 12–28.
The metaphors of painting and combing used by the female falcon to describe the faithless tercelet imply the 'cosmetically-achieved artificiality' (p 20) of words and appearance that she failed to recognize in her lover.

596 Conner, Edwin Lee. '*The Squire's Tale* and Its Teller: Medieval Tradition and Chaucer's Artistry of Allusion.' 1985. See **217**.
The Squire's portrait and tale are as closely related as any in *CT*. An examination of the medieval ages of man tradition shows that the Squire's *radix* trait is adolescence. *SqT* is at once an expression of the Squire's immaturity, his need for discipline and interior growth, and an exemplary fiction 'directed toward the young, and those who teach the young' (p 255). In Part 1, various signs indicate Chaucer's (but not the Squire's) intention to provide a spiritual level of meaning focused on the stranger knight's four gifts. The four objects symbolize the four cardinal virtues necessary for the soul's maturity in God. This interpretation of the gifts is the heart of a symbolic action – the *moto spiritale* of the Squire's soul – that displaces plot as the tale's center of interest. In Part 2, allusions to devotional tradition sustain the spiritual level of meaning through a prolonged analogy with the Crucifixion (figured in the parallel between the falcon and the pelican-as-Christ and in the reference to the dry tree) and the Compassion of the Virgin (represented by Canacee's pity). These allusions point up a contrast between the 'sentimental carnality' of the falcon and her tercelet and Christian faith, hope, and charity (p 212). The Squire produces an unintentional burlesque of a tale of martyrdom to love like those in *LGW*; the analogous examples of Dido, Sigune in Wolfram von Eschenbach's *Parzival,* and Dante's Francesca

da Rimini (the latter recalled specifically by a sustained pattern of references to *Inferno* 5) suggest the kind of love that Chaucer comically depicts. In the light of contemporary chronicles, *SqT* may also be intended to satirize the decadence of the court of Richard II and its 'boy king' on the eve of the Deposition.

597 David, Alfred. 'Recycling *Anelida and Arcite*: Chaucer as a Source for Chaucer.' *SAC. Proceedings, No 1, 1984: Reconstructing Chaucer*. Ed. Paul Strohm and Thomas J. Heffernan. Knoxville, TN: New Chaucer Society, 1985. Pp 105–15.

The falcon's story in *SqT* is *Anel* 'recycled – with feathers' (p 110). In reworking this 'source,' Chaucer eliminated the epic frame, and introduced in Part 1 'a fluid naturalism that validates the romance world' (p 111). The old story is distanced from us, first through the tale of Cambyuskan, second through the falcon's narrative, 'a frame within a frame' (p 112). Unlike the narrator of *Anel*, the Squire treats his tale of betrayed love with detached humor; 'the transformation of the characters into birds suggests … that tragedy viewed from a higher perspective turns into comedy' (p 113).

598 Lawton, David. *Chaucer's Narrators*. Chaucer Studies 13. Cambridge: Brewer, 1985.

Ch. 5, 'The Literary History of the Squire's Tale' (pp 106–29), distinguishes four phases in the tale's reception. The Renaissance view is marked by reverence for Chaucer and regret that he left the tale unfinished; the late Augustan and Romantic view emphasizes the sublime and romantic aspects of Part 1 and generally deprecates the episode of Canacee and the falcon; late nineteenth- and early twentieth-century scholarship concentrates on source study, illuminating the tale's structure in the process; in the criticism of the last forty years, 'preconceptions derived from the novel have joined forces uneasily with sustained close reading' (p 107). Beginning with Stillwell (**446**), modern commentary has concerned itself with the tale's tone. But what Stillwell saw as Chaucer's playful humor becomes in later interpretations irony directed at the Squire's moral failings and his incompetence as a storyteller. The decline in *SqT*'s popularity and the distortions in its critical appreciation may be traced to the inappropriate application of the Kittredgean dramatic principle. The evidence produced by Jones (**133**, **174**), Lowes (**147**), and others that 'Chaucer at one stage designed a complete plot for what he left an unfinished fragment' (p 117) calls into question the belief that *SqT* is 'dramatically' interrupted by the Franklin. Moreover, those passages of rhetorical excess often attributed to the Squire's 'psychological maladjustment' (p 115) or artistic incapacity are better explained by the notion of 'parodic tone' (p 114). The closest parallel to the tone of *SqT* can be found in Ariosto, whose treatment of the chivalric world is 'self-consciously literary … even at times zany' (p 123); Renaissance readers of *SqT* would have

seen Chaucer, like his Italian successor, as having undertaken 'a romance of truly epic proportions' (p 123). *SqT* may have been composed in the early 1380s, and hence may not have been designed originally for its place in *CT*. Blake's suggestion (**102**) that the ascription of *SqT* to its present narrator is not Chaucer's but that of his fifteenth-century editors 'confirms the wisdom of earlier generations that concentrated on the Tale, not the teller' (p 127). The 'curious and cursory' introduction to *SqT* (lines 1–8) may be the work of Thomas Hoccleve, 'the best writer of Chaucerian lines after Chaucer' (p 127); the passage's emphasis on *wille* recalls a favorite Hocclevian topos. See **784**.
• Review by Helen Cooper, *RES* n.s. 38 (1987), 382–3: Lawton makes a strong case for Chaucer's having originally intended to complete *SqT*, and 'outlines a plausible ending that avoids the incest which Squire-bashing critics have been eager to perceive in the final lines of the summary' (p 382).
• Review by A.S.G. Edwards, *ES* 68 (1987), 280–3: 'The longest chapter deals with the literary history of *SqT* – a chapter which not simply invokes, but emulates Spenser in its ramifications, ramifications which lead far away from narrative tone to Hoccleve, John Lane, the textual tradition of *CT* and Milton's praise of Chaucer' (p 282).
• Review by Dieter Mehl, *Anglia* 106 (1988), 507–10: Lawton argues convincingly that Chaucer may not have intended *SqT* for its present speaker, and that the concept of the 'unreliable narrator' is not a useful one for understanding the special qualities of the tale.
• Review by Jonathan W. Nicholls, *MLR* 83 (1988), 663–4: Although it does little to advance the book's thesis, Lawton's chapter on *SqT* offers a 'robust reassessment' of the tale and the reasons for its appeal to Spenser and Milton (p 664).
• Review by C. David Benson, *Speculum* 64 (1989), 182–3: Lawton's 'excellent, if somewhat peripheral' essay contains an effective comparison of *SqT* to *Orlando Furioso* and the intriguing suggestion that Hoccleve may have written the introductory link (p 183).

599 Mandel, Jerome. 'Courtly Love in the *Canterbury Tales*.' *ChauR* 19 (1985), 277–89.
The Squire's depiction of *amour courtois* as a relationship between birds undercuts the possibility of a serious exploration of courtly love. The spectacle of the lovelorn falcon wrapped in bandages and put in a decorated cage next to Canacee's bed reveals the comic disparity between the avian world and the human world. 'No matter how gorgeous it is, no courtly lover recuperates in a bird-cage' (p 280).

600 Middleton, Anne. 'War by Other Means: Marriage and Chivalry in Chaucer.' *SAC. Proceedings, No. 1, 1984: Reconstructing Chaucer*. Ed. Paul Strohm and Thomas J. Heffernan. Knoxville, TN: New Chaucer Society, 1985. Pp 119–33.
Chaucer thematizes chivalric representation in *SqT*; the magical gifts pre-

sented at Cambyuskan's birthday feast are read by his courtiers 'as rhetorical devices in material form, silent arguments in the "illusion of power."' 'Gentil' behavior in the tale is 'the art of deploying expressive representations, and ethical responsibility is simply a form of aesthetic responsiveness, a capacity for wonder' (p 129).

601 Pearsall, Derek. *The Canterbury Tales*. London: George Allen and Unwin, 1985.
SqT embodies traditional romance values, although the handling of supernatural machinery (e.g., the magic horse) is touched by a spirit of skepticism or rationalization. The ironic reading of the tale as a manifestation of the youthful Squire's ineptness as a narrator is methodologically suspect; the tale's awkwardnesses are 'laid more appropriately at Chaucer's door than at the Squire's' (p 142). The story of the betrayed falcon is 'told with sympathy and poignancy ... it is hard to see how Chaucer could have returned to the first part of the tale after this' (p 142). The Squire's concluding promise of what is to come is difficult to take seriously; it may be that Chaucer, 'returning to the story he left unfinished ... adapted it to *CT* by adding an impossible scenario for its continuation and then having it "dramatically" interrupted' (p 143).

602 Spearing, A.C. *Medieval to Renaissance in English Poetry*. Cambridge: Cambridge UP, 1985.
Although not sharply satiric of romance in the manner of *Thop*, *SqT* displays the 'pleasures and limits' of the genre (p 36). A synthetic text with no single identifiable source, it embodies the complications of plot and leisurely narration typical of courtly romance in the thirteenth and fourteenth centuries, developed 'as a means of conspicuous consumption of its public's ample spare time' (p 37). *SqT* reflects its teller's youth and taste for excess; 'it is delightfully appropriate that it should be terminated by the shooting down in mid-sentence of Apollo, the god of poetic inspiration, on his way into the mansion of Mercury, the god of eloquence' (p 37).

603 Baker, Donald C. 'William Thynne's Printing of the *Squire's Tale*: Manuscripts and Printer's Copy.' *SB* 39 (1986), 125–32.
In preparing his 1532 edition of *CT*, William Thynne consulted MSS as well as printed texts. For *SqT*, he probably used one or more MSS closely related to Delamere (Dl), McCormick (Mc), and Rawlinson Poet. 141 (Ra^1), and, for the latter stages of the poem, a MS or MSS from the Rawlinson Poet. 149 (Ra^2) Hatton Donat. (Ht) group. For Thynne's copy from printed texts, Pynson's second edition (PN^2), perhaps in conjunction with the second Caxton edition (CX^2) and Wynkyn de Worde (WN), is a likely candidate.

604 Burnley, J.D. 'Curial Prose in England.' *Speculum* 61 (1986), 593–614.
The speech of the stranger knight in *SqT* is much indebted to the elaborate curial style developed for public documents in the fourteenth century (p 604). The approval given to the knight's performance reflects the importance

of the impression made by the messenger himself (p 595).

605 Burrow, J.A. *The Ages of Man: A Study of Medieval Writing and Thought*. New York: Oxford UP, 1986.

The Squire's youth and his status as 'a lovyere and a lusty bacheler' (I.80) are reflected in his tale, which concerns three young Tartars; even their father, King Cambyuskan, is 'assimilated to the prevailing youthfulness' (p 171).

606 ———. 'The *Canterbury Tales* I: Romance.' In *The Cambridge Chaucer Companion*. Ed. Piero Boitani and Jill Mann. Cambridge: Cambridge UP, 1986. 2nd ed., *The Cambridge Companion to Chaucer*. 2003. Pp 109–24/pp 143–59. Excerpts in *Readings on the Canterbury Tales*. Ed. Don Nardo. San Diego, CA: Greenhaven, 1997. Pp 109–16.

Spenser's and Milton's admiration of *SqT* make one hesitate to accept the modern view that the tale is unworthy of its teller. It contains some of Chaucer's richest passages of poetic narrative: Canacee's walk at dawn, the arrival of the Arabian emissary at the Tartar feast, and especially the account of the feast's conclusion, with its 'powerful narcotic effect' (p 116/p 150). The goodnight kiss bestowed with 'galpyng mouth' by Sleep and received by the revelers with an answering yawn anticipates the 'more famous infectious yawn' (p 116/p 150) that concludes Pope's *Dunciad*. See **784**.

607 Haas, Renate. 'Chaucer's Use of the Lament for the Dead.' In *Chaucer in the Eighties*. Ed. Julian N. Wasserman and Robert H. Blanch. Syracuse, NY: Syracuse UP, 1986. Pp 23–37.

The falcon's lament for her lost love borrows elements from the lament for the dead. The mixing of modes demonstrates the magnitude of the bird's grief, and also underlines the artificiality of the lament. The stylized complaint, moving to Canacee and her ladies, strikes the reader as bathetic; Chaucer is distinguishing here between 'a sentimental fictive audience and a real one' (p 27).

608 Kelly, Henry Ansgar. *Chaucer and the Cult of Saint Valentine*. Davis Medieval Texts and Studies 5. Leiden: Brill, 1986.

The magic ring in *SqT* 'set Chaucer off on a sentimental avian romance that must be ranked among the worst narrative sequences he ever wrote' (p 7). The description of Cambyuskan's birthday celebration on 'the laste Idus of March, after the yeer' (line 47) provides evidence that Chaucer could imagine a spring-like March – at least in the Orient (pp 20–1).

609 Knight, Stephen. 'Chaucer's Religious *Canterbury Tales*.' In *Medieval English Religious and Ethical Literature: Essays in Honour of G.H. Russell*. Ed. Gregory Kratzmann and James Simpson. Cambridge: Brewer, 1986. Pp 156–66.

SqT accepts the values of courtly culture as an absolute; it is 'a deliberately overblown construction which falters of its own inauthenticity and inertia' (p 161).

610 ———. *Geoffrey Chaucer*. Oxford: Blackwell, 1986.

The Squire 'is an ineffectual ideologue for his own status, and offers no more than a brief and florid cultural diversion, a literary equivalent of his embroidered vest' (p 117).

611 Mehl, Dieter. *Geoffrey Chaucer: An Introduction to his Narrative Poetry*. Cambridge: Cambridge UP, 1986. Rev. and expanded translation of Geoffrey Chaucer. *Eine Einführung seine erzählenden Dichtungen* (Berlin: Schmidt, 1973). Although we cannot be certain whether the Franklin's words to the Squire were meant to serve as a dramatic interruption of the narrative, *SqT* is effectively complete in that it successfully characterizes its teller and presents all the important elements of a specific type of romance – the indiscriminate amassing of adventures and wonders that naïve listeners expected of the form. The use of an animal fable makes it difficult for us to take seriously the courtly pathos of Part 2; in addition, the Squire's idea of courtly love focuses on its 'superficial symptoms,' and the falcon's use of the image of the caged bird seems almost like 'an involuntary admission ... that her lover felt his devotion to be a kind of imprisonment' (p 164). The Squire seems unaware of the potential comedy of his material. But the tale's ironies should not be overstressed. Its central purpose is not to hold the Squire up to ridicule, nor should it be read as 'the dramatic monologue of a sharply drawn individual' (p 163). Chaucer is less concerned with mocking courtly conventions than with reviewing the traditions and possibilities of courtly narrative; the Franklin's response to the Squire's performance 'shows that one listener at least is sincerely impressed by the surface splendour of the story' (p 165).
• Review by C. David Benson, *SAC* 10 (1988), 174–7: Mehl's reading of *SqT* does justice both to the tale's genuine charm and to its limitations, and shows us why it appealed to Spenser and Milton (p 176).

612 Miller, Robert P. 'Chaucer's Rhetorical Rendition of Mind: *The Squire's Tale*.' In *Chaucer and the Craft of Fiction*. Ed. Leigh A. Arrathoon. Rochester, MN: Solaris, 1986. Pp 219–40.
SqT renders rhetorically the characteristics of the Squire's portrait: thematically, it treats fashionable but superficial manners and frivolities; structurally, it lacks a clear purpose and inner direction; stylistically, it is self-consciously concerned with appearance. Rather than simply mocking the romance genre, as Stillwell (**446**) suggests, *SqT*'s artistic infelicities represent dramatically 'the as-yet-unstructured mind of the narrator' (p 221). In striving to emulate his father's rhetoric, the Squire misconstrues the style and sentiments of *KnT*; he similarly distorts Boethius in the falcon's speech about 'propre kynde' (line 610). Although the Squire condemns the 'lewed peple' (line 221) for their skeptical attitude toward the strange knight's gifts, his own admiration of the magical and the marvelous marks him as one who prefers illusion to reality, and values Art above Nature.

613 Minnis, A.J. 'From Medieval to Renaissance? Chaucer's Position on Past

Gentility.' *PBA* 72 (1986), 205–46.
In contrast to the Franklin's nervous assertion of the superiority of Christian truths to pagan beliefs, the Squire praises Cambyuskan for acting in accordance with the best law available to him, and treats magic as a fact of pagan life (pp 236–7).

614 Payne, Robert O. *Geoffrey Chaucer*. 2nd ed. Boston: Twayne, 1986.
'It is nearly impossible to guess how *SqT* might fit into any conjectural thematic, stylistic, or generic associational pattern that might structure *CT*' (p 125).

615 Rogers, William E. *Upon the Ways: The Structure of The Canterbury Tales*. English Literary Studies Monographs 36. Victoria, BC: ELS, 1986.
SqT can be read as a rejection of the irony and cynicism of *MerT*, but is more immediately concerned with 'the central theme of fragments III–V – the value and significance of human experience' (p 71). Contrasting the courtiers' superficial reaction to the magic gifts with Canacee's empathetic response to falcon's sad story, the tale shows us that 'experience can have value only to the extent that one is capable ... of valid contemplation' (p 72). The Squire's frequent use of *occupatio* reinforces the importance of immediate experience and proper contemplation 'by telling us, in essence, "You had to be there"' (p 72). Yet the Squire's privileging of presence ultimately creates a world which is 'all phenomenon and no law ... No principle gives coherence to events or makes distinctions of relative importance' (p 73).

616 Benson, Larry D., gen. ed. *The Riverside Chaucer*. 1987. See **108**.
The Squire's taste in chivalric romance is as much in accord with the latest fashions as is his elegant dress. Chaucer probably intended the tale to be unfinished, at least once it was assigned to the Squire (p 13).

617 Bishop, Ian. *The Narrative Art of the Canterbury Tales: A Critical Study of the Major Poems*. London: Dent, 1987.
SqT is not intended to expose the incompetence of its teller, but is rather a sympathetic portrait of its youthful narrator's imaginative universe. The poem's two parts encapsulate the Squire's response to the 'masculine and public' and the 'feminine and intimate' aspects of romance, respectively (p 50). The account of Cambyuskan's birthday feast, which recalls the opening scene of *SGGK*, combines the Squire's attraction to oriental exoticism with his nostalgia for Arthurian legend. Canacee embodies his ideal of a young woman; by leaving her on the brink of a world of painful experience, the Squire shows himself to be 'the true son of his father' (p 51).

618 Blamires, Alcuin. *The Canterbury Tales*. London: Macmillan; Atlantic Highlands, NJ: Humanities Press, 1987.
The falcon's account of the deceptive tercel is Chaucer's most elaborate presentation of 'counterfeit intent ... small wonder that the Squire imagines elsewhere in his tale a magic mirror – portable lie-detector – in which you

can see "openly" a man's ulterior intentions toward you' (p 59).

619 De Weever, Jacqueline. *Chaucer Name Dictionary: A Guide to Astrological, Biblical, Historical, Literary, and Mythological Names in the Works of Geoffrey Chaucer*. New York: Garland, 1987.
Names in *SqT* that fall under the categories listed in the title are explicated (*Pegasee* [line 207] is omitted). Entries include biographical, historical, and mythological information; references to Chaucer's use of the name; etymologies and variant spellings; and bibliographical references. Place names are excluded.

620 Gray, Douglas. 'Chaucer and *Gentilesse*.' In *One Hundred Years of English Studies in Dutch Universities*. Ed. G.H.V. Bunt, E.S. Kooper, J.L. Mackenzie, and D.R.M. Wilkinson. Amsterdam: Rodopi, 1987. Pp 1–27.
Although the falcon's tale is about false *gentilesse*, she eloquently expresses the close association between *gentilesse* and *pitee* in her praise of Canacee's compassion (p 23).

621 Howard, Donald R. *Chaucer: His Life, His Works, His World*. New York: Dutton, 1987.
Phase Two of the composition of *CT* (ca 1389–96) includes 'tales ineptly told' (p 445): *Thop, MkT, SqT,* and possibly *PrT*. The Squire shows himself unable to handle his complex narrative; his rhetorical ineptness is part of the tale's appeal. It is possible that the Franklin's words of praise are intended as 'a kindly interruption to get the Squire out of the labyrinth he has entered' (p 446).

622 Jordan, Carmel. 'Soviet Archeology and the Setting of the *Squire's Tale*.' *ChauR* 22 (1987), 128–40.
Soviet archeological excavations reveal close correspondences between the historical city of Sarai, the imperial capital of the Golden Horde in Russia during the fourteenth century, and the setting of *SqT*. From the mid-thirteenth century to the end of the fourteenth century, Sarai was renowned for the beauty of its architecture and for the opulence of its court spectacles, which featured magical entertainments and optical illusions. Objects with mystical connotations, including magnificent rings and mirrors, were among the artifacts found in the city's ruins; mysteriously inscribed chalices, crucibles, and pipes also suggest an interest in alchemical pursuits. Two horses, gifts to the Khans at Cambaluc and Sarai from Pope Benedict XII, were the occasion for an ode in which a 'Heavenly Horse' is described as having flown magically across the seas to reach the Khan. Discoveries of workshops devoted to the manufacture of equestrian articles reveal ornately decorated brass or iron horse armor; covered almost completely with armor in the Mongol fashion, horses would have appeared, like the steed in *SqT*, to be made of metal. Chaucer's knowledge of Sarai could have come from his association with Genoese merchants; the Genoese had strong trade relations

with the Mongol empire, an embassy at Sarai, and a large resident population in the capital city.

623 Lawler, Traugott. 'Deconstructing *The Canterbury Tales*: Con.' *SAC Proceedings, No. 2, 1986. Fifth International Congress, 20–23 March 1986, Philadelphia, Pennsylvania.* Ed. John V. Fleming and Thomas J. Heffernan. Knoxville, TN: New Chaucer Society, 1987. Pp 83–91. Repr. in *Critical Essays on Chaucer's Canterbury Tales* (see **390**). Pp 222–9.

The confusions in the falcon's simile comparing the faithless tercelet to a caged bird who returns to the woods may be read as deconstructing a series of binary oppositions (e.g., male/female, nature/art, social status/moral worth), showing them to be the author's or society's constructions, and perhaps revealing as well Chaucer's anxieties about such issues as gender and *gentilesse*. Additionally, these oppositions and contradictions mirror the larger division of the tale into two thematically and stylistically contrasted parts. The discontinuities of the simile are, however, repaired through Canacee's sympathetic listening to the falcon's speech. Like deconstruction, *SqT* opens up gaps and discloses differences; but it then attempts to bridge those gaps. 'Where Chaucer parts company with Derrida is in his willingness to give us narratives of presence and closure: in place of the deconstructionist's skepticism, he offers us faith' (p 90).

624 Quinn, William A. 'Chaucer's Janglerye.' *Viator* 18 (1987), 309–20.

In *SqT*, *janglerye* (lines 220, 261) is produced by 'unstable knowledge' (p 317) – the mysterious gifts of the stranger knight, the causes of natural phenomena. Only true knowledge terminates *janglyng* (line 257), which, 'like the Squire himself … needs to be silenced because it never stops of its own accord' (p 317).

625 Seymour, M.C. 'Hypothesis, Hyperbole, and the Hengwrt Manuscript of the *Canterbury Tales*.' *ES* 68 (1987), 214–19.

Blake's suggestion (**558**) that *SqT* was incomplete because Chaucer had not finished it ignores the 'clear satiric pointers' (p 216) that reveal the tale to be a parody of courtly romance, dramatically interrupted by the Franklin.

626 Stone, Brian. *Chaucer*. Harmondsworth, UK: Penguin, 1987.

The Squire attempts to emulate the high style of his father's narrative; had he been allowed to continue, he might have produced an interlaced romance involving the stranger knight's gifts. The falcon's true passion and fidelity in Part 2 serves an indirect riposte to *MerT* (p 106).

627 Item cancelled.

628 Brewer, Derek S. 'Orality and Literacy in Chaucer.' In *Mündlichkeit und Schriftlichkeit im englischen Mittelater*. Ed. Willi Erzgräber and Sabine Volk. ScriptOralia 5. Tübingen: Narr, 1988. Pp 85–119.

The wordplay on *stile* and *style* (line 105–6) – perhaps more properly called a 'jingle or word-echo than a pun' – proclaims 'in a characteristic Chaucerian paradox the simplicity of his own style in a way that is not itself simple' (p 95).

629 Brunetti, Giuseppe. *Sui Canterbury Tales*. Padova: Unipress, 1988.
SqT is incomplete, but Chaucer may have intended to develop the story of Cambyuskan and his three sons into an interlaced romance, a genre more traditional than that employed by the Knight in his tale (p 7).

630 Coote, Stephen. *English Literature of the Middle Ages*. London: Penguin, 1988.
Chaucer may have intended *SqT* as a satire of the excessive narrative complexity of much medieval romance. The Squire himself is somewhat bewildered by the fertility of his own invention (p 197).

631 Davenport, W.A. *Chaucer: Complaint and Narrative*. Cambridge: Brewer, 1988.
SqT belongs among the 'Composites of Courtly Romance' (p 41), late fourteenth- and fifteenth-century works that employ segments of earlier romances as building blocks and favor multiple plots, exotic settings, and magical objects. The composite nature of *SqT* is also evident in its combining of human and animal characters, and in its juxtaposition of the public narrative of Part 1 with the private lyric complaint of Part 2. Part 1 is itself further 'mixed' by the shifting of the narrative between full engagement with the scene and gestures of distancing and withdrawal (e.g., in the Squire's frequent use of *occupatio*). This sophisticated rhetorical strategy 'asks for our interest and yet allows us to limit it, assess it, recognise its ironies' (p 43). The characteristic qualities of Part 1 emerge in lines 275–87, 'the most striking instance of Chaucer's use of a voice which is specifically "not Squire"' (p 46). By reading such a moment as a demonstration of the Squire's inadequacies as a storyteller, we miss the 'knowing, nostalgic quality of the composition,' which at once evokes the world of romance and expresses the narrator's alienation from that world, turning it into 'a distant dance of phantoms and shadows of the imagination' (p 46). Canacee's rising at dawn 'is a modified, feminine version of the beginning of a romance quest' (p 46), which modulates into the world of dream poem and fable with the appearance of the talking bird. Like Part 1, the falcon scene mixes seriousness and detachment; the familiar motifs of the complaint are mingled with 'hints of burlesque' (p 47). The logical development of the story would involve the love of Canacee and the stranger knight of Part 1. But Canacee 'is caught in the results of Chaucer's compositeness' (p 49), displaced from the role of heroine into that of confidante. The Canacee–falcon episode – like *SqT* as a whole – fails to reconcile romance narrative with lyrical *dit*, and 'is left dangling between stools' (p 49).
• Review by Alfred David, *SAC* 12 (1990), 269–71: The book's strength lies in its notion of Chaucer working through artistic problems in his poetry. Davenport's reading of *SqT* as a dual structure – a narrative introducing a potentially long romance, linked to a lyric tale told by the falcon to Canacee

– 'brings out the story's true charm and virtuosity and rescues it from interpretations attempting to read it as a deliberately botched effort to make fun of the Squire's ineptitude' (p 270).

632 Fyler, John. 'Domesticating the Exotic in the *Squire's Tale.*' *ELH* 55 (1988), 1–26. Repr. in *Chaucer's Cultural Geography*. Ed. Kathryn Lynch. New York: Routledge, 2002. Pp 32–55.
SqT simultaneously examines the distinctive concerns of romance narrative – 'questions of identity ... distinctions between self and other; the difficulties of making discriminations in a mysterious, magical world' (p 2) – and the Squire's own motives as a storyteller. The stranger knight's gifts offer a means of recapturing an unfallen world of freshness and wholeness. But 'alienation and disenchantment' (p 4) enter the tale in the skeptical crowd's refusal to grant the objects their exotic otherness, in the Squire's own ambivalence about the Tartar court, and his repeated reductions of the marvelous to the mundane. The pattern of 'marvels debunked and fresh beginnings aborted' (p 10) calls into question the Squire's innocence as a narrator of romance. Each of his three attempts to enter into a point of view outside his own – as a Christian European imagining a heathen Tartar, a human being imagining a bird, and a man imagining a woman – is colored by self-absorption and self-interest: Cambyuskan's court is at once 'comfortably familiar and convincingly exotic' (p 13); the 'imperfect homology between human and avian terms' (p 15) produces jarringly comic effects in Canacee's interview with the falcon, especially in the latter's Boethian exemplum; and the Squire's 'extreme partisanship on behalf of women' (p 18) is rendered suspect by his own amorous interests. *SqT*'s romance trappings comment primarily on the Squire's own behavior as a lover. But Chaucer also manipulates generic conventions to explore his favorite myth of the Golden Age and declining world; the tale shows 'how fully romance reflects a basic human desire for reintegration, for abolishing the distance caused by alienating categories; and it also shows how vigorously such categories resist their own dissolution' (p 21).

633 North, J.D. *Chaucer's Universe*. Oxford: Clarendon; New York: Oxford UP, 1988. Repr. with additional preliminary matter and corrections, 1990.
Embedded in the planetary events described in Part 1 of *SqT* are both astronomical indications of a particular day and year (15 March 1383) and, below the surface, 'an allegory of extraordinary richness' (p 264). Cambyuskan is associated with Mars, the stranger knight with Mercury, the steed of brass with the Sun (as well as with the constellation Pegasus and medieval astronomical timepieces), Canacee with the star δ Piscium and her attendants with 'the stars forming the fishing line in the constellation of Pisces' (p 280), the *knotte* that will conclude Canacee's walk (line 401–8) with another star in Pisces, and Algarsyf with Jupiter. Lines 671–2 describe the Sun's entrance

into the domicile of Mercury (i.e., the sign of Gemini). In 1383, this situation obtained on May 13, when Saturn and Venus would have been in almost precise conjunction, a configuration which was thought to portend marriages of kin. Recognizing that 'the planets on that day spelled out a message of incest' (p 284), the Franklin interrupts the Squire to forestall a tale unfit for the pilgrim audience. The precision of the astronomical references bespeaks Chaucer's intimate knowledge of the subject. But he is also a 'master of concealment' (p 285), encoding within his narrative a cryptic astronomical subtext that would have engaged his audience even if they lacked the key to deciphering it. The peregrine falcon corresponds to Vega, the chief star in the constellation Lyra, sometimes glossed as 'Vultur Cadens'; the falcon, who at first sits 'ful hye' over Canacee's head (line 411), is subsequently referred to four times as falling (lines 431, 442, 464, 473). The tercelet may be identified with the planet Mercury, whose movements are 'analogous to the to-ing and fro-ing of the false lover' (1990, xiii).

• Review by Angus Clarke, *N&Q* n.s. 37 (1990), 76: 'North offers ... an elegantly suggestive explanation for the abrupt ending of *SqT*' (p 76).

• Review by M.C. Seymour, *ES* 71 (1990), 67–70: '*SqT* is a romantic spoof ... the astronomical elements ... must be part of the spoof. In concentrating so informedly on the astronomy, North has failed to see the wood for the trees' (p 68). North's 'equations' (p 69) seem remarkably distant from the tale's parodic intent.

• Review by Linda Ehrsam Voigts, *Isis* 81 (1990), 567–9: North's analyses of *SqT* and *Mars* reveal a high level of astronomical expertise, and are 'the most satisfying treatments I have read' (p 568).

• Review by Caroline D. Eckhardt, *Speculum* 66 (1991), 928–30: North's shifting of his earlier conclusions (see **503**) about the astronomical sources of the names of Canacee and her brothers is 'slightly disconcerting. However, it is much to North's credit that he himself points out the variations in his readings and explains why his choices among alternative allegories have changed' (p 929).

• Review by Daniel J. Ransom, *ANQ* n.s. 4 (1991), 33–7: Some of North's more oblique astrological allegories (e.g., his rejection of the traditional connection of the *knotte* with Horace's *nodus* in favor of supposed reference to a star in Pisces) suggest that he may simply be 'making an occult science of serendipity' (p 36).

634 Strauss, Jennifer. '"I kan nat seye": The Rhetoric of Narratorial Self-Consciousness in Chaucer, especially in *The Canterbury Tales*.' *AUMLA* 69 (1988), 164–79.

The Squire exhibits 'a consciousness of rhetoric together with an uneasiness in handling it' (p 169); the summary of coming attractions near the end of Part 2 is 'a kind of reverse *occupatio*, threatening to leave out nothing in an unwitting parody of the narrative elephantiasis that sometimes affects medieval romance' (p 170).

635 Cooper, Helen. *The Canterbury Tales*. Oxford Guides to Chaucer. Oxford: Clarendon, 1989; pbk ed., 1991. 2nd ed., 1996.

The discussion of *SqT* treats the Prologue, date and text, genre, sources and analogues, structure, themes, the tale in context, and style. The content of the Prologue, which in Hg and other MSS is used to link *MerT* with *FranT*, suggests that Chaucer wrote it with the Merchant and Squire in mind; the migration of the passage around *CT* is probably due to its having been written on a separate leaf. Attempts to date the tale have been inconclusive. Arguments from the quality of the poetry are generally tendentious. The allusion to Boethius in Part 2 would seem to eliminate a very early date; the interest in rhetorical practice, shared with *ClT* and *FranT*, may indicate that *SqT* was written during the main period of composition of *CT*. Also problematic is *SqT*'s place in the *CT* sequence; the order adopted by most editors (*ClT–MerT–SqT–FranT*) appears in relatively few MSS, though they include El and the early Harley 7334. The MSS afford no clue as to whether *SqT* was left unfinished, deliberately broken off, or whether the later pages were lost from the original exemplar. *SqT* is a romance, similar to the lengthy interlaced romances most common in French but of which some fourteenth-century English examples survive. If the tale was intended as a parody of romance, 'there is not a great difference between the original romances and the parody ... Worse examples were written with a straight face' (p 219). Cooper summarizes scholarship on the French and Oriental analogues of *SqT*, concluding that Chaucer was probably 'aware of the Oriental origins of the various elements of the tale and assembled them deliberately' (p 220). Although Chaucer's knowledge of the French analogues is 'empirically more likely' (p 219) than his familiarity with the Oriental materials, the relation between the two parts of the tale is more typical of Oriental than of Western interlaced stories. The most obvious analogues to Part 2 are Chaucer's own writings: 'the whole falcon episode could be described as being by the *Parliament* out of *Anelida*' (p 222). The tale's two parts are different in subject matter and style, and also in point of view: Part 1 tells a story, Part 2 tells of a story being told. If Chaucer had completed *SqT*, the flashback of Part 2 would presumably have been completed as a direct narrative, connected with the material introduced in Part 1. The tale's major themes are 'marvels, faithfulness in love, *gentillesse*' (p 223). The flawed treatment of this subject matter that has troubled modern readers is less likely to represent Chaucer's portrait of the Squire's immaturity than to reflect the tendency, common in romance, to treat all issues with a comparable degree of seriousness. This 'stylistic flattening' (p 225) distinguishes *SqT* from more nuanced kinds of romance narration (e.g., *KnT* and, especially, *FranT*) in which *gentilesse* and the mar-

velous are treated with a depth and structural cohesion unmatched in the preceding tale. The Squire lacks a sense of cause and effect, concentrating on the present moment to the detriment of the story's logical progression. His favorite stylistic mode is the superlative, an imitation (rather than, as in *Thop,* a parody) of a popular romance style that reveals the limitations of that style – its 'concentration on manner at the expense of matter' (p 229).
• Review by C. David Benson, *SAC* 13 (1991), 183–6: Cooper sensibly points out that *SqT*'s exploration of the limitations of romance does not turn the tale into parody. Like Ariosto, Chaucer could mingle mockery with high sophistication (p 185).

636 DiMarco, Vincent Joseph. 'The Historical Basis of Chaucer's Squire's Tale.' *Edebiyât* n.s. 1 (1989), 1–22. Repr. in Lynch, ed., *Chaucer's Cultural Geography* (see **632**). Pp 56–75.
The romantic circumstances surrounding the events of *SqT* are modeled on contemporary geographical and political realities. The kingdom of 'Arabe and of Inde' (line 110), whose ruler sends an emissary to Cambyuskan's court, would have been identified in Chaucer's day with Middle India or India Minor, the area encompassing southern Arabia, which from 1252 to 1382 was ruled by the Bahri Mamluks at Cairo. The emissary's appearance at 'Sarray, in the land of Tartarye' (line 9) seems to foreshadow Canacee's betrothal. The relations of the Mamluk sultan el-Melik en-Nasir (ruled 1291–2, 1298–1308, 1309–40) and Özbeg [Uzbek] Khan (ruled 1313–41) of the Golden Horde included the marriage of the Tartar princess Tulunbeg to Nasir in an attempt to formalize the Mamluk–Mongol alliance; the situation in *SqT* reflects the strength of Mamluk Egypt and the shrewdness of its foreign policy. Nasir's diplomacy created a coalition that shattered the 'European dream of a Mongol–Christian alliance to defeat Egypt and regain the Holy Land' (p 131). It is ironic that the tale told by the son of the crusading Knight depicts the circumstances that hint at the ultimate failure of later crusading enterprises. Yet *SqT* presents a sympathetic portrait of the sophistication and political acumen of 'infidel' culture. (In an Appendix, DiMarco proposes a derivation of the name *Cambyuskan* from *Khan Usbekkan.)

637 Edwards, Robert R. 'The Failure of Invention: Chaucer's Squire's Tale.' In *Ratio and Invention: A Study of Medieval Lyric and Narrative*. Nashville, TN: Vanderbilt UP, 1989. Pp 131–45.
SqT is a failed attempt to synthesize narrative form with new or unconventional subject matter. Chaucer attempts to give new configurations to the traditions of medieval romance, as in the translation, in the opening scene, of an Arthurian court to the Orient. He is unable, however, to control the rich possibilities of his materials, and fragments his narrative with repeated professions of inadequacy. The eloquent stranger knight who visits Cambyuskan's court represents one version of the Squire's ideal poet–craftsman.

We also evaluate the Squire's performance in relation to that of his father; in contrast to *KnT*, *SqT* collapses rather than sustains 'hierarchies of value' (p 139). The distinction between mysterious powers and human achievements, for example, is blurred in the empirical magic that governs the operation of the knight's three gifts. The view of magic in *SqT* is 'closer to the emergent tradition of experimental science than to the standard conventions of late medieval romance' (p 141). But Chaucer's poetic experiment with mechanical magic 'fails ... because he does not discover the *interior sententia* that produces a unified narrative' (p 144).

• Review by Catherine Batt, *MLR* 86 (1991), 962–3: The 'able study' of *SqT* fails to account for the organizational strategies 'most remarkable for their interplay of lyric and narrative referents' (p 963).

638 Ferster, Judith. 'Writing on the Ground: Interpretation in Chester Play XII.' In *Sign, Sentence, Discourse: Language in Medieval Thought and Literature*. Ed. Julian N. Wasserman and Lois Roney. Syracuse, NY: Syracuse UP, 1989. Pp 179–93.

In the debate over the significance of the brass steed, the chaos of multiple interpretations prevails until the stranger knight explains how to work it, but not how it works: 'authority steps in with instruction and evasion. The moment is emblematic of the structure of *CT* as a whole, a chorus of voices presenting a world view in a contest never finished and never judged, but closed by the instructions and evasions of *Ret*, and by its deference to God' (p 188).

639 Osborn, Marijane. 'The Squire's "Steed of Brass" as Astrolabe: Some Implications for *The Canterbury Tales*.' In *Hermeneutics and Medieval Culture*. Ed. Patrick Gallacher and Helen Damico. Albany: State U of New York P, 1989. Pp 121–31.

See **730**.

640 Seymour, M.C. 'Some Satiric Pointers in the *Squire's Tale*.' *ES* 70 (1989), 311–14.

SqT – '*Thop* writ large' (p 313) – parodies courtly romance. In the obtuse narrator, we see Chaucer recalling an earlier self, shaped by memories of the 'metrical extravagances' (p 312) he produced in Prince Lionel's household. Foremost among the tale's unambiguous satiric markers are 'the Squire's rhetorical advances and collapses, his total inability to hold a narrative line, his empty fluency of comment and detail' (p 312). The parody in Part 2 is 'gloriously expansive' (p 312); that in Part 1 is more subtly developed. (Seymour comments on the satiric content of lines 47, 51, 81, 90, 142, 246, and 272.) See **690**.

641 Strohm, Paul. *Social Chaucer*. Cambridge, MA: Harvard UP, 1989.

The crowd's response to the magical gifts at Cambyuskan's feast seems to present a diversity of views. But the Squire's skepticism about marvels and his scorn for the ignorance of the viewers undercuts the potential 'polyvocality' (p 170) of the discourse, replacing it with his own singlemindedness.

642 Wetherbee, Winthrop. *Geoffrey Chaucer: The Canterbury Tales.* Cambridge: Cambridge UP, 1989.
SqT calls into question its teller's courtly idealism. The Squire fails to examine his value system; in the 'hermetic' (p 49) world of his tale, the entrance of a stranger knight does not – as it does in *SGGK* – lead to a 'testing confrontation' (p 47) with a more complex reality. The idealizing tone of *SqT* is constantly undercut by 'oddly mundane details' (p 47) that have no apparent purpose other than as a manifestation of the Squire's taste for novelty. Although the note of idealism is more consistently sustained in the Canacee–falcon idyll, this episode comes close to depicting gentility as an intrinsically empty notion and representing the rhetoric of *gentilesse* as merely the self-indulgent cultivation of fine feelings. The falcon's 'disoriented and arbitrary' (p 49) discourse, with its mishandling of Boethius's bird simile, 'illustrates the danger of viewing life through the Squire's courtly vision: a world confected entirely out of the values and trappings of courtliness can become itself a cage, divorced from reality like the beautiful birdhouse Canacee creates for the falcon' (p 49).

643 White, Hugh. 'Chaucer Compromising Nature.' *RES* n.s. 40 (1989), 157–78. See **716**.

The Squire's Tale, 1990–1999

644 Ganim, John. *Chaucerian Theatricality.* Princeton, NJ: Princeton UP, 1990.
In the Squire's narrative, as in those of the Clerk and the Franklin, sophisticated literary values are imperfectly integrated with an older stratum of popular and folk themes; the Squire is uncertain about, even embarrassed by, the status of the magical in his tale. The Squire's taciturn preamble to his tale embodies both the virtues and the limitations of courtliness, which cannot indulge in praise of the self. In his afterword to *SqT*, the Franklin uses the Squire as the model of courtliness against which he judges his own son, thereby historicizing the Squire's values and performance (pp 92–8).

645 Spearing, A.C. 'Rewriting romance: Chaucer's and Dryden's *Wife of Bath's Tale.*' In *Chaucer Traditions: Studies in Honour of Derek Brewer*. 1990. See **227**. Pp 234–48.
SqT is a 'critical rewriting' of romance, 'a generous and affectionate burlesque of all that is most complicated, sentimental, and unrealistic in courtly romance' (p 234).

646 Tigges, Wim. 'Romance and Parody.' In *Companion to Middle English Romance*. Ed. Henk Aertsen and Alasdair A. MacDonald. Amsterdam: VU UP,

1990. Pp 129–51.

In *SqT*, the conventions of the supernatural come under attack; the magical objects in Part 1 'are not so much ridiculed as reasoned away' (p 138).

647 Wicher, Andrzej. 'A Discussion of the Archetype of the Supernatural Husband and the Supernatural Wife as It Appears in some of Geoffrey Chaucer's *Canterbury Tales*.' *REALB* 7 (1990), 19–60.

The betrayed falcon's story in *SqT* may be read as a modified version of the folktale of the man who becomes the lover of a fairy woman, spends some time with her in fairyland, and then abandons her by returning to his own land. Chaucer's falcons do not seem to be human beings metamorphosed by magic, a circumstance that apparently prevents any solution to the she-falcon's plight along the lines of the transformation of the old hag in *WBT*.

648 Brewer, Derek S. 'Feasts in England and English Literature in the Fourteenth Century.' In *Feste und Feiern im Mittelalter. Paderborner Symposion des Mediävistenverbandes*. Ed. Detlef Altenburg, Jörg Jarnut, and H.-H. Steinhoff. Sigmaringen: Thorbecke, 1991. Pp 13–26.

Chaucer is more interested in the personal relationships of the participants in Cambyuskan's birthday feast than in the splendid food, drink, and appurtenances, which are dismissed with some impatience (p 22).

649 Brown, Peter, and Andrew Butcher. *The Age of Saturn: Literature and History in the Canterbury Tales*. Oxford: Blackwell, 1991.

In contrast to the Franklin, whose command of language is acquired rather than innate, the Squire deploys the arts of rhetoric as an aspect of his gentility. The Squire uses rhetorical tropes as 'weapons of social status' (p 69); combined with his inadequacies as a narrator, his social pretensions alienate his listeners and necessitate the Franklin's interruption. Echoing contemporary criticisms of aristocratic cultural values, Part 2 of *SqT* tells a story of 'chivalric betrayal' (p 70) in which gentility itself is seen as endangered.

650 Burrow, J.A. 'The Biennial Chaucer Lecture: Poems Without Endings.' *SAC* 13 (1991), 17–37.

Early readers of *SqT* – scribes, printers, editors, and continuators – assume that the tale is incomplete, either because Chaucer never finished it or because the conclusion has been lost; their comments and continuations attest to their unhappiness with what the textual tradition has left us. Many modern critics, on the other hand, find the tale satisfactory as it stands, viewing it as 'a deliberately botched job, designed to be cut off, like *Thop*, once the satiric point has been made' (pp 30–1). The admiring testimony of earlier readers should make us wary of such judgments, which reflect the legacy of the Romantic taste for the fragmentary, the modern suspicion of closure, and the unwillingness of scholars to admit 'the accidental and the contingent … disinclination or distraction or death' (p 36) into discussions of poems.

651 Frese, Dolores Warwick. *An Ars Legendi for Chaucer's Canterbury Tales:*

Re-Constructive Reading. Gainesville: U of Florida P, 1991.
El represents Chaucer's own final plan for *CT*, recoverable from the 'ingenious textual systematics' (p 2) of the poem itself, which disclose the 'hermeneutical intent of [Chaucer's] literate aesthetics' (p 172). *SqT*'s astronomical and astrological references reveal the tale's '"midday" status' (p 167); counting *GP* as the first 'tale' (and omitting *CYT*, a late addition), the story of the '"yong son[n]e"' stands as the twelfth of the twenty-four tales (p 168). *SqT*'s central place in Chaucer's 'cosmographic *involucrum*' (p 171) is further reinforced by analogies between the *hors* (line 208) that can carry its rider anywhere in the cosmos within twenty-four hours and the poet's literary 'hors' (or *horae*) of the twenty-four tales (p 170); by the 'seel and ... bond' (line 131) employed by the horse's creator, recalling the techniques of poetic *conjointure* (p 171); by the allusion to Gawain, whose shield (in *SGGK*) depicts an 'endless knot' parallel to the hermeneutical *knotte* (line 401) of the Squire's narration; and by the tale's final, fragmentary lines (lines 671–2), in which, as the Squire's 'Phaetonically divine chariot of the sun [is] depicted in its pretentious ascent to the heights of mercurial eloquence ... the poetic text ... slyly predicts its own imminent disappearance' (p 173).

652 Fyler, John. 'Man, Men, and Women in Chaucer's Poetry.' In *The Olde Daunce: Love, Friendship, Sex, and Marriage in the Medieval World*. Ed. Robert R. Edwards and Stephen Spector. Albany: State U of New York P, 1991. Pp 154–76.
See **632**.

653 Gittes, Katharine S. *Framing the Canterbury Tales: Chaucer and the Medieval Frame Narrative Tradition*. New York: Greenwood, 1991.
The Franklin's interruption of the Squire indicates that the tale is intentionally incomplete; like most medieval frame narratives, *SqT* is fragmentary and open-ended (p 111). The Squire's choice of subject portrays him as a romantic, while his inefficient use of *occupatio* contrasts him with his father; the Knight is a 'polished raconteur,' the Squire 'earnest, but unpolished' (p 131).

654 Hill, John M. *Chaucerian Belief: The Poetics of Reverence and Delight*. New Haven, CT: Yale UP, 1991.
SqT reveals its teller as youthful and somewhat inexperienced, but 'workmanlike and appropriately conscious of his limitations' (p 83). He prefers to honor beauty and the marvelous for what they are rather than engaging in fruitless speculation about their origins and workings. Like the narrator of *BD*, 'he has trouble feeling anything at all strongly' (p 84); having himself not yet loved and lost, he fails to value the sentiments expressed by the stricken falcon. As the Franklin realizes, the Squire is likely to deepen as he matures; an understanding of the relation between the stranger knight's gifts and the power of rhetoric or of the questions of truth and interpretation

raised by the falcon's narrative may well lie in his future. For now, however, 'his telling and the artifice of the tale remain a gilded cage that confines rather than opens up its material' (p 85).

• Review by Edward E. Foster, *PhilosLit* 15 (1991), 367–8: In his comments on *SqT* and *FranT*, Hill 'offers not interpretations that flow from his thesis but plot summaries accompanied by assertions about meaning which provide useful occasions to speculate about "knowing feelingly"' (p 368).

• Review by Dolores Warwick Frese, *CY* 2 (1995), 172–9: Hill's linking of the Squire's and Franklin's performances, each of which 'stops short of any sufficient sorting out of truth and falsehood,' is 'particularly acute' (pp 176–7).

655 Mann, Jill. 'Chaucer and the "Woman Question."' In *This Noble Craft: Proceedings of the Xth Research Symposium of the Dutch and Belgian University Teachers of Old and Middle English and Historical Linguistics, Utrecht, 19–20 January 1989*. Ed. Erik Kooper. Amsterdam: Rodopi, 1991. Pp 173–88.
See **729**.

656 ———. *Geoffrey Chaucer*. Atlantic Highlands, NJ: Humanities Press International, 1991.
See **729**.

657 Owen, Charles A., Jr. 'The Falcon's Complaint in The Squire's Tale.' In *Rebels and Rivals: The Contestive Spirit in the Canterbury Tales*. Ed. Susanna Greer Fein, David Raybin, and Peter C. Braeger. Studies in Medieval Culture 29. Kalamazoo: Medieval Institute Publications, 1991. Pp 173–88.
Although similar in certain respects to the complaints of Mars (*Mars*) and Anelida (*Anel*), the falcon's lament goes beyond its analogues in depicting the speaker's emotional development. The falcon begins her speech with fierce animus against her faithless lover, but ends with a recognition that his behavior is natural for male creatures and that her despair cannot be assuaged by remembering him as a base deceiver. In the act of recounting her suffering, the falcon experiences an emotional purgation; the imagery, syntax, and patterns of allusion in her lament reflect this transformation of thought and feeling.

• Review by Peggy A. Knapp, *SAC* 14 (1992), 124–6: Owen's 'meticulous' reading uncovers the 'subtle complexity' of an often-neglected episode (p 125).

658 ———. *The Manuscripts of The Canterbury Tales*. Chaucer Studies 17. Cambridge: Brewer, 1991.
The spaces left for large initials in Harley 7335 sometimes indicate an intelligent response to the text: a space occurs, for example, at the first mention of the falcon in *SqT*. The compilers also left a blank page and two leaves (later excised) for the missing conclusion of the tale (p 73).

659 Patterson, Lee. *Chaucer and the Subject of History*. Madison: U of Wisconsin P, 1991.
The falcon's Boethian exemplum of the caged bird, comic in its immediate

effect, also poses a serious question about the redemption of natural man. In *SqT*, the redemptive powers of culture – in the form of *gentilesse* – are 'tested and found wanting' (p 73).

660 Potter, Russell A. 'Chaucer and the Authority of Language: The Politics and Poetics of the Vernacular in Late Medieval England.' *Assays* 6 (1991), 73–91.
The Squire's comment on the insufficiency of his English to describe Canacee's beauty (lines 34–7) suggests a contrast between the elaborate and mannered vocabularies of French romance and the comparatively narrow rhetorical range of his native tongue. *SqT* satirizes 'the discursive *dissonance* that results from the translation of romance conventions for an English-speaking audience' (p 83).

661 Wimsatt, James I. *Chaucer and His French Contemporaries: Natural Music in the Fourteenth Century*. Toronto: U of Toronto P, 1991.
The falcon's lament in *SqT* – a reprise of the betrayed lover's tale told several times by Machaut and by the younger Chaucer – comes closer to the contemporary French tradition than does any other narrative in *CT*. Yet the speech is not a full-fledged *dit amoureux*, since it lacks extended lyric passages characteristic of the genre; 'it is as if Anelida had told her story without delivering her complaint' (p 170).

661a Dorrance, Nina Helen. 'Chaucerian Pathos.' PhD diss., University of Virginia, 1992. Dir. A.C. Spearing. See also *DAI*–A 53/08 (1993): 2807.
The secular scene of pathos in Part 2 of *SqT* is detached from the context that might make it intelligible; its 'free-floating' character makes it resistant to interpretation (pp 43–4). The tale may be seen as 'a beautiful artifact ... [that] acquires privilege precisely because of its distinctively imaginary qualities,' a 'cognitive universe' independent of 'the rules that govern other parts of our lives' (pp 286–7). A 'newly autonomous version of poetry,' *SqT* 'may be Chaucer's most radically secular and innovative text' (p 287).

662 Hansen, Elaine Tuttle. *Chaucer and the Fictions of Gender*. Berkeley: U of California P, 1992.
SqT responds to *MerT*'s questioning of gender differences and the possibility of feminine virtue by restoring one version of the ideal heroine in the victimized falcon; in doing so, however, the tale creates a troubling image of male falseness and hypocrisy (p 268).

663 Lee, Brian S. 'The Question of Closure in Fragment V of *The Canterbury Tales*.' *YES* 22 (1992), 190–200.
SqT is an exercise in circularity and recommencement, characterized by 'roundabout inconclusion' (p 193). Its events and speeches break off with the expectation that they will eventually resume; 'only if we expect a narration should we get impatient' (p 195). The Squire's style recalls that of oral exposition, suited to a community 'where time is not money, and a rapid end to the subject at hand is neither envisaged nor desired' (p 195). In contrast,

FranT implies a literate readership, and brings its actions and discourse to significant closure. In his handling of Dorigen's Complaint, for example, Chaucer combats Dorigen's resistance to closure by bringing to an end, with Arveragus's return, a speech 'which the character uttering it wishes to make interminable' (p 198). Aurelius's two speeches to Dorigen are superficially circuitous like the speech of the Squire's ambassadorial knight, but in fact they build steadily up to their devastating conclusions. 'As satisfyingly whole as the Squire's was inconclusive' (p 190), the Franklin's narrative provides a rhetorical completion of *SqT*.

664 Mandel, Jerome. *Geoffrey Chaucer: Building the Fragments of the Canterbury Tales*. Rutherford, NJ: Fairleigh Dickinson UP; London: Associated University Presses, 1992.

Alone among the *CT* fragments, Fragment V contains two thoroughly pagan tales. Among the themes that contribute to the fragment's unity are dance (linked in both tales with dangerous deception), references to death and wounds, astrology (associated with magic and the marvelous), and illusion (the disappearance of the rocks in *FranT*; the four gifts and the deceptive tercelet in *SqT*). Several themes unify the tales by contrast: troth (with the exception of the tercelet's vow, pledges are honored in *SqT*; in *FranT*, none of the promises is fulfilled); and *gentilesse* – in Part 2 of *SqT*, connected with courtly love and a 'façade for disillusion' (p 100), in *FranT*, a mark of nobility and generosity. The fundamental structure of Fragment V is chiasmus: *SqT* opens with the giving of gifts to Cambyuskan and ends with the courtly love adventure of the unhappy falcon; *FranT* begins with the courtly love adventure of the unhappy Dorigen and ends with gifts of human generosity that in turn reflect the Christian gifts implicit in the reference (lines 1244–55) to the Christmas season. The tales' treatment of time is also chiastic: the pagan spring of Cambyuskan's birthday at the beginning of *SqT* balances the Christian winter of the Nativity near the conclusion of *FranT*. Characterization provides a final means of unity: the tercelet in *SqT* shares traits with Aurelius and Arveragus, while Dorigen and the falcon are drawn together by contrast (compared to Canacee, who represents a norm for womanly behavior, the falcon is shown to be more 'mesurable' than the heroine of *FranT*).

• Review by Vincent DiMarco, *Speculum* 69 (1994), 831–3: Mandel's discovery of a chiasmic relationship between *SqT* and *FranT* places structure at cross purposes with theme, reversing the pattern of deterioration and decay for which he has argued (p 833).

• Review by Helen Cooper, *RES* n.s. 46 (1995), 398–9: Even when his parallels are well demonstrated – as in the cross references between *SqT* and *FranT* – Mandel never suggests why they should matter. And some of his examples contradict each other: *SqT* and *FranT* are said to be 'thoroughly pagan,' but later contrasted by way of *FranT*'s 'orthodox Christian scheme' (p 399).

665 Pearsall, Derek. *The Life of Geoffrey Chaucer: A Critical Biography*. Oxford: Blackwell, 1992.
Of *CT*, only *CkT*, *Thop*, and *SqT* lack a known source or well-attested analogue, perhaps indicating Chaucer's lack of interest in literary originality. *CkT* is left deliberately unfinished; *Thop* is open parody; *SqT*, 'begun with the best of intentions, draws attention more and more to its own tendency to stray from the point ... and to ramify uncontrollably' (p 241).

666 Richmond, Velma Bourgeois. *Geoffrey Chaucer*. New York: Continuum, 1992.
SqT contains memorable details, but is structurally diffuse, anticipating the form of late-medieval composite romances like *Valentine and Orson*. Chaucer was more at home in sharply focused stories (pp 69–72).

667 Sharon-Zisser, Shirley. 'The *Squire's Tale* and the Limits of Non-Mimetic Fiction.' *ChauR* 26 (1992), 377–94.
A concentration on the tale itself rather than on the relation of tale and teller reveals *SqT* to be a dramatization of the interplay between two modes of nonmimetic narrative: the fantastic and the metafictional. *SqT* contains two incongruous categories of the fantastic: the marvelous, exemplified by the knight's gifts, which project a 'transcendence toward an ideal reality,' and the 'ontological transgression' exemplified by the knight himself, which erodes and scrutinizes dominant cultural orders (p 383). The tale's metafictional dimension also involves two conflicting sub-modes. The 'thematic' mode, comprised of elements that have textuality as their subject, is present in the courtiers' responses to the knight's gifts – treated as problems of interpretation to be elucidated by previously encountered texts – and in the Squire's conception of rhetoric as an 'absolute correspondence between an utterance and its referent' (p 383). This ideal is undercut, however, by 'structural,' or self-reflexive, metafiction, which foregrounds the speaker's mediating role, turning attention away from the discourse to its utterer, and thus highlighting the materiality rather than the transparency of language. The oscillation within and between the two dimensions of *SqT* creates an analogous swerving in the reader, who is pulled between mutually exclusive ways of reading the tale. Those who seek mimetic wholeness by referring the tale's effects to the Squire himself only confirm its nonmimeticism, admitting, in effect, that all other links to an external reality are blocked. 'If "about" nothing else, [*SqT*] is about its own limits' (p 393).

668 Goodman, Jennifer R. 'Dorigen and the Falcon: The Element of Despair in Chaucer's *Squire's* and *Franklin's Tales*.' In *Representations of the Feminine in the Middle Ages*. Ed. Bonnie Wheeler. Dallas, TX: Academia, 1993. Pp 69–89.
Dorigen and the abandoned falcon are both victims of despair, brought on by 'los of love' (line 450), whether through physical separation or rejection. By contrast, Aurelius, whose despair is in some ways analogous to Dorigen's, has had no experience of previous fulfillment. All three characters must be

saved by *fortitudo* – the virtue opposed to despair – in the form of magnanimity. Canacee's pity for the falcon suggests a possible happy ending; Arveragus's generosity moves Aurelius from the fantasy of his self-created love story into the world of adult responsibility. Dorigen's despair necessitates forceful action on her husband's part; his command that she keep her promise to Aurelius serves to shake her out of her emotional paralysis. Dorigen is saved from unwilling adultery by the overpowering '"feminine"' (p 87) need to speak that compels her to reveal her husband's command to the squire and thus arouse his compassion.

669 Lionarons, Joyce Tally. 'Magic, Machines, and Deception: Technology in the *Canterbury Tales*.' *ChauR* 27 (1993), 377–86. Excerpts in *Readings on the Canterbury Tales*. 1997. See **606**. Pp 101–8.
Chaucer blurs the line between magic and technology in *CT*; both depend on hidden knowledge, which in turn allows each to abet fraud and trickery. The horse of brass in *SqT* resembles real and fictional medieval automata, but the observers in Cambyuskan's court attribute its workings to magic. The esoteric knowledge required to make or operate the horse and the other gifts raises the suspicion that they may be employed by the learned to deceive the ignorant.

670 Crane, Susan. *Gender and Romance in Chaucer's Canterbury Tales*. Princeton, NJ: Princeton UP, 1994.
Part 2 of *SqT* posits a distinctively feminine sensibility manifested by compassion and closeness to the natural world. In its revisions of its sources in Boethius and *RR*, the falcon's caged bird simile rehabilitates women's merit and illustrates harmful masculine inconstancy by 'ascribing to men a paradoxical, disunified nature reminiscent of that ascribed to women in romance' (p 71). The falcon's self-wounding expresses both a close association between femininity and the body and the falcon's 'profound helplessness in the face of events' (p 76). The transference from Cambyuskan to Canacee of the magical mirror brought by the stranger knight marks a shift from public masculine to private feminine concern (p 134). In her relation to clerical magic, Canacee moves toward 'subjective knowledge of relationships … rather than toward a masculine appropriation of the exotic for self-advancement' (p 145).

671 Crepin, André. 'L'Exotisme dans le Conte de l'Ecuyer des *Canterbury Tales*.' In *Nouveaux mondes et mondes nouveaux au Moyen Age: Actes du Colloque du Centre d'Etudes Médiévales de l'Université de Picardie Jules Verne, Amiens, mars 1992*. Ed. Danielle Buschinger and Wolfgang Spiewok. Griefswalder Beiträge zum Mittelalter 22; Wodan, 37. Griefswald: Reineke, 1994. Pp 29–34.
The 'parfum exotique' (p 29) of *SqT* arises from a number of details: place names, personal names derived from Arabic astronomy, hints of incest, and echoes of Western writings on the Orient. The most potent sources of the

tale's exoticism are its narrative structure – a frame story on the model of *The Thousand and One Nights* – and its incompleteness, deliberately designed by the Squire to sharpen our curiosity, 'à l'orientale' (p 33).

672 Fyler, John. 'Chaucerian Romance and the World Beyond Europe.' In *Literary Aspects of Courtly Culture: Selected Papers from the Seventh Triennial Congress of the Courtly Literature Society, University of Massachusetts, Amherst, USA, 27 July–1 August 1992*. Ed. Donald Maddox and Sara Sturm-Maddox. Cambridge: Brewer, 1994. Pp 257–63.

In contrast to the xenophobia and parochialism exhibited by the narrators of *PrT* and *MLT*, the Squire embraces 'exotic otherness' (p 258). Even as *SqT* attempts to assimilate the Other, however, it demonstrates the difficulty of bridging gaps between European and Tartar, human beings and birds, men and women.

673 Hardman, Phillipa. 'Chaucer's Man of Sorrows: Secular Images of Pity in the *Book of the Duchess*, the *Squire's Tale*, and *Troilus and Criseyde*.' *JEGP* 93 (1994), 204–27.

The physical description of the peregrine falcon – the blood of her wounds streaming down the tree, her self-laceration with her beak, recalling the mythical behavior of the pelican as an image of Christ – evokes a comparison with the suffering Man of Sorrows. By presenting the falcon as a 'secular *imago pietatis*' (p 225), Chaucer emphasizes the noble compassion of Canacee's emotional response to the bird's plight.

674 Jost, Jean E. 'Potency and Power: Chaucer's Aristocrats and Their Linguistic Superiority.' In *The Rusted Hauberk: Feudal Ideas of Order and Their Decline*. Ed. Liam O. Purdom and Cindy L. Vitto. Gainesville: UP of Florida, 1994. Pp 49–76.

In contrast to *KnT*, in which the teller's certainty about the efficacy of language is shown to be warranted, the Squire's incoherent and rambling narrative belies his 'innate confidence in himself,' a quality evident in the 'disingenuous humility' (p 68) of his assertions of linguistic insufficiency.

674a Boenig, Robert. *Chaucer and the Mystics: The Canterbury Tales and the Genre of Devotional Prose*. Lewisburg, PA: Bucknell UP, 1995.

'Chaucer himself' is the only poet 'less adept than the Squire' (p 157). In *Thop*, Chaucer 'lives in the same realm of poetic ineptitude' as the Squire; neither exerts narrative control over his materials (pp 158–9). Moreover, the narrator of *Thop* – a 'bumbler of hyper-Squirean proportions' – has in common with his creator 'at least one disturbing fact ...: the tendency to break off before completing a work' (p 164).

675 Chance, Jane. *The Mythographic Chaucer: The Fabulation of Sexual Politics*. Minneapolis: U of Minnesota P, 1995.

The Squire's allusions to the fall of Troy – the steed of brass is compared to the Trojan horse, the deceptive tercelet to 'Parys of Troye' (line 548) – remind us that 'deceit draws forth deceit' (p 33). But the tale offers positive images that counter the discourse of deceit: the steed is also compared to Pegasus, the winged horse of the poetic imagination, 'to suggest that art grows out of, and transmutes, suffering and anxiety, in order to transcend human limitations' (p 34).

676 Edwards, A.S.G. 'Chaucer from Manuscript to Print: The Social Text and the Critical Text.' *Mosaic* 28:4 (1995), 1–12.
In early printed editions of Chaucer's works, explicits or other editorial interventions were regularly employed to indicate endings for fragmentary tales (e.g., those of the Cook and the Monk), as well as for other incomplete works like *LGW*. 'Only occasionally did the scrupulous editor feel forced to acknowledge an intractable problem, as Thynne did with the *Squire's Tale*: "There can be founde no more of this foresaid tale whiche hathe ben sought in dyuers places"' (p 5).

676a Hasegawa, Kazuko. 'A Study of Chaucer's Description of Sounds.' *Research Bulletin of Otemae Junior College* 15 (1995), 64–80.
Includes an account of the relation between verb tense and narrative action in lines 42–6 and 56–61 (p 72).

677 Kaylor, Noel Harold, Jr. 'The Orientation of Chaucer's *Canterbury Tales*.' *MedPers* 10 (1995), 133–47.
The presentation of the steed of brass to the Khan at Sarray reveals a 'hierarchy of the exotic' (p 136). In contrast to Western culture, Tartary is already exotic, but an object from India is more exotic still. The comparison to the Trojan horse signals the potential danger in the foreignness of Indian and Tartar culture.

678 Klassen, Norman. *Chaucer on Love, Knowledge and Sight*. Cambridge: Brewer, 1995.
SqT brings together the popular – the expectations of romance – and the learned, including a parody of learning. The list of authorities in lines 232–5 represents the range of contemporary optical learning, which in Chaucer's time had become a symbol of knowledge (pp 39–40).

679 Lynch, Kathryn L. 'East Meets West in Chaucer's Squire's and Franklin's Tales.' *Speculum* 70 (1995), 530–51. Repr. in Lynch, ed., *Chaucer's Cultural Geography* (see **632**). Pp 76–101.
Central to *SqT* and its reception is the tale's Orientalism, its 'aura of exotic alterity' (p 531). *SqT*'s narrative logic is 'a logic of the feminine East, morally relativistic, sexually deviant, building to a potentially incestuous climax' (p 538). These sexual improprieties are mirrored in the tale's narrative improprieties; its open-endedness and associative linkage of episodes, characteristic of the Oriental tale, is pushed to a new level of excess in which Chaucer 'out-Easts the East' (p 541). The Squire's sympathies with Eastern cultural difference are blunted by his introduction of courtly and Western motifs,

especially in his treatment of Canacee and the falcon in Part 2. The tale's vacillation between Western and Eastern modes destabilizes the narrative itself and the gender distinctions required by the marriage plot. The Franklin's 'interruption' of the tale, and his dismantling in his own tale of the Squire's argument about women, power, and the East, may be read as responses to *SqT*'s oscillation between East and West, masculine and feminine.

680 Scala, Elizabeth. 'Canacee and the Chaucer Canon: Incest and Other Unnarratables.' *ChauR* 30 (1995), 15–39.
See **731**.

681 Weisl, Angela Jane. *Conquering the Reign of Femeny: Gender and Genre in Chaucer's Romance*. Chaucer Studies 22. Woodbridge, UK: Brewer, 1995.
Although the Squire attempts to cram every possible romance motif into his narrative, the tale finally eschews 'romance necessity' (p 51) and hence falters. The *locus amoenus* into which Canacee wanders in Part 2 is not a place where the heroine falls in love, but rather the scene of a lesson about the perils of the romance plot for women. United by a private language, Canacee and the betrayed falcon examine male courtly discourse and discover its falsity. The *mewe* that Canacee builds for the falcon 'is a physical *Legend of Good Women*, warning women, as the falcon's lay warns Canacee, of the false nature of men and the dangers of love' (p 67). Canacee's failure to enter into the romance plot arrests the tale's narrative movement; 'without a woman at its center, coerced into the roles that the genre defines for her, the romance becomes a kind of stuck record' (p 69).

682 Astell, Ann W. *Chaucer and the Universe of Learning*. Ithaca, NY: Cornell UP, 1996.
The tales of Fragment V exemplify an 'Epicurean grammatical *regimen* especially associated with the antigamous inversion of courtly love' (p 174). *SqT* focuses on grammatical, not rhetorical, practice; the Squire's wish to speak the language of gentility leads him into the 'social ungrammaticalities' (p 175) of courtly love. While condemning her duplicitous lover, the falcon also indicts herself as guilty of 'the inversion of social grammar through a seductive courtly subterfuge' (p 176).

683 Axton, Richard. 'Chaucer and the Idea of the Theatrical Performance.' In *'Divers toyes mengled': Essays on Medieval and Renaissance Culture, in Honour of André Lascombes*. Ed. Michel Bitot. Tours: Université François Rabelais, 1996. Pp 83–100.
The courtiers' comments on the horse of brass in Part 1 of *SqT* and the account of the tregetours' performances in *FranT* reflect Chaucer's interest in three essential aspects of drama: the importance of specialized place, of specialized verbal performance, and of spectacle (p 87).

684 DiMarco, Vincent. 'The Dialogue of Science and Magic in Chaucer's *Squire's Tale*.' In *Dialogische Strukturen/Dialogic Structures. Festchrift für Willi Erzgräber* *zum 70. Geburtstag*. Ed. Thomas Kuhn and Ursula Schaefer. Tübingen: Narr, 1996. Pp 50–68.

In their conventional links with black magic, the powers of divination, locomotion, healing, and knowledge embodied in the mirror, horse, sword, and ring, respectively, possess 'overwhelmingly pejorative' resonances (p 52). Chaucer purges his versions of these powers of both necromantic and moralized Christian associations. 'There is *no* magic in *SqT*' (p 55); the descriptions by critics of the devices as magic gifts misappropriate a discourse that both the narrator and Chaucer seek to disparage. Within the tale, the interpretation of the gifts as magical is the product of *lewed* (line 221) observers who fail to understand their scientific or technological basis; like Aquinas, among others, the Squire emphasizes 'the knowable causes of seemingly wondrous phenomena' (p 58). In the accounts of each of the gifts, myth and legend are rationalized scientifically; the doctrine of 'the multiplication of species, whereby substances and qualities were believed to send out likenesses of themselves' (p 63), serves as a general explanation for the effects of the individual devices.

685 Grudin, Michaela Paasche. *Chaucer and the Politics of Discourse*. Columbia: U of South Carolina P, 1996.

Taken together, *SqT* and *FranT* constitute 'a poetic essay on the uses and misuses of discourse' (p 114). The stranger knight's gifts in *SqT* are 'visual emblems of the power of discourse' (p 118), connected in various ways with human understanding and communication. The gifts are framed on the one hand by the eloquence of the strange knight, with its consonance of words and deeds, and on the other by the duplicitous tercelet's depraved imitation of virtuous discourse. Recalling the model of rhetoric expressed by Cicero and inherited by the Italian humanists, the version of discourse embodied in the gifts suggests that true eloquence transcends mere style and is a powerful political tool. The Squire's own self-conscious and sometimes clumsy exposition calls attention 'not only to the importance of eloquence, but to the manifold difficulties in gaining it' (p 129).

• Review by John M. Ganim, *SoAR* 62 (1997), 109–11: Taken together, *SqT* and *FranT* function in Grudin's scheme as an essay on the misuses of language rather than as 'the failed experiment and successful solution respectively that criticism has traditionally assumed' (p 110).

• Review by Edwin D. Craun, *MÆ* 67 (1998), 137–8: The paired reading of *SqT* and *FranT* is animated by 'sophisticated analysis of the role of the listener, of speech as an infinitely variable transaction between speaker and listener' (p 138).

686 Koff, Leonard Michael. '"Awak!": Chaucer Translates Bird Song.' In *The Medieval Translator. Traduire au Moyen Age*. Vol. 5. Ed. Roger Ellis and René Tixier. [Turnhout, Belgium]: Brepols, 1996. Pp 390–417.

Canacee's ring, which allows her to understand what birds say, is 'an instrument of wish-fulfillment, of restorative magic' (p 391). In *SqT*, 'objects of magic are made present in our vacant world … in order to make it magical again' (p 413n).

687 Olsen, Alexandra H. 'The Rise of the Middle Class in Middle English Literature.' *InG* 17 (1996), 51–7.
SqT's opulence 'makes it attractive to all who profited from the commercial revolution and are flattered by the attention of royalty' (p 54).

687a Shibata, Takeo. 'Chaucer and the Affected Modesty Topos.' *Review of Kobe Shinwa Women's University* 30 (1996), A103–25.
Includes comments on the Squire's use of the affected modesty topos in lines 35–41 and 105–6. (Full text at http://ci.nii.ac.jp/els/110006606898.pdf?id=ART0008574171&type=pdf&lang=en&host=cinii&order_no=&ppv_type=0&lang_sw=&no=1457233200&cp=. In Japanese.)

688 Simpson, James. 'Desire and the scriptural texts: Will as reader in *Piers Plowman*.' In *Criticism and Dissent in the Middle Ages*. Ed. Rita Copeland. Cambridge: Cambridge UP, 1996. Pp 215–43.
SqT is generated out of the mutual desire of the teller and audience (the Host); the Squire's reference to his own good will as teller (lines 1–8) reflects the growing concern with the moral status of the author in the late Middle Ages (p 218).

689 Tinkle, Theresa. *Medieval Venuses and Cupids: Sexuality, Hermeneutics, and English Poetry*. Stanford, CA: Stanford UP, 1996.
Lines 270–4 depict Venus as a planetary force, affecting the physical and psychic orientation of those born under her influence. 'The idea of "children of the planet" here seems a consummate eastern and aristocratic fiction, a fable about oriental sensuality and magic and nobility' (p 148).

690 DiMarco, Vincent. 'Supposed Satiric Pointers in Chaucer's *Squire's Tale*.' *ES* 78 (1997), 330–3.
Commenting on lines 47, 76–88, 243–6, and 272, DiMarco argues that what Seymour (**640**) regards as signs of the Squire's ineptness as a narrator may more accurately be read as Chaucer's unparodic manipulation of convention or as the Squire's grounding of his romantic fiction in scientific and historical reality. 'One can only wonder how much in the Squire's intriguing fiction has yet to be properly understood, much less fully appreciated' (p 333).

691 Gutiérrez Arranz, José Maria. 'The Precepts of Epistolary Discourse and Letters in Geoffrey Chaucer's *The Canterbury Tales*.' In *Proceedings of the 9th International Conference of the Spanish Society for Medieval Language and Literature*. Ed. Margarita Giménez Bon and Vickie Olsen. [San Sebastián]: SELIM, 1997. Pp 140–5.
The discourse of the strange knight in Part 1 of *SqT* is a clear example of the high style that belongs to the world of elevated people and things.

692 Heffernan, Carol. 'Chaucer's *Squire's Tale*: The Poetics of Interlace or the "Well of English Undefiled."' *ChauR* 32 (1997), 32–45.
See **736**.

693 Jacobs, Nicholas. 'Ricardian Romance? Critiques and Vindications.' In *Essays on Ricardian Literature. In Honour of J.A. Burrow*. Ed. A.J. Minnis, Charlotte C. Morse, and Thorlac Turville-Petre. Oxford: Clarendon, 1997. Pp 203–21.
Although *SqT* is not a parody of romance in the manner of *Thop*, some aspects of the tale suggest that Chaucer did not intend it to be taken with complete seriousness. The promised complexity of structure – perhaps that of the frame tale – would seem to be beyond the Squire's capacities. His rhetorical disclaimers highlight his genuine limitations as a narrator, while his anthropomorphic tropes often court absurdity (e.g., in the falcon's comparison of the tercelet to a tiger who falls on his knees like a human being). Like *NPT*, the falcon episode contrasts the avian nature of the speaker with her inflated rhetoric – perhaps a gentle send-up of the conventions of the love-vision. If *SqT* was conceived as a frame tale, the untold episodes might have been intended to anthologize burlesques of different poetic genres, of which romance would have been one example.

694 Kamowski, William. 'Trading the "Knotte" for Loose Ends: The *Squire's Tale* and the Poetics of Chaucerian Fragments.' *Style* 31 (1997), 391–412.
SqT is not only a fragment within a fragment, but it is also internally fragmentary: 'the Squire leaves incomplete nearly everything he discusses' (p 392). The tale's incompleteness prompts the reader to flesh it out by filling in textual gaps or by conceptualizing a whole from clues that imply a structure; these clues include 'the inception of the frame tale, concerning the gifts brought to court ... the embedded narrative about Canacee and the falcon; and ... the Squire's concluding projections for continuing the tale' (p 396). In providing multiple perspectives on its own fragmentary status, *SqT* is 'a rhetorical miniature of the *CT*, which is likewise a framed composite incomplete at several narrative levels' (p 398). *SqT* shares with Romantic fragments (e.g., Coleridge's 'Kubla Khan') a 'sense of the infinite' (p 399) that answers the audience's desire to sustain the experience of the text. It also reflects the medieval receptiveness to fragmentary texts and open-ended fictions, and invites other writers to continue the tale. The Squire's projection of further adventures at the end of Part 2 can be read as Chaucer's signal that he is not going to finish his tale, a gesture that parallels the poet's leave-taking in *Ret*; both *SqT* and *CT* appear to be 'intentional fragment[s]' (p 406).

695 Minnis, A.J. 'Looking for a Sign: The Quest for Nominalism in Chaucer and Langland.' In *Essays on Ricardian Literature. In Honour of J.A. Burrow*. 1997. See **693**. Pp 142–78.
The Squire's praise of the pagan Cambyuskan for keeping the law of the religion into which he was born is compared with Romans 2:14–15, and with

commentaries by John of Wales and Walter Hilton on virtuous pagans who are nevertheless barred from salvation (pp 142–3, 147–8).

696 Taylor, Paul Beekman. 'Chaucer's Strategies of Translation,' *CY* 4 (1997), 1–19.
See **702**.

697 Burnley, David. *Courtliness and Literature in Medieval England.* London: Longman, 1998.
The speech of the strange knight who enters Cambyuskan's court shows him to be clerically educated. Chaucer's 'admittedly inadequate account of his performance' (p 114) is a verse pastiche of the sort of official letter in curial style that would at this period have been written in French.

697a Dane, Joseph A. *Who is Buried in Chaucer's Tomb?: Studies in the Reception of Chaucer's Book.* East Lansing: Michigan State UP, 1998.
Strohm's reading (**512**) of John Duxworth's gloss on *SqT* – 'Ista fabula est valde absurda in terminis' – is not accurate. It is not the tale itself that is labeled 'absurd,' but rather the *termini,* which here refers to the words in which the tale is written (p 201).

698 Davenport, W.A. *Chaucer and His English Contemporaries: Prologue and Tale in The Canterbury Tales.* New York: St Martin's, 1998.
In a tale less dependent on traceable sources than most of *CT,* we can see more clearly what Chaucer comes up with when he is inventing his plot material. After an opening scene that rivals the episode of the Green Knight's appearance in Camelot in *SGGK,* the poem changes gears and becomes a courtly complaint; masculine adventure gives way to feminine pathos and the language of dream poetry (pp 130–1).

699 Fredell, Joel. 'Paraphs and Patterns: Two Early Forms of the *Canterbury Tales.*' *EBSN* 3:2 (1998), n.p.
See **711**.

700 Fyler, John. 'Froissart and Chaucer.' In *Froissart Across the Genres.* Ed. Donald Maddox and Sara Sturm-Maddox. Gainesville: UP of Florida, 1998. Pp 195–218.
Acutely aware of his own belatedness, the Squire debunks the chivalric past in his tale; he relocates chivalry in the nearly contemporary, exotic otherness of Cambyuskan's court, and worries about explaining magic away, of dispelling the exotic by domesticating it. By contrast, the Franklin sets his tale in the pagan past; he links magic with the self-regarding *fin'amor* that threatens true *gentilesse* and the amorous ideal that the Franklin associates with the Golden Age. The episode of the 'Voyage en Béarn' in Froissart's *Chroniques* may be read as a fusion of *SqT* and *FranT*. 'It shares their concern with the chivalric, the exotic, belatedness, the mysterious and the magical, the Golden Age, and the threats to it of contingency and death' (p 202).

701 Johnston, Andrew James. 'Chaucer, Galilei, Brecht: Sprache und Diskurs im

Leben des Galilei.' In *Bertolt Brecht (1898–1956)*. Ed. Walter Delbar and Jörg Döring. Berlin: Weidler, 1998. Pp 239–64.

Chaucer's uneasiness about scientific knowledge as a social ideal is reflected in the narrator's scorn for the response of the 'diverse folk' (line 202) at Cambyuskan's court to the magical gifts. The episode stages a conflict between a naïve confidence in rationality, which is perceived as vulgar, and aristocratic virtue, which grants the miraculous its place. The latter ability distinguishes the noble from the non-noble. Curiosity about scientific knowledge, on the other hand, especially when clothed in the garb of academic authority, opens itself to the charge of pedantry, a deadly trait in the Squire's elegant courtly world.

702 Taylor, Paul Beekman. *Chaucer Translator*. Lanham, MD: UP of America, 1998.

For Chaucer, *translatio* is both a natural movement and an artificial one. Canacee's ring is a 'translating machine' (p 11) that has the power to transpose avian complaints into the artful language of human *courtoisie*, a process that, ironically, moves Canacee to imprison the falcon in a cage just as the translation has already imprisoned the bird in language. The steed of brass is also a device of transport or translation that operates through a combination of nature, in the form of human desire, and art, in the form of the horse's mechanism.

703 Ambrisco, Alan Scott. *Medieval Man-eaters: Cannibalism and Community in Middle English Literature (John Gower, Geoffrey Chaucer)*. PhD diss., Indiana University, 1999. Dir. Lawrence M. Clopper. Ann Arbor, MI: University Microfilms International, 1999. See also *DAI*–A 60/05 (1999): 1569.

See **740**.

704 Condren, Edward I. *Chaucer and the Energy of Creation: The Design and Organization of the Canterbury Tales*. Gainesville: UP of Florida, 1999.

In combination, the four magical objects brought by the stranger knight into Cambyuskan's court 'would overcome all the physical limitations that make life and social interaction problematic' (p 151). Properly employed, they would have protected the falcon against the tercelet's verbal deceptions, and would have prevented as well misunderstandings and miscommunications in several of the tales that precede *SqT*. 'The magical properties of these objects direct attention to what has been impeding the progress of all the relationships throughout this lengthy section of the *Canterbury Tales*, that people use language in formulaic ways, without ever saying exactly what they mean or meaning exactly what they say' (p 152).

705 Haas, Kurtis B. 'Rhetoric, Romance and the Structure of Authority in the *Canterbury Tales*.' PhD diss., University of Nebraska, 1999. Dir. Paul Olson. See also *DAI*–A 59/08 (1999): 2970.

Ch. 3, 'Of Anglis and of Slye Reflexiouns: What Rhetoric Reveals to the Squire' (pp 75–100), argues that a budding self-consciousness about both rhetoric and romance form marks the Squire's narrative. The chapter uses Bakhtinian insights into language to examine the ways in which rhetorical tropes lead the Squire to move from the monological poetic typical of romance to a heteroglossic narrative that he ultimately abandons. For example, the modesty topos at one point causes the Squire to recognize that he is translating a speaker from a tale that he is translating in the first place, describing a foreign voice within an environment already foreign to his own experience. Such insights created by the forms of the *artes poeticae* continue in a variety of ways until the tale becomes too dangerous and unpleasant for the Squire to finish or for the company to hear.

706 Houwen, L.A.J.R. '*Exemplum et Similitudo*: Natural Law in the *Manciple's Tale* and the *Squire's Tale*.' In *Chaucer in Perspective: Middle English Essays in Honour of Norman Blake*. Ed. Geoffrey Lester. Sheffield, UK: Sheffield Academic Press, 1999. Pp 100–17.

The medieval Aristotelian theory of natural law helps us to understand why Chaucer inserted the exempla of the caged bird into *SqT* and *ManT*. For Aquinas, natural law was essentially a moral law: when people follow the natural inclinations they share with animals without allowing them to be controlled by reason, they are denying their true nature. Such behavior characterizes the tercelet in *SqT* and Phoebus's wife in *ManT*: both take pleasure in novelty and choose socially inferior lovers. 'At the narrative level Chaucer's *exempla* provide the motivation for the immoral behaviour of the tercelet and Coronis, but at an ethical level they question and criticize these same actions' (p 115).

The Squire's Tale, 2000–2005

707 Akbari, Suzanne Conklin. 'From Due East to True North: Orientalism and Orientation.' In *The Postcolonial Middle Ages*. Ed. Jeffrey Jerome Cohen. The New Middle Ages. New York: St Martin's, 2000. Pp 19–34.

SqT and *FranT* participate in the medieval construction of the Orient as hot and the Occident as cold. Cambyuskan and his daughter Canacee are associated with the sun and its heat (see lines 263–7, 385), while the pale sun in *FranT* (line 1249) 'coldly illuminates a world where fraternal exchange takes precedence over carnal desire' (p 30).

708 Andrew, Malcolm, and A.C. Cawley, eds. *Geoffrey Chaucer: Three Tales of Love and Chivalry*. 2000. See **125**.

Parts 1 and 2 of *SqT* are only tenuously related, illustrating the tendency of romance to be loosely constructed and episodic in form and content. The Squire's unfulfilled promise of coming attractions has been read as a satiric comment both on the discursive qualities of the genre and on the youthful teller's failure to select and discriminate (xvi).

709 Crane, Susan. 'Duxworth Redux: The Paris Manuscript of the *Canterbury Tales*.' In *Manuscript, Narrative, Lexicon: Essays in Literary and Cultural Transmission in Honor of Whitney F. Bolton*. Ed. Robert Boenig and Kathleen Davis. Lewisburg, PA: Bucknell UP; London: Associated University Presses, 2000. Pp 17–44.
Questions Crow's belief (**441**) that Jean d'Angoulême controlled the hand of the scribe John Duxworth. Many features of the Paris MS seem to reflect Duxworth's sense of his role as that of *compilator*. His omission or shortening of all of the fragmentary tales (including *SqT*), for example, may testify to his belief that Chaucer himself was dissatisfied with them.

710 Dane, Joseph A. '"Tyl Mercurius House He Flye": Early Printed Texts and Critical Readings of the *Squire's Tale*.' *ChauR* 34 (2000), 309–16.
The early printed texts of *CT* (up to Thynne's 1532 edition) fail to support the modern reading of *SqT* as interrupted by the Franklin; in these editions, *SqT* is presented as 'unfinished, incomplete, or simply missing' (p 311). The twentieth-century reading of *SqT* as parody, which requires 'a great deal of textual self-reflection' (p 314), is not the one represented in early Chaucer books.

711 Fredell, Joel. 'The Lowly Paraf: Transmitting Manuscript Design in *The Canterbury Tales*.' *SAC* 22 (2000), 213–80.
Distinguishing among MSS of *CT* that exhibit 'sparse' and 'dense' patterns of glossing – in particular the use of the paraf as an internal text divider – Fredell observes that for *SqT*, two 'sparse' MSS (Oxford, Corpus Christi College MS 198 and Lansdowne MS 851) offer 'a few dutiful glosses with no connection to a literary/critical agenda' (p 250), while two 'dense' MSS (Hg and El) are attentive in their glossing and use of parafs to the tale's 'romance wisdom' (p 249), dividing it 'into an intricate series of plot shifts and points of sapiental *gravitas*' (p 250).

712 Maíz Arévalo, Carmen. 'El Sistema Dialogal en los "Canterbury Tales."' Doctoral diss., Universidad Complutense de Madrid. Departamento de Filología Inglesa, 2000. Dir. Inés Ana María Pinto Muñoz. See http://biblioteca.ucm.es/tesis/fll/ucm-t25279.pdf.
This sociolinguistic study of the ways in which linguistic behavior enables individual characterizations of the pilgrim speakers, expresses both ideological tensions and group connections among the pilgrims, and creates social dialects, draws several examples from *SqT*.

713 Partridge, Stephen. 'Minding the Gaps: Interpreting the Manuscript Evidence of the *Cook's Tale* and the *Squire's Tale*.' In *The English Medieval Book: Studies in Memory of Jeremy Griffiths*. Ed. A.S.G. Edwards, Vincent Gillespie, and Ralph Hanna. London: British Library, 2000. Pp 51–85.
An examination of the physical makeup of *CT* MSS and of typical scribal

practice in Chaucerian and non-Chaucerian MSS suggests that Chaucer may have released *CkT* and *SqT* into the scribal medium in their unfinished state. In particular, the blank spaces following the tales and the notes on the tales' incompleteness may originate with Chaucer rather than with his scribes. The manuscripts tell us nothing about what Chaucer had in mind for the tales; rather they tell us that he meant these two incomplete tales to be included in the collection and that he 'understood the text to be discontinuous where each of them breaks off' (p 75). Despite ingenious arguments that *SqT* is tactfully broken off by the Franklin, the MS evidence suggests that both Chaucer and his scribes understood it differently from both the complete tales and from *Thop* and *MkT* – the two clearly interrupted tales.

714 Phillips, Helen. *An Introduction to the Canterbury Tales: Reading, Fiction, Context*. New York: St Martin's, 2000.
SqT is self-conscious about its own narrative machinery, but 'this particular machine ... goes nowhere' (p 134). Taken as a sequence, *SqT* and *FranT* develop together the themes of *gentilesse* and virtue. Chaucer may deliberately have left *SqT* unfinished, with the suggestion, in the Franklin's remarks to the Squire, that the continuance of the tale should be left to the imagination; '*SqT* is as *gentil*, as promising, and as unfinished as the Squire himself is' (p 135).

714a Scala, Elizabeth. 'The Deconstructure of the *Canterbury Tales*.' *Journal x: A Journal of Culture and Criticism* 4 (2000), 171–90.
In contrast to Harry Bailly's interruption of *Thop*, the Franklin's words following *SqT* 'say nothing explicitly disruptive to the Squire' (p 176). Scala notes a logical inconsistency between Cooper's (**581**) comparison of *CT*'s structure to that of a good interlaced romance and her assertion that, in *SqT*, Chaucer is implicitly passing judgment on the entire genre (p 177). Scala also argues for treating the gaps at the end of *CkT* and *SqT* not as lacks that need to be filled or explained away, but as part of the text (p 179). Responding to the employment of the Knight's 'rhetorical control' as a 'yardstick for the other secular tales, most notably the Squire's,' Scala claims that the Squire is in fact 'an archetypal narrator' whose tale demonstrates how narrative is 'founded upon particular acts of exclusion' (p 184).

715 Stevens, Martin. 'Chaucer's "Bad Art": The Interrupted Tales.' In *The Rhetorical Poetics of the Middle Ages: Reconstructive Polyphony. Essays in Honor of Robert O. Payne*. Ed. John M. Hill and Deborah M. Sinnreich-Levi. Madison, NJ: Fairleigh Dickinson UP; London: Associated University Presses, 2000. Pp 130–48.
The interrupted tales (*Thop, MkT,* and perhaps *SqT*) provide us with an index to Chaucer's self-conscious act of narration. If we read *SqT* as deliberately broken off by the Franklin, the interruption calls attention to 'the pointed disjunction between the incompetent teller and the competence of his story'

(p 145) – a 'failed interlaced romance' (p 144) in which dazzling invention is undercut by incompetent rhetoric.

716 White, Hugh. *Nature, Sex, and Goodness in a Medieval Literary Tradition*. Oxford: Oxford UP, 2000.
Adapting Boethius's image of the caged bird (*Consol* 3.m2) – a figure for the return to nature as something good – in *ManT* and *SqT*, Chaucer 'completely subverts' the passage's original drift (p 225). In *SqT* (lines 607–20), '"kynde" drags down rather than elevates [and] "gentil" blood is unable to refine raw nature' (p 228). One can attribute this unflattering view of nature to the hawk's personal distress, but she may also be 'voicing, albeit perhaps in rather an overwrought manner, a perfectly legitimate opinion' (p 229).

717 Yamamoto, Dorothy. *The Boundaries of the Human in Medieval English Literature*. Oxford: Oxford UP, 2000.
Although birds and the highborn Canacee share 'an elevated appreciation of love and of its discourse' (p 37), we are reminded of the distance between the bodies of birds and those of humans in Canacee's failure to catch the falcon when she drops from the bough, in the simile of the weeping tiger, and in the image of the faithless tercelet falling on his knees. 'Despite Canacee's willing sympathy, where bodies are concerned she and the falcon appear to be slightly out of sync with one another' (p 38).

718 Collette, Carolyn P., and Vincent J. DiMarco. 'The Matter of Armenia in the Age of Chaucer.' *SAC* 23 (2001), 317–58.
The imagery of *Anel* offers correlations with three of the four magical gifts in *SqT*; the latter depict successful resolutions of issues left tragic or unresolved in *Anel*. If the history of Anelida – the sorrowful 'quene / Of Ermony' (lines 71–2) – is read in the light of the thirteenth- and fourteenth-century history of Lesser Armenia, *Anel* 'must break off without a clear hope of a happy resolution, while *The Squire's Tale*, related from the perspective of the Mamluk-Mongol alliance,' points toward reunion and reconciliation (p 332).

719 Fields, Peter John. *Craft and Anti-Craft in Chaucer's Canterbury Tales*. Studies in Medieval Literature 19. Lewiston, NY: Mellen, 2001.
Chaucer's interest in craft goes beyond mere technical prowess. In *CT*, the word denotes human efforts to control the world through personal experience and learned tradition. In *SqT*, the stranger knight is the Squire's alter-ego, and his gifts are a means by which the Squire cultivates favor within the royal court. But the knight's ultimate contempt for his auditors (as in his refusal to explain the 'craft' that lies behind the workings of the brass horse) betrays the Squire's uneasiness about his own position. As a youthful *bacheler* subordinate to his father, he expresses by way of the knight's speech 'a secret ... grudge against medieval courtship and marriage, both of which effectively exclude many young men' (p 130). Forced to engage in duplicity like the tercelet in the second part of his tale, the Squire 'yearns for some-

thing clearly out of reach and hoarded by ... all-powerful elders, even as he envisions unparalleled tools that should conceivably ensure success' (p 137).

720 Fradenburg, L.O. Aranye. 'Passare il tempo. La storicità del "romance" medievale.' In *Il romanzo.* Volume 1: *La cultura di romanzo.* Ed. Franco Moretti. Turin: Einaudi, 2001. Pp 227–43.
For this essay in English, see **742**.

721 Johnston, Andrew James. *Clerks and Courtiers: Chaucer, Late Medieval Literature, and the State Formation Process.* Anglistische Forschungen 302. Heidelberg: Winter, 2001.
In his treatment of the problematic relation between human and avian behavior in the hawk's narrative, the Squire subjects courtly ritual to satiric scrutiny. The misinterpretation of the Boethian passage, for example – in which *gentilesse* is implicitly compared to straw and in which the falcon becomes so 'ridiculously humanized' that it rejects its avian nature (p 89) – serves in part to interrogate the aristocratic code of values. And in his choice of the falcon – a hunting bird tamed by its human masters – the Squire uses aristocratic symbolism against itself, drawing an analogy between the human social group and 'the bird of prey [that] has lost its function' (p 92). But the Squire's attack on the political and social structures of late medieval England is 'strangely ineffective' (p 99). His unrelentingly negative approach implies that his ideal aristocratic world is irreparably lost, leaving him only with impotent irony and 'disillusioned sarcasm' (p 98) when he realizes that 'his dreams cannot come true' (p 99).

722 Lightsey, Scott. 'Chaucer's Secular Marvels and the Medieval Economy of Wonder.' *SAC* 23 (2001), 289–316. Repr. in Lightsey, *Manmade Marvels in Medieval Culture and Literature.* New York: Palgrave Macmillan, 2007. Pp 55–80.
In Part 1 of *SqT,* Chaucer uses romance to depict an inquiry into the nature of courtly *mirabilia.* The courtiers' reading of the gifts brought by the stranger knight encompasses the aristocratic view of these marvels as objects of wonderment, but also a more skeptical mechanistic view from the sciences and the crafts-classes. Curiosity about marvels is presented as a kind of courtly entertainment; speculation about the brass steed begins with the horse's classical antecedents, but moves quickly to a realm closer to home: perhaps the steed is produced by sleight-of-hand like that practiced by 'jogelours ... at thise feestes greete' (line 219). The ring resists explanation as magic or technology; the courtiers' biblical analogues seem to suggest divine origin. In this, Chaucer conforms to contemporary practice, which exempted divine interventions from empirical analysis.

723 Osborn, Marijane. 'Learning How to Use the Astrolabe While Finding Chaucer's Meaning.' *Al-Māsaq* 13 (2001), 1–24.
See **730**.

724 Rudd, Gillian. *The Complete Critical Guide to Geoffrey Chaucer.* London: Routledge, 2001.

The 'jumble of elements' in the tale might be taken either as an indication of the Squire's inexperience as a narrator or as an aspect of the intricate interweaving of motifs in romance (p 129). The desire for *newefangelnesse* (a variety of restlessness or instability) manifested in the tercel's behavior in Part 2 may be intended to recall the brass horse in Part 1, which draws the courtiers' fascinated attention, only to vanish without a trace (pp 129–30).

725 Schildgen, Brenda Deen. *Pagans, Tartars, Moslems, and Jews in Chaucer's Canterbury Tales*. Gainesville: UP of Florida, 2001.

The Squire's representation of the Tartar court reflects his Epicureanism. He rejects the idea of fate or predestination (Cambyuskan's family is associated with the stars, but its actions are independent of any causation), Cambyuskan's birthday feast celebrates pleasure as an end in itself, and the account of the stranger knight's gifts shows respect for the workings of empirical science. The Squire's version of Tartary elides the cultural differences between East and West, assimilating the Tartar 'other' to the familiar world of Arthurian romance. As a representative of the noble classes, the Squire 'uses literature or storytelling to marginalize history' (p 47).

• Review by John C. Hirsh, *MÆ* 72 (2003), 136: 'Locating in the Knight's Tale and the Squire's Tale a responsiveness to Christian and pagan, ancient and modern, Schildgen produces a compelling reading of cultural difference which invests the tales with a powerful responsiveness to contemporary philosophical and narrative constructions.'

726 Yager, Susan. 'Chaucer's *Peple* and *Folk*.' *JEGP* 100 (2001), 211–23.

Chaucer distinguishes between *peple* and *folk*, the former being (in, e.g., *Bo*, *TC*, and *KnT*) 'vocal and emotional.' In *SqT*, the onlookers who gossip about the strange knight's gifts are referred to as *peple* four times within sixty lines describing the public's inability to judge (p 219 and n).

727 Bleeth, Kenneth. 'Orientalism and the Critical History of the *Squire's Tale*.' In *Chaucer's Cultural Geography*. 2002. See **632**. Pp 21–31.

Orientalist discourse – the ways of imagining and describing the East that have been given their most influential formulation in Edward Said's *Orientalism* (1978) – has left its mark on the study of *SqT*'s genre, theme, structure, style, sources, and narrative voice. From the eighteenth century through the 1970s, Orientalist assumptions remain largely unexamined in critical commentary on the tale. More recent assessments of the poem engage directly with the issues raised by Said's work, sometimes complicating and interrogating Said's own views.

728 Kordecki, Lesley. 'Chaucer's *Squire's Tale*: Animal Discourse, Women, and Subjectivity.' *ChauR* 36 (2002), 277–97.

See **751**.

729 Mann, Jill. *Feminizing Chaucer*. Chaucer Studies 30. Cambridge: Brewer, 2002.

In the female falcon's lament over her lover's desertion, Chaucer adds to his Boethian source an identification of man's 'propre kynde' as *newefangelnesse*: Chaucer sees betrayal in love as 'the bitterest manifestation' (p 18) of the fundamental human capacity for change. The falcon's account of her former amorous bliss embodies Chaucer's ideal of harmonious unity in love: the 'spontaneous fusion of two wills into one' (p 51; cf. p 84). This ideal is parodied in the mechanical obedience of wife to husband in the Merchant's marriage encomium (IV.1337–54), a passage that nevertheless contains a faintly nostalgic memory of the original.

729a Monz, Dominic. *Gentilesse und gentils. Der weltliche Adel und seine Werte in Geoffrey Chaucers Canterbury Tales*. Regensburger Skripten zur Literaturwissenschaft 23. Regensburg: Braun, 2002.
SqT is a charming but technically and intellectually deficient narrative that exposes its teller's misguided vanity. Its faults make it more likely that the tale is deliberately interrupted by the Franklin than that Chaucer simply left it unfinished. Although the Squire identifies with the knightly virtues enumerated in his tale, his concept of *gentilesse,* which he defines as nobility of ancestry, is limited, especially in contrast to his father's treatment of the same quality. The absurd, class-conscious bird fable reduces its own social views to a kind of 'humbug' (p 144), while the Squire's earlier depiction of the Tartar court insults his own audience. The admiring references to Gawain and Lancelot, on their surface modesty *topoi,* in fact reveal the Squire's insincerity, since he sees himself in these heroic figures. The vices targeted in the narrative – jealousy, falsehood, hypocrisy, and *newefangelnesse* – are precisely the faults of the Squire and the tale he tells; no distance exists between the narrator and his discourse (pp 137–46).

730 Osborn, Marijane. *Time and the Astrolabe in The Canterbury Tales*. Norman: U of Oklahoma P, 2002.
In none of the analogues to *SqT* is the magic steed made of brass. The stranger knight's steed of brass represents the brass astrolabe, which, like the horse, can carry its user through the cosmos 'in the space of o day natureel' (line 116). In support of the identification of the two objects, Osborn cites the description in *Astr* of a 'large pyn' that must be turned (cf. lines 315–16) and a wedge or knob 'which that is cleped the hors' at the center of the instrument. In addition to designating the pin or wedge, the Arabic word *alpheraz* is also a star name, associated with the constellation Pegasus, which is in turn linked with the date of King Cambyuskan's birthday. The astrolabe appears in *SqT* only in its disguise as the brass steed, but the latter is shown to be more than it seems through the comparison (lines 306–7) to the Trojan horse (pp 34–54). Repunctuated as a list, lines 48–51 simply elaborate the date of Cambyuskan's birthday and alert the reader to the astrolabic reference in Part 1 (pp 70–2). The Squire's incomplete chronographia (am-

biguous in both its syntactic and semantic structures) in Part 3 (lines 673–4) is – despite 'bothersome but not irrefutable evidence' (p 110) against the hypothesis – a 'double dating device, offering a date within the tale and one outside it' (i.e., in the 'real' world of the pilgrimage) (p 107). The dating may also have an allegorical significance, since Mercury (line 672) is associated with clerks (cf. *WBP* lines 697–705), and the Franklin (who, according to one reading, interrupts the Squire at this point in his story) proceeds to tell a tale that 'exalts' a clerk among his social superiors (p 109).

• Review by Keith Snedegar, *Isis* 95 (2004), 694–5: Osborn's correlation between *SqT*'s steed of brass and the astrolabe is a 'tantalizing' instance of Chaucer's suggestively concealed references to the astrolabe in his works (p 695).

• Review by Chauncey Wood, *Speculum* 80 (2005), 536–9: 'While the similarities of brass, "horse," and Arabic origin between the gift and the instrument are promising, the astrolabe is essentially a measuring device, so the parallels between the two are tenuous' (p 538).

731 Scala, Elizabeth. *Absent Narratives, Manuscript Textuality, and Literary Structure in Late Medieval England*. The New Middle Ages. New York: Palgrave Macmillan, 2002.

The critical response to *SqT* may be understood as a 'textual effect of the tale' (p 83), specifically of its unnarrated story of incest, which has generated an anxiety in the poem's readers and editors that has provoked them into 'evasive action' (p 85), admitting the incest story into the tale only to omit it. The absent story foregrounds the larger gap at the center of the tale – the absence of a coherent plot or governing significance. By putting off the incest story suggested by *SqT*, readers enact the tale's own more explicit deferrals of its subject(s). Textual absences (emblematized in the blank space that follow the fragmentary story in several MSS) have become part of *SqT*'s text. The Squire frequently comments on what he has left out, calling attention to the gaps in his story and dwelling on 'the way meaning is inevitably lost, told but fallen away' (p 91). Always in quest of its own subject (a quest repeated in the poem's critical reception), *SqT* becomes 'a story about Chaucer's storytelling' (p 92). In his constant return to, and recycling of, the beginning of his tale, the Squire displays his unfulfilled desire to uncover the origins of his romance, an act of 'eternal regress' (p 94) replicated in the interest shown by the tale's critics in the missing '"incest" narrative at the story's "source"' (p 97). Although denigrated by most modern critics, *SqT* is a paradigm of Chaucer's handling of narrative, in particular its processing of history and memory.

732 Ambrisco, Alan Scott. 'Teaching the *Squire's Tale* as an Exercise in Literary History.' *SMART* 10:1 (2003): 5–18.

The author teaches *SqT* 'not as a settled text, but as a fluid one' (p 6). He begins with attention to matters of tone, structure, and unity, and moves on to explorations of the relation of teller and tale, rhetoric, the tale as fragment, the Franklin's comments, and the tale's editing and its placement within *CT.* He then moves beyond formal and thematic issues by providing an historical context and a sense of the poem's textual environment by way of *Mandeville's Travels,* readings in Edward Said's *Orientalism,* and an examination of medieval *mappaemundi.* Students discover that, in contrast to (say) Mandeville, *SqT* domesticates exotic elements. They also see that the tale is unified by its treatment of language; the flawed rhetoric of Part 1 is contrasted to the presentation of English 'as a vehicle for perfect communication' in Part 2 (p 140).

733 Cohen, Jeffrey Jerome. *Medieval Identity Machines.* Medieval Cultures 35. Minneapolis: U of Minnesota P, 2003.
The narrator of *SqT* 'refuses to abandon multiple pleasures for a diminished knightly stability'; the tale fails because it wanders through a world of objects regulated by inhuman agency, of nonnormative sexuality, and of stories that resist closure (p 67).

734 Di Rocco, Emilia. *Chaucer: Guida ai "Canterbury Tales."* Rome: Carocci, 2003.
The falcon's simile of the caged bird comments obliquely on the vanity of the courtly world as presented by the Squire in Part 1 of his tale. A world comprised entirely of the values and ornaments of the courtly milieu may itself become a kind of cage (p 61).

735 Gray, Douglas. 'The Squire's Tale.' In *The Oxford Companion to Chaucer.* Ed. Douglas Gray. Oxford: Oxford UP, 2003. Pp 449–50.
Attempts by modern critics to find *SqT* parodic or ironic, or a reflection of its teller's inadequacies, are 'both dubious and dangerous.' Perhaps the Squire begins to gets 'lost in the labyrinth' of his leisurely and digressive narrative, but any possible irony is carefully controlled, and not destructive (p 449).

736 Heffernan, Carol F. *The Orient in Chaucer and Medieval Romance.* Woodbridge, UK: Boydell and Brewer, 2003.
SqT's structure, that of the interlaced romance, links it with European literary tradition rather than with the Oriental analogues uncovered by earlier scholars. The narrative doubles back upon itself (e.g., the focus on Canacee in Part 2 recalls the previous references to her in Part 1) in the manner of many European romance plots. The Squire's references to the *knotte* of his tale (lines 401, 407) draw attention to the complexity and length of romance interlace, which at its best is fastened together into some form of meaningful unity. The Squire is trying his hand at a narrative form associated with the world of chivalry he aspires to; he expresses the Eastern frame structure by means of the interlaced form of French romances popular at court. But *SqT* parodies neither the teller nor the genre; at most, the Franklin's cutting off of the tale is Chaucer's joke on himself, his recognition that he has attempted a

mode of romance for which he is temperamentally unsuited.

• Review by Donald L. Hoffman, *Arthuriana* 14 (2004), 100–2: Although it contains some imaginative suggestions about Eastern influences on *SqT*, Heffernan's discussion 'has been almost completely superseded' by Vincent DiMarco's chapter on the tale in the new *Sources and Analogues of the Canterbury Tales* (**242**) (p 102).

• Review by Elizabeth Archibald, *MÆ* 75 (2006), 328–9: To claim that Chaucer 'quickly discovered that interlace was not his forte' is inadequate as a response to the tale's apparent incompleteness, nor does the author make sufficient use of recent discussions of Chaucer's attitude toward romance, a genre which he often treats ironically, or even critically.

737 Hughes, Alan. *Signs and Circumstances: A Study of Allegory in Chaucer's Canterbury Tales*. Pentrefoelas, Wales: AlaNia, 2003.

Hughes reads the tale as an historical allegory in which the falcon's plight represents Queen Anne's 'anguished realization that King Richard has betrayed her trust in the genuineness of his love' (p 72).

738 Lynch, Kathryn L. 'Team Teaching the Literature of the European and Islamic Middle Ages: The European Perspective.' In *Medieval Cultures in Contact*. Ed. Richard Gyug. Fordham Series in Medieval Studies. New York: Fordham UP, 2003. Pp 213–22.

Describes a team-taught course offered at Wellesley College ('Images of the Other in the European and Islamic Middle Ages') that includes *SqT* and *FranT*.

739 Vial, Claire. 'Chaucer et la danse de Vénus ou les délices d'adultère.' In *Enfers et délices à la Renaissance*. Ed. François Laroque and Franck Lessay. Paris: Presses Sorbonne Nouvelle, 2003. Pp 119–34.

In Chaucer's narrative poetry, Venus appears as a double-sided figure whose dance among the lovers she ostensibly protects could adumbrate either the pleasures of mutual love or the torments of a cuckolded husband. In the banquet scene in *SqT* (lines 268–88) she appears as the protectress of love; the dance of Venus is perfectly in accordance with the rules of courtly chivalry (pp 122–3).

740 Ambrisco, Alan Scott. '"It lyth nat in my tonge': Occupatio and Otherness in the *Squire's Tale*.' *ChauR* 38 (2004), 205–28.

The rhetorical failures in Part 1 of *SqT* – in particular the Squire's excessive use of *occupatio* – suppress ethnic and cultural difference and encourage the poem's audience to adopt the position of the Mongols. At the same time, the poem overemphasizes the exoticism of the emissary from the King of Araby and India, employing the rule of the excluded middle to move the stranger knight into the space of the Other and the Europeans/Mongols into the place of the self. In Part 2, the Squire no longer uses *occupatio*; the tale of Canacee and the falcon constitutes 'a fantasy of linguistic competence' in which English 'claims immediate access not just to another culture, but to another species' (p 216). This fantasy goes beyond the matter of the narrator's linguistic ability; it 'reflects and refutes fears about the status of the English language, about its worth as a vehicle of translation' (p 219). The figure of Canacee, however, resists appropriation, stubbornly asserting her alterity as an 'incalculable object' who remains 'uncontrolled, unmarried, unwestern, uneastern, and unassimilated' (p 222).

741 Fichte, Joerg O. 'Rome and Its Anti-Pole in the *Man of Law's* and the *Second Nun's Tale*: *Christendom* and *Hethenesse*.' *Anglia* 122 (2004), 225–49.
The portrait of Cambyuskan – an intellectually astute, morally perfect pagan ruler – participates in the late medieval tradition exemplified by *Mandeville's Travels*, in which the Khan is so powerful that his conversion to Christianity could change the world (pp 238–9).

742 Fradenburg, L.O. Aranye. 'Simply Marvelous.' *SAC* 26 (2004), 1–27.
The responses of Cambyuskan's courtiers to the brass horse and the other gifts of the stranger knight in *SqT* show 'how absorbing wonder can be' (p 7) and how it takes place on the edge of the known and the unknown and on the border between technology and magic. 'Gawain might be long-lost in Faerye, but the new knight (who stands in the place of Green Knight) can be even more polite than Gawain, and have cooler stuff' (p 8).

743 Saunders, Corinne. 'Chaucer's Romances.' In *A Companion to Romance from Classical to Contemporary*. Ed. Corinne Saunders. Malden, MA: Blackwell, 2004. Pp 85–103.
Part 1 of *SqT* seems a self-conscious weaving together of traditional romance motifs, especially those that engage with the marvelous. But Chaucer complicates our acceptance of marvels by introducing references to astrology, natural sciences, and human debate and inquiry. The second part of the tale, although it contains elements of burlesque, overwhelmingly emphasizes lament, 'the pure expression of emotion and suffering' (p 90).

744 ———. 'Magic, Science and Romance: Chaucer and the Supernatural.' In *Medieval English Literary and Cultural Studies. SELIM XV.* Ed. Juan Camilo Conde Silvestre and Maria Nila Vásquez González. [Murcia: Universidad de Murcia], 2004. Pp 121–43.
Although *SqT* includes the familiar romance convention of unexplained magical objects, the Squire's self-conscious rhetoric and his uncourtly asides undercut the ethos of the marvelous, as does the emphasis on astrology, natural sciences, and human inquiry; Part 1 of the tale 'seems to offer an ironic comment on romance naïveté' (p 135). In Part 2, however, the genuineness of magical objects is reasserted. The ring that allows Canacee to understand the speech of birds is neither an illusion nor an explicable mechanical device, retrospectively making it likely that the steed of brass will actually fly and 'be magical in a profound way' (p 136).

745 Mann, Jill, ed. *Geoffrey Chaucer: The Canterbury Tales*. 2005. See **128**.

Although *SqT* is unfinished, it embodies some central Chaucerian topics and contains significant connections with other tales – for example, the themes of betrayal and of the ineradicability of natural instinct. The latter (see, e.g., IX.87–95) appears as *newefangelnesse* (line 610), which in its benign form is the *pitee* (line 479) that characterizes Canacee's *gentil herte* (lines 451, 479) and that of Theseus in *KnT*.

746 Van Dyke, Carolynn. *Chaucer's Agents: Cause and Representation in Chaucerian Narrative*. Madison, NJ: Fairleigh Dickinson UP, 2005.
SqT offers a 'disjointed representation of animal agency' (p 85). Rather than linking animal and human species, Canacee's ring, which purportedly allows her to understand the language of birds, produces a version of the falcon 'so anthropomorphic that its avian original cannot be imagined' (p 83). The Boethian simile of the caged bird (lines 607–17) blurs the distinction between birds and humans so fully that its 'only stable meaning … resides … in its referential instability' (p 84). The narrator's rhetoric – he purports to make himself transparent even as he calls attention to the processes of storytelling – demonstrates his 'duplicitous agency' (p 86), as does his supposed neutrality about other cultures; 'like the birds' conversation, the customs of Tartary and Arabia turn out to be those of medieval Europe' (p 86).

The Squire's Tale, 2006–2013

The following fourteen entries move beyond the volume's 2005 cut-off date to recognize a significant development in recent commentary on *SqT*. Although Canacee's encounter with the falcon in Part 2 of the poem has been the subject of a number of careful and sympathetic investigations (e.g., **632**, **657**, **668**, **670**, **693**, **717**, **721**, **729**, **746**), the items in this section mark the first sustained engagement by students of *SqT* with the work in critical animal studies that has produced new paradigms for the interpretation of animal–human relations in a wide range of literary texts (see p 16).

747 Crane, Susan. 'For the Birds.' *SAC* 29 (2007), 23–41.
In *SqT*, Chaucer places cross-species contact in frameworks of gentility, femininity, and adventure that are central to romance. Crane examines species difference from three perspectives: the falcon's symbolism, her relation to the exotic, and 'cross-species compassion' (p 27). The bird's symbolic associations with nobility validate Canacee's 'human merit from beyond the realm of the human' (p 30), participating in a 'symbolic loop' in which Canacee's '"similitude" to the falcon is a mutually reinforcing proof of their shared superiority' (p 29). Chaucer also aligns species difference with cultural difference, translating orientalism (which familiarizes the exotic in order to mas-

ter it) into cross-species terms that render the falcon so like a courtly lady that her alien species seems 'acceptable and even familiar' (p 31). Invoking the meanings of *kynde* as (1) the hierarchy of created things and as (2) kindness and benevolence, Chaucer privileges the latter over the former, raising the question of whether kindness should transcend species lines as well as human differences. The 'contradiction of hospitality' (p 38), in which the hosted becomes hostage to the ways of the host, is embodied in the mews that Canacee creates for the peregrine – an effort at 'hosting that transcends appropriation' (p 40). The mixed success of this project can be taken to represent Chaucer's own artistic challenge as he attempts to do justice both to 'the strangeness and [to] the proximity of another species' (p 41).

748 Lillvis, Kristen. '"Be war by me": Fearing the *Newefangelnesse* of Female Autonomy in the Squire's Tale.' *Genre: An International Journal of Literature and the Arts* 28 (2008), 51–68.

Although overtly concerned with male *newefangelnesse*, Part 2 of *SqT* also warns females of the dangers attendant on freedom and novelty. Canacee displays autonomy by leaving her father's court in the early morning. In doing so, she encounters 'an example of the negative consequences of female autonomy' (p 61) in the falcon; venturing far from her birthplace, the bird becomes a victim of her lover's infidelity. Canacee responds by constructing a *mewe* to confine the falcon and to warn the bird – and, by extension, herself – of the perils of life beyond the cage. Held within these interiors, both Canacee and the falcon fit the Squire's ideal of womanhood and stand as his counterexamples to the freewheeling Wife of Bath.

749 Cooper-Rompato, Christine F. *The Gift of Tongues: Women's Xenoglossia in the Later Middle Ages.* University Park: Pennsylvania State UP, 2010.

Ch. 4, 'Women's Miraculous Translation in Chaucer's *Canterbury Tales*' (pp 143–88), argues that *SqT* explores 'the possibilities and impossibilities of translation' (p 176). In the masculine realm of Cambyuskan's court, translation is 'difficult, competitive, and imperfect' (p 177). In the feminized world of bedroom and park in Part 2, exact translation becomes possible through the agency of Canacee's magical ring, which enables her to communicate perfectly with a non-human creature. But in representing bird-speech as exactly like human speech and experience, the poet unnerves us. In proposing an exact equivalence between the two realms of language the narrator ignores the ramifications of such an act of translation, leaving us 'strangely sensitized to his insensitivity' (p 185).

750 Mann, Jill. *From Aesop to Reynard: Beast Literature in Medieval England.* New York: Oxford UP, 2010.

The tale of the three ravens in *The Seven Sages of Rome*, in which a boy's ability to understand avian speech allows him insight into the feelings of the birds themselves, provides the nearest parallel among animal tales Chaucer might have known to Canacee's encounter with the female falcon in Part 2 of *SqT*. Canacee's communication with the bird is made possible not only by her magic ring but also by the natural principle of *pitee*. The love affair with the tercel narrated by the female falcon reproduces on the avian plane the passionate mutual commitment of human lovers, but it also replicates human treachery. Using the Boethian image of the bird in the cage to explain her lover's betrayal, the falcon shifts the emphasis of Boethius's figure (and perhaps Jean de Meun's appropriation of it) to suggest that both human and avian infidelity result from a desire for *newefangelnesse*, the propensity to change that, along with *pitee*, forms the natural bond between bird and human (pp 200–6).

750a Williams, Tara. 'Magic, Spectacle, and Morality in the Fourteenth Century.' *New Medieval Literatures* 12 (2010), 179–208.
Of the objects introduced by the stranger knight, it is the ring that embodies magic's moral dimension. The ring's magic allows both Canacee and the reader access to the falcon's tale of betrayal, not simply by translating animal speech, but by enabling comprehension of the speaker's motivations. Had Canacee overheard the vows of the falcon's lover while wearing the ring, she would have understood 'his "entente," which he concealed so skilfully from the falcon' (p 207). The one-sided communication between the falcon and the tercelet is contrasted with the genuine rapport between the falcon and Canacee, enabled by the ring's magic. 'Magic … is moral in *SqT* because it facilitates true communication' (p 209).

751 Kordecki, Lesley. *Ecofeminist Subjectivities: Chaucer's Talking Birds*. The New Middle Ages. New York: Palgrave Macmillan, 2011.
Ch. 3, 'The *Squire's Tale*: Romancing Animal Magic' (pp 77–176), argues that, in *SqT*, Chaucer constructs human subjectivity through representations of animals and animal discourse. The brass horse in Part 1 functions as an icon of masculine magic and masculine subjectivity; in Part 2, the betrayed falcon transfers the narrative into the discourse of a stylized romance heroine. The narrative aborts itself because the masculine writer cannot fully imagine an animal other. The falcon must be a woman who conforms to the passive marginality of a lady in romance. Traditional notions of species and genre block Chaucer's full resolution of this imagined world.

752 Crane, Susan. 'Chivalry and the Pre/Postmodern.' *postmedieval: a journal of medieval cultural studies* 2 (2011), 68–87.
Medieval sources celebrate the integration in knighthood of arms, man, and horse, both as a feat of technology and as a 'mutually enhancing coordination between noble warrior and noble beast' (p 70). Although the steed of brass in *SqT* appears to be a 'fully technologized horse,' it proves to be more than a mechanism (p 78). The role of natural magic in its creation, the creature's response to the human voice, the shift from *it* to *hym* and *his* in

the description of the horse, the epithets 'horsly' and 'quyk of ÿe' (line 194), and the comparison to two prestigious breeds – the Lombard steed and the courser (lines 193, 195) – all contribute to a sense that the brass steed is not simply a product of human mechanical ingenuity, but rather that 'it flickers with the living physicality that chivalric ideology values in horses' (p 82).

753 Schotland, Sara Deutch. 'Talking Bird and Gentle Heart: Female Homosocial Bonding in the Squire's Tale.' In *Friendship in the Middle Ages and Early Modern Age: Explorations of a Fundamental Ethical Discourse.* Ed. Albrecht Classen and Marilyn Sandidge. Fundamentals of Medieval and Early Modern Culture 6. Berlin: de Gruyter, 2011. Pp 525–41.

'A rare portrayal of female homosocial bonding' (p 525), Part 2 of *SqT* depicts sympathy for women betrayed by men and emphasizes the value of female friendship as a defensive strategy. Canacee demonstrates considerable agency in her response to the formel's tragic tale, offering advice about male treachery and expressing sympathy in an ekphrastic depiction of male faithlessness on the exterior of the *mewe* (line 643) that she constructs for the injured bird. The ethics of care manifested in Canacee's actions has implications that extend beyond her succoring of a particular creature. Rather than estranging us from the formel, as some critics have argued, the tale's anthropomorphosis 'invites us to sympathize with "the other," whether species, nationality, or gender' (p 539).

754 Gutmann, Sara. 'Chaucer's Chicks: Feminism and Falconry in "The Knight's Tale," "The Squire's Tale," and *The Parliament of Fowls.*' In *Rethinking Chaucerian Beasts.* Ed. Carolynn Van Dyke. The New Middle Ages. New York: Palgrave Macmillan, 2012. Pp 69–83.

Part 2 of *SqT* holds out the promise of a world of female cross-species companionship beyond the masculine world of Cambyuskan's court in Part 1 of the tale. 'The peregrine, like Canacee, inhabits a space between human and animal, tame but wild, useful but dangerous in her potential to disrupt the masculine prerogative' (p 77). But Canacee's women, who respond to the peregrine's distress with physical remedies rather than with consolatory discourse, and Canacee herself, whose construction of the mews domesticates the falcon in her world of feminine virtue and modesty, close off the possibility of genuine interspecies communication. The human-animal fusion so highly valued in the masculine body of the knight becomes problematic when attempted by a woman.

754a Kiser, Lisa J. 'The Animals That Therefore They Were: Some Chaucerian Animal/Human Relationships." *SAC* 34 (2012), 311–17.

The Squire's steed of brass prefigures 'the later Cartesian "animal machines" that theorized and then repressed animal suffering into invisibility' (p 316). Privileged and not yet disenchanted, the Squire inhabits 'a psychic world where easily acquired tech support seems to be all one needs to ensure immortality' (p 317).

755 Schotland, Sara Deutch. 'Avian Hybridity in "The Squire's Tale": Uses of Anthropomorphism.' 2012. See **754**. Pp 115–30.
The hybridity of the falcon and tercelet – divided creatures with primarily avian form but with human linguistic capabilities – allows anthropomorphism to work positively in Part 2 of *SqT*. The avian element in the birds' hybridity shows that communication can occur across barriers of rank, language, and species. The human element in the falcon's hybridity enables friendship between women in a dangerous world. The friendship is not mere social dalliance; it takes the form of the comfort Canacee provides to rescue the falcon from suicidal despair. The falcon's warnings to Canacee about male treachery and Canacee's nursing of the wounded bird create a relationship of reciprocal compassion that anticipates the 'ethics of care' advocated by Carol Gilligan.

756 Stock, Lorraine Kochanske. 'Foiled by Fowl: The Squire's Peregrine Falcon and the Franklin's Dorigen.' 2012. See **754**. Pp 85–100.
Reversing the figural relation common in anthropomorphism in which animal activities reflect and comment on human behavior, the human activities in *FranT* parody those of the birds in *SqT*. The textual and situational parallels between the falcon episode in *SqT* and *FranT* – the contracts between two pairs of lovers, the departure of the male figure and the females' subsequent philosophical reflections, the females' despair and contemplation of suicide – provide a context for evaluating the genuineness of character and action in *FranT*. In each instance, particularly in the falcon's and Dorigen's suicidal laments, the bird's grief seems the more authentic and Dorigen's distress an 'anemic parody' in which she is '"foiled" (in the sense of both "contrasted" and "confounded") by the Squire's fowl' (p 98).
• Review of Van Dyke, *Rethinking Chaucerian Beasts* (see **754**) by Barbara Newman, *TMR* (July 2013), n.p.: 'In asking us to sympathize profoundly with a seduced and abandoned bird while we only smile at Dorigen, whose plight is of her own making, Chaucer – or Stock – pushes the envelope of empathy well beyond its normal bounds.'

756a Crane, Susan. 'A Cautionary Elephant.' *SS* 41 (2013), 29–39.
See **747**.

757 ———. *Animal Encounters: Contracts and Concepts in Medieval Britain*. Philadelphia: U of Pennsylvania P, 2013.
Ch. 5, 'Falcon and Princess' (pp 120–36) and ch. 6, 'Knight and Horse' (pp 137–68), incorporate lightly revised versions of **747** and **752** respectively.

℘ *The Squire–Franklin Link* (V.673–708)

The longstanding tradition of interpreting the links between the tales as episodes in a roadside drama has led some critics to claim that the Franklin's words to the Squire constitute a tactful interruption of a performance that threatens to run on indefinitely. Although these readers have demonstrated much ingenuity in providing stage directions for the Franklin's supposed breaking off of the younger man's narrative, commentators less wedded to a dramatic interpretation of the links point out that the Franklin's address to the Squire differs significantly from the two unequivocal interruptions – of *Sir Thopas* by the Host and of *The Monk's Tale* by the Knight – elsewhere in *The Canterbury Tales* (see **480**, **500**, **713**, **765**, **781**, **783**). Skepticism about the 'interruption' theory has been abetted by bibliographical and codicological scholarship on the ending of *The Squire's Tale* that makes a persuasive case for understanding the passage as intended for a completed tale (see pp 18–19). Differences of opinion about the sort of speech act represented by the Franklin's initial words to the Squire characterize interpretations of the link as a whole as well. The Franklin's comparison of the Squire to his own wastrel son and his interchange with the Host have generated a range of readings that, in recent years, have abandoned a narrow emphasis on the Franklin's supposed social climbing for a more nuanced understanding of the passage in the context of fourteenth-century gentry culture (see **786**, **792**, **793**, **794**).

For additional comments on *Sq–FranL* embedded in discussions of *SqT* and *FranT*, see **75**, **102r**, **366**, **378**, **394**, **402**, **442**, **447**, **451**, **453**, **456**, **471**, **474**, **480**, **483**, **487**, **490**, **493**, **500**, **502**, **505**, **506**, **514**, **546**, **548**, **554**, **563**, **574**, **577**, **581**, **588**, **591**, **593**, **611**, **621**, **625**, **633**, **633r**, **644**, **649**, **653**, **654**, **679**, **710**, **713**, **714**, **714a**, **715**, **729a**, **730**, **736**, **805**, **819**, **845**, **864**, **872**, **909**, **929**, **946**, **955**, **958**, **965**, **969**, **1013**, **1016**, **1028**, **1030**, **1049**, **1067**, **1136**, **1142**, **1152**, **1164**, **1183**, **1198**, **1235**, **1266**, **1276**, **1308**, **1309**, **1317**, **1337**, **1395**, **1433**, **1444**, **1496**.

758 Kittredge, George Lyman. 'Chaucer's Discussion of Marriage.' 1912. See **390**. The Franklin has been especially impressed by the Squire's treatment of *gentilesse*. 'And the reason for his enthusiasm soon appears. He is … the kind of man that may hope to found a family, the kind of man from whose ranks the

English nobility has been constantly recruited. And that such is his ambition comes out naïvely and with a certain pathos in what he goes on to say: "I wish my son were like you" … It is the contrast between the Squire and his own son … that has led the Franklin's thoughts to *gentillesse*, a subject which is ever in his mind' (pp 458–9).

759 ———. *Chaucer and his Poetry*. Cambridge, MA: Harvard UP, 1915. Repr. with an introduction by B.J. Whiting, 1970. Repr. [Whitefish, MT]: Kessinger, 2004; Danvers, MA: General Books, 2009.
Feeling that the theme of marriage has run its course, the Host calls on the Squire for a love story, which would be a 'welcome relief' from the marriage debate. The Franklin admires *SqT* as much for its teller's 'eloquent style and courtly bearing' as for its substance; 'he has a son whose low tastes are a grief to him, and he compliments the Squire on his "gentillesse," contrasting him rather piteously with the ungracious heir, who will be rich some day, but has no wish to grow up a gentleman' (p 204). The Squire has displayed his familiarity with the precepts of oratory in his description of the stranger knight's speech. In praising the Squire's *eloquence* (line 678), the Franklin uses the term in its technical sense – 'elegance and elevation of phrase' (p 13) – and is so impressed that he disclaims any knowledge of rhetorical colors when he tells his own tale.

760 Chesterton, G.K. *Chaucer*. New York: Farrar and Rinehart; London: Faber and Faber, 1932/1948. Numerous reprs including New York: Sheed and Ward, 1956.
The Franklin's words to the Squire demonstrate Chaucer's novelistic genius. The Franklin's praise of the Squire's exemplary performance leads him to 'the lamentable subject of his absent and unpresentable offspring,' who would be unlikely to trouble himself by telling an entertaining story to the assembled company. This 'living incident … comes straight out of the things that really happen. It is as quiet and as real as Jane Austen' (p 176).

761 Kase, C. Robert. 'Observations on the Shifting Positions of Groups G and DE in the Manuscripts of the *Canterbury Tales*.' In Russell Krauss, Haldeen Braddy, and C. Robert Kase, *Three Chaucer Studies*. New York: Oxford UP, 1932. Pp 1–89 [sections not consecutively paginated].
Lines 673–708 make dramatic and thematic sense as the Franklin's response to the Squire; the adaptation of the link to the Merchant that appears in twenty-two MSS is dramatically inappropriate. The passage follows *SqT* in all of the MSS in which it appears, suggesting that it was intended as an endlink to *SqT*. In thirty-two MSS, *MLE* introduces *SqT*, with the Squire forestalling the Parson's tale telling at II.1179. The passage is dramatically appropriate as a Man of Law–Squire link, suggesting that Chaucer originally intended it to introduce the Squire; Brown (**388**) is cited as corroboration of the genuineness of the Man of Law–Squire sequence. If Chaucer had once intended *SqT*

to follow *MLT*, Kittredge's theory of Fragment F (V) as the culmination of a Marriage Group (**805**) needs reexamination. Fragment F contributes little to the marriage debate: the Squire tells a tale of courtly love; the Franklin focuses primarily on *gentilesse*; Dorigen and Aurelius, *FranT*'s two principal characters, are not married, nor does the Franklin refer to his own marriage; there is no reference in either *SqT* or *FranT* to *WBT, ClT*, or *MerT*; *FranT* is followed by *SNT*, a story of an unconsummated marriage. See **422**, **762**, **846**.
• Review by J. Koch, *ESt* 67 (1932–3), 405–11: It is unlikely that Chaucer would have put the coarse language that concludes *MLE* in the mouth of the courtly Squire (p 410).
• Review by Robert K. Root, *MLN* 48 (1933), 465–70: Kase's argument that *MLE* was designed to introduce *SqT* is not compelling; the tone of the passage is inappropriate for the fastidious young Squire.
• Review by B.J. Whiting, *Speculum* 8 (1933), 531–8: Kase argues unconvincingly for the dramatic appropriateness of *MLE* to the Squire, and his attempt to emend Kittredge's scheme fails to persuade. *Gentilesse* is as definite a link among the four tales as the subject of marriage itself, while the unfinished state of *SqT* leaves open the question of what Chaucer might have put in it.

762 Tatlock, John Strong Perry. 'The Canterbury Tales in 1400.' 1935. See **424**.
Kase's argument (**761**) for the Squire as the speaker of *MLE* is not persuasive; the passage's rude tone is inappropriate for the courteous Squire, and the young man is unlikely to swear by his living father's soul (pp 115–16n).

763 Kolinsky, Muriel. 'Pronouns of Address and the Status of Pilgrims in the *Canterbury Tales*.' *PLL* 3 (summer supplement, 1967), 40–8.
The pronoun of address in the Host's 'Straw for youre gentillesse!' (line 695) is ironically derisive; the Host normally uses the *thou* form in addressing the Franklin. The Franklin uses eleven *thou*'s to the Squire, then wishes that his son 'were a man of swich discrecioun / As that ye been!' (lines 685–6). The switch from *thou* to *ye* could be attributed to the Franklin's state of mind as he compares the Squire's *gentilesse* with his own son's lack of it.

764 Duncan, Charles F., Jr. '"Straw for Youre Gentilesse": The Gentle Franklin's Interruption of the Squire.' *ChauR* 5 (1970), 161–4.
The difference in social status prevents the Host from interrupting the Squire's inept tale; the Franklin's social position uniquely suits him for bridging the gap between *cherl* and *gentil* without offending anyone. His fulsome praise of the Squire's *gentilesse* is a tactfully ironic reminder that the young man 'has acted churlishly in subjecting his quite captive audience to boredom' (p 163). The Host's rude outburst to the Franklin expresses his pique at having had his authority undercut, but it also provides the opening the Franklin needs to begin his own tale. Of the three 'interruptions' in *CT* – the Host's of Chaucer, the Knight's of the Monk, and the Franklin's of the Squire – only the last demonstrates genuine social finesse. See **765**.

765 Clark, John W. '*Does* the Franklin Interrupt the Squire?' *ChauR* 7 (1972), 160–1.
The Franklin's words to the Squire are unlikely to have been intended as a dramatic interruption, as Duncan (**764**) maintains. The Franklin would probably have liked *SqT*; his code of *gentilesse* would have included 'reluctance to interrupt' (p 161); his words sound like a compliment elicited by a completed tale; the logical place for an interruption is at the end of the second part of the tale, not two lines into the third. See **500**.

766 Fisher, John H. 'Chaucer's Last Revision of the "Canterbury Tales."' *MLR* 67 (1972), 241–51.
The Franklin's effusive praise of the Squire's confused performance 'reeks of servile toadying to the aristocracy' (p 250).

767 Kaske, Robert E. 'Chaucer's Marriage Group.' In *Chaucer the Love Poet*. Ed. Jerome Mitchell and William Provost. Athens: U of Georgia P, 1973. Pp 45–65.
The Franklin tactfully interrupts *SqT* by 'smothering the teller with praise.' Like *Thop*, which is clearly interrupted by the Host, *SqT* breaks off near the beginning of an episode closely following a catalogue of adventurous tales, and ends 'in the midst of a clause beginning with the word *Til*' (p 57).

768 Reinecke, George F. 'Speculation, Intention, and the Teaching of Chaucer.' In *The Learned and the Lewed: Studies in Chaucer and Medieval Literature*. 1974. See **528**. Pp 81–93.
If the Franklin's words to the Squire are read as a means of cutting off *SqT* by assuming it has ended, we can see a 'gradation in courtesy' from the Host's vulgar interruption of *Thop* to the Knight's directness in stinting *MkT* to the 'subtlety and elegance' (p 87) of the Franklin's comments. But such an interpretation contradicts our sense of the Franklin's relation to the Squire; his admiration for the young man is reflected in the contrast with his own profligate son and in the portrait of the squire Aurelius as a noble courtly lover.

769 Kee, Kenneth. 'Illusion and Reality in Chaucer's Franklin's Tale.' *ESC* 1 (1975), 1–12.
The Franklin's admiration for the Squire's gentility provides a key to his own performance. In his tale, the Franklin seeks to promote his interest in *gentilesse* by echoing the ideas, phraseology, and rhetorical figures of *SqT* and by writing a romance, which, like *SqT*, 'presents an idealized view of reality' (p 5).

770 Harrington, Norman T. 'Experience, Art, and the Framing of the *Canterbury Tales*.' *ChauR* 10 (1975–6), 187–200.
In contrast to the Squire's 'easy eloquence,' the 'flat, prosy accents' (p 196) of the Franklin's response to *SqT* remind us of the social and educational gap that separates the two pilgrims. The Franklin's diction at once exposes his attachment to material things and manifests his yearning for the courtly values of *SqT*.

771 Johnson, Judith A. '*Ye* and *Thou* Among the Canterbury Pilgrims.' *MichA* 10 (1977), 71–6.
The Franklin's use of *thou* to the Squire is 'a *faux pas,* and a bad one' (p 73). The Host rebukes the Franklin's breach of good manners by switching his form of address from *ye* to *thou.*

772 Reiss, Edmund. 'Chaucer and his Audience.' *ChauR* 14 (1980), 390–402.
The Franklin's 'warped view' of *gentilesse* as expressed in his words to the Squire makes the Host's reprimand 'doubly ironic,' since the Host is un*gentil* himself (p 394).

773 Blake, N.F. 'On Editing the *Canterbury Tales.*' In *Medieval Studies for J.A.W. Bennett. Aetatis Suae LXX.* Ed. P.L. Heyworth. Oxford: Clarendon, 1981. Pp 101–19.
The Merchant–Franklin Link in Hg is spurious, copied on a single sheet and inserted between *MerT* and *FranT.* When the sequence was rearranged in El, the entire passage was moved, with the references to the Franklin replaced by those to the Squire.

774 Owen, Charles A., Jr. 'A Certein Nombre of Conclusiouns: The Nature and Nurture of Children in Chaucer.' *ChauR* 16 (1981), 60–75.
SqT reminds the Franklin of his own failure as a father. In contrast to the Squire – a model son – his own son has rebelled against his authority. Only time, and his son's character, will determine the outcome of the young man's career; the Franklin himself can do nothing.

775 Specht, Henrik. *Chaucer's Franklin in the Canterbury Tales: The Social and Literary Background of a Chaucerian Character.* Publications of the Department of English, University of Copenhagen, Second Series, vol. 10. Copenhagen: Akademisk Forlag, 1981.
The Franklin's response to *SqT* is a 'delicate rescue operation' (p 154) designed to save the Squire from further entanglement in a project that has gotten out of hand. After interrupting the Squire in midsentence, the Franklin diplomatically shifts his focus from the actual performance to the good intentions that lie behind it. The Franklin's remarks on his son focus on the nature of true *gentilesse.* The Host's words at lines 695–8 are not a rebuke directed solely the Franklin; they are probably addressed to both the Franklin and the Squire, and satirize the Host's boorishness. The Franklin's response to the Host is suave and dignified, ironically exposing Harry's high opinion of himself as a literary critic. His noble conduct in *Sq–FranL* confirms the attractive *GP* portrait and 'forms a worthy illustration of his own ideal of gentilesse' (p 164). See Gopen (**1124r**) and Powell (**1124r**).

776 Ando, Mitsunobu. '"Straw for youre gentilesse!": "Gentilesse" and the Pilgrim Franklin.' *Shuryu* 43 (1982), 21–41.
Not seen. Listed in *BPMELLJ* (1983), p 141. In Japanese.

777 Higgs, Elton D. 'The Old Order and the "Newe World" in the General Prologue to the Canterbury Tales.' *HLQ* 45 (1982), 155–73.

The Franklin's grasp of gentility is superficial; the prologue to his tale demonstrates his failure to realize that 'mere association with the "proper" crowd cannot endow him or his son with an aura of nobility' (p 164).

778 Iwasaki, Haruo. '"Not worth a straw" and Similar Idioms.' *KWSC* 1 (1984), 33–49.

Includes a commentary on the Host's 'Straw for youre gentillesse!' (line 695). (Not seen. Listed in *BPMELLJ* [1994], p 80.)

779 Schless, Howard H. *Chaucer and Dante: A Revaluation*. 1984. See **215**.

The Franklin's response to *SqT* shows how little he knows of the true *gentilesse* of the spirit as Dante defines it. For the Franklin, *gentilesse* is the good breeding exemplified by the courtly Squire, which he wishes for his own son. Questions Bethel's assertion (**271**) that the Franklin's recognition 'that "gentilesse" and truth are not intimately related' (p 204) is a legacy from Dante. The Franklin's version of this idea would seem closer to that in *RR* (lines 2181–2202). The Franklin's *gentilesse* centers on 'a social graciousness that at its height becomes magnanimity, but … is never a mark of divine grace' (p 204), as in Dante (pp 199–200, 203–6).

780 Storm, Melvin. 'Chaucer's Franklin and Distraint of Knighthood.' *ChauR* 19 (1984), 162–8.

In stating that he would rather have a son with the Squire's virtues than 'twenty pound worth lond' (line 683), the Franklin alludes to the writs of distraint of knighthood initiated in England during the thirteenth century, under which all landholders whose holdings yielded £20 of annual income were called upon to become knights. The Franklin is in effect saying 'I would rather have a son of knightly virtue than be given the amount of land that would once have made me a knight,' a statement that at once rejects position for inner *gentilesse* and implies that possession, 'which the Franklin here disparages but clearly values and even flaunts in practice, has in the past been the basis for the granting of rank' (p 166).

781 Lawton, David. *Chaucer's Narrators*. 1985. See **598**.

Dramatic readings of *SqT* refuse to contemplate that the tale was left unfinished by Chaucer. When compared to the unequivocal interruptions elsewhere in *CT* (e.g., the cutting off of *MkT* by the Knight), the Franklin's words to the Squire do not read like an interruption (p 115).

781a Burrow, J.A. 'The *Canterbury Tales* I: Romance.' In *The Cambridge Chaucer Companion*. 1986. 2nd ed., *The Cambridge Companion to Chaucer*. 2003. See **606**.

The Franklin's words to the Squire do not sound like an interruption. It is better to suppose (as Spenser did) that the remainder of the tale is lost, or that (in Milton's words) Chaucer left the tale 'half-told' (p 115/pp 149–50).

782 Ellis, Roger. *Patterns of Religious Narrative in the Canterbury Tales*. London: Croom Helm; Totowa, NJ: Barnes and Noble, 1986.

The comment on the unfinished *SqT* is assigned to the Franklin in El, and to the Merchant in Hg. The exchange between the Host and the Squire before the latter's tale in El appears as an exchange between the Host and Franklin in Hg, and introduces *FranT*. These examples show 'how notional the tie between tale and teller could be ... they lead to the conclusion that not the individual but the type is being realised ... In the first instance, the type is an older, socially self-conscious person' (p 19) who perhaps envies the youthful representative of a class higher than his own; in the second, someone sufficiently high on the social ladder to evoke the Host's good manners.

783 Seaman, David M. '"The Wordes of the Frankleyn to the Squier": An Interruption?' *ELN* 24 (1986), 12–18.
The 'unequivocal interruptions' (p 15) in *CT* – the Host's interruption of *Thop* and the Knight's of *MkT* – share several traits: they are delivered from a position of authority, they are not ambiguous, they are marked as interruptions by scribal glosses, both Host and Knight give reasons for their actions, and both use similar language ('namoore of this') that appears as a formula for interruptions elsewhere in *CT*. The words of the Franklin that follow *SqT* exhibit none of these features, and are 'less likely to be an interruption than an end comment' (p 16). But *SqT* was not necessarily meant to be completed; the passage in question may have been written before *SqT*, or was perhaps intended to come after an interruption by someone other than the Franklin. See **784**.

784 Blake, N.F. 'The Manuscripts and Textual Tradition of the Canterbury Tales Again.' *PoeticaT* 28 (1988), 6–15.
Commentators on *CT* have not taken sufficiently into account recent work on the manuscripts, in particular the implications of the probable primacy of Hg. In suggesting that the link after *SqT* may have been written before the tale itself, Seaman (**783**) is 'apparently ignorant of the proposal that this link was written after the tales were arranged in Hg to fill a gap that was created by placing the tales in a sequence of tale-link-tale-link' (p 8). Burrow's contention (**606**) that Chaucer intended *SqT* and *FranT* to stand side by side is weakened by his admission that the Franklin does not interrupt *SqT*; 'if the tale was never completed, one might wonder whether a following link commenting on the tale would have been written' by the original author (p 11). If, as Lawton (**598**) suggests, the lines that appear in El as the introduction to *SqT* and in Hg as part of the Merchant–Franklin Link were written by Hoccleve, the argument that the passage as it appears in El was Chaucer's original form ceases to be valid, along with its corollary that the Ellesmere tale order is also Chaucerian.

784a Brewer, Derek S. *An Introduction to Chaucer*. 1984. 2nd ed., *A New Introduction to Chaucer*. 1998. See **586**.
The Franklin's effusive praise 'is perhaps meant to stifle any continuation'

of *SqT* (p 332).

785 Koff, Leonard Michael. *Chaucer and the Art of Storytelling*. Berkeley: U of California P, 1988.
In contrast to the Franklin's diplomatic praise of *SqT*, the Host's words to the Franklin are rude; the interchange reveals 'the Franklin's poise and the Host's imbalance' (p 202). In dismissing the Franklin's wish that his son might have heard and profited from *SqT*, the Host may be sensing contradictions in the Franklin's attitude toward material wealth; he scorns *possessioun* (line 686) but also laments his son's mishandling of his possessions (pp 201–2).

786 Cooper, Helen. *The Canterbury Tales*. 1989. See **635**.
Although the tone of the Franklin's words to the Squire differs from that of the other unequivocal interruptions in *CT*, the Franklin is a *gentil* speaking to another *gentil*, and he addresses the Squire with the tact and courtesy required by the occasion, praising the performance as if it were complete. Since franklins were long-established *gentils*, the Franklin's stress on *gentilesse* should not be interpreted as a sign of social climbing – although the Franklin does dwell on the topic at somewhat excessive length.

787 Ganim, John M. 'Forms of Talk in The Canterbury Tales.' *PoeticaT* 34 (1991), 88–99.
The interchange between the Franklin and Harry Bailly dramatizes the distinction between unselfconscious 'talk' and the more elevated practice of comuning (cf. line 693). In switching from the former to the latter, Harry 'describes the act of tale-telling in the same contract-like way that the Franklin himself will describe "gentilesse" in the tale' (p 95). But the Franklin backs down, acknowledging that he has not yet earned the right to commune with the Squire; his earlier remarks were just talk.

788 Miller, Clarence H. 'Three Phrases in The Canterbury Tales: "youre dyvynytee" (FrT III–D 1512), "youre gentillesse" (SqT V–F 695), "Goode lief" (Pro WBT III–D 431).' *N&Q* n.s. 39 (1992), 152–5.
The Host's 'Straw for youre gentillesse!' is derisive, a deliberate violation of the polite use of the second-person plural for ironic effect. In his response, the Franklin may also be using the polite form ironically.

789 Spearing, A.C., ed. *The Franklin's Prologue and Tale from the Canterbury Tales by Geoffrey Chaucer*. 1966/1994. See **86**.
It seems likely that Chaucer meant to have the Franklin interrupt the Squire – tactfully, but with the tact of a man determined to assert his own social position. In contrasting the Squire's *vertu* and *gentilesse* with his own son's dissoluteness, the Franklin exposes 'muddled values with no awareness of what he is doing' (1994, p 74).

790 Laskaya, Anne. *Chaucer's Approach to Gender in the Canterbury Tales*. Chaucer Studies 23. Woodbridge, UK: Brewer, 1995.

Harry Bailly's response to the Franklin's hopes for his son's reform shows that he prefers 'gamesmanship' to *gentilesse* (p 190).

791 Andrew, Malcolm, ed. *Geoffrey Chaucer: Three Tales of Love and Chivalry.* 2000. See **125**.
The Franklin's interruption of the Squire's rambling narrative – apparently pretending that he believes the younger man to have finished his tale – is 'a remarkable feat of tactful manipulation,' perhaps something the Franklin learned from his public life as an MP and a JP. The Franklin further displays his social skills by glossing over the Host's irritation at his dwelling on *gentilesse,* defusing a potentially awkward moment in the introduction to his own tale (xvi).

791a Mazzon, Gabriella. 'Social relations and Forms of Address in the *Canterbury Tales.*' In *The History of English in a Social Context: A Contribution to Historical Sociolinguistics.* Ed. Dieter Kastrovsky and Arthur Mettinger. Berlin: de Gruyter, 2000. Pp 135–68.
The asymmetric switching between *thou* and *you* forms of address in the Harry Bailly's interchange with the Franklin (lines 696–704) reveals a clear imposition of authority on the part of the Host, who ranks lower than the Franklin on the social ladder.

792 Smith, D. Vance. *Arts of Possession: The Middle English Household Imaginary.* Medieval Cultures 33. Minneapolis: U of Minnesota P, 2003.
In dismissing *possessioun* while citing precisely the sum that would make him liable for distraint of knighthood (lines 983–7), the Franklin 'makes his oath espousing virtue into ... a false rendering.' And in expressing his desire that his son might learn virtue from a 'gentil wight' rather than from 'a page' (lines 692–3), he indicts the young man for exactly those wasteful practices commonly associated with the gentility (pp 40–1).

793 Keen, Maurice. 'Chivalry.' In *Gentry Culture in Late Medieval England.* Ed. Raluca Radulescu and Alison Truelove. Manchester, UK: Manchester UP, 2005. Pp 35–49.
In Chaucer's day, the international chivalry of the Knight and the regional society and local government of the Franklin were 'overlapping worlds.' In his words to the Squire, the Franklin wishes for his son the *gentilesse* of one born to a higher degree rather than a standard of his own; 'he wished to see him look and live like a knight's son, not like a bumpkin with too much money' (p 37). Had the Franklin founded a gentry lineage, the Squire's *gentilesse* would have rubbed off, if not yet fully on the Franklin's son, then probably on his grandson in the next generation (p 47).

794 Mann, Jill, ed. *Geoffrey Chaucer: The Canterbury Tales.* 2005. See **128**.
The Franklin's words imply that the Squire has finished his tale; they do not support the suggestion that he is interrupting the young man in midstream. The Franklin's concern with his son's lack of *gentilesse* may be more

plausibly taken as a version of the country gentry's lament over the younger generation's dissipated ways than as a sign of the Franklin's aspirations to a higher social stratum (p 949).

ꙮ *The Franklin's Tale*: 1894–2005

See also **200, 246, 253, 283, 285, 289, 296, 298, 300, 301, 315, 328, 332, 335, 340, 345, 352, 355, 356, 357, 359, 360, 363, 365, 367, 371, 372, 400, 452, 494, 515, 517, 530, 539, 567, 581, 591, 635, 649, 654, 663, 664, 668, 679, 683, 700, 707, 714, 756, 761, 1741, 1789, 1863.**

The Franklin's Tale, 1894–1949

795 Skeat, Walter W., ed. *The Complete Works of Geoffrey Chaucer, Edited from Numerous Manuscripts*. 1894–7. See **4**.
Among Skeat's notes to *FranT*, the following have attracted comment. 'Withouten coppe' (line 942) signifies that Aurelius 'drank his penance in full measure, not by small quantities at a time' (5:389–90). The original sense of *tregetoure* (line 1141) was 'one who caused rapid changes, by help of some mechanical contrivance' (5:392). Skeat's comments on the clerk's astrological calculations (lines 1273–96) are notably detailed (5:393–5).

796 Ker, William Paton. 'Chaucer.' In *Essays on Medieval English Literature*. London: Macmillan, 1905. Pp 76–100.
FranT includes superstitions uncharacteristic of Chaucer's more complex poetry. It revolves around 'the point of honour,' on which 'the virtue of patience, the virtue of truth, are ... impaled, crying out for some gentle casuist to come and put them out of their torment' (p 99).

797 Root, Robert Kilburn. *The Poetry of Chaucer*. 1906/1922. See **378**.
The Franklin laments his son's behavior as a 'Toledo oil-magnate' might 'bewail the vicious tendencies of the son whom he is lavishly maintaining at Yale or Harvard' (p 273). The source of *FranT* is probably a French fabliau, the model as well for Menedon's tale in *Fil*. Although the sense of honor that demands the fulfillment of Dorigen's pledge is 'hyperquixotic' (p 276), Arveragus's action is nonetheless justified; it is a noble deed that begets nobility in others. (Revised edition contains additional bibliography, pp 294–300.)

798 Hinckley, Henry Barrett. *Notes on Chaucer: A Commentary on the Prolog and Six Canterbury Tales*. 1907. See **380**.

Chaucer's source for *FranT* was probably a Latin version of a Breton story, supplemented by *Fil*. Stylistic lapses and structural uncertainties point to an early date of composition, not later than 1380. Like *ClT*, *FranT* exalts a single virtue, appealing to a 'sentimental standard' (p 239) of *trouthe* rather than to common sense. Numerous words and lines are annotated, including *Cithero* (line 722; a popular association of *Cicero* with *Cithaeron*?); *Kayrrud* (line 808; 'the coast of Brittany has been slowly sinking beneath the sea ever since the dawn of history ... perhaps the site of Chaucer's *Kayrrud* is now submerged'); 'withouten coppe' (line 942; 'he drank, not of the cup of sorrow, but of the fountain-head'); lines 992–8 (the removal of the rocks is a 'happier invention' than the creation of a garden in winter, as the former suggests Dorigen's solicitude for her absent husband); 'this is as muche ... nyght' (line 1018; 'is not this curiously abrupt line a mark of immaturity in the poet's art?'); 'his herte' (line 1260; 'that is, the Magician's heart. I do not believe that Aurelius threatened to commit suicide. Such a threat would not have troubled a magician in medieval Europe, whatever effect it might have produced in Japan'); lines 1367–1456 (the catalogue of virtuous women 'was evidently written in order to conciliate the prejudices that the conduct of Dorigene was likely to arouse especially among the more devoted adherents of the Church'); 'cropen out of the grounde' (line 1614; the ancients believed that men were originally sprung from the earth, from rocks or from trees) (pp 237–60).

799 Hammond, Eleanor Prescott. *Chaucer: A Bibliographical Manual*. 1908. See **382**.
Discusses *FranT*'s position in the MSS (pp 310–11), lists editions, modernizations, and translations, and summarizes previous scholarship on the tale's sources and analogues and date (p 314).

800 Koellreutter, Maria. *Das Privatleben in England nach der Dichtungen von Chaucer, Gower, und Langland*. Halle: Karras, 1908.
Lines 1472–4 are cited as an example of *you* as the form of address of husband to wife in courtly circles and among socially conscious bourgeois (p 96).

801 Hart, Walter Morris. 'The Franklin's Tale.' In *Haverford Essays: Studies in Modern Literature Prepared by Some Former Pupils of Francis B. Gummere*. Haverford, PA: Haverford College, 1909. Repr. Freeport, NY: Books for Libraries, 1967. Pp 183–204.
FranT is dramatically conceived, appropriate to the character of its teller. Although the Franklin calls it a Breton lay, he does not invest it with the trappings of Celtic faerie; its settings are vaguely conceived and described, and its characters are dimly visualized. Although *FranT* is memorable for 'the dramatic ... expression of all degrees of joy and sorrow,' its central motif is not an emotion but a concept: 'the contagious influence of good' (p 207). *FranT* shares details of setting, plot, theme, and characterization with

the Breton lays, but the contrasts are more striking than the parallels. *FranT* lacks the vividly pictured backgrounds and developed social settings of the lays, its characters are more subtly drawn, and it differs from the lays in its skepticism about the supernatural and its concern with a moral concept. The tale is closely connected with the pilgrimage frame. It springs from the Franklin's 'good-natured rivalry' (p 233) with the Squire, and two of its characters – the knight Arveragus and the squire Aurelius – 'are more or less accurate portraits of Canterbury Pilgrims' (p 233). *FranT* is also integrated into *CT* by means of common themes: the interest in astrology, the question of marital relations, the borrowings, in Dorigen's Complaint, from *Jov*, 'the favorite book of the Wife of Bath's fifth husband' (p 234).

802 Corson, Hiram. *Index of Proper Names and Subjects to Chaucer's Canterbury Tales together with Comparisons and Similes, Metaphors and Proverbs, Maxims, etc., in the Same*. 1911. See **389**.
The index of names and subjects (including scriptural quotations and allusions) is followed by separate listings of comparisons and similes (two in *FranT*); metaphors (one in *FranT*); proverbs, maxims, and sententious expressions (two in *FranT*); prayers, entreaties, and imprecations (one in *FranT*).

803 Douady, Jules. *La Mer et les Poètes Anglais*. Paris: Hachette, 1912.
Chaucer's interest in astronomy is evident in *Astr*; in *FranT*, however, he rejects genuine learning for illusionistic magic. If, instead of resorting to implausible hocus-pocus, the clerk had used his books to predict a high tide that would have covered the coastal rocks, he would have been recognized for his mastery of true science (p 42).

804 Ker, William Paton. *Medieval English Literature*. London: Oxford UP, 1912; pbk ed. (with bibliographical notes), 1969. Also published as *English Literature: Medieval*. London: Oxford UP; New York: Holt, 1912. Numerous reprs, including Folcroft, PA: Folcroft, 1977.
Chaucer's use of a popular medieval convention in which a single obligation is regarded as if it were the only rule of conduct is a partial obstacle to the success of *ClT* and *FranT*. In the latter, Chaucer is 'confined to a problem under strict rules, a drama of difficulties without character' (p 134).

805 Kittredge, George Lyman. 'Chaucer's Discussion of Marriage.' 1912. See **390**.
The Franklin's admiration for the *gentilesse* expressed by the Squire in his tale reveals his own social ambition, which 'comes out naïvely and with a certain pathos' (p 24) in his comparison of the Squire and his own son. He 'takes delicate vengeance' (p 26) on the Host's repudiation of the topic of *gentilesse* by telling a story in which the three male characters exemplify that quality. The Wife of Bath's disquisition on *gentilesse* is doubtless lingering in the Franklin's mind, and his tale responds to the discussion of marriage that she has set in motion. The Franklin's theory of marriage depends upon the presence of both *gentilesse* and love on both sides; he offers this ideal as

the basis of a happy married life. In so doing, he repudiates the one-sided unions depicted by the Wife of Bath and the Clerk. He also 'boldly challenges' the view that chivalric love is incompatible with the mastery that accompanies marriage; 'the difficulty about mastery vanishes when mutual love and forbearance' are made the guiding principles of a marriage (p 33). The Franklin brings the marriage debate to a satisfactory conclusion, and proposes a solution that we 'need not hesitate ... to accept ... as that which Geoffrey Chaucer the man accepted for his own part ... A better has never been devised or imagined' (p 33). See **761**, **845**, **867**, **910**, **973**, **977**, **987**, **1072**, **1196**, **1238r**, **1358**.

806 Schofield, William Henry. *Chivalry in English Literature: Chaucer, Malory, Spenser and Shakespeare*. 1912. See **391**.
FranT treats 'ideal love, with its concomitant fidelity to troth' (p 52). After we read the tale, 'our English word "betrothed" renews its medieval significance; it implies a chivalric obligation' (p 54).

807 Dodd, William George. *Courtly Love in Chaucer and Gower*. 1913. See **392**.
Lists instances of conventional love language and courtly terminology in *FranT*. The wooing of Dorigen by Aurelius recalls the situation described by many of the troubadours, but Chaucer departs from the usual courtly denouement by having Dorigen reject her suitor (pp 248–50).

808 Koch, J. 'Textkritische bemerkungen zu Chaucers *Canterbury Tales*.' 1913. See **393**.
Textual notes on lines 725, 950, 1150, 1455–6, 1493–8, and 1540 (pp 380–2).

809 Meyer, Emil. *Die Charakterzeichnung bei Chaucer*. Studien zur Englischen Philologie 48. Halle: Niemeyer, 1913.
Characterization in *FranT* is primarily a function of plot; the noble-mindedness of the characters at once creates and resolves their dilemmas (p 52).

810 Tatlock, John Strong Perry. 'Astrology and Magic in Chaucer's *Franklin's Tale*.' In *Anniversary Papers by Colleagues and Pupils of George Lyman Kittredge*. Ed. F.N. Robinson et al. Boston: Ginn, 1913. Repr. New York: Russell and Russell, 1967. Pp 339–50.
'The most subtly interesting person in the tale' (p 340), the Orléans clerk is well-versed in astronomy and astrological magic. The moon, his planet of choice, was thought to be especially favorable to magical illusions. At the time of his activities, the moon was likely to have been full, in the sign of Cancer, in the term of Jupiter or Venus, and in the ascendant – a set of circumstances unusually potent for the clerk's magical practices. The clerk's attention to the moon's mansions suggests that these divisions of its monthly path were connected with the production of illusions. The magician may have chosen a mansion whose influence reinforced his other rites, which might have included the charms and spirits of natural magic, and perhaps the sacrifices and incantations associated with necromancy as well. The es-

teem with which this practitioner of forbidden arts is portrayed accords well with the tale's setting in pagan antiquity.

811 Tupper, Frederick. 'Saint Venus and the Canterbury Pilgrims.' *Nation* 97 (1913), 354–6.
If Fragment C (VI) is placed after *FranT*, 'we may then regard the Doctor's story of oppressed virginity courting death rather than disgrace, as directly inspired by the country gentleman's many illustrations of this pathetic theme' (p 355).

811a Hadow, Grace E. *Chaucer and His Times*. 1914. See **394**.
'One of the most perfect pictures of married life at its best,' *FranT* gives dramatic substance to the narrator's axioms about true love and forbearance. Dorigen's confidence in her husband's honor almost makes us forget the unlikeliness of the situation (pp 128–9).

811b Nitze, William Albert. 'The Romance of Erec, Son of Lac.' *MP* 11 (1914), 445–89.
At the beginning of his discussion of *Erec*, Nitze quotes *FranT*, lines 745–52, as an expression of the 'fundamental issue' of Chrétien's poem (p 447). Although the ideal marriage must include both love and forbearance, the husband must keep the name of *soveraynetee* (line 751), in accordance with the orthodox doctrine that husbands must rule. Since Enide has been the innocent cause of his disgrace, 'it is only natural that Erec, wounded in his pride, should turn against the cause of his dishonor, blameless as Enide really is' (p 448).

812 Tatlock, John Strong Perry. *The Scene of the Franklin's Tale Visited*. Chaucer Society Publications, Second Series, 51. London: Kegan Paul, Trench, Trübner; Oxford: Oxford UP, 1914.
Pedmark (line 801) is the Pointe de Penmarch in Brittany, the southern cape encircled by a chain of dark granitic rocks, dangerous to sailors. The low, flat coast at Penmarch does not correspond to the high shore on which Dorigen wanders; the first localizer of the tale probably 'drew somewhat on his imagination' (p 9). *Kayrrud* (line 808) signifies 'red mansion' or 'village' in Breton, and is likely to have designated a place that once contained Gallo-Roman ruins. The form of the word suggests that it was not derived from a French source. Chaucer's care in placing his story in Roman times is indicated by place names (e.g., *Armorik*, line 729), personal names, and numerous pagan details. The poem's ancient setting reflects Chaucer's wish to present a fully imagined account of astrology and magic, while at the same time distancing himself as a contemporary Christian from such heathen practices. Unwilling to mar the poem's noble tone by representing the magician as 'a shabby and knavish *déclassé*,' he nevertheless expresses 'the incredulity and disgust he felt for such arts in his own day' (pp 36–7). *Dorigen* may be derived from 'Dorguen' or 'Droguen,' the name of the wife of Alain I, the ninth-century

king of Brittany. Chaucer's choice of Orléans – world famous as a law school by the end of the thirteenth century – may also have been dictated by its association with occult studies, and by its popularity as a place of study among medieval Bretons. Schofield's argument for the Celtic origin of *FranT* by way of a Breton lay (**246**) is less persuasive than Rajna's claim (**249**) for *Fil* as Chaucer's primary source. The details from Geoffrey of Monmouth cited by Schofield as evidence of the tale's Celtic roots would have been directly available to Chaucer from *HRB*. Paradoxically, the exactness of the topography in *FranT* argues against a Breton lay as Chaucer's source; the French lays are notably spare in their use of local detail. 'The fact is that *FranT* is too Breton for a Breton lay' (p 75).

• Review by J. Koch, *ESt* 49 (1915–16), 437–40: Although Tatlock maintains that the very precision of the Breton elements in *FranT* argues against a Breton source, Chaucer is unlikely to have conducted extensive research in order to trick his audience into believing in the historical authenticity of his tale. Nor does Tatlock's tracing of the names of the characters to *HRB* provide a conclusive refutation of Schofield's argument for a Breton source. *FranT* would seem to be based on a Breton lay that came to England in a French or Latin form.

• Review by William Paton Ker, *MLR* 12 (1917), 84–5: Tatlock's view of the genesis of *FranT* – that the poet borrows the name of Breton lay for a story that he has taken from Geoffrey of Monmouth and Boccaccio in part because the tale is a short one, in part because he wants the black rocks of Penmarch for his scenery – seems probable, and speaks to Chaucer's command of artifice.

813 Tupper, Frederick. 'Chaucer and the Seven Deadly Sins.' *PMLA* 29 (1914), 93–128.
See **811**.

814 Heidrich, Käte. *Das geographische Weltbild des späteren englischen Mittelalters mit besonderer Berücksichtigung der Vorstellungen Chaucer's und seiner Zeitgenossen*. 1915. See **395**.
Includes brief discussions of place names in *FranT*, beginning with *Pernaso* (line 721) and ending with *Tolletanes* (line 1273).

815 Kittredge, George Lyman. *Chaucer and his Poetry*. 1915. See **759**. Excerpts repr. in *The Canterbury Tales: Nine Tales and the General Prologue* (see **111**). Pp 539–46.
Kittredge's comments on *FranT* present the substance of his earlier argument (**805**) with some additions and rephrasing. The Franklin resumes the debate on matrimony and 'carries it to a triumphant conclusion' (p 205). Although the old tale that the Franklin employs throws no light on the problem of sovereignty in marriage, the Franklin puts this subject at the center of his retelling, devoting almost a hundred lines, 'without a particle of verbiage,'

to his theory of marriage (p 209). The Franklin's personal credibility ('he is no cloistered rhetorician, but a ruddy, white-bearded vavasour') compels us to 'lend a credent ear' to his proposed solution (p 210). 'The thing is possible. The problem need puzzle us no longer' (p 210). See **818**.

816 Wells, John Edwin. *A Manual of Writings in Middle English, 1050–1400*. 1916. See **398**.

The spirit and tone of *FranT* accord with the noble sentiments expressed about sovereignty in marriage, patience, and *gentilesse*. Perhaps Chaucer intended an unwritten endlink to the tale to comprise a discussion of the Franklin's final question about generosity. The tale's style and appearance in the MSS suggests that it is one of the last composed of the *CT* (pp 735–7). Surveys scholarship on the place of Fragment V (F) in the MSS (pp 732–3) and supplies bibliographical references (p 880). Nine supplements (1919–52) take the survey of scholarship through 1945.

817 Baum, Paull F. 'Notes on Chaucer.' 1917. See **399**.

Although most editions extend it to line 1544, Aurelius's farewell speech to Dorigen ends at 1540. The following four lines, which call attention to the squire's generosity and refer to Dorigen in the third person, are inappropriate for Aurelius, and should be assigned to the Franklin.

818 Hinckley, Henry Barrett. 'The Debate on Marriage in the *Canterbury Tales*.' *PMLA* 32 (1917), 292–305. Repr. in *Chaucer: Modern Essays in Criticism* (see **381**). Pp 216–25.

Disputing Kittredge's belief (**815**) that *WBT, ClT, MerT,* and *FranT* constitute a coherent Marriage Group, Hinckley argues that *FranT* exhibits few if any significant links with any tale preceding *SqT*. *FranT* is not primarily concerned with matrimony; it can be better understood as a medieval version of Cicero's *De amicitia*. Kittredge's characterization of *FranT* as a 'triumphant conclusion' of the marriage debate fails to take into account Cecilia's unconsummated marriage in *SNT*, 'which might easily be drawn into the debate by just such processes of reasoning as those by which the debate itself has been constructed' (p 303).

819 Jefferson, Bernard L. *Chaucer and the Consolation of Philosophy of Boethius*. 1917. See **151**.

The Franklin's comments on true *gentilesse* in *Sq–FranL* reveal the influence of Dante and of Boethius's treatment of *gentilesse* in *Consol* 3.m6 (p 102). Palamon's address to the cruel gods in *KnT* (I.1303–23) and Dorigen's lament over the rocks are derived from *Consol* 1.m5. In both passages, Chaucer's characters leave to the wisdom of clerks the answers that Dame Philosophy explains in full and to Boethius's satisfaction (pp 69–71).

820 Hinckley, Henry Barrett. 'Chauceriana.' 1918. See **401**.

FranT's beauty is that of the naïve Italian Renaissance primitives. The tale's naïve features include the literal interpretation of Dorigen's playful promise, the attribution of the final meeting of Dorigen and Aurelius to chance, and the absence of shock or amusement at Arveragus's threatening of Dorigen with death if she discloses their secret.

821 Grimm, Florence M. *Astronomical Lore in Chaucer*. University of Nebraska Studies in Language, Literature and Criticism 2. Lincoln, NE: n.p., 1919. Repr. New York: AMS, 1970.
Chaucer gives *FranT* a pagan setting to express the scorn he feels for certain contemporary superstitions without debasing the character of the clerk. The tale's astrological passages do not suggest total disbelief on Chaucer's part; like Dante, he was interested in astrology's philosophical aspects, even while distancing himself from its shady practices (p 58).

822 Jack, Adolphus Alfred. *A Commentary on the Poetry of Chaucer and Spenser*. 1920. See **402**.
The conclusion of *FranT* is 'fearfully unreal ... Aurelius was willing to compel Dorigen. Why then should he be moved by the husband? Only if you are to look on the wife as a chattel. Thus in Chaucer the flow of mediaeval manners, the prevailing conception, is constant, even when, as here, the ideal is that of mediaeval chivalry' (pp 105–6).

823 Wedel, T.O. *The Mediæval Attitude Toward Astrology, Particularly in England*. Yale Studies in English 60. New Haven, CT: Yale UP, 1920. Numerous reprs, including Hamden, CT: Archon, 1968.
The Franklin's condemnation of astrological magic contains 'nothing ... that is strikingly divergent from the general tenor of enlightened opinion in the fourteenth century' (p 150). Although Chaucer acknowledged the ecclesiastical hostility toward magic in the persons of the Parson and the Franklin, 'he accepted a moderate judicial astrology ... without protest' (p 150).

824 Brusendorff, Aage. *The Chaucer Tradition*. London: Oxford UP; Copenhagen: Branner, 1925. Repr. Gloucester, MA: Peter Smith, 1965.
Lines 1455–6 appear only in El, accompanied by a Latin marginal note giving sources for a more elaborate listing of virtuous wives, of which Chaucer produced only this single couplet (p 82). Lines 2493–8 (also unique to El) have the character of a later addition, perhaps generated by the oral nature of Chaucer's presentation (p 83). The description of Aurelius's love poetry (lines 947–8), similar in phrasing to Alceste's listing of Chaucer's amorous lyrics in *LGW* (F410–1, 420), suggests that the latter passage is formulaic rather than an accurate record of Chaucer's lost minor poems (p 432).

825 Gerould, Gordon Hall. 'The Social Status of Chaucer's Franklin.' *PMLA* 41 (1926), 262–79. Repr. with revisions in Gerould, *Chaucerian Essays*. Princeton, NJ: Princeton UP; London: Oxford UP, 1952. Repr. New York: Russell and Russell, 1968. Pp 33–54.
The Franklin's disclaimers about his knowledge of rhetoric are the 'half-humorous deprecations of a person who made no pretence of clerkly lore' (p

264), although his tale shows sufficient learning. See **1067**, **1124r**.

826 Manly, John Matthews. 'Chaucer and the Rhetoricians.' 1926. See **406**.
'A fine story finely told is nearly spoiled by one hundred lines of rhetorical *exempla*' (p 112). Chaucer tries to give this 'astonishing fad' dramatic motivation by inserting the series of twenty-one consecutive instances into Dorigen's complaint against Fortune (p 105). But any reader, 'modern or medieval,' would have been more powerfully moved if Dorigen had been allowed to express 'the real feelings appropriate to her character and situation' (p 112).

827 Royster, James F. 'Chaucer's "Colle Tregetour."' *SP* 23 (1926), 380–4.
A passage from the earliest extant French conversation manual, *La Maniere de language qui t'enseigners bien adroit parler et escrire doulz francois selon l'usage et la coustume de France* (1396), linking Orléans with necromancy, is cited in connection with Aurelius's visit to the city to seek out the clerkly magician. The squire's name is perhaps based on the form of the city's name (*Aurelians* or *Aurelianus*) attested in the French treatise.

828 Baldwin, Charles Sears. 'Cicero on Parnassus.' *PMLA* 42 (1927), 106–12.
The conjunction of Cicero and Parnassus in the Franklin's disclaimer of knowledge of 'colours of rethoryk' (line 726) is part of Chaucer's criticism – evident also in *HF, SqT, ClT,* and *NPT* – of the application of rhetoric to narrative recommended in the twelfth- and thirteenth-century compositional manuals.

829 Cowling, George H. *Chaucer*. 1927. See **408**.
FranT is 'a picture of a perfect marriage and a riddle in comparative liberality' (p 175). The tale's wise solution shows that the opinions on marriage in *WBT, ClT,* and *MerT* were 'deliberate jests' (p 176).

830 Praz, Mario. 'Chaucer and the Great Italian Writers of the Trecento (II).' *MC* 6 (1927), 131–57. Repr. in Praz, *The Flaming Heart*. Garden City, NY: Doubleday, 1958; repr. Gloucester, MA: Peter Smith, 1966, pp 29–89; in Praz, *Machiavelli in Inghilterra ed altri saggi sui rapporti letterari anglo-italiani*. Florence: Sansoni, 1962, pp 29–61; and in *Chaucer: The Critical Heritage* (see **390**), 2:403–29.
Cithero (line 722) is not the Franklin's blunder; confusion between 'Cithero' and 'Cicero' can be ascribed to phonetic variation (pp 132–3). The wife's request to her suitor in *Fil* for a garden blooming in midwinter is an arbitrary impossibility. The task Dorigen sets for Aurelius – the removal of the dangerous coastal rocks – is really a vow of loyalty to Arveragus: she is ready to bind herself to a condition which, if fulfilled, will lead to her husband's safety (p 155n).

831 Buck, Howard. 'Chaucer's Use of Feminine Rhyme.' *MP* 26 (1928–9), 13–14.
'In Chaucer, the feminine rhyme is at the very least upon an equal footing' with the masculine (p 13). Feminine rhymes in Chaucer tend to form in clusters. *FranT* lines 729–40, 855–68, and 1373–86 are cited examples of passages

in *CT* with a least ten consecutive feminine rhymes.

832 Getty, Agnes K. 'Chaucer's Changing Conceptions of the Humble Lover.' 1929. See **412**.
Aurelius's behavior is wholly conventional; he becomes a puppet moved by the code of love. Chaucer's apparent sympathy with the squire's distress dissolves when, at lines 1084–6, he 'forcibly drops him' (p 214), effectively undermining the elements of idealized love in Aurelius's conduct for the remainder of the tale.

833 Naunin, Traugott. *Der Einfluss der mittelalterlichen Rhetorik auf Chaucers Dichtung*. 1929. See **413**.
FranT is cited to illustrate the poet's direct commentary on medieval rhetoric (lines 719–26), his use of *apostrophe*, his mimicry of school rhetoric (lines 1016–18), and his failure to integrate a long series of exempla into the fabric of his narrative (lines 1367–1456).

834 Vallese, Tarquinio. *Goffredo Chaucer visto da un italiano*. 1930. See **415**.
Chaucer surpasses Boccaccio in his evocation of pathos; Dorigen's wavering between fear and hope, her melancholy, her inexperience, and her sincerity have no parallels in Boccaccio's treatment of his heroine in *Fil* (pp 122–3).

835 Engel, Hildegard. *Structure and Plot in Chaucer's Canterbury Tales*. 1931. See **416**.
The tale's key ideas of truth and magnanimity are enriched by psychological realism in the delineation of character, which includes the capacity for self-denial (p 54).

836 Patch, Howard Rollin. 'Chauceriana.' *ESt* 65 (1931), 351–9.
'Beste farynge' (line 932) probably denotes physical appearance rather than behavior.

837 Baldwin, Charles Sears. *Three Medieval Centuries of Literature in England, 1100–1400*. Boston: Little, Brown, 1932. Repr. New York: Phaeton, 1968.
Like *PardT, FranT* is 'composed by scenes not merely in a series, but in a compelling order ... its critical scene [Arveragus's interview with Dorigen after his return home] functions as the turning-point of a play' (p 214).

838 Dempster, Germaine. *Dramatic Irony in Chaucer*. 1932. See **276**.
Dramatic irony exists in *FranT* in the gap between the expectations of the three male characters and the tale's denouement. The best stroke of irony is Dorigen's attempt to discourage Aurelius, which gives him a right to claim her love. In contrast to the task set by the weakly characterized heroine of *Fil*, Dorigen's request that Aurelius remove the rocks from the Breton coast expresses her fear for her beloved husband's safety, and hence deepens the pathos of the plot's ironic twist (pp 62–7/pp 306–11).

839 Getty, Agnes K. 'The Mediæval–Modern Conflict in Chaucer's Poetry.' 1932. See **417**.
The piling up of authorities is one of Chaucer's 'mediæval' characteristics.

He tells *FranT* with 'modern' economy until he reaches Dorigen's Complaint; her 'endless parade of learning' reminds us that 'Dorigen is but Chaucer after all' (p 397).

840 McCormick, William, with the assistance of Janet Heseltine. *The Manuscripts of Chaucer's Canterbury Tales, a Critical Description of Their Contents.* 1933. See **419**.
Describes the contents of fifty-seven complete or virtually complete copies of *CT* (including Caxton's first and second printed editions) and twenty-eight defective MSS. For *FranT*, the details noted include omitted lines, conflated lines, blank lines, anticipated lines, transposed lines, missing passages, missing headlinks, the presence and omission of special capitals, and scribal rubrics. The rubrics include the following descriptions of the tale: *fabula de la Frankleyn* (p 4 et passim), *the Frankleyns tale* (p 16 et passim), *fabula sua de la Rokkes de Britayne* (p 114 et passim), *the tale of the Frankeleyn* (p 141 et passim), *the Frankelens tale of the Knyght Arveragus and Dame Dorygene his wyff and the noble Philosophre of Orlyaunce* (p 517).

841 Tuve, Rosemond. *Seasons and Months: Studies in a Tradition of Middle English Poetry*. 1933. See **420**.
Cites parallels between the Franklin's winter description (lines 1243–55) and representations of the seasons in medieval art (pp 123–4).

842 Whiting, B.J. *Chaucer's Use of Proverbs*. 1934. See **423**.
FranT contains two proverbs (lines 764–7, 1472) and two sententious remarks (lines 773–5, 829–31).

843 Goffin, R.C. 'Chaucer and Elocution.' *MÆ* 4 (1935), 127–42.
Dorigen's catalogue of virtuous heroines is an instance of Chaucer's ironic treatment of lists of exempla from antiquity. Dorigen 'pauses, though only for a moment, to reflect: "what sholde I mo examples heer-of sayn ...? I wol conclude ..." But her memory seems refreshed by the interval, and off she starts again, recounting examples for another thirty lines!' (pp 141–2).

844 Harrison, Benjamin Samuel. 'The Rhetorical Inconsistency of Chaucer's Franklin.' *SP* 32 (1935), 55–61.
The Franklin's statement that he 'lerned nevere rethorik' (line 719) is belied by the presence in his tale of at least seventy of the rhetorical colors prescribed in *Ad Herennium* and the medieval Latin compositional manuals. Three possible reasons for this inconsistency are suggested: the disclaimer may be a conventional modesty prologue – 'a meaningless gesture' (p 60); Chaucer may have written the tale before assigning it to the Franklin, and neglected to make tale and Prologue agree; Chaucer may be 'playing with us in the spirit of a Shakespearian Puck. He fools us into expecting a plain tale and then surprises us with one highly ornate and literary' (p 61).

845 Lyons, Clifford P. 'The Marriage Debate in the *Canterbury Tales*.' *ELH* 2 (1935), 252–62.

The examination of marital sovereignty in *WBT*, *ClT*, *MerT*, and *FranT* does not imply, as Kittredge (**390**, **805**) maintains, a debate on marriage among the pilgrims. The Franklin's words to the Squire and his introductory apology give his fellow pilgrims no reason to suspect that he is about to resolve a knotty problem about marriage, and his concluding question to the tale's listeners has to do with *gentilesse*, not with marriage.

846 Tatlock, John Strong Perry. 'The *Canterbury Tales* in 1400.' 1935. See **424**.
Responding to Kase (**761**), Tatlock notes specific echoes in *FranT* of *WBP*, *WBT*, *ClT*, and *MerT*. 'The debate on marriage was held in mind in [*FranT*] as much as one need expect; Chaucer was writing tales, not polemics' (p 116n).

847 Dempster, Germaine. 'Chaucer at Work on the Complaint in *The Franklin's Tale*.' *MLN* 52 (1937), 16–23.
A comparison of the order of the exempla in lines 1367–1458 with *Jov* suggests that Chaucer originally may have contemplated ending Dorigen's Complaint either at lines 1412–13 or at line 1424, but that he later returned to Jerome's letter, sifting it for additional material. A marginal gloss (perhaps Chaucer's own) in El implies that the poet viewed the additions as improvements. But lines 1425–56 display 'perfunctoriness and lack of interest' on Chaucer's part, 'a degree of *negligence* and *rape*, not to say boredom' rarely evident elsewhere in his works (p 22). See **289**, **298**, **850**, **912**.

848 Hawkins, Laurence Faulkner. *The Place of Group F in the Canterbury Chronology*. 1937. See **428**.
FranT contains crudities of plot and characterization that suggest artistic immaturity; its romantic, serious tone is characteristic of Chaucer's earlier writings. *FranT*'s literary filiations (Machaut, Jean de Meun, Boethius, Boccaccio) place it, like *SqT*, in the mid-1380s, a date supported as well by its close thematic relation to *KnT*, *TC*, and *Anel*. Parallels with *WBP*, *WBT*, and *MerT* suggest the chronological priority of *FranT*. There is no evidence that *FranT* was revised in order to serve as the conclusion to the marriage debate; the Franklin's introductory discussion of marriage shows by its use of Machaut and Jean de Meun that it belongs to the same early period as the rest of the tale. Dorigen's Complaint, however, was probably inserted at a later date.

• Review by Dorothy Everett, *YWES* 18 (1937), 79: Although Hawkins's argument for *FranT*'s date of composition may be correct, he has hardly proved his case.

• Review by M.B. Ruud, *MLN* 54 (1939), 140–2: *FranT*'s possible date of composition has little relevance to the problem of the Marriage Group. 'What difference does it make when the tales were written, if they do in fact bear on the question of "maistrie" in marriage?' (p 142).

See also **428r**.

849 Whitmore, Sister Mary E. *Medieval English Domestic Life and Amusements in the Works of Chaucer*. 1937. See **431**.

Given the cost of books in Chaucer's time, it is unlikely that the clerk's *studie* (line 1214) was wholly devoted to books; it was probably a combination of chamber and study (pp 43–4).

850 Dempster, Germaine. 'A Further Note on Dorigen's *Exempla.*' *MLN* 54 (1939), 137–8.

The placement of one of the Ellesmere glosses (see **847**) opposite line 1392 (or, in one case, 1395) in five MSS of *CT* may reflect an early, short form of Dorigen's Complaint. Chaucer may at one point have considered ending the passage at line 1398 or thereabouts.

851 Héraucourt, Will. *Die Wertwelt Chaucers, die Wertwelt einer Zeitwende.* 1939. See **434**.

Cites some seventy lines from *FranT* in this study of Chaucer's value system, organized around four cardinal virtues: wisdom, justice, valor, and moderation. Chaucer's use of terms in *FranT* (e.g., *blisse, suffraunce, trouthe, libertee, pitee*) is compared with his use of these terms elsewhere in his writings. The numerous appearances of *gentil* and its variants make *FranT* 'ein Hohes Lied auf *gentilesse*' (p 57).

852 Patch, Howard Rollin. *On Rereading Chaucer*. Cambridge, MA: Harvard UP, 1939.

In adapting *Fil* in *FranT*, Chaucer might have retained the lady's request that her suitor produce a garden blooming in January, thereby establishing parallels with *MerT*. But the task of removing the rocks more truly symbolizes Dorigen's love for her husband, and emphasizes this love rather than Aurelius's courtly desire (pp 220–1). Dramatic irony appears in *FranT* in the mutual promise of Dorigen and Arveragus to avoid *maistrye*, which is subsequently undercut by Arveragus's insistence that Dorigen commit adultery, and by our knowledge, in advance, that Aurelius will release Dorigen from her vow, an instance of irony that is 'positive, hopeful, implying better things than the characters expect' (p 226).

853 Chambers, R.W. 'Geoffrey Chaucer: Spring-Tide of English Poetry.' *TLS*, 20 April 1940.

Compares *FranT* to *SGGK*. Like Dorigen, Gawain is trapped by enchantment, but it never occurs to him to break his tryst.

854 Shelly, Percy Van Dyke. *The Living Chaucer*. 1940. See **437**.

The comment on Dorigen and Arveragus's domestic arrangement goes beyond questions of married life and gives us the Franklin's – or Chaucer's – views on human relations in general. In insisting that women desire liberty as much as men and are not to be kept in servitude, Chaucer is 'well in advance of his age' (p 283).

855 Vallese, Tarquinio. *La Poesia di Chaucer*. 1941/1946. See **439**.

See **834**.

856 Crow, Martin Michael. 'John of Angoulême and His Chaucer Manuscript.'

1942. See **441**.
In the manuscript of *CT* owned by John, count of Angoulême (a royal prisoner in England from 1412 to 1445), two spurious lines are introduced after line 784: 'But every wrong mot redressid be / Sum what by pacience and not al by cruelte.' Perhaps these lines were composed by Angoulême as an expression of 'the prisoner's philosophy' (p 97).

857 Long, E. Hudson. 'Chaucer as a Master of the Short Story.' *DelNotes* 16 (1943), 11–29.
As a 'continuous action centered about a single situation in which the characters reveal themselves' (p 25), *FranT* is both a well-told short story and an affirmation of human nobility.

857a Speirs, John. 'Chaucer (III): The Canterbury Tales (II).' *Scrutiny* 12 (Winter 1943), 35–57.
See **876**.

858 Utley, Francis Lee. *The Crooked Rib: An Analytical Index to the Argument about Women in English and Scots Literature to the End of the Year 1568.* Columbus: Ohio State UP, 1944.
The marriage in *FranT* violates the codes of courtly love and misogynistic satire in order to transcend them. The idea of partnership in marriage is present in medieval religious writing, but 'Chaucer was the first layman to make it palatable as a theory to laymen' (p 262).

859 French, W.H. '*The Franklin's Tale*, line 942.' *MLN* 60 (1945), 477–80.
'Withouten coppe he drank al his penaunce' is glossed by expressions connecting drinking with suffering sorrow in love, which in turn was often described as *penance*. To 'drink penance' would be to suffer inwardly – no cup would be needed. Line 942 might be paraphrased 'In secrecy he suffered bitter pain from love' (p 480).

860 Castelli, Alberto. *Geoffrey Chaucer*. 1946. See **444**.
The apparent contradiction between the Franklin's rhetorically accomplished tale and his professions of ignorance in his Prologue is not Chaucer's joke on the pilgrim narrator, but rather the Franklin's own irony. The tale's learning appears, inter alia, in its numerous classical and mythological allusions, which, as is common in Chaucer's poetry, illustrate moments of sadness or suffering. These allusions reflect the feeling of tragic fatality diffused throughout *FranT*, culminating in Dorigen's two monologues (pp 78–81).

861 Chute, Marchette. *Geoffrey Chaucer of England*. 1946. See **445**.
FranT brings the discussion of marriage to an 'adult, civilized conclusion': the Franklin corrects the Wife of Bath's ideas about sovereignty, provides a sympathetic view of the need for patience as an alternative to Griselda's 'somewhat feeble-minded fortitude,' and offers in his tale of a knight, a lady, and a lovesick squire an optimistic response to the Merchant's bitter treatment of a similar story (pp 289–90).

862 Praz, Mario. *Geoffrey Chaucer e i racconti di Canterbury*. Rome: Edizioni Italiane, 1947.
Although Chaucer bases *FranT* on Boccaccio, the story's atmosphere is that of a Breton lay. The tale teaches the virtues of fidelity and courtesy, embodied in the ideal union of Dorigen and Arveragus (p 136). See **312**.

863 Sledd, James. 'Dorigen's Complaint.' *MP* 45 (1947), 36–45.
Dorigen's Complaint is not, as has been argued, a flaw in the design of *FranT*. The evidence for its supposed lack of unity can be refuted, as can the claim that it exhibits a progressive deterioration of style and content. A deeply pathetic complaint would have thrown into disarray the tale's careful tonal balance. The passage is 'a deliberate bit of rhetorical extravagance, intended … as an assurance that all shall yet go well' (p 42); Dorigen is like the heroine of a child's story, with its inevitable happy ending. As she moves through her increasingly lengthy and increasingly irrelevant roll call of heroines, a potentially tragic tale becomes tragicomic, and we begin to suspect that this is another occasion when her husband will have to intervene. *FranP*, with its simultaneous display and denial of rhetorical skill, prepares us for the 'humorous incongruity' of Dorigen's rhetorical flights, which prevents her grief from becoming too painful, while the Franklin's distancing of himself and us from heathen illusion reminds us that 'if we are safe, so Dorigen must be' (p 45).

864 Hulbert, J.R. 'The *Canterbury Tales* and their Narrators.' *SP* 45 (1948), 565–77.
Although the *Sq–FranL* prepares us for *FranT*, the tale is an unlikely choice for the earthy landowner depicted in *GP*.

865 Coghill, Nevill. *The Poet Chaucer*. 1949/1967. See **447**.
FranT is Chaucer's 'last word and summary' (p 170) on the problem of reconciling courtly love and marriage. But the true subject of the tale is noble behavior, specifically how generosity can manifest itself in any walk of life: 'it is not a class prerogative' (p 171).

866 Pratt, Robert Armstrong. 'The Importance of Manuscripts for the Study of Medieval Education, as Revealed by the Learning of Chaucer.' *Progress of Medieval and Renaissance Studies in the United States and Canada* 20 (1949), 43–51.
The form *Cithero* (cf. line 722) is found in Latin manuscripts of Chaucer's time and earlier; it occurs frequently in texts of Walter Map's *Valerius ad Rufinum*.

The Franklin's Tale, 1950–1959

867 Lawrence, William Witherle. *Chaucer and the Canterbury Tales*. 1950. See **450**.
Agrees with Kittredge (**805**) that the discussion of marriage in *CT* is 'design-

edly resumed and closed' (p 143) in *FranT* with the solution that mutual forbearance is the key to marital happiness. Such a focus is the best explanation of the detailed account of Dorigen and Arveragus's marital arrangement, a passage otherwise not necessary to the story.

868 Thomas, Mary Edith. *Medieval Skepticism and Chaucer*. New York: William-Frederick, 1950. Repr. New York: Cooper Square, 1971.
Dorigen, unable to comprehend the purpose of the black rocks, is compared with Julian of Norwich (*XVI Revelations of Divine Love*): 'I wondered why, by the great aforesaid wisdom of God, the beginning of sin was not letted, for then thought me that all should have been well' (p 128).

869 Albrecht, W.P. 'The Sermon on Gentilesse.' *CE* 12 (1951), 459.
The marriage of the knight and the Loathly Lady in *WBT* looks as if it will turn out to be more like that of Dorigen and Arveragus than those of the Wife of Bath and her five husbands. The Loathly Lady's at least partial relinquishment of mastery in marriage recalls Dorigen's similar renunciation (lines 758–9).

870 Holman, C. Hugh. 'Courtly Love in the Merchant's and Franklin's Tales.' *ELH* 18 (1951), 241–52. Repr. in *Chaucer: Modern Essays in Criticism* (see **381**). Pp 240–50.
MerT and *FranT* are 'recto and verso of the same page' (p 243), embodying complementary aspects of Chaucer's depiction of courtly love. In *MerT*, the courtly code serves as a façade for Damian and May's lust and for their deception of January. Although its dignified tone is strikingly different from the embittered pessimism of *MerT*, *FranT* also embodies a critique of *amour courtois*. The tale begins by rejecting the idea that ideal love is extramarital; Dorigen and Arveragus's happy marriage is threatened by the forces of courtly love in the form of Aurelius; Dorigen's protestation to Aurelius of her love for her husband is 'utter treason to the religion of love' (p 250); Arveragus, who refuses to be jealous of his wife, also behaves in a manner foreign to courtly love doctrine. The differences of characterization and plot that exist within the parallels between *MerT* and *FranT* enforce a contrast between 'those who make of marriage something noble and splendid [to] achieve enviable happiness' and 'those who seek pleasure in the pattern of lust or of courtly love' (p 252) and achieve only illusory felicity. See **917**.

871 Kane, George. *Middle English Literature: A Critical Study of the Romances, the Religious Lyrics, Piers Plowman*. London: Methuen, 1951. Repr. Folcroft, PA: Folcroft, 1969.
Impressive as are the externals of presentation in *FranT*, its greatest strength lies in the characterization of Dorigen and Arveragus, whose decency and integrity are depicted by Chaucer with unusual care and psychological plausibility. 'The rhetoric of *FranT* may commend it to the historian of such matters, but the behaviour of Dorigen and her husband in their predicament

is what makes it attractive to the common reader' (p 87).

872 Lumiansky, Robert M. 'The Character and Performance of Chaucer's Franklin.' *UTQ* 20 (1951), 344–56.
FranT reflects both the narrator's grounding in the 'practical everyday world' (p 345) and his wish for advancement among the gentry. These double concerns are present in his flattery of the Squire and his interaction with the Host, and in his Prologue, in which an interest in *gentilesse* and the high style exists side-by-side with less elevated matters and diction. The marriage contract of Dorigen and Arveragus is an odd combination of courtly love language and the terms and concepts of bourgeois wedlock, capped by 'a fine example of double-talk' in which the Franklin comments on the wisdom of the arrangement (p 352). All elements of the tale mirror the two sides of the Franklin's nature; in her Complaint, for example, Dorigen's testing of high courtly behavior is followed by her adoption of the more realistic solution of informing her husband of her plight 'in true wifely fashion' (p 354). The juxtaposition of courtly and down-to-earth elements has been seen as incongruous. But it is just this incongruity that suits the tale to the Franklin's own divided nature.

873 Madeleva, Sister M. *A Lost Language and Other Essays on Chaucer*. New York: Sheed and Ward, 1951.
Dorigen's lament over the black rocks, in its 'candid, conversational attitude toward God,' illustrates Chaucer's 'maturer attitude toward prayer. To appreciate how robust an attitude this is one should read beside it Tennyson's lovely, languorous *Sweet and Low*' (p 23).

874 Malone, Kemp. *Chapters on Chaucer*. 1951. See **451**.
The Host's discourtesy to the Franklin and the Franklin's humble response are equally untrue to life; 'on an actual pilgrimage in fourteenth-century England ... no innkeeper would have dreamt of behaving this way towards a gentleman, and if he did behave so no gentleman would have put up with it' (pp 192–3). The comedy here is based on a deliberate disregard for the 'realities of social intercourse' (p 193). *FranT* is suitable for one of the gentles among the pilgrims, but has no particular relevance to the Franklin as an individual. The Franklin is Chaucer's mouthpiece; his tale illuminates his social milieu rather than his personality.

875 Neville, Marie. 'The Function of the *Squire's Tale* in the Canterbury Scheme.' 1951. See **452**.
SqT anticipates *FranT* in its treatment of *gentilesse* as the source of compassion and in the falcon's credo of mutual forbearance in love. *FranT* is 'a direct result of the ideal of love suggested by the Squire' (p 179), and was probably intended as a compliment to the younger pilgrim.

876 Speirs, John. *Chaucer the Maker*. 1951. See **454**.
The happy marriage of Dorigen and Arveragus seems initially imperiled by

the black rocks, the irrationality of which particularly disturbs Dorigen. But the rocks only symbolize the larger forces that prevent perfect happiness in the world. The relationship of husband and wife seems threatened by Aurelius's desire and the clerk's magic. In the winter description (lines 1243–55), however, the Franklin shows us that 'even in the dead season life and reality are still at the root of the world ... The robust figure of Janus ... has here a suddenly invigorating effect. He is seen as a contemporary English yeoman by a Yule fire. He draws his strength and significance from both the immediately observed world of English agricultural life and the mythological world. His substantiality makes the decisive contrast with the magician's illusions' (pp 166–7).

877 Bloomfield, Morton W. 'Chaucer's Sense of History.' 1952. See **455**.
The archaizing details in *FranT* emphasize the pastness of the tale's fantastic events and the difference between those days and Chaucer's own. Chaucer 'turned to the past in order to make his *Tale* palatable, and in so doing reveals an awareness of the problem of time and credibility' (p 307).

878 Preston, Raymond. *Chaucer*. 1952. See **456**.
FranT is about manners, and is suited to the character of its teller, who 'might in our own day be a comfortable don of an ancient college ... telling his story with mellow vinous satisfaction' (p 274). Yet the tale is a serious one, raising questions similar to those in *KnT* about the '*raison d'être* of suffering' and 'the relativity of evil' (p 275). At the tale's conclusion, however, 'it is as if the pieces are knocked down and the game is over' (p 276); we are not expected to ponder the Franklin's final *demande* with undue seriousness.

879 Blenner-Hassett, Roland. 'Autobiographical Aspects of Chaucer's Franklin.' *Speculum* 28 (1953), 791–800.
The Franklin's legal training (perhaps a reflection of Chaucer's own) is reflected in the language of his tale, in which the idioms of contractual law serve to represent the rituals of courtly love and to 'inform the poem with an air of added seriousness' (p 793). The tale's legally inflected terminology centers on the keeping of promises, culminating in Aurelius's release of Dorigen from her vow (lines 1533–6). Aurelius couches his generosity in phrases associated with the 'quit-claim,' verbal formulas that appear as well in Cecilia Chaumpaigne's release of Chaucer from her suit for rape, in consideration of a monetary payment. The clerk's forgiveness of Aurelius's debt (lines 1613–15) is a 'deliberate burlesque' of the language used by Aurelius to Dorigen (p 800). Taken together, the two passages show Chaucer the poet converting into art the sordid and disquieting associations that the 'quit-claim' must have had for Chaucer the man.

880 Brewer, Derek S. *Chaucer*. 1953/1960/1973. See **457**.
The Franklin tells 'what is perhaps the pleasantest tale in the whole series' (p 170); in contrast to *MerT*, *FranT* exalts 'humanity and decency of spirit'

(p 171). Compared to the lady's demand in Boccaccio for a spring garden in winter, Dorigen's request that Aurelius remove the coastal rocks is 'more natural to the lady's character, more profound in irony, more poetical in that it makes a more searching comment on the nature of life ... An ingenious anecdote is raised to a drama of human hopes and fears, of enmeshed motives and events' (p 172). *FranT* shows that 'the physical materiality of the world, as represented by the rocks, may be harsh, but if you deny it you lose the spiritual values of love and faith' (1973, p 179). When the rocks are seemingly covered by the sea, appearance takes over from reality, threatening Dorigen's moral integrity; 'reality is better than illusion, even when painful' (1973, p 179). *FranT*'s subject is 'trouthe's superiority to honour' (1973, p 195). In the conflict of mutually incompatible values, the deeper, less tangible virtue prevails. The 1973 edition illustrates playing at 'ches and tables' (line 900) and Janus 'with double berd' (line 1252) from medieval manuscripts.

881 Dempster, Germaine. 'A Period in the Development of the *Canterbury Tales* Marriage Group and of Blocks B² and C.' 1953. See **458**.
Chaucer established a relation between the Marriage Group and *Mel*, *ClT*, and *NPT* and put Fragments B² and C in their final forms in the 'middle third of the Canterbury period' (p 1154). Although *FranT* was conceived as a conclusion to the Marriage Group, it had probably not been written or even planned at the beginning of this period.

882 Hunter, William B., Jr. 'Canterbury Tales, V, 1031ff.' *MLN* 68 (1953), 174.
Because he wishes to violate Dorigen's chastity, Aurelius could not address his prayer directly to Lucina, who in one of her guises is also Diana, goddess of chastity. He therefore prays to Apollo, asking his help in influencing his sister to produce a high tide that will cover the rocks.

883 Owen, Charles A., Jr. 'The Crucial Passages in Five of the *Canterbury Tales*: A Study in Irony and Symbol.' *JEGP* 52 (1953), 294–311. Repr. in *Chaucer: Modern Essays in Criticism* (see **381**), pp 251–70; in *Critical Essays on Chaucer's Canterbury Tales* (see **390**), pp 51–66; and in *Discussions of the Canterbury Tales* (see **455**), pp 79–89.
In her promise to love Aurelius if he removes the rocks from the coast of Brittany, Dorigen unwittingly transforms the rocks' symbolic meaning: initially a menace to her husband's life, their permanence is now a guarantee of her enduring love for Arveragus. Their changed significance is underlined by Aurelius's prayer for the removal of the rocks, an event that would now endanger the marriage of Dorigen and Arveragus. Like the rocks, the real obstacles to the consummation of Aurelius's desire only appear to have vanished in the wake of the magician's activities; 'they are the honor, the decency, the gentility of all the people involved,' and Dorigen and Arveragus's love for one another (p 297). Dorigen's promise to Aurelius is also an expres-

sion of superficial *gentilesse*; she knows in her heart that the disappearance of the rocks is against the order of nature, but 'even while accepting the natural order, she is shirking a part of her duty in the moral' (p 297).

884 Kökeritz, Helge. 'Rhetorical Word-Play in Chaucer.' 1954. See **460**.
'Colours ... colours' (lines 723–6) is an instance of repetition that results in real punning (p 950).

885 Prins, A.A. 'Notes on the Canterbury Tales (3).' *ES* 35 (1954), 158–62.
Tregetoures (lines 1141, 1143) are not, as Skeat (**4**) states, 'magicians who perform mechanical tricks,' but rather magicians who cause 'hallucinations or collective apparitions' (p 161). The performance of the *tregetour* is compared to the Indian rope trick, in which 'the operator succeeds in instilling the *idea* of the rope' into the minds of his audience, much as a hypnotist does (p 132).

886 Schaar, Claes. *Some Types of Narrative in Chaucer's Poetry*. 1954. See **461**.
Chaucer uses 'close chronological narrative' (a detailed account of the chain of events falling within a brief period) in lines 1166–75, the account of Aurelius's brother's search for and subsequent meeting with the Orléans clerk (pp 153–4).

887 Lumiansky, Robert M. *Of Sondry Folk: The Dramatic Principle in the Canterbury Tales*. 1955. See **462**.
'The Franklin' (pp 180–93) is a revised version of **872**.

888 Magoun, Francis P., Jr. 'Canterbury Tales, F 1541–44.' *MLN* 70 (1955), 173.
Lines 1541–4, printed by Skeat (**4**), Pollard (**6**), Manly (**47**) and Robinson (**55**) as part of Aurelius's preceding speech to Dorigen, are probably the words of the Franklin himself. There is no need to place this passage after line 1550, as Manly and Rickert (**61**) suggest.

889 Savage, James E. 'The Marriage Problem in "The Canterbury Tales."' *MQ* 9 (1955), 27–9.
The Franklin's deployment of the words *love* and *lovere* (associated with *amour courtois*) and *housbonde* and *wyf* underscores his reconciliation of courtly love with marriage.

890 Schaar, Claes. *The Golden Mirror: Studies in Chaucer's Descriptive Technique and its Literary Background*. 1955. See **463**.
Emotion in *FranT* is depicted more frequently by 'behaviouristic description' (p 81), focused on bodily or facial expression of feeling, than by descriptions of purely internal states. In contrast to *Fil*, in which signs of emotion are relatively infrequent, *FranT* contains numerous comments on the characters' feelings or behavior (pp 79–82). Character portraits in *FranT* are generally idealized, recalling the style of portraiture in the Breton lays (pp 231, 347–8). Depictions of nature combine idealizing and impressionistic description; the account of the garden is compared with passages in Boccaccio and Machaut (pp 417–19).

891 Baum, Paull F. 'Chaucer's Puns.' 1956. See **465**.

Sleep (line 721) may suggest sleeping with one of the Muses; the repetition of *armes* (lines 1091–2) may imply a slight touch of sarcasm.

892 Chute, Marchette. 'On the Pleasure of Meeting Chaucer.' *EJ* 45 (1956), 373–94. *FranT* contains Chaucer's 'own point of view on marriage' (p 379).

893 Coghill, Nevill. *Geoffrey Chaucer*. 1956. See **466**.
FranT embodies the 'wise equability and kindliness that is so great an attribute of Chaucer's mind'; the address to the company at lines 761–70 manifests a 'Chaucerian wisdom' that suits the Franklin's sanguine temperament (pp 45–6).

894 Kleinstück, Johannes Walter. *Chaucers Stellung in der Mittelalterlichen Literatur*. 1956. See **467**.
Chrétien de Troyes' comment on Yvain and Gauvain in the penultimate episode of *Yvain* ('Tant sont andui franc et jantil') finds a parallel in Chaucer's use of *gentil* and *fre* at the conclusion of *FranT* (p 16). A comparison of Aurelius's releasing of Dorigen from her vow with the analogous scene in *Fil* reveals Chaucer's detailed representation of the experience of compassion for another (pp 63–4).

895 Mroczkowski, Przemysław. *Opowieści Kanterberyjskie na tle Epoki*. 1956. See **468**.
The Franklin desires to ascend in the social hierarchy: he finds mere wealth insufficient. Aurelius's release of Dorigen from her promise emphasizes the nobility of one lower in social rank than a knight. This allows the Franklin to show that the aristocracy does not have a monopoly on nobleness of character. Problems in the moral construction of the tale – Arveragus's tacit expectation that Aurelius will act nobly, the latter's intransigence in the face of Dorigen's despair and the fact that only her husband's magnanimity makes him relent – expose the Franklin's lack of expertise in the subtleties of the aristocratic ethos. He understands, however, that magnanimity can appear only where there is freedom of choice (pp 283–94).

896 Schlauch, Margaret. *English Medieval Literature and its Social Foundations*. 1956. See **469**.
FranT mediates between two extremes of domination in marriage. Chaucer shapes his plot to 'exemplify an ideal for marriage relations of his own time – an ideal which was far from realisation under normal conditions' (pp 263–4).

897 Frye, Northrop. *Anatomy of Criticism: Four Essays*. Princeton, NJ: Princeton UP, 1957.
The 'mature innocent wisdom' of *FranT* belongs to the fifth phase of romance, a 'reflective, idyllic view of experience from above … the mood is a contemplative withdrawal from or sequel to action rather than a youthful preparation for it' (p 202).

897a Quinn, Dorothy MacKay. 'The Medieval Extracurriculum: The Orléans Example.' *MQ* 10 (1957), 120–32.

The tone of the episode in the clerk's house suggests that 'such things were not unusual at Orléans, and that if one needed a magician, Orléans was the place to look for one' (pp 130–1).

898 Slaughter, Eugene Edward. *Virtue According to Love—in Chaucer*. 1957. See **470**.
Analyzes the medieval ideas of love and virtue, both earthly and spiritual. Love is an axis with charity and cupidity as its two poles; the goodness or badness of a desire depends on the system of virtues invoked. *FranT* is 'syncretistic': the heroic, courtly, and religio-philosophic systems combine harmoniously to provide the theory of love and marriage exemplified in the marriage of Arveragus and Dorigen. The virtues and vices mentioned in *FranT* are listed and classified (pp 236–7).

899 Baum, Paull F. *Chaucer: A Critical Appreciation*. Durham, NC: Duke UP, 1958.
Dorigen 'misses being a tragic figure, but misses only narrowly' (p 124). The other characters are less successfully handled; Arveragus, in particular, is sacrificed to a limited concept of *trouthe*. *FranT* exhibits a conflict between intermittently realistic characterization and implausible motives and actions: 'the more Chaucer did to make it humanly interesting and not merely an artificial confection, the more he exposed the underlying fallacies ... the greater the air of naturalness such a story is given, the greater the risk of exposing its unnaturalness' (p 129). *FranT* is not a serious representation of actual life; 'it is more like what the French call *littérature* ... by turning it all into a game or riddle at the end, [Chaucer] ... may have hinted ... that we should regard the tale as something from the realm of the higher nonsense' (p 132).

900 Donaldson, E. Talbot, ed. *Chaucer's Poetry: An Anthology for the Modern Reader*. 1958/1975. See **71**.
FranT has less to do with marriage than with the virtues of *trouthe* and *fredom* upon which an ideal marriage must depend. Dorigen exhibits an uncompromising idealism that nearly undoes her; in a 'delightfully feminine' speech about the rocks, she calls upon Nature to reorganize the world according to her notion of how it should be (p 924). Confronted with Aurelius's unwelcome advances, she 'makes an analogy between his bad behavior and nature's,' and in her vow to love him if he removes the rocks, she 'promises to be untrue to her own nature if Aurelius manages to rearrange creation' (p 925). His use of illusion turns an illusory evil into a real one; ironically, Dorigen's idealism creates a situation where she must act in direct opposition to it. In insisting that Dorigen keep her promise, Arveragus knows that 'an ideal has no relevance unless we are willing to sacrifice our whole world to it' (p 925). The solution to Dorigen's dilemma is foreshadowed in the winter description preceding the account of the removal of the rocks; the moment when Nature seems most sterile is also the season when Christ redeemed the dead and fulfilled the Old Law with the New, just as, in the poem, the Christian virtue of *fredom* fulfills the Old Testament contractual

law of *trouthe.* Although *FranT* is not directly based on any extant Breton lay, it is written in the spirit of the lays; 'it might be said that even if there had been no genre of the Breton lay before Chaucer, *FranT* would have established one' (p 926). In its spirit of optimism and its translation of courtly idealism into a happy marriage, the tale reflects its teller's sanguine nature and his bourgeois aspirations to aristocratic values. Chaucer's admiration for the Franklin does not, however, blind him to his quirks, most amusingly his unaristocratic preoccupation with the value of money.

901 Loomis, Laura Hibbard. 'Secular Dramatics in the Royal Palace, Paris, 1378, 1389, and Chaucer's "Tregetoures."' *Speculum* 33 (1958), 242–55. Repr. in Laura Hibbard Loomis, *Adventures in the Middle Ages: A Memorial Collection of Essays and Studies.* [No ed.] New York: Franklin, 1962. Pp 274–92.

The *Chronique de Charles V* contains a detailed account of a feast given by the French king on 6 January 1378, at the Palais de la Cité for the emperor Charles IV. The subject of the *entremés* performed between the courses of the banquet was an historical one, the conquest of Jerusalem in 1099 by Godfrey of Bouillon. The entertainment included a boat floating upon water and a castle under siege; these stage properties were moved about by men concealed within. The Fall of Troy formed the subject of an *entremés* at a royal banquet in 1389; Froissart's account notes a stage city, a ship, and a pavilion. The parallels between these performances and the scenic marvels reported by Aurelius's brother suggest that the *tregetoures* who produced the latter were not magicians, but mechanical artisans. See **1215**.

902 Mroczkowski, Przemysław. 'Medieval Art and Aesthetics in *The Canterbury Tales.*' *Speculum* 33 (1958), 204–21.

Cites parallels in the visual arts to the Franklin's winter description (lines 1243–55).

903 Owen, Charles A., Jr. 'The Development of the *Canterbury Tales.*' 1958. See **473**.

Although the treatment of marital sovereignty suggests that *FranT* was intended as a response to the position taken by the Wife of Bath in the latter part of her Prologue and her Tale, other aspects of the tale (e.g., the dependence of Dorigen's lament on *Jov* and the genre of the complaint itself) are characteristic of an earlier period of composition, when Chaucer conceived of *CT* as 'a more varied *LGW*' (p 467).

904 Benjamin, Edwin B. 'The Concept of Order in the *Franklin's Tale.*' *PQ* 38 (1959), 119–24.

Disorder arises in *FranT* from the moral weakness of the characters. In protesting God's creation of the rocks, Dorigen, 'in her unaggressive feminine way' (p 120), is guilty of the sin of pride; Aurelius displays a moral flaw similar to Dorigen's in wishing to change the order to things to suit his desires. Aurelius's attempt to alter the laws of nature through magic produces a state of chaos. Order is restored when Arveragus, insisting with 'manly firmness' (p 123) that Dorigen keep her promise to Aurelius, sets an example of self-sacrifice that proves infectious. Dorigen, however, 'does not come out too well … but she is only a daughter of Eve' (p 123). In 'one of the most philosophical of the *CT*' (p 119), the narrator handles his subject with delicacy and restraint; 'we can recognize Satan when he squats by our head in the form of a toad … It is less easy to spot him … in the neurotic fancies of a pretty woman' (p 124). See **917**.

905 Mason, H.A. *Humanism and Poetry in the Early Tudor Period*. London: Routledge and Kegan Paul, 1959.
Aurelius's amorous complaints show that by Chaucer's day there was a well-established traditional vocabulary for handling courtly love, 'part translation from the French, part native coinage, part borrowed from the "popular" … love conventions' (p 160).

906 Nathan, Norman. 'Pronouns of Address in the "Canterbury Tales."' *MS* 21 (1959), 193–201.
Chaucer varies from the standard distinction between *thou* (informal) and *ye* (formal) in addresses to the Christian Deity and pagan gods in *KnT* and *FranT*, suggesting that there was 'no firmly established usage in addressing a deity' (p 194). *FranT* is 'otherwise perfect in its usage' (p 194).

907 Nicolson, Marjorie Hope. *Mountain Gloom and Mountain Glory: The Development of the Aesthetics of the Infinite*. Ithaca, NY: Cornell UP, 1959.
Dorigen's seacoast lament echoes earlier theological speculation that rocks and mountains are the result of God's curse upon the earth after the Fall and the Flood (p 96).

908 Wickham, Glynne. *Early English Stages, 1300–1660*. Vol. 1: *1300 to 1576*. London: Routledge and Kegan Paul; New York: Columbia UP, 1959.
Cites accounts of court entertainments that parallel the *apparences* created by *tregetoures* (lines 1138–51) (pp 212–16).

The Franklin's Tale, 1960–1969

909 Hodgson, Phyllis, ed. *The Franklin's Tale*. 1960. See **74**.
The Franklin's class consciousness is expressed in his admiration of the Squire's accomplishments. His good-humored response to the Host's rude comments demonstrates the tact that has brought him worldly success; his experience in jurisdiction qualifies him to resolve the arguments about love and marriage set out in the preceding tales. The Franklin's literary interests are in keeping with his character; of the country rather than the court and thus unfamiliar with the latest narrative fashions, he adopts the 'rather outmoded form' of the Breton lay, and views the extravagances of aristocratic

romance through the lens of practical common sense (p 13).

910 Howard, Donald R. 'The Conclusion of the Marriage Group: Chaucer and the Human Condition.' *MP* 57 (1960), 223–32.
In arguing that the Franklin's portrait of domestic concord represents 'what Chaucer thought about marriage,' Kittredge (**805**) overlooks the possibility that the poet may have intended *FranT* to be followed either by *PhyT* or by *SNT* in the tale-telling sequence. Both of these tales – the former about virginity and the latter about a chaste marriage – offer alternatives to the Franklin's worldly compromise between courtly love and husbandly authority, which is far from consistent with the Church's counsels of Christian perfection. The parallels between *FranT* and *SNT* (the heroines' noble birth, the marriage vow) set into high relief 'the great weakness in the Franklyn's solution as the Church would see it – that it allows a purely domestic comfort to replace the Christian ideals of self-abnegation' (p 229). Although Chaucer was clearly attracted to the Franklin's view of marriage, his apparent consideration of *PhyT* and *SNT* as appropriate tales to follow *FranT* shows that he never abandoned the more orthodox position.

911 Whittock, Trevor G. 'The Marriage Debate II.' *Theoria* 15 (1960), 43–53.
The black rocks represent Dorigen's anxieties about her husband's safety, Aurelius's unconscious desires, and, more generally, suffering and evil in life. In making her promise to the squire, Dorigen attempts to dispel her fears and wish them away; the consequences of her vow reveal a pattern of justice that punishes those who rebel against the order of nature. In his prayers and use of magic, Aurelius escapes into fantasy. Arveragus's invocation of *trouthe* includes not only Dorigen's obligation to honor her promise, but refers back as well to 'the whole indulgence in wishful-thinking and illusion in her and Aurelius' (p 52).

912 Baker, Donald C. 'A Crux in Chaucer's *Franklin's Tale*: Dorigen's Complaint.' *JEGP* 60 (1961), 56–64.
The first part of Dorigen's Complaint reflects her division of virtuous women into two groups: maidens who killed themselves rather than be dishonored, and wives who did the same thing. The exempla in the second half of the Complaint comprise Chaucer's (or the Franklin's) categories: women who committed suicide *before* being ravished, those who killed themselves *after* being raped, and those who were 'simply faithful and exemplary wives and sweethearts' (p 62). The organization of the Complaint bespeaks careful artistry on Chaucer's part rather than the ad hoc use of *Jov* that Dempster (**847**) envisions. Offering Dorigen not one but three possible courses of action, the passage at once conveys her internal struggle and looks forward to the moral of the tale, in which Dorigen's faith in her husband's wisdom prompts her to leave her fate in his hands. See **298**.

913 Kee, Kenneth. 'Two Chaucerian Gardens.' *MS* 23 (1961), 154–62.

The garden in *MerT* carries with it expectations, realized in the course of the tale, of 'adultery, the Fall, and unbridled sexuality' (p 161). The description of the garden in *FranT* links it as well with Eden and the *paradis d'amour*. But Chaucer suppresses the implications of the garden tradition by having Aurelius renounce his claims to Dorigen before they reach the garden. 'Thus the shadows cast by both the love garden and the Garden of Eden are lifted. Courtly love and the Fall are held in abeyance and Dorigen returns to her husband Arveragus as innocent in body and heart as when she left him' (p 162).

914 Loomis, Roger Sherman. 'Was Chaucer a Free Thinker?' In *Studies in Medieval Literature in Honor of Professor Albert Croll Baugh*. Ed. MacEdward Leach. Philadelphia: U of Pennsylvania P, 1961. Pp 21–41. Repr. in Robert Sherman Loomis, *Studies in Medieval Literature: A Memorial Collection of Essays*. New York: Franklin, 1970. Pp 289–312.

Dorigen's attempt to reconcile the Creator's benevolence with the hostility of the created world in her speech about the rocks reflects Chaucer's own obsession, in his late thirties, with disturbing theological and metaphysical issues.

915 Magoun, Francis P., Jr. *A Chaucer Gazetteer*. 1961. See **475**.

Alphabetized entries on Chaucer's place names include etymologies, variant manuscript spellings, brief discussions of the names' use in Chaucer's works, ancient, medieval, and modern geographical information, and citations of scholarship. The entry on *Orliens*, for example, cites Hermann Gröhler, *Über Ursprung und Bedeutung der französischen Ortsnamen* (1913) on the connection with the Roman *Aurelia*, later *Aurelianus*, and observes that the accidental relationship of the name with that of Dorigen's suitor would have been unnoticed by Chaucer. The book conflates Magoun's articles on Chaucerian place names in *MS* 15 (1953), 107–36; 16 (1954), 131–56; and 17 (1955), 117–42.

916 Stevens, John E. *Music & Poetry in the Early Tudor Court*. London: Methuen, 1961.

Aurelius's *compleynyng* (line 945) is cited as an example of the courtly love lyric as enigma – 'a riddling, or dark, way of conveying your thoughts to someone who is, or pretends to be, your lover' (p 216).

917 Mallikarjunan, S. 'On Three Interpretations of Chaucer's *The Franklin's Tale*.' *IJES* 3 (1962), 1–11.

In focusing on 'a confusion or a conflict of conventions' (p 6) in *FranT* and undervaluing or disregarding the Franklin's concluding question, the interpretations of Holman (**870**), Lumiansky (**872**), and Benjamin (**904**) reduce the tale to pointlessness. Read rightly as a narrative of courtly love, *FranT* is dramatically and structurally harmonious, and appropriately capped by the *demande d'amour*.

918 Robertson, D.W., Jr. *A Preface to Chaucer: Studies in Medieval Perspectives.* Princeton, NJ: Princeton UP, 1962/1970; pbk ed., 1969.
Dorigen's catalogue of virtuous women is irrelevant to her situation; in spite of the principles adduced in her exempla, she goes to Aurelius with the consent of her husband (p 274). The Franklin's concept of *gentilesse* 'reflects the entirely superficial nobility of a wealthy man of the middle class' (p 276); his wish to maintain the delights of Cupid within marriage aligns him with January and the Wife of Bath. Love inspired by Cupid is traditionally represented as servitude, not as freedom. The Franklin's endorsement of equality in marriage is consistent with his class outlook and his 'irrepressible Epicurean optimism', factors that account for the supposed 'modernity' of his views (p 470). 'But Chaucer had no way of knowing that the spiritual descendants of the Franklin would one day rule the world' (p 472). See **1201r**, **1438**.
• Review by R.E. Kaske, *ELH* 30 (1963), 175–92: Rather than embodying a superficially worldly view of the marriage bond, as Robertson maintains, *FranT* is 'a calculated antithesis to *MerT*, presumably reflecting some sort of marital "ideal"' (p 180n).
• Review by F. Parmisano, O.P., *MÆ* 35 (1966), 273–9: Although Robertson believes that the marriage equality theme in *FranT* runs counter to the medieval doctrine of the husband's sovereignty, the notion that the husband should be both servant and lord 'is the perfect expression of the Christian ideal of sovereignty' (p 278). Nor was this idea peculiar to the rising bourgeoisie, as Robertson claims; it can be found in Chrétien's *Cligés*, in *RR*, and in Nicholas of Oresme.

919 Beck, Richard J. 'Educational Expectations and Rhetorical Result in *The Canterbury Tales*.' 1963. See **476**.
The rhetorical dimension of *FranT* 'is a case of double-bluff' (p 253). The Prologue shifts readers' expectations several times, from a learned, to a plain, and then to an overly ornate tale by an ironical teller. The Franklin's 'very disclaimer is as bret-full of rhetorical devices as the Pardoner's wallet was of pardons!' (p 253).

920 Payne, Robert O. *The Key of Remembrance: A Study of Chaucer's Poetics.* 1963. See **477**.
Chaucer discovers a general set of aesthetic principles rather than specific compositional techniques in the writers of the past; in his Prologue, the Franklin lumps together the Breton lays and Cicero's rhetoric as if they were the same thing and then excuses himself from employing verbal arts in his tale (pp 84–5).

921 Pratt, Robert Armstrong. 'Saint Jerome in Jankyn's Book of Wikked Wyves.' *Criticism* 5 (1963), 316–22.
Jov, excerpts from which appear in manuscripts corresponding to Jankyn's 'book of wikked wyves' (III.685) as described by the Wife of Bath, is also the

source for Dorigen's catalogue of virtuous women. The latter passage may be read as 'a series of resounding blows aimed directly at the Wife of Bath' (p 320) in which the behavior of exemplary women 'puts to shame the Wife of Bath's callousness, lasciviousness, and promiscuity' (p 321).

922 Bloomfield, Morton W. 'Authenticating Realism and the Realism of Chaucer.' *Thought* 39 (1964), 335–58. Repr. in Bloomfield, *Essays and Explorations: Studies in Ideas, Language, and Literature* (see **455**), pp 174–98, and in *Geoffrey Chaucer* (see **483**), pp 210–33.
FranT 'is by no means fundamentally realistic. It is set in pagan Brittany and depends on magic for the success of the story' (p 350).

923 Bowden, Muriel. *A Reader's Guide to Geoffrey Chaucer*. 1964. See **478**.
The chivalric nature of *FranT* fits the character of its teller, and is manifested in the emphasis on Dorigen's keeping of her word and in the high-minded actions of the male characters at the tale's conclusion. The tale places the 'old' – courtly love – against the 'new,' in which sinless physical love could exist within marriage (pp 34–9).

924 Broadbent, J.B. *Poetic Love*. London: Chatto and Windus, 1964; New York: Barnes and Noble, 1965.
FranT offers an idealized solution to the problem of power in love; Dorigen and Arveragus's decision to preserve in marriage the freedom of romantic love preserves marriage against romantic dangers (pp 54–5).

925 Corsa, Helen Storm. *Chaucer: Poet of Mirth and Morality*. 1964. See **479**.
The Franklin suggests that good and evil depend upon the nature of the doer; despite the presence of magic, the events in *FranT* are caused by human beings. The tale, which ends happily after the threat of disaster, summarizes Chaucer's comic view of life. Its teller is a man of honest simplicity, conscious of his audience and direct in his response to the natural world and human nature. His narrative translates abstract values into actualities, putting to the test the innate goodness of his characters. But the Franklin's idealism is neither sentimental nor naïve; human goodness does not predetermine happiness or guarantee right action. *FranT* corroborates the Wife of Bath's thesis that *gentilesse* arises from noble deeds; a possible tragic outcome is averted by compassion and responsible action. The human goodness on display in *FranT* is 'as much a part of Chaucer's realistically comic vision' (p 181) as are the worldviews of the other marriage tales.

926 Gaylord, Alan. 'The Promises in *The Franklin's Tale*.' *ELH* 31 (1964), 331–65. Repr. in *Geoffrey Chaucer* (see **483**). Pp 300–35.
FranT reveals in its treatment of promises the inadequacy of the Franklin's understanding of gentle behavior. The Franklin wishes us to believe that the tale's promises exemplify *gentilesse* in action, Arveragus's commitment to *trouthe* – the keeping of promises – generating a chain reaction of *gentil* acts. But the Franklin's intended interpretation elides the conflict between the

sacred trothplight of marriage and Dorigen's foolish promise to Aurelius. Moreover, by insisting that Dorigen keep her *trouthe* to the squire, Arveragus is breaking his earlier promise not to exercise mastery over his wife. In her initial interchange with Aurelius, Dorigen makes her intentions perfectly clear. Her 'promise' isn't a promise; Aurelius interprets it as binding because it has been put into words. As the Franklin understands the courtly code, words have a life of their own; he exhibits a 'fanatical literalism' that disregards *entente* (p 347). Dorigen does not fulfill her promise to 'love [Aurelius] best of any man' (line 997), nor does Aurelius actually remove the coastal rocks. 'The final irony is that no one keeps this promise which was never really made' (p 348). Ambrose, Augustine, *ParsT,* and Robert of Brunne's *Handlyng Synne* counsel that rash promises ought not to be kept, and that 'breaking a contract made in sin ... cannot be called a sin at all' (p 351). Breton lays that include impossible tasks differ from *FranT* in that the tasks are overcome in actuality, by a hero who takes them seriously from the start. In the debate concerning liberality that follows Menedon's *questione* in *Fil,* Fiammetta makes it clear that the lady's promise to her suitor amounted to nothing because it contradicted her prior marriage vow. Chaucer's changes in his source illustrate the moral absurdity at the heart of the *questione*'s dilemma, and demonstrate that he and Boccaccio share the same position on the invalidity of rash promises. Chaucer expected his audience to recognize 'the ludicrous ethical acrobatics' that the Franklin's characters perform (p 365). If *FranT* provides an answer to the marriage debate, it does so 'in spite of and not because of the Franklin's philosophy' (p 365).

927 Greaves, Margaret. *The Blazon of Honour: A Study in Renaissance Magnanimity*. London: Methuen; New York: Barnes and Noble, 1964.
Aurelius's refusal to hold Dorigen to her promise and his recollection of the demands of *gentilesse* 'deserve that lovely medieval word "solempne"; there is something of fine ceremony in his withdrawal, the joyful seriousness of one who partakes in a ritual demanded by high custom' (p 42).

928 Howard, Edwin H. *Geoffrey Chaucer*. 1964. See **480**.
The main theme of the tale is neither courtly love nor sovereignty, but honor. The concluding question is really a way of asking which character acted most honorably (pp 157–8).

929 Huppé, Bernard F. *A Reading of the Canterbury Tales*. Albany: State U of New York P, 1964/1967.
The Franklin's words to the Squire reveal his snobbishness and the superficiality of his concept of *gentilesse.* The Franklin tells his tale to compliment the Squire and to show off his own courtesy, but the courteous marriage he envisions offers an inadequate solution to the issues raised by the other tales in the Marriage Group. Neither Arveragus nor the squire exhibits true generosity. In relinquishing husbandly control in his marriage contract,

Arveragus surrenders his reason to his will. In sending Dorigen to Aurelius, Arveragus is not giving up his right to his wife because he has none to give up. In remaining lovers and using their marriage as a secret disguise for their passion, Dorigen and Arveragus violate God's moral order; the confusion Dorigen sees in the black rocks reflects the perverseness of her marriage, and causes her to make her perilous bargain with Aurelius. The latter's title to Dorigen is based on illusion, and his supposed act of generosity is 'a forswearing of a fraudulent claim' (p 173). Only the clerk has acted generously. The tale's conclusion suggests that the Franklin does not understand the implications of his own narrative; 'there is no way in marriage but the hard, laborious way which the Parson prescribes. All else is illusion' (p 174).

• Review by Albert C. Baugh, *ES* 48 (1967), 435–8: Huppé's argument – that the marriage of Dorigen and Arveragus is merely a cloak to hide their passion from the world, that neither Arveragus nor Aurelius was acting generously at the conclusion of the story, and that the Franklin fails to understand the implications of his own tale – 'seems particularly perverse' (p 437). 'Huppé has such gifts as a special pleader that the reader who does not know *FranT* at first hand may be persuaded by his reading of it' (p 438).

• Review by A.C. Spearing, *MÆ* 36 (1967), 195–9: Huppé's attempt to find hidden symbolism in *FranT*'s rocks is weakened by the poem's emphasis on the rocks' literal reality: 'they simply exist; that is why they are so dangerous' (p 197).

930 Masui, Michio. *The Structure of Chaucer's Rime-Words: An Exploration into the Poetic Language of Chaucer.* 1964. See **481**.
The repetition of the phrase 'rokkes blake' in rhyme position in the early part of the tale (lines 859–60, 867–8, 891–2) gives it symbolic weight as the story develops (p 282).

931 Murphy, James J. 'A New Look at Chaucer and the Rhetoricians.' 1964. See **482**.
The Franklin equates *rethorik* (line 719) with 'poetic,' or the art of imaginative writing. His use of Cicero's full name may be intended as word play, punning on 'Mount Cithaeron': lines 722–3 would then be paraphrased as 'I never slept on Mount Parnassus or studied Mount Cithaeron Cicero' (p 10).

932 Presson, Robert K. 'The Aesthetics of Chaucer's Art of Contrast.' *EM* 15 (1964), 9–23.
CT contains a number of situations in which 'a traditional answer to a question is not acceptable for the nonce anyway' (p 19). In Dorigen's speech on the rocks 'an ancient question is raised but no traditional answer is acceptable' (p 19).

933 Spearing, A.C. *Criticism and Medieval Poetry*. London: Arnold, 1964.
The Franklin undercuts his claim that he knows nothing of rhetoric with his accomplished use of *circumlocutio* in his tale, and by his hints (as in line 1018)

that he is precisely aware of what he is doing (pp 55–6).

934 Walter, Gertrud. *Grundtypen der Erzähl- und Darstellungstechnik bei Chaucer.* 1964. See **484**.

The narrator's laconic comment on Dorigen's sorrow (lines 817–21) is colored with irony; his use of the historical present emphasizes the continuous nature of her grief (pp 70–1). *FranT* contains several short scenes of vivid dialogue (lines 1209–18, 1463–89, 1576–1619) that recall the fabliaux in their representation of natural speech and stand in contrast to the tale's longer rhetorical monologues; Chaucer may have added these scenes in revising an earlier version of the tale (p 86). The ironic treatment of Dorigen earlier in the tale is reflected in the handling of her Complaint; the dramatic beginning of the monologue is dissipated in the long list of exempla, and the conclusion constitutes a fading out rather than a climax (p 106).

935 Burrow, J.A. *A Reading of Sir Gawain and the Green Knight*. London: Routledge and Kegan Paul, 1965.

Dorigen's promise to Aurelius was made 'in pley' (line 988), and Aurelius fulfilled his part of the bargain by magical means. Although either of these considerations might be thought sufficient to invalidate the squire's claim, their availability 'makes Dorigen's truth the more notable and praiseworthy ... [Chaucer] simply assumes that it is right and noble of her not to entertain such thoughts' (p 25).

936 David, Alfred. 'Sentimental Comedy in the *Franklin's Tale*.' *AnM* 6 (1965), 19–27.

The Franklin's social theories – marriage based on mutual forbearance and honor based on reciprocal trust – appeal to us because they are our own, but they would not necessarily have been accepted by the Knight and the Squire, whom the Franklin intends to compliment in his tale. The Franklin's chivalry is 'a watered-down version of the old-fashioned kind' (p 21); in writing his romance, 'he ingeniously transforms the aristocratic ideals of love and nobility into something that conforms more comfortably to his own values' (p 23). In contrast to *KnT*, which treats love as an overpowering force subject to hierarchical principles, *FranT* endorses reason over passion, and proposes 'an ideal of love that is in essence democratic' (p 25). The Franklin also eschews the violent solutions of chivalric romance: 'a generous heart may accomplish as much as feats of arms' (p 26). In suggesting that virtue and reason will prevail, *FranT* reveals its kinship with eighteenth-century sentimental comedy, in which potentially tragic plots are happily resolved through noble behavior.

937 Gray, Paul Edward. 'Synthesis and the Double Standard in the *Franklin's Tale*.' *TSLL* 7 (1965), 213–24.

Dorigen and Arveragus's agreement to marry and remain courtly lovers indicates 'their desire to have things both ways, to mix the world of God with the world of men' (p 217). According to the Franklin, this mixture is an unqualified success. But the tale itself refutes his vision. Like the Franklin, Dorigen attempts to fuse two worlds in her playful promise to Aurelius: she 'wishes to combine the "fruyt" of the rocks ... with the "chaf" of the courtly garden' (p 221). Subsequent events, however, reveal that this attempted synthesis is in fact a dichotomy. Although Arveragus, upholding the double standard on which he based his marriage, urges Dorigen to preserve her courtly *trouthe* to Aurelius, the latter's decision to release her from her vow represents 'an unqualified capitulation of courtly ideals to those of marriage' (p 223). Thus the Franklin 'unwittingly presides over the dissolution of his own theory' (p 223).

938 Hodge, James L. 'The Marriage Group: Precarious Equilibrium.' *ES* 46 (1965), 289–300.
The Franklin's 'conclusion' to the marriage debate favors neither marriage nor courtly love, but rather suggests the impossibility of living up to the ideals of either system. Although the Franklin would seem suited to reconciling the practical and courtly worlds, his tale undercuts the values he hopes to support: Aurelius and the clerk deal in illusion, while Arveragus and Dorigen, conforming to an 'unreal system of ethics' (p 297), deny their basic instincts. The climax of *FranT* – Arveragus's command to Dorigen to fulfill her bargain with Aurelius – is a 'more damaging indictment of marriage and courtly love than the Merchant has presented' (p 298), in part because of the Franklin's benign intentions. The symbol of the rocks provides a clue to Chaucer's attitude: the illusion for which Dorigen's honor will be sacrificed is no more compelling than January's acceptance of May's explanation of the pear-tree episode.

939 Holbrook, David. *The Quest for Love*. University: U of Alabama P, 1965.
FranT expresses the poet's dissatisfaction with the cynical treatment of marriage in *MerT*; notably free from irony, it represents Chaucer's most mature presentation of civilized values, comparable to that in Shakespeare's late plays. The tale celebrates '"curtesy" ... in the sense of yielding generously to other creatures, and thus escaping from the destructive forces of egotism, isolation in the self, cut off from the relationship with the "other"' (p 117). Aurelius's decision to release Dorigen from her promise is 'perhaps the most moving point in all of Chaucer's work' (p 124).

940 Knox, Norman. 'The Satiric Pattern of *The Canterbury Tales*.' In *Six Satirists*. Ed. A. Fred Sochatoff. Carnegie Series in English 9. Pittsburgh: Carnegie Institute of Technology, 1965. Pp 17–34.
FranT involves the same adulterous triangle as the fabliaux, but focuses on ideals of behavior rather than emotions; 'all the characters leave the stage feeling very noble indeed' (p 18).

941 Moorman, Charles. 'The Philosophical Knights of *The Canterbury Tales*.' *SAQ*

64 (1965), 87–99.
See **964**.

942 Ruggiers, Paul G. *The Art of The Canterbury Tales*. Madison: U of Wisconsin P, 1965; pbk ed., 1967. Pp 226–37 ('The Franklin's Tale') repr. in *Geoffrey Chaucer: A Critical Anthology* (see **411**). Pp 276–85.
FranT's moral point has to do with the extension of personal integrity beyond marriage into other human relationships. By acting generously for the sake of preserving his wife's good word, Arveragus sets in motion a widening circle of charitable actions outside his marriage. Dorigen and Arveragus's marriage contract goes beyond any purely courtly love tradition, presenting a relationship that anticipates the mutual tolerance demonstrated in the tale's concluding actions. The marriage also exists in the context of a Boethian 'lawe of love' (line 798) which insists on the 'terrible burden of freedom' (p 230). The problem of evil (raised in Dorigen's Boethian meditation on the rocks), of personal freedom and responsibility, is put to the test in the scene in the garden, in Aurelius's assault on marriage in his temptation of Dorigen and in her promise to the squire. Love has made Dorigen free, and in her Complaint she is confronted with the terrible freedom to choose death or dishonor. The solution to her dilemma grows less out of the personal traits of the poem's agents than out of the needs of plot and theme; the male characters' willingness to conform to the principles of honor and generosity impart to the tale the tone of moral romance and Christian comedy. Far from being a blemish on the tale's structure, the behavior of the squire and the magician demonstrates the cycles of generosity enabled by Arveragus's devotion to an ideal of behavior. The tale draws a parallel between the magician and God Himself; the clerk 'verges upon the creator-poet shaping the stuff of dreams and mere appearance to create a reality' (p 233). Poetic faith leads to another kind of faith, in which the spiritual order impinges upon man's sensual nature and upon the social and mundane spheres. In contrast to the garden in *MerT*, the Franklin's garden produces only the semblance of a Fall, out of which arises 'a generous vindication of the rule of love' (p 236). See **1123**.

943 Silvia, Daniel S., Jr. 'Glosses to the *Canterbury Tales* from St. Jerome's *Epistola Adversus Jovinianum*.' *SP* 62 (1965), 28–39.
Two of the glosses to *FranT* in El and Additional 35286 are probably Chaucer's notes to himself, indicating material from *Jov* that he might later use for further revision of Dorigen's Complaint. Silvia disagrees with Manly (**61**) about the inappropriateness to the Complaint of the subjects mentioned in the glosses; none of the women alluded to in the final glosses are any less appropriate for inclusion than Valeria, Rhodogune, and Bilia (lines 1453–6).

944 Utley, Francis Lee. 'Some Implications of Chaucer's Folktales.' *Laographia* 22 (1965), 588–99.

Of the examples of the folktale Chaucer assigns to the Franklin (Aarne–Thompson No. 976, 'Which was the Noblest Act?'), only eleven out of seventeen are oral, and none of them is Celtic, a statistic that confirms the accepted derivation of *FranT* from Boccaccio rather than from a lost Breton lay. The usual term for the folktale, 'The Damsel's Rash Promise,' errs in focusing on the tale's heroine; 'the real issue is the nobility of the men ... the wife is but a pawn' (p 593). The male characters who compete in courtesy are usually a bridegroom, a lover, and a robber; in replacing the robber with a magician, Chaucer turns the tale into a comment on appearance and reality, 'especially fitting to be told by that sanguine and deluded Epicurean, the Franklin' (p 593).

945 Williams, George. *A New View of Chaucer*. 1965. See **489**.
In Aurelius's desire for Dorigen and Arveragus's response, Chaucer may be depicting his own 'courtly love' for Blanche of Lancaster and John of Gaunt's 'attitude (poetically exaggerated, no doubt) toward his wife's humble lover' (p 161).

946 Berger, Harry, Jr. 'The F-Fragment of the *Canterbury Tales*: Part I.' 1966. See **490**.
In his response to the Squire and in his own tale, the Franklin emphasizes the dangers of narcissism that attend the innocence of youth. His patient reply to the Host's aggression demonstrates that the courtly game is one that franklins can play as well as aristocrats. In his Prologue, the Franklin presents the world of the 'olde gentil Britouns' (line 709) as a 'golden-age *pleasaunce*' (p 99) which must be modified if it is to be recovered. By characterizing his tale as a Breton lay, the Franklin promises a meditation on this form of literary entertainment in the economy of life. Even as he apologizes for his ignorance of rhetoric, he resorts to rhetorical colors; 'as with his other pleasures, he indulges himself and then qualifies his indulgence' (p 101). His disclaimer seems a deliberate echo of the Squire – not in mockery, but as 'a more controlled and mature use of the strategy' (p 102). See **957**.

947 Hackethal, Marietta. *Aufbau und Erzählstruktur der Erzählungen Chaucers*. Ludwig-Maximilians-Universität diss. 1966. Dir. W. Clemen and H. Kuhn. Published Munich, 1966.
Instances of the deferred beginning of an action (lines 925–64), the interlacing of several distinct actions (lines 1019–1102), and the spoken remark that generates an action (lines 995–7) are cited from *FranT*.

948 Hoffman, Richard L. *Ovid and the Canterbury Tales*. 1966. See **192**.
Arveragus's marriage contract, in which he becomes Dorigen's 'servant in fact and lord in name alone' (p 167), violates the sacramental ordering of Christian wedlock. His command that Dorigen commit adultery rather than break her sworn word demonstrates both his and the Franklin's 'shallow morality' (p 168). The Franklin's feeble moral sense is further exposed by his

closing question about generosity; none of the characters is truly *fre.*

949 Joseph, Gerhard. 'The *Franklin's Tale*: Chaucer's Theodicy.' *ChauR* 1 (1966), 20–32.

Told from 'an overtly Christian point of view' (p 29), *FranT* 'illuminate[s] the divine plan which permits evil to darken the human comedy' (p 21). Dorigen's questioning of the rocks is a failure of moral imagination that leads to her chastisement and, ultimately, to the revelation of the providential purpose of the apparent hostility of nature. The garden mirrors Dorigen's faulty comprehension of God's *purveiaunce;* in making her promise to Aurelius, she becomes caught up in the garden's superficial courtliness, thus encouraging Aurelius's cupidinous desires. In seeking out the Orléans clerk, Aurelius moves from the garden of *cupiditas* to the 'Augustinian city of man' (p 27); the magician's images expose Aurelius's paradise as a place 'in which all creatures are at war in an amoral wilderness' (p 28). And when Aurelius announces the disappearance of the rocks, Dorigen's contemplation of suicide repeats the pagan failure of *pacience* that had earlier led her to question God's wisdom. This despair is answered by the descent of gratuitous providential grace; as Dorigen and Aurelius make their way toward the garden, Aurelius chooses to abstain from his lust. The Franklin's narrative answers Dorigen's Complaint by creating the conditions under which man may 'freely choose between the garden of fleshly desire and the city of God' (p 31). Treating *gentilesse* within the context of Christian theology, the tale may be read as a 'parable justifying the ways of God to men' (p 32).

950 Kee, Kenneth, ed. *Geoffrey Chaucer: A Selection of His Works.* 1966. See **87**.

If the nuptial agreement of Dorigen and Arveragus constitutes what in the minds of some critics seems an ideal marriage, it is difficult to understand why this ideal solution to the dilemma of marital sovereignty should run into serious difficulties. Although Dorigen desires the liberty of a courtly mistress, she 'exhibits a pitiful incapacity for exercising the responsibilities of that liberty' (p 145). The crisis in the marriage is resolved only by forces external to the two marriage partners. Like *MerT, FranT* contains a garden, but neither the paradisal nor the hellish connotations of the garden in the earlier tale are realized in *FranT*. Dorigen's springtime vow to Aurelius to love him best if he removes the coastal rocks may represent 'some kind of unconscious vernal acquiescence on her part,' but the wintry setting of the occasion on which she must keep her promise brings with it a 'sobering realization' of the implications of that promise (pp 145–6). The tale's concluding *demande d'amour* diverts us from the narrative's moral implications to the solution of a riddle to which there is no definitive answer.

951 Kelly, Francis J. 'Chaucer's Franklin's Tale, F. 942.' *Expl* 24 (1966), no. 81.

In line 942 ('Withouten coppe he drank al his penaunce'), *withouten* should be glossed as 'outside of,' a reference to the custom of pouring the last drop of one's cup on the thumbnail (i.e., *supernaculum*), then licking it off, to signify that the drink was good to the last drop. Aurelius 'drank all his penance *supernaculum*, i.e., until the last drop of penance was outside of the cup, or completely.'

952 Mann, Lindsay A. '"Gentilesse" and the Franklin's Tale.' *SP* 63 (1966), 10–29. Although it plays down the external or formal aspects of *gentilesse*, *FranT* touches on all of the other qualities traditionally associated with the ideal: loyalty, compassion, humility, generosity, cheerfulness, concern with reputation, patience, and love. Loyalty (*trouthe*) and love are the most important of these qualities; the others play a subordinate role. *Gentilesse* in *FranT* is finally neither Christian nor courtly; the poem 'looks to this world,' and 'implies a transformation of courtly and Christian ideals to practical life in this world' (p 25).

953 Muscatine, Charles. '*The Canterbury Tales*: Style of the Man and Style of the Work.' In *Chaucer and Chaucerians: Critical Studies in Middle English Literature*. Ed. Derek S. Brewer. University: U of Alabama P, 1966. Pp 88–113. Repr. in *Medieval Literature, Style, and Culture: Essays by Charles Muscatine* (see **516**). Pp 1–25.
In the 'gratuitous exempla' of Dorigen's Complaint, 'sententiousness jostles art a little harder than we should like' (p 94).

954 Severs, J. Burke. 'Appropriateness of Character to Plot in the "Franklin's Tale."' In *Studies in Language and Literature in Honour of Margaret Schlauch*. Ed. Mieczysław Brahmer, Stanisław Helsztyński, and Julian Krzyżanowski. Warsaw: PNW – Polish Scientific Publishers, 1966. Repr. New York: Russell and Russell, 1971. Pp 385–96.
Chaucer takes pains early in *FranT* to portray characters whose actions will seem credible as the tale develops. The marriage contract establishes Arveragus's generosity, his high sense of honor, his need to avoid public shame, and his forswearing of jealousy – all qualities manifested later in the tale; in a similar fashion, the passage foreshadows Dorigen's absolute fidelity to her husband. In Aurelius and the clerk, we also see character fitted to plot: both men exhibit traits that render plausible their generous responses at the tale's conclusion. The characters are not simply idealized types; Arveragus's actions are unconventional, as is Dorigen's 'overpassionate response to circumstances' (p 392).

955 Spearing, A.C., ed. *The Franklin's Prologue and Tale from the Canterbury Tales by Geoffrey Chaucer*. 1966/1994. See **86**.
Many of the characteristics touched on in the *GP* portrait of the Franklin are reflected in the tale (e.g., his love of good living). The Franklin's interruption of the Squire is brilliantly tactful. But the Franklin's remarks are also patronizing, demonstrating his determination to assert his own social standing. His denigration of his own son in contrast to the Squire and his somewhat

obsessive focus on *gentilesse* depict a man uneasy about his relationship to the chivalric world represented by the Knight and the Squire. Despite the Franklin's identification of his tale as a Breton lay, the similarities to known examples of this genre are mostly superficial ones. With the possible exception of the two English lays in the Auchinleck MS, there is no evidence that Chaucer had read any of the Breton lays. The closest parallels to *FranT* are *Fil* and *Dec* 10.5. Although Chaucer may have read either or both, there is no sign that he wrote with a copy of Boccaccio before him. Chaucer's identification of *FranT* as a Breton lay may have been prompted by his desire to make the old-fashioned Franklin choose a genre that had lost its vogue, or by his wish to give the black rocks – a real topographical feature of coastal Brittany – a correspondingly full Breton setting. In his Prologue, the Franklin disclaims knowledge of rhetoric even while displaying it. This 'masterpiece of rhetorical trickery' (p 19) is an example of mock modesty through which the Franklin can reveal his true learning to the more perceptive pilgrims, and – for Chaucer and us – an exposé of the Franklin's ostentation that keeps him from being truly *gentil*. The Franklin's secret pride in his rhetorical skill also appears in his tale, particularly in the periphrasis describing nightfall (lines 1015–18), and in Dorigen's elaborate and overlong Complaint. The Franklin's three main themes are *trouthe*, marriage, and *gentilesse*. His treatment of convention can be seen in the character of Aurelius and in the description of the garden, which combines elements of the courtly paradise of love with echoes of Eden. Convention is augmented by realistic touches, notably in the speeches and actions of Dorigen and Aurelius. The symbolic function of the black rocks also changes under the pressure of realistic human emotions. The clerk's magic is treated as a scientific process; its ambiguity produces the effect of removing the rocks while reminding us that Aurelius is still pursuing an illusion. The tale's many doubts and ambiguities do not, however, turn it into a 'problem-poem'; Dorigen's speech questioning God's Providence is a loose end in *FranT*, which elsewhere is kept below the level of the disturbingly problematic. (For Spearing's completely rewritten introduction to the 1994 edition, see **1339**.)

956 Wood, Chauncey. 'Of Time and Tide in the *Franklin's Tale*.' *PQ* 45 (1966), 688–711.

The medieval theory of the annual period of the tides as developed in commentaries on Aristotle argues that the highest tides occur in winter rather than summer, at a period after the solstice that corresponds to the December date given for the magician's activities (lines 1243–5). If the Orléans clerk only predicted a high tide, his deceptiveness in fulfilling his bargain with Aurelius calls his *gentilesse* into question, and in turn that of the tale's other characters. Infatuated with the world of romance, the Franklin fails to see the limitations of the actors in his tale. His blindness about moral issues extends to his attitude toward magic as well; although he seems to reject the clerk's astrology, his 'casual dismissal of magic is given the lie by his enthusiasm for its effects' (p 708). At the tale's center is the Franklin's 'self-delusion about appearance and reality, illusion and truth' (p 709).

957 Berger, Harry, Jr. 'The F-Fragment of the *Canterbury Tales*: Part II.' *ChauR* 1 (1967), 135–56. Repr. as 'Pleasure and Responsibility in the Franklin's Tale' in *Geoffrey Chaucer's "The Canterbury Tales": A Casebook.* Ed. Lee Patterson. Oxford: Oxford UP, 2007. Pp 137–57.

The Franklin's soft-focus presentation of Dorigen and Arveragus and his symbolically expressive handling of description reveal both his attraction to his subjects and his need to keep his material from seeming too real. The sea and the rocks 'both cause and express Dorigen's lack of *pacience*'; in retreating to the garden, she moves from 'the symbol of pure pain to the symbol of pure pleasure' (p 137). The garden also symbolizes Aurelius's obsessive desire; the Franklin's feelings about courtly gardens and lovers can be inferred from the *GP* portrait, where his tendency to self-indulgence is 'fitted into the wider frame of social and natural order' (p 139). The word *vitaille* (line 904) encompasses life's essential needs in a general sense. The contrast between rhetoric as *vitaille* and as magic and fantasy forms the basis for the 'pattern ... of withdrawal and return' that marks the overall narrative shape of *FranT* as well as of its subsequences (p 140). Connected to this pattern is the Franklin's shift in focus from his audience to his subject and back again. The tale, which is 'about the functions and dangers of recreation, is itself an exemplary recreative act' (p 141). Concerned with the proper balance between work and play, the Franklin finds Arveragus's chivalric *labour* (line 812) 'too purely self-directed' (p 142), while the tale's serious trouble is caused by Dorigen's playful response to Aurelius. The Franklin is at pains to distinguish proper from improper uses of magic – on the one hand, the recreative uses of magic as part of a social occasion, on the other, magic as pagan *folye* (line 1131) that produces only disruptive illusions. In his account of the magician's domestic arrangements and clerkly possessions, the Franklin seems to be identifying with his character. The narcissistic and escapist tendencies to which magic, courtly love, and fiction appeal are thus given 'qualified approval' (p 148) as elements of social experience. The winter description (lines 1243–55) serves as an 'emblem ... of the Franklin's view of life,' with the 'Franklin-like Janus' succeeding the 'Squire-like Phoebus ... in the sequence of life and experience' (p 149). The Franklin's balanced sense of life's rhythms underscores the extent to which the excessive behavior of some of the characters violates these norms. The clerk's illusion-making activities symbolize dangerous human tendencies, but the Franklin also displays a 'grudging admiration' (p 152) for his craft. Dorigen's prolix Complaint is contrasted with the Franklin's concern for his obligations to his audience;

after her monologue, the Franklin increases the pace of the narrative, and shifts his attention from his tale to his listeners. The closing *demande* translates a private, aristocratic idyll into the practical sphere of public activity. Having indulged his fantasy and provided entertainment for his audience and himself, the Franklin directly engages his auditors, and offers *vitaille* – something 'relevant and instructive' (p 156) – only at the very close of his tale. See **946**.

958 Burlin, Robert B. 'The Art of Chaucer's Franklin.' *Neophil* 51 (1967), 55–73. Repr. with revisions in *Chaucer—The Canterbury Tales: A Casebook*. 1974. See **390**. Pp 183–208.
The Franklin's social insecurity, hinted at in *GP* and foregrounded in his comments on his son's lack of *gentilesse*, governs genre, style, and theme in his tale. He tells a Breton lay, a genre that would have seemed outmoded to Chaucer's audience. Ostentatious and occasionally clumsy, his rhetorical flights suggest a man imperfectly schooled in the verbal arts; Dorigen's Complaint is an especially egregious instance of failed rhetorical control. The Franklin's handling of character also reveals a narrator ill suited to the kind of tale he has chosen to tell: Dorigen, Arveragus, and Aurelius are 'elegant but artificial puppets pieced together from bits of faded but noble romances' (p 67). Although the Franklin's overt intentions are easy to isolate, 'Chaucer has made the poem do more than he permitted the Franklin to see' (p 71). The latter's 'myopia' (p 71) manifests itself in the tale's metaphysical dimensions – centered around Dorigen's and Aurelius's foolish dissatisfaction with God's creation, in the form of the black rocks – and in the ironic implications (unrecognized by the teller) of the discourse on patience. Like Dorigen, the Franklin 'places personal well-being above a humble respect for the established order ... [his] excessive concern for "gentillesse" ... is merely another kind of dissatisfaction with things as they are' (p 72). The tale's 'submerged theme' is the Franklin's own 'imperfect virtue' (p 72).

959 Fifield, Merle. 'Chaucer the Theater-goer.' 1967. See **494**.
The *tregetoures* recalled by Aurelius's brother are masters of stage illusion who create visual effects paralleled in accounts of fourteenth-century English and continental court revels. The sample performance offered to Aurelius by the clerk likewise includes elements familiar from contemporary outdoor pageants and indoor entertainments, and is ordered like a masque: it entertains the visitors until supper is ready, it includes a joust, and it ends with a dance.

960 Gardner, John. 'The Case Against the "Bradshaw Shift"; or, the Mystery of the Manuscript in the Trunk.' 1967. See **495**.
Fragments II–V (B^1–D–E–F) of *CT* constitute a coherent thematic block; *FranT* contains themes – mutual obligation, patient endurance, appearance and reality – introduced in previous tales. 'The final word in the argument –

the wise resolution of the demands of orthodoxy and of medieval emotional experience – is given to a sort of buffoon, the social climbing, slightly befuddled Franklin' (p 104).

961 Hatton, Thomas J. 'Magic and Honor in *The Franklin's Tale.*' *PLL* 3 (summer supplement, 1967), 179–81.
Two passages in Froissart's *Chronicles* provide contexts for an evaluation of the behavior of the clerk and Arveragus in *FranT*. In the first passage, a deceptive magician is beheaded; 'if one reads the magic of Chaucer's magician as like that of the Duke of Anjou's magician, the former would appear to deserve a different payment from the one Aurelius contemplates giving him' (p 180). In the second passage, a husband avenges the honor of his wife (who has been raped by a squire) in a trial by combat. Hatton contrasts his actions with those of Arveragus, who is willing to sacrifice his wife's honor for a vow made in jest.

962 Hoffman, Richard L. 'Jephthah's Daughter and Chaucer's Virginia.' *ChauR* 2 (1967), 20–31.
Jephthah's vow (Judges 11), recalled by Virginia before her death in *PhyT* (VI.240–1) and glossed by medieval exegetes as rash and foolish, is paralleled in Dorigen's promise to Aurelius. As in Virginia's case, Dorigen's vow seems to necessitate a choice between voluntary death and sexual dishonor. But the women cited by Dorigen in her Complaint were truly chaste, whereas Dorigen's dilemma is brought about by a conditional vow to commit adultery.

963 Howard, Ronnalie Roper. 'Appearance, Reality, and the Ideal in Chaucer's *Franklin's Tale.*' *BSUF* 8:3 (1967), 40–4.
The blurring of appearance and reality in *FranT* makes it difficult to maintain conventional ideals of conduct. Dorigen and Arveragus reject both Christian and courtly ideals in their marriage, but the new ideal they create involves a conflict between appearance – Arveragus's 'name of soveraynetee' (line 751) – and reality. The illusion created by the magician stands as a paradigm for other dangerous illusions: the rocks appear to be a threat, but are less harmful in reality than after they seem to disappear; the garden is more dangerous than the sea coast; Dorigen's jest to Aurelius seems to him to be a vow; Arveragus is pushed to rash behavior in attempting to maintain the 'illusion' of sovereignty for the world's eyes. The Franklin's concluding question concerns *gentilesse,* and is 'a kind of joke': none of the characters is truly noble (p 44). 'The tale shows a world in which no ideal holds at all times, in which life is too complex to admit of any one predetermined code of action'; in such a world, patience with human frailty is a necessity (p 44).

964 Moorman, Charles. *A Knyght Ther Was: The Evolution of the Knight in Literature.* Lexington: U of Kentucky P, 1967.
The essential conflict in *FranT* stems from Dorigen and Arveragus's attempt

to carry the practices of courtly love into marriage. The tale revolves around Arveragus's realization of 'the essential dishonesty of the chivalric code,' exposing the immorality of courtly values and praising the bourgeois ideal of marriage (pp 93–4). Like *WBT, FranT* achieves its happy ending through the intervention of a *deus ex machina* and the conversion of the hero from false chivalry to a more practical set of values.

• Review by Georgia Ronan Crampton, *CL* 21 (1969), 266–71: Moorman misrepresents the balance in the marriage of Dorigen and Arveragus between the latter's courtly submissiveness and his husbandly authority. Nor does the tale avoid tragedy through a *deus ex machina*; it is the human response of Aurelius that secures the happy ending.

965 Peck, Russell A. 'Sovereignty and the Two Worlds of the *Franklin's Tale*.' *ChauR* 1 (1967), 253–71.

FranT's central theme is the difficulty of perceiving truth in a world of illusions. The tale is set at the center of two corresponding worlds: the timeless and spaceless world of God and the bounded and temporal world observable by human senses. Ideally, the marriage of Dorigen and Arveragus should reflect the divine order. If this correspondence is disturbed, frustration and confusion follow. The tale's characters, and its teller as well, fail to see beyond appearances and project their private desires upon reality. The Franklin's self-deception is evident in his comments to the Squire and the introduction to his tale; he is 'not the man he thinks he is' (p 259), and this lack of self-knowledge is manifested in his tale, particularly in Arveragus's preoccupation with his public image. In relinquishing his responsibilities as head of the household, Arveragus leaves Dorigen to her own inadequate devices; isolated from reality, she 'plays sovereign with God' (p 263) in her speech about the rocks (paralleled in Aurelius's self-regarding prayer to Apollo) and undergoes a kind of fall from paradise in the May garden. In obeying her husband and returning to the garden, 'the scene of her crime' (p 269), to face the consequences, Dorigen reaffirms right order and allows the two worlds of the poem to be reconciled. This spiritual rebirth is underlined by Christian and classical allusions, including the placement of Dorigen's return to the garden on the eve of Epiphany.

966 Silvia, Daniel S., Jr. 'Geoffrey Chaucer on the Subject of Men, Women, Marriage, and *Gentilesse*.' *RLV* 33 (1967), 227–36.

Accepting the Bradshaw ordering of *CT*, Silvia posits a discussion of marriage running from *Mel* through *FranT*. In *Mel*, mutual aid and advice provide a solution to marital distress. In *NPT, WBT, ClT,* and *MerT*, Chaucer gives a hearing to the possible objections that might be raised to the solution offered in *Mel*; in each of these tales, one of the mates asserts sovereignty to the disadvantage of the other. *FranT* concludes the discussion by presenting a relationship similar to that in *Mel*, but with the important difference that

Arveragus and Dorigen pledge mutual forbearance at the beginning of their marriage. Their relationship is based on *gentilesse*, which is the true subject of the marriage tales. (For an earlier version of this material, see **298**.)

967 Böker, Uwe. *Studien zu Chaucers Franklin's Tale.* University of Regensburg diss. 1968. Dir. K.H. Göller and O. Hietsch. Regensburg: n.p., 1968.
An investigation of the relationship between 'Erzählzeit' and 'erzählte Zeit' and between various dialogues and rhetorical devices shows that the story maintains dramatic tension throughout, and that the Franklin leads his narrative towards the climax of a threefold denouement. The poem is constructed symmetrically about an axis, formed by three monologues – Dorigen's lament over the rocks, Aurelius's prayer to Apollo, and Dorigen's Complaint. The Franklin's excessive admiration for an ancient feudal system and his eagerness to display *largesse* and *gentilesse* suggests that he is not a naturally born member of the gentry. He is an Epicurean in the medieval sense of the word, more like Jovinian than the latter's opponent Jerome, whom he quotes. The Franklin foregrounds his ideals of knightly courtesy in the tale's setting, names, and key terms. But his preference for *amour courtois* clashes with Christian ideals, and prevents us from taking the Franklin's attitudes as Chaucer's. Neither Arveragus nor Dorigen is morally free. The former's exaggeratedly chivalric behavior leaves his wife unprotected, and his sending of Dorigen to Aurelius is no act of generosity but a sign of his superficiality. Dorigen also displays a superficial and schematic view of the universe; she is unable to fit life's hazards into God's plan of salvation. Her lack of suspicion and innocence become weaknesses and lead to her thoughtless promise to Aurelius. The latter is the only character in the tale who changes his attitudes toward himself, nature, and God. Initially a courtly lover of the idolatrous school, Aurelius undergoes a transformation by renouncing his claim to Dorigen and recognizing his guilt. In this way his liberality becomes an act of moral freedom. The rocks provide a connection with the overall theme of *CT*, the pilgrimage to the heavenly Jerusalem. The rocks represent dangers but also unalterable creation. Magic and illusion only make them seem to disappear; the world remains as it is, and man has to accept it to become mature and free.

968 Brewer, Derek S. 'Class Distinction in Chaucer.' *Speculum* 43 (1968), 290–305.
Chaucer takes the notion of *degree* seriously – but not too seriously. It is a worldly thing, as the Franklin shows in noting that Arveragus keeps 'the name of soveraynetee … for shame of his degree' (lines 751–2).

969 Lawlor, John. *Chaucer*. London: Hutchinson, 1968; New York: Harper, 1969.
The Franklin's interruption of the Squire, his interchange with Harry Bailly, and his disclaimer of rhetorical skill mark him as an 'unpolished but quietly enthusiastic advocate of fine behaviour' (p 134). As an observer of idealized life, the narrator of *FranT* (linked to but not identical with the pilgrim depict-

ed in *GP*), strives to protect the happiness of Dorigen and Arveragus from over-intent scrutiny. The Franklin does not offer a solution to the debate on *maistrye;* his tale is directed towards 'the vindication of *gentillesse* from the standpoint of innocent *auctoritee*' (p 143). The Franklin's role as narrator is one that Chaucer often takes as well – slightly simple-minded, diffident in expressing his own views. This pose of 'artful inadequacy' (p 153) keeps the story at a remove from the narrator, and grants his characters an independence apart from his control. Yet the Franklin is 'not all amiable incompetence' (p 154). Although the poem's set speeches seem dutiful rather than deeply felt, he can hardly be equaled for the powerful brief phrase or telling silence; at these latter moments, the narrator's simplicity of statement carries the weight of the story. The Franklin's regard for his audience parallels his sympathy for his characters. In contrast to the narrator of *TC,* who finds himself in 'an unhappily predestined position,' the Franklin 'constitutes a benevolent Providence, steering his story to a happy ending' (p 158). The winter vignette (lines 1252–5) is a comforting reminder that whatever may happen in apparent defiance of the natural order will bring no permanent harm. *FranT* comes as close as we can imagine to the *comedye* promised at the end of *TC.*

970 Miller, Robert P. 'Allegory in the Canterbury Tales.' In *A Companion to Chaucer Studies*. 1968/1979. See **500**. Pp 268–90/pp 326–51.
In *FranT,* Chaucer adapts the allegorical framework of his Boccaccian source (in which the three men represent the worldly sins enumerated in 1 John 2:16) to create, in his three male characters, embodiments of the Franklin's own Epicurean worldliness.

971 Milosh, Joseph. 'Chaucer's Too-Well Told *Franklin's Tale*: A Problem of Characterization.' *WSL* 5 (1968), 1–11.
What seem like inconsistencies in characterization – Arveragus's transformation from a 'cardboard character' to an 'emotionally real' figure (p 5), conflicting assessments of Dorigen's mental abilities, Aurelius's sudden about-face in the tale's final scene – can be explained by the requirements of *FranT*'s genre, the *demande d'amour*. Hints of psychological complexity within a form that usually produces two-dimensional characters have puzzled critics and generated conflicting interpretations. A simpler explanation is Chaucer's imagination, which produces depth in a genre that would have stifled creativity in a lesser poet.

971a Rodax, Yvonne. *The Real and the Ideal in the Novella of Italy, France, and England. Four Centuries of Change in the Boccaccian Tale*. 1968. See **498a**.
The supernatural in *FranT* is 'allied with the moral powers of the universe.' Embodying conflicting values, the tale nevertheless reaches a solution 'satisfactory to humanist, to courtly lover and Christian alike' (p 15).

972 Severs, J. Burke. 'The Tales of Romance.' In *A Companion to Chaucer Studies*.

1968/1979. See **500**. Pp 229–46/pp 269–95.

Chaucer derived his understanding of the Breton lay from the poems in the Auchinleck MS; in reading *Sir Orfeo*, he would have identified the theme of the married lovers with the Breton lay. When he found in *Fil* elements like those in *Sir Orfeo*, he associated Boccaccio's tale with the Breton lay. Severs surveys the critical reception of *FranT* since Kittredge (**805**). Critics who see the tale as morally absurd and the Franklin as shallow ignore the 'obvious meaning' of the tale and read into it 'private views' unsanctioned by 'the tale itself' (p 237).

973 Wagenknecht, Edward C. *The Personality of Chaucer*. 1968. See **501**.

Questions Kittredge's view of *FranT* (**805**) as the harmonious conclusion of the debate about marital sovereignty. The tale's subject is not domination in marriage but 'the sanctity of the pledged word' (p 100). And Arveragus does exhibit *maistrye* when he commands Dorigen to keep her promise. Chaucer understood women as few writers have, and was able to see the world through their eyes. Dorigen's speech about the rocks is characteristic: 'since [clerks] are not women, they cannot know what a woman feels, and so their knowledge is more or less irrelevant after all' (p 137).

974 Whittock, Trevor. *A Reading of the Canterbury Tales*. 1968. See **502**.

See **911**.

975 Anderson, George K. 'Chaucer: A Suggested Portrait.' In *Medieval Drama: A Collection of Festival Papers*. Ed. William A. Selz. Festival Papers, vol. 3. Vermillion: University of South Dakota, 1969. Pp 84–95.

Chaucer's unhappiness with the institution of marriage may explain the structural weaknesses of *FranT*; 'it is difficult to write *con amore* about anything to which one is not emotionally and intellectually committed' (p 91).

976 Beidler, Peter. 'The Pairing of the *Franklin's Tale* and the *Physician's Tale*.' *ChauR* 3 (1969), 275–9.

A comparison of *FranT* and *PhyT* suggests that the tales are deliberately juxtaposed in the *CT* sequence. Both tales concern a man smitten with desire for a woman who is not, at first, aware that she is desired. More significant is the contrast between the Franklin's heroine and Virginia, 'strong in all the ways in which … Dorigen is weak' (p 276). Unlike Dorigen, Virginia willingly chooses death over dishonor; although Dorigen wishes to be like the women she mentions in her speech, she lacks the courage to act. Virginia's unwavering virtue casts into its proper light Dorigen's moral confusion.

977 Howard, Donald R., ed. *Geoffrey Chaucer, The Canterbury Tales. A Selection*. 1969. See **90**.

Questions Kittredge's idea (**805**) that the Franklin's view of marriage was intended as Chaucer's final word on the subject; 'there is something faintly ludicrous about the Franklin's literal-minded characters and the fantastical situation they get involved in.' Moreover, 'the Franklin's own character makes him an unlikely mouthpiece for serious views' (xxix). The value he places on mutual concession in marriage was to become the bourgeois ideal; 'if Chaucer did not agree with it, he at least saw it coming' (xxx).

978 Kearney, Anthony M. 'Truth and Illusion in *The Franklin's Tale.*' *EIC* 19 (1969), 245–53.
FranT moves beyond the initial theoretical assumptions about marriage embodied in Dorigen and Arveragus's contract to more practical concerns. Much of the tale's irony is at Dorigen's expense: she lacks patience, 'tends to retreat from the harsh blows of Fortune' (p 248), and enters the world of illusion in her promise to Aurelius, whose own impatience and querulousness are exaggerated versions of the same qualities in Dorigen. Both characters are 'brought to good sense' (p 249) by the idealized figure of Arveragus, whose actions imply Chaucer's belief in the value of wise husbandly sovereignty in marriage. At the end of the tale, 'with the wife looking to the husband, the squire to the knight, and the clerk to the squire, we have a fine tableau of social and moral order' (pp 251–2). See **981**.

979 Knight, Stephen. 'Rhetoric and Poetry in the *Franklin's Tale.*' *ChauR* 4 (1969), 14–30.
Simple identification of rhetorical tropes is inadequate for an analysis of Chaucer's poetry; one must consider the relation of language and meaning. The tale's narrative is for the most part presented in long, fluent verse paragraphs, an 'urbane and supple' medium (p 19) that calls attention to those passages where Chaucer departs from it. The Franklin's 'blunt style,' Dorigen's 'varying and emotional style,' and Aurelius's 'circumlocutory tendencies' are essential to our sense of their characters (p 25). Chaucer's use of rhetorical devices allows us to see the excesses of Dorigen and Aurelius, as well as the Franklin's inadequacies. Towards the end of the tale, however, 'bravura effects' are replaced by a simpler style, appropriate to the story's 'quiet happy ending' (p 29).

980 North, J.D. 'Kalenderes enlumyned ben they: Some Astronomical Themes in Chaucer.' *RES* n.s. 20 (1969), 129–54, 257–83, 418–44.
The calendrical structure of *FranT* hangs on two dates – 6 May (line 906) and a date in early January when the clerk works his magic. A consideration of astronomical evidence points to 1389 as the most probable year in Chaucer's lifetime for the 6 May date; the configuration of the planets makes it suitable for Aurelius's first declaration of love (e.g., the Sun's presence in the domicile of Venus suggests a reason for Aurelius's prayer asking for Apollo's intercession on his behalf). The state of the heavens on 10 January 1392, makes this date appropriate for the clerk's magic. For example, Mercury (the planet of craft and learning, representing the subtle clerk) and Mars (representing the squire) were only a degree or so apart on this date. The 'thridde nyght' (line 1459) on which Arveragus returns to Dorigen would be that of 14 Jan-

uary; Jupiter, 'an astrologically irresistible candidate for Arveragus,' could rest content that the malevolent influences of 10 January were now 'fighting it out amongst themselves' (p 266).

The Franklin's Tale, 1970–1979

981 Colmer, Dorothy. '*The Franklin's Tale*: A Palimpsest Reading.' *EIC* 20 (1970), 375–80.

Kearney (**978**) attributes to Chaucer attitudes that are properly the Franklin's; Arveragus's 'geniality, love of domestic order, [and] regard for appearances' are the Franklin's own characteristics (p 378). The tale's idealized picture of domestic peace runs up against the courtly assumptions of the source story; because the Franklin treats his characters alternately as real people and as romance stereotypes, he is unable to develop an argument through characterization. The Franklin's narrative is superimposed upon the tale's Boccaccian source; the human and realistic qualities of the former stand out 'fresh and sharp against the tarnished finery' of the latter (p 379). See **993**.

982 Galewski, Barbro. *Simplicity and Directness in Chaucer's Canterbury Tales*. University of Uppsala diss. 1970. Published Uppsala, 1970.

Arveragus and Dorigen stand out as the best examples of Chaucerian *gentilesse*. Dorigen's conception of honor, or 'female chivalry,' is the tale's essence. When this idea becomes too strict, or threatens to seem inhuman, '"gentillesse" surges in like a wave of freshness' (p 124).

983 Golding, M.R. 'The Importance of Keeping "Trouthe" in *The Franklin's Tale*.' *MÆ* 39 (1970), 306–12.

FranT is concerned with two kinds of honor – that of the tale's story world and that demanded by real life. The narrative plays ironically with reversals of illusion and reality. The rocks, for example, represent a reality that Dorigen cannot comprehend; when, in accordance with her wish, they seem to disappear, their disappearance creates a 'moral chaos' that threatens the very values she had hoped to safeguard (p 309). In its treatment of *trouthe*, the tale comes out on the side of reality. Dorigen's keeping of her *trouthe* to Aurelius involves an acceptance of responsibility for her actions that is 'consonant with the demands of real life rather than with the fulfilling of a test-case' (p 312).

984 Hoy, Michael, and Michael Stevens. *Chaucer's Major Tales*. London: Bailey, 1970. Repr. New York: Schocken, 1983.

Treats the resolution of the issues raised earlier in the marriage debate; the significance of the courtly love convention; the tale's geographical setting; rhetoric and the use of exempla; the Boethian sources of Dorigen's lament over the rocks and the shifting symbolism of the rocks; *gentilesse* (Arveragus, in his insistence that Dorigen keep her promise, fulfills most completely the *gentil* ideal); and the Franklin as a narrator who takes 'an ambiguous Janus-like stand' (p 97) on the issues of courtly love versus Christian marriage and science versus magic (pp 79–101).

985 Nist, John. 'Chaucer's Apostrophic Mode in *The Canterbury Tales.*' *TSL* 15 (1970), 85–98.
Apostrophe in *FranT* reveals the teller's 'serene sensibility' (p 93). Dorigen's initial apostrophe lamenting the existence of the rocks generates subsequent apostrophic passages – Aurelius's prayer to Apollo and his lament about his financial straits, Dorigen's complaint to Fortune – in which the characters 'vent their rage for order and come to be stilled in the final peace of the Franklin's ultimate moral vision: Whose honor-keeping heart is indeed the most generous?' (p 93).

986 Pearsall, Derek. '*The Canterbury Tales.*' 1970/1986. See **505**.
Chaucer brings humane significance to *FranT*'s fairy-tale plot by turning it into a tragicomedy. Dorigen's 'faintly comic' Complaint detaches us from her plight and enables the poet to move from the touching seriousness of the first part of the tale to the playfulness of its conclusion; this 'delicacy of disengagement' accounts for *FranT*'s success (p 183/p 256).

987 Woo, Constance, and William Matthews. 'The Spiritual Purpose of the *Canterbury Tales.*' *Comitatus* 1 (1970), 85–109.
FranT 'is not Chaucer's solution, as Kittredge [**805**] seemed to think. Such gentilesse, such consideration, is not to be found this side of heaven' (p 104).

988 Wood, Chauncey. *Chaucer and the Country of the Stars: Poetic Uses of Astrological Imagery.* 1970. See **508**.
See **956**.
• Review in *TLS*, 2 October 1970: Despite his 'admirable learning,' Wood 'seems not to like poetry much, and to have a taste for simplistic moralizing ... He cannot decide whether the lovely passage in *FranT* 1243–55 is a parody, or just simply bad poetry. Later he describes himself as – like the Franklin – one of "we burel folk", the sort of people who don't understand highly-wrought feelings or poetry. One is tempted to agree.'

989 Coghill, Nevill. *Chaucer's Idea of What is Noble.* London: Engish Association, 1971. Repr. in *The Collected Papers of Nevill Coghill, Shakespearean and Medievalist* (see **466**). Pp 54–73.
FranT shows how *trouthe* and *fredom* inhere in *gentilesse,* and shows that all classes have an equal capacity for that virtue; 'neither birth nor wealth have anything to do with it' (p 12).
• Review by Derek S. Brewer, *MÆ* 12 (1973), 117: *KnT* and *FranT* are now often represented as 'jokes, satires against their tellers.' Coghill's view will seem old-fashioned in comparison, but it is 'essentially the truer, and will eventually prevail, however modified by proper qualification' (p 117).

990 Doltas, Dilek. 'The Discussion of Love and Marriage in "The Canterbury Tales."' *Haceteppe Bulletin of Social Sciences and Humanities* 3 (1971), 157–75.
The reader of *MerT* and *FranT* feels as if the same plot is being enacted by two different sets of characters, the first 'a collection of lost souls,' the second unfailingly noble and *gentil* (p 172). *FranT* criticizes courtly love conventions, particularly the claims that true love and marriage are incompatible and that jealousy is a necessary part of a love relationship. In asserting the 'glory of conjugal love,' *FranT* teaches virtues that come close to man's love of God (p 173).

991 Hoffman, Richard L. '*The Canterbury Tales*.' In *Critical Approaches to Six Major English Works: Beowulf through Paradise Lost*. Ed. R.M. Lumiansky and Herschel Baker. Philadelphia: U of Pennsylvania P, 1971. Pp 41–80.
If *FranT* is read as Chaucer's final word on marriage, then the poet must have been '"ahead" of his age in philosophy ... a "free-thinker" in religion, and ... a rather dangerous man to know should he meet your wife in a mood to make outrageous bargains with her' (pp 69–70).

992 Hussey, Stanley S. *Chaucer: An Introduction*. London: Methuen, 1971.
The real concern of *FranT* is not character but plot: will Aurelius be able to remove the black rocks, and if he does, will Dorigen keep her word? Arveragus's command to Dorigen to keep her promise is unlikely as psychology, but consistent with the Franklin's preoccupation with *gentilesse* (pp 135–40).

993 Kearney, Anthony M. 'The *Franklin's Tale*.' *EIC* 21 (1971), 109–11.
Responding to Colmer (**981**), Kearney questions whether it is possible to distinguish between the creative 'tale' and the conventional 'source,' expresses doubt that the Franklin (rather than Chaucer) is responsible for the tale's inconsistencies, and suggests that Colmer has offered us 'a tale without a consistent parable or theme' in which Chaucer is merely playing games with his readers (p 111).

994 Murtaugh, Daniel. 'Women and Geoffrey Chaucer.' *ELH* 38 (1971), 473–92. Repr. in *Geoffrey Chaucer* (see **483**). Pp 336–56.
The movement of *FranT* toward an 'exorcism of fantasy' can be seen in Chaucer's treatment of the garden he inherited from *Fil*. In the latter, the lady's demand that her would-be lover produce a spring garden in winter suggests a kind of romantic frivolity on her part; in *FranT*, the garden is transformed into a symbol of Aurelius's illusions of adulterous love. In her Complaint, Dorigen recycles Jerome's celebration of women for their willingness to destroy themselves in the name of chastity. The real threat to Dorigen's marriage comes not from the coastal rocks, 'but from two complementary fantasies: a courtly lover's dream of her beauty and a celibate propagandist's dream of her virtue' (p 490). In his response to Dorigen's plight, Arveragus 'denies the validity of the dilemma' (p 491), making it clear that spiritual integrity – the devotion to *trouthe* – rather than the physical integri-

ty of her body is the real basis of their marriage. And '*trouthe* begets *fredom*' in the subsequent episode: '*because* Arveragus and Dorigen free themselves from the patristic view of womanly virtue, *therefore* Aurelius frees himself from the courtly, adulterous view of love' (p 491).

995 Robinson, Ian. *Chaucer's Prosody: A Study of the Middle English Verse Tradition.* Cambridge: Cambridge UP, 1971.
Trouthe is defined in *FranT* by its connection with the narrative; 'following the story and understanding the word fall together' (p 33). In contrast to the Squire, who sometimes drops his final –e's in 'immature haste,' the Franklin sounds his –e's as befits his 'mature seniority' (p 103). The Franklin also employs variable stress for dramatic effect, as in the variation between *vitaille* as an iamb (line 904) and a trochee (lines 1186, 1618) (p 127).

996 Rowland, Beryl. *Blind Beasts: Chaucer's Animal World.* 1971. See **511**.
The deer hunt summoned up by the magician is used to 'override the discretion of Aurelius. The squire, who has seen his own pastimes of the chase and of love so strikingly depicted, recklessly promises to buy magic for a sum which he later realizes will beggar him' (p 63).

997 Sastri, H.N.L. 'The Treatment of Marriage in Chaucer.' *Journal of the Karnatak University. Humanities* 15 (1971), 51–67.
In *FranT,* courtly love stands in opposition to the values of marriage. In contrast to the other Marriage Group tales, *FranT* depicts a union in which mutual love and *gentilesse* bring happiness for both husband and wife.

998 Bloomfield, Morton W. 'The Gloomy Chaucer.' In *Veins of Humor*. Ed. Harry Levin. Harvard English Studies 3. Cambridge, MA: Harvard UP, 1972. Pp 57–68. Repr. in *Light of Learning: Selected Essays of Morton W. Bloomfield, 1970–1986*. Ed. Elizabeth Walsh and Susie M. Barrett. New York: Lang, 1993. Pp 83–93.
Lines 1493–8 exemplify the Chaucerian-persona strategy of answering a querulous objector: 'a group of querulous objectors is told to wait a little before they leap to criticize, for the tale is not yet finished' (p 63).

999 Burnley, J.D. 'Chaucer's Art of Verbal Allusion: Two Notes.' *Neophil* 56 (1972), 93–9.
'Places delitables' (line 899) corresponds precisely to *locus amoenus* in the Latin rhetorical manuals. In conjunction with *peynted* (line 907) – a technical term of rhetorical *descriptio* – 'places delitables' is being used in a double sense, 'as simple description and as allusion to the techniques of rhetoric' (p 95).

1000 Eliason, Norman E. *The Language of Chaucer's Poetry: An Appraisal of the Verse, Style, and Structure.* 1972. See **514**.
Dorigen's complaint against the black rocks is neither foolish nor impious; it is the natural response of a faithful wife. Her promise to Aurelius is not rash or frivolous, but a tactful attempt to relieve his embarrassment. The

Franklin himself is an admirable character; his concern for getting ahead in the world 'is the time-honored motivation of the bourgeois class from the Middle Ages, when they first got up enough backbone to try it, down to the present moment' (p 88). The conclusion, although satisfactory for the tale, is not satisfactory as a culmination of the Marriage Group (p 171).

• Review by Theodore Stroud, *MP* 72 (1974), 60–70: Eliason's view that the Franklin's claim of rhetorical incompetence and his highly rhetorical narrative is a deliberate mismatch of teller and tale overlooks the probability that the Franklin's disclaimer is 'humorously self-deprecatory' (p 62), demonstrating his desire to toady up to the Squire.

1001 Fisher, John H. 'Chaucer's Last Revision of the "Canterbury Tales."' 1972. See **766**.

The 'Sunday School virtue' of *FranT* will prevail if people behave decently, but we know that life is not so simple – 'except in a Breton lay' (p 250).

1002 Hume, Kathryn. 'The Pagan Setting of the *Franklin's Tale* and the Sources of Dorigen's Cosmology.' *SN* 44 (1972), 289–94.

The apparently Christian commonplaces of Dorigen's lament over the rocks – eternal God, *purveyaunce*, a fair creation in which man (made in God's image) is the fairest part – can be found in Chaucer's 'two favorite repositories of "pagan" thought' (p 290), Ovid's *Metamorphoses* and *Consol*. If Dorigen's cosmology is pagan in keeping with the tale's setting, then 'Christian theological censure' (p 289) of the protagonists is inappropriate. And if the characters are exempt from condemnation, then no blame should attach to the teller for his choice of tale – a choice taken by Christianizing critics as a symptom of the Franklin's defective notion of *gentilesse*. 'There is no immorality to the lesson that *gentil* generosity and selflessness can solve apparently hopeless tangles. A Christian listener is entirely free to extract further guides to conduct from the story, but such lessons are extrinsic to the characters in the tale' (p 294).

1003 ———. 'Why Chaucer Calls the *Franklin's Tale* a Breton Lai.' *PQ* 51 (1972), 365–79.

Three essential features of the Breton lay as they appear in the works of Marie de France and her imitators are present in *FranT*: the concern with love and *gentilesse*, the use of magic as a plot device, and an a-Christian ethic. Although evidence for the familiarity of Chaucer's audience with the form is somewhat scant, his labeling of *FranT* as a Breton lay presumes some prior knowledge on his readers' part. By assigning his tale to this genre, Chaucer may have been attempting to anticipate and nullify his audience's objections to two aspects of the plot – magic and the husband's consent to his wife's adultery – present in his source. The pagan setting of the Breton lay and its concern with *courtoisie* rather than Christian morality would have justified Chaucer's use of the potentially offensive elements contained in the narrative he inherited from Boccaccio.

1004 Kean, P.M. *Chaucer and the Making of English Poetry.* 2 vols. Vol. 2: *The Art of Narrative.* 1972. See **515**.

FranT gives us Chaucer's norm for marriage in which a sound balance between partners has been achieved. Responding to Jean de Meun's satirical account of male mastery, the Franklin attempts to reconcile service and lordship, and equates the permanent companionship of wedlock with *amicitia* rather than with *amor.* When this ideal union is threatened by Dorigen's foolish promise, Arveragus's response exemplifies Jean's 'humane conception of the lasting love in which reason has a share' (p 147). Dorigen's troubles derive from her lack of patience and her wish to eliminate Fortune's power in the case of the rocks. She is later subjected to Fortune's influence, which is in turn 'defeated by the very qualities of generosity and forbearance on which the marriage is built' (p 148).

1005 Robinson, Ian. *Chaucer and the English Tradition.* 1972. See **517**.

The tone that predominates throughout the first three-quarters of *FranT* is typical of Chaucer's softer mood. The opening of the tale gives the impression of the Franklin's 'benign uninvolvement' (p 185) with the courtship and marriage of Dorigen and Arveragus; the doctrinal discussion seems more real than the characters. The best parts of the earlier sections of the tale treat the stock figures 'with a light dusting of irony' (p 187); the irony goes hand in hand with a dreamlike unreality that pervades the scene in the garden, and the handling of magic. This unreality sets us up by contrast for the test to which Dorigen and Arveragus are subjected, and which changes their sense of the contract they have made. Dorigen's recognition that the apparent disappearance of the black rocks is contrary to natural processes marks her awakening to reality, as her marriage is brought into collision with genuine adversity. In her interview with Arveragus and his insistence, in the name of *trouthe,* that she keep her promise to Aurelius, 'the tale suddenly wakes right out of its cosiness into a human situation as convincing as anything in *Women in Love*' (p 193). *Trouthe,* which in the marriage contract had guaranteed the safety of love, is now the very quality that puts that safety at risk. But by daring and keeping this second *trouthe,* Dorigen and Arveragus subject their relationship to an adventurousness that they had previously tried to keep out of their marriage. In surviving this test, the marriage becomes 'fully real' (p 193) in a way it had not been before.

• Review by Marjory Rigby, *RES* n.s. 24 (1973), 321–3: Robinson's comparison with *Women in Love* serves only to demonstrate how little the Franklin is concerned with the problems of marriage. The description of the marriage after the crisis, in which Robinson finds 'new depth and richness,' hardly differs from the opening description (p 323).

1006 Ross, Thomas W. *Chaucer's Bawdy.* 1972. See **518**.

Includes entries on *coppe* (line 942; since Aurelius 'does not gain the love of Dorigen, it might well mean the vagina'); *daunce* and *juste* (the conjunction of the two words in line 1098 suggests an erotic double meaning); and *oppressed* (line 1435; 'a rather pompous euphemism for "raped"').

1007 Roucaute, Danielle. 'Champ semantique de l'érotique dans les *Contes de Canterbury* de Chaucer.' *CahiersE* 1 (1972), 3–24.
The repetition of synonyms in line 819 does not simply illustrate the rhetorical figure of *amplificatio*, but also intensifies the reader's response to the feeling depicted in the passage.

1008 Brewer, Derek S. 'Honour in Chaucer.' *E&S* 26 (1973), 1–19. Repr. with additions in Brewer, *Tradition and Innovation in Chaucer* (see **523**). Pp 89–109.
FranT is 'explicitly about *trouthe*'s superiority to honour' (p 16). In the marriage arrangement, Arveragus retains the appearance of sovereignty because of his honor as a knight; his proper concern for knightly honor also prompts his quest to seek worship in arms. In making her bargain with Aurelius, Dorigen promises dishonor for honorable reasons. When Arveragus decides that Dorigen must fulfill her promise, he gives up honor so that she may keep her *trouthe*; 'she has to accept her own dishonor because it would be dishonorable not to' (p 17). 'Honour as a social virtue, and honour as chastity and possession, are subordinated to honour as obedience to a high moral ideal, perforce an inner, indeed, a spiritual value' (p 18).

1009 Eliason, Norman E. 'Personal Names in the *Canterbury Tales*.' *Names* 21 (1973), 137–52.
Like *Aurelius, Arveragus* is a Latin name, thus presumably pronounced with a hard *g*, as may also be the case with the *g* in *Dorigen*.

1010 Faulkner, Dewey R. 'Introduction.' In *Twentieth-Century Interpretations of the Pardoner's Tale*. Ed. Dewey R. Faulkner. Englewood Cliffs, NJ: Prentice-Hall, 1973. Pp 1–14.
The Franklin's view of evil resembles that which Mrs Shelley attributed to Percy Shelley: that 'evil is not inherent in the system of the creation, but an accident that might be expelled' (p 6). The Physician, who includes in his tale several deliberate parallels to *FranT*, responds to the Franklin's optimism by representing man as 'a pawn in a cosmic battle between good and evil' (p 7).

1011 Herz, Judith Scherer. 'A Syncretic Reading of *The Franklin's Tale*.' *RUO* 43 (1973), 587–601.
Chaucer's main concern in *FranT* is 'our uncertainty of response' (p 601). The tale encourages conflicting reactions to character, plot, and motivation without insisting that we choose between them; Dorigen's reaction to the rocks, for example, is 'both neurasthenic and natural' (p 593) and the tale itself is 'at once a romance and … anti-romance' (p 595). The Orléans clerk, 'both charlatan and "creator-poet"' (p 598), embodies the poem's ambiva-

lences; like Shakespeare's Prospero, he 'develops the magician-artist metaphor and ... suggests the terrifying ambiguities of creation – and its fragility' (pp 599–600).

1012 Kaske, Robert E. 'Chaucer's Marriage Group.' In *Chaucer the Love Poet*. 1973. See **767**.

The 'statically ideal' marriage at the beginning of *FranT* – an attempt to combine the best aspects of courtly love and Christian wedlock – is complicated by Dorigen and Arveragus's '"overdrawing"' on courtly love behavior (p 59), especially in Dorigen's promise to Aurelius. Her vow is one instance of the '"feminine flightiness"' (p 61) that she displays elsewhere in the tale – in her meditation on the black rocks, in her Complaint, and in her response to Aurelius when they meet on the way to the garden, a speech that sounds 'like nothing so much as the lament of a little girl who has just broken her doll' (p 62). In commanding Dorigen to keep her promise to the squire, Arveragus, 'an extraordinarily wise and idealistic man' (p 63), sees further than we and Dorigen do, and anticipates the tale's happy ending. Ostensibly about generosity, this ending is in reality about superior male wisdom, and thus provides a contrast to the conclusion of *WBT*. 'Covertly undemocratic' (p 65), it shows Chaucer to be a product of the culture that nurtured him.

1013 Knight, Stephen. *The Poetry of the Canterbury Tales*. 1973. See **521**.

The hint of pretension in *Sq–FranL* and *FranP* is not a criticism or a full characterization of the Franklin. In the tale itself, plot, characterization, and style are handled with notable skill. Knight comments on the relation of style and meaning in the scene of Dorigen's response to the rocks, the encounter in the garden, Aurelius's reaction to Dorigen's promise, the scene in the clerk's house, Aurelius's announcement that the rocks have disappeared, Dorigen's reaction to this announcement and her Complaint, her explanation of her plight to Arveragus, Arveragus's response, and the tale's concluding episodes. 'Central to the poem's meaning is the use of a courtly and complex style which reveals emotion, passion, and unreal attitudes and a straightforward style which represents self-control, reality and integrity' (p 115). The Franklin, briskly characterized in the preliminaries to his tale, recedes into the background for the bulk of the narrative, and reemerges in the question about *gentilesse* at the very end, thus reasserting the framework of *CT* as a whole.

1014 ———. *Rymyng Craftily: Meaning in Chaucer's Poetry*. Sydney and London: Angus and Robertson, 1973. Repr. Atlantic Highlands, NJ: Humanities Press, 1976.

A detailed commentary on style – syntax, diction, rhetorical and metrical patterns – as it creates the Franklin's personality within his tale and shapes the tale's characters and actions. Dorigen is depicted as a woman of somewhat unstable mentality whose 'equilibrium is easily overthrown by circumstance' (p 190). Aurelius, an impressive figure on his first appearance, is later gently mocked for his passivity and courtly excesses, and rehabilitated in the tale's concluding episode. The Franklin himself seems initially 'a man of some simplicity' (p 184), but there is more to him than we at first imagined: his voice is at different points clumsily self-conscious, unobtrusively subservient to his narrative, and rhetorically flamboyant. He emerges as 'a personality within the tale who yet does not dominate the tale itself' (p 204).

1015 Kohl, Stephan. *Wissenschaft und Dichtung bei Chaucer: Dargestellt hauptsächlich am Beispiel der Medizin.* Frankfurt am Main: Akademische Verlagsgesellschaft, 1973.

In *MilT* and *FranT*, a belief in astrology is linked with erotic desire and hence with the blurring of judgment. Excessively concerned with his wife, John the carpenter does not ask about the scientific foundations of Nicholas's prophecy; Aurelius's understanding of astrology is likewise limited. Both men are interested in astrology only insofar as it serves a practical purpose. Blindly focused on ends rather than means, Aurelius risks involving himself with black magic. Although Chaucer probably did not share the Franklin's unqualified disapproval of astrology, both *MilT* and *FranT* seem to endorse the Christian position on the dangers of a purely utilitarian use of science (pp 164–75).

1016 Pearcy, Roy J. 'Chaucer's Franklin and the Literary Vavasour.' *ChauR* 8 (1973), 33–59.

Chaucer's description of the Franklin as 'worthy vavasour' (I.360) links him with depictions of vavasors in romance (as local landholders who offered hospitality to knights errant) and fabliau (as practical, sometimes mercenary, figures). This double tradition throws light both on the Franklin's desire for solidarity with the Squire and on the Host's rude remark about his *gentillesse* (line 695). Similarly, the Franklin's decision to narrate a lay – a genre somewhat old-fashioned and debased by the fourteenth century – reflects his nostalgic attachment to the noble life as well as his bourgeois origins. The vision of *FranT* is 'charmingly benign, but it is also narrowly and artificially utopian' (p 52); its teller is less an exemplar of the rising middle class than 'the figural representative of an age wistfully asserting spiritual allegiance with an antique chivalric world whose values are rapidly becoming anachronistic' (p 53).

1017 Pearsall, Derek, and Elizabeth Salter. *Landscapes and Seasons of the Medieval World*. Toronto: U of Toronto P, 1973.

The Edenic May garden in *FranT* is far from paradisal in its implications; having retreated to it from the seashore and its black rocks, Dorigen is led into making a bargain far more sinister than she realizes (pp 99–100). The Franklin's winter vignette (lines 1243–55) charts symbolically 'the passage of unthinking confidence into stern reparation; what is promised carelessly in

May is demanded in December' (p 151).

1018 Stevens, John E. *Medieval Romance: Themes and Approaches*. 1973. See **522**.
FranT is not primarily a poem in praise of marriage. Rather, the marriage of Dorigen and Arveragus is one example of a relationship based on *trouthe*. *Trouthe* means at least four things in the tale: a pledged word, personal integrity, loyalty, and transcendental reality. This last meaning – Boethian and Christian – is not overtly present in the poem, but it lies behind the Franklin's conception of *trouthe* as the necessary foundation of *gentil* behavior (pp 62–6).

1019 Tripp, Raymond P., Jr. 'The Franklin's Solution to the Marriage Debate.' In *New Views on Chaucer: Essays in Generative Criticism*. Ed. William C. Johnson, Jr. and Loren C. Gruber. Denver, CO: Society for New Language Study, 1973. Pp 35–41.
The Franklin's '*non*-solution' (p 35) to the marriage debate is Dorigen and Arveragus's renouncing of sex in their marriage, a possibility hinted at by verbal ambiguities (e.g., *pryvely* [line 741], 'day ne nyght' [line 746], 'the *name* of soveraynetee' [line 751]); by Arveragus's preference of martial exploits to domesticity; and by the construing of lines 668–70 to mean that women and men desire *libertee* from the constraints of *kynde* (i.e., from their physical natures). But the tale demonstrates the dangers of denying the sexual instinct. Dorigen's interest in sex, repressed but evident in her 'compulsive concern' with the 'suggestively phallic' black rocks and 'her obsession with the "bodys of mankinde"' (p 39), produces her teasing promise to Aurelius, which in turn compels Arveragus to exert absolute *maistrye* over his wife. Creating characters who oppose their personalities to the 'generic powers of life itself,' Chaucer shows us 'an "ideal" marriage that crashes on the murderous rocks of suppression' (p 40).

1020 Wright, Constance S. 'On the Franklin's Prologue, 716–21, Persius, and the Continuity of the Mannerist Style.' *PQ* 52 (1973), 739–46.
Rude and *excused*, employed by the Franklin in his disclaimer of rhetorical skill (lines 716–21), are paralleled in classical and medieval examples of the affected modesty topos. Line 721 – 'I sleep nevere on the Mount Pernaso' – is probably not a direct quotation from Persius (see **142**), but rather Chaucer's version of a formula frequently used by medieval Latin writers to contrast pagan rhetorical embellishment with unadorned Christian truth. 'In the best mannerist tradition the Franklin will proceed to belie his statement about his lack of rhetorical accomplishment by his florid rhetorical practice' (p 745).

1021 Bennett, J.A.W. *Chaucer at Oxford and at Cambridge*. Toronto: U of Toronto P; Oxford: Oxford UP, 1974.
The books given by Bishop William Reed to several Oxford colleges include copies of works that Chaucer may have read. Merton College C.2.10, a collection of works of Arabic astronomy, includes the Tables of Toledo,

the 'tables Tolletanes' of the Orléans clerk (line 1273). Reed prepared tables corrected for the meridian of Oxford, just as the clerk's tables were corrected for the longitude of Orléans (p 74).

1022 Beston, John B. 'How Much Was Known of the Breton Lai in Fourteenth-Century England?' In *The Learned and the Lewed: Studies in Chaucer and Medieval Literature*. 1974. See **528**. Pp 319–36.
The comments on the Breton lay in *FranP* are 'vague and inaccurate' (p 329), corroborating the impression derived from the other English lays that the form was never as popular in England as it had been in France. By injecting his own common sense into the world of the 'olde gentil Britouns' (line 709), both in his Prologue and in his treatment of Aurelius's love longing, the Franklin deflates the romantic atmosphere he strives for.

1023 Brewer, Derek S. 'Towards a Chaucerian Poetic.' 1974. See **524**.
Distinguishes between horizontal context, which refers to the sequence of events in a narrative, and vertical context, which cuts across the horizontal line and refers to traditional topoi, the audience, or the general point of the work. Dorigen's Complaint exists primarily in a vertical context; neither naturalistically expressive nor symbolic, it is a 'rhetorical marker to elaborate on Dorigen's situation, to generalise it within a long tradition, and also to isolate it' (p 242).

1024 Diekstra, F.N.M. *Chaucer's Quizzical Mode of Exemplification*. Nijmegen: Dekker and Van de Vegt, 1974.
The Franklin's closing question is an example of Chaucer's fondness for 'the incongruous application of a *sentence* to material that does not warrant it' (p 6). Despite the 'basic frivolousness' (p 9) of the Franklin's question, many commentators have gravely taken it up. Chaucer would have been amused at such solemn attempts to answer a tongue-in-cheek clerkly riddle.

1025 Dillon, Bert. *A Chaucer Dictionary: Proper Names and Allusions (Excluding Place Names)*. 1974. See **525**.
Entries for the proper names in *FranT*, arranged alphabetically, give variant spellings, identification, references to other literary works and scholarly studies, and a list of occurrences in Chaucer's works. Also included are authors and texts used by Chaucer, with a list of specific indebtednesses (e.g., the entry for Alanus de Insulis, *Anticlaudianus*, cites three passages from *FranT*).

1026 Elliott, Ralph V.W. *Chaucer's English*. 1974. See **526**.
Chaucer probably exploited the newly popular pronunciation of long [u] as [iu] for comic effect, as in the Franklin's 'vulgar' pronunciation of *excused* and *rude* in line 718 (pp 35–6). Chaucer's landscape descriptions (e.g., that of the garden in *FranT*) are generally 'insipid and uninteresting, because the poet prefers the superlatives of advertisers' English to the eclectic diction of the alliterative masters' (p 105). In contrast to the 'genuine English land-

scape' of the *Gawain* poet's wintry scenery, the rocks along the Breton coast are 'a Gothic picture to evoke a mood' (p 108). Lines 1015–18 recall *Bo* 1.m6: 'Whan that the hevy sterre of the Cancre eschaufeth by the bemes of Phebus (that is to seyn, whan that Phebus the sonne is in the sygne of the Cancre ...)' (pp 297–8). The economy of language with which the Franklin depicts Dorigen's response to the disappearance of the rocks (lines 1338–41) is all the more effective in contrast to the previous display of astronomical jargon (p 366). The Franklin is *burel* (line 716) not (as he would have us believe) because he is uneducated, but rather in the sense in which the friar in *SumT* uses the word: 'burell folk' (III.1874) may live lavishly, yet still lack essential spiritual and moral qualities (p 407).

1027 Engelhardt, George J. 'The Lay Pilgrims of the *Canterbury Tales*: A Study in Ethology.' *MS* 36 (1974), 278–330.
The Franklin is 'a parody of the magnanimous man' (p 325); his tale reflects his personality. The terms of Arveragus and Dorigen's 'acephalous union' (p 326) contradict the tenets of medieval Christian matrimony. Arveragus's insistence that Dorigen fulfill her promise to Aurelius shows his lack of discretion as well as his imperceptiveness; he should have suspected that the squire carried out his task by fraudulent means. 'The absurdity pervading this apologue of specious magnanimity and illusory justice is consummated in the question posed at the end by the Franklin as if to a court of love' (p 328); in reality, none of the participants is *fre*.

1028 Lenaghan, R.T. 'The Clerk of Venus: Chaucer and Medieval Romance.' In *The Learned and the Lewed: Studies in Chaucer and Medieval Literature*. 1974. See **528**. Pp 31–43.
In his response to *SqT*, the Franklin assumes that romance is a genre suited to the display of learned skills that testify to the acquisition of *gentilesse*. His own version of romance is concerned as much with dialectics as with marriage – Boccaccio's magician is described as a clerk, and the closing *demande* recalls the debates of clerks and knights.

1029 Reiss, Edmund. 'Chaucer's Courtly Love.' In *The Learned and the Lewed: Studies in Chaucer and Medieval Literature*. 1974. See **533**. Pp 95–111.
FranT is less about love than about sovereignty. When the crisis comes, the 'facile solution' (p 100) of equality in marriage breaks down as Arveragus asserts *maistrye* over his wife.

1030 Robertson, D.W., Jr. 'Chaucer's Franklin and his Tale.' *Costerus* n.s. 1 (1974), 1–26. Repr. with addenda in Robertson, *Essays in Medieval Culture*. Princeton, NJ: Princeton UP, 1980. Pp 273–90.
The *GP* portrait of the Franklin as a self-indulgent follower of Epicurus and the superficiality of his comments to the Squire prepare us for a tale in which appearances count for more than truth or virtue. The 'Epicurean marital arrangement' (p 12) of Dorigen and Arveragus contradicts the hierarchical

idea of marriage spelled out by St Paul; the principle that love and *maistrye* are incompatible, 'if applied rigorously, would have undermined the entire structure of Chaucer's society' (pp 12–13), while the Franklin's attempt to rationalize his couple's marriage agreement results in 'an amusingly verbose flurry of illogicality' (p 17). The actions of the characters are marked by literalism, reflecting the Franklin's own preoccupation with externals; in their failure to see beyond surface meanings, they are 'all little images of himself' (p 23). Arveragus is 'satisfied with the appearance of honor ... just as he was satisfied with an appearance of husbandly status in the first place' (p 24). And the supposed generosity of the men in the tale's final scene is undercut by their lack of a genuine claim to the things they give up. In his handling of his story as in his own life, the Franklin is 'self-deluded' (p 26), and skilled at using words to hide the truth. See **1203**.

• Review by Valerie Adams, *TLS*, 9 January 1981: 'Robertson's view of medieval people as not troubled by moral uncertainties prevents him from thinking that their literature could be concerned with difficulties in coping with moral problems. He sees only verbal trickery in *FranT*.'

1031 Scott, A.F. *Who's Who in Chaucer*. 1974. See **535**.
The names of characters and historical and mythological personages in *FranT* are briefly glossed, along with other names of people and animals in Chaucer's writings.

1032 Severs, J. Burke. 'Chaucer's Clerks.' In *Chaucer and Middle English Studies in Honour of Rossell Hope Robbins*. 1974. See **523**. Pp 140–52.
Chaucer's depiction of the Orléans clerk incorporates realistic details about the university in the fourteenth century. Orléans had an official reputation as a center of legal studies, and an unofficial reputation as a hotbed of necromantic pursuits.

1033 White, Gertrude M. '*The Franklin's Tale*: Chaucer or the Critics.' *PMLA* 89 (1974), 454–62.
In contrast to the marriage in *MerT*, which is based on the desire for possession, the union of Dorigen and Arveragus demonstrates the truth and generosity of the participants. Arveragus, who is 'presented almost as abstractly as a figure in a morality play' (p 461), abjures sovereignty in favor of the authority of an ideal that is opposed to his own interests as a husband; he chooses the 'new covenant of love and truth' over 'possession and the law' (p 456). Dorigen, although she questions the operations of providence, also accepts and submits to the demands of reality and truth. And Aurelius is ultimately 'a much better kind of man than his actual conduct would suggest' (p 458). The Franklin's treatment of *gentilesse*, *fredom*, *honour*, and *curteisie* parallels the representation of these virtues as standards of moral measurement elsewhere in *CT*. The tale's moral viewpoint is also consistent with that of *Truth*, *Gent*, and *Sted*, which engage directly the question of 'how life is

to be lived in the wilderness of this world' (p 460). The real magic of *FranT* is not that of the Orléans clerk, but rather Arveragus's *trouthe,* which asserts the value of an ideal in a universe full of physical and moral menace.

1034 Brody, Saul N. 'The Comic Rejection of Courtly Love.' 1975. See **536**.
Although Dorigen and Arveragus are an exemplary courtly couple in their willingness to sacrifice themselves for a principle, we recognize that real people, as opposed to fictional characters, cannot live up to this ideal. Chaucer finally rejects courtly idealism 'not because it is in itself unworthy but because it has no place in the world he knows' (p 254).

1035 Dean, Nancy. 'Chaucerian Attitudes toward Joy with Particular Consideration of the *Nun's Priest's Tale.*' *MÆ* 44 (1975), 1–13.
In *FranT,* the word *blisse* is always used to describe worldly rather than spiritual joys.

1036 Foley, Michael. 'Irony and Plot in the Franklin's Tale.' *EQ* 7 (1975), 49–55.
A thread of irony runs through the rising action of *FranT*'s plot, increasing as each of the three main characters betrays the tenets of *gentilesse.* In her lament over the rocks, Dorigen lacks the patience extolled by the Franklin, while her later Complaint is 'a masterpiece of chaos' (p 52). Aurelius, initially presented as a noble squire, reveals himself as a hypocrite and 'a new tempter serpent' in the garden (p 51). Arveragus's insistence that Dorigen fulfill her promise reveals 'astonishing blindness' (p 53). Aurelius's release of Dorigen from her nonexistent vow is ironical as well, while the tale's crowning irony is the Franklin's own incomprehension of the *gentilesse* that he thinks he so ardently admires.

1037 Hanning, Robert W. 'The Theme of Art and Life in Chaucer's Poetry.' In *Geoffrey Chaucer.* Ed. George D. Economou. New York: McGraw-Hill, 1975. Pp 15–36.
FranT 'solicits difficult questions from us about art's response to the harsh facts of life' (p 34). The tale includes numerous images of art, but art cannot finally destroy evil or grief. The Franklin's own art is powerful but limited; although he manipulates his plot and characters to provide a happy ending, the black rocks remain as a reminder of 'recalcitrant experience with its potential for calamity that art can hide, but not, alas, destroy' (p 34).

1038 Hieatt, A. Kent. *Chaucer, Spenser, Milton: Mythopoeic Continuities and Transformations.* 1975. See **200**.
The marriage of Dorigen and Arveragus succeeds because they have chosen each other freely; this freedom of choice overrides the social disparity of the knight and the highborn lady (p 63). Central to *FranT* is the concept of friendship in love; the concord based on the freedom exercised by both parties is an implicit criticism of the Wife of Bath's advocacy of female mastery and an implicit affirmation of the Boethian theme of love and friendship in *KnT.* The Franklin's remarks on patience and *suffraunce* reflect Theseus's

frame of mind in Part 2 of *KnT* and define the behavior of the married pair in the ensuing tale – in Arveragus's response to Dorigen's foolish vow, and in Dorigen's willingness to step down the social ladder in marrying Arveragus (pp 68–72).

1039 Jameson, Hunter T. *Moral Seriousness in the Canterbury Tales: Human Conduct and Providential Order in the Knight's Tale, Franklin's Tale, and Parson's Tale.* PhD diss., Indiana University, 1975. Dir. Alfred David. Ann Arbor, MI: University Microfilms International, 1976. See also *DAI*–A 36/11 (1976): 7437.
Ch. 3 (pp 67–113) argues that *FranT*, like *KnT*, examines human conduct in relation to providence. In each, the benignity of the providential plan is questioned (e.g., in Dorigen's lament over the rocks). *FranT* shows the difficulties resulting from Dorigen's doubts about providential goodness, but also supplies a solution for them in the practice of *gentilesse* and in *trouthe*-keeping. The idealism of *FranT* and the failure of the characters to realize that providence sanctions certain types of human conduct keep the tale from providing a definitive solution to the question of human action within a providential order.

1040 Jordan, Robert M. 'Chaucerian Romance?' *YFS* 51 (1975), 223–34.
FranT 'displays a richer *conjointure* than *WBT*, though it is based on a similarly folkloristic *conte* ... and is similarly concerned with a problem of courtly ethics' (p 228). The tale's scenes and episodes 'enable Chaucer to delve into a variety of problems germane to the courtly ethos and more or less relevant to the basic *conte* of the Damsel's Rash Promise' (p 232).

1041 ———. 'A Question of Genre: Five Chaucerian Romances.' 1975. See **539**.
'Compositional technique' (p 81) makes a better criterion than subject matter in determining whether *SqT*, *WBT*, *KnT*, *FranT*, and *Thop* qualify as romances. In *FranT*, Chaucer weaves 'a complex *conjointure*' (p 94) over the simple 'Damsel's Rash Promise' folktale which enables him to examine in depth the ethical implications of *trouthe*, *fredom*, *franchise*, and *gentilesse*. 'For such an analytical purpose ... the principles of inorganic composition are very well suited' (p 94).

1042 Kee, Kenneth. 'Illusion and Reality in Chaucer's Franklin's Tale.' 1975. See **769**.
Franklin intrudes into his story with unusual frequency. His effort to control the reception of his tale stems in part from his equivocal social status, which accounts for his concern with *gentilesse*, the code of conduct appropriate to the class he aspires to. Among the narrative intrusions that assert the Franklin's pretensions to *gentilesse* are his disclaimer of knowledge of the suspect science of astrology and the 'diversionary' (p 7) asides (e.g., lines 1493–8, and the final *demande*) that prevent us from examining too closely the tale's moral issues. The Franklin also seeks to promote his interest in *gentilesse* by echoing the ideas, phraseology, and rhetorical figures of *SqT* and by writing

a romance which, like *SqT*, presents an 'idealized view of reality' (p 5). His concern with *trouthe* (he uses the word more than any other pilgrim) is another manifestation of his desire to please the gentlefolk on the pilgrimage. The appearance of the word elsewhere in the *CT* in ignoble contexts, however, somewhat tarnishes the glamor of the virtue extolled by the Franklin.

1043 Kelly, Henry Ansgar. *Love and Marriage in the Age of Chaucer*. Ithaca, NY: Cornell UP, 1975.
Dorigen and Arveragus enter into a marriage contract without public witnesses. Although Chaucer does not elaborate, 'presumably they make their marriage public, however that was done in the vaguely pre-Christian setting of the story' (p 191).

1044 Kurokawa, Kusue. 'The Franklin's "gentillesse."' *Transactions of the Kawamura Junior College Department of English Language and Literature* 8 (1975), 1–28.
Not seen. Listed in *BPMELLJ* (1983), p 145.

1045 Mannucci, Loretta Valtz. *Fourteenth Century England and the Canterbury Tales*. Milan: Coopli, Istituto Universitario Lingue Moderne, 1975.
FranT, although about a knight and his lady, reflects a middle-class view of marriage. 'The idea that a woman has a personality and a dignity of her own, that she desires liberty, is part of the dawning protestant puritan mentality and goes along with the idea of the wife as partner and of the nuclear family as the community of choice' (p 136).

1046 Miskimin, Alice S. *The Renaissance Chaucer*. 1975. See **201**.
The Franklin's 'elegantly humble denial' of rhetorical expertise (lines 716–28) 'includes all three of Cicero's names, and the Muses by metonymy; his flowers are *flores* by both synecdoche and pun ... [His] pedantic self-deprecation ... invites speculation on deceptive poetic artifice itself' (p 122).

1047 Pearcy, Roy J. 'A Pun in the "Franklin's Tale" 942: "Withouten coppe he drank al his penaunce."' *N&Q* n.s. 22 (1975), 198.
Proposes a derivation of *coppe* from Latin *culpa*, 'guilt, sinfulness, culpability.' Line 942 would then be glossed: 'guiltless he endured all his penance.' See **1232**.

1048 Cooper, Helen. 'Magic That Does Not Work.' 1976. See **543**.
In contrast to the magic in Chaucer's Boccaccian source, which produces a real spring garden in winter, the clerk's arts in *FranT* create an illusion that the rocks have disappeared. The issue in Chaucer's tale is not whether the magic has worked or not, but how people behave in the face of the apparent miracle; 'the most striking incident of the poem is something of a non-event physically, and it is the emotional and human significance that counts' (p 141).

1049 David, Alfred. *The Strumpet Muse: Art and Morals in Chaucer's Poetry*. 1976. See **544**.
The benevolent Franklin's solution to all human problems is the use of rea-

son. But we see the limitations of his reasoned ideal of *gentilesse* even before his tale begins; although he believes that virtue can be learned, he has evidently been unsuccessful in impressing his son with his own teaching and example. In contrast to the Knight's belief in order as hierarchy, the Franklin's vision of ideal human conduct is essentially democratic, based on contracts entered into by free and equal parties. His tale turns on a series of such agreements; the dilemmas that arise in the keeping of them, the Franklin believes, should be resolved through reason rather than by feats of arms. But the *fredom* apparently demonstrated by men at the end of the tale founders on the objection that each has given up something that never rightly belonged to him. Unlike the sacrifices recalled by the poem's Christian allusions, those in *FranT* are not real sacrifices, and the reciprocal acts of renunciation that produce the tale's happy ending 'are clearly a fantasy' (p 190). Despite the superficiality that links the Franklin's art with that of the clerk, however, the tale's generosity of spirit compels us to suspend our disbelief.

1050 Howard, Donald R. *The Idea of the Canterbury Tales*. 1976. See **545**.
FranT is unlikely to have been intended to settle the *CT* marriage debate; the Franklin's views on wedlock are inconsistent with what the Church taught and his personal limitations undercut his authority as a possible spokesman for the poet's own views. The Franklin's naïveté is reflected in the earnest and literal-minded Aurelius, with whom he in part identifies, and in the equally literal-minded behavior of Dorigen and Arveragus in the matter of her promise to the squire. The flurry of *gentilesse* with which the tale ends is a '"country-squire"' version' of the aristocratic virtue, a mark of the social ambitions that 'could … be viewed with irony by real lords and ladies or by the new men of the age like Chaucer' (pp 270–1). See **1373**.
• Review by Jill Mann. 1978. See **545r**: Among the instances of Howard's disengagement from the tales he writes about is his claim that 'in the midst of our sympathy for Arveragus's agonised response to Dorigen's dilemma, we can find it "amusing" that he can (allegedly) contradict' his earlier agreement of mutual concession by giving his wife a direct order (p 357).

1051 Koretsky, Allen C. 'The Heroes of Chaucer's Romances.' *AnM* 17 (1976), 22–47.
In his romances, Chaucer deemphasizes military activity and random adventures in favor of 'plots which lead to moments of moral crisis for the protagonists' (p 46). The purpose of Arveragus's quest for 'worshipe and honour' (line 811) is to set the stage for Aurelius's temptation of Dorigen and the subsequent ethical dilemma. Arveragus's trial is an emotional and moral one, not a test of prowess.

1052 Mitchell, Susan. 'Deception and Self-Deception in "The Franklin's Tale."' *PMR* 1 (1976), 67–72.

Dorigen's plight results from her inadequate knowledge of herself. St Augustine and Hugh of Saint-Victor are cited on knowledge of the microcosm – oneself – as the necessary first step to knowledge of the macrocosm; the self-knowledge that teaches man his place in the universe 'serves as a safeguard against ... the egocentricity displayed by Dorigen' (p 69) in her wish that the black rocks disappear. Dorigen's difficulty in knowing herself is also evident in her conflicting desires. In her promise to Aurelius, she speaks both as a faithful bourgeois wife and as a courtly lady; the ambiguity of her answer to the squire 'mirrors her divided self' (p 71). In the tale's concluding scenes, Dorigen attains two pieces of self-knowledge: that her desire to obey her husband supersedes all other desires and that she is as chaste a spouse as any of the women named in her exempla. Aurelius's encounter with a Dorigen 'shorn of all pretenses and illusions' sets off a chain reaction of new knowledge as well as one of good deeds (p 71).

1053 Salter, Elizabeth, and Derek Pearsall. 'Chaucer's Realism.' In *English Poetry.* Ed. Alan Sinfield. London: Sussex, 1976. Pp 36–51.
Chaucer's challenge in *FranT* is to reconcile the expectation of realism established in the first part of the story with the 'romantic congratulatory quality' of the last part (p 47). The transition from realism to conventionalism can be seen in Dorigen's Complaint, in which she appears less as a 'real person' than a 'participant in a story' (p 48); in the neglect of such details as the unlikeliness in December of a romantic assignation in a garden; and, especially, in the Franklin's reminder to his listeners that all will turn out happily in the end.

1054 Zacher, Christian K. *Curiosity and Pilgrimage: The Literature of Discovery in Fourteenth-Century England.* Baltimore, MD: Johns Hopkins UP, 1976.
Dorigen's irresponsible offer to Aurelius is appropriately made in a garden *curiously* (line 909) wrought by man's hand. Unwilling to accept God's wisdom and stability because He tolerates *confusion* (line 869), Dorigen 'grows inquisitive about God's mysteries and dares Aurelius to alter nature; wise and stable justice demands that she be repaid and trapped by the effects of "artes that been curious"' (p 111).

1055 Bachman, W. Bryant, Jr. '"To Maken Illusioun": The Philosophy of Magic and the Magic of Philosophy in the *Franklin's Tale.*' *ChauR* 12 (1977), 55–67.
FranT presents magic as the equivalent of Boethian philosophy: both can make illusory evil disappear. In *Consol,* evil is denied a place in the providential scheme; the experiential world, where disorder often exceeds order, is inherently illusory. Initially, *FranT* seems to favor the reality of experience: Dorigen's promise to Aurelius is based on her belief in the presence of evil in the black rocks. Magic, however, alters the characters' perception of reality. When the rocks disappear, 'what is reality in the Boethian world becomes in the world of this tale illusion ... the tale certainly questions, if it

does not actually parody, its Boethian frame' (p 62). In a world in which illusion making is comparable to Boethian cosmology, and which demonstrates the 'susceptibility of human perception to manipulation' (p 64), the only constant is control of one's own will, affirmed in Arveragus's insistence that Dorigen be true to her promise.

1056 Burlin, Robert B. *Chaucerian Fiction*. Princeton, NJ: Princeton UP, 1977.
The first part (pp 195–207) of Ch. 11, 'The Franklin and the Merchant: "We Seken Faste After Felicitee,"' is a revised version of **958**.

• Review by Gloria Cigman, *RES* n.s. 29 (1978), 469–70: Burlin's argument that we see, '"over Chaucer's shoulder,"' the gap between the Franklin's intention to tell an elevated tale and the travesty of nobility that he in fact creates 'is a particularly fruitful departure from ... tradition' (p 470).

• Review by Judson Boyce Allen, *Speculum* 54 (1979), 116–8: Burlin's indictment of the Franklin for presuming that nobility can be put on like 'the cloak of rhetoric' manifests an 'unmedieval distrust' of rhetorical art (p 117).

• Review by Lee Patterson, *UTQ* 48 (1979), 263–82: In Burlin's commentary, 'the Franklin becomes a suburban boor and his tale an inadvertent burlesque of *nobilitas*, despite the fact that Boccaccio used just this tale to demonstrate the quintessence of the same virtue' (p 277)

• Review by Robert M. Jordan, *Rev* 2 (1980): 'What Burlin sees as flaws or ineffectual elements in the narrative are ... interpreted, by a process of imaginative transference, as facets of the personality of the narrator' (pp 62–3).

1057 Diamond, Arlyn. 'Chaucer's Women and Women's Chaucer.' In *The Authority of Experience: Essays in Feminist Criticism*. Ed. Arlyn Diamond and Lee R. Edwards. Amherst: U of Massachusetts P, 1977. Pp 60–83.
The solutions offered by the Franklin to the dilemmas posed by the Marriage Group are not real solutions. The appealingly idealistic terms of Dorigen and Arveragus's marriage contract are undercut by Arveragus's unwillingness, at the conclusion of the tale, to give up mastery over his wife; Aurelius and the magician also assume that Arveragus has the right to determine Dorigen's fate. The Franklin, 'having apparently forgotten that love cannot be constrained, winds up his tale in naïve admiration for the largesse of the male characters' (p 82).

1058 Fisher, John H., ed. *The Complete Poetry and Prose of Geoffrey Chaucer*. 1977/1989. See **96**.
FranT appears to provide a resolution to the marriage argument, but the tale's simplistic *moralitee* is complicated by unanswered questions, ethical ambiguities, and hints of satire in the treatment of Arveragus's chivalry, Aurelius's courtly passion, Dorigen's ability to act, and the magician's illusions (p 187).

1059 Gardner, John. *The Life and Times of Chaucer*. New York: Knopf, 1977.
FranT forms part of an imperfect debate on government in *CT*. 'The husband

... works with full authority granted him by his wife and aimed at her benefit, exactly the arrangement recommended by the English political theorist Henry Bracton, who defines "the king's pleasure" not as the king's private wish but the welfare of his bride the state' (p 290).

1060 ———. *The Poetry of Chaucer*. 1977. See **549**.
FranT reintroduces most of the motifs of the preceding Marriage Group tales in support of an orthodox position on marriage, tempered by the Wife of Bath's 'sensuality and worldliness' (p 290). Arveragus's concept of *trouthe* shows him caught up in the letter of the law, and is finally as hollow as the Franklin's idea of *gentilesse*. It is providence, not her husband's actions, that saves Dorigen.

1061 Lucas, Angela M. 'Chaucer's *Franklin's Tale*: The Case of the Unreliable Narrator.' *MayR* 3 (1977), 3–19.
Taking its cue from the Franklin's regard for worldly pleasure as the highest good (I.335–8), *FranT* reveals its narrator as socially pretentious, ethically muddled, and artistically inept. His naïve preoccupation with *gentilesse* leads him to emphasize appearance over substance; he misuses the *gentil* art of rhetoric and displays his ignorance of astrological terminology; he announces his tale as a Breton lay, although it conforms neither to the letter nor the spirit of this genre; he is confused about the courtly notions of honor and the keeping of one's promise, and ignorant of the true goals of the knightly life. His desire to synthesize Christian matrimony and courtly love generates impossible contradictions, producing moral absurdity when Arveragus, ignoring the *trouthe* of the marriage contract, orders his wife to keep her meaningless *trouthe* to Aurelius. In his failure to see the inconsistencies of his own positions, the Franklin joins the company of other unreliable pilgrim narrators.

1062 Morgan, Gerald. 'A Defence of Dorigen's Complaint.' *MÆ* 46 (1977), 77–97.
A moral and rhetorical rather than a psychological reading of Dorigen's Complaint allows us to see its decorum within the thematic structure of *FranT*. Dorigen's dilemma arises from the apparent subversion of the providential order; thus we feel the justice of her outcry against a Fortune that seems to have been elevated to the status of a final principle in human affairs. Her Complaint focuses attention on three key concepts in the tale's moral universe: the first seven exempla concern chastity, the following sequence (lines 1424–41) illustrates the principle of fidelity, and the final set (lines 1442–56) exemplifies 'the honour that feminine virtue brings with it' (p 91). These are the guiding principles that inform Dorigen's relationship with her husband. Arveragus's response to her dilemma, especially his insistence on the primacy of *trouthe,* demonstrates his profound understanding of the moral issues raised by the Complaint.

1063 Neumann, Fritz-Wilhelm. *Chaucer: Symbole der Initiation im Troilus-Roman.*

Studien zur englischen Literatur 17. Bonn: Bouvier, 1977.
In the tradition of erotic poetry, the garden symbolizes *luxuria*. But this symbolic use derives from a form of pedagogy alien to the erotic tradition, with the consequence that courtly love and adultery are equated, and the didactic impact on the squire Aurelius is located on another level (p 39).

1064 Owen, Charles A., Jr. *Pilgrimage and Storytelling in The Canterbury Tales: The Dialectic of "Ernest" and "Game."* 1977. See **551**.
The tale's central image of the rocks is transformed in Dorigen's promise to Aurelius from a useless element in God's creation into a symbol of the strength of her marriage. Aurelius's plea to Apollo to cover the rocks, with its insistent paganism, and his syntactically tortured announcement to Dorigen that the rocks have been removed reflect his implicit awareness of the obstacles to his desires. The final obstacle is Arveragus's 'respect for his wife as an independent human being whose obligations are as binding as his own' (p 208). The Franklin's use of the 'firm, cold image' of the rocks and his recognition that 'all men need "suffraunce"' mitigate possible charges of smugness or self-satisfaction (p 209).
• Review by Thomas J. Garbáty, *SAC* 2 (1980), 196–202: Owen's 'straight' reading of *FranT* is 'more satisfying than recent criticism which sees Arveragus as a male tyrant and the Franklin smug and lacking in true *gentilesse*' (p 201).

1065 Pichaske, David R. *The Movement of the Canterbury Tales: Chaucer's Literary Pilgrimage.* 1977. See **552**.
The relationship between Dorigen and Aurelius established at the tale's beginning is not restored at the end of the tale; it is precisely the nature of this initial relationship that precipitates near-tragedy, and which must be corrected. The marriage contract entails the complete submission of Arveragus to Dorigen. But neither Christian marriage nor true *gentilesse* works this way. The vulnerability of the marriage manifests itself in Dorigen's actions when Arveragus departs for two years. In her enervation and her confused indictment of providence in her lament over the coastal rocks, and, later, in the disorganized list of pagan heroines in her Complaint, she proves herself unworthy of Arveragus's submission. The plot begins to mend when Arveragus reclaims the authority he had forsworn in the earlier marriage agreement; 'with this assertion of male dominance, the marriage and surrounding social relationships evidence a marked return to health' (p 109). Arveragus's actions reestablish marriage as a metaphor of harmony in the metaphysical realm, as an assertion of Divine Providence and of God's good order.

1066 Pison, Thomas. 'Liminality in *The Canterbury Tales*.' *Genre* 10 (1977), 157–71.
The Canterbury narratives reflect 'the tripartite division within the ritual process … separation, liminality, and reaggregation' (p 164). The Franklin separates from the real world one of its components – the courtly-love trian-

gle; within the bounds of his tale, he questions fundamental tenets of social structure (e.g., that true love is extramarital); and he returns the fiction to reality in his concluding question to his audience.

1067 Schaefer, Ursula. *Höfisch–ritterlich Dichtung und sozialhistorische Realität: Literatursoziologische Studien zum Verhältnis von Adelsstruktur, Ritterideal und Dichtung bei Geoffrey Chaucer.* Neue Studien zur Anglistik und Amerikanstik 10. Frankfurt: Lang, 1977.

The Franklin is not, as Gerould (**825**) asserts, a member of the gentry, but rather belongs to a class immediately below the gentry. His 'Fy on possessioun, / But if a man be vertuous withal!' (lines 686–7) reflects the ambivalence toward *gentilesse* among the late-medieval aristocracy. On the one hand, property seems to be a qualification for *gentil* status; on the other, *gentilesse* seems to be a quality that only the virtuous can possess. The Franklin's remarks in *Sq–FranL* thus reflect three aspects of *gentilesse*: aristocracy through wealth, nobility through virtue, and courtly behavior as something that can be learned. The *gentilesse* that lies at the center of *FranT* is a nobility of soul that is available only to those of aristocratic birth. In contrast to *MilT*, a contemporary tale in which noncourtly people aspire to courtliness, Chaucer sets *FranT* in the distant past, thus preserving, through a nostalgic evocation of the good old days of the ancient Bretons, the social exclusivity of *gentilesse*.

1068 Strohm, Paul. 'Chaucer's Audience.' *L&H* 5 (1977), 26–41.

Chaucer concludes his debates not with definitive answers but with an acknowledgment of competing points of view. Although Dorigen and Arveragus's marriage pact seems to resolve the issues of the marriage debate, Chaucer's final statement about marriage involves recognition of the clashing perspectives of all the participants in the discussion.

1069 ———. 'The Origin and Meaning of Middle English *Romaunce*.' *Genre* 10 (1977), 1–28.

While the Breton elements in *FranT* are factitious, the genre of the Breton lay is itself 'fundamentally bogus'; Chaucer's imitation of the lay is no less authoritative than Marie de France's 'fabrication of an entire tradition' (p 27). Chaucer's interest in a form popular in England in the early fourteenth century reveals 'a quality of antiquarianism, of anachronism' (p 27) that suits the character and the aspirations of the old-fashioned Franklin.

1070 Whitlark, James S. 'Chaucer and the Pagan Gods.' *AnM* 18 (1977), 65–75.

Chaucer uses the pagan gods in *FranT* to highlight Christian meaning and underline the Franklin's worldliness. In Dorigen and Arveragus's marriage, biblical patriarchy is rejected in favor of the equality favored by 'the God of Love' (line 765); Aurelius prays to the pagan gods to further his carnal passion, and thanks Venus when the magician creates his illusion. The conclusion of the tale, however, seems 'almost Christian' (p 68). Arveragus's invocation of God (line 1475) is rewarded when Aurelius releases Dorigen from her promise, and the clerk in turn releases Aurelius 'in a speech with such biblical echoes as the Pauline expletive "but God forbede"' (line 1610) (p 69).

1071 Yoder, Emily K. 'Chaucer and the "Breton" Lay.' *ChauR* 12 (1977), 74–7.
The *Britouns* to whom the Franklin refers as the composers of *layes* (lines 709–10) are not the inhabitants of Brittany, but of Britain.

1072 Berggren, Ruth. 'Who *Really* is the Advocate of Equality in the Marriage Group?' *MSE* 6:1–2 (1978), 25–36.
The Wife of Bath, not the Franklin (as Kittredge [**805**] maintains), is the advocate of marital equality in the Marriage Group tales. *ClT*, *MerT*, and *FranT* represent three refutations of the Wife's argument, embodying, respectively, three views of women: 'that they should be docile dears; that they are deceitful sluts; and that they are incompetent' (p 35). The Franklin presents Dorigen and Arveragus's contract as a failed 'hypothetical experiment in women's rights in marriage' (p 34); having entangled herself in an impossible dilemma of conflicting obligations, Dorigen finds herself dependent on the generosity of three men. 'Was it not absurd,' the Franklin implies, 'to believe that a woman could avoid such dilemmas if left to think for herself?' (p 34).

1073 Cosmos, Spencer. 'Toward a Visual Stylistics: Assent and Denial in Chaucer.' *VLang* 12 (1978), 406–27.
An analysis of spelling variations in Chaucer's poetry that distinguish between the implications of *no/nay* and *yis/yea*. Examples from *FranT* include lines 992–1001, 1232–4, 1364–6, 1467–73, and 1587–90.

1074 Erzgräber, Willi. 'Langland–Gower–Chaucer.' In *Europäisches Spätmittelalter*. Ed. Willi Erzgräber. Neues Handbuch der Literaturwissenschaft 8. Weisbaden: Akademische Verlagsgesellschaft Athenaion, 1978. Pp 221–74.
The conflicts in *FranT* between aristocratic and bourgeois values and between courtly and Christian conceptions of love were of special concern to Chaucer's audience. Chaucer presents these conflicts from the Franklin's point of view even as it transcends the limitations of his perspective.

1075 Frazier, J. Terry. 'The Digression on Marriage in the *Franklin's Tale*.' *SAB* 43 (1978), 75–85.
The account of Dorigen and Arveragus's marriage arrangement has no functional value in the story. By the end of the tale, when Arveragus asserts *maistrye* in commanding Dorigen to fulfill her promise to Aurelius, the Franklin seems to have forgotten about the original agreement. 'The digression on the ideal marriage arrangement participates primarily in the sphere of pilgrim interaction, not in the tale proper' (p 84). Interrupted in his remarks on *gentilesse* by the Host, who insists that he tell his tale 'withouten wordes mo' (line 702), the Franklin disguises his contribution to the *maistrye* debate as part of his narrative.

1076 Luengo, Anthony E. 'Magic and Illusion in *The Franklin's Tale.*' *JEGP* 77 (1978), 1–16.

The 'diverse apparences' (line 1140) conjured up by the Orléans clerk are stage magic – analogous to the *automates* described in accounts of courtly entertainments – rather than astrological magic. Similarly, the supposed removal of the rocks is produced by purely scientific means: the clerk has calculated a high tide that will cover the rocks, and his astrological terminology is 'so much hocus-pocus' (p 12). Neither the tale's major characters nor the Franklin himself recognize the true nature of these illusions; their 'myopia' (p 12) is a measure of the limitations of their moral conduct throughout the tale, which consistently fails to distinguish between appearance and reality.

1077 Manning, Stephen. 'Rhetoric as Therapy: The Man in Black, Dorigen, and Chauntecleer.' *KPAB* 5 (1978), 19–25.

In her Complaint, Dorigen gradually shifts from a close identification with ladies who killed themselves rather than suffering shame to a playfully self-conscious listing of exempla. Her rhetorical game allows her to distance herself from her plight, and thus to talk herself out of committing suicide.

1078 Middleton, Anne. 'The Idea of Public Poetry in the Reign of Richard II.' *Speculum* 53 (1978), 94–114. Repr. in *Medieval English Poetry.* Ed. Stephanie Trigg. London: Longman, 1993, pp 24–46, and in Middleton, *Chaucer, Langland, and Fourteenth-Century Literary History.* Ed. Steven Justice. Variorum Collected Studies Series. Farnham, UK: Ashgate, 2013, pp 1–25.

The 'practical, worldly, plain, public-spirited, and peace-loving' (p 96) voice of public poetry in the Ricardian period, characteristic of Langland and Gower, is audible as well in *FranT*. The Franklin's self-deprecation about his lack of eloquence becomes in his tale an undertone of skepticism about the power of such eloquence (especially as manifested in the rhetoric of courtly love) to create illusion. The Franklin's notion of '"suffraunce"... is not the grand passion of self-immolation, but mutual tolerance, compassion, forgiveness' (p 112).

1079 Miller, Robert P. 'Augustinian Wisdom and Eloquence in the F-Fragment of the *Canterbury Tales.*' 1978. See **555**.

Cicero's ideal of rhetoric, which links Wisdom and Eloquence, was transformed by St Augustine into a Christian *sermo humilis,* which took revelation rather than public display as its end. Although the Franklin's disclaimer of eloquence in his Prologue would seem to favor an Augustinian attitude toward language, the speaker's worldly aspirations show that his rhetorical modesty is only a pose. The Augustinian distinction between the letter of the Old Law and the spirit of the New Law forms a context for the constellation of associations between the Franklin and the law, all of which reveal the superficiality of his Epicurean revisions of divine wisdom. The Franklin's commitment to *verba* rather than inner meaning is evident in the tale's emphasis on *name* (e.g., line 751) and on preserving appearances, most notably in Arveragus's invocation of *trouthe* to salvage his public reputation. Dorigen's lament over the rocks and the artificial garden to which her friends lead her are both manifestations of Epicurean rhetoric, structures designed to avoid painful realities. The tale's protagonists disguise their essential worldliness in rhetorical modes (chivalric honor, courteous love, and clerical brotherhood) that are undermined by their actions. *FranT* may be 'Chaucer's most sophisticated effort in reproducing the language of unregenerate human thought, the *sapientia* which appears in the eyes of God as *stultitia*' (p 265). As in *SqT*, the genuine magic of Christian revelation is replaced in *FranT* by deceptive fictional magic; in the latter, however, magic functions more ominously as a version of clerical eloquence designed to disguise reality and to promote temporal profit and pleasure. The Franklin's Epicurean rhetoric 'is a refined, experienced, worldly version of the Squire's naïve and dreamy art' (p 267).

1080 Roth, Elizabeth. 'On the Wife of Bath's Embarrassing Question.' *ANQ* 17 (1978), 54–5.
Fisher (**96**) glosses *wys* in III.117 ('And of so parfit wys a wight ywroght') as either an adjective ('wise') or a noun ('manner'). The former interpretation is supported by Dorigen's 'parfit wys God' (line 871).

1081 Andersen, Wallis May. *Rhetoric and Poetics in the Canterbury Tales: the Knight, the Squire, and the Franklin.* 1979. See **557.**
An examination of Chaucer's use of rhetoric in three tales as a device for characterizing the pilgrim narrators; the relationship among the tales suggests that *CT* is a debate on poetics. Ch. 4, 'The Franklin as Poet' (pp 146–94), argues that the Franklin's use of rhetorical colors – although not inept, as some critics have maintained – reveals him as aspiring to aristocratic values that he fails to attain because of his practical bourgeois mentality.

1082 Burnley, J.D. *Chaucer's Language and the Philosophers' Tradition.* 1979. See **559.**
The image of the pagan gods as tyrannous rulers in *KnT* is compared with Dorigen's speech on divine dispensation. The black rocks would have presented no problem to Palamon and Arcite, who knew their gods were tyrants. But Dorigen seems to accept the Christian doctrine of a just and loving God and cannot reconcile this notion with the existence of the threat to her husband's life posed by the rocks (pp 38–9).

1082a Escribano, F. Javier Sánchez. 'Los Maridos en the Canterbury Tales.' *CIF* 5 (1979), 129–44.
The husband in *FranT* becomes the model for the behavior of the other men; we see Arveragus's commitment to *trouthe*, his generosity, and his *gentilesse* in Aurelius, who frees Dorigen from her promise to him, and in the clerk, who forgives Aurelius's debt (p 141).

1083 Fujimoto, Masashi. 'A Reading of Chaucer's "The Franklin's Tale."' *The Bul-*

letin of the Faculty of Literature of Tokai University 32 (1979), 123–42.
Chaucer's view of *gentilesse* sharply contrasts with that of the teller of *FranT*. High comedy develops in the course of the Franklin's performance. Full text at http://ci.nii.ac.jp/els/110000195399.pdf?id=ART0000562682&-type=pdf&lang=en&host=cinii&order_no=&ppv_type=0&lang_sw=&no=1449937044&cp=. (In Japanese. Annotation from *SAC* 4 [1982], 220.)

1084 Gilbert, A.J. *Literary Language from Chaucer to Johnson.* London: Macmillan, 1979.
Aurelius's announcement to Dorigen that the rocks have disappeared (lines 1311–38) and Shakespeare's Sonnet 1 are compared as examples of the middle style. Both are petitions to social superiors, but the Chaucerian passage is 'more diffuse and periphrastic,' its syntax 'elegant but easy' – as befits a speech designed to be heard rather than read (p 21).

1085 Heffernan, Carol Falvo. 'Wells and Streams in Three Chaucerian Gardens.' *PLL* 15 (1979), 339–56.
Dorigen's literal fear that the rocks along the coast of Brittany will endanger her husband is echoed on the level of allusion by the symbolism of the rock as a sign of the Church, with its sacrament of marriage. In wishing the rocks away, Dorigen ironically intuits the threat to her marriage that will surface in her encounter with Aurelius in the Edenic garden. Her promise to love Aurelius if he removes the rocks shows her unconsciously articulating the removal of the moral teachings of the Church that secure her fidelity. But the Church's teachings are not abrogated; 'the rocks are there and so is the moral order. She who was more faithful than Eve is saved' (p 354).

1086 Luecke, Janemarie. 'Dorigen: Marriage Model or Male Fantasy.' *JWSL* 1 (1979), 107–21.
Dorigen must be viewed as she existed in the minds of poet, narrator and audience, not as a medieval wife as she existed in reality. A comparison with two historical women – Margaret Paston and Christine de Pizan – shows Dorigen to be repressed, childish, and incapable of acting without her husband. Such a woman would attract a husband who, like Arveragus, responds to her passivity; they are 'made for each other' (p 117), a couple whose marriage is more like a children's game than a union of adults. If she is presented as an ideal wife, Dorigen is the product of Chaucer's 'male fantasy' (p 118) rather than of the sensitivity to lived experience evident elsewhere in his poetry.

1087 Manning, Stephen. 'Rhetoric, Game, Morality, and Geoffrey Chaucer.' *SAC* 1 (1979), 105–18.
FranT contains four primary games: the initial game of courtship and marriage, the game of courtly love, a game of magic, and a 'courtesy match.' The remaining games – Dorigen's two laments – are solitary ones that provide transitions between the major games. The game structure parallels the plot

structure. The Franklin's final question invites us to imitate the play world of the tale. 'The games of *FranT* thus become their own meaning' (p 116).

1088 McCall, John P. *Chaucer Among the Gods: The Poetics of Classical Myth*. University Park: Pennsylvania State UP, 1979.
Despite the Franklin's claims that heathen practices defy the processes of nature, there is nothing unnatural in *FranT*; its classical divinities are 'reassuringly natural' (p 135), its magic is rhetorical artifice, and its astrology predicts the workings of nature. 'Although *FranT* should be read in terms of its ancient setting and pagan worship, the only thing they tell us is that ... mythological prayer and heathen illusion ... must finally succumb to nature's own normality' (p 134). The classical exempla that make up Dorigen's Complaint engage serious issues, but the speech 'becomes "comical" in context because nothing comes of it' (p 145).

1089 McMillan, Ann Hunter. *'Evere an Hundred Goode Ageyn Oon Badde': Catalogues of Good Women in Medieval Literature.* PhD diss., Indiana University, 1979. Dir. E. Talbot Donaldson. Ann Arbor, MI: University Microfilms International, 1979.
The attribute shared by the women in Dorigen's catalogue of virtuous heroines is not genuine *trouthe,* which involves a conscious act of will, but rather physical integrity. Accustomed to modeling her behavior on the example of the heroines of romance and mythology, Dorigen finds herself in a predicament when these examples urge her to suicide. The Franklin suggests the inappropriateness of these models by showing us 'a woman trying to follow rules which are inhumane in the extreme' (p 192).

1090 Mehl, Dieter. 'Chaucer, Geoffrey.' In *Enzyklopädie des Märchens*. 1979. See **562**.
FranT praises a utopian marriage founded on love, respect, and trust that culminates in a question about whose action is the noblest. The socially ambitious Franklin attempts to make a claim for *gentilesse* as a quality not reserved solely for the aristocracy.

1091 Richmond, Velma B. 'Pacience in Adversitee: Chaucer's Presentation of Marriage.' *Viator* 10 (1979), 323–54.
FranT states explicitly what has been implied in the other marriage tales: that love and force are mutually exclusive. All is not perfection in the union of Dorigen and Arveragus; generosity and merciful behavior in one character produce kindness in another. See **1373**.

1092 Item cancelled.

1093 Satow, Tsutomu. *Sentence and Solaas: Thematic Development and Narrative Technique in the Canterbury Tales.* 1979. See **563**.
Discusses the Franklin's concept of an ideal marriage, the symbolism of the rocks, Aurelius's character and his connection with the pilgrim Squire, parallels and contrasts with *MerT* (the love triangle, the garden), the role of illusion and magic, the nature of Dorigen's promise, *gentilesse* and *trouthe,*

and the optimistic tone of the tale (pp 200–19).

1094 Sleeth, Charles R. 'Astrology as a Bone of Contention between the Man of Law and the Franklin.' *ChauN* 1:1 (Winter 1979), 20–1.
The Man of Law's condemnation of those who have access to astrological knowledge but fail to use it (II.311–15) may have exasperated the Franklin, whose own comments on the worthlessness of astrology may be read as a comment on 'his old friend's refusal to recognize that he is toying with the raw materials of damnation' (p 20).

1095 Windeatt, Barry. 'Gesture in Chaucer.' *M&H* n.s. 9 (1979), 143–61.
The lowered gaze in Chaucer is often a sign of inner activity. On the cliffs Dorigen looks down because she is starting to think, not because she attempting to view the rocks.

1096 Woolf, Rosemary. 'Moral Chaucer and Kindly Gower.' In *J.R.R. Tolkien, Scholar and Storyteller: Essays in Memoriam*. 1979. See **561**. Pp 221–45.
Chaucer's 'moral tact' (p 241) in *FranT* is evident in his handling of Dorigen's promise (for the sake of the plot, it must be treated as binding, but Christianity and common sense indicate that it is not); in the Franklin's 'dramatically uneasy attempt to deflect judgment' (p 241) on Arveragus's insistence that Dorigen keep her word; in two passages relating to Dorigen's actions that may have been later additions to the tale (lines 1001–5, 1541–4); and in the shifting of some of responsibility for furthering Aurelius's adulterous liaison to the latter's brother.

The Franklin's Tale, 1980–1989

1097 Aers, David. *Chaucer, Langland, and the Creative Imagination*. London: Routledge and Kegan Paul, 1980.
FranT embodies both a vision of noncoercive personal relations founded on mutual love and a meditation on the problems presented by such utopianism. The courtship of Dorigen and Arveragus brackets economic, patriarchal, and Christian determinations over the institution of marriage. But the narrator's language (e.g., lines 792–8) introduces confusions that point to the difficulties inherent in such a vision. The tale itself perpetuates received categories and traditional ideologies even as it wishes to transcend them. Dorigen accepts male myths concerning women and wifely obedience; Arveragus, who earlier had attempted to initiate mutuality in his relationship with Dorigen, responds to her plight with a display of 'the unreflexive masculine egotism habitual in the traditional culture' (p 166). The poem does not stop at pointing out the errors of its characters, nor does it simply document the 'wretched collapse' of the Franklin's utopian aspirations (p 167). Rather, the poem's 'cosy and evasive' conclusion reveals the Franklin's

'refusal to concentrate on the power of dominant tradition and attitudes to resist and pervert utopian alternatives, his refusal to accept the poem's disclosure of this power and its human consequences' (p 168). See **1179**.
• Review by Jill Mann, *Encounter* 55 (1980), 60–4: In freezing the narrative into two contrasting moral tableaux (the opening marriage contract and the crisis of Arveragus's response), Aers ignores the poet's use of 'narrative expectation as a way of indicating the persistence of change even when events have apparently reached a standstill' (p 63).

1098 Clarke, Leonard W. *The Astronomy and Astrology of Geoffrey Chaucer (with Special Reference to The Frankleyns Tale)*. Ickenham, UK: Clarke, n.d. [1980–1989?].
Clarke, senior narrator at the London Planetarium, comments on Aurelius's prayer to Phebus for an extended spring flood (unworkable because, 'if the moon always remained full, there would certainly always be a spring flood somewhere' – but not necessarily in Brittany [p 11]), and explicates several aspects of the clerk's astrological calculations (lines 1273–96) – the moon's mansions, 'tables Tolletanes,' 'rootes,' 'geeris,' 'equacиouns,' 'face,' and 'terme.'

1099 Crepin, André. '"Sustres and paramours": sexe et domination dans les *Contes de Cantorbéry.*' *Caliban* 17, *Annales Publiées Trimestriellement par L'Université de Toulouse–Le Mirail* n.s. 16:1 (1980), 3–21.
FranT provides a positive instance of the Parson's condemnation of worldly desire. In Aurelius's conversion by Arveragus's generosity, bodily desire is not negated, but transcended.

1100 Fichte, Joerg O. *Chaucer's 'Art Poetical': A Study in Chaucerian Poetics.* Tübingen: Narr, 1980.
The Franklin's noble ideal, set forth in lines 744–52 and reiterated in lines 791–8, fails in the end, when it is sacrificed to 'an inhuman, abstract principle of truth. Only by the demonstration of Aurelius's "routhe," set against Arveragus's concept of "trouthe," is Arveragus and Dorigen's marriage saved through the intercession of an outsider' (p 100).

1101 Fukushi, Naoko. 'Chaucer's "Franklin's Tale" and "Gentilesse."' *Sophia English Language and Literature Research* 5 (1980), 1–17.
Not seen. Listed in *BPMELLJ* (1983), p 142. See also http://repository.cc.sophia.ac.jp/dspace/handle/123456789/20287. In Japanese.

1102 Heffernan, Carol Falvo. 'The Two Gardens of The Franklin's Tale.' In *Court and Poet: Selected Proceedings of the Third Congress of the International Courtly Literature Society, Liverpool, 1980*. Ed. Glyn S. Burgess, A.D. Deyermond, W.H. Jackson, A.D. Mills, and P.T. Ricketts. ARCA: Classical and Medieval Texts, Papers, and Monographs 5. Liverpool, UK: Cairns, 1981. Pp 177–88.
Dorigen comes to the garden of love from an Edenic 'conjugal garden' (p 177), transformed into a '*hortus interruptus*' (p 178) by Arveragus's departure for England. The rocks are in part a projection of Dorigen's fears, in part an

allusion to the sanctity of marriage. In the tale's second garden, Aurelius is the serpent–tempter to Dorigen's Eve; her condition that he remove the rocks suggests the 'removal of the ecclesiastical imperatives that underlie the sacrament of marriage' (p 183). Having apparently failed in the courtly garden, Aurelius seeks to control the waters of the conjugal garden by manipulating the sun and the moon – in Christian allegorical terms, 'to interfere with the relationship between Christ and His Church whose union is the metaphysical version of that between man and wife' (p 184). He strikes a Faustian bargain with the Orléans clerk; an earlier reference to the twenty-eight mansions of the moon – 'a period that coincides with the female menstrual cycle' (p 186) – reveals that Aurelius's goal is a purely sexual one; 'the life-giving waters of the conjugal garden are the woman's private parts ... to which ... only a husband has access' (p 186). But the tale's celestial forces operate independently of the magician; the real magic occurs when Aurelius 'mysteriously ... becomes open to Luna's more spiritual waters' (p 187), frees Dorigen from her promise, and allows the grace of the conjugal garden to reassert itself.

1103 Kane, George. *The Liberating Truth: The Concept of Integrity in Chaucer's Writings.* London: Athlone, 1980. Repr. in Kane, *Chaucer and Langland: Historical and Textual Approaches.* Berkeley: U of California P, 1989. Pp 46–62.
FranT illustrates a moral choice made in blindness. The tale's pagan characters understand imperfectly by fourteenth-century standards; Arveragus's difficulty comes from not knowing that an oath to commit sin is not binding. Yet *trouthe* has a compelling power, even in a pagan setting. 'The initially limited expression of *trouthe,* "fidelity to a pledge" ... comes to seem to have the dimensions of integrity, "the character of uncorrupted virtue, especially in relation to truth and fair dealing"' (p 19).

1104 Klene, Jean, C.S.C. 'Chaucer's Contribution to a Popular Topos: The World Upside-Down.' *Viator* 11 (1980), 321–34.
FranT dramatizes the rhetorical device of *impossibilia* in Aurelius's apparent fulfillment of Dorigen's request for the removal of the rocks. 'Characters do seem to solve the impossible, at least for the time being' (p 326).

1105 Knight, Stephen. 'Chaucer and the Sociology of Literature.' *SAC* 2 (1980), 15–51.
The solution to conflict suggested by the Franklin's final question belies the 'uneasy nature' of the tale's comic end, manifested in the address to the audience at lines 1493–8 (p 35).

1106 ———. 'Ideology in "The Franklin's Tale."' *Parergon* 28 (1980), 3–35.
FranT both recognizes and rejects antihegemonic forces in the socio-economic context. Hegemony, embodied in Arveragus, undergoes challenges from Aurelius and from the clerk's magic; the restoration of hierarchical order at the tale's conclusion neutralizes these threats. The ideological plot also sets

the orderly forces of public acts against private scenes that create disorder. Dorigen's social position empowers her promise to Aurelius, but her lack of actual authority leaves room for resolution by a greater authority. Dorigen 'figures forth feeling' (p 6), but in the scene where Arveragus sends her to Aurelius in the name of *trouthe*, emotion is appropriated to Arveragus; in a 'classic piece of hegemonic absorption' (p 7), Dorigen's threatening feminine viewpoint is used to contain the threat. Aurelius's threat to hegemony is neatly resolved when Aurelius adopts Arveragus's values through imitation. The threat posed by Aurelius is strengthened by his business relationship with the magician, 'an intellectual, professional, cash-related force … disapproved by the hegemonic church' (p 11). The Franklin associates himself with the aristocracy, but is linked with the clerk as well; he thus 'mildly represents and stoutly resists the threats that Arveragus figurally defeats' (p 12). The story pattern of *FranT* reveals parallels with Celtic narratives and their later French analogues in which a knight wins a fairy mistress and property rights. The character names in the tale also point to a Celtic source, connecting it to a narrative of conflict over and through a property-figuring woman of fairy power. The tale's style and structure operate to enforce its ideological subtext. Arveragus's stylistic invisibility, for example, bespeaks his power, his 'absence of accidentals' (p 21). The 'quibbling rhetoric' (p 21) of the discussion of marriage brings the relationship of Dorigen and Arveragus into question, while the presence of Janus, rather than an actual local lord, as supervisor of the scene (lines 1243–55) exemplifies 'ideological concealment' (p 22). The values of Arveragus, the tale's decisive character, are external to the action, creating a vertical structure that operates through a horizontally linked plot. Mimesis of character and action realizes the underlying ideological pattern in which privatized forces 'disturb but finally yield to the calm, external, static, aristocratic system' (p 25). Dorigen's Complaint, for example, enacts both masculine hegemony and Dorigen's self-destructive isolation. Aurelius and the magician are socially isolated as well. The one character whose actions are not shown to be isolative and threatening is Arveragus; he is an externalized figure of authority against whom the others react and by whom they are contained. Textual features (the scribal variants in line 1467, the narrator's comment at lines 1493–8, present in only two MSS) demonstrate 'strain as [the poem] forecloses a threat' (p 31). Through the figure of Dorigen, the text 'indicates that its confident dismissal of threats to hegemony is not all it has to say … *CT* as a whole has the same force' (p 31).

1107 Lawler, Traugott. *The One and the Many in the Canterbury Tales.* 1980. See **564**. The ideals expressed by the Franklin in his tale are moderated by 'subversive patterns' (p 80) produced by 'generic stereotypes' (p 74). Dorigen's constancy is qualified by her emotionality and 'sliding heart' (p 77); the narrative falls into a fabliau-like pattern in which a lady becomes a pawn in a competition of *quiting* among a knight, a squire, and a clerk; despite its appearance of a command, Arveragus's insistence that Dorigen keep her promise to Aurelius is actually 'a typical granting of maistrie to a woman' (p 79). The marriage in *FranT* is not fully harmonious; it is 'purgatorial at best, and certainly not paradise' (p 80).

• Review by S.S. Hussey, *YES* 13 (1983), 297–8: The search for stereotypes can lead to a denial of a character's individuality, as in Lawler's commentary on Dorigen; she would not have seen herself as analogous either to the Wife of Bath or to Alison in *MilT* (p 297).

1108 Middleton, Anne. 'Chaucer's "New Men" and the Good of Literature in the *Canterbury Tales*.' In *Literature and Society*. Ed. Edward W. Said. Baltimore, MD: Johns Hopkins UP, 1980. Pp 15–56. Repr. in Middleton, *Chaucer, Langland, and Fourteenth-Century Literary History* (see **1078**). Pp 27–60.

The Franklin shares with the Man of Law, the Monk, the Clerk, and the Squire the view that 'the good of a story lies not only in the exemplary virtues it depicts ... but in the virtues required to derive pleasure from it' (p 16). A member of an ascendant social group, the Franklin is conscious of the problematic status of chivalric manners and of the relation of his own social identity to his literary performance. Like the Squire, the Franklin values the capacity of the human mind to respond feelingly to new occasions. But he also warns us that the making of worldly appearances – both by magic and by artful social gestures – can create dangerous 'monstres and mervailles' (line 1344). The Franklin offers no practical solutions to the dilemmas he raises. Stories are for him 'social parables whose power lies in the quality of talk they create. Like a good host's leading questions, they invite us to put examined, conscious human bonds in place of unexamined ritual' (p 44).

1109 Miller, Robert P. 'The Epicurean Homily on Marriage by Chaucer's Franklin.' *Mediaevalia* 6 (1980), 151–86.

The doctrine of the Franklin's marriage homily (lines 761–86) is appropriate to a son of Epicurus, who substitutes worldly felicity for genuine virtue as embodied in Christian doctrine. It is based in part on Ami's advice to the Amant in *RR*, which involves a misrepresentation of the prelapsarian state as a garden of Epicurean delights, and runs counter to the counsel both of Jean de Meun's Raison and Boethius's Lady Philosophy. The Franklin's remarks on personal freedom also recall the discourse of Jean de Meun's La Vieille, whose vision of *fredom* is simply an unrestrained opportunity to pursue sensual self-gratification. Although the Franklin's seemingly Stoical advice – 'Lerneth to suffre' (line 777) – would appear to be at odds with Epicureanism, he is in reality saying that 'husbands must learn to *condone*, or *permit*, the "freedom" which their wives naturally desire' (p 177). The Franklin's language, which superficially sounds reasonable but in fact involves a profound rejection of reason, is characteristic of Epicurean sophistry.

1110 Morgan, Gerald, ed. *The Franklin's Tale from The Canterbury Tales*. 1980. See **103**.
Our understanding of *FranT* has been hampered by the attempt to read it as an expression of the Franklin's old-fashioned tastes, an approach that fails to account, inter alia, for the tale's rhetorical elaborateness. The Franklin's social position as a representative of the lowest rank of the class of gentles accounts for his consciousness of class and for his sense of the community of class, with its emphasis on shared nobility. The marriage of Dorigen and Arveragus is defined in terms of service prompted by generosity and sustained by fidelity; the potential conflict between courtly service before marriage and husbandly authority within it is resolved by the concept of mutual service. Morgan's commentary on the tale's meaning, focusing on Dorigen's Complaint, is a reworking of **1062**.

1111 Reiss, Edmund. 'Chaucer and his Audience.' 1980. See **772**.
The Franklin's concluding question about *gentilesse* is a false dilemma, since none of the characters has given up what was rightly his. Chaucer's audience would not have viewed the question as worthy of serious consideration.

1112 Roy, Bruno. 'The Household Encyclopedia as Magic Kit: Medieval Popular Interest in Pranks and Illusions.' *JPC* 14 (1980), 60–9.
According to Joseph Strutt (1749–1802), the Franklin's description of illusions produced by *tregetoures* exemplifies the credulousness of medieval spectators in an age when the principles of natural philosophy were very little known. In fact, the public went to such entertainers deliberately to be amused and deceived.

1112a Sargent-Baur, Barbara Nelson. 'Erec's Enide: "sa fame ou s'amie"?' *RPhil* (1980), 373–87.
FranT involves a compromise on the part of the man between the public self of the husband and the private self of the lover. The two roles can be maintained only through role-playing, in which the relations between a man and a woman according to the conventions of *fin'amor* are self-consciously constructed in opposition to those of legal and social reality (p 383).

1113 Schuman, Samuel. 'Man, Magician, Poet, God—An Image in Medieval, Renaissance, and Modern Literature.' *Cithara* 19:2 (1980), 40–54.
Examines the image of the artist as magician–god in *FranT*, *The Tempest*, and Nabokov's *Lolita*. *FranT* focuses on the 'functions and disfunctions of illusions,' contrasting 'the dangerous illusions of the lovers with the saving illusions of the magician' (p 43). In the scene of illusion making in the clerk's house, the 'imaginative efforts of the poem's magician character' (p 43) are related to those of the poem's creator. Like Chaucer's clerk, Shakespeare's Prospero is a bookish sorcerer who creates illusions that, paradoxically, free the play's characters from their own distorted visions. In *The Tempest*, the magician is 'a clear symbol of the creative artist' (p 47), a connection only

hinted at by Chaucer.

1114 Allen, Judson Boyce, and Theresa Anne Moritz. *A Distinction of Stories: The Medieval Unity of Chaucer's Fair Chain of Narratives for Canterbury.* 1981. See **567**.

Read as one of the 'tales of magic' (*SNT, SqT, WBT, SumT, FrT, PhyT, PardT*), in which things are not as they seem, *FranT* reveals the 'fundamental disorderliness' (p 148) of its characters' attitudes; Dorigen's questioning of God's creation of the rocks contains a wish for 'the magical power to overcome all naturally imposed obstacles to private desire and private good' (p 149). Any personal desire expressed in *FranT*, if given free rein, 'would ... upset the *totam machinam mundi*' (p 150).

• Review by Emerson Brown, *JEGP* 81 (1982), 554–6: The placement of *FranT* in a group that has *SNT* as its 'incipit tale' is 'especially productive,' demonstrating that Dorigen's sense of the order of things (e.g., her desire for a miracle that will overcome natural evil) is 'really appropriate to, and workable for, the saint' (p 556).

1115 Barney, Stephen A. 'Suddenness and Process in Chaucer.' *ChauR* 16 (1981), 18–37.

In Chaucer's works, the process of time opposes the twists and turns of Fortune. Dorigen's excessive grief over the absence of her husband is assuaged 'by proces' (line 829), by 'mere passive abiding' (p 31).

1116 Benson, Robert G. *Medieval Body Language: A Study of the Use of Gesture in Chaucer's Poetry.* Copenhagen: Rosenkilde and Bagger, 1981.

Several moments in *FranT* (lines 842, 864, 894, 1309, 1353, 1545) are cited as examples of 'gestures in prepositional phrases which seem to be only formulaic fillers' (p 62).

1117 Brown, Emerson. 'What is Chaucer Doing with the Physician and His Tale?' *PQ* 60 (1981), 129–49.

FranT, which introduces questions about the causes of evil but glosses them over, is linked with *PhyT* and *PardT* as a 'triad of variations on the theme of causality' (p 142).

1118 Carruthers, Mary J. 'The Gentilesse of Chaucer's Franklin.' *Criticism* 23 (1981), 283–300.

Both 'convincingly plausible and impossibly idealized' (p 284), Chaucer's Franklin is a man of social dignity and privilege whose *gentilesse* is manifested primarily in worthy actions and virtuous behavior, as in the generosity that associates him with 'an antique social ideal' (p 290). The epithet *vavasour* (I.360) identifies the Franklin as a representative of old-fashioned goodness. His values are especially on display in the crux of his tale, Arveragus's response to Dorigen's dilemma. For Arveragus, 'Dorigen's integrity is sacred and must be kept before all else'; sending her to Aurelius is 'an act of moral courage' that gives primacy to *trouthe* and honor (p 295). The tale's 'moral opprobrium' (p 297) falls on Aurelius, whose faith in illusion and appearance is contrasted with Arveragus's (and the Franklin's) respect for integrity. The Franklin's social optimism is, finally, qualified by an air of nostalgia and unreality, a recognition of the 'limiting sentimentality' (p 300) that marked the *gentilesse* of the fourteenth-century English gentry.

1119 Chamberlain, David. 'Musical Signs and Symbols in Chaucer: Convention and Originality.' In *Signs and Symbols in Chaucer's Poetry*. 1981. See **571**.
Aurelius's elaborate music (lines 929–30, 947–50) may imply a contrast to David, the greatest singer of scriptural tradition. His music's extravagance, however, suggests the misguided nature of his passion.

1120 Collins, Marie. 'Love, Nature and Law in the Poetry of Gower and Chaucer.' In *Court and Poet: Selected Proceedings of the Third Congress of the International Courtly Literature Society, Liverpool, 1980*. 1981. See **1102**. Pp 113–28.
When Aurelius renounces his claim to Dorigen in 'elaborately legal terms recalling the laws of both God and man' (p 125), he formally undoes a morally perverted contract and reasserts the dominion of reason over passion. His magnanimous act 'exemplifies the optimistic principle stated by Aquinas that Natural Law cannot be totally abolished from the human heart' (p 125).

1121 Cooper, Helen. 'The Girl with Two Lovers: Four Canterbury Tales.' In *Medieval Studies for J.A.W. Bennett. Aetatis Suae LXX*. 1981. See **773**. Pp 65–79.
A shared plot motif – the story of the girl with two lovers – is the basis for specific episodes, images, and themes that are mirrored or distorted among *KnT*, *MilT*, *MerT*, and *FranT*. The cross linkings include the treatment of the gods, the imagery of gardens and the seasons, the theme of marriage, and the role of chance. The Franklin's handling of these motifs underlines the centrality in his tale of feelings rather than events, human relationships rather than metaphysical correspondences.

1122 Rogers, H.L. 'The Tales of the Merchant and the Franklin: Text and Interpretation.' In *Studies in Chaucer*. Ed. G.A. Wilkes and A.P. Riemer. Sydney Studies in English. Sydney: University of Sydney, 1981. Pp 3–27.
The narrative voice of *FranT* is that of the poet Chaucer – 'poised, detached, and amused' (p 17). In designating his poem as a Breton lay, the narrator reminds us that he does not belong in this world of 'once upon a time'; we are never allowed to suspend our disbelief. He links Aurelius and Dorigen, and is critical of both: 'in money matters as in love, [Aurelius] is more promise than performance' (p 19), while Dorigen manifests some of Criseyde's fearfulness and instability. Arveragus and the clerk are associated in their rationality, a contrast to the extravagances of the squire and the lady. Dorigen's speech about the rocks is a 'patchwork of philosophical ideas which Dorigen … finally abandons in a cloud of unknowing' (p 22). *FranT* is 'very much a man's tale' (p 22), offering no support either for the Wife of Bath's doctrines or for modern notions of equality; the tale is less about love and marriage

than about the ideals of *trouthe, pitee,* and *gentilesse,* which the narrator presents with his 'ironical but charitable cast of mind' (p 21).

1123 Sola Buil, Ricardo. *Dinamica Social en los "Canterbury Tales."* Zaragoza: Universidad de Zaragoza, 1981.

In asserting that the virtues inherent in the marriage of Dorigen and Arveragus extend beyond their domestic situation into other social spheres, Ruggiers (**942**) is theorizing about love rather than describing the Franklin's vision of matrimony. The Franklin proposes not a traditional Christian–bourgeois marriage, but a conjunction of two distinct and incompatible conventions, presented not as facts but as linguistic modes of understanding. From the Franklin's perspective, the virtue of *gentilesse* serves as the ground on which characters as different as Dorigen, Arveragus, and the clerk can exercise the same social virtue (pp 95–7).

1124 Specht, Henrik. *Chaucer's Franklin in the Canterbury Tales: The Social and Literary Background of a Chaucerian Character.* 1981. See **775**.

Specht examines the legal, economic, and social status of franklins in late medieval England, concluding that 'the fourteenth century franklins, or the more prominent part of their number, were ... members of the country gentry' (p 100). The *GP* portrait shows almost conclusively that Chaucer's Franklin was 'a worthy and fairly unexceptional representative' (p 181) of his class. The final two sections of Ch. 8 (pp 153–78) treat *Sq–FranL* and *FranT.* The union of Dorigen and Arveragus is based on mutual love, respect, trust, and, above all, the exercise of patience and restraint. The latter two qualities are exalted in the first two stanzas of *Truth;* this Boethian lyric is 'the most reliable guide to Chaucer's poetic and moral intentions in *FranT*' (p 170), echoing in particular Arveragus's idealistic belief in the power of *trouthe,* both in its philosophical and religious senses and in its everyday sense of good faith in human relationships. Had Chaucer written a link in which the pilgrims debated the Franklin's final *demande,* one of the *gentils* would doubtless have attributed the highest degree of *fredom* to Dorigen's noble – though still imperfect – husband. The tale demonstrates *gentilesse* in action; its moral is that *gentilesse* – nobility of conduct supported by traditional Christian doctrine – can be practiced at all levels of society by all sorts of men. That such values as fidelity to one's word, generosity, sympathy, and patience have so prominent a place in *FranT* suggests that 'the Franklin was to some extent intended as Chaucer's mouthpiece' (p 175).

• Review by G.C. Britton, *N&Q* n.s. 30 (1983), 72–3: The value of Specht's book lies in its accumulation of nonliterary evidence that the status of a franklin in the fourteenth century was not to be distinguished from that of a gentleman.

• Review by George D. Gopen, *JEGP* 82 (1983), 436–9: The main strength of Specht's book is in its documentation of conclusions about the Franklin's social status first set out by Gerould (**825**) and long accepted by many Chaucerians. Despite the mostly derivative nature of this study, Specht makes some new contributions (e.g., his interpretation of the Host's 'Straw for youre gentillesse!' [line 695]). In general, however, he fails to distinguish between historical fact and literary interpretation.

• Review by Gerald Morgan, *MÆ* 52 (1983), 125–6: Despite the weakness of some of the critical assumptions from which his analysis proceeds, 'it is to be hoped that [Specht's] lucid and well-documented book will decently put to rest the erroneous opinion of the Franklin as a social upstart and the literary interpretations that have been spawned by it' (p 125).

• Review by Marianne Powell, *OL* 38 (1983), 280–1: Specht's argument that the Franklin should be included among the *gentils* is precise and well-documented, and provides a convincing explanation of the Franklin's interruption of the Squire and his response to the Host's rebuke as acts of *gentilesse*.

• Review by M. Teresa Tavormina, *Speculum* 58 (1983), 825–7: Specht reads *FranT* with open sympathy, as a straightforward demonstration of the admirable ideals subscribed to by both the Franklin and Chaucer. Even those who prefer 'darker and more ambiguous readings' (p 827) of the tale will need to take into account Specht's conclusions about the Franklin's social status.

• Review by D.C. Fowler, *MP* 81 (1984), 407–14: Specht's 'impressive' evidence for the Franklin's high social standing underlies his 'sensible and persuasive' reading of *FranT* as a demonstration of '*gentillesse* in action … Using the same documentary evidence, and with careful attention to tone, Specht has presented a challenge that the historical critics [who take a pejorative view of the Franklin and his tale] may well wish to ponder' (p 411).

• Review by Phillipa Hardman, *RES* n.s. 35 (1984), 528–9: Specht makes a plausible case that franklins were ranked among the *gentils* of medieval society, and that the Franklin's handling of the tale's moral problems would have enjoyed Chaucer's approval. It is less certain, however, that the Boethian ballads that Specht takes as exemplifying the Chaucerian ethos are more personal than any of Chaucer's other works.

• Review by Jason Reakes, *Anglia* 102 (1984), 218–22: Specht draws parallels between the ethos of *FranT* and three of Chaucer's lyrics; the 'sincerity of tone' (p 221) that marks *Truth* is not self-evident in the tale.

1125 Starkey, David. 'The age of the household: politics, society and the arts c. 1350–c.1550.' In *The Later Middle Ages*. Ed. Stephen Metcalf. New York: Holmes and Meier, 1981. Pp 225–90.

FranT demonstrates the difficulty of reconciling the courtly convention of the lady's superiority with the mastery of the husband implied in the marriage contract. '"Servant in love and lord in mariage" … seems to be meant as an ideal paradox' (p 241).

1126 Watanabe, Ikuo. '*The Franklin's Tale*: A Narrative.' *Journal of Tenri University*

33 (1981), 91–109.
In spite of its appearance as a tragedy, the tale by the sanguine Franklin quickly arrives at the conclusion of a happy exemplum. It is the narrator himself who most keenly enjoys the tale. In Japanese. (Not seen. Annotation from *SAC* 5 [1983], 250.)

1127 Barney, Stephen A. 'Chaucer's Lists.' In *The Wisdom of Poetry: Essays in Early Literature in Honor of Morton W. Bloomfield*. Ed. Larry D. Benson and Siegfried Wenzel. Kalamazoo, MI: Medieval Institute Publications, 1982. Pp 189–223.
Dorigen's catalogue of virtuous women – the 'arch-series of exempla' (p 195) outside of Chaucer's prose works – can be taken to represent the sorts of things that can go wrong with a list.

1128 Bloomfield, Morton W. 'The Franklin's Tale: A Story of Unanswered Questions.' In *Acts of Interpretation: The Text in Its Contexts, 700–1600. Essays on Medieval and Renaissance Literature in Honor of E. Talbot Donaldson*. Ed. Mary J. Carruthers and Elizabeth D. Kirk. Norman, OK: Pilgrim, 1982. Pp 189–98. Repr. in *Light of Learning: Selected Essays of Morton W. Bloomfield, 1970–1986* (see **998**). Pp 53–62.
FranT contains three unanswered questions: Dorigen's questioning of God's wisdom in creating the black rocks, Aurelius's request to Apollo to remove the rocks by a miracle, and the Franklin's concluding *demande,* directed at the tale's audience. The final question – 'which was the moste fre?' (line 1622) – is far less weighty than Dorigen's question about the rocks; the disparity in the questions' importance may be seen as a structural flaw in the tale. If we read the Franklin's question primarily as a means of emphasizing the potential generosity of human nature, however, Dorigen's earlier query about God's Providence appears in a new light: 'this question which led to an elaborate plot which teetered on the edge of the tragic finally leads to happiness' (p 197). See **1236**.

1129 Brewer, Derek S. 'The Archaic and the Modern.' In Brewer, *Tradition and Innovation in Chaucer*. 1982. See **523**. Pp 1–21.
FranT embodies the archaic belief that cosmology, morality, and personal relationships are all part of the same general system. The illusion that the rocks are gone endangers Dorigen's relationship with her husband; the structure of the story depends on a recognition of the connection between the rocks, Dorigen's faithfulness, and Arveragus's honor. 'An event in the physical world is one in the social and moral world ... Nothing is context-free or self-enclosed' (p 5).

1130 Burrow, J.A. *Medieval Writers and Their Work: Middle English Literature and its Background, 1100–1500*. 1982. See **579**.
The Franklin announces his tale as a Breton lay, but at least one of the traditional characteristics of the genre – the 'Celtic passion for magic and faerie' (p 81) – is weakened in *FranT;* the marvel of the disappearing rocks is ratio-

nalized through its association with the bookish calculations of the Orléans clerk.

1131 Eade, J.C. '"We ben to lewed or to slowe": Chaucer's Astronomy and Audience Participation.' *SAC* 4 (1982), 53–82.
Traditionally regarded as obscure, the Franklin's description of the clerk's astrological activities (lines 1273–93) is in fact orderly and comprehensible, couched in the common language of medieval astronomy. The syntax of the passage gives it a logical air that seems to reflect a knowledge of what the clerk's procedure is; in the first phase of his operations, for example, the clerk converts his date and employs the sections of the Toledo Tables that deal with centers, arguments, and proportions. Eade questions Skeat's contention (*A Treatise on the Astrolabe*, EETS ES 16 [London: Trübner, 1872], lx) that by finding out where Alnath was, the clerk was discovering the extent of the precession of the equinoxes; we should regard Alnath not as the star of that name in the constellation Aries, but as the moon's first mansion, an identification supported by a gloss in El. The determining of which of its mansions the moon occupies is workaday astronomical calculation, and would have been so recognized by any moderately learned contemporary; hence Chaucer adds the 'othere [unspecified] observaunces' (line 1291) that the clerk needs to close the credibility gap, at once impressing the layman with his technical jargon and protecting himself from the experts by leaving vague exactly what these other *observaunces* were.

1132 Kossick, Shirley. 'Love, Sex and Marriage in the Merchant's and Franklin's Tales.' *Communiqué* 7:1 (1982), 25–38.
The fabliau form of *MerT* emphasizes the less-than-noble conduct of its characters; the Franklin, in keeping with his social station, chooses the more refined form of the Breton lay. Dorigen's Complaint centers around the issues of chastity and fidelity, themes treated humorously in *MerT*. The squire Damian is satirized by the Merchant; Aurelius, his counterpart in *FranT*, is treated almost without irony. In contrast to the Merchant, who savagely debunks the deficiencies of courtly love, the Franklin, although he implicitly condemns the adulterous nature of *amour courtois*, also depicts its capacity to refine its adherents in Aurelius's transformation at the end of the tale. The failure of a marriage based on selfishness and sovereignty in *MerT* is contrasted with the mutual respect evident in the idealized marriage in *FranT*.

1133 Mann, Jill. 'Chaucerian Themes and Style in the *Franklin's Tale*.' In *The New Pelican Guide to English Literature*. Ed. Boris Ford. Vol. 1, Part 1: *Medieval Literature: Chaucer and the Alliterative Tradition*. Harmondsworth, UK: Penguin, 1982. Pp 133–53. Repr. in Mann, *Life in Words: Essays on Chaucer, the Gawain-Poet, and Malory*. Ed. Mark David Rasmussen. Toronto: U of Toronto P, 2014. Pp 62–79.
The opening episodes of *FranT* connect the situation of Dorigen and

Arveragus with general human experience, thus intensifying the narrative's claims on the reader. Like several of *CT, FranT* is concerned with 'the ideal of patience and the problems of time and change' (p 133). Human stability may be disturbed by influences both inside and outside of the self; the maintenance of harmony in a relationship requires constant adaptation, as in the 'wys accord' (line 791) of Dorigen and Arveragus's marriage agreement, which depicts not equality but alternation in the exercise and surrender of power. When her happiness changes to grief after the departure of Arveragus, Dorigen's experience is placed in a general context of human suffering and framed by the traditional wisdom that time heals, thus enabling us to 'appreciate not only what is pitiable about Dorigen's misery but also the inevitability of its alleviation' (p 141). The surrender that, paradoxically, leads to the release of power, seen initially in the foregoing of *maistrye* that wins for Arveragus his wife's promise of truth and fidelity, appears again near the tale's conclusion, when Arveragus allows *aventure* – the power of chance – to take its course by subduing his own claims and wishes. Illustrating the command 'lerneth to suffre' (line 777), Arveragus '"suffers" in the double sense of enduing pain and "allowing"' (p 150). In response to the intensity of Dorigen's surrender to the situation in which she has been trapped, Aurelius is moved to match Arveragus's surrender with his own; 'allowing' the marriage of Dorigen and Arveragus its own being, he also exercises patience and 'suffers' it. The tale's astrological and performative magic suggests the illusory quality of Aurelius's power over Dorigen. 'The real magic [in *FranT*] is Aurelius's change of heart' (p 151).

1134 Rudat, Wolfgang E.H. 'Aurelius' Quest for *Grace*: Sexuality and the Marriage Debate in the *Franklin's Tale.*' *CEA* 45 (1982), 16–21.
Dorigen makes her promise to Aurelius out of sexual frustration. 'When Arveragus, forsaking the *labour* of Venus for that of Mars to spend two years away from Dorigen, becomes remiss in his payments to his wife, she offers her love to Aurelius' (p 18). Aurelius's decision to give up his claim to Dorigen arises not from *gentilesse,* but because he has been 'psychologically castrat[ed]' (p 19) by Arveragus's order that Dorigen keep her promise. Rendered sexually powerless, Aurelius becomes obsessed with money, replacing his quest for Dorigen's *grace* with his need for 'bettre grace' (line 1566) from the magician. The latter, however, destroys Aurelius's worth as a human being by suggesting that the squire pretend never to have made an agreement with him. 'The point which the Franklin seems to be making … is a moral one: the adulterous pursuit leads to the loss of self-worth' (p 21).

1135 Steiner, Wendy. *The Colors of Rhetoric: Problems in the Relation between Modern Literature and Painting.* Chicago: U of Chicago P, 1982.
FranT relates truth to figuration, and to the creative power of God, nature, and man. The creator leaves his mark on his creation, and knowing how to

read that mark (as Dorigen does not in the case of the rocks) keeps one in touch with the truth. In making her promise based on the belief that it could not be fulfilled, Dorigen divorces her word from reality and from herself, and thus releases language's mischief-making potential. As the Franklin suggests in his Prologue, the colors of the meadow and the colors of paint are safe to know, but the colors of rhetoric are too tricky to keep under control. But the Franklin is a master of rhetoric in his tale, thus suggesting that it is only through figuration that truth is possible (pp 221–6).

1136 Traversi, Derek. '*The Franklin's Tale*.' In *The Literary Imagination: Studies in Dante, Chaucer, and Shakespeare*. Newark: U of Delaware P; London: Associated University Presses, 1982. Pp 87–119.
Setting the Franklin's idealism against the Host's realism, the exchange on the subject of *gentilesse* in *Sq–FranL* establishes a key concern of the tale that follows. The ambiguities and contradictions of the marriage contract compel us to ask whether such a relationship, suitable to an idealized work of fiction or to clerkly theory, would not constitute an evasion of responsibility in the real world. Such evasions of reality are evident not only in Arveragus's renunciation of the hard decisions that daily life places upon him, but also in Dorigen's excessive grief at Arveragus's departure and in her questioning of the order of the cosmos, and in Aurelius's attempt to satisfy his impossible desire for Dorigen by embracing magical arts. The tale's magic is pure illusion, a fantasy world in which the real is remolded to correspond more closely to men's desires; the visit to the clerk's house is clothed in an atmosphere of romance set in deliberate contrast to everyday reality. Yet harsh reality (heralded by the description of winter in lines 1250–5) reasserts itself, and with it impending tragedy in the form of Dorigen's weighing, in her Complaint, of dishonor against suicide. Arveragus's response to his wife's plight reflects a complacency that seems to echo the note of unreality elsewhere in the poem. But his recognition of the primacy of *trouthe* provides a turning point in the tale's moral trajectory; *trouthe* signifies 'the trust upon which all valid relations between human beings must rest' (p 114) and, as a complement, 'the acceptance of the permanent, unchanging reality of things as they are' (p 115). The series of renunciations set in motion by Arveragus's *trouthe* restores the proper balance of the marriage. The Franklin's concluding question is not intended to provoke a formal answer to the issues raised by the tale or by the ongoing marriage debate; if answers exist, they belong to an order beyond the tales themselves, 'in the true and final reality that is the end of the "pilgrimage"' (p 117).

1137 Ando, Mitsunobu.'"Pitee Renneth Soone in Gentil Herte": "Pity" and "Gentilesse" in Chaucer's Works.' *Bulletin of Aichi Institute of Technology. Part A.* 18 (1983), 43–8.
In *KnT, MerT,* and *FranT,* Chaucer depicts *pitee* as a component of *genti-*

lesse. Chaucer's insistence on the necessity of *pitee* for *gentil* behavior may be understood in the light of the Parson's claim that *pitee* is the essence of Christ and His religion. (Not seen. Annotation from http://ci.nii.ac.jp/naid/110000043133. In Japanese.)

1137a Barbeito Varela, José Manuel. 'Dos problemas formales en *The Canterbury Tales.*' *Atlantis* 5 (1983), 39–53.
In forgoing his claim to Dorigen, Aurelius not only secures his personal salvation, but also establishes the foundation for an ideal world. Aurelius exists in a false world. When he recognizes the existence of a real world, he immediately behaves well and renounces possession of Dorigen. Chaucer understands the dramatic weakness of Aurelius's sudden realization and tries to reinforce its plausibility by presenting it as a chain: the magician also sees reality and acts accordingly, relieving Aurelius of his debt (pp 52–3).

1138 Bishop, Ian. 'Chaucer and the Rhetoric of Consolation.' *MÆ* 52 (1983), 38–50.
Dorigen's lament over the black rocks is a 'failed consolation' (p 45). While Dorigen rejects the traditional consolation of clerks concerning the ultimate illusoriness of unpleasant worldly phenomena, she is still suffering from a *fantasye* (misconception, illusion) that later brings about her dangerous promise to love Aurelius if he removes the rocks.

1139 Brewer, Derek S. *English Gothic Literature*. New York: Schocken, 1983.
The moral of *FranT* is that 'we cannot avoid risks in life, and we should not manipulate the environment or we shall find disagreeable consequences' (p 122).

1140 Brown, Emerson. 'Chaucer and a Proper Name: January in the *Merchant's Tale.*' *Names* 31 (1983), 79–87.
The seasonal vignette in *FranT* (lines 1243–55) 'brings together several mutually supporting associations: cold, winter, Janus the god, January the month, January the character, the Merchant, the Franklin, wine, swine, rich living in general and Epicureanism in particular' (p 86). The passage underlines the Franklin's Epicureanism as announced in *GP* and contributes to the worldly atmosphere of the tale.

1141 Cooper, Helen. *The Structure of the Canterbury Tales.* 1983. See **581**.
Among the tales, *FranT* comes closest to fulfilling the romance ideal, increasingly questioned in the late fourteenth century, of man's perfectibility. The story's theme – that virtue is independent of class status – need not be read as an ironic reflection of the Franklin's social ambitions; the tale reflects little of its teller's putative psychology. More significant are its connections (e.g., the virtue of hospitality) and contrasts, both structural and thematic, with *SqT*. 'Given the Franklin's Tale, the Squire's does not need to be finished. The narrative may be incomplete, but its themes are taken over and concluded with the profundity that the Squire's Tale could never have achieved' (p 154).

1142 Ginsberg, Warren. 'The Lineaments of Desire: Wish-Fulfillment in Chaucer's Marriage Group.' *Criticism* 25 (1983), 197–210.
The Franklin projects himself into others. Concerned that his son may not embody the *gentilesse* he values, he shapes the characters of his tale to reflect aspects of himself: Aurelius displays some of 'the attributes of a seasoned gentleman' (p 205); Arveragus shares the Franklin's devotion to *trouthe*; the clerk shares his passion for food; Dorigen's grief (lines 817–21) 'is rendered in terms that suit the Franklin better than they suit her … No matter which character we say was the most "fre," the Franklin would have us choose some aspect of himself' (p 206).

1143 Hamel, Mary. 'The *Franklin's Tale* and Chrétien de Troyes.' *ChauR* 17 (1983), 316–31.
The possible influence of Chrétien's *Cligès* on *FranT* is suggested by two verbal correspondences and several more general thematic parallels. The latter instances (which in Chrétien contains details present in Chaucer but not in *Fil*) include the impossible condition for the granting of love; the use of magic for the fulfillment of that condition; the resort to death as an escape from a regretted vow; the 'mistress and wife' marriage contract; and the hero's journey to Britain to seek renown in arms. Chrétien's romance may have influenced Chaucer's treatment of the theme of illusion and the escape from reality. But the French poet's characters are never awakened to reality, whereas Aurelius transcends 'his enslavement by a literary code of ideal behavior' (p 329) and glimpses a truer ideal of *caritas*.

1144 Hanna, Ralph, III. 'Unlocking What's Locked: Gawain's Green Girdle.' *Viator* 14 (1983), 289–302.
At the end of his tale, the Franklin 'eschews explicit interpretation' (p 301). In soliciting an audience evaluation that is potentially diverse, his final question 'posits a colloquy in which no definitive answer may be forthcoming' (p 301).

1145 Kanno, Masahiko. '*The Franklin's Tale* – Aurelius's *gentilesse*.' *SFLL*19 (1983), 85–98.
In Japanese, with an English summary. For this essay in English, see **1284**.

1146 Knight, Stephen. 'Textual Variants: Textual Variance.' *SoRA* 16 (1983), 44–54.
Rejects the possibility of tracing the genetic relations of Chaucer's manuscripts, proposing instead an editorial principle based on choosing those variants that produce 'the maximum possible historical tension' (p 49). Using examples from his edition-in-progress of *FranT* for the Chaucer Variorum (see **98**), Knight defends 'frendly wyse' (line 1467) and *serement* (line 1534) as readings that 'load the text most strongly with ideology' (p 49). See **1162, 1184, 1206**.

1147 Lucas, Angela M. 'Astronomy, Astrology and Magic in Chaucer's *Franklin's Tale*.' *MayR* 8 (1983), 5–16.

The Franklin's faulty knowledge of and conflicting attitudes toward astrology and astronomy produce bogus science in his tale. Aurelius prays to Apollo for a natural miracle, a prolonged high tide that will cover the rocks. The references to *tregetoures'* tricks, however, depict nature manipulated by illusion and human artifice, an association that in turn colors the account of the clerk's calculations, in which the Franklin employs astrological terms with 'only the faintest idea of their meaning' (p 10). Despite the Franklin's show of learning, the tale's seasonal references imply that the rocks temporarily disappear not through magical means, but as the result of a high tide. Astrological magic is also rendered suspect by the clerk's consultation of his 'tables Tolletanes' (line 1273) after (rather than before) he finds a propitious moment for making his experiment. The tale's sham astrology not only invalidates the clerk's claim to his fee and Aurelius's claim to Dorigen, but also exposes the Franklin's pretensions and superficiality.

1148 Magnus, Laury. 'The Hem of Philosophy: Free and Bound Motifs in the *Franklin's Tale.*' *Assays* 2 (1983), 3–18.

Drawing on Boris Tomashevsky's distinction between free and bound motifs (the latter are essential to the orderly progression of the narrative; the former may be omitted without disturbing the causal–chronological sequence of events), Magnus proposes that the seemingly free elements in *FranT* – Dorigen's lament over the rocks and her complaint against Fortune, the Franklin's commentary on the action and his addresses to the audience – are transformed into bound motifs; the elements of Boethian philosophy introduced in these apparent digressions become essential to the tale's denouement.

• Review by Daniel J. Ransom, *SAC* 6 (1984), 199–202: Magnus's essay lacks a clear thesis; its obfuscations conceal an implausible argument about the thematizing of the theory and practice of writing in *FranT*.

1149 Mathewson, Effie Jean. 'The Illusion of Morality in *The Franklin's Tale.*' *MÆ* 52 (1983), 27–37.

Dorigen's Complaint is a 'rote recital, a kind of catechism of virtuous womanhood' (p 28) that she only partly understands. Dorigen's promise that she will love Aurelius 'best of any man' (line 997), understood by the tale's main characters to mean that she should sleep with the squire, is an evasive euphemism characteristic of the spirit of *FranT* as a whole. Arveragus's *trouthe* – a knightly concept appropriate to his masculine world – does not fit Dorigen, whose moral experience is restricted to maidenly and wifely virtues. Arveragus's seemingly high-minded morality, moreover, demonstrates a concern for loss of public reputation that is manifested as well in his marriage agreement. This contract fails to work in practice because the partners are unequal; instinctively submissive, Dorigen is unable to make use of the freedom she is granted. Neither Arveragus nor Aurelius fulfills the role of the courtly lover; their actions and pronouncements exhibit 'the literal-minded … morality of the stock market' (p 35). The potential nobility of the final competition in *gentilesse* is undercut by each man's self-interest, and ultimately reflects upon the Franklin himself, whose tale succeeds in demonstrating only a 'wistful yearning' (p 36) for *fredom*.

1150 Pearsall, Derek. 'Gardens as Symbol and Setting in Late Medieval Poetry.' In *Medieval Gardens*. Ed. Elisabeth B. Macdougall. Washington, DC: Dumbarton Oaks, 1983. Pp 235–51.
The garden in *FranT* is both literal and symbolic, part of the play of meanings in which the literal and dramatic presses against and renders vulnerable the element of fantasy in the story.

1151 Ruggiers, Paul G. 'Platonic Forms in Chaucer.' *ChauR* 17 (1983), 366–81.
'Withouten coppe he drank al his penaunce' (line 942) suggests the pagan term *poculum mortis*, the cup of death, and the Christian term *calyx passionis*, the chalice of suffering. The figure of drinking a draught of pain recalls the scene of Christ's Passion, and brings to Chaucer's line 'the weight of victimization, lonely suffering, and death' (p 370).

1152 Saul, Nigel. 'The Social Status of Chaucer's Franklin: A Reconsideration.' *MÆ* 52 (1983), 10–26.
Chaucer's portrait of the Franklin is 'a parody of a *parvenu*' (p 22). His praise of the Squire – so effusive as to seem patronizing – suggests a man uncertain of his status in the world, an uncertainty reflected his tale, which represents *gentilesse* as a quality dependent not on noble birth but on one's manners and behavior.

1153 Ames, Ruth M. *God's Plenty: Chaucer's Christian Humanism*. 1984. See **584**.
The marriage in *FranT* is presented without irony, and comes closer than any other in *CT* to portraying a balance of carnal and spiritual love (pp 134–7).

1154 Amoils, E.R. 'The Lady, the "Lemman" and the Saint: Some Images of Womanhood in Chaucer's "Canterbury Tales."' In *Middeleeuse Studies/Medieval Studies 1984*. Ed. C.J. Conradie. Johannesburg: Rands Afrikaans University, 1984. Pp 3–21.
Like Emelye in *KnT*, Dorigen retains in the marriage relationship the status of 'lady,' the woman who is idealized and worshiped by her lover. Both tales demonstrate that this elevated status is not incompatible with marriage in *gentil* society.

1155 Bergner, Heinz. 'Der gelöste Konflikt. Zu Chaucers "Franklin's Tale."' In *Liebe–Ehe–Ehebruch in der Literatur des Mittelalters: Vorträge des Symposiums vom 13. bis 16. Juni 1983 am Institut für Deutsche Sprache und Mittelalterliche Literatur der Justus Liebig-Universität Giessen*. Ed. Xenja von Ertzdorff and Marianne Wynn. Beiträge zur deutschen Philologie 58. Giessen: Schmitz, 1984. Pp 140–7.
Clerical marriage doctrine in the late Middle Ages provided clear legal

guidelines for a legitimate union that were notably attentive to the practicalities of wedlock. Along with the genre of the narrative lay, which dramatizes moments of crisis in human relationships, late medieval marriage law provides a context for our interpretation of a secular, humanistically oriented tale that foregrounds ethical and legal doctrines rather than Christian principles. Aurelius's pursuit of Dorigen goes against marriage law as well as courtly ideals. Arveragus's actions at the tale's conclusion offer no real alternative to the squire's plan. According to the understanding of marriage in Chaucer's time, Arveragus had no right to send Dorigen to Aurelius; in insisting that she obey his demands, he is shown as caught up in his unreflective aristocratic thinking about marriage. For Arveragus, *trouthe* is a marker of his social class, and does not refer to his relationship to his wife. It is only through the freely expressed pity of Aurelius, who in the tale's final episode undergoes a shift in consciousness, that a solution comes about. In a traditional society, in which even dubious law can claim legitimate status, freedom from the constricting limitations of such a system can be found only in the morally responsible realization of forces that grow up naturally.

1156 Brewer, Derek S. *An Introduction to Chaucer.* 1984. 2nd ed., *A New Introduction to Chaucer.* 1998. See **586**.

The values the tale teaches are part of each other, but also in conflict: Dorigen's *trouthe* to her husband conflicts with her *trouthe* to her plighted word, Arveragus sacrifices his own honor to its deeper aspect as integrity – the keeping of one's promises. While articulating 'modern' sentiments (e.g., Dorigen's questioning of the purpose of the rocks), Chaucer also affirms 'his traditional, archaic feeling for the unity of experience' (p 232): good and evil are inextricably linked in this world. The ironic reading of *FranT* as a send-up of its teller results from ignorance or disregard of the tale's historical dimension, particularly of the value traditionally attributed to chastity and honor. Material new to the revised edition concerns *FranT*'s originality ('not comedy, not exactly romance, certainly not satire, nor irony, yet with elements of all these,' p 333), its unabashed celebration of *trouthe* and *gentilesse*, the centrality of the passage (lines 777–86) on *suffraunce* ('the foundation stone of the story ... said by the poet,' p 333), and the unironical treatment of Arveragus's need to pursue honor in arms.

1157 Diekstra, F.N.M. 'Some Recent Books on Chaucer.' *ES* 65 (1984), 555–69.

Questions the thesis of A.J. Minnis, *Chaucer and Pagan Antiquity* (Cambridge: Brewer, 1982) that Chaucer 'practised a consistent antiquarian precision' (p 562). The deliberately restricted point-of-view of much of the Boethian philosophizing in *CT* depicts 'misguided souls' attempting to rationalize or in a state of turmoil. Dorigen's Complaint, for example, 'serves emotional purposes ... more vital than any concern for accurate rendering of classical paganism' (p 562).

1158 Eade, J.C. *The Forgotten Sky: A Guide to Astrology in English Literature.* 1984. See **587**.
See **1131**. Commenting on lines 1245–9, Eade calculates that in the latitude of London, 'the sun's altitude at noon on midsummer's day will be 60° 30′, and its altitude at noon on mid-winter's day will be a mere 14° 30′ ... Its nearness to the horizon at the winter solstice is indeed likely to give it a coppery colour' (p 115).

1159 Hussey, Stanley S. 'Chaucer and Character.' In *Medieval Studies Conference, Aachen, 1983: Language and Literature.* Bamberger Beiträge zur Englischen Sprachwissenschaft 15. Frankfurt am Main: Lang, 1984. Pp 121–30.
Although *FranT* doesn't offer much in the way of characterization as we now understand it, Chaucer's handling of Dorigen's promise to Aurelius shows him complicating the stock figure bequeathed to him in the other versions of the story.

1160 Lane, Robert. '*The Franklin's Tale*: Of Marriage and Meaning.' In *Portraits of Marriage in Literature.* Ed. Anne C. Hargrove and Maurine Magliocco. Macomb: Western Illinois University, 1984. Pp 107–24.
The Franklin's discourse on marriage (lines 761–84) brings together apparently disparate elements around a new model of marriage based on mutuality. Classical and medieval thinking about friendship and patience helps amplify the traits that are essential to a relationship based on responsiveness to others. These traits are the foundation both of the mutual relationship presented and the process of creating meaning through speech. The balance of the tale recounts the failure of the characters to bring about the mutuality so central to the marriage discourse. Dorigen's *defaute* (line 790), her lack of a firm sense of self, makes her vulnerable to Aurelius's aggressive reading of her playful promise; deprived of their proper context – her intentions when she uttered them – her words assume 'an independent reality' (p 118). Arveragus's allegiance to the values of chivalry and masculine honor renders him deaf to Dorigen's plight; in asserting the centrality of *trouthe*, 'he merely imports a concept from the world of knights ... and imposes it on the situation with epigrammatic directness' (p 119). Dorigen, Arveragus, and, initially, Aurelius are unable to engage in interactions that produce a shared understanding of each other's words. It is only in Aurelius's final conversation with Dorigen that questions, sympathetic listening, and shared speech produce compassionate understanding of another.

1161 Lee, Anne Thompson. '"A Woman True and Fair": Chaucer's Portrayal of Dorigen in the *Franklin's Tale*.' *ChauR* 19 (1984), 169–78.
Dorigen – 'a genuinely good, loving, and lovable woman' (p 169) – is at the center of *FranT*. The tale is not about an ideal union, but about the lived experience of marriage, examined from a woman's perspective. We empathize with Dorigen's despair after Arveragus leaves her; her lament about

the rocks may be 'philosophically narrow' (p 172), but her energy in questioning God's Providence and her realization that she is living in a man's world create intuitive sympathy in the reader. Dorigen's love for Arveragus and her consequent desire to see the rocks disappear override all other considerations in her interchange with Aurelius; following her playful promise, she responds to him with 'uncourtly bluntness,' and places a positive emphasis on her wifely subservience to her husband (p 173). When the tale moves away from Dorigen – as in Aurelius's overlong prayer to Apollo – it begins to falter. Chaucer's attempt to 'clothe Dorigen in the dusty garb of rhetoric' (p 174) in her Complaint is also a misstep. Unlike the classical heroines to whom she compares herself, Dorigen responds to her plight not with suicide, but rather by exhibiting loyalty and deference to her husband. Dorigen's obedience to his command exemplifies her own version of *trouthe*. Compared with Dorigen's 'loving integrity,' the ethical abstractions enacted by the three men at the end of the tale are 'shadowy chimaeras' (p 177).

1162 Love, Harold. 'Sir Walter Greg and the Chaucerian Force Field.' *BBSANZ* 28 (1984), 73–81.
Knight's employment of a Marxist interpretation of medieval society as an editorial tool (**1146**) will render his edition-in-progress of *FranT* less useful than one edited along traditional lines; 'the text becomes a twentieth-century artefact, not a medieval one' (p 80). See **1184**.

1163 Mann, Jill. 'Proverbial Wisdom in the *Ysengrimus*.' *NLH* 16 (1984), 93–109.
The Franklin's celebration of patience (lines 771–80) shows a proverb – 'Patience conquers all' – making itself at home in both popular and learned contexts. The passage's colloquial tone suggests common speech, but 'as thise clerkes seyn' and the Latin origin of the proverb ('Patiencia vincit omnia') link it as well with written tradition.

1164 Rudat, Wolfgang E.H. '*Gentillesse* and the Marriage Debate in the *Franklin's Tale*: Chaucer's Squires and the Question of Nobility.' 1984. See **589**.
The Franklin's final *demande* is not merely rhetorical; it is intended to provoke the reader to answer the questions about *gentilesse* raised by the tale, and to decide whether the Franklin's narrative resolves the marriage debate. Aurelius releases Dorigen from her vow not out of true *gentilesse*, but rather to give the impression that he possesses that quality; outmaneuvered by Arveragus, the pity he feels is really for himself. After Dorigen makes her rash promise, Aurelius is motivated not by sexual desire, but by desire for *maistrye* over her; once Arveragus orders her to fulfill her promise, the challenge of *maistrye* is gone. Aurelius's exchange with the magician is an attempt to outmaneuver him by forcing him to join the socio-moral competition instituted by Arveragus. The magician's response shows 'utter contempt' (p 457) for the squire; the former does not even pretend to perform a 'gentil dede' (line 1611). Although Dorigen is not usually credited with the

gift of wit, her Complaint is a witty rhetorical move designed to preserve her chastity by delaying action until Arveragus returns. In their exchange after Arveragus has returned, husband and wife reach a mutual understanding by means of 'benign mutual manipulation' (p 462). They behave not like members of the nobility, but as 'mere human beings' (p 463) who exhibit *suffrance* (line 788) toward each other's errors. Aurelius functions in the tale to expose false ideals of *gentilesse* and, ultimately, to strengthen Arveragus and Dorigen's marriage. The flattering irony with which the Franklin treats the pilgrim Squire in his comment on his tale anticipates his concluding question about which character was 'the mooste fre' (line 1622): in contrast to the squire Aurelius's false *gentilesse* and the 'manipulative, practical' use of *gentilesse* by Dorigen and Arveragus, only the magician, with his 'earned *gentilesse*,' stands out as truly *fre* (p 470).

1165 Schmidt, Gary D. 'The Marriage Irony in the Tales of the Merchant and the Franklin.' In *Portraits of Marriage in Literature*. 1984. See **1160**. Pp 97–105.
In both *FranT* and *MerT*, the ostensible concern with *maistrye* is forced in to the background by extraneous issues. Where it does appear, it is dealt with summarily. Although the Franklin seems to have aspirations to courtliness, his tale attacks the courtly ideal, which continues to intrude into the marriage relationship. The difficulties created by attempting to combine courtly love and wedlock are seen in the behavior of Arveragus, who strives to maintain the name of husband while prolonging the courtly relationship, and in Dorigen, who also plays the wife and the lady; in the scene in the garden, she adopts the role of a 'courtly temptress, beguiling and enticing at the same time that she presumes to reject [Aurelius]' (p 103). In the tale's penultimate scene, the mask of the courtly world drops; Arveragus's glibness vanishes, and he is suddenly a husband, although no more ideal as a husband than he was as a courtly lover. True *gentilesse* is demonstrated by the behavior of Aurelius and the magician in the tale's final scene; the term applies here not to courtly values, but to the performance of good deeds – although the Franklin seems unaware of this shift in definition.

1166 Item cancelled.

1167 Smith, Eric. *A Dictionary of Classical Reference in English Poetry*. 1984. See **592**.
Lists classical references in some eighty English poets, with paragraphs of background material at the beginning of each entry and an index of poems, poets, and references. Thirty-seven classical references are cited from *FranT*.

1168 Blake, N.F. *The Textual Tradition of the Canterbury Tales*. 1985. See **594**.
In copying *FranT*, the scribe of Corpus Christi College, Oxford, MS 198 omitted or rearranged details that offended his sense of decorum – references to suicide, magic, breaches of the marriage code, and the account of Aurelius's conversion to virtuousness (p 107).

1169 Braswell, Mary Flowers. 'The Magic of Machinery: A Context for Chaucer's

Franklin's Tale.' Mosaic 18 (1985), 101–10.

The magic tricks in *FranT* parallel contemporary accounts of automated devices such as those used in court entertainments or in the park of the Dukes of Burgundy at Hesdin in Artois. Several of the feats performed by the *tregetoures* – the name suggests 'one who creates an illusion of magic with his machines' (p 106) – have analogues in records of medieval English pageantry, while the clerk's illusions might well have been accomplished by means of mechanical devices. Chaucer's position as Clerk of the King's Works and his authorship of *Astr* and (perhaps) *Equat* attest to his own mechanical expertise. If *CT* were mimed or performed with props, Chaucer might have 'orchestrated his own special magic show' (p 107) in presenting *FranT*.

1170 Brewer, Derek S. 'The Reconstruction of Chaucer.' In *Studies in the Age of Chaucer. Proceedings, No. 1, 1984: Reconstructing Chaucer*. Ed. Paul Strohm and Thomas J. Heffernan. Knoxville, TN: New Chaucer Society, 1985. Pp 3–19.

The material existence of the black rocks guarantees the moral qualities of honor and chastity. When the rocks' physical substance is hidden by illusion, the moral values are also endangered.

1171 Burguera Nadal, Maria Luisa. 'El *Franklin's Tale* de Chaucer, desde una perspectiva semiótica.' *Caligrama* 2 (1985), 213–18.

Analyzes *FranT* using Tzvetan Todorov's division of a text into its semantic, morphosyntactical, and rhetorical aspects (*Théorie de la littérature*). The semantic aspect enumerates content – the themes of happy marriage, courtly love, sexual aggression, and loyalty to one's plighted word. The morphosyntactical aspect treats sequences of action, which allow us to deduce the characters of the actors in relation to the poem's cultural values. The rhetorical aspect concerns the relations among author, narrator, literary source (the Breton *lai*), and the poem's audience.

1172 Frese, Dolores Warwick. 'Chaucer's *Canterbury Tales* and the Arthurian Tradition: Thematic Transmissions/Aesthetic Transpositions.' In *Actes du 14e Congrès International Arthurien*. Ed. Charles Foulon et al. Rennes: Presses Universitaires, 1985. Pp 184–207.

The magician's performance for Aurelius constitutes 'a basic catalogue of Arthurian romance materials' (p 187) which are acknowledged to belong to a time and place different from those of the Franklin's project. The description of the Franklin as a 'worthy vavasour' (I.360) alerts the reader of Arthurian romance to his role – traditional for literary *vavasours* – in assisting young knights in their quest for honor, a function the Franklin fulfills both for Arveragus and the pilgrim Squire. The question that concludes *FranT* combines the flavor of a Christian parable of forgiveness (e.g., Luke 7:41–3) with the courtly *demande d'amour*, 'effecting a *molte bele conjointure* of old law and new – theological and narratological' (p 191).

1173 Jacobs, Kathryn. 'The Marriage Contract of the *Franklin's Tale*: The Remaking of Society.' *ChauR* 20 (1985), 132–43.

The mutual submission and self-denial in the marriage of Dorigen and Arveragus is intended as a model for the poem's audience. Arveragus's insistence that Dorigen keep her vow to Aurelius is not an assertion of husbandly authority but a recognition of the superior authority of an ideal opposed to his personal interests; his grief in making his sacrifice humanizes him and makes him a figure worthy of emulation. The marriage is the most significant of several beneficent social ties in the tale, which are in turn contrasted with Aurelius's self-interested contracts with Dorigen and the clerk. In moving away from the legalistic and mercantile terms of these contracts, the tale's conclusion is designed 'to initiate the creation of an ideal society by beginning to make the audience into one' (p 142).

1174 Lawton, David. *Chaucer's Narrators*. 1985. See **598**.

Critics who read *FranT* as an expression of the Franklin's personality are divided about whether the tale reveals the teller's 'charming modesty' or his 'downright dishonesty' (p 98). But there is little in the tale to support a psychological or dramatic reading of narratorial persona; 'the frame does not occlude or inhabit the picture' (p 99).

1175 Mandel, Jerome. 'Courtly Love in the *Canterbury Tales*.' 1985. See **599**.

In *FranT*, courtly love serves merely as an adornment to a story of married love. Aurelius, 'the most courtly lover in *CT*' (p 281), is also the tale's villain, the obstacle to Dorigen and Arveragus's harmonious union. Courtly love is 'antagonistic to happiness'; 'it functions only to make the adversary's behavior explicable in terms of a code of behavior which even the lovers … seem to have outgrown through marriage' (p 282).

1176 McGerr, Rosemarie Potz. 'Retraction and Memory: Retrospective Structure in the *Canterbury Tales*.' *CL* 37 (1985), 97–113.

In lines 1493–8, the narrator gives us an explicit warning against hasty judgment. 'The point that the poem as a whole seems to make is that one should suspend judgment until all the evidence has been presented'; only the complete picture will show each part in relation to the others (p 109).

1177 Middleton, Anne. 'War by Other Means: Marriage and Chivalry in Chaucer.' 1985. See **600**.

The Franklin distinguishes between social empathy and wonder; the latter, associated with magic and theatrical performance, is depicted as destroying rather than creating communal accord. In *FranT*, patience and pity are the true forms of natural magic; both are produced through horizontal bonds of accommodation rather than emanating from a higher authority. Wherever rhetoric creates illusion in *FranT*, the rhetorical arts are those of chivalric self-representation. The view of magic as theatrical illusion and political persuasion, unique to Chaucer's version of the tale, is contrasted with the 'shared discourse' (p 133) based on mutual understanding of the common world, that lies at the heart of the Franklin's representation of noble conduct.

1178 Nicholson, R.H. '*Sir Orfeo*: A "Kinges Noote."' 1985. See **338**.
'Every surviving Middle English lai clearly contains two linked plots ... composing a narrative history of an individual hero to form the romance' (p 171). Chaucer responds to this structural pattern in *FranT* by presenting the first narrative phase as a 'Planct Dorigen' (p 172), in which his heroine laments but survives Arveragus's absence; in the second phase, she escapes the consequences of her promise to Aurelius, and is reunited with her husband.

1179 Pearsall, Derek. *The Canterbury Tales*. 1985. See **601**.
In altering and deepening characterization and the nature of the lady's promise as they appear in *Fil*, Chaucer transforms *FranT* into a romance. Identifying his tale as a Breton lay, Chaucer underlines its pre-Christian setting and creates a sense of distance and remoteness. Although there is a speaking voice in the tale – that of a plain man who disclaims hyperbolic rhetoric, is impatient with extravagant emotion, and is skeptical of astrological mumbo-jumbo – the narrative is not primarily an expression of the Franklin's character, as commentaries generated by a 'jaundiced reading' of the *GP* portrait of the Franklin as a self-satisfied Epicurean would have us believe (p 148). The 'problem' of *FranT* resides rather in 'the discrepancy ... between the story ... and the ideal virtues of truth and *gentillesse* that it purports to be a triumphant vindication of' (p 150). These difficulties are most clearly visible in the tale's denouement, where Arveragus's actions defy a naturalistic reading; 'the world in which such acts are admired is not the world of ordinary reality' (p 152). For much of the tale, the high degree of dramatic realism suggests domestic tragedy rather than romance. In the final scene, Chaucer shifts back to the romance mode. Dorigen's Complaint, an isolated rhetorical set piece in which she 'behaves like the melodramatic heroine of a bad Italian opera,' distances us from possible tragedy, as does the narrator's assurance (lines 1493–8) that all will turn out for the best, in accordance with the proper genre of the story (p 155). In insisting on a literal reading of Arveragus's command that Dorigen keep her promise, Aers (**1097**) (in addition to ironizing the role of the Franklin) fails to acknowledge that 'romance has its own kind of access to reality' (p 157). In traditional stories, a promise kept is often a reassurance of the primacy of civilized values over the blind forces of nature, a perception encoded in the 'extraordinarily evocative' seasonal passage (lines 1243–55) (p 158). The conclusion of the tale shows how trust and the voluntary surrender of the self breeds further trust. Patience and *suffraunce* are Chaucer's way of talking about 'the willing embrace of the will of another as a means to strengthening the bond of love' (p 160).

1180 Rosenberg, Bruce A. 'Medieval Popular Literature: Folkloric Studies.' In *The*

Popular Literature of Medieval England. Ed. Thomas J. Heffernan. Tennessee Studies in Literature 28. Knoxville: U of Tennessee P, 1985. Pp 61–84.
In folk tradition, dinners are traditionally convened to consummate business agreements. In *FranT*, Chaucer shows the clerk and Aurelius dining together before they discuss terms to suggest that 'the deal's conclusion was forgone ... Aurelius has already, in his own mind, agreed in advance to whatever the magician will ask' (p 81).

1181 Smallwood, T.M. 'Chaucer's Distinctive Digressions.' *SP* 82 (1985), 437–49.
The Franklin's remarks on *maistrye* and patience (lines 761–86) conform to a pattern evident in *WBT*, *MerT*, *PhyT*, *PardT*, and *ManT*, in which Chaucer breaks off the narrative shortly after it begins to insert a substantial digression. These digressions present generalized wisdom; they rarely advance the story line, and contribute little to our sense of an individualized narrator.

1182 Spearing, A.C. 'Literal and Figurative in *The Book of the Duchess*.' In *SAC. Proceedings, No. 1, 1984: Reconstructing Chaucer*. 1985. See **600**. Pp 165–71.
The courtly love lyric is at once a way of expressing and not expressing the *sentement* that is its source. Aurelius conceals his feelings in his love songs (lines 943–5), and the passage in which he finally discloses that he has made the black rocks disappear is 'a masterpiece of deferral, holding back the literal statement that "the rokkes been aweye" (line 1338) until the final words of a speech of twenty-eight lines' (pp 167–8). See also **1220**, pp 96–8.

1183 ———. *Medieval to Renaissance in English Poetry*. Cambridge: Cambridge UP, 1985.
In *FranT*, romance wonders are reduced to science or illusion (p 39). Dorigen's questioning of God's creation of the rocks strikes 'an interrogative mood ... recurrent in Chaucer, and not only among pagans' (p. 56). Although the Franklin feels aggrieved that his son does not possess the *vertu* that he inwardly believes himself to possess, his tale argues that *gentilesse* is not derived from birth (p 98). Dorigen's Complaint is 'a form of evasion of reality ... a substitute for action' (p 185).
• Review by A.J. Minnis, *SAC* 9 (1987), 253–60: The views of Chaucer's pagan characters are not necessarily his own. 'To prove that Chaucer used his pagan worlds to interrogate his Christian God would require the powers of a clairvoyant rather than those of a critic' (p 258).

1184 Trigg, Stephanie. 'The Politics of Editing Medieval Texts: Knight's Quest and Love's Complaint.' *BBSANZ* 29 (1985), 15–22.
In his description of editorial principles for his proposed edition of *FranT*, Knight (**1146**) is unclear about what is meant by '"historical tension."' It is equally unclear what Love (**1162**), in his critique of Knight, means by a '"twentieth-century artefact," and how he can possibly hope to have anything else' (p 21).

1185 Utsugi, Takeshi. '*Gentilesse* in Chaucer's *The Franklin's Tale*.' *Kagoshima Keidai*

Ronshu (International University of Kagoshima, Japan) 25 (1985), 99–127. Full text at http://ci.nii.ac.jp/els/110004672316.pdf?id=ART0007405732&type=pdf&lang=en&host=cinii&order_no=&ppv_type=0&. In Japanese.

1186 Aers, David. *Chaucer*. Atlantic Highlands, NJ: Humanities Press, 1986.
Although *FranT* opens with an attempt to express an ideal of marriage as a mutual, noncoercive relationship, we are not shown a realization of this ideal. When Arveragus tells Dorigen that 'she owes it to "Trouthe" to allow [Aurelius] to "screw" her' (p 88), he acts stupidly as well as immorally; his command displays 'unregenerate egotism' (p 89). The closing prediction of the marriage's blissful future suggests that egotism can be transcended. But the absence of any depiction of Arveragus's regeneration creates skepticism about the conventional romance ending; it seems 'a depressingly superficial evasion' (p 91) of the problems raised by the poem.

1187 Boitani, Piero. *English Medieval Narrative in the Thirteenth and Fourteenth Centuries.* 1986. See **578**.
Like *WBT* and *NPT, FranT* is a *tour de force* in which source, theme, and stylistic register blend together to create 'an absolutely unique idiom' (p 250). The central theme of the tale is less the relationship of individuals to each other than the conflict of the ideals that the characters embody. The tale's construction exemplifies '*ordo artificialis* that comes as close as possible to the *naturalis*, with a beginning, middle, and end that would have pleased Aristotle' (p 257).

1188 Brewer, Derek S. 'Chaucer's poetic style.' In *The Cambridge Chaucer Companion*. 1986. See **606**. Pp 227–42.
The description of the garden in *FranT* (lines 906–13) exemplifies Chaucer's use of 'repetition with variation ... to complain that such a style is diffuse would be the same as complaining that there are too many trills and *reprises* in a Mozart aria' (p 232–3).

1189 Burger, Douglas A. 'The *Cosa Impossibile* of *Il Filocolo* and the *Impossible* of The *Franklin's Tale*.' In *Chaucer and the Craft of Fiction*. 1986. See **612**.
Chaucer's alterations of and additions to Menedon's story generate complexities and ironies not found in Boccaccio's work. In requiring her unwelcome suitor to produce a springtime garden in January, Boccaccio's heroine is motivated by 'self-protective expediency' (p 170); in contrast, Dorigen's request for the removal of the coastal rocks manifests her care for Arveragus's well-being. The pagan magic in *Fil* brings about a genuine rejuvenation of nature; the magic of the Orléans clerk, condemned by the Franklin as 'supersticious cursednesse' (line 1272), produces an unnatural illusion that weakens the clerk's claim to being the 'mooste fre' (line 1622) and taints Aurelius's motives by association. Boccaccio's lady fears her husband's jealousy and anger; the focus of Dorigen's concern is her own dishonor – for her a matter of life and death. In commanding his wife to keep her vow, the hus-

band in Menedon's tale stresses the lover's deserts; Arveragus is concerned about Dorigen's *trouthe*. Chaucer's changes to his source deepen the portrait of marriage, raise complex moral and ethical issues, fill out our sense of the story's narrator, and unsettle interpretive certainties.

1190 Burrow, J.A. 'The *Canterbury Tales* I: Romance.' In *The Cambridge Chaucer Companion*. 1986. 2nd ed., *The Cambridge Companion to Chaucer*. 2003. See **606**.
The principle that 'love wol nat been constreyned by maistrye' (line 764) extends beyond the marriage of Dorigen and Arveragus; Aurelius, too, gives up *maistrye* in freeing Dorigen from her promise. Aurelius's refusal to constrain Dorigen's love is related to patterns of *gentil* behavior elsewhere in medieval romance. In *SGGK*, a potential adversary waives his rights and releases Gawain from his obligation; at the end of *WBT*, the knight's submission triggers the old hag's decision to give up her claim to one-sided *maistrye*. Far from betraying the Franklin's uneasiness about his social status, the tale 'may claim to express more fully than any other Middle English poem that generous and humane spirit which marks the best medieval courtly writing' (p 120/p 154). See **784**.

1191 De Weever, Jacqueline. 'Chaucer's Moon: *Cinthia, Diana, Latona, Lucina, Proserpina*.' *Names* 34 (1986), 154–74.
Aurelius invokes Lucina, who as a planet controls the tides, and links her with another of her manifestations – Proserpina, queen of the dark realm. But in *FranT*, events are controlled by human decisions, not by planetary intervention.

1192 Ferster, Judith. 'Interpretation and Imitation in Chaucer's Franklin's Tale.' In *Medieval Literature: Criticism, Ideology and History*. Ed. David Aers. New York: St Martin's, 1986. Pp 148–68.
FranT examines 'the interpretation of stories and the imitation that stories often inspire' (p 154). Dorigen's dilemma – despite her clear understanding of Aurelius's wishes and his understanding of her refusal – comes from imitation (her vow mirrors the false courtly atmosphere of the garden) and interpretation (Aurelius interprets her as a woman who has made a binding promise). The Franklin attempts to protect his audience from the illusions generated by interpretation and imitation: he calls our attention to the fictionality of his tale and makes us conscious of our role as interpreters. In his frequent addresses to his audience, 'he suppresses the fiction in favour of the reality of the pilgrims … He thus emphasises the interpretive community that surrounds his tale – the social context that gives it meaning' (p 163).

1193 Green, Donald C. 'The Semantics of Power: *Maistrie* and *Soveraynte*e in *The Canterbury Tales*.' *MP* 84 (1986), 18–23.
Arveragus's knightly and husbandly roles require public acknowledgment that he is head of the household; within the marriage, he is in courtly service – but not in *servage* (line 795) – to his wife.

1194 Hansen, Bert. 'The Complementarity of Science and Magic before the Scientific Revolution.' *AS* 74 (1986), 128–36.
In *FranT*, 'the power to create illusion and the power to produce physical change are not easily distinguished' (p 130). It is a modern rather than a medieval assumption that 'magical effects cannot be real and what is real cannot be magical' (pp 130–1).

1195 Jost, Jean E. 'Forswearing in Chaucer's *Pardoner's* and *Franklin's Tales*: A Recurring Motif of Tale and Teller.' *MedPers* 1 (1986), 75–88.
Dorigen and Arveragus make their marital vow without considering its possible consequences. Arveragus's behavior extenuates the blame that might otherwise accrue to Dorigen's later vow to Aurelius; distraught at her husband's extended absence, she is vulnerable to Aurelius's plea. The same pity that moves Dorigen to make her promise to Aurelius motivates his brother's engagement of the magician, and thus leads to Aurelius's promise to pay the latter a huge sum. Arveragus's insistence that his wife fulfill her bargain with the squire ignores her personal anguish, and reflects the Franklin's own literal-mindedness. The ensuing crisis can be resolved only through generosity, in the form of freeing the 'none-too-wise but good-willed' cast of characters from their 'foolish and exorbitantly high-priced vows' (p 87).

1196 Knight, Stephen. 'Chaucer's Religious Canterbury Tales.' In *Medieval English Religious and Ethical Literature: Essays in Honour of G.H. Russell.* 1986. See **609**.
Like many medieval romances, *FranT* creates threats for male aristocratic patriarchy and resolves them conservatively. 'The tale is hardly the sonorous ending to a "marriage group" that Kittredge [**805**] dreamed into being as part of his humanistic and novelistic re-reading of the *Tales*' (p 161). Despite the protestations of mutuality, the marriage of Dorigen and Arveragus 'must adopt an authoritarian structure in order to survive' (p 161).

1197 ———. *Geoffrey Chaucer*. 1986. See **610**.
FranT 'is one of the most thorough pieces of conservative secular ideology in the whole Tales' (p 118). Threats to patriarchal aristocracy – loss of a wife to another man, the independent role of a woman, the threat to the established order from financial power and the new professional classes – are resolved by reasserting the feudal status quo: Aurelius and the magician give up their claims, while Dorigen's potential independence, asserted in her questioning of God's Providence and her authoritative rejection of Aurelius, is contained at the end of the tale when Arveragus asserts 'an essentially austere patriarchal control' (p 123).

1198 Mehl, Dieter. *Geoffrey Chaucer: An Introduction to his Narrative Poetry.* 1986. See **611**.
The Franklin, sincerely but perhaps too easily impressed by the surface splendor of *SqT*, tells a tale in which the courtly surface is contrasted with a rather simple-minded morality. The Franklin is not Chaucer's mouth-

piece, nor is his tale intended as a solution to the problems raised by the Marriage Group tales. The narrator's mentality is revealed in Dorigen and Arveragus's marriage contract, well-intentioned but unrealizable in practice. The tale's actors are themselves less important than the test situations in which they are placed; their dilemmas and their responses to them (e.g., Dorigen's Complaint) are 'artificially contrived' (p 168), and the reader has little doubt that the tale will end happily. Although the Franklin wishes to present Arveragus's decision that Dorigen keep her promise to Aurelius as an exemplary one that embodies true *gentilesse,* he 'has but a faint idea of the complexity of the problems he has raised' (p 169). Similarly, the Franklin wishes to invest his tale with moral and philosophical depth; we may find his treatment of these matters inadequate, but the sincerity and intensity invested in pursuing moral questions distinguishes *FranT* from the romances of the Squire and the Wife of Bath.

1199 Minnis, A.J. 'From Medieval to Renaissance? Chaucer's Position on Past Gentility.' 1986. See **613**.

FranT is 'a story of pagan nobles who all turn out to be noble pagans' (p 235). Dorigen's protest against the rocks – the product of emotion rather than reason – places her in the position of the tortured Boethius persona in need of instruction and healing, and is not meant to convey Chaucer's own doubts about the cosmic order. The convergence of pagan and Christian attitudes in *FranT* has 'more in common with the values of late medieval classicism than those of early Renaissance humanism' (p 218); the virtue of the tale's characters is portrayed as universal even as their culture is depicted as circumscribed. In contrast to the sorcerer in *Fil,* Chaucer's clerk is an honorable figure – noble by birth and 'something of a scientist' (p 225) – whose astrological activities predict rather than exploit natural processes; the Franklin's attack on 'supersticious cursednesse' (line 1272) 'sounds rather like a nervous over-reaction' (pp 225–6). Both Aurelius and Dorigen exhibit moral nobility. The portrait of the former is 'a masterpiece of tact' (p 228). Dorigen's behavior is neither blameworthy nor blasphemous; her Complaint is in keeping with pagan criteria of virtue, and, viewed from the standpoint of her time and place, her protest against the rocks evinces impressive enlightenment. As a noble pagan, Arveragus acts with the highest motives available to him. His willingness to sacrifice his wife in the service of *trouthe* reflects an absoluteness that has outraged some modern readers. Yet (as his weeping reveals) Arveragus is not inhuman. The pagan tales of the aristocratic Knight and Squire are 'models of historical reconstruction and cultural relativity' (p 237). In contrast, the limitations of the Franklin's character and status affect his presentation of the past; the values of his tale are 'to some extent at variance with the values of its teller' (p 237).

1200 Morgan, Gerald. 'Boccaccio's *Filocolo* and the Moral Argument of the *Frank-*

lin's Tale.' *ChauR* 20 (1986), 285–306. Excerpts in *Chaucer: Contemporary Critical Essays*. Ed. Valerie Allen and Ares Axiotis. New York: St Martin's, 1996. Pp 63–76.

Based on the judgment of Fiametta in *Fil* that the knight was the most generous, Arveragus's generosity in sending his wife to Aurelius is a *donnée* of the tale; it is not Chaucer's personal opinion, much less that of the Franklin. Modern commentators critical of Arveragus's behavior invert the medieval privileging of action over character, and set their own moral values above the meaning of a text built on different principles. Through verbal parallels, Chaucer establishes a moral equivalency between Dorigen's marriage promise to Arveragus and her promise to Aurelius, an equality underlined by oaths that establish not merely Dorigen's fidelity to human contracts, but also her reverence toward God. Arveragus's invocation of *trouthe* (line 1479) affirms the fundamental principle of obligation inherent in Dorigen's promise; his insistence that she keep her word is 'not a command, but an expression of moral solidarity with his wife' (p 294). Judged by the medieval criteria for valid oaths, Dorigen's promise to Aurelius is not defective in any respect. There is no doubt about her intentions, she doesn't wish to deceive or toy with Aurelius, and she shows herself to be neither foolish nor unfaithful to her husband. Since this second promise does not contradict the first, we cannot expect Dorigen to revoke it. Her inability, in her Complaint, to carry through her contemplated suicide is not 'feminine frailty,' but a testimony to her moral integrity: 'the horror of infidelity is matched by a corresponding horror of suicide' (p 298). Arveragus's response to his wife's plight is based on the centrality of honor in the chivalric code. His love for honor runs so deep that he can set it above the fear of shame, although he takes care to safeguard his public reputation by enjoining his wife to secrecy. His act of generosity is that of a loving husband, built on love of friendship rather than love of desire. Aware that his wife's moral integrity is at stake, Arveragus seeks to unite his will with hers; he is thus bound by the promise she has made. Although the Franklin's final question asks us to adjudicate between the generosity of the husband, the lover, and the magician, we are not asked to discriminate between the virtue of husband and wife, who are united in the love of friendship.

1201 Olson, Paul A. *The Canterbury Tales and the Good Society*. Princeton, NJ: Princeton UP, 1986.

The Franklin tells an Epicurean tale in which suffering and evil are eliminated, and delight experienced without pain. The marriage agreement of Dorigen and Arveragus is based on the Franklin's faulty understanding of the nature of lordship: 'the ordinary franklin knew that his freedom did not derive from the lord's having only "the name of soveraynetee" ... but on both lord and man pledging and keeping a lifelong fealty and troth' (pp

268–9). Dorigen's 'denial of the divine troth represented by the existence of pain … reflects the Franklin's general confusion of genuine troth and its polite semblance' (p 271). The generosity of the characters at the tale's conclusion exists only on the surface; in making Arveragus the poem's hero, the Franklin defines his own sense of honor as that of 'the "good old boy" who can play St. Julian in Epicurus's country where every human prospect pleases and only Truth is vile' (pp 273–4).

• Review by Glending Olson, *Speculum* 63 (1988), 972–4: Olson's 'Franklin bashing' will feel familiar to readers of D.W. Robertson's commentaries (p 973).

1202 Payne, Robert O. *Geoffrey Chaucer*. 2nd ed. Boston: Twayne, 1986.

FranT is about the testing of an apparently ideal marriage, but the manner of the testing is 'strangely artificial,' like 'the riddling games of logical evasion' in the medieval French *demandes d'amour* and 'some courses in twentieth-century law schools' (p 127). At the end of the tale, we are uncertain about exactly which aspects of love or marriage have been tested.

1203 Pearsall, Derek. 'Chaucer's Poetry and its Modern Commentators: The Necessity of History.' In *Medieval Literature: Criticism, Ideology and History*. 1986. See **1192**. Pp 123–47.

'The Franklin … is identified by Robertson [**1030**] … as a social upstart, not because this is the necessary conclusion from the available evidence … but because it suits Robertson's interpretation of *FranT* to see the teller as a *parvenu* who is as flawed morally as he is unstable socially' (p 139).

1204 Rogers, William E. *Upon the Ways: The Structure of The Canterbury Tales*. 1986. See **615**.

The Franklin's idealism answers the Merchant's cynicism; in its treatment of *trouthe* as something to be acted upon rather than simply contemplated, *FranT* also responds to *SqT*. Everyone in the tale learns something from the experience, the primary significance of which is to dispel illusion. The rocks in the tale represent the problem of evil. The ease with which they, and the questions that they raise, are made to disappear suggests that *FranT* 'is, like the art of the clerk of Orléans, superficial' (p 78).

1205 Shoaf, R.A. 'Chaucer and Medusa: The *Franklin's Tale*.' *ChauR* 21 (1986), 274–90. Excerpts in *Chaucer: Contemporary Critical Essays*. 1996. See **1200**. Pp 242–52.

A pun in *astoned* (line 1339) – 'namely, *a-stoned*, that is, "turned to stone"' (p 275) – encourages us to read *FranT* as an essay on 'Epicureanism, petrifaction, illusion, surfaces, and magic' (p 274). In the episode of *Inferno* 9 in which the pilgrim is in danger of being turned to stone by Medusa's glance, Dante addresses those readers who can penetrate beneath the stony surface of his text. In a parallel fashion, *FranT* exposes the literalism of its teller, whose self-presentation and treatment of his narrative produces the illusion of depth, but who in fact wishes his readers to focus on the surface, lest we see him for 'the hollow man he really is' (p 280). The Franklin's attraction to surfaces is attributable to his Epicureanism, which privileges the evidence of the senses, and to his anxiety about his social status. Placing himself and his preferred interpretations at the center of the tale, he attempts to 'detour our interrogation of the signifier' (p 281), to prevent us from recognizing, for example, that the seemingly noble and generous Arveragus is in reality 'a self-serving hypocrite' (p 281). In striving for originality – the power to treat the reader as a *tabula rasa* on which he can impress his own desired significance – the Franklin discloses his fear of the 'vivifying of the letter' (p 283), the tropes of true poetry that destabilize the signifier. He is thus unlike Chaucer, who felt no need to assert his originality, to compete with his precursors as the Franklin does with the Knight. See **1260**, **1453**.

1206 Trigg, Stephanie. 'The Signature of the Editor: Towards a Theory of Editorial Intention.' *Meridian* 5 (1986), 169–74.
Knight's reconstruction of Chaucer's text on the principle of maximum historical tension (**1146**) paves the way for a feminist editorial practice. For Knight's 'frendly wyse' in line 1467, a feminist editor might print the variant 'husbound wyse,' which provides an 'ironic reminder that regardless of any private agreement made between the parties, the social formulas and conventions still prevail' (p 173).

1207 Tripp, Raymond P., Jr. 'The Darker Side to Absalon's Dawn Visit.' *ChauR* 20 (1986), 207–12.
'Offending against love's rules calls forth life's darker, destructive side' (p 208). Dorigen and Arveragus err in attempting to contain eros within the limits of a rational contract. The result is a narrowly avoided marital disaster, culminating in Arveragus's threat to kill his wife in order to save his own reputation.

1208 Benson, Larry D., gen. ed. *The Riverside Chaucer*. 1987. See **108**.
Although the Franklin gives his tale an authentically Breton setting, it differs in many respects from the usual Breton lay. The marriage contract of Dorigen and Arveragus is well suited to the Franklin, who prizes domestic comfort. Like many of the other tales in Fragments III–V, *FranT* turns on a problem of *troth* (p 14).

1209 Bishop, Ian. *The Narrative Art of the Canterbury Tales: A Critical Study of the Major Poems*. 1987. See **617**.
Dorigen's 'essential life is internal' (p 140), expressed primarily in soliloquy. Her lament over the rocks gives voice to a fantasy that is both obsession and illusion. Although Dorigen's arraigning of God's wisdom would have been condemned by Boethius and Augustine, Nominalists such as William of Occam and Robert Holcot might have taken a sympathetic view of her reliance on faith rather than on clerkly arguments. The *accord* of Dorigen and

Arveragus depends on mutual trust rather than legal arrangements; their marriage weathers the crisis because their love is genuine. Arveragus's insistence that Dorigen keep her promise to Aurelius would be implausible in a realistic novel; in the Franklin's romance, however, Dorigen's plight, engineered by 'outrage against the laws of nature' (p 144), can be undone only by something equally outrageous. In Jungian terms, Aurelius has projected his own *anima* onto his beloved; in the context of *fin'amor*, he sees himself as a lover in the mold of Tristan or Lancelot. But in *FranT*, the bond of *fin'amor* exists between the married pair, while it is the lover who attempts to impose legal conditions on his lady.

1210 Blamires, Alcuin. *The Canterbury Tales*. 1987. See **618**.
Dorigen's conditioning by her culture emerges in the 'near-brutal candor' with which she states that her husband possesses her body whenever he wishes to (p 34). In her promise to Aurelius, Dorigen 'muddies her own *entente* with a "playful" promise, only too easily misconstrued into earnest' (p 63). Her fear of the rocks is a classic example of Chaucer's exploration of *fantasye*; Dorigen's obsession with the rocks and her desire for them to sink 'becomes the condition upon which she cryptically half-offers her love to her suitor Aurelius' (p 72). Chaucer contrasts Dorigen's and Aurelius's 'introverted, obsessive characters' with 'the uncluttered mind' of Arveragus; he is not *ymaginatyf* (line 1094), and doesn't 'crowd his brain with unbalancing fancies' (p 74).

1211 Buffoni, Franco. 'L'elemento "magico" nei *Canterbury Tales* di Geoffrey Chaucer.' *Lingua e letteratura* 5 (1987), 38–49.
See **1277**.

1212 De Weever, Jacqueline. *Chaucer Name Dictionary: A Guide to Astrological, Biblical, Historical, Literary, and Mythological Names in the Works of Geoffrey Chaucer*. 1987. See **619**.
Names in *FranT* that fall under the categories enumerated in the title are explicated. Entries include biographical, historical, and mythological information; references to Chaucer's use of the name; etymologies and variant spellings; and bibliographical references. Place names are excluded.

1213 Fyler, John M. 'Love and Degree in the *Franklin's Tale*.' *ChauR* 21 (1987), 321–37.
When Arveragus asks for 'the name of soveraynetee, / That wolde he have for shame of his degree' (lines 751–2), 'for shame' should be glossed as 'from a sense of shame.' Arveragus is ashamed because of his relatively *low* social status, for which the name of sovereignty will provide partial compensation. When (as in Walter's marriage to Griselda in *ClT*) the sexual hierarchy is lined up with those of social rank, the temptations of power become too great; Arveragus's arrangement 'is designed to avoid a milder version of Griselda's situation' (p 328). At the beginning and the end of his tale, 'the

Franklin gestures from within a world of hierarchies to a world before degree' (p 330), a version of the Golden Age marked in the tale by the contrast between plain speaking (associated with clearsightedness and innocence) and rhetorical skill (associated with illusion and self-deception), and by Chaucer's placement of his narrative in a pagan past governed by natural law. This choice of setting 'protects [the tale's] ideal of innocence and unworldly naïveté against our normally more cynical responses' (p 333), and provides a context within which Arveragus and Dorigen create an ideal of marriage that attempts to achieve the equality of the Golden Age 'within the contingencies of the fallen world' (p 334).

1214 Gray, Douglas. 'Chaucer and *Gentilesse.*' In *One Hundred Years of English Studies in Dutch Universities.* 1987. See **620**.
The marriage of Dorigen and Arveragus is an example of ideal *gentilesse,* and sets us up for the tale's subsequent demonstrations of *gentilesse* as profoundly moral. The competition in *gentilesse* between the squire and the clerk recalls the lingering class suggestions of the word 'even as the fiction is destroying them ... no one in this optimistic mood says "straw for your gentillesse!"' (p 25). *Gentilesse* in *FranT* is an exemplary quality as in *ClT,* but more fully humanized; linked with love as in *WBT,* it has a wider ethical range than it does it the earlier tale.

1215 Greene, Thomas M. 'Magic and Festivity in the Renaissance Court: The 1987 Josephine Waters Bennett Lecture.' *RenQ* 40 (1987), 636–59.
Questions Loomis's view (**901**) that the *tregetoures* recalled by Aurelius's brother were mechanical artisans rather than magicians. Even though Chaucer and his audience probably knew of historical analogues to the spectacle described, this knowledge 'did not damage the miraculous wonderment of the allegedly magical show' (p 640).

1216 Howard, Donald R. *Chaucer: His Life, His Works, His World.* 1987. See **621**.
FranT is framed by two compromises: that of Dorigen and Arveragus in their marriage agreement and the mutual concessions of the three male parties at the end of the tale. Chaucer suggests that such compromise is possible by linking key events and images – the black rocks, Dorigen's promise to Aurelius, the garden – with illusion, and by assigning the tale to an appealing figure who might well understand the secret of success in marriage. 'But it is possible to see the Franklin as naïve and so to read his optimistic tale with skepticism ... The ambiguous *FranT* is a clear-headed, positive notion about mutuality in marriage – pushed away in caution or in doubt' (p 434).

1217 Kirby, I.J. 'The Scene of the Franklin's Tale Revisited.' In *Studies in Honour of René Derolez.* Ed. A.M. Simon-Vandenbergen. Ghent: Seminarie voor Engelse en Oud-Germaanse Taalkunde R.U.G., 1987. Pp 283–92.
Kayrrud (line 808), the home of Arveragus, may be a variant of **Keriu* or **Kairiud* (Phillipps MS 8137 has *caere iuda* at line 808), a misreading by Chau-

cer or an intermediate source of *Kériti*, the name of a fishing village in Penmarch that overlooks the chain of coastal rocks. See **1445**.

1218 Lee, Brian S. 'The Position and Purpose of the *Physician's Tale*.' *ChauR* 22 (1987), 141–60.
Both *PhyT* and *FranT* (juxtaposed in some *CT* MSS) investigate the theme of responsibility. Chaucer may have drawn attention to Arveragus's risky conduct in sending Dorigen to Aurelius because he was about to present, in *PhyT*, a situation in which Arveragus's choice would have been the wrong one. *PhyT* may be seen as addressing the question: 'What would have happened if Aurelius had not been "fre" at all?' (p 150).

1219 Seymour, M.C. 'Hypothesis, Hyperbole, and the Hengwrt Manuscript of the *Canterbury Tales*.' 1987. See **625**.
Disputes Blake's contention (**102**) that lines 1455–6 (present in El but not in Hg) are unoriginal. The concluding couplet of Dorigen's list of virtuous wives is unlikely to be an interpolation, since all three names (Bilyea, Rodogone, Valeria) are also found in *Jov*, Chaucer's source for the whole catalogue; a motive for such an addition would be hard to imagine.

1220 Spearing, A.C. *Readings in Medieval Poetry*. Cambridge: Cambridge UP, 1987.
The 'restricted codes' of the OFr. *Chanson de Roland*, in which discourse silently accepts and transmits communal values, are contrasted with the 'elaborated codes' of the scene of Aurelius's final encounter with Dorigen (lines 1499–1525), in which the conflicting values and individual subjectivities of the characters are fully represented (pp 121–3).

1221 Stone, Brian. *Chaucer*. 1987. See **626**.
FranT's subject is 'the operation under stress of a marriage founded on multiple mutual promises' (pp 108–9). Although some critics have been troubled by Arveragus's insistence that Dorigen keep her promise to Aurelius, the context of mutual promises necessitates his action, 'which has the ring of emotional truth and the sanction of the logic by which the two live in trust. It is a transcendence of sharing, and immensely painful to both' (p 110).

1222 Williams, David. *The Canterbury Tales: A Literary Pilgrimage*. Twayne's Masterwork Studies 4. Boston: Hall, 1987.
In his life, the Franklin attempts to disguise his social climbing as true nobility. In his tale, he plays a similar game of 'concealing and revealing' (p 45) – concealing under false signs of nobility the true worth that the perceptive reader will presumably recognize. The Franklin's self-serving intention is to show that 'the least socially distinguished [character] is the most noble' (p 47), but (like the rocks temporarily disguised by the clerk's magic) the Franklin's false values lurk beneath his artful rhetoric.

1223 Wurtele, Douglas J. 'Chaucer's Franklin and the Truth about "Trouthe."' *ESC* 13 (1987), 359–74.
The ongoing debate about the rightness or wrongness of Arveragus's insis-

tence that Dorigen keep her promise to Aurelius results from the Franklin's own polarizing of the issue in his closing *demande d'amour,* which invites us to take sides in 'pursuing a rational answer to the problem' (p 362). The limitations of both the 'legalistic' argument (in which Arveragus – and by extension the Franklin – is faulted for a too-literal reading of the importance of oath keeping) and the 'subjective' view (which lauds Arveragus and his creator for valuing the claims of chivalric honor over those of law) suggest that Chaucer wishes his audience to see beyond these two extremes to a tertium quid: Arveragus should have consulted his wife's wishes in the matter, a response that would conform both to the courtly love code in Arveragus's deference to his lady's desires and to the Christian ethic, 'for it is inconceivable that Dorigen would opt for unfaithfulness' (p 370).

1224 Kellogg, Judith L. '"Large and Fre": The Influence of Middle English Romance on Chaucer's Chivalric Language.' *Allegorica* 9 (1987–8), 221–48.
The Franklin's understanding of noble behavior reflects that of the audience of ME metrical romance, who wished to be entertained with the same fare as their social betters, but who failed to comprehend gentle behavior. Although the Franklin believes that Arveragus, Aurelius, and the clerk are all worthy candidates for the title of 'mooste fre,' their language and actions undercut their claims to true nobility. Arveragus is concerned more with appearances than with the sacred values of marriage; Aurelius's courtly wooing is discredited by his manipulativeness and mercantile outlook. The clerk – 'the most honest of a dishonest lot' (p 238) – nevertheless deals in deception. Dorigen's ethical ideals have the potential to transcend those of the male character, but she is marginalized by the tale.

1225 Banerjee, Jacqueline. 'Chaucer and the Courtly Love Debate.' *Kobe Jogakuin Daigaku Ronshu* [Kobe College Studies] 34:3 (1988), 1–14.
The Franklin's solution to the problems of love and marriage previously aired in *CT* is a pragmatic one, based neither on courtly adulation of the woman nor on a modern concept of equality, 'but on male "lordshipe" informed with courtly "gentillesse"' (p 11).

1226 Blake, N.F. 'Literary and Other Languages in Middle English.' In *Genres, Themes, and Images in English Literature: From the Fourteen to the Fifteenth Century*. Ed. Piero Boitani and Anna Torti. Tübinger Beiträge zur Anglistik 11. Tübingen: Narr, 1988. Pp 166–85.
In El, Dorigen's list of faithful women ends with three further examples (lines 1455–6) not found in Hg or other early MSS. The addition, presumably scribal, suggests that 'some scribes thought that catalogues were literary highlights and should be improved where possible' (p 183).

1227 Brewer, Derek S. 'Orality and Literacy in Chaucer.' In *Mundlichkeit und Schriftlichkeit im englischen Mittelalter*. 1988. See **628**.
See **1188**.

1228 Brunetti, Giuseppe. *Sui Canterbury Tales*. 1988. See **629**.
In contrast to Theseus's final speech in *KnT*, Dorigen's Complaint feels disproportionately long; its extended list of exempla is more appropriate to a learned compilation (in the voice of the narrator) than to a lament (in the voice of the heroine) (p 7). *ShT* can be read as a negative reflection of *FranT* in which the courtly is transformed into the mercantile: a free gift becomes an exchange, *trouthe* becomes *chevyssaunce*, and fidelity to one's word becomes a confidence game. The fabliau's private domestic space appears in *FranT* as a psychological interior space, a realm of intimate feelings (pp 15–17). The natural landscape reappears and is transformed in the tale's theater of the mind. The sea and the rocks, which carry figural meanings before Dorigen encounters them, are initially objects onto which she displaces her turbulent emotions; when she makes the rocks the focus of her 'impossible request,' they become symbols of her marital fidelity. Her proposal to Aurelius implies that the laws of nature would need to change before she would be untrue to her husband, and thus anticipates Arveragus's later invocation of *trouthe* as absolute and immutable (pp 74–5).

1229 Coote, Stephen. *English Literature of the Middle Ages*. 1988. See **630**.
FranT explores the implications of two central aspects of *gentilesse*: *fredom* and *trouthe*. In wishing for the disappearance of the black rocks, Dorigen fails to understand the truth by which the Creator orders the universe; in making her vow to Aurelius, she also jeopardizes her freedom. Aurelius's reliance on magic to remove the rocks sets 'diabolic illusion' against 'divine truth' (p 198). The potential danger of magical illusions is defused, however, by *gentil* actions, specifically Arveragus's reassertion of the *trouthe* that underlies the sanctified vows of marriage.

1230 Davenport, W.A. *Chaucer: Complaint and Narrative*. 1988. See **631**.
Chaucer's reimagining of *Fil* produces a narrative of greater moral complexity. Chaucer's alterations of and additions to his source include the references to Breton tradition, which allow the poet to mix stock figures of contemporary literature with echoes of ancient chronicle; the combining of the story of Dorigen and Arveragus's separation and reunion with that of Aurelius's love quest; the extending of the abstract liberality of the husband in *Fil* to the condition of the marriage itself; the symbolism of the rocks; the exploration of the ethical dimension of Dorigen's behavior, which becomes as important as male honor and generosity; and the open-endedness of the concluding *demande*. The tale's three rhetorical passages of direct speech draw out the narrative's moral implications and allow time for the story to gain due weight. Dorigen's address to God establishes her seriousness, the unintellectual quality of her mind, and her vulnerability; without engaging directly with God's foreknowledge and man's free will, her speech explores one aspect of the question of moral freedom central to the tale. Aurelius's prayer

to Apollo is 'complaint unreasonably used,' a desperate plea for a 'pagan, unnatural miracle,' prefaced by bathos and finished off by the narrator's 'dismissive scorn' (p 190). In her Complaint to Fortune, Dorigen reaches out from a condition of disorder for fixed rules of behavior, even as her rhetoric of repetition enacts the closing off of possibilities for the speaker. The speech suspends the poem's action, introduces a moral question waiting to be resolved, and prepares us for seriousness of the later ethical point about *trouthe*. In the Franklin's 'inexplicable fusion' (p 194) of pagan and Christian elements, magic is treated as 'modern intellectual paganism' (p 195) which, combined with Aurelius's recourse to primitive forces of nature, opposes the Christian values of fidelity, honesty, and truth present in the behavior of Arveragus and Dorigen.

• Review by Catherine Batt, *English* 38 (1989), 69–76: In Davenport's sensitive account of *FranT*, complaint emerges as central to the representation of Dorigen's vulnerability. His discussion of the tale's idealized language 'leads us to wonder to what extent husband and wife are victims of the rhetoric they use' (p 76).

• Review by N.F. Blake, *ES* 71 (1990), 66–7: Davenport makes a strong case for the linking of complaint and narrative, but he spends more time analysing the tale as a whole than considering the role of complaint within it.

• Review by J.D. Burnley, *RES* n.s. 41 (1990), 549–51: Davenport's comparison of *FranT* with its Boccaccian precursor is a valuable interpretive aid, and the role of complaint in moral exploration is effectively demonstrated.

• Review by Dieter Mehl, *Anglia* 109 (1991), 191–4: In focusing on the function of complaint, Davenport occasionally loses sight of the tale's central themes. His argument that the complaints complicate the ethical issues that Chaucer inherited from Boccaccio is convincing, although the discussion would have profited from a firmer editorial hand.

1231 Harrington, David V. 'Redefining the Middle English Breton Lay.' *M&H* n.s. 16 (1988), 73–95.

The ME Breton lays are distinguished by a shared set of social and ethical values: the major characters undergo suffering that serves as a test of character; the suffering is resolved by mutual aid rather than individual effort; the happy endings encourage a positive faith that gentle, peaceful values are shared by others and can prevail. In addition, the ME poets use the term 'Breton lay' not descriptively, 'but as an honorific to confer prestige' (p 80). *FranT* exhibits all of these characteristics. In his Prologue, the Franklin emphasizes the *gentil* lineage of the form; Aurelius, Dorigen, and Arveragus experience suffering; the characters' difficulties are resolved by acts of generosity, repentance, and forgiveness; and the Franklin's final question encourages his audience to 'scrutinize the ethical implications of each character's sacrifice' (p 91).

1232 Hill, Archibald A. 'Chaucer and the Pun-Hunters: Some Points of Caution.' In *On Language: Rhetorica, Phonologica, Syntactica. A Festschrift for Robert P. Stockwell from his Friends and Colleagues*. Ed. Caroline Duncan-Rose and Theo Venneman. London: Routledge, 1988. Pp 66–78.
Pearcy's suggestion (**1047**) that *coppe* (line 942) is a pun on Latin *culpa* is ruled out by the difference in pronunciation, spelling, and language. Foreign words, 'normally at the outer fringes of consciousness,' are unlikely to appear in puns (p 70).

1233 Hornsby, Joseph Allen. *Chaucer and the Law*. Norman, OK: Pilgrim, 1988.
The canon law of agreements provides an important perspective on the promises in *FranT*. In Dorigen and Arveragus's marriage contract, *trouthe* is used in a specific legal sense that 'manifests the intention to be seriously bound by that agreement' (p 52). In contrast to this pledge, Dorigen's vow to Aurelius is 'a false sign rendered legally impotent as a means to secure a promise' (p 53). In holding Dorigen to this empty promise, Aurelius must rely on an illusory standard of conduct for exacting her performance of the agreement. Arveragus's problematic response to her dilemma is based on a 'literalist's reading' of the significance of *trouthe* (p 54); his insistence that she honor her invalid agreement bespeaks the disordered condition of a pre-Christian world where true bonds are treated lightly and false bonds granted undue significance. Rather than endorsing a clear standard of conduct, *FranT* suggests the ambivalence of codes of value and the slipperiness of verbal signs. The agreement that Aurelius makes with the clerk satisfies all the requirements needed to bring an action of debt in the royal courts. Aurelius's release of Dorigen from her promise and the clerk's release of Aurelius from his debt 'mimic the formulaic language of legally valid quitclaims' (p 85).

• Review by George D. Gopen, *SAC* 11 (1989), 241–7: 'By passing judgment on whether ... the characters in *FranT* "actually" had binding contracts or not, [Hornsby] ignores entirely the question of what *should* happen when people make rash promises to each other, leaving us instead with an implied conclusion that Dorigen would have been better off had she taken herself not to the garden, but to the nearest lawyer's office' (pp 243–4).

• Review by Henry A. Kelly, *Speculum* 65 (1990), 429–32: 'In dealing with the promises made in *FranT*, Hornsby acknowledges ... that one should not "look at Arveragus's decision with a cold and legal eye and disregard the ethos of Romance which obviously colors how we should regard it" ... but his own interpretation calls for such a decontextualized view' (p 430).

• Review by Thomas L. Reed, Jr., *Envoi* 2 (1990), 367–73: Hornsby's account of the relation between intent and obligation in *FranT* and its connection with the tale's treatment of language is 'sensitive, informed, and attractive' (p 370).

• Review by Wendy Scase, *N&Q* n.s. 37 (1990), 215–17: In his use of canon law to elucidate *FranT*, Hornsby makes little mention of the literary transmutation of the medieval courts of law into the 'court of love' implied by the Franklin's concluding question (p 217).
• Review by John A. Alford, *JEGP* 90 (1991), 241–3: Hornsby's discussion of promises in *GP* and *FranT* exemplify the book's major weakness, its failure to adequately relate the legal elements in Chaucer's writings to a literary context.
• Review by Marie Axton, *YES* 22 (1991), 333–5: Hornsby is interesting on intention in canon law; he exonerates Dorigen from her unintended bargain, but fails to convincingly explain Arveragus's holding his wife to the letter rather than the intention of her agreement.

1234 James, Max H. 'Chaucer's "Contemporary" Search for *Steadfastnesse* and *Trouthe*.' *CSR* 18 (1988), 118–35.
FranT examines the degree to which humans can imitate 'the providential pattern of steadfastness, faithfulness, and truth' (p 132). Dorigen and Arveragus steadfastly maintain their initial pledge to each other; Dorigen's playful promise to Aurelius is in reality proof of her profound devotion to her absent husband. The tale portrays a shame culture, in which nothing is more important than one's plighted word. Arveragus's insistence that Dorigen keep her *trouthe* not only exemplifies his belief that she must be responsible for her actions, but also demonstrates, in its subsequent effect on Aurelius and the magician, that 'truth/trust is the bond cementing all of society' (p 134).

1235 Kendrick, Laura. *Chaucerian Play: Comedy and Control in the Canterbury Tales.* Berkeley: U of California P, 1988.
The Host's 'Straw for youre gentillesse!' (line 695) is equivocal, both facetiously courteous (Harry either literally or figuratively hands the Franklin a straw, signifying that it is his turn to tell a story) and derogatory ('[I don't give a] straw for your gentility'). Both the polite and impolite senses are supported by the larger context of the subsequent exchange between Host and Franklin (pp 107–9). *FranT* is among those tales that 'deconstruct themselves' (p 117). Dorigen's playful promise is milked for its pathos in her long Complaint, which in due course is turned into 'a game of deciding which of three men gave up the most, who was most generous … in a more vulgar, materialistic sense of the word' (p 117).

1236 Koff, Leonard Michael. *Chaucer and the Art of Storytelling*. 1988. See **785**.
Chaucer encourages readings that give his texts a place in our history as well as in their own. Dorigen's complaint to Fortune 'puts her in a context that is intentionally multiple,' encouraging our assessment of speaker and action (p 190). Arveragus's response to Dorigen's dilemma requires speculation, at once personal and historical, about his motives and about our own. The

textual abbreviations and omissions in lines 1460–9 compel us to rehearse to ourselves the circumstances of Dorigen's fate, and to imagine the subtexts of Arveragus's overt remarks. His response in lines 1472–86 is 'complex, not simply husbandly'; its complexity arises from what is left unsaid (p 192). And this complexity transforms Aurelius, who, like us, finds Arveragus's embodiment of seemingly irreconcilable difficulties a source of wonder. In acknowledging both Arveragus's *gentilesse* and Dorigen's *distresse* (lines 1526–7), Aurelius also acknowledges 'our several responses to idealism' (p 197). The magician is a kind of Franklin in his Epicurean hospitality and self-possession; like the Franklin, the magician 'appropriates images of history ... to share ... on his own spectacular terms' (p 200). Bloomfield's reading of *FranT* (**1128**) represents 'the kind of ahistorical criticism that, despite itself, gives us speculative, metaphysical connections' – in contrast to narrower historicist questions about the fictional Franklin's social status (p 204).

1237 Laird, Edgar S. 'Astronomical "Proporcioneles" in Chaucer's *Franklin's Tale.*' *ELN* 25:3 (March 1988), 23–6.
The clerk's *proporcioneles* (line 1278) corresponds to the term *minuta proportionalia,* found in advanced astronomical texts in Latin, and to 'proporcional minutis' in late fourteenth-century English astronomical treatises.

1238 North, J.D. *Chaucer's Universe.* 1988. See **633**.
Despite the his professed ignorance of the subject, the Franklin 'utters not a word of astrology or astronomy that is less than precise' (p 439); his account of the clerk's calculations (lines 1273–84), for example, is error free. *Alnath* (line 1281) refers to the lunar mansions rather than to the star (pp 153–6). The 'book ... of magyk natureel' (lines 1124–5) describing the moon's mansions may be connected in Chaucer's mind with the treatise by one 'Gergis' or 'Gergith' which relates the lunar mansions to the practice of magic (pp 251–4). Aurelius's reference to the 'opposicioun ... in the signe ... of the Leon' in his prayer to Apollo (lines 1058–9) leaves it unclear whether the sun or the moon is in Leo. The idea of 'synchronous lunae-solar motion' was probably original with Chaucer, although he may have known the authoritative discussion of tides in Albumasar's *Introductorium* (p 425). The association of natural magic and stage illusions should be attributed to the ignorance of Aurelius's brother. The stage tricks are 'a mere curtain-raiser' to the genuine astrological magic performed by the clerk, who achieves what he set out to do (p 427). The tale's astronomical indications allow us to place the removal of the rocks either in December or January. Considering dates in which the moon and the sun were either in opposition or in conjunction (both related to tidal effects) in the period between 1375 and 1400, 25 December 1387, seems the most likely candidate for the removal of the rocks. Other indications (the sun in his own domicile and in the term of Venus; the moon at opposition in Aquarius – a water sign – as well as in the face

and term of Venus) point to 22 July 1385 as the likely date for Aurelius's prayer to Apollo. Moreover, the total eclipse of the moon on that date adds a double meaning to lines 1074–5: 'the Moon at the time of the eclipse would have been in a truly "dirke regioun", for she would have been in the Earth's shadow, and would at that time have been "under the ground", from a London perspective' (p 441). The astrological framework supporting *FranT* is 'essentially simple: a prayer to the Sun, at a time when Jupiter was conjoined with Venus, asking for a miracle during the eclipse of the Moon beneath the ground, at a time when Jupiter was to be in friendly aspect with Venus ... The removal of the rocks when Mercury and Venus are conjoined, but when Jupiter is in unfriendly aspect with both. The rocks, removed on Christmas day, were gone for "a wyke or tweye" – perhaps until twelfth night' (p 442). The clerk's practices are 'theologically suspect,' something other than benign natural magic (p 257). In distancing himself from such activities, the Franklin adopts a stance that was probably close to Chaucer's own. In wishing away the rocks – a significant part of God's universe – Dorigen threatens her own well-being by enabling a world created by the subtle clerk in which, under the terms of her contract, she is in the power of Aurelius.

• Review by Sigmund Eisner, *SAC* 12 (1990), 317–19: 'North's conclusion that the Franklin echoes Chaucer himself is reminiscent of ... Kittredge's and like Kittredge's is open to question ... this reviewer finds it difficult to maintain that the Franklin, that middle-class advocate of deception in marriage, does indeed speak for Chaucer' (p 319).

• Review by Michael W. Twomey, *Anglia* 109 (1991), 186–90: Ch. 6, an excursus on Dorigen's wish to change the order of the universe by removing the rocks from the coast of Brittany, could have been reduced to its last paragraph and inserted into the chapter on *FranT* with no loss (p 190).

1239 Saito, Tomoko. 'Women in Chaucer's Works (5) – Dorigen.' *Kōnan daigaku bungaku kai ronshū* [Journal of the Literary Society of Konan University] 65 (1988), 42–53.

Although the theme of the tale is *gentilesse,* none of the three men is gentle, and Dorigen suffers from the egoistic behavior of Arveragus and Aurelius. Dorigen is not a wise wife but an ordinary woman. (Not seen. Annotation from *BPMELLJ* [1994], p 95.)

1240 Scott, Anne Marie. *"Do nu as þu sedes": Word and Deed in King Horn, Havelok the Dane, and the Franklin's Tale.* PhD diss., Brown University, 1988. Dir. Elizabeth Kirk. Ann Arbor, MI: University Microfilms International, 1988. See also *DAI*–A 49/08: 2214.

Ch. 3, 'Words, Worlds, and the Pursuit of Happiness in The Franklin's Tale' (pp 106–56), argues that, in *FranT,* 'ideal communication must take into account words left *unspoken,* that ideal actions are modified by the acknowledgment of human emotion, and that an ideal worlds can be created through the ability to perceive fresh meaning in conventional words and "werks"' (p 107).

1241 Shoaf, R.A. 'The Play of Puns in Late Middle English Poetry: Concerning Juxtology.' In *On Puns: The Foundation of Letters*. Ed. Jonathan Culler. Oxford: Blackwell, 1988. Pp 49–61.
See **1205**.

1242 Strauss, Jennifer. '"I kan nat seye": The Rhetoric of Narratorial Self-Consciousness in Chaucer, especially in *The Canterbury Tales*.' 1988. See **634**.
The Franklin's disclaimer of competence in using the colors of rhetoric is subverted by his highly rhetorical tale. Unlike *SqT*, however, *FranT* 'survives its narratorial excesses' (p 172); language is shown to be both slippery and subject to abuse, but nevertheless able to convey truth.

1243 Zong-qi, Cai. 'Fragments I–II and III–V in *The Canterbury Tales*: A Re-examination of the Idea of the "Marriage Group."' *Comitatus* 19 (1988), 80–98.
The treatment of marriage in *CT* is an extended discussion beginning from issues raised in Fragments I–II. *FranT* concludes this discussion by integrating themes and plot motifs and advocating 'meaningful moderation' (p 93). The Franklin's solution is a compromise among all the versions of matrimony previously examined, achieved by avoiding their extremes and retaining their reasonable elements.

1244 Delany, Sheila. 'Difference and the Difference It Makes: Sex and Gender in Chaucer's Poetry.' *Florilegium* 10 (1988–91), 83–92. Repr. in *A Wyf Ther Was: Essays in Honour of Paule Mertens-Fonk*. Ed. Juliette Dor. Liège: Université de Liège, 1992. Pp 103–11.
Dorigen and Arveragus's marriage agreement seems to eliminate oppressive husbandly authority. By the end of the tale, however, the contract's promise of mutuality has failed. Dorigen depends on Arveragus to resolve her dilemma, and he does so in authoritarian terms. 'We have been invited first to sympathize with the impulse to an ideal sexual egalitarianism, then reminded in the narrative that social life is not after all ideal' (p 90).

1245 Brooke, Christopher N.L. *The Medieval Idea of Marriage*. Oxford: Oxford UP, 1989.
FranT has been read as an ideal portrait of marriage. But this view can be sustained only if we ignore the harsh – even cynical – aspects of the tale: the deception of Dorigen, her contemplation of suicide, and the ambivalence of the final question (pp 219–20).

1246 Canfield, J. Douglas. *Word as Bond in English Literature from the Middle Ages to the Restoration*. Philadelphia: U of Pennsylvania P, 1989.
In promising to love Aurelius if he removes the rocks, Dorigen unintentionally breaks *trouthe* both with Arveragus and with God, whose wisdom in creating the rocks she distrusts. Her error is made right by the generosity of Arveragus, who responds to her plight not by taking vengeance but by

showing patience and forgiveness. The absurdity of Arveragus's sending his wife to commit adultery in order to keep her *trouthe* is only apparent; a symbolic reading of his language shows him putting faith in God's mercy, a faith that is vindicated by the *grace* (lines 1508, 1566) that manifests itself in the selfless actions of Aurelius and the clerk in the tale's concluding episode (pp 45–52).

1247 Charnes, Linda. '"This Werk Unresonable": Narrative Frustration and Generic Redistribution in Chaucer's *Franklin's Tale*.' *ChauR* 23 (1989), 300–15. *FranT* undermines the viability of heroic and romance themes and reevaluates their relation to human experience through the use of three structural paradigms: narrative pacing, repression and substitution, and generic redistribution. The tale conjures and rejects violence in narrative gaps generated by the techniques of distance (which gives rise to a space for violence) and delay (which produces the expectation that violence will occur). Two opposing time systems emerge in the tale: Arveragus's is compressed (reflecting the Franklin's imaginative distance from the world of the knight errant), while Dorigen's is expanded (reflecting the Franklin's sympathy with the domestic). Yet the Franklin accepts 'generic exigency' – Arveragus's commitment to his chivalric adventures – as 'natural,' while representing Dorigen's emotional response to his absence as 'unnatural' (p 304). Dorigen redeploys her suffering through a series of substitutions in which her anger at Arveragus is displaced onto the rocks and her frustration at his physical and emotional absence played out in her dalliance with Aurelius, Arveragus's narrative stand-in. Each character occupies a different generic space. Although Chaucer understands the comic possibilities of the skewing of genres, the Franklin does not. His 'generic ineptitude' (p 312) emerges, for example, in the conflicting roles occupied by Dorigen. Finding a *trouthe* common to disparate generic values emerges as the tale's final quest. In the concluding episodes, the characters become members of a 'homogeneous generic community' (p 313). *FranT* demonstrates how generic conventions can falsify, but also reaffirms their redemptive possibilities.

1248 Cooper, Helen. *The Canterbury Tales*. 1989. See **635**.
The chapter on *FranT* treats *Sq–FranL*, date and text, genre, sources and analogues, structure, themes, the tale in context, and style. *FranT* almost certainly dates from the high period of Chaucer's work on *CT*. Two passages (lines 1455–6 and 1493–8) appear only in El and one other manuscript. Glosses are almost entirely limited to Dorigen's Complaint, and may well go back to Chaucer. Like other Breton lays in French and English, *FranT* is short in length and scope, recounts a group of related episodes rather than a series of adventures, and focuses more on emotion than on event. Chaucer's tale does not share with the French lays a Breton or Celtic origin; its closest analogues are found in Boccaccio (see **345**). *FranT*'s generic stylization makes

the improbability of the plot less troublesome, as does its association with a genre in which magic is commonplace. The plot is symmetrical, falling into two halves that mirror each other around a midpoint. The tale moves from happiness and virtue to increasing uncertainty to a point where illusion dominates, and then gradually back toward equilibrium; such a pattern imitates the seasonal cycle of romance, with winter, which looks both ways in the figure of Janus, at the center. Interpretations that see the Franklin as a superficial parvenu and those that read the marriage of Dorigen and Arveragus as a violation of the tenets of Christian orthodoxy are derived from assumptions that lie outside the tale. The story 'flies in the face of conventional morality' (p 237) and is set up as a test case, with Dorigen's rash promise as a condition of the narrative. At the end of the tale, generosity prevails because the three men give up what they could rightfully claim as theirs. Arveragus's concern with honor is a proper one in the chivalric world; his one act of *maistrye* is an attempt to protect Dorigen's reputation as well as his own. The tale's concern with *trouthe* is underlined by the centrality of *illusioun, trouthe*'s opposite. The tale's universe is a Christian one, but the semipagan setting prevents us from judging the characters by Christian criteria; they are allowed space to exercise their natural virtue. *FranT*'s two great principles are *pacience* and *gentilesse*; it is virtue, rather than plot, that produces the happy ending. *FranT* is usually read in relation to the other tales of the Marriage Group, but its thematic connections extend beyond these three narratives. The virtues of Dorigen and Arveragus's marriage are a model for all human relationships. *FranT* bears particular affinities with *SqT* (revisiting the latter's romance motifs as 'matters of real human import,' p 241), with *KnT* (in its treatment of providence and male friendship), and especially with *MerT* (in a precise series of contrasts of plot and theme). The tale's narrative voice rarely calls attention to itself; neither 'single [n]or stable' (p 244), it is continuously modulated in accordance with the immediate subject. Each of the tale's main characters is accorded a specific idiom. Aurelius's mode is 'exaggeration,' almost always with a 'slight distance between statement and tone' (p 243). Arveragus is treated seriously, in both narrative and speech, while Dorigen's idiom lies somewhere between the two. The garden description (lines 907–22) and the representation of the clerk's illusions as material objects suggest that it is 'things' in *FranT* that are unstable, whereas the tale's absolutes are moral qualities.

• Review by Monica McAlpine, *CE* 54 (1992), 595–602: Although Cooper generally avoids scholarly controversies, she defends the values of *trouthe* and *gentilesse* in *FranT* 'against both too-cynical and too-moralistic interpretations' (p 597).

1249 Fyler, John M. 'Love and the Declining World: Ovid, Genesis, and Chaucer.' *Mediaevalia* 13 (1989, for 1987), 295–307.

In his gestures toward the Golden Age, Chaucer manifests a distrust of rhetorical ornament as a sign of the fallen world. The Franklin's representation of a marriage of equals that recalls a time before sexual hierarchies existed is paralleled by his distrust of elaborate rhetoric and its capacity for deception.

1250 Kim, Hyonjin. '"What is this world?": the Knight's Tale, the Man of Law's Tale, the Franklin's Tale, the Physician's Tale e natanan Chaucer eui yeoksakwan.' ['"What is this world?": Chaucer's historical insight in the Knight's Tale, the Man of Law's Tale, the Franklin's Tale, and the Physician's Tale.'] *ESK* 14 (1989), 1–22.

Not seen. Listed in *ABELL* 65 (1993), 221. In Korean.

1251 Kim, Jong-Hwan. 'Dramatic Irony in Chaucer's *The Franklin's Tale*.' *JELL* 35 (1989), 3–12.

Chaucer employs dramatic irony to satirize the Franklin's misuse of rhetoric and the characters' moral absurdities. Although the Franklin labels his speech as 'bare and pleyn' (line 720), it reflects not the genuine modesty of the Augustinian *sermo humilis*, but the affected humility recommended by Cicero as a way of pleasing one's audience. His tale foregrounds the discrepancy between appearance and reality in its treatment of the characters' promises. Although the story ends by praising the generosity of the participants, Dorigen and Arveragus break their marriage vow by taking seriously Dorigen's promise to Aurelius, which contradicts her allegiance to her husband, while Aurelius does not fulfill his promise to Dorigen because he fails to remove the rocks 'stoon by stoon' (line 993), and, in addition, is unable to keep his contract with the magician. The final irony lies in the Franklin's ignorance of his failure as a story teller; he intends his tale to be an example of ideal conduct, but it is in fact 'a pseudo-exposition of "gentilesse"' that avoids the moral issues it raises (p 11).

1252 Patterson, Lee. '"What Man Artow?": Authorial Self-Definition in *The Tale of Sir Thopas* and *The Tale of Melibee*.' *SAC* 11 (1989), 117–75.

In *FranT*, 'fantasy and magic ... come finally to allow for acts of generosity that show human beings at their best – a best that may well be itself only a fiction (the tale is after all a Breton lay, an explicitly fantastic form) but which claims the power to solicit from its readers similar acts of generosity' (p 128). *FranT* and *WBT* 'bespeak ... a heavy Chaucerian investment in the power of the fictive, the fantastic, and the wish-fulfilling' (p 128).

1253 Shoaf, R.A. 'Medieval Studies After Derrida After Heidegger.' In *Sign, Sentence, Discourse: Language in Medieval Thought and Literature*. 1989. See **638**. Pp 9–30.

See **1205**.

1254 Singer, Margaret. '*Aventure* or *grace*: Lucky in Love in the *Franklin's Tale*?' In *Words and Wordsmiths: a volume for H.L. Rogers*. Ed. Geraldine Barnes, John Gunn, Sonya Jensen, and Lee Jobling. Sydney: Department of English, Uni-

versity of Sydney, 1989. Pp 112–18.
An examination of other uses of *aventure* and *grace* in Chaucer's works suggests that both words connote 'luck' or 'chance' in line 1508. Aurelius's meeting Dorigen is typical of a tale in which a character's attribution of an event to fate, providence, or fortune is frequently undercut by the reader's perception that it is merely a stroke of luck.

1255 Stephens, John, and Marcella Ryan. 'Metafictional Strategies and the Theme of Sexual Power in The Wife of Bath's and Franklin's Tales.' *NMS* 33 (1989), 56–75. Repr. in *Chaucer: The Canterbury Tales.* Ed. Steve Ellis. Longman Critical Readers. London: Longman, 1998. Pp 147–68.
An approach to *WBT* and *FranT* that locates itself outside habits of male reading and examines the tales' metafictional dimensions reveals a bleak picture of male–female relations. Dorigen's desires are defined by structures of male authority, including structures of language. The power relationship between the sexes is analogous to the text/reader relationship; like Dorigen, the reader may be dominated and even violated. *FranT*'s extreme linguistic self-consciousness is echoed at the narrative level by episodes in which concealment and illusion-making become metafictional. Aurelius hides his true *entente* from Dorigen, a naïve reader who interprets language at face value. The clerk's magic threatens to entrap both Dorigen and the reader; his art 'glosses over' the black rocks, 'the covert meanings which rise up to subvert the text' (p 67). Throughout *CT*, Chaucer stages parallels between the poet's power over language and women's creative verbal power. In contrast to the old woman in *WBT*, however, Dorigen 'is sentenced ... to channel her creativity into silent suffering' (p 73).

1256 Strohm, Paul. *Social Chaucer*. 1989. See **641**.
The virtue of *trouthe* is preserved in *FranT* 'by severing it from the outworn and unworkable restrictions of the sworn oath and by grounding it on natural and more generally available qualities of *franchise* and *gentillesse*' (p 105). Although the tale's characters seek at the outset to regulate their interactions by sworn relations of a traditional, quasi-feudal kind, oaths are ultimately treated not as timeless and immutable, but as finite contracts, subject to renegotiation and even outright abandonment. The Franklin, 'whose whole life expresses a desire to set others at their ease,' elevates 'human solidarity' over 'sterile and restrictive covenants' (p 106), and espouses virtues open to all levels of society, thereby engaging issues of pressing importance for the middle social strata to which Chaucer, most of Chaucer's audience, and the Franklin himself belong.
• Review by Britton J. Harwood, *SAC* 13 (1991), 245–50: Although Strohm's criticism is in general 'highly reliable ... few readers will be persuaded by his interpretation of *FranT*' (p 250).
• Review by Lee Patterson, *Speculum* 67 (1992), 485–8: Strohm's analysis of

the 'much-analyzed *FranT* ... will do much to put the criticism of that often-misunderstood text on a sound footing' (p 486).

1257 Veldhoen, N.H.G.E. '"Which was the mooste fre": Chaucer's realistic humour and insight into human nature, as shown in The Frankeleyns Tale.' In *In Other Words: Transcultural Studies in Philology, Translation, and Lexicology Presented to Hans Heinrich Meier on the Occasion of His Sixty-fifth Birthday*. Ed. J. Lachlan Mackenzie and Richard Todd. Dordrecht: Foris, 1989. Pp 107–16.
The Franklin's concluding question is not rhetorical; it is intended to be answered. Dorigen and the magician must be ruled out as candidates; the former is 'held up for commiseration, not for either admiration or rejection' (p 108), the latter is a subsidiary character not directly involved in the love plot. The choice of the husband in *Fil* as the most generous suggests that Arveragus is the upholder of honor in *FranT*. But the squire Aurelius, presented with greater vividness than the other characters, may well be the Franklin's real favorite, especially in light of his demonstrated fondness for the pilgrim Squire. The answer to the Franklin's question is a double one: officially, the husband is 'the mooste fre'; in his heart, the Franklin chooses the young lover.

1258 Wetherbee, Winthrop. *Chaucer: The Canterbury Tales*. 1989. See **642**.
Things are either real or artificial in *FranT*. The courtship and marriage of Dorigen and Arveragus are idealized; Arveragus's departure for England, Dorigen's lament over the rocks, and her vow to Aurelius in the garden are shaped by chivalric and courtly conventions. Aurelius, dislocated from reality, 'exists only to play the lovesick squire' (p 51). In contrast, the tableaux produced for Aurelius by the clerk comment shrewdly on the 'self-absorption' (p 53) of the chivalric and courtly ways of life, while the images of natural process in Franklin's winter vignette foreground 'the lack of real purpose in the lives of the protagonists' (p 53). This unreality becomes even plainer as the narrative nears its climax – in Dorigen's operatic and ineffectual Complaint, or in our awareness that Arveragus, in commanding his wife to keep her promise to the squire, 'is treating his own marriage and Aurelius's fantastically contrived idyll with equal seriousness' (p 55). Although the tale's conclusion calls into question courtly and chivalric idealism, it also reminds us (especially in the clerk's refusal to claim payment for his work) that 'without courtesy the social world becomes chaotic and inhuman' (p 55).

1259 Speed, Diane. 'Character and Circumstance in *The Franklin's Tale.*' *SSEng* 15 (1989–90), 3–30.
By introducing his tale as a Breton lay and indulging in a falsely modest disclaimer about his limitations as a rhetorician, the Franklin sends a 'duplex message ... a romantic fairytale is to be presented as an intellectual exercise' (p 4). The tale takes up the challenges of this seemingly impossible task by posing a series of problems, to be worked out in terms of the 'logical and

generic possibilities of the roles played by the characters at different stages' (p 4). The course of the narrative is determined by Dorigen and Arveragus's marriage relationship; by the courtly love relationship of Dorigen and Aurelius; by the business relationship between Aurelius and the clerk; and, finally, by the new relationships instituted by the competition in *gentilesse*, which resolves the other three.

The Franklin's Tale, 1990–1999

1260 Booker, M. Keith. 'Postmodernism in Medieval England: Chaucer, Pynchon, Joyce and the Poetics of Fission.' *Exemplaria* 2 (1990), 563–94.
The pun on *astoned* (line 1339) noted by Shoaf (**1205**) and linked by him to the Medusa episode in *Inferno* 9 initiates a 'chain reaction of meaning' (p 573) that transcends authorial intention. The pun proleptically evokes Wallace Stevens's 'The Man on the Dump' ('stanza my stone') and radiates internally through Chaucer's works to make connections between the magic of *FranT* and the philosopher's stone in *CYT*, and with the 'stalwart "stoons"' (p 574) of the Nun's Priest that Harry Bailly blesses in the epilogue to *NPT*. 'In this case, being "astoned" thus implies that Dorigen is, as we might say in postmodern vulgar parlance, fucked – and potentially in more ways than one' (p 574).

1261 Crane, Susan. 'The Franklin as Dorigen.' *ChauR* 24 (1990), 236–52.
'In important narrative respects, the Franklin is himself Dorigen' (p 243). Dorigen's marginalized status as a woman is analogous to the Franklin's social position as a gentle at the periphery of gentility. Both Dorigen and the Franklin wish to revise their status. Both characters confront courtly and clerical traditions – Dorigen in her unconventional marriage and in her rejection of clerkly wisdom in her response to the rocks, the Franklin in his revisions of the romance plot and in his condemnation of the clerk's natural magic. But in both cases their attempted manipulations of these traditions fail, and they are compelled to accept circumstances they wished to avoid. Dorigen and the Franklin at once resist and are drawn to romance conventions; both subject themselves to the command of the romance hero Arveragus – Dorigen by going to Aurelius, the Franklin by endorsing his hero's wisdom for the conduct of his plot. 'The precariousness of the Franklin's status,' echoed in Dorigen's role, 'comments on romance's literary authority and on the power of its hierarchies to disenfranchise by measures of gender and class' (p 250). See **670**.

1262 Delany, Sheila. 'Strategies of Silence in the Wife of Bath's Recital.' In *Medieval Literary Politics: Shapes of Ideology*. Manchester: Manchester UP, 1990. Pp 112–29.

To attempt to answer the question posed at the end of *FranT* (line 1622) and determine which man was most *fre* is to accept the premise that a woman is 'an object without will or moral responsibility' (p 126).

1263 Edwards, A.S.G. 'Chaucer and the Poetics of Utterance.' In *Poetics: Theory and Practice in Medieval Literature*. The J.A.W. Bennett Memorial Lectures, Seventh Series, Perugia, 1990. Ed. Piero Boitani and Anna Torti. Cambridge: Brewer, 1991. Pp 57–67.

Structured around a series of promises that cannot all be faithfully adhered to, *FranT* concludes with deeds which 'exempt all the characters from the consequences of ill-considered verbal agreements none wishes to fulfill' (p 59).

1264 Fischer, Andreas. 'Story and Discourse in *Sir Gawain* and *The Franklin's Tale*.' In *Anglistentag 1989 Würzburg: Proceedings*. Ed. Rüdinger Ahrens. Tübingen: Niemeyer, 1990. Pp 310–19.

FranT and *SGGK* are chivalric romances, contain folk motifs freshly reworked, incorporate elements of the fantastic, and show chivalric virtues – especially *trouthe* or *trawthe* – being put to the test. Dorigen and Gawain both make two promises of *trouthe*, the second invalidating the first; in both cases, the resulting conflict is resolved happily. But the happy endings conceal critiques of the chivalric code. Dorigen's dilemma arises from her inability to accept imperfection, symbolized in the story by the black rocks; 'like Gawain she falls short of her own high principles' (p 316). Three conflicting evaluations of Gawain's conduct – his own, the Green Knight's, and that of Arthur's court – are paralleled by three unanswered questions in *FranT*: which of the three men was 'the mooste fre' (line 1622)? The Franklin's silence on this issue points to the greater question of 'Dorigen's quandary and of the values that caused it' (p 316). Both poems test codes of behavior, and reveal them to be 'as difficult and dangerous as they are ideal and admirable' (p 318).

1265 Fleming, John V. *Classical Imitation and Interpretation in Chaucer's Troilus*. Lincoln: U of Nebraska P, 1990.

The Franklin 'knows approximately as much about moral philosophy as a hog knows about Christmas ... "Trouthe is the hyeste thyng that man may kepe" ... is to be sure a stark and pagan avowal, but do not call it *gentilesse*' (p 172).

1266 Ganim, John M. *Chaucerian Theatricality*. 1990. See **644**.

Like the Clerk and the Squire, the Franklin is explicitly aware of the self-consciously literary nature of his enterprise. In *FranP*, oral transmission is cited as evidence not of folk roots, but of the noble origin of stories; the values of *FranT* itself, in reality transmitted through folk tale, are presented as derived from the courtly world. The Franklin's obsession with the sources of his story reflects Chaucer's own 'struggle with the multifarious forces of literary culture' (p 96). In his afterword to *SqT*, the Franklin treats the Squire as a model for behavior, turning the latter's life into a text. In using the young man as the pattern of courtliness against which he judges his own son, the Franklin historicizes the Squire's values and performance.

1267 Holley, Linda Tarte. *Chaucer's Measuring Eye*. Houston, TX: Rice UP, 1990.
Words shape illusion in *FranT*. The rocks seem to disappear under the influence of the magician's language; Dorigen in turn believes what she 'sees' that this language has wrought (p 11).

1268 Kawasaki, Masatoshi. 'The Topography of the *Franklin's Tale*: the meaning of *gardyn*.' *Studies in British and American Literature* (Komazawa University, Japan) 25 (1990), 1–18.
Full text at http://wwwelib.komazawa-u.ac.jp/cgi-bin/retrieve/sr_bookview.cgi/U_CHARSET.utf-8/XC00014511/Body/KJ00004486419.html. In Japanese.

1269 Kelly, Henry Ansgar. Review of Hornsby (**1233**). *Speculum* 65 (1990), 429–32.
The marriage of Arveragus and Dorigen is 'the clearest example in Chaucer of a true clandestine marriage, with full consent on both sides' (p 431).

1270 Kessel-Brown, Deirdre. 'The Emotional Landscape of the Forest in the Medieval Love Lament.' *MÆ* 59 (1990), 228–45.
In medieval texts, the forest appears as a setting, both literal and metaphorical, for those wounded by love. In *FranT*, the lovesick Aurelius is described as a victim of a forest hunt (lines 1111–22); the clerk's magic (lines 1189–94) reveals to him this 'wounded' state (p 238).

1271 Knapp, Peggy. *Chaucer and the Social Contest*. New York: Routledge, Chapman and Hall, 1990.
Having attempted through their unconventional marriage agreement to 'subvert the normal force of institutions' (p 104), Arveragus and Dorigen find themselves thrown back on the power of their private promises. The tale asks whether their good intentions can grapple with the difficulties these private agreements have created, and answers in the affirmative: by not pressing his rights of lordship, Arveragus makes *fredom* into an 'irresistible force,' and the Franklin's fiction comes out on the side of 'personal intervention in the legal structures by which society is organized' (p 105).
• Review by Britton J. Harwood, *Speculum* 68 (1993), 818–22: Knapp's notion that Dorigen and Arveragus aggressively subvert institutional norms is 'very doubtful' (p 820).

1272 Leicester, H. Marshall. *The Disenchanted Self: Representing Subjectivity in the Canterbury Tales*. Berkeley: U of California P, 1990.
In contrast to the *demande* at the end of Part I of *KnT*, which serves primarily to emphasize the inconsequentiality of the narrative thus far, the Franklin's concluding question is a 'genuinely social act' (p 243), an attempt to give the story fulfillment in the community of the pilgrims.

1273 Lucas, Peter J. 'Chaucer's Franklin's *Dorigen*: Her Name.' *N&Q* n.s. 37 (1990),

398–400.

Droguen (or *Dorguen*), the Breton royal name that has been proposed as a source for the name of Chaucer's heroine, is a scribalism for *Ohurgeun,* the correct name of the wife of Alain I, ninth-century Duke of Brittany. The scribal error may have been influenced by the currency of *Droguen* as a man's name. The inappropriateness of *Dorigen* as a woman's name is 'in tension with the apparent approval with which the Franklin … presents *Dorigen* as an authentic woman's name' (pp 399–400).

1274 Martin, Priscilla. *Chaucer's Women: Nuns, Wives, and Amazons.* Iowa City: U of Iowa P, 1990.

FranT is 'perhaps the most ambiguous' of *CT;* rather than ending a debate, it 'begins with a "solution" and ends with a question' (p 123). Arveragus initially has difficulty combining the various roles he is required to play; in sending Dorigen to Aurelius at the story's conclusion, he simultaneously relinquishes and asserts power over his wife. Dorigen's enactment of the role of the faithful wife in her encounter with Aurelius is compromised by her wish to be 'nice … as if Daunger had briefly assumed the guise of Fair Welcome' (pp 125–6). Aurelius, introduced as the ideal servant of Venus, is degraded by his love; his speech to Dorigen announcing the rocks' disappearance is 'a thoroughly slimy performance,' alternating between 'a smooth courtly surface and a threatening ultimatum' (p 126). The tale avoids the absolutes of tragedy for the 'fluidities of romance or the deflations of comedy' (p 129); the poem's compromises display an element of common sense, a reflection of the Franklin's character and social status.

• Review by Joerg O. Fichte, *Anglia* 109 (1991), 194–7: Martin's treatment of the relation of teller and tale (e.g., her view of *FranT* as a direct reflection of the Franklin's character) is insufficiently attentive to recent work on Chaucer's narrative strategies.

1275 Wicher, Andrzej. 'A Discussion of the Archetype of the Supernatural Husband and the Supernatural Wife as It Appears in some of Geoffrey Chaucer's *Canterbury Tales.*' 1990. See **647**.

FranT may be read as a truncated version of the folktale of the Supernatural Husband (e.g., 'Cupid and Psyche'); the heroine's transgression is forgiven, and her punishment forestalled by *gentilesse* and *fredom,* which consist in part in 'a refusal to act on the spur of the moment or comply with the logic of the immediate circumstances' (p 46). The three male characters represent 'three avatars of the supernatural husband' (p 47), transformed by the rationalistic spirit of the tale, in which Dorigen's misfortunes appear to be engineered by fate rather than anyone's devilish malice. In contrast to characters in the *Märchen* tradition, the main actors of *FranT* are 'unaccomplished and halfhearted,' a reflection of the critical analysis of and gradual abandonment of the 'superlative' style and dogma of the folktale in *CT* (p 49).

1276 Brown, Peter, and Andrew Butcher. *The Age of Saturn: Literature and History in the Canterbury Tales*. 1991. See **649**.

The Franklin's seemingly ironic reply to the Squire's speech veils a desire to emulate the young aristocrat's fine words; the Franklin 'aspires to that very rank from which, by birth, he is excluded' (p 75). This mixed response foreshadows the Franklin's ambivalent attitude toward rhetoric in his tale. The tale's most ornate rhetoric is given to Dorigen and Aurelius, the major aristocratic protagonists. Their bravura complaints are 'empty breath, fanciful attempts to conjure a desired end result out of nothing but the power of words' (p 78). Likewise, Aurelius's wooing speeches are almost comic in their formulaic predictability. Just as the Franklin undercuts the false rhetoric of aristocratic role-playing, he exposes the esoteric language of the world of learning, even as he demonstrates his knowledge of and a hint of admiration for the clerk's astrological jargon. The alternative to courtly and learned rhetoric is the plain style of Arveragus, whose authority lies not in his words, but in himself. Arveragus begins from a social position inferior to that of his wife, but establishes his claim to moral superiority through his actions. The tale can thus be read as a consolation to that kind of man (e.g., the Franklin) marginalized by his place in the social hierarchy. The Franklin contrasts the courtly world's unreality with a 'real' world in which suffering is a necessity and actions often speak louder than words. He frames the make-believe world of the romance with the 'honesty to truth' world of Arveragus (p 90). *FranT* is a romance that is not allowed to happen; the critique of aristocratic values achieved through rhetoric is thus supplemented with a critique of such attitudes achieved through genre. The tale is a study of the *mentalité* of two members of the nobility who have lost their sense of reality within their enclosed world. Dorigen projects her anxieties into the visual world (she encounters the rocks 'as if meeting ... an alter ego'); the meaning of experience is for her a construct generated by attitudes characteristic of the noble classes (p 95). Dorigen's susceptibility to *impressiouns* is paralleled by Aurelius's suggestibility to magical illusions. The tale's magic lies in the mind of the beholder, figuring forth Aurelius's heart's desire in evanescent courtly images. Lines 761–98 explore the wider implications of the marriage of Dorigen and Arveragus. The passage's culminating language of paradox points to the complexity and the fragility of the marriage arrangement; it is a 'humble ... accord' more for Arveragus than for Dorigen, and a *wys* arrangement for Dorigen, who keeps the continued service of a lover-husband and a husband who is lord in name only. The deliberate parallelism between the story of the falcon in *SqT* and the story of Arveragus in *FranT* sets two views of social and political order against each other. For the Squire, right order implies the hierarchical separation of the nobility from the lower orders (the crisis is precipitated by the seduction of the tercelet by the newfangled kite); for the Franklin, right order is established not by blood or traditional rank, but by inherent *gentilesse*. Yet the Franklin launches his alternative vision from within the ethical codes of aristocratic society. Arveragus's anguish in sending Dorigen to fulfill her promise tells us that, having achieved the public social status that he sought, Arveragus now faces private shame; his tears manifest 'the painful duality which the aristocratic system' (p 113) imposes on husband and wife for the unconventional nature of their marriage.

• Review by P.R. Cross, *L&H* (3rd ser.) 2 (1993), 87–9: In a 'masterly' (p 88) chapter on *SqT* and *FranT*, the authors explore the relation between the text's ambivalences and the phenomenon of upward social mobility. But they are perhaps too willing to equate the Franklin's voice and social position with Chaucer's own.

1277 Buffoni, Franco. *I racconti di Canterbury: un'opera unitaria.* Milan: Guerini, 1991.

Chaucer treats the clerk's astrology seriously; as a result of his activities, the rocks are invisible to sight. From the clerk's point of view, the event is produced by *magik* (line 1295); from Aurelius's perspective, it is 'this myracle' (line 1299) (p 134).

1278 Dane, Joseph A. 'Double Truth in Chaucer's *Franklin's Tale*.' *SN* 63 (1991), 161–7.

In late ME, *trouthe* had two potentially contradictory meanings: (1) fidelity (cf. ModE *troth*) and (2) factuality (cf. ModE *truth*). A third sense – 'linguistic truth' – mediates this double meaning. The interpretive issues that surround Arveragus's 'Trouthe is the hyeste thyng that man may kepe' (line 1479) depend upon these multiple meanings: 'Truth is the highest thing' refers to sense 2, but to talk of 'keeping' truth invokes sense 1. Dorigen's trust in personal relations prevents her from ascertaining whether the rocks have really disappeared (truth as factuality) or whether Aurelius's statement that they have disappeared (linguistic truth) is correct. *FranT* depends 'not only on ignorance of facts ... but on ignorance of the way language works in relation to those facts' (p 164). Dorigen intends her statement that she will love Aurelius best when the rocks disappear as a rejection. 'But so locked is she in archaic *trouthe* (fidelity), she can neither grasp linguistic truth (what she means) nor even factual truth (what is the case with those rocks)' (p 164).

1279 Donnelly, Colleen. 'Silence or Shame: How Women's Speech Contributes to Generic Conventionality and Generic Complexity in *The Canterbury Tales*.' *Lang&S* 24 (1991), 433–43.

Dorigen's words show how women's speech can be potentially dangerous to social order and romance conventions. If she were made to keep her promise to Aurelius and cuckold her husband, romance would become fabliau. Her dilemma illustrates what can happen when women's language is not carefully monitored. Her words create the problem, which is avoided only through the kindness of men.

1280 Elliott, Ralph V.W. 'Chaucer's Landscapes: Language and Style.' In *Language and Style in English Literature: Essays in Honour of Michio Masui*. Ed. Michio Kawai. Tokyo: Eihosha, 1991. Pp 74–95.
The rocky coast of Brittany in *FranT* is a rare Chaucerian example of a natural scene drawn from what may have been first-hand observation. The Franklin's winter vignette, a 'homely Dutch interior' (p 92), anticipates the concluding song in Shakespeare's *Love's Labours Lost*.

1281 Fyler, John M. 'Man, Men, and Women in Chaucer's Poetry.' In *The Olde Daunce: Love, Friendship, Sex, and Marriage in the Medieval World*. 1991. See **652**.
Dorigen's list of virtuous women in her situation who chose to kill themselves, drawn from St Jerome's antifeminist *Jov*, has the effect of 'an unconvincing recital of rote knowledge'; a simple inversion of Jankyn's Book of Wicked Wives in *WBP*, also much indebted to Jerome, the list suggests that for Chaucer 'antifeminism and an unworldly standard of female virtue are opposite sides of the same coin' (pp 164–5).

1282 Gaylord, Alan. 'From Dorigen to the Vavasour: Reading Backwards.' In *The Olde Daunce: Love, Friendship, Sex, and Marriage in the Medieval World*. 1991. See **652**. Pp 177–200.
FranT invites two complementary kinds of reading: '"reading forwards"' – 'unscrolling a text as if it were being … listened to' – and '"reading backwards"' – an 'activity of resistance' (p 179). Read forwards, lines 1537–52 focus attention on what happens next; individual characters and voices (including the Franklin's) are subordinated to narrative momentum. In contrast, lines 1490–1502 encourage us to read backwards, calling attention to the Franklin at work behind the scenes, and generating comparisons and reflections; it 'turns us into readers more than listeners' (p 183). Read forwards, Dorigen's lament over the rocks is emotional rather than intellectual in its impact, producing sympathy with the speaker's plight. Read backwards, the passage points beyond the character of Dorigen and puts us in touch with 'the vavasorial temper,' which 'gesture[s] toward philosophy on the way to comforts untested by … true pain' (p 188). For a backwards-reading critic, the account of Dorigen and Arveragus's marriage agreement (lines 792–805) offers 'a warm feeling, at best,' a version of *gentilesse* that can be renamed 'gentleniceness' (p 193). The rhetorical play in *FranP* encourages the audience to feel included in the game. But the Franklin 'plays to win'; his aim is 'total control,' and we respond to our loss of readerly freedom by 'de-authoriz[ing] the Franklin' (p 196). A backwards reading interrogates the gaps in the Franklin's self-presentation and the questions raised by the *GP* portrait, especially the implications of *vavasour* (I.360), which makes us examine the Franklin's relation to Chaucer, and to ourselves as 'citizens of

the New World' (p 198). 'The vavasorial vision of life asks for credit on the basis of a smile and a shoeshine,' an 'insupportable fiction of prosperity' encouraged by too exclusively forwards reading (p 200).

1283 Hill, John M. *Chaucerian Belief: The Poetics of Reverence and Delight*. 1991. See **654**.
The role of feeling in *FranT* has been underestimated. The Franklin's marvels are not magical toys, but rather involve noble sympathies and feelings. Feeling, in the form of *pitee, pacience,* and, especially, *suffraunce,* is central to Dorigen and Arveragus's contract; the latter is 'the central wit of their marriage, setting all else into motion' (p 88). Commentators have been needlessly hard on Aurelius, whose actions must be viewed in the context of his extreme despair; he insists that Dorigen keep her word 'out of ... pain and wretchedness, not out of a devotion to sexual gratification' (p 90). And when, in the tale's penultimate scene, he sees her misery, 'feeling triumphs,' moving the squire to wonder, compassion, and a change of heart (p 91).
• Review by Edward E. Foster, *PhilosLit* 15 (1995), 367–8: see **654r**.
• Review by Dolores Warwick Frese, *CY* 2 (1995), 172–9: see **654r**.

1284 Kanno, Masahiko. 'The Franklin's Tale: Transformation of Aurelius.' In *Language and Style in English Literature: Essays in Honour of Michio Masui*. 1991. See **1280**. Pp 306–21. Repr. in Kanno, *Studies in Chaucer's Words: A Contextual and Semantic Approach*. [Tokyo]: Eihōsha, 1996. Pp 70–84.
Employing a variety of rhetorical devices (e.g., *polyptoton, metonymy, traductio*), *FranT* foregrounds moral terms (e.g., *gentil, fre, vertu, trouthe*) and their derivatives. As the tale moves from the world of *fantasye* to the world of *trouthe*, Aurelius – who in the first half of the tale is devoid of generosity but able to insist on his rights – is transformed into a *gentil* squire who enacts the virtue of *franchise* in freeing Dorigen from her obligation to him. See **1145**.

1285 Kolve, V.A. 'Rocky Shores and Pleasure Gardens: Poetry vs. Magic in Chaucer's *Franklin's Tale*.' In *Poetics: Theory and Practice in Medieval English Literature*. 1990. See **1263**. Pp 165–95. Repr. in Kolve, *Telling Images: Chaucer and the Imagery of Narrative II*. Stanford, CA: Stanford UP, 2009. Pp 171–98.
FranT's narrative moves through, and its meaning depends on, three major places: the rocks, the garden, and the clerk's study. Although they are made to stand for something by the despairing Dorigen, 'the rocks must be seen as no more than rocks' (p 169n). The artful pleasure garden is set in 'binary opposition' to the rocks: 'what one includes the other excludes, and vice versa' (p 172). The book-lined study is the locus of '*real* illusion' (p 185), a space where, through magic of some sort, Aurelius is deceived into believing that his desires can be fulfilled. (In contrast, the *apparences* created by the *tregetoures* delight their audiences by means of mime and mechanical devices.) It is against the learned clerk's magic that Chaucer sets his own art. Unlike the clerk, who produces for Aurelius the dangerous illusion of 'a world without

moral consequence' (p 191), Chaucer includes within his own tale both rocks and garden – the extremes of unmitigated despair and pure pleasure – to 'express a dialectical truth, setting the two side by side, in appropriate scale and balance' (p 193). Despite the apparent similarities of the two arts, poetic fiction finally can be distinguished by its 'truth-telling potential' (p 195) from other sorts of magic and illusion.

• Review of *Telling Images* by Alcuin Blamires, *JEGP* 110 (2011), 407–9: Kolve 'develops a whole nuanced statement of Chaucerian "poetics" from his meditation on garden, rocks, and the clerk-magician's production of illusions among books in The Franklin's Tale' (p 408).

1286 Lucas, Angela M., and Peter J. Lucas. 'The Presentation of Marriage and Love in Chaucer's *Franklin's Tale.*' *ES* 72 (1991), 501–2.

A close examination of Dorigen and Arveragus's marriage agreement reveals it to be 'muddled in conception [and] adopted for inappropriate reasons' (p 512). The pilgrim narrator's credibility as a spokesman for marriage is undermined by the marriage's secrecy, the husband's foregoing of *maistrye* in a Christian union, the misapplication of medieval doctrines of patience, and the unconvincing attempt to reconcile Christian marriage with *amour courtois*. The Franklin's misuse of proverbial material and the original contexts of his allusions to Ovid and *RR* show him making 'statements which belie true knowledge of the authorities he refers to' (p 506). Difficulties inevitably arise when the Franklin's version of marriage is put to the test; 'Dorigen and Arveragus are trapped not by their love but by the way their love is presented' (p 512). See **1359**.

1287 Lucas, Peter J. 'The Setting in Brittany of Chaucer's *Franklin's Tale.*' *PoeticaT* 33 (1991), 19–29.

FranT's setting in Brittany, although visually vivid, is (in part) topographically inaccurate; *Kayrrud* (line 808) and *Armorik* (line 729) are archaic forms; Arveragus's departure from Brittany to England to seek chivalric adventures reverses romance convention and would have seemed laughable to an English audience. The inconsistencies and inaccuracies in the Franklin's treatment of Brittany tell us something about his character – his willingness to play with familiar facts in order to impress, and his old-fashioned and provincial tastes.

1288 Mann, Jill. *Geoffrey Chaucer*. 1991. See **656**.

See **1450**.

• Review by Derek S. Brewer, *MÆ* 61 (1992), 320–1: In Mann's sympathetic and insightful discussion, Dorigen's plight and the tale itself 'are rightly taken to be without irony' (p 320).

• Review by Susan K. Hagen, *SAC* 14 (1992), 177–80: In Mann's reading of the denouement of *FranT*, 'the female-identified virtue of patience replaces the more conventional male regard for "trouthe" as the motivator of Arveragus's actions' (p 178). But these actions are still troubling, especially in light of the narrator's own insistence that 'patience sometimes means not being avenged on ... people who speak amiss' (pp 178–9).

• Review by Valerie Allen, *RES* n.s. 44 (1993), 405–6: Mann argues that 'Chaucer celebrates an ideal married love in terms of a mutuality that takes some of the sting out of the external structures of gendered oppression' (p 405). Her interpretation of *FranT* in the light of this thesis convinces in its own terms, but it fails to answer the questions raised by the Marxist–feminist criticism of ideology.

• Review by Joerg O. Fichte, *Anglia* 112 (1994), 175–7: Mann's view of the marriage in *FranT* as an ideal partnership is contradicted by Arveragus's exercise of mastery in the poem's penultimate scene. It is inaccurate to speak of 'Arveragus's *non*-coerciveness'; salvation for this marriage comes from Aurelius's pity for Dorigen's plight.

1289 Noji, Kaoru. 'A Reading of Chaucer's *Franklin's Tale*: The Different Understanding of "trouthe" in Ideal Marriage.' *BYWJC* 3 (1991), 245–62.
FranT reveals gaps between the intents of the poet and the pilgrim narrator, and between Dorigen's and Arveragus's understanding of *trouthe*. For Dorigen, *trouthe* means loyalty in conjugal love; for Arveragus, it means the public aspect of keeping a covenant. Behind the ideal marriage described by the Franklin lies a 'natural difference of attitude between a husband and a wife' that is implicitly recognized by Chaucer (p 259).

1290 Patterson, Lee. *Chaucer and the Subject of History*. 1991. See **659**.
Arveragus's invocation of the sacredness of *trouthe* echoes a familiar chivalric sentiment, but emphasizes personal integrity rather than public honor (p 196). In promoting the aristocratic virtue of *gentilesse* from a position outside a specific social location, the Franklin, like the Wife of Bath, gives voice to the bourgeois belief that true value and true selves are not socially determined (p 324).

1291 Seaman, David M. '"As thynketh you": Conflicting Evidence and the Interpretation of *The Franklin's Tale*.' *M&H* 17 (1991), 41–58.
Our response to the Franklin's concluding question, and to the issues raised in *FranT* more generally, is dictated not by the text alone, but also by our own expectations and desires. Decisions about the tale cannot be made by invoking the personality of the teller; the narrative voice is more often generic than individual. The narration mixes modes and value systems; the tale's promises are rendered ambiguous through qualifying clauses and by the availability of conflicting contexts (e.g., Church doctrine, legal theory, common sense, the generic expectations of romance) that produce differing interpretations. The text provides support for two contrary positions on Arveragus's command to Dorigen, and embeds her *trouthe*-keeping in a paradox: in keeping the *trouthe* of her promise to Aurelius, she would be break-

ing the *trouthe* of her marriage vow. The final question about *fredom* is not an inevitable one, nor does it imply a single answer; in gesturing towards the decision-making process itself rather than the comparative generosity of the characters, its second clause – 'as thynketh yow'(line 1622) – is the more important to the operation of *FranT*.

1292 Sturges, Robert S. *Medieval Interpretation: Models of Reading in Literary Narrative, 1100–1500.* Carbondale: Southern Illinois Press, 1991.
The concluding question in *FranT* invites a multiplicity of interpretations; any view that the reader supplies can be supplemented or contradicted by others (pp 174–5).

1293 Taylor, Paul Beekman. 'The Uncourteous Knights of *The Canterbury Tales*.' *ES* 72 (1991), 209–18.
FranT parodies *KnT*'s concern with order. Whereas Theseus binds together the cosmic and the human, the Franklin's plot proceeds by 'a succession of untyings' (p 212): Arveragus surrenders his natural superiority over his wife in all matters except public posture, and releases her from a sacred marital contract to honor a frivolous promise. In contrast to Theseus's revelation of a universe governed by providential design, the characters in *FranT* are returned to order by 'gratuitous and contingent repudiations of bonds' (p 213).

1294 Wimsatt, James I. *Chaucer and His French Contemporaries: Natural Music in the Fourteenth Century.* 1991. See **661**.
The Franklin's comment on the accord between Dorigen and Arveragus, where neither assumes *maistrye,* is paralleled in Machaut's *Remède de Fortune,* where the lady lectures Amant on mastery. The language associated with Aurelius and his love for Dorigen also echoes the Middle French lyric tradition. One of Chaucer's last significant reflections on French court poetry, *FranT* presents it as a medium suitable for depicting lovers of the gentle class (pp 171–2).

1295 ———. 'Reason, Machaut, and the Franklin.' In *The Olde Daunce: Love, Friendship, Sex, and Marriage in the Medieval World*. 1991. See **652**. Pp 201–10.
The Franklin's view of marriage as a partnership of *freendes* (line 762) has been criticized as inappropriate to a medieval marital situation, in which the husband should maintain lordship. Yet ancient and medieval commentaries on friendship – Cicero's *De amicitia,* Aelred of Rievaulx's *De spirituali amicitia,* and Reason's speech in *RR* – provide a precedent for representing the marital relationship as friendship and for Dorigen and Arveragus treating each other as equals. In Machaut's *Remède de Fortune,* moreover, friendship between the sexes is possible both in courtship and in marriage. Although his tale does not represent the ideal answer to the marriage problem, the Franklin's beliefs on the incompatibility of love and *maistrye* agree with 'the greatest medieval authorities on friendship and marriage, and certainly ap-

peals to common sense' (p 210).

1296 Blake, N.F. 'The Literary Language.' In *The Cambridge History of the English Language.* Vol. 2, *1066–1476.* Ed. Norman Blake. Cambridge: Cambridge UP, 1992. Pp 500–40.

In *FranT*, the polite *you* form is used by all the aristocratic characters among themselves. The clerk's use of *thou* in his final speech to Aurelius may indicate his social status; although he behaves magnanimously in waiving his fee, his speech reveals him to be of a different class.

1297 Brown, Carole Koepke. '"It Is True Art to Conceal Art": The Episodic Structure of Chaucer's *Franklin's Tale.*' *ChauR* 27 (1992), 162–85.

FranT is structured by an 'alternating parallelism' consisting of a thrice-repeated triad (ABC) in which 'A stands for a major *trouthe,* B for a major *complainte,* and C for the help a compassionate character gives to a destitute character' (p 165). The tale's nine major episodes are linked by 'the cohesive logic of a causal progression' (p 166). In omitting the episodes featuring magic from this alternating parallelism, Chaucer directs the reader's attention to human response rather than supernatural machinery as the moving force in the tale. The orderly pattern of three-times-three heightens the poem's Boethian emphasis on a benign providence that governs cosmic and human affairs. While the three *trouthe*s and the three complaints form descending patterns (the former from a marriage covenant to a promise in play to a business transaction; the latter addressed to God, to planets, and to Fortune), the three 'compassionate helper' episodes increase in complexity and intensity, culminating in the *gentil* act of Arveragus that brings the narrative of *gentilesse* to closure.

1298 Collette, Carolyn. 'Seeing and Believing in the *Franklin's Tale.*' *ChauR* 26 (1992), 395–410.

FranT's stress on seeing and believing, manifested in a sustained pattern of sight imagery, may be understood in the light of late-medieval discussions of optics, faculty psychology, and magic. Things seen were thought to impress images or *phantasms* on the brain; the human will was responsible for making use of these images for good or ill. Dorigen's 'derke fantasye' (line 844) about the rocks demonstrates how images produced by sense experience may multiply and become dangerous when not controlled. Dorigen's will, weakened by her separation from her husband, fails to relegate the *phantasms* to their proper place in the cosmos. Her long rehearsal of classical women who chose death before dishonor is also a result of her disordered will working upon *phantasms* produced in the brain by reading or hearing. Failures of the will and the sense of sight help to explain the tale's ambiguity about whether the rocks are truly gone or only seem to be gone; observers subject to weaknesses of perception and judgment might mistakenly attribute naturally occurring events to necromancy and astrological magic.

1299 Hagstrum, Jean H. *Esteem Enlivened by Desire: The Couple from Homer to Shakespeare.* Chicago: U of Chicago P, 1992.
The Franklin begins his tale with a lofty ideal of marriage that is then modified and darkened by reality; magic and naïveté of mind and character are summoned, with scant conviction, to untie the knotty problems that reality poses (pp 268–9).

1300 Hansen, Elaine Tuttle. *Chaucer and the Fictions of Gender*. 1992. See **662**.
The Franklin responds to *MerT* and *SqT* by attempting to restore proper gender difference and by offering a more positive ideal of proper masculinity. The Franklin and Dorigen share a marginal status, but the tale's feminized narrator is identified with male interests. In the first half of the narrative, Dorigen is shown to have 'dangerous and storyworthy powers' (p 272) in the intensity of her devotion to the absent Arveragus, in her questioning of God's wisdom, and particularly in her complex response to Aurelius's importunities, all of which demonstrate the 'implicit dangers of ungoverned female subjectivity and sexuality' (p 273). Dorigen's promise to Aurelius to love him best asserts her right to control her own body and her own word, it threatens Arveragus by revealing similarities with his young rival, it threatens Aurelius by making light of his passions, and it imperils class and gender distinctions. Dorigen's cancellation of her promise (lines 1003–5) is even more troubling; in implying that Aurelius's real pleasure is in challenging and supplanting his male rival, she reveals the homosocial subtext beneath the courtly scenario that 'turns out to be the gist of the tale as a whole' (p 276). For her overt statement of the covert rules of the courtly game, Dorigen must be contained and punished. The rocks, which 'may be taken as … an objective correlative of masculine fantasies about the monstrosity of female sexuality' (p 277), are made to seem an illusion, a feat that returns Dorigen to her proper feminine position: paralyzed, and in need of the corrective guidance of husband and lover. Because both husband and lover are generous, the possibility of violence against women – raised in Dorigen's Complaint and in Arveragus's response to Dorigen's confession (lines 1481–3) – is threatened but averted. At the tale's end, the dangers of traffic in women are safely sidestepped as male virtue asserts the *gentil* idea of keeping one's word.

1301 Haruta, Setsuko. 'Chaucer and "Courtly Love."' In *Kotoba to Bungaku to Bunka to: Ando Sadao Hakushi Taikan Kinen Ronbunshu* [Language, literature, and culture: essays to honor Sadao Ando]. Ed. Masachiyo Amano et al. Tokyo: Eicho-sha Shiusha, 1992. Pp 305–14.
Courtly love is 'misunderstood, distorted, and vulgarized' by the non-aristocratic Franklin (p 311). In the marriage agreement of Dorigen and Arveragus, a chivalric love relationship is subjected to 'bourgeois *bon sens*,' the *trouthe* invoked by Arveragus in sending his wife to Aurelius amounts to

'keeping a business contract,' and the lady's love is finally made equivalent to a thousand pounds of gold (pp 310–11).

1302 Lee, Brian S. 'The Question of Closure in Fragment V of *The Canterbury Tales*.' 1992.
See **663**.

1303 Mandel, Jerome. *Geoffrey Chaucer: Building the Fragments of the Canterbury Tales*. 1992. See **664**.
Alone among the *CT* fragments, Fragment V contains two thoroughly pagan tales. Among the themes that contribute to the fragment's unity are dance (linked in both tales with dangerous deception), references to death and wounds, astrology (associated with magic and the marvelous), and illusion (the disappearance of the rocks in *FranT*; the four gifts and the deceptive tercelet in *SqT*). Several themes unify the tales by contrast: troth (with the exception of the tercelet's vow, pledges are honored in *SqT*; in *FranT*, none of the promises is fulfilled) and *gentilesse* (in Part 2 of *SqT*, connected with courtly love and a 'façade for disillusion' [p 100]; in *FranT*, a mark of nobility and generosity). The fundamental structure of Fragment V is chiasmus: *SqT* opens with the giving of gifts to Cambyuskan and ends with the courtly love adventure of the unhappy falcon; *FranT* begins with the courtly love adventure of the unhappy Dorigen and ends with gifts of human generosity that in turn reflect the Christian gifts implicit in the allusion (lines 1243–55) to the Christmas season. The tales' treatment of time is also chiastic: the pagan spring of Cambyuskan's birthday at the beginning of *SqT* (lines 47–57) balances the Christian winter of the Nativity near the conclusion of *FranT* (lines 1243–55). Characterization provides a final means of unity: the tercelet in *SqT* shares traits with Aurelius and Arveragus, while Dorigen and the falcon are drawn together by contrast (compared to Canacee, who represents a norm for womanly behavior, the falcon is shown to be more *mesurable* than the heroine of *FranT*).
• Review by Vincent DiMarco, *Speculum* 69 (1994), 831–3: Mandel's discovery of a chiasmic relationship between *SqT* and *FranT* places structure at cross-purposes with theme, reversing the pattern of deterioration and decay for which Mandel has argued (p 833).
• Review by Peter Robinson, *N&Q* n.s. 41 (1994), 90: 'To read *FranT* purely in relation to *SqT*, … ignoring the links concerning the themes of gentilesse, illusion, marriage, and sovereignty between *FranT* and all the other tales that do not happen to be in the same fragment, is to impoverish our reading.'
• Review by Helen Cooper. 1995. See **664r**.

1304 Martin, Ellen E. 'The Romance of Anxiety in Chaucer's Franklin's Tale.' In *Voices in Translation: The Authority of "Olde Bookes" in Medieval Literature. Essays in Honor of Helaine Newstead*. Ed. Deborah M. Sinnreich-Levi and Gale Sigal. New York: AMS, 1992. Pp 117–36.

FranT undoes the notion of fidelity and intention by generating, in the story's concluding question, an 'interminable debate' over reading the characters; in addition, the characters undo themselves in the course of interpreting themselves or being interpreted by others (p 118). Anxiety over the nonidentical self and the interpretation of figurative texts are parallel manifestations of the gaps in our system of signifieds and signifiers. The story of Arveragus and Dorigen shows how no real sovereignty exists without being attached to some distorting Name of sovereignty (as in Lacan's Name-of-the-Father). Although Dorigen and Arveragus come to recognize that sovereignty is not a desirable possession, the gap reflected in the maturing self is the site of anxiety and desire. The self invests various objects, people, ideas, and actions with its hopes and fears – most powerfully in the coastal rocks, which figure Dorigen's 'intensely ambivalent mix of desire and fear towards her husband and towards herself as a wife' (p 121) and in the 'splitting of the spouse,' the doubling of the hero into Arveragus and Aurelius, and subsequently into Apollo, Aurelius's brother, and the magician (p 125). The anxiety of self-fashioning in the characters belongs as well to the text and our reading of it. 'Anxiety is : to the subject's contrivance of self :: as interpretation is : to the text of fable' (p 133).

1305 Pearsall, Derek. *The Life of Geoffrey Chaucer: A Critical Biography*. 1992. See **665**. *FranT* explores some of the consequences of social change and mobility, embodied in the figure of the Franklin himself. The tale offers a new way of thinking about social relationships, in which conflict is resolved by means of mutual forbearance, not just between the sexes, but also between social classes (pp 246–7). Attractive as it is, however, the ideal of mutual tolerance advanced in the tale is 'deeply compromised by being transferred from a discussion of *amicitia* ... to the discussion of marriage' (p 261). At the end of the story, the husband's power is not relinquished, only suspended; the male values of honor and shame lie behind Arveragus's insistence that Dorigen keep her promise, and the three official competitors for the title of 'mooste fre' (line 1622) are men. Yet Chaucer treats the matter of *gentilesse* playfully in the conundrum that ends the tale, and adds the suggestion that 'the true hero of *gentillesse* is a heroine, that is, Dorigen' (p 151).

1306 Raybin, David. '"Wommen, of kynde, desiren libertee": Rereading Dorigen, Rereading Marriage.' *ChauR* 27 (1992), 65–86.
Although Dorigen is often seen as a passive sufferer, *FranT* insists on her independence and agency. The tale makes an implicit distinction between authority (the structural position that confers status to one's assertions) and power (the actual ability to impose one's will); Dorigen's subservient social position does not prevent her from making decisions that affect herself and those around her. The ambiguities of the speech in which Arveragus releases Dorigen from strict obedience to her marriage vow leaves the choice of

action up to Dorigen; she decides what her husband's words mean. We see Dorigen making independent decisions in her Complaint, challenging patriarchal assumptions about women's place by walking into the 'quykkest strete' (line 1502) and manipulating Aurelius with her half-madness when she meets him on the way to the garden. The tale affirms the need for absolute freedom of choice for both men and women. Dorigen is the 'mooste fre' (line 1622) in a double sense: in her generosity of spirit and in her self-determination.

1307 Richmond, Velma B. *Geoffrey Chaucer*. 1992. See **666**.
FranT's happy ending (which connects it to several of the lays in the Auchinleck MS) is cumulative, 'a kind of great chain of behaving well' (p 76) in which one person's generosity inspires another's. The tale's core values are easy to define, but less easy to embody; illusions constantly threaten the characters' perceptions of reality. In its contrast of extravagant rhetoric and plain speech, the poem's language serves to reinforce its warning against appearances, 'the simple being surer than the grand apostrophes' (p 79).

1308 Saul, Nigel. 'Chaucer and Gentility.' In *Chaucer's England: Literature in Historical Context*. Ed. Barbara A. Hanawalt. Medieval Studies at Minnesota 4. Minneapolis: U of Minnesota P, 1992. Pp 41–55.
Doubtful of his own possession of gentility on grounds of rank or inherited wealth, the Franklin is concerned that his son will squander any chance of acquiring it by his manner of life. In his tale, he demonstrates through Aurelius's release of Dorigen from her promise that gentility is dependent not on birth but on behavior; a humble esquire is as capable of keeping *trouthe* as is a knight.

1309 Straus, Barrie Ruth. '"Truth" and "Woman" in Chaucer's Franklin's Tale.' *Exemplaria* 4 (1992), 135–68.
Although the Franklin's masculinist discourse privileges a notion of truth as constant and attainable and a notion of woman as an object similarly to be possessed and kept separate from the concept 'man,' his words suggest the limitations of this discourse, revealing the interrelatedness of truth, freedom, and woman. The problematic structure of truth is exemplified in *Sq–FranL* and *FranP*: the Franklin's promise to tell his tale is both 'serious and playful' (p 141) shows him both obeying and disobeying the Host; the apparent opposition between rhetoric and his own plain speaking is presented in language that undercuts this opposition. His tale is framed by and frames other impossible promises. The initial promises about sovereignty and marriage present multiple interpretive difficulties: deciding who is obeying whom, decoding key terms, distinguishing between appearance and reality. Dorigen's promise to love Aurelius if he removes the black rocks is 'impossible' not only in the nature of the task, but also in its interpretive puzzles – the mixing of play and seriousness, of rhetoric and

plain speech, and in Dorigen's replacement of the condition that Aurelius remove the rocks in reality with a condition based on perception: that 'ther nys no stoon ysene' (line 996). The homoerotic economy of *FranT* employs women's bodies as the site of masculine exchange. In his response to Dorigen's dilemma, Arveragus seems more concerned with his relationship to other men than with his relation to his wife. His claim that 'Trouthe is the hyeste thyng that man may kepe' (line 1479) 'enjoin[s] Dorigen to act like a man' (p 157). In doing so, Dorigen perpetuates masculine desire and order. Yet she also operates differently from the men in her lack of knowledge of 'appearance' and in her ignorance of clerkly learning. Although masculine learning maintains that appearance and truth are separate, the tale dissolves this binary, suggesting that men as well as women are unable to distinguish between the two. In his claim to speak plainly and eschew eloquence, the Franklin promises a truth beyond appearances. But his words reveal the mutual contamination of the two categories, as well as the rhetorical nature of all language.

1310 Wimsatt, James I. 'The Wife of Bath, the Franklin, and the Rhetoric of St. Jerome.' In *A Wyf Ther Was: Essays in Honour of Paule Mertens-Fonk*. 1992. See **1244**. Pp 275–81.

In contrast to the Wife of Bath, who undermines Jerome's rhetoric about virginity and marriage with her own rhetoric, the Franklin uses dramatic means to call into question the extreme solution found in the examples of female virtue from *Jov* cited by Dorigen in her Complaint. Although Jerome tells Dorigen that death is preferable to loss of chastity, Arveragus (and, by implication, the Franklin) advocates a more moderate course of action. But neither the Wife nor the Franklin is Chaucer's spokesperson; adopting a dialogic mode, the poet allows each voice to speak for itself, encouraging readers to decide for themselves where justice lies.

1311 Barnett, Pamela E. '"And shortly for to seyn they were aton": Chaucer's Deflection of Rape in the *Reeve's* and *Franklin's Tales*.' *WS* 22 (1993), 145–62.

Dorigen and Arveragus's marriage only seems to confer agency on Dorigen; the scenario of 'eroticize[d] dominance and submission' (p 155) implicit in the marriage agreement sets the stage for the possibility of rape when Arveragus sends his wife to Aurelius. The 'absence of pre-copulatory behavior' (p 157) in Dorigen's earlier relations with Aurelius makes clear her distaste for the idea of a sexual encounter. Her refusal is couched in metaphorical language that is not 'univocal, singular, patriarchal' (p 157). But her playful words are nevertheless interpreted literally by Aurelius 'with the intent to coerce' (p 158), although the squire employs the conventions of *fin'amor* to mystify his menacing desires. The trickery of the clerk's magic is of a piece with Aurelius's 'soothing rhetorical maneuvers' (p 158). The tale's conclusion enforces the patriarchal paradigm in which the husband holds his wife as property. The 'mystifying discourse of masculine gift-giving' (p 160) deflects our recognition that Dorigen is an object of exchange; the word *fre* is used mostly in reference to generosity with material goods. The 'remarkable absence' (p 161) of a discussion of rape in *FranT* is proof that the potential rape scenario has been successfully deflected; in its place, the Franklin offers the 'false and ridiculous' (p 161) notion that *trouthe* is the central issue here.

1312 Bleeth, Kenneth A. 'The Rocks and the Garden: The Limits of Illusion in Chaucer's *Franklin's Tale.*' *ES* 74 (1993), 113–23.

Initially, the rocks and the garden are scenes of personal obsession: the rocks both cause and symbolize Dorigen's paralyzing anxieties about her husband's safety, the garden is the setting for Aurelius's courtly fantasies. Dorigen attempts to distance herself from the game of love in her playfully parodic response to Aurelius's amorous rhetoric. But the entrance of magic into the tale intertwines both rocks and garden even more complexly with illusion. Almost from the beginning of the tale, however, the Franklin depicts the limits and the dangers of private obsessions embodying singular desires. Asserting the counterclaims of common sense and mutual understanding, he prepares us for the exorcism of illusion that arises from communicative speech and sympathetic listening in the poem's concluding episode.

1313 Børch, Marianne Novrup. *Chaucer's Poetics: Seeing and Asking*. University of Odense diss. 1993. 2 vols. Published Bagsværd: Eget, 1993.

Chaucer mixes Christian and pagan in *FranT* to explore an analogy between human love and divine grace. Initially, Dorigen and Arveragus are unable to distinguish letter from spirit; they think of love as physical possession. The tale's other characters also fail to understand the spiritual aspect of social relationships. Dorigen's and Aurelius's monologues expose their moral innocence and immaturity. By the end of the tale, however, each of the characters becomes less blinded by a false image of self and learns to separate the spiritual values latent in their social roles from the roles themselves. The tale's events teach the characters to be free, a freedom marked by patience, the ability to dispense with the absolute, and the capacity for change. Dorigen and Arveragus are pagans, but they develop psychologically toward an unillusioned worldview that the Franklin identifies as Christian. In the tale's closing *demande,* the question of 'who' matters less than the nature of freedom itself.

1314 Bowman, Mary R. '"Half as she were mad": Dorigen in the Male World of the *Franklin's Tale.*' *ChauR* 27 (1993), 239–51.

Dorigen's agency and subjectivity are subordinated to the values of the male characters and the male narrator. Yet it is possible, by reading against the grain of the narrative, to elicit Dorigen's feelings and motivations. For the men in *FranT,* public virtues take precedence over personal relationships.

To Dorigen, however, the values cherished by the male characters 'either are meaningless or bear a different interpretation' (p 246); the ideal of *trouthe* embodied in Arveragus's sending Dorigen to Aurelius is for Dorigen inadequate compensation for an act of marital unfaithfulness. It is in her expressions of grief that Dorigen is able to shape a self within the tale's male discourse; in her Complaint and her lament over the rocks, the meanings of male-authored texts (*Jov* and *Consol*) change when they are spoken in a different voice. The two laments exemplify the 'bi-valent quality of Dorigen's representation' (p 250), as 'a passive figure in a male-dominated world and a speaking subject with an identity of her own' (p 244).

1315 Dillon, Janette. *Geoffrey Chaucer*. New York: St Martin's, 1993.
The behavior of Chaucer's knights is often open to doubt. Arveragus's two-year disappearance to pursue military honor exposes his wife to the attentions of an unwelcome suitor. He invokes *trouthe* in insisting that she keep her promise to Aurelius, but his application of this knightly principle is grounded upon tyranny and deceit. The tale smooths over the cracks opened up by Arveragus's behavior, but its aura of fairy tale leaves hanging questions of how knights and ladies should behave and whether their ideals are viable ones (pp 52–3).

1316 Goodman, Jennifer R. 'Dorigen and the Falcon: The Element of Despair in Chaucer's *Squire's* and *Franklin's Tales*.' In *Representations of the Feminine in the Middle Ages*. 1993. See **668**.
See **668**.

1317 Green, Joe. 'Chaucer's Genial Franklin.' *PVR* 21 (Winter 1993), 6–16.
GP, *Sq–FranL*, and *FranP* show the Franklin to be an uncritical idealist, obsessed with maintaining appearances. In his tale, his shallowness takes the form of a superficial understanding of *gentilesse* and a belief in the power of illusion to bring happiness.

1318 Hallissy, Margaret. *Clean Maids, True Wives, Steadfast Widows: Chaucer's Women and Medieval Codes of Conduct.* Westport, CT; London: Greenwood, 1993.
FranT represents men and women as equally capable of all virtues. In his marriage contract, Arveragus honors the notion of a woman's independent will. Although the freedom Dorigen enjoys is not absolute, their marriage begins as a relationship of equals. At the moment of crisis, however, Dorigen reverts to the traditional model for women's behavior. She sees her alternatives either as death or dishonor; in turning to Arveragus for counsel, she may be viewed as shifting the responsibility for a decision onto him, in keeping with the conventional hierarchical formula. Yet she is also asking him to act like the partner he had promised to be. Arveragus's intervention in his wife's decision has been read both as a violation of Dorigen's freedom and a tribute to her integrity. Although both of these arguments make valid points, Arveragus has nevertheless achieved a redefinition of virtue: 'he has

encouraged his wife to demonstrate a "male" virtue, *trouthe,* and has himself practiced a "female" virtue, self-sacrifice and abnegation' (p 40). Such 'innovative behavior' (p 40) decisively breaks down the 'simple binary moral categories' (p 35) that governed the traditional paradigm for marriage in the Middle Ages.

1319 Kim, Jae-Hwan. 'Chaucer's View of Marriage: Centered on the "Franklin's Tale."' *MESt* 1 (1993), 77–93.
Through the tale Chaucer tries to show that the vision of an idealistic marriage cannot be realized without dialectical processes between the present and the idealistic perspective. (Not seen. Summary from http://hompi.sogang.ac.kr/anthony/mesak/Chbiblio.htm. In Korean.)

1320 Lionarons, Joyce Tally. 'Magic, Machines, and Deception: Technology in the *Canterbury Tales.*' 1993. See **669**.
The Franklin never reveals exactly how the clerk creates the illusion of the rocks' disappearance, but the tale hints (e.g., in the description of the entertainments staged by the *tregetoures*) that his magic may be mechanical rather than supernatural. The clerk's skills, moreover, are employed to bring about 'an unnatural and immoral state of affairs' (p 382); like *SqT, FranT* reveals a distrust of technology that involves esoteric knowledge and can therefore be used to fool the uninitiated.

1321 Mertens-Fonck, Paule. 'Le Franklin et la doctrine d'Epicure dans les *Contes de Canterbury.*' In *Etudes de linguistique et de littérature en l'honneur d'André Crépin.* Ed. Danielle Buschinger and Wolfgang Spiewok. Griefswald: Reineke, 1993. Pp 273–80.
The portrait of the Franklin in *GP* reveals him as a true disciple of Epicurus, for whom pleasure – the absence of physical suffering and moral perturbation – is the highest good. The doctrines of Epicurus are on display in the Franklin's disdain of rhetoric and in several of his tale's thematic strands: the preference for *quiete* and *reste* (line 760) over movement and adventure, the association of the sea with moral turbulence, the courtly garden as an antitype of Epicurus's garden of wisdom, Dorigen's shock at the modification of natural processes in the disappearance of the rocks, and in her avoidance of suicide. In the tale's final scene, courtly perspectives give way to a humanist doctrine that rejects illusion in favor of a wisdom that examines the true conditions of human happiness.

1322 Morse, Ruth. 'Absolute Tragedy: Allusions and Avoidances.' *PoeticaT* 38 (1993), 1–17.
We respond to Dorigen's indecision in the final lines of her lament over the rocks by 'sympathiz[ing] with her while feeling slightly her superior'; her concern for her husband's safety disarms any criticism for her failure to pursue her argument to its logical conclusion (p 15).

1323 Penninger, Frieda Elaine. *Chaucer's Troilus and Criseyde and The Knight's Tale:*

Fictions Used. Lanham, MD: UP of America, 1993.
In asking which of the three men in his tale was 'the mooste fre' (line 1622), the Franklin fails to point out that 'they all make free with the wife, who … is not free' (p 78).

1324 Petty, George R., Jr. 'Power, Deceit, and Misinterpretation: Uncooperative Speech in the *Canterbury Tales.*' *ChauR* 27 (1993), 413–23.
Aurelius's wooing of Dorigen is based on a series of 'performative misinterpretations' (p 415) in which he deliberately misconstrues the intent of her words and sets a linguistic trap from which she is not linguistically sophisticated enough to escape. Arveragus also avails himself of linguistic misconstruction when, in line 1479, he interprets the 'troth' that Dorigen has pledged 'not in the courtly love context but in a larger ethical context,' thus forcing Aurelius to contend with a 'textual repertoire' different from the one he had originally intended (p 416).

1325 Wheeler, Bonnie. '*Trouthe* Without Consequences: Rhetoric and Gender in Chaucer's *Franklin's Tale.*' In *Representations of the Feminine in the Middle Ages.* 1993. See **668**. Pp 91–116.
Metonymy – suggesting rather than defining causal relationships – creates fissures that are a defining feature of *FranT*. Such gaps threaten to disclose presumptions that privilege dominant class and gender systems, unmasking chivalric romance as an encoding of sexual exploitation and mapping the stress of economic and class competition in the tale's courtly world. In embellishing his tale with the colors of rhetoric, the Franklin overlays the story with metonymic decoration, producing 'chains of discrete narrative sequences [that] resist intellectually persuasive coherence' (p 98). The opening disquisition on marriage and patience, for example, may be read as a 'disorderly metonymic mélange' in which Dorigen is required to enact a 'logical lie' which the Franklin labels as a 'happy paradox' (pp 99–100). The Franklin's rhetoric evokes both sympathy for and distance from Dorigen's misery after Arveragus's departure; she is depicted as both rational and hysterical. Each of Dorigen's three replies to Aurelius's entreaties engages a distinct rhetoric – the rhetoric of contracts (lines 980–7); the rhetoric of chivalric love (lines 989–98); and in the third reply (lines 1000–5), a 'crude and uncourtly question' that enables her to say 'no' uncategorically only by moving beyond the first two rhetorical frames permitted by her class, her gender, and her husband (p 107). Arveragus's reported reflections on Dorigen's behavior in his absence (lines 1094–7) – the most overlooked piece of the tale's metonymic narrative – represent our sole access to Arveragus's inner thoughts, even as they sustain several contradictory interpretations. In promising to love Aurelius 'best of any man' (line 997) if he removes the coastal rocks, Dorigen would seem to be pledging 'the movement of her heart' (p 112). But she does not love Aurelius better than she loves her hus-

band, hence her *trouthe*-plighting implicitly reduces idealized love to the act of physical possession. The effect of this exchange is 'a thorough dissection of *fin'amors*' (p 114) in which textual slippages metonymically expose the Franklin's 'failure to recognize a spiritual ground to romantic love' (p 116). On a metatextual level, Chaucer's reluctance to derive coherent *sentence* from his tale 'problematizes ideas of art's *solaas*' (p 116).

1326 Arnovick, Leslie K. 'Dorigen's Promise and Scholar's Premise: The Orality of the Speech Act in the *Franklin's Tale*.' In *Oral Poetics in Middle English Poetry*. Ed. Mark C. Amodio. New York: Garland, 1994. Pp 125–47.
Linguistic, legal, and folkloric contexts inform the orality of Dorigen's garden conversation with Aurelius and produce the interpretive tensions within it. As a speech act, Dorigen's discourse – taken in its entirety – constitutes a rejection, an assertion of her intention *not* to love Aurelius. Within the discourse, however, lines 989–98 represent a secondary speech act which compromises the first; 'the propositional content of Dorigen's secondary utterance completely conforms to that required for promises' (p 136). Yet the linguistic soundness of this secondary proposal is itself undercut by the legal definitions for invalid promises (e.g., when they necessitate an immoral action). In the world of the folktale from which the plot of *FranT* is ultimately derived, however, 'promises made insincerely and rashly do obligate their speakers' (p 140). The critical disagreements about the status of Dorigen's promise reflect the contradictory nature of the evidence and Chaucer's playful refusal to rest in any single interpretation.

1327 Braswell, Mary Flowers. 'Chaucer's "Court Baron": Law and *The Canterbury Tales*.' *SAC* 16 (1994), 29–44.
The role of the reader or hearer of *FranT* is that of a pleader in a court of law, articulating and arguing a response to the facts presented. The tale's concluding question is, like a legal text, open to a rich variety of interpretations. It is unlikely that those members of Chaucer's audience with legal training would have been expected to treat this question as a simple *demande d'amour*.

1328 Brown, Peter. *Chaucer at Work: The Making of the Canterbury Tales*. London: Longman, 1994.
The Franklin's treatment of patience is compared to the representation of the virtue in the alliterative *Patience*, where it entails the willing acceptance of suffering and the tempering of irascible tendencies. In the account of Dorigen and Arveragus's marriage agreement, Arveragus demonstrates patience, but we note the absence of any reference to the virtue in Dorigen's disposition. Dorigen's resistance to patience is exemplified in her response to the coastal rocks; the space into which she stares is 'the void of her own identity' (p 146), threatened by her impatient response to Arveragus's absence. Dorigen's loss of patience is also a loss of faith; her self-doubt suggests connections with the confusion of Hell. The moral chaos into which

her ungoverned reaction to the rocks leads her is averted at the conclusion of the tale only through mutual acts of patience and charity on the part of each of the poem's four main characters (pp 138–51).

1329 Calin, William. *The French Tradition and the Literature of Medieval England.* Toronto: U of Toronto P, 1994.
FranT is 'French in essence' (p 354), closer to Marie de France and Chrétien de Troyes than to the narratives of the Auchinleck MS. The questions about the place of *fin'amor* within marriage had been raised by Chrétien; the Franklin's modesty prologue, the tale's setting, magic, rendering of sentiment, and focus on one archetypal image (the rocks) qualify *FranT* as a true Breton lay (pp 347–56).
• Review by Edward E. Foster, *PhilosLit* 19 (1995), 400–1: Calin's emphasis on French intertexuality in *FranT* leads to a reading that too easily dismisses both Robertsonian and ironic alternatives (p 401).

1330 Crane, Susan. *Gender and Romance in Chaucer's Canterbury Tales.* 1994. See **670**.
Relatedness as a characteristic of the romance hero's identity is manifested in the doubling of Arveragus in Aurelius, revealing each man's identity as contingent on public norms and perceptions (p 7). *FranT* internalizes judicial procedures by submitting characters who are concerned with governing themselves to the judgment of the audience; the legal terminology present in the tale's dialogue incorporates public standards of reliability into personal behavior (p 37). The erotic triangle of Arveragus, Aurelius, and Dorigen 'is more the focus of development for the tale than is the relation of either man to the woman in question' (p 49). The gap between Dorigen's desire to refuse Aurelius and his response to her words as 'an enigmatic encouragement' (p 61) illustrate the difficulty of expressing resistance to courtship in romance. Dorigen's promise is neither rash nor flirtatious; rather, her wish to discourage Aurelius is at odds with a courtly discourse that admits no language of refusal. In distorting and exaggerating the scripted feminine role in courtship, Dorigen both clarifies and resists the restrictions under which she speaks. Chaucer characterizes the Franklin by his liminal status, which comes to resemble Dorigen's ambivalent social position. 'The resemblances between them allow Chaucer to relate estate to gender identity' (p 102; for an earlier version of this argument, see **1261**). In contrast to the tale's other characters, Dorigen and the Franklin allow themselves to be swept along in the flow of events. In her Complaint, Dorigen acknowledges and repeats Jerome's text, but manifests a passive resistance by reciting the exempla long enough to elude their instruction to kill herself (p 111). The Franklin treats the clerk's activities from a double perspective typical of the presentation of clerical magic in romance, which at once strives to 'preserve wonder from the demystifications of the ignorant' and assumes an attitude of detachment and even condemnation (p 141). Through magic, Aurelius and the clerk at-

tempt to control the feminized exotic and incorporate it into identity. Clerical magic also seems to promise an escape from male rivalry by producing a miracle that temporarily places the squire beyond the reach of competition. But magic – exposed as illusion and entangling Aurelius in further competition among men – does not finally provide freedom from personal contingencies; the tale rejects transcendent magical solutions in favor of communal values (pp 146–8). Dorigen's conflict between a bodily faith – her chastity – and a faith to pledged word, evident especially in her Complaint and her pained acceptance of Arveragus's command to keep *trouthe,* reveals 'a feminine sensibility that opposes but finally participates in the tale's predominantly masculine negotiations' (p 202).

• Review by Catherine Batt, *MLR* 92 (1997), 168–9: Crane's astute chapter on the relation of social roles and sexuality places perhaps too much emphasis on the correlation between Dorigen's and the Franklin's marginalization, while neglecting the role of language in the romance's construction of morality and systems of social exchange.

• Review by Sheila Fisher, *MP* 95 (1997), 87–91: Crane's reading of Dorigen's Complaint is notable for its originality and interest. In identifying Dorigen with the Franklin, however, Crane elides the masculine privilege accessible to the Franklin but denied to Dorigen because of her gender.

1331 Justman, Stewart. 'Trade as Pudendum: Chaucer's Wife of Bath.' *ChauR* 28 (1994), 344–52.

The Franklin purports to harmonize the romantic and realistic modes that the Wife of Bath cannot, imagining the ennobling passion of love within the constraints of marriage. At the end of the tale, however, women and self-interest are conspicuously left out, a double exclusion that 'confirms the identity of women and commerce that produces the speech of the Wife of Bath' (p 351).

1332 Kearney, John. 'Chaucer's "Franklin's Tale": "Trouthe", "Routhe" and the "Rokkes Blakke."' *South African Journal of Medieval and Renaissance Studies* 4:1 (1994), 95–107. Repr. in *'Tis all in peeces, all cohaerence gone': Change and Medieval and Renaissance Studies.* Ed. Rosemary Gray and Estelle Maré. Pretoria: University of South Africa, 1995. Pp 146–53.

Trouthe implies unchanging commitment. Yet in its sense of 'the truth of the world as it is' (p 96), it also betokens openness to the unfolding consequences of time (which includes the rocks). The fantasies – a form of *untrouthe* – that beset both Dorigen and Aurelius reveal a degree of resistance to both forms of *trouthe.* The consequences of this resistance, however, lead Dorigen and Aurelius, through suffering, to a reawakened sense of *trouthe,* accompanied in both cases by a shift in feeling. Aurelius's appreciation of the *trouthe* of Dorigen's suffering, of Arveragus's generosity, and thus of the nature of their bond, prompts him to show *routhe.* Prolonged misery leads Dorigen from the inappropriate *routhe* she initially showed Aurelius to an even deeper level of marital devotion. The escalation of *untrouthe* as the tale unfolds is finally outweighed by a succession of acts of *routhe*. At the heart of the tale lies a belief in the union of *trouthe* and *routhe*.

1333 Lee, Monika H. 'Concepts of Truth in Fourteenth-Century English Poetry.' *ELWIU* 21 (1994), 152–65.
Although the importance placed on Dorigen's keeping of her vow may seem incomprehensible to a modern reader, the significance of communal bonds and obligations built into an oral promise would have outweighed considerations of personal freedom and autonomy for a medieval audience.

1334 Lynch, Andrew. '"Be War, Ye Wemen": Problems of Genre and the Gendered Audience in Chaucer and Henryson.' In *Constructing Gender: Feminism and Literary Studies*. Ed. Hilary Fraser and R.S. White. Nedlands: U of Western Australia P, 1994. Pp 19–38.
Aurelius's use of 'atemporal, performative lyric conventions' within the context of a temporal narrative make his love complaint (lines 1311–38) seem 'almost wholly solipsistic' rather than addressed to Dorigen (p 27).

1335 Mosser, Daniel W. 'Reading and Editing the Canterbury Tales: Past, Present, and Future (?).' *Text* 7 (1994), 201–32.
As an example of the difference it makes to read a text in a particular manuscript as opposed to a modern edition, Mosser cites the presentation of Dorigen's Complaint (lines 1425–56) in El, where it is accompanied by a dense series of glosses incorporated into an elaborate decorative program in multicolored inks. 'The cumulative effect is spectacular' and emphasizes 'the presentation of the work as a *compilatio*' that draws attention to the range of authorities being employed (p 207).

1336 Peck, Russell A. 'The Phenomenology of Make Believe in Gower's *Confessio Amantis*.' *SP* 91 (1994), 250–69.
Gower is concerned with 'what goes on inside Amans' head amidst the flux of phenomena. What is in the lover's head is fiction. That is, one does not have rocks in one's head, unless one is Dorigen, and even there the rocks are ideas of rocks, which may be a greater problem than real rocks' (p 256).

1337 Riddy, Felicity. 'Engendering Pity in the *Franklin's Tale*.' In *Feminist Readings in Middle English Literature: The Wife of Bath and All Her Sect*. Ed. Ruth Evans and Lesley Johnson. London: Routledge, 1994. Pp 54–71.
In the Franklin's *gentil* discourse, *fredom*, *trouthe*, and *pitee* are both gendered and elements in a class myth. For men, demonstrating pity and being pitied are positions of power, whereas the pathos that attaches to Dorigen is a masculinist strategy that trivializes her. The male courtly lover's need for the woman to be inaccessible may account for the tale's ambivalence toward Dorigen and for its backing off from a sexual denouement. To cast Dorigen as a sexual victim, moreover, would represent Aurelius as a rapist (cf. the

examples in Dorigen's Complaint), and thus undercut the myth of aristocracy served by the Franklin's fiction. The narrative's courtly tone is in part maintained by the appeal to *trouthe*; yet the distraught Dorigen seems barely capable of comprehending this courtly imperative, and her distress allows Aurelius to manifest a show of *pitee*, which defines him as a gentleman – Dorigen's humiliation enables the men to display their *gentilesse*. The seemingly idealized reciprocity of Arveragus and Dorigen's marriage contract masks the fact that the male lover's *servage* is in reality a kind of lordship; when Arveragus seems to violate the spirit of the marriage agreement by commanding Dorigen to sleep with Aurelius, 'he is in fact simply exercising the reserved powers of the male which he had never surrendered' (p 63). Similarly, Aurelius's courtly abasement before Dorigen exists alongside veiled threats. When the tale shifts away from Dorigen at its close, back to the competition among men that was established in the class-based interchange between the Host and the Franklin in *Sq–FranL*, 'there is an attempt to reclaim "fredom" as a class- and gender-exclusive social skill' (p 65). See **1450**.

1338 Roney, Lois. 'Chaucer Subjectivizes the Oath: Depicting the Fall from Feudalism into Individualism in the *Canterbury Tales*.' In *The Rusted Hauberk: Feudal Ideas of Order and Their Decline*. 1994. See **674**. Pp 269–98.
Dorigen's oath to Aurelius is a focal point of *FranT*'s examination of the 'problematics of intention' (p 283). The innocence of Dorigen's original intent is played off against the binding force of her spoken words. Although we never doubt the nature of her intentions, intentions may nevertheless in time become ephemeral, difficult to recall, whereas spoken oaths should be 'unequivocal, unchanging, and life-long' (p 283).

1339 Spearing, A.C., ed. *The Franklin's Prologue and Tale from the Canterbury Tales by Geoffrey Chaucer*. Rev. ed., 1994. See **86**.
By invoking 'thise olde gentil Britouns' (line 709), the Franklin defies the Host's prohibition on further discussion of *gentilesse*; his subsequent denial of knowledge of rhetoric is in reality 'a masterpiece of rhetorical skill' which links eloquence and *gentilesse* as a claim to high social rank (p 75). The explicit themes of *FranT* are marriage, *trouthe*, and *gentilesse*. The tale seems to propose a mean between the extremes of wifely and husbandly dominance present in *WBT* and *ClT*, respectively, and to defend marriage against the Merchant's cynicism. But it does so by allowing us to draw our own conclusions about marriage rather than by offering definitive solutions to the problems raised by the preceding tales. The debate about marriage has centered on the question of *maistrye*; the Franklin removes the issue of power from the equation, focusing rather on the need for equality between husband and wife, and for *pacience* (line 773) and *suffrance* (line 788). Yet the tale can be read as testing the idealism of the marriage arrangement by exposing its 'risky

impracticability' (p 24). Exercising her *libertee* (line 768) by promising herself to Aurelius if he will ensure Arveragus's safe return, Dorigen paradoxically creates the possibility that her husband will be cuckolded. And under pressure of this crisis, Arveragus reassumes the traditional role as the 'head' of his wife, allowing *maistrye* to reenter the marriage. The most important invocation of *trouthe* occurs when Arveragus tells Dorigen that she must hold her promise to Aurelius because 'Trouthe is the hyeste thyng that man may kepe' (line 1479). Arveragus's emotion keeps his *sententia* from seeming a pat statement of a general principle. Its force is complicated, moreover, by questions involving the validity of Dorigen's initial promise; as with marriage, Chaucer 'leaves us with uncertainty rather than with … unequivocal doctrine' (p 31). The component parts of *gentilesse* – *trouthe*, compassion, graciousness, generosity, cheerfulness, concern for reputation, moderation, and the capacity for romantic love – are all present in the tale's characters. In *FranT*, *gentilesse* is an ethical quality that bears no necessary relation to high birth. Arveragus and Dorigen are noble pagans, '*gentil* gentiles' (p 40), analogous to the Jews who, before Christ's coming, sought spiritual liberation by means of the covenant with Jehovah. But adherence to *trouthe* alone cannot make gentiles into free men; true freedom is gained by going beyond the letter of covenants, as in the free acts of releasing at the conclusion of the tale. The movement from *trouthe* to *gentilesse* or *franchise* does not, however, involve the abandoning of *trouthe*. As the New Law of Christianity fulfilled rather than destroyed the Old Law, pagan mythology gives way, in the midwinter setting for the clerk's miracle (lines 1243–55), to the announcement of '"Nowel"' (line 1255) with its allusion to Christ's birth. Of the tale's characters, Arveragus develops least; he is the embodiment of *trouthe*, which by its nature is unchanging. Aurelius, Dorigen, and the clerk initially interest us primarily as 'units in a familiar pattern'; as the tale proceeds, this conventionality develops into something 'more inward and … more individual' (p 44). Although Aurelius enters the tale as a generic lovesick squire, aspects of his inner life are gradually revealed in his speech and its bodily accompaniments, and finally, in a moment of self-recognition and existential choice that precedes speech. Dorigen's questioning of God's creation of the black rocks marshals its Boethian content to present an argument about divine providence, but it also expresses intense personal feeling. The rocks are the imaginative center of the speech, the symbol of some flaw in the divinely ordered course of nature. They are juxtaposed with the human artifice of the garden to which the distraught Dorigen is led by her friends; the meaning of both settings changes in relation to events. Dorigen's 101-line *compleynt* addressed to Fortune has been thought a miscalculation on Chaucer's part. But its very length and the increasing distance between Dorigen's examples of virtuous women and her own circumstances may be part of its purpose;

we see Dorigen '[falling] short of the heroism she so vividly imagines, and [using] words as a way of *not* dealing with her real situation' (p 57). It is not easy to arrive at a comprehensive assessment of Dorigen's role in the tale. Although feminist readings have noted that Dorigen is treated like an object of exchange in a narrative focused on male generosity, it seems unlikely that Chaucer wished to question what we now call patriarchy. The tale's magic is purposefully ambiguous; it is both science and illusion, at once producing the effect of removing the rocks and indicating that Aurelius is pursuing a fantasy. The clerk exists on a plane higher than that of the other characters. His magic shapes the story, suggesting a role parallel to the poet's own; like Chaucer, the clerk is a prosperous professional, a man whose status depends on skill rather than birth, and an artist who derives images of romantic love from books. The *GP* portrait of the Franklin, *Sq–FranL,* and *FranP* introduce topics – the Franklin's hospitality and love of food, *gentilesse,* rhetoric – that resurface in *FranT.* But the connections between teller and tale cannot be stabilized into a set of values attributable to the Franklin; as in most of *CT,* narratorial voice and position in *FranT* are 'fluctuating and inconsistent' (p 76).

1340 Stone, Gregory. *The Death of the Troubadour: The Late Medieval Resistance to the Renaissance.* Philadelphia: U of Pennsylvania P, 1994.
Chaucer consistently represents the voice of the courtly lover as impersonal or plural, as in Aurelius's veiling of his desire for Dorigen in nonexpressive public song (lines 943–5). When the impasse of Aurelius's public performance is replaced by the lyric discourse of his later plea to Dorigen (lines 972–8), his 'previously generalized voice is made singular' (p 152).

1341 Arfin, William. 'Chaucerian Choice: Formal and Thematic Considerations in the *Wife of Bath's Tale.*' *CR* 35 (1995), 64–80.
FranT can be considered at the level of moral experiment; we must project ourselves into the narrative and imagine our own reactions to the options.

1342 Boenig, Robert. *Chaucer and the Mystics: The Canterbury Tales and the Genre of Devotional Prose.* 1995. See **674a**.
Dorigen's self-punishing behavior after Arveragus's departure is an ironic version of the physical deprivations of female medieval mystics. Dorigen weeps, fasts, and wakes 'not to escape an earthly husband in favor of a heavenly but to protest against her earthly husband's absence' (p 140). Whereas the written lives of medieval religious women were intended to provide models for their readers, Dorigen 'fragments' the stories of the virtuous women she cites in her Complaint, 'divorcing motive from paradigmatic situation' (p 144).

1343 Chance, Jane. *The Mythographic Chaucer: The Fabulation of Sexual Politics.* 1995. See **675**.
In *FranT,* Chaucer deploys the figures of Echo and Narcissus to undercut the aristocratic exposition of love as *free* (line 767) – without constraint –

which becomes, like Dorigen's obsession with the rocks, a 'derke fantasye' (line 844) impossible to maintain. Arveragus is a self-deluded Narcissus, enclosed in his chivalric egotism and blind to his wife's needs and desires. Aurelius, who compares himself to Echo, functions as Arveragus's double; in wooing Dorigen, the squire imitates the knight's private role in a thinly disguised act of homosocial bonding. In her lack of traditional role models, Dorigen seems a 'pale reflection of the desire of her husband' (p 253), an image of a shadowy Narcissus who doesn't know himself. Ironically, however, she is also the character potentially most free. Seeing no way out of her agreement with Aurelius, she resorts in her Complaint to the feminizing traditions of classical antiquity – examples of 'heroic women ... empowered in sexual situations outside their control' (p 257). Her posture as Narcissus's image reflects her need for a self beyond the limits of masculine desire. A model for this self exists in the moon, associated with Narcissus in the mythographic tradition, instrumental in making the rocks disappear, and thus (despite Aurelius's and the clerk's attempts to manipulate the cosmos) 'empowering Dorigen to reconstruct herself' (p 259). Chaucer's treatment of mythographic material demonstrates Dorigen's freedom in shaping an identity for herself 'outside the patriarchal binarism of the myth of Echo and Narcissus' (p 262).

1344 Edwards, Robert R. 'Some Pious Talk About Marriage: Two Speeches from the *Canterbury Tales*.' In *Matrons and Marginal Women in Medieval Society*. Ed. Robert R. Edwards and Vickie Ziegler. Woodbridge: Boydell, 1995. Pp 111–27.

The marriage encomium in *MerT* (IV.1267–1392) and the Franklin's speech on marital values (lines 761–90) bring to the surface conflicting cultural traditions that inform medieval doctrine about marriage. The Franklin's speech is organized around the themes of friendship, patience, and temperance; on the surface, it appears to redefine love away from appetite and power toward an ideal of reciprocity. The mixed reception of the passage among modern readers, however, points to its problematic nature, in part a result of Chaucer's transposition of Boccaccio's aristocratic story into a different social milieu, in part a result of conflicts among the sources and traditions embodied in the speech. The Franklin's argument for *libertee*, for example, draws on a passage in *RR* that links freedom with natural appetite rather than with mutual obligation; his discourse on friendship is complicated by its allusions to the classical doctrine of accord between noble males (rather than married partners) and by its goal of *prosperitee*, a value discredited in Cicero's commentary on *amicitia*. The tales that follow the speeches give 'paradoxical illustrations of their doctrines' (p 127), as in the Franklin's final question about *fredom*, which speaks only of the male characters.

1345 Hallissy, Margaret. *A Companion to Chaucer's Canterbury Tales*. Westport, CT:

Greenwood, 1995.
FranT challenges the medieval principle that chastity is a woman's only important virtue. In maintaining that *trouthe*, not chastity, is the highest good, Arveragus goes against prevailing cultural norms, earning for himself the title of 'mooste fre' (line 1622), and advancing Chaucer's belief that 'men and women are equally capable of all virtues, with no virtue seen as gender-specific' (p 203).

1346 Jacobs, Kathryn. 'Rewriting the Marriage Contract: Adultery in the *Canterbury Tales*.' *ChauR* 29 (1995), 337–47.
FranT is a test case designed to try Chaucer's 'qualified approval of adultery' (p 344). Like the merchant in *ShT*, obsessed with his money, Arveragus neglects his wife to pursue his professional labors. He recognizes the effect of his neglect when he commands Dorigen to keep her promise to Aurelius: 'he has not provided her with the consolation of his presence, and therefore yields her up under all the impetus of his own moral imperative' (p 346). Although Aurelius releases Dorigen from her vow, *FranT* 'portrays adultery as a moral alternative available to good people whose spouses have not lived up to their part of the marriage contract' (p 346).

1347 Laskaya, Anne. *Chaucer's Approach to Gender in the Canterbury Tales*. 1995. See **790**.
The 'clerkly reputation for sexual scheming' (p 112) in *CT* is exemplified in the actions of the Orléans magician, whose attempts to aid Aurelius in deceiving Dorigen also involve his obscuring God's creation, in the form of the black rocks. *FranT* questions assumptions about male domination and female submission. The marriage contract of Dorigen and Arveragus posits equality; the comedy of Dorigen's Complaint implies the inappropriateness of suicide as a means of preserving integrity. Although Dorigen conforms to men's desires, her conformity is made to appear ridiculous – as in her jesting promise to Aurelius, her failure to challenge his claim that the rocks have disappeared, and her immediate submission to her husband's insistence that she keep her word to Aurelius (pp 161–2).

1348 ———, and Eve Salisbury, eds. *The Middle English Breton Lays*. Kalamazoo, MI: Medieval Institute Publications, 1995.
In invoking the 'olde gentil Britouns' (line 709), Chaucer is reclaiming a tradition that had migrated with the ancient Celts from Britain to Brittany (p 7).

1349 Lucas, Angela. 'Keeping Up Appearances: Chaucer's Franklin and the Magic of the Breton Lay Genre.' In *Literature and the Supernatural: Essays for the Maynooth Bicentenary*. Ed. Brian Cosgrove. Blackrock, Co. Dublin: Columba, 1995. Pp 11–32.
The Franklin's misunderstanding of the generic characteristics of the Breton lay he purports to tell begins with his blurring, in his Prologue, of the traditional distinction between oral/musical lays and the short narrative poems

of the sort made familiar by Marie de France. His claim to be telling a Breton lay is further undercut by his handling of almost all of the conventional motifs of the lay (the setting, the rash promise, magic, the impossible task, the love triangle, love and marriage), into which he introduces 'complexities and ironies [that] remove *FranT* from any place beside known Breton Lays' (p 28). The Franklin's choice of genre may be his attempt to tell the most refined tale he can, but his ignorance of the contents of the lays suggests 'a man out of touch with the ways and interests of the nobility, while attempting to ape those ways' (p 29).

1350 Lynch, Kathryn L. 'East Meets West in Chaucer's Squire's and Franklin's Tales.' 1995. See **679**.

FranT may be read as a response to the oscillations between East and West, feminine and masculine, that characterize *SqT*. The Franklin tells a specifically British tale; its allusions to *HRB* link it to a respected British foundation myth. Although Dorigen seems to embody 'the threat of the exotic' (p 545), she is not allowed to realize the full possibilities of female autonomy. Her playful promise to Aurelius generates the action that sends the squire to Orléans and puts him in touch with forms of exotic magic associated with the East. But the Franklin strives to bring the wonders of the Orient under Occidental control, scorning the clerk's astrology and shifting the tale's setting from the 'morally ambiguous' Orléans to the 'hypermasculine, native hearth' (p 547) evoked in the winter description (lines 1243–55). Dorigen's Complaint leads nowhere, and in the tale's final episodes, she is 'spoken through by the male characters' (p 549); Aurelius's compassion is produced not by Dorigen's distress, but by Arveragus's *gentilesse*. The Franklin's concluding question may appear to open up the tale to discussion, but in reality closes it down: none of the characters is *fre*. This control and reduction of outcomes typifies the Franklin's entire narrative method, 'which is as far from Eastern openness as imaginable' (pp 549–50).

1351 Minnis, A.J. *The Shorter Poems*. Oxford Guides to Chaucer. Oxford: Clarendon, 1995.

If Arveragus's absence had been permanent rather than temporary, Dorigen would partly be reenacting the role of Queen Alcyone in respect of her beloved husband King Ceyx in *BD* (p 147).

1352 Pearsall, Derek. '*The Franklin's Tale,* Line 1469: Forms of Address in Chaucer.' *SAC* 17 (1995), 69–78.

Arveragus's response after Dorigen has told him of her promise to Aurelius – 'Is ther oght elles, Dorigen, but this?' (line 1469) – treats the matter as a serious one; Arveragus is attempting to ascertain whether his wife has told him the whole truth, the complete story. His instinctive assumption of authority is evident in his use of the unadorned vocative *Dorigen* (a form of address not normally used in Chaucer by a courtly lover to a lady); in his movement from the formal or polite plural to the singular second-person pronoun (lines 1481–3); and in his 'bare appellation "wyf"' (p 77) in line 1472. Arveragus's language in this passage show him adopting, with 'the unself-consciousness of ingrained habit' (p 77), forms of address suited to a relationship quite different from the one he swore to when he married Dorigen.

1353 Scott, Anne. '"Considerynge the Beste on Every Syde": Ethics, Empathy, and Epistemology in the *Franklin's Tale.*' *ChauR* 29 (1995), 390–415.
The interpretive cruxes in *FranT* inhere in the ways in which the characters present and act upon their perceptions, moral principles, and emotions. Dorigen and, especially, Arveragus, perceive the world in binary categories; both are uncomfortable with ambiguity. In his response to Dorigen's plight, Arveragus places a high value on abstract universals, but his defense against 'disrupted hierarchies' exposes Dorigen to the 'evil of separation, loss of relation, and loss of human connection' (pp 398–9). In contrast to Arveragus, Dorigen, especially in her complaint against the rocks, characterizes herself as a '"subjectivist" knower' (p 399) who depends on intuitive and sensory perceptions to the exclusion of rational or universalizing reasoning. Her reliance on the inner world of feeling leaves her vulnerable to emotional and visual deception. For most of the tale, Aurelius shares with Dorigen an imagination that overwhelms intellect and hence undermines his capacity for moral judgment. In the final episode, however, Aurelius demonstrates 'constructivist' knowing (p 407) that reintegrates the tale's more limited forms of knowing into a more effective process of moral reasoning. Although none of the characters achieves a complete balance of perceptions, the aggregate of their epistemic views suggests the broad expanse of, and a possible model for, interpersonal encounters.

1354 Van Dyke, Carolynn. 'The Clerk's and Franklin's Subjected Subjects.' *SAC* 17 (1995), 45–68.
ClT and *FranT* display a similar thematic and structural incoherence because they both equivocate about the possibility of female agency. In adapting his Boccaccian source, Chaucer expands the role of the lady in an apparent attempt to make Dorigen comparable to the male characters in moral agency. But her agency is paradoxical, resulting primarily in inaction; 'her deliberations all end in culs-de-sac' (p 62). The initial marriage agreement, moreover, waffles about the proper limits of male *maistrye,* and thus anticipates the tale's ending, which (despite the Franklin's claims for the universal applicability of his themes) leaves Dorigen out of its question about *fredom.* From one viewpoint the divided tales of the Clerk and Franklin silence female agents. But because we cannot place them clearly in the poem's allegorical schemes, we generate psychological readings, which, however problematic, attest to 'the force of the unresolved counter tales in which women

are protagonists' (p 68). (For a revised version of this material, see **1506**.)

1355 Weisl, Angela Jane. *Conquering the Reign of Femeny: Gender and Genre in Chaucer's Romance*. 1995. See **681**. Excerpts in *Chaucer*. Ed. Corinne Saunders. Blackwell Guides to Criticism. Oxford: Blackwell, 2001. Pp 300–6.

FranT begins with a compressed lay, which ends in a happy marriage. By beginning at the end, however, the tale must continue beyond the 'happily ever after' ending prescribed by the genre; in so doing, Chaucer exposes the problematic nature of such endings. Dorigen and Arveragus's marriage contract, which seeks to reconcile courtly love service with marital power structures, reveals the impossibility of bringing together these two worlds into a single whole. The tale's romance genre is 'ultimately about male concerns and male desires' (p 109), and Dorigen is constrained within it. Deprived of agency in her marriage, she is subsequently interpreted by Aurelius as a courtly lady; 'the erotic plot is the only one available to her' (p 109). When the tale moves from the private space of the garden into the public world of commerce and contracts, Dorigen is transformed into an object of exchange among men. And when the clerk – 'a palpable symbol of masculine discourse and power' (p 111) – deploys illusion to beguile Dorigen, she loses even the minimal autonomy she had previously enjoyed. Arveragus, reasserting the sovereignty he had earlier abjured, denies her subjectivity by sending her off to keep her promise to Aurelius. The concluding description of Arveragus and Dorigen (lines 1551–5) defines her entirely through her relationship to him, while the tale's final episode is concerned wholly with male *gentilesse*. Although *FranT* considers women's power and autonomy, the genre's traditional values ultimately reassert themselves in 'male dominance and female submission' (p 117).

1356 Yager, Susan. 'Boethius, Philosophy, and Chaucer's "Marriage Group."' *CarmP* 4 (1995), 77–89.

In *WBT*, *MerT*, and (to a lesser extent) *ClT*, wives emerge as powerful figures because of their resemblance to Boethius's Lady Philosophy. In contrast, Dorigen resembles Boethius in Book 1 of *Consol* rather than Philosophy; her speech about the rocks, which echoes *Consol*, repeats the errors of Boethius. Unlike Boethius, however, she receives no aid from a Philosophy figure, and remains the least powerful of the wives in the Marriage Group tales.

1357 Astell, Ann W. *Chaucer and the Universe of Learning*. 1996. See **682**.

The Franklin's attempt to speak the language of gentility leads him into 'the social ungrammaticalities of courtly love and female *regimen*' (p 175). Dorigen and Arveragus join in an 'ungrammatical marriage where the male is subjected to the female subject' (p 176); Dorigen's 'ungrammatical' (p 176) reply to Aurelius in the garden, simultaneously a promise and a denial, leads to Aurelius's claim – at once true and false – that the rocks have disappeared; the poem's last word belongs to the clerk, who specializes in substituting illusion for reality. *FranT* 'typifies both a female grammar, in which predicates become subjects, and an allied Epicurean *grammatica* in which words constitute reality' (p 177).

1358 Ellis, Steve. *Geoffrey Chaucer*. Plymouth, UK: Northcote, 1996.
Kittredge's view (**805**) that *FranT* offers a solution to the questions about marriage initially raised by the Wife of Bath is undermined by the tale itself, in which the husband does in fact exercise dominance over his wife. In addition, the Franklin's 'fantasy romance' (p 37) can hardly provide an answer to the socio-economic problems of medieval marriage central to the Wife's discourse. The so-called Marriage Group tales touch on issues that go well beyond the marriage debate; *FranT,* for example, satirizes the exemplum tradition in Dorigen's long catalogue of virtuous women (pp 37–8).

1359 Flake, Timothy H. 'Love, *Trouthe,* and the Happy Ending of the *Franklin's Tale.*' *ES* 77 (1996), 209–26.
Far from being incoherent, as the Lucases argue (**1286**), the marriage of Dorigen and Arveragus expresses the freedom and love brought about by the power of *trouthe.* The lovers' response to the crisis created by Dorigen's rash promise proves their loyalty to the spirit of their vows, moves the story from tragedy to comedy, establishes the ascendancy of *trouthe* over illusion, and converts the squire and the magician to the rule of *gentilesse.* Arveragus's command that Dorigen keep her promise in the name of *trouthe* does not compromise the story's integrity. His concept of *trouthe* grows out of his respect for the freedom of Dorigen's will. Her will, her confidence to act, was grounded on the apparent permanence of the black rocks; with their removal, her 'will is in a sense forfeit' (p 220), and she shifts the responsibility to act onto Arveragus. His action, in turn, converts Dorigen's 'immature and sentimental will' (p 219) into a mature and sober one, based on a clear understanding of *trouthe.*

1360 Friedman, John B. 'Dorigen's "Grisly Rokkes Blake" Again.' *ChauR* 31 (1996), 133–44.
In speaking of the rocks in *FranT,* both the major characters and the narrator note their cthonic nature, associate them with a pre-Christian or actively anti-Christian point of view, and personify them as diabolical and supernatural. The rocks become the focus of Dorigen's fears of the malign forces in the universe that threaten her peace of mind and her marital happiness. The rocks' function in the tale suggests that Chaucer may have expected his audience to connect them with the megalithic menhirs and dolmens along the lower coast of Brittany, which were believed in the Middle Ages to be the work of giants, sorcerers, and demons. The ordinary rocks, dangerous to sailors, would then be linked with the rocks dangerous to 'spiritual mariners'; their 'inexplicable purpose and origins created ... deep unease in Christians' (p 142) and thus color by association Dorigen's vision of a cos-

mos that menaces both her love and her faith.

1361 Grudin, Michaela Paasche. *Chaucer and the Politics of Discourse*. 1996. See **685**.
Taken together, *SqT* and *FranT* constitute 'a poetic essay on the uses and misuses of discourse' (p 114). In her promise to Aurelius, Dorigen speaks amiss without intending to do so. Aurelius deliberately misinterprets Dorigen's words, ignoring their spirit and attending only to their letter. When he conveys to Dorigen the results of the magician's labor, Aurelius's speech 'imitates on a rhetorical level the self-serving craft of the magician' (p 132). In the tale's final episode, however, the proper relation between words and deeds, discourse and reality, is restored.

1362 Kitson, Annabella. 'Astrology and English Literature.' *ContempR* 269 (1996), 200–7.
The astrology in *FranT* is associated with dark deeds. It is therefore striking that Chaucer wove it into a tale of 'moral gentleness' (p 202).

1363 Koff, Leonard Michael. '"Awak!": Chaucer Translates Bird Song.' In *The Medieval Translator. Traduire au Moyen Age*. 1996. See **686**.
Dorigen's promise to love Aurelius if he removes the rocks and Aurelius's response enact the disjunction between language and truth that is the substance of much of Chaucer's art. In projecting onto the hateful rocks her desire for her husband to return, Dorigen is implicitly telling Aurelius that she does not wish to love him. Aurelius, however, reads her similitude literally, hearing only what he wants to hear, and equating form or surface with content.

1363a Larson, Leah Jean. *Love, Troth and Magnanimity: The Weltanschauung of the Breton Lay from Marie de France to Chaucer*. PhD diss., University of Southwestern Louisiana, 1996. Dir. W. Bryant Bachman. Ann Arbor, MI: University Microfilms International, 1996.
Ch. 3, 'The *Franklin's Tale*: Chaucer's Breton Lay' (pp 130–63), argues that in refashioning Boccaccio's love question on the model of a Breton lay, Chaucer foregrounds the values of 'troth-keeping, magnanimity, and ... egalitarian love' inherent in the latter genre (p 163).

1364 Léon Sendra, Antonio R. *Ensayos Chaucerienses*. Córdoba: Universidad de Córdoba, 1996.
Despite the difficulties that threaten the marriage of Dorigen and Arveragus, the stability of their relationship is safeguarded by a mutual loyalty that consists of respecting the desire of the other. Both characters act as free beings – Dorigen in her ability to confess her dilemma to Arveragus, Arveragus in his acknowledgment of Dorigen's duty toward herself in fulfilling her promise to Aurelius. *Trouthe,* a key term here as elsewhere in Chaucer's works, stands for the nucleus of one's personality. Being true to oneself implies being faithful to another. The tale's happy ending reinforces the message that a successful marriage rests on the mutual respect of two human beings

faithful to their own selves (pp 127–30).

1365 Lim, Hye-Soon. '*Gentil* and *fre* in "The Franklin's Tale." *MESt* 4 (1996), 149–73.

Gentil and *fre* are almost cognate in *FranT,* but the word *gentil* is higher. By using *fre* in his final question, the Franklin betrays a lack of understanding of his own tale. (Not seen. Summary from http://hompi.sogang.ac.kr/anthony/mesak/Chbiblio.htm. In Korean.)

1366 McEntire, Sandra J. 'Illusions and Interpretation in the *Franklin's Tale.*' *ChauR* 31 (1996), 145–63.

Menedon's tale in *Fil* examines the romance ideals in which love can flourish and suggests that male honor is underpinned by and indebted to female virtue. In his rewriting of Boccaccio's narrative, Chaucer veils the original genre and meaning of the tale to call into question the hermeneutics of interpretation. Although the Franklin's ostensible subjects are marriage and sovereignty, he is actually promoting another agenda, that of bonding with the male pilgrims in order to achieve equality with the best of them. In pursuing this goal, he deprives Dorigen of control over her words and of her ability to interpret her own experience; through clerkly illusion, she is made to see what men intend her to see. Where Boccaccio's magician effects an Ovidian transformation of nature, the magic of Chaucer's clerk is ultimately nothing more than wordplay, under which Dorigen collapses. A second veiling of Dorigen takes place when Arveragus, invoking the *trouthe* kept and defined by men, takes from Dorigen the ability to act by commanding her to go to Aurelius; Dorigen, not Arveragus, is about to be *ystiked* (line 1476), both through physical victimization and mental, spiritual, and rhetorical violation. The game played out in the final scenes is one of 'male bonded one-upmanship' in which Dorigen is reduced to a commodity of exchange among the male characters (p 155). The tale is not, however, primarily about the victimization of woman by men. Chaucer's concern is rather with the illusions created by art and artifice, and the dangers of reading too literally (as Aurelius reads Dorigen's promise) or too metaphorically (the Franklin reads Dorigen as a sign of a woman who has usurped her place). The allusion to Christmas and Epiphany in the cry of '"Nowel"' (line 1255) juxtaposes the tale's pagan events with a moment in salvation history when false powers and magic are to be rejected. In *FranT,* illusions arise not from magic but from misinterpretation; by encouraging us to look beyond the Franklin's stated subjects, Chaucer asks us to examine the kinds of interpretations we reach, how we read, and what we believe of what we read.

1367 McKinley, Kathryn L. 'The Silenced Knight: Questions of Power and Reciprocity in *The Wife of Bath's Tale.*' *ChauR* 30 (1996), 359–73.

The ending of *WBT* parallels that of *FranT*; in each, a character (the knight) or characters (Arveragus and Dorigen) resign themselves to making an almost impossible sacrifice and are thereby released from having to fulfill it.

1368 Parry, Joseph D. 'Dorigen, Narration, and Coming Home in the *Franklin's Tale*.' *ChauR* 20 (1996), 262–93.
For Arveragus, the physical world of *FranT* is a space of free mobility; his home is a place of self-definition. For Dorigen, home represents proximity to her husband; she is denied physical mobility, and in Arveragus's absence, the local landscape becomes a place of pain, isolation, and fear. After Arveragus returns home, the tale shifts to the less visually detailed landscape of the characters' psyches. The male characters – especially Aurelius – exercise freedom of choice and achieve upward social mobility in the tale's privileging of honor, even as the narration displaces Dorigen from the tale's center. Yet Dorigen's extended recounting of the histories of noble women from *Jov* allows her a kind of space in the act of narration itself; in her Complaint, she exercises the power of deferral, choosing not to choose between the options of sexual disgrace and suicide. The *hoom* (line 1346) where she engages in her monologue is an interior landscape in which she explores a world she knows how to read. Whereas Aurelius's dwelling is the scene of his disabling two-years' love sickness and the magician's *hoom* (line 1185) is the site of illusion, Dorigen 'realizes her most moral self at her home' (p 288). In this, she is like the author of *CT*; 'both Dorigen and Chaucer inhabit a world where one lives by and because of one's acts of narration' (p 289).

1369 Pulham, Carol A. 'Promises, Promises: Dorigen's Dilemma Revisited.' *ChauR* 31 (1996), 76–86.
During the Middle Ages' transition to literacy, the binding nature of the written text was initially transferred to oral communication. Thus Dorigen's promise to Aurelius would have had a force not evident to a modern reader. Viewed as a lie, her promise would function as a kind of fiction and hence would be subject to misinterpretation. Although Arveragus's command that Dorigen commit adultery rather than breaking her promise has been criticized, it can be seen as the lesser of two evils. By telling her to go to Aurelius, Arveragus has released Dorigen from her marriage vow; his solution observes 'the letter, not the spirit' of her promise to the squire, while maintaining 'the spirit, not the letter' of her earlier vow to himself (p 80). Medieval views of adultery, moreover, offer mitigations of Dorigen's offense – for example, in their restriction of the sin to pleasurable sex. According to the 'utilitarian' (p 83) philosophy of promising, the greater the expectations raised by the promise and the greater the efforts of the promisee to bring about the necessary conditions, the greater the obligation of the promisor to keep the promise. Aurelius's dedication to the task of removing the rocks may thus be seen as changing 'the circumstance of the promise from a joking one to a serious one' (p 84), and placing Dorigen under an increased obligation to fulfill her part of the bargain.

1369a Shibata, Takeo. 'Chaucer and the Affected Modesty Topos.' 1996. See **687a**.
Includes comments on the Franklin's use of the affected modesty topos in lines 716–28. Full text at http://ci.nii.ac.jp/els/110006606898.pdf?id=ART0008574171&type=pdf&lang=en&host=cinii&order_no=&ppv_type=0&lang_sw=&no=1457233200&cp=. In Japanese.

1370 Sigal, Gale. *Erotic Dawn-Songs of the Middle Ages: Voicing the Lyric Lady*. Gainesville: UP of Florida, 1996.
The Franklin's belief that love can exist only in a relationship of equality and freedom is problematized when applied to marriage; in the course of the story, Dorigen's ostensible equality is eroded as she is traded between men. Although *fin'amor* is represented as a volitional relationship, marriage creates obligation and inequality (pp 105–7).

1371 Taylor, Paul Beekman. *Chaucer's Chain of Love*. Madison, NJ: Fairleigh Dickinson UP; London: Associated University Presses, 1996.
Words in *FranT* mask appetite as harmonious union in Dorigen and Arveragus's marriage contract, express blasphemous wishes in the 'Christian' (p 93) Dorigen's seaside address to God, shape a 'cosmos of desire' (p 96) in Dorigen's promise to Aurelius and his subsequent prayer, collaborate with magic to create illusion, and function as a 'verbal charm' (p 99) in Dorigen's Complaint. Arveragus's words restore order. In responding to Arveragus's *gentilesse* rather than to Dorigen's distracted words, Aurelius is freed from his obsession with possessing her body, and is in turn released from his debt by the clerk. 'Dorigen's eye and mouth may not have served reason,' but her 'inconsiderate words are occasion for three men to move their own spirits higher on the chain of love' (p 100).
• Review by Janette Dillon, *MLR* 94 (1999), 156–7: The Robertsonian influence, productive in Taylor's early chapters, produces strained readings elsewhere, as in the peculiar argument about illusory words in *FranT*.

1372 Thompson, N.S. *Chaucer, Boccaccio, and the Debate of Love: A Comparative Study of The Decameron and The Canterbury Tales*. 1996. See **357**.
The generic puzzle of *FranT* lies in its combination of elements of the courtly debate poem with a moral exemplum. This dual perspective reflects the mutual influence of Menedon's story in *Fil* and *Dec* 10.5; the tale retains the 'unworldly, timeless, and abstract quality' of the former and the 'realistic and exemplary nature' of the latter (p 264). Both Boccaccio (in *Dec*) and Chaucer take a narrative of courtly love and use it as a vehicle for a tale 'whose morality goes beyond the bounds of *fin amor*' (p 264). Like Messer Ansaldo (*Dec*), who moves from passionate desire to charitable love, Aurelius undergoes a transformation in the poem's final episode; *trouthe* and *routhe* (lines 1529–30) are released from the courtly code to signify, respectively, the sacredness of the marriage vow and Dorigen's personal integrity, and Aurelius's 'genuine human compassion' (p 267).

• Review by Janet Smarr, *JEGP* 97 (1998), 241–3: In Thompson's chapter on *FranT* and its analogues, it is unclear how *trouthe* refers to the marriage vow rather than to Dorigen's promise, how the Franklin's final question is not about generosity but about spousal support, and how *Dec* 10.5 exemplifies mutuality in marriage.

1373 Arlandi, Juan Ramírez. 'Reconsiderations on the Theme of Marriage in The Canterbury Tales.' In *Proceedings of the 9th International Conference of the Spanish Society for Medieval Language and Literature*. 1997. See **691**. Pp 247–52.
The readings of *FranT* proposed by Kittredge (**805**), Howard (**1050**), and Richmond (**1091**) are limited by the authors' restriction of their argument to selected tales, especially those of Kittredge's Marriage Group. A more adequate context would include all of the narratives in *CT* that touch on marriage.

1374 Hillman, Richard. *Self-Speaking in Medieval and Modern English Drama*. New York: St Martin's, 1997.
Dorigen's lament over the rocks has intriguing implications for the connection between soliloquy and subjectivity, intimating that Dorigen is punished both for the content of her monologue (its rejection of patriarchally mediated truth) and for its form (its rejection of mediated speech) (pp 51–2).

1375 Howes, Laura L. *Chaucer's Gardens and the Language of Convention*. Gainesville: UP of Florida, 1997.
The garden in which Dorigen makes her promise to Aurelius literalizes and makes visible her conventional role. Created by 'craft of mannes hand' (line 909), the pleasure park at once reminds Dorigen of her absent husband and serves as the site of Aurelius's wooing, thus representing her conflicting roles as wife and courtly lady. By participating in the verbal play expected of the latter, Dorigen unwittingly compromises her marriage vow, and is subsequently ordered by her husband – who invokes a limited conception of *trouthe* – to commit adultery against her will. We are asked to decide which of the male characters is the 'mooste fre,' or generous (line 1622). In contrast, Dorigen is the least free – the most restricted – character in the tale (pp 102–9).

• Review by Kenneth Bleeth, *Speculum* 74 (1999), 434–6: Howes's pages on the *CT* make a valuable contribution to the reexamination of women and space in medieval culture. Because gardens are only one thread in the tales' thematic and linguistic tapestries, however, treating them in isolation from other images makes for certain thinness in the commentary.

• Review by Peter Brown, *RES* n.s. 50 (1999), 366–9: Arveragus's neglect of the private garden-centered world of his loving wife is a function of the value system he serves rather than (as Howes argues) an indictment of his attitude towards marital responsibility.

1376 Kawasaki, Tadashi Shun. 'The Significance of the Garden as a Place from

Boccaccio to Chaucer.' *Studies in British and American Literature* (Komazawa University) 32 (1997), 1–13.
Full text at http://ci.nii.ac.jp/els/110006159508.pdf?id=ART0008126226&-type=pdf&lang=en&host=cinii&order_no=&ppv_type=0&lang_sw=&no=1392583375&cp=. In Japanese.

1377 McGregor, Francine. 'What of Dorigen? Agency and Ambivalence in the *Franklin's Tale.*' *ChauR* 31 (1997), 365–78.
FranT contains competing narratives about Dorigen: one diminishes her as the independent woman that the narrator theorizes about in his remarks on women's need for *libertee* (line 768); the other presents her as a vital figure and a dynamic presence in the tale. The introduction to the poem appears to grant Dorigen agency, but simultaneously undermines her capacity for action by suggesting Arveragus's continued *maistrye*. The marriage arrangement anticipates the 'bias toward the masculine' (p 369) in the tale's final episode: Dorigen's intent is subsumed in Arveragus's focus on the letter of her promise, while Aurelius reads her distress as an expression of her husband's shame. Dorigen does attempt to exercise power within the social structures that govern her: she rejects her friends' consolation, and asserts her will in her initial encounter with Aurelius by inscribing her priorities on the stable medium of the coastal rocks. When the clerk creates the illusion that the rocks have disappeared, however, she is rendered powerless; she is further deprived of agency by Arveragus's transformation of the fiction of her inability to intend or act into a reality. The tale's 'great feat of illusion' (p 377) is to treat a 'trewe wyf' (line 758) as one who has made a promise to be untrue and then focusing on men's *gentilesse* as the force that finally enables her be *trewe*.

1378 Taylor, Mark N. 'Servant and Lord/Lady and Wife: The *Franklin's Tale* and Traditions of Courtly and Conjugal Love.' *ChauR* 32 (1997), 64–81.
The marriage of Dorigen and Arveragus is best understood as proceeding from the antiadultery tradition, as exemplified in Marcabru's representation of *fin'amor* as 'a reciprocal relationship based on mutual constancy' (p 69) and Chrétien de Troyes' promotion of marriage in *Erec et Enide* and *Cligés* as the 'ideal locus of *fin'amor*' in which the adulterous ideal of love is reconfigured through an integration of erotic love and Christian virtue (p 70). The antiadultery texts establish *topoi* germane to *FranT* (e.g., female constancy) and throw light on the behavior of Aurelius (a type of the false lover) and Arveragus, whose refusal to exercise mastery over his wife reflects the ideals of *fin'amor*.

1379 Travis, Peter W. 'Chaucer's Heliotropes and the Poetics of Metaphor.' *Speculum* 72 (1997), 399–427.
The Franklin problematizes his claim that he knows nothing about rhetoric (lines 719–26) by embedding his demurral concerning the proper under-

standing of *colours* in a passage that itself illustrates metaphor's complex linguistic and epistemological nature.

1380 Yoon, Hee-Oyck. 'The Debate on Marriage in the Marriage Group of *The Canterbury Tales*.' *Humanities Research* (Institute of Humanities, Yeungnam University) 19 (1997), 161–76.
In contrast to the preceding tales in the Marriage Group, *FranT* represents marriage as a partnership of equals. Chaucer emphasizes mutual faith and trust, treating the subject of mastery as irrelevant to the marriage debate.

1381 Besserman, Lawrence. *Chaucer's Biblical Poetics*. Norman: U of Oklahoma P, 1998.
In her lament over the rocks, Dorigen obliquely alludes to the topos of the Book of Nature, traditionally contrasted with the Book of Scripture. Although her words evoke one of the two poles of this fundamental dyad of Christian metaphysics, she is a pagan who cannot fully understand the truth to which her words are pointing (pp 15–16).

1382 Bisson, Lillian M. *Chaucer and the Late Medieval World*. New York: St Martin's, 1998.
Although Dorigen and Arveragus promise mutuality in their marriage agreement, their personal relationship exists in a social matrix that requires the husband to retain the appearance of sovereignty. The promise is thus compromised; by the end of the tale, Dorigen has lost much her autonomy, and become an instrument by which the three males assert their claims to noble behavior (pp 236–7).

1383 Item cancelled.

1384 Burnley, David. *Courtliness and Literature in Medieval England*. London: Longman, 1998.
In its conflict between personal interest and courtly proprieties, evident in its elaborately indirect syntax, Aurelius's request that Dorigen keep her promise to him (lines 1308–18) is 'a masterpiece of tortuous casuistry' (p 109).

1385 Davenport, W.A. *Chaucer and His English Contemporaries: Prologue and Tale in The Canterbury Tales*. 1998. See **698**.
FranP, enriched by comments on technical uses of language, prepares us, in the Franklin's courtesy of speech and behavior, for the old-fashioned tale to follow (pp 43–4). In the tale, the role of the romance hero is diminished or diverted. Neither Arveragus nor Aurelius is the story's most noble character; Dorigen and the magician emerge as the dominant figures (p 117). In identifying *FranT* as a Breton lay, Chaucer connects his narrative with traditional motifs even while transforming them; the landscape, for example, becomes a symbolic locus, full of iconographic meaning. Chaucer's main transformations of his material are rhetorical, centered in the three complaints that mark the tale's three phases: 'marriage and anxiety' (Dorigen's speech ar-

raigning the Almighty for his creation of the rocks), 'the fervent impulses of disruptive love' (Aurelius's prayer to the pagan gods), and 'the tense interplay of promises' (Dorigen's Complaint) (p 127). The idea of a Breton lay enabled Chaucer to create a literary hybrid that moves his narrative away from the rationality of his Boccaccian source and allows him to introduce contradictory elements into his story.

1386 Englade, Emilio. '"Straw for Youre Gentillesse!" Masculine Identity, Honor, and Dorigen.' *PMAM* 5 (1998), 34–57.

The mutual freedom envisioned in Dorigen and Arveragus's idealized marriage is gradually eroded by the masculine quest for honor and status. Georges Bataille's concept of 'expenditure' – the giving away of excess goods in order to gain social prestige – helps us understand the Franklin's representation of this quest; both he and the clerk are associated with lavish hospitality that forms their primary claim to social respectability. The rivalry among the men in the tale creates a bond among them in which there is no place for Dorigen. Aurelius's wooing of Dorigen, for example, is fueled as much by his identification with Arveragus as by his desire for the lady. Although the Franklin uses the clerk and his illusions as a scapegoat, all the male characters must share the responsibility for the suffering that arises in the narrative. The tale's basic conflict between the private world of individual freedom and the public world of honor requires a symbiosis of these two realities for its resolution. But Arveragus is unable to bridge this gap; the prospect of the loss of public honor compels him to deprive Dorigen of the last vestiges of her freedom. The apparent harmony of the tale's conclusion is 'built on a foundation of sand' (p 49); Arveragus's sacrifice of his wife, motivated by desperation rather than generosity, shows the masculine ideal of honor to be 'mere pretence, appearance without substance' (p 50).

1387 Fyler, John. 'Froissart and Chaucer.' In *Froissart Across the Genres*. 1998. See **700**.

See **1281**.

1388 Gravlee, Cynthia A. 'Presence, Absence, and Difference: Reception and Deception in *The Franklin's Tale*.' In *Desiring Discourse: The Literature of Love, Ovid through Chaucer*. Ed. James J. Paxson and Cynthia A. Gravlee. Selinsgrove, PA: Susquehanna UP; London: Associated University Presses, 1998. Pp 77–87.

FranT outwits its teller by thwarting the Franklin's efforts to define appropriate ethical behavior. Concepts such as truth, honor, freedom, and courtesy are continually displaced by their absent opposites. The characters' actions contradict their self-images as well as the Franklin's judgments of them. None of the tale's actors is truly concerned with mutuality in relationships; none exhibits true patience; and all (including the Franklin) suffer from illusion. The tale's true subject is not marriage, but rather 'the illusory nature of rhetoric and the difficulty of establishing univocal truth or of bringing any issue to complete closure' (p 185).

• Review by John Fyler, *Speculum* 77 (2002), 964–6: Gravlee's discovery of thoroughgoing irony in her examination of motive in *FranT* is less than persuasive.

• Review by Ralph Hexter, *ILCT* 7 (2001), 555–61: Although Gravlee's reading of the tale makes its case for deception, it is not clear how her chapter is related to the governing theme of the collection.

1389 Lipton, Emma. '"Affections of the Mind": The Politics of Marriage in Late Medieval English Literature.' PhD diss., Duke University, 1998. Dir. Lee Patterson. ProQuest (304430715). See also *DAI*–A 60/01 (1999): 123.

Ch. 1, 'Married Friendship: An Ideology for the Franklin' (pp 14–66), argues that the portrait of marriage in *FranT* develops an ideology for the emergent class of the teller. The Franklin represents the new socially mobile middle strata of society; his role as a civil servant makes him a symbol of the growth of government and civic ideology in the later Middle Ages. The tale appropriates models of love and marriage found in the romance, a mainstay of aristocratic literary ideology, and gives them a form more suitable to civil society. In the process, the tale valorizes the male civic virtues of mutuality, free will and choice, virtues that are emphasized in the classical friendship tradition. The Franklin's focus on male bonding at the end of the tale and his failure to address Arveragus's violence towards his wife suggests that he may be more invested in using marriage to articulate a horizontal ideology of social equality and in reformulating the social order than in constructing truly egalitarian gender relations. (This material forms the basis for Ch. 1, 'Married Friendship: An Ideology for the Franklin,' in Lipton, *Affections of the Mind: The Politics of Sacramental Marriage in Late Medieval English Literature* [Notre Dame, IN: U of Notre Dame P, 2007], pp 21–50.)

• Review by Conor McCarthy, *MÆ* 78 (2009), 143–4: Lipton's suggestion that *FranT* stands in contrast to anti-matrimonial poems written for friends seems undermined by Chaucer's authorship of just such a poem, *Lenvoy de Chaucer a Bukton*. And the tale's difficult conclusion poses a challenge to Lipton's claim that the final relationship between knight, squire, and clerk constitutes a social ideal.

1390 Rossi-Reder, Andrea. 'Male Movement and Female Fixity in the *Franklin's Tale* and *Il Filocolo*.' In *Masculinities in Chaucer: Approaches to Maleness in the Canterbury Tales and Troilus and Criseyde*. Ed. Peter G. Beidler. Cambridge: Brewer, 1998. Pp 105–16.

In Menedon's tale in *Fil*, men are constantly on the move, usually in an attempt to attract the *donna*'s attention. Men are also on the move in *FranT*, but their movements take place outside the domestic sphere, whereas women's movements, confined to enclosed, domestic spaces, are severely limited.

The limited mobility of Boccaccio's *donna* limits her characterization, but Chaucer places Dorigen at the center of the tale despite her lack of physical movement in the story. The reader is granted insight into Dorigen's mental movements and into the plans that she makes in private. These plans produce as much result as the obvious place-to-place movements of the men in the tale. Masculine agency in Chaucer involves physical mobility, while female agency entails intellectual movement and allows Dorigen relief from her rock-like fixity.

1391 Russell, J. Stephen. *Chaucer and the Trivium: The Mindsong of the Canterbury Tales.* Gainesville: UP of Florida, 1998.
Dorigen and Arveragus's marital agreement is cited as an example of 'perilous naming' in *CT*: the Franklin's juggling of terminology in this passage invests and reinvests the characters with 'absolute, almost allegorical identities' (p 210) and gives to the act of naming a quasimagical power.

1392 Sutcliffe, Joe. '"The Franklin's Tale": Christianity versus Paganism and Magic.' *ER* 9 (1998), 12–14.
FranT is an essentially Christian story that celebrates the power of God's grace and the virtues of patience, compassion, and forgiveness, in contrast to the pagan world and the power of magic. The contrast appears in the Franklin's condemnations of magic, in the role of providence, in the symbolism of the black rocks, in the characters' display of forgiveness, and in the opposition between marriage and courtly love.

1393 Weisl, Angela Jane. '"Quiting" Eve: Violence Against Women in the *Canterbury Tales*.' In *Violence Against Women in Medieval Texts.* Ed. Anna Roberts. Gainesville: UP of Florida, 1998. Pp 116–36.
Although nothing violent happens to Dorigen, we are reminded that it may and can: the black rocks symbolize dangers that may befall her, and her list of women who would rather die than be unfaithful is 'a literary history of women's destruction.' Dorigen is lucky, but Chaucer shows 'how easily she might not have been' (p 122).

1394 Wright, Michael J. 'Isolation and Individuality in the Franklin's Tale.' *SN* 70 (1998), 181–6.
Dorigen's individuality in *FranT* – she is a pagan who argues herself into belief in a proto-Christian God, a woman with a *trouthe* to keep rather than a conventionally chaste wife – also isolates her: she is deprived of the moral advice of the confessor that a Christian woman would have, and of the physical protection of a stereotypical vengeful spouse. Moreover, her treatment of Aurelius as an individual, with his own feelings to consider, generates her problematic promise. *FranT* celebrates 'the power of individuals to fashion their own lives' while making visible 'the costs and threats of individuality' (p 184).

1395 Condren, Edward I. *Chaucer and the Energy of Creation: The Design and Orga-*

nization of the Canterbury Tales. 1999. See **704**.

The Franklin's 'superficial sensibility,' initially demonstrated in his remarks to the Squire, his devaluing of his son, and his self-deprecating disclaimer of rhetorical knowledge, is manifested in the 'literary naïveté' (p 155) of this tale. His privileging of 'surface appearance' (p 157) shapes Dorigen and Arveragus's marriage contract; the speech and activities of the squire Aurelius; and Dorigen's confusion of symbol and fact in her lament over the rocks, her promise to Aurelius, and her protracted list of virtuous heroines. The distortion of reality by appearance is especially evident in the tale's penultimate scene, in which Arveragus, concerned with his own reputation, reduces Dorigen to a piece of property, just as the Franklin had earlier reduced his son to a possession by comparing his value to that of a parcel of land. For both Arveragus and his pilgrim creator, 'all is for show' (p 163). In his simplistic view of the world, the Franklin celebrates the trappings of *gentilesse*, but fails to understand its essence.

1396 De la Cruz Cabanillas, Isabel. 'Estereotipos Femeninos y Sexismo en *The Canterbury Tales*.' In *El Sexismo en el Lenguaje*. Ed. Maria Dolores Fernández de la Torre Madueño, Antonia María Medina Guerra, and Lidiz Taillefer de Haya. 2 vols. Málaga: Servicio de Publicaciones de Ediciones de la Diputación de Málaga, 1999. 1:261–70.

Like Custance (*MLT*) and Griselda (*ClT*), Dorigen embodies all the virtues proper to an ideal wife: submission, patience, obedience, loyalty, and fidelity (p 267).

1397 Dessart, James Marie Thomas. 'Rolled On Many a Tongue: The Ironic Convergence of Women, Authority, and Language in Five of Geoffrey Chaucer's Works.' PhD diss., University of Kentucky, 1999. Dir. Kevin S. Kiernan. See also *DAI*–A 60/01 (1999): 123.

Ch. 4, 'Speaking Amiss: Interpretation in the *Franklin's Tale*' (pp 101–23), argues that the Franklin's biases affect his story, that the characters' definitions of key concepts like *trouthe* are problematic, and that multiple interpretations are possible at all levels of the tale. The tale demonstrates the Franklin's assertion that that speech can often go 'amys' (line 780).

1398 Foster, Edward E. *Understanding Chaucer's Intellectual and Interpretative World: Nominalist Fiction*. Lewiston, NY: Mellen, 1999.

The Franklin fails to provide adequate resolutions to the issues raised in the previous tales in the so-called Marriage Group and to the questions – about appearance and reality, fraud and cynicism – peculiar to his own tale. As 'a coda on the problem of interpretation itself' (p 120), *FranT* raises 'the level of our epistemological perplexity' (p 127).

1399 Green, Richard Firth. *A Crisis of Truth: Literature and Law in Ricardian England*. Philadelphia: U of Pennsylvania P, 1999.

In Arveragus's invocation of Dorigen's *trouthe* (lines 1476–9), the legal sense would seem to be uppermost, but by associating *trouthe* with self-sacrifice, Chaucer 'pushes ethical considerations beyond the limits of an honor code' (p 16). A medieval reader might have viewed an unmarried Dorigen as obliged to keep her promise to Aurelius, on the grounds that sexual irregularity carries with it less opprobrium than oath breaking. But Chaucer sets Dorigen's promise to the squire against her marriage vow, thus dramatizing 'the clash between ostensible moral duty and private oath-keeping' (p 333). Faced with the impossible task of reconciling these two imperatives, Chaucer places his tale in an idealized fairy-tale past, a world where 'the equation of truth and honor' can be made to seem unproblematic; 'the less Dorigen is legally bound by her promise, the more honor she is finally able to demonstrate by keeping it' (p 334).

• Review by Anne Hudson, *MÆ* 69 (2000), 304–5: Green's commentaries 'do not offer easy answers: the discussion of the status of Dorigen's promise to Aurelius offers intriguing suggestions about the differing attitudes that might be taken to it in various contemporary legal forums, but leaves us to decide whether Chaucer prefers any one of them' (p 304).

1400 Greenberg, Nina Manasan. 'Dorigen as Enigma: The Production of Meaning in the *Franklin's Tale.*' *ChauR* 33 (1999), 329–49.

Dorigen's absence from the question that concludes *FranT* is the enigma that generates the central interpretive issues raised by the Franklin's narrative. Decisions to enter into contracts are informed by differing conceptions of the Real; Dorigen's 'unfleshly, ethereal promise' to 'love [Aurelius] best' (line 997) if he removes the coastal rocks is reinterpreted by her husband and her would-be lover according to the masculinist discourse that views a woman's body as a commodity (p 335). The privileging of the masculine in Arveragus's response to Dorigen's crisis demonstrates that 'there is no place within the parameters of the language of dominant (phallogocentric) economy for woman as subject' (p 339). Arveragus's exertion of the *maistrye* that he had previously forsworn is possible because the marriage contract is empty of meaning; the initial authority granted to Dorigen is a pseudo-power insofar as it lies outside of the realm of public patriarchal discourse. The Franklin could not have included Dorigen in his final *demande* without upsetting the order of the patriarchal economy. But this strategy is ultimately unsuccessful: 'Dorigen's presence speaks too loudly throughout the text to be silenced simply because she is left out of a question at the end' (p 344).

1401 Haas, Kurtis B. 'Rhetoric, Romance and the Structure of Authority in the *Canterbury Tales.*' 1999. See **705**.

Ch. 4, '*The Franklin's Tale* and the Medieval Trivium: A Call for Critical Thinking' (pp 101–24), connects the Franklin's rhetorical obsession with the linguistic incompetence of the tale's aristocratic characters. Dorigen and Arveragus fail to implement even the most rudimentary aspects of thinking inculcated by the trivium. This failure is juxtaposed with the clerk's use of the more scientific quadrivium to perpetrate fraud upon Dorigen. The tale contains echoes of John of Salisbury's *Metalogicon*, which sees the dominance of the quadrivium as a threat to clear thinking. Drawing on Paulo Freire's notion of education as a means of identifying and grappling with 'limit-situations,' Haas reads *FranT* as serving notice that fourteenth-century aristocrats may lack the thinking skills necessary to act well or wisely in the limit-situations facing them in their changing culture.

1402 Jacobs, Kathryn. 'Marriage Ceremonies and Property in *The Canterbury Tales*.' *Mediaevalia* 22 (1999), 245–63.
In several of the *CT*, Chaucer links wifely prosperity with the rights bestowed upon her in a proper church wedding. *FranT*, in which Dorigen ultimately thrives despite the apparent lack of a church marriage ceremony, would seem to be the exception that proves the rule. But given the dangers that Dorigen narrowly escapes, the tale is hardly a convincing exploration of the 'conditions under which legal safeguards can be dispensed with' (p 260). A 'fairy tale with a sense of unease behind it' (p 260), *FranT* has little application to people living in a less idealized world.

1403 Kline, Barbara. 'Scribal Agendas and the Text of Chaucer's Tales in British Library Harley MS 7333.' In *Rewriting Chaucer: Culture, Authority, and the Idea of the Authentic Text, 1400–1602*. Ed. Thomas A. Prendergast and Barbara Kline. Columbus: Ohio State UP, 1999. Pp 116–44.
Harley MS 7333, copied at Leicester Abbey by Augustinian canons, omits Dorigen's contemplation of her own suicide (lines 1422–3). Although both suicide and magic were forbidden by the Church, the references to magic are not tampered with. It is difficult to recover a consistent scribal agenda based on the canons' ideology (p 128).

1404 Roney, Lois. '"Abuse of Innocents" as a Theme in *The Canterbury Tales*: Dorigen as Instance.' *InParen* 1 (1999), 18–33.
Dorigen is a 'wimp' (p 18) because, although she is educable, she has never learned how to mediate between conflicting ethical claims, having been excluded, as a woman, from serious moral reasoning. Dorigen's innocence of worldly knowledge is a deficiency. Chaucer encourages the reader to question the social practices that kept women in a condition of debilitating innocence, unable to defend themselves against 'the Aureliuses of this world, and worse' (p 29).

1405 Spearing, A.C. 'Classical Antiquity in Chaucer's Chivalric Romances.' In *Chivalry, Knighthood, and War in the Middle Ages*. Ed. Susan J. Ridyard. Sewanee, TN: U of the South P, 1999. Pp 53–73.
Dorigen's catalogue of twenty-two pagan ladies who died rather than be dishonored may suggest that suicide, even for pagans, is a sign of female weakness, or, alternatively, that for women in the pagan world, suicide

might in certain circumstances be the only way of retaining moral integrity. With its 'long, passionate, aria-like speeches,' *FranT* is 'operatic' in character (p 64). *FranT* may be compared with Shakespeare's *Cymbeline.* Both are 'Celto-Roman tragi-comic fantasias' played out against a historical drama that occurs behind the scenes – 'the transition from paganism to Christianity' (p 65).

1406 Youmans, Karen DeMent. *Chaucer and the Rhetorical Limits of Exemplary Literature.* PhD diss., University of North Texas, 1999. Dir. James Landman and Peter Richardson. Ann Arbor, MI: University Microfilms International, 1999. See also *DAI*–A 60/05 (1999): 1549.

Ch. 5, 'Chaucer's Staged Readings of Exemplary Literature' (pp 112–39), argues that Chaucer examines the rhetorical flexibility and persuasive limits of exemplary literature not only through his own creation of exemplary texts, but also through staged readings of exempla. In her Complaint, Dorigen (unlike other readers and interpreters of exemplary texts like the Wife of Bath) approaches her legendary with an earnest desire for moral guidance. But the narratives themselves, by creating further ethical confusion and anxiety, 'intensify Dorigen's moral paralysis' (p 133).

1407 Yu, Je-Boon. 'Chaucer's Women: His Feminist/Anti-Feminist Vision.' *British and American Language and Literature* (Saehan English Language Institute, Korea) 41 (1999), 155–71.

To acknowledge that women 'desiren libertee' (line 768) is to accept women as independent individuals who are the equal of men. Unlike the other tales of the Marriage Group, *FranT* examines honor (a quality normally associated with men) as a key facet of Dorigen's trial. Far from depriving her of freedom, Arveragus's advice that Dorigen must preserve her honor by keeping her promise to Aurelius allows her to take full responsibility in exercising her *libertee.*

The Franklin's Tale, 2000–2005

1408 Andrew, Malcolm, ed. *Geoffrey Chaucer: Three Tales of Love and Chivalry.* 2000. See **125**.

FranT is concerned with the ethics of behavior within a loving marriage, a subject unusual for romance, which usually treats the processes of wooing rather than the trials of married life. The marriage arrangement of Dorigen and Arveragus is based on mutual respect and forbearance, with the husband forgoing the dominance that is normally his due. The tale tests this arrangement by means of a plot that may seem contrived, but which nevertheless addresses fundamental human values and principles (xvi–xvii).

1409 Archibald, Elizabeth. 'The Breton Lay in Middle English: Genre, Transmission, and the Franklin's Tale.' In *Medieval Insular Romance: Translation and Innovation*. Ed. Judith Weiss, Jennifer Fellows, and Morgan Dickson. Woodbridge, UK: Brewer, 2000. Pp 55–70.

Breton lays in French may have been more widely read and recited in thirteenth- and fourteenth-century England than has generally been supposed. In contrast to many of the French lays, none of the extant ME Breton lays focuses on adultery. In introducing *FranT* as a French-style Breton lay, Chaucer raises and then undercuts generic expectations by telling a story of a happily married woman who rejects an unwanted suitor and is then faced with the horrifying prospect of sleeping with him at her husband's urging. Two of the three set complaints in *FranT* are spoken by Dorigen. Chaucer's use of the term *lay* (line 710) in connection with the genre of the complaint in *FranT* and elsewhere suggests that he thought of complaints – especially by women – as characteristic of the Breton lay.

1410 Bowers, John M. 'Chaucer after Smithfield: From Postcolonial Writer to Imperialist Author.' In *The Postcolonial Middle Ages*. 2000. See **707**. Pp 53–66.

Chaucer's choice of Brittany as the setting for *FranT* reflects the duchy's Celtic origins and its cultural and political separateness from France. Arveragus's quest for honor in arms takes place in a kindred land – 'in Engelond that cleped was eek Briteyne' (line 810). The French town of Orléans, on the other hand, is a zone of instability, uncertainty, and illusion.

1411 Burnley, David. 'Language.' In *A Companion to Chaucer*. 2000. See **237**. Pp 235–50.

Lines 1571–1619 are examined as an example of Chaucer's grammar, syntax, and lexical borrowing. The passage reflects the clerk's character and idiom.

1412 Crane, Susan. 'Duxworth Redux: The Paris Manuscript of the *Canterbury Tales*.' In *Manuscript, Narrative, Lexicon: Essays on Literary and Cultural Transmission in Honor of Whitney F. Bolton*. 2000. See **709**.

Questions Crow's belief (**441**) that Jean d'Angoulême controlled the hand of the scribe John Duxworth. Many features of the Paris MS may reflect Duxworth's sense of his role as that of *compilator*. For example, the incorporation of Latin glosses into the text of Dorigen's Complaint mirrors Dorigen's deference to authority even while echoing, in the difference in scripts, 'the tale's problematic differentiation between what Dorigen cites and what she herself does with regard to suicide' (p 31).

1413 Cullen, Dolores L. *Chaucer's Pilgrims: The Allegory*. Santa Barbara, CA: Fithian, 2000.

The Franklin's association with the god Jupiter, established in *GP*, continues in *FranP*, in wordplay on *burel* (line 716) as 'a ray of light'; in the 'flicker' of an allusion to Mount Olympus in line 721; and in the Franklin's lack of knowledge of Cicero, 'a mere mortal [who] came into being long after the Franklin/Jupiter took charge' (p 239).

1414 Eaton, R.D. 'Narrative Closure in Chaucer's Franklin's Tale.' *Neophil* 84 (2000), 309–21.

FranT's happy ending, in which the narrative undoes itself, should cause us to be suspicious of the teller's values and motives. At the end, we see the principal characters carrying on as if the earlier unpleasantness had never happened, while our attention is directed away from the blameworthy behavior we have just witnessed and toward the final state of happiness. When we look beyond the tale's optimism, we see a world that is isolated and isolating, weighed down and limited by the physical, the material, and the sensual. The tale's subject is man's vulnerability to himself – the ways in which the connection between self and body weakens man's moral strength and his capacity for spiritual fulfillment.

1415 Fredell, Joel. 'The Lowly Paraf: Transmitting Manuscript Design in *The Canterbury Tales*.' 2000. See **711**.

Reproductions of parallel passages from Dorigen's Complaint in Cambridge University Dd.4.24 (Dd) and Oxford, Corpus Christi College 198 (Cp) show Dd marking Dorigen's exempla of virtuous suicides with a paraf, whereas in Cp no such markers are used. Dd distinguishes each exemplum as a separate pearl of wisdom; Cp 'preserves the purity of the text column and the narrative integrity of the speech as a whole' (p 217). In El, Hg, and Dd, *KnT*, *SqT*, and *FranT* are the most heavily flagged tales; bits of magic and mythology (in *FranT*, the clerk's illusions) are singled out for attention. See **699**.

1416 Fyler, John M. 'Pagan Survivals.' In *A Companion to Chaucer*. 2000. See **237**. Pp 349–59.

Astrology and magic in *FranT* are aligned with other versions of delusion and self-delusion, notably Aurelius's devotion to the fantasy of adulterous love. In the context of the Franklin's comments about heathen folly and illusion, the seasonal vignette (lines 1243–55) symbolically reenacts 'the progress from Old Law to New Law, from the Old Testament to the new dispensation of mercy and grace' (p 357), figured in the tale by Aurelius's releasing of Dorigen from her vow and the magician's releasing of Aurelius from his payment.

1417 Glanz, James. 'In Chaucer Tale, a Clue to an Astronomic Reality.' *NYT*, 7 March 2000, late ed.: F6.

Summarizes **1421**. The weakest link in Olson's argument is that Chaucer knew about the rare astronomical event, since it occurred around the year of his birth. (See also 'In "The Canterbury Tales," Clues to a Rare Celestial Event.' *Pittsburgh Post–Gazette*, 13 March 2000: A-10.)

1418 Hamaguchi, Keiko. 'In Defense of Dorigen: Dorigen's Complaint in the *Franklin's Tale*.' In *Fiction and Truth: Essays on the* [*sic*] *Fourteenth-Century English Literature*. Ed. Hisao Tsuru. Tokyo: Kirihara Shoten, 2000. Pp 195–211.

Reading the exempla in Dorigen's Complaint as instances of 'trafficking in women' compels us to question interpretations of the passage as a comic interlude. Although suicide to preserve chastity was permissible in pagan cultures, 'Dorigen is ... a Catholic woman' (p 201). Dorigen's dilemma – a choice between the sin of adultery and the sin of suicide – reflects the same dilemma that the Christian fathers grappled with when they examined this subject; Augustine, Jerome, and Ambrose 'taught that suicide is unlawful, yet they were still indecisive when they evaluated the women who chose death to protect their chastity' (p 205). Dorigen's final instances of women who were famous for their chastity may suggest her desperate hope for an alternative solution that might avoid both adultery and suicide. Arveragus's speech and actions ignore Dorigen's dilemma and perpetuate the trafficking in female bodies suffered by the pagan women of her exempla. The Complaint underscores the cruelty of Arveragus's decision and the callousness of Aurelius's claim. The Franklin's concluding question about generosity is perhaps an 'ironic joke' aimed at the three men (p 211).

1419 Higgs, Elton D. 'Temporal and Spiritual Indebtedness in the *Canterbury Tales*.' In *New Perspectives on Middle English Texts. A Festschrift for R.A. Waldron*. Ed. Susan Powell and Jeremy J. Smith. Cambridge: Brewer, 2000. Pp 151–67.

Although the characters in *FranT* involve themselves in problematic kinds of indebtedness, the Franklin, who is 'constitutionally unable to encompass a sordid or tragic view of life' (p 165), is sanguine rather than cynical about the possibility of conflicting interests being worked out. He believes that any debt incurred in honor and free will can transcend human frailties and produce harmonious resolutions that move beyond possessions and social status.

1419a Nesmith, Jeff. 'Eclipse may explain story in "The Canterbury Tales."' *Austin American Statesman* [Austin, TX], 11 March 2000: A28.

Summarizes **1421**.

1420 Noji, Kaoru. 'Chaucer's View of Women: Dorigen, Griselda, Wife of Bath.' In *Fiction and Truth: Essays on the* [*sic*] *Fourteenth-Century English Literature*. See **1418**. Pp 19–34.

The three female voices of Dorigen, Griselda, and the Wife of Bath ironically expose Chaucer's hierarchical view of women. (Not seen. Annotation from *SAC* 24 [2002], 501.)

1421 Olson, Donald W., Edgar Laird, and Thomas E. Lytle. 'High Tides and *The Canterbury Tales*.' *S&T* 99:4 (April 2000), 44–9.

The high tide that covers the rocks along the coast of Brittany may reflect a rare astronomical configuration – an eclipse with the earth near perihelion and the moon near perigree – and an exceptionally high tide that actually occurred on 19 December 1340, just after the winter solstice and with the sun in Capricorn (cf. lines 1245–9). The clerk's calculations enable him to predict the tide, and to pretend that he caused it. See **1417, 1419a, 1424, 1449a**.

1422 Phillips, Helen. *An Introduction to the Canterbury Tales: Reading, Fiction, Context*. 2000. See **714**.
FranT is an 'issue-raising fable' (p 142) that poses problems rather than supplying answers. But the effect of the tale's aporias and unresolved issues is not self-cancelling; rather, they lead to an awareness of incompatible value systems coexisting within the text. In contrast to *WBT* and *ClT*, the themes of nobility and generosity in *FranT* are set in relation to money; the clerk's act of generosity, for example, while signifying 'a sort of entry into the knightly class' (p 141), is also related to the economic basis of this speaker's rank: he earns his money from his *craft* and his *travaille* (line 1616–19). Chaucer may have recast Boccaccio's narrative as a Breton lay because, like Marie's lays, the tale centers on magic and the power of human generosity.

1423 ———. 'Love.' In *A Companion to Chaucer*. 2000. See **237**. Pp 281–95.
Lines 729–802 construct a view of marriage centered on love, friendship, consent, and respect for the other partner, but the passage also contains counterelements that are essentially conservative, in which the wife voluntarily accepts the subordinate role. The 'voluntary obedience' model entails unanswered questions that produce some 'distinctly confusing writing' (e.g., lines 751–2); in the passage as a whole, 'liberal and illiberal principles are in conflict' (p 288).

1424 Sincell, Mark. 'Science, Not Fiction, in a Canterbury Tale.' 8 March 2000. *Science Now*. [Washington, DC]: American Association for the Advancement of Science. 9 June 2006. <http://sciencenow.sciencemag.org>.
Summarizes **1421**, noting that there is no way of determining whether Chaucer repeated the clerk's calculations.

1425 Sweeney, Michelle. *Magic in Medieval Romance from Chrétien de Troyes to Chaucer*. Dublin: Four Courts, 2000.
In contrast to the romances of Chrétien de Troyes and the Breton lays, in which magic generally reveals something about a particular character, *FranT* shows magic affecting an entire community. The Franklin's 'magyk natureel' (line 1125) moves away from the idea of magic as demonically inspired, and toward the belief that man has power over the natural world. The tale's magic raises questions about man's power to control his own fate and about the relation of the gods to man-made illusions; it also reveals the vulnerabilities of the characters who come in contact with it. In the tale's conclusion, Aurelius gains control over his superiors by using magical illusion; 'magic in this context evokes a potentially explosive debate concerning social status and the qualifications for entry into the ranks of the political and influential' (p 168).
• Review by Ardis Butterfield, *Speculum* 77 (2002), 998–9: Sweeney's mixing

of social and intellectual history, French reference, and analysis of magic as illusion yields a fresh view of *FranT* (p 999).

1426 Wheatley, Edward. 'Modes of Representation.' In *A Companion to Chaucer*. 2000. See **237**. Pp 296–311.
'A moment of considerable psychological realism' occurs in Arveragus's response to Dorigen's account of her promise to Aurelius (lines 1474–84). His 'genuine anguish,' followed by his reassumption of the *maistrye* that he had previous forsworn and his threat to kill Dorigen if she divulges their secret, are in contrast both to the apparent nonchalance of his own initial response and to 'uncomfortably idealized' reactions of the husband in Chaucer's sources, *Fil* and *Dec* 10.5 (p 309).

1427 Zangen, Britta. 'Frauen(körper) in der patriarchalen Welt des Mittelalters: Chaucers *Canterbury Tales*.' In *Sprachformen des Körpers in Kunst und Wissenschaft*. Ed. Gabriele Genge. Tubingen: Francke, 2000. Pp 244–58.
In the opening discussion of marital relations in *FranT*, the nature of a husband's *lordshipe* (line 743) over his wife remains an open question. Later, however, Dorigen defines a husband as a man who has power over his wife's sexual body (line 1005), a view corroborated when Arveragus orders Dorigen to yield her body to Aurelius in repayment for a promise that she had made in jest.

1428 Braswell, Mary Flowers. *Chaucer's "Legal Fiction": Reading the Records*. Teaneck, NJ: Fairleigh Dickinson UP; London: Associated University Presses, 2001.
FranT is steeped in law and legal terminology. In asking 'Which was the mooste fre?' (line 1622), Chaucer insists that his audience become pleaders in a legal case, arguing and articulating a response to the facts that he has provided (pp 77–9).

1429 Collette, Carolyn P. *Species, Phantasms, and Images: Vision and Medieval Psychology in The Canterbury Tales*. Ann Arbor: U of Michigan P, 2001.
Ch. 3, 'Tales of Marriage, *Fantasye*, and *Wille*' (pp 60–98), incorporates **1298** in revised form.

1430 Desens, Marliss C. 'Marrying Down: Negotiating a More Equal Marriage on the English Renaissance Stage.' *MRDE* 14 (2001), 227–55.
The class difference between Arveragus, a lowly knight, and Dorigen, a woman of high degree, allows them to create a nonhierarchical relationship that conforms only outwardly to society's gender paradigms (p 228).

1431 Fields, Peter John. *Craft and Anti-Craft in Chaucer's Canterbury Tales*. See **719**.
Several episodes in *FranT* (Dorigen's two monologues, her interchange with Arveragus on the subject of her promise to Aurelius) reveal that 'in Chaucer's world, nothing is as it seems, and simple assumptions must convolute and accommodate a reality that is increasingly the creature and inadvertent invention of our own conceptions' (p 18). 'The *complex craft* of self-mystifi-

cation and authority' present in *FranT* and elsewhere in Chaucer's works is traceable to the 'humanist ambiguity' of Geoffrey of Vinsauf's *Poetria Nova* (pp 388–95).

1432 Jacobs, Kathryn. *Marriage Contracts from Chaucer to the Renaissance Stage.* Gainesville: UP of Florida, 2001.

Incorporates **1173**, **1346**, and **1402** in revised form.

1433 Johnston, Andrew James. *Clerks and Courtiers: Chaucer, Late Medieval Literature, and the State Formation Process.* 2001. See **721**.

In his response to *SqT* and in his own tale, the Franklin attempts to 'contain the Squire's destructive criticism and re-construct an ideologically coherent aristocratic world-picture' (p 100). Although he praises the Squire's tale telling, the Franklin's reference to the Squire's youth serves as a mild rebuke and hints at a generational conflict. Similarities of theme in *SqT* and *FranT* highlight the differences in the tellers' value-systems. The Squire treats courtly love irreverently, while the Franklin describes an ideal merging of *fin'amor* and Christian marriage. The glamorous magic of *SqT* is reduced in *FranT* to a 'symbol of disenchantment' (p 103), a scientific commodity antithetical to the world of chivalric culture. The Brittany of *FranT* is 'the true space of romance' (p 103), whereas the Squire's Tartary is marked by 'superficial exoticism' (p 104). The Franklin responds to the Squire's 'frivolous devaluation of aristocratic culture' (p 105) by constructing a stable image of the noble life. But he does so only by depoliticizing this world 'to an extent impressive even by romance standards' (p 110).

• Review by David N. DeVries, *TMR* (May 2001), n.p.: According to Johnston, the Franklin tells a cautionary tale as a criticism of the present with the state formation process running rampant over the accepted verities. The Franklin's imagination, Johnston claims, retreats to a time before clerkly contamination had corrupted the social system. But this argument is problematic because the Franklin is neither consistent nor insistent in his criticism of the clerkly class.

1434 Lightsey, Scott. 'Chaucer's Secular Marvels and the Medieval Economy of Wonder.' 2001. See **722**.

In *FranT,* Aurelius and his brother find that 'marvels made subject to commodification and trade lose their mystery and become mundane objects of curiosity' (p 305). The garden arrayed 'by craft of mannes hand' (line 909) recalls the artificial reproductions of romance motifs in actual medieval gardens and anticipates the man-made *mirabilia* that appear later in the tale. In exposing the financial motives and means of execution that lie behind the marvels performed for Aurelius, Chaucer dispels their sense of wonder. In a like fashion, the books in the clerk's study emphasize his immersion in science rather than in demonology. We are aware of the 'astronomical and astrological mechanics' (p 307) that allow him to control nature; only

Dorigen, ignorant of Aurelius's bargain with the clerk, displays the traditional romance sense of *admiratio* – e.g., 'It is agayns the proces of nature' (line 1345) – when confronted with the rocks' disappearance.

1435 Maíz Arévalo, Carmen. 'El Sistema Dialogal en los "Canterbury Tales."' 2000. See **712**.

This sociolinguistic study of the ways in which linguistic behavior enables individual characterizations of the pilgrim speakers, expresses both ideological tensions and group connections among the pilgrims, and creates social dialects draws several examples from *FranT.*

1436 Mann, Jill. 'Wife-Swapping in Medieval Literature.' *Viator* 12 (2001), 92–112. See **1450**.

1437 Mehl, Dieter. *English Literature in the Age of Chaucer.* Harlow, UK: Longman, 2001.

It is difficult to speak of the narrator's character in *FranT*, because the MSS suggest that Chaucer had not arrived at a final ascription to a particular pilgrim. The marriage depicted at the beginning of the tale bears a 'suspicious resemblance' to January's dream of blissful wedlock in *MerT*, but the Franklin apparently believes in the reality of this idealized fantasy (p 47). The Franklin's hint of a happy ending (lines 1493–8) may seem a cheap way of justifying a questionable decision on Arveragus's part, but his point seems to be that one noble act will, against all odds, generate another. Such a claim may exemplify naïve optimism; the Franklin trusts that there is a perfect answer to every moral dilemma if one follows the rules of *gentilesse*. The question that ends the tale, however, is open-ended, reminding us that there is no single ideal solution to the ethical questions raised by the plot.

1438 Morgan, Gerald. 'Experience and the Judgement of Poetry: A Reconsideration of "The Franklin's Tale."' *MÆ* 70 (2001), 204–25.

A true understanding of *FranT* rests on an admiration for chivalric values and an acceptance of obedience as the proper duty of a wife. The marriage of Dorigen and Arveragus is based on an ideal of mutual service and love and on each partner's respect for the other's free will – both central tenets of Christian marriage that inform this ostensibly pagan tale. In accepting the validity of Dorigen's promise to Aurelius and in sending his wife to the squire, Arveragus refuses to infringe on Dorigen's autonomy. His apparent exercise of *maistrye* is in fact in accordance with her will, just as his concern with public reputation manifests care for his wife's honor more than for his own. Dorigen's wifely humility is a sign of her love and fidelity and is in accordance with the wife's vow of obedience in the Christian marriage ceremony. Hers is true rather than false obedience, a moral virtue actively willed by the obedient person. Arveragus does not (*pace* Robertson [**918**]) send Dorigen off to commit adultery; in treating her as an equal rather than as an inferior, he regards her oath to Aurelius to be 'as binding as any he might give … as a knight' (p 219). The self-sacrificing generosity of the husband is the only means by which the tale's moral dilemma can be resolved and in it lies 'the true meaning of love' (p 220).

1439 Oldmixon, Katherine Durham. 'Otherworlds/Otherness: The Cultural Politics of Exoticism in Middle English "Breton" Lays.' PhD diss., University of Texas at Austin, 2001. Dir. Thomas Cable and Geraldine Heng. ProQuest (54223235). See also *DAI*–A 65/11 (2005): 4189.
Ch. 4, 'Chaucer's "Derke Fantasye": The Lay of Dorigen' (pp 258–324), examines Chaucer's choice of genre, the tale's presentation of gender and class politics, and the implications of its concluding question.

1440 Ronquist, E.C. 'The Franklin, Epicurus, and the Play of Values.' In *Chaucer and Language: Essays in Honour of Douglas Wurtele*. Ed. Robert Myles and David Williams. Montreal: McGill-Queen's UP, 2001. Pp 44–60.
The Franklin's treatment of young people, rhetoric, natural perfection, and acts of promising in his tale 'reveals a more subtle character than his portrait in the *GP* would suggest' (p 57).

1441 Rudd, Gillian. *The Complete Critical Guide to Geoffrey Chaucer*. 2001. See **724**.
FranT continues the debate on *gentilesse* and the discussion of marriage introduced in previous tales. The crux of the tale is the matter of *trouthe*, both in relation to Dorigen's promise to Aurelius and to the actions of the men in the story. The tale's genre leads us to expect magic, but unlike the unquestionable marvels in *SqT*, the disappearance of the rocks in *FranT* may be genuine magic or simply the product of advanced learning (pp 130–2).

1442 Saunders, Corinne J. *Rape and Ravishment in the Literature of Medieval England.* Cambridge: Brewer, 2001.
The image of threatened rape in *FranT* is less a matter of physical than of verbal constraint. The potential shame of Dorigen submitting herself to Aurelius aligns her with the classical victims of rape whom she cites in her lament. But the emphasis is finally not so much on 'the permanence of physical pollution and shame as on the social implications of force and consent, and on the transformative power of virtue' (p 295).

1443 Schildgen, Brenda Deen. *Pagans, Tartars, Moslems, and Jews in Chaucer's Canterbury Tales*. 2001. See **725**.
FranT represents pagan difference by way of philosophical discourse. Arveragus and the clerk adhere to an Epicurean value system (e.g., a belief in free will, hardheaded empiricism), Dorigen reflects the ideals of the 'virtuous Stoic pagan' (p 76), Aurelius's moral ethos includes several pagan philosophies (particularly the Epicurean search after pleasure), and the Franklin himself expresses a pagan philosophical pluralism that nowhere defers to Christian morals or ethics. Dorigen's narrative tests both Stoicism and Epicureanism – she does not 'lerne to suffre' (line 777) in Stoic fashion, and she gives away her free will when she marries. The oaths in the tale reflect folk

conventions; they exist outside the Judaeo-Christian tradition, and contradict as well the Stoic and Epicurean philosophies debated in the tale.
• Review by Warren Ginsberg, *C&L* 51 (2002), 667: While acknowledging the force of Schildgen's arguments that the Franklin rehabilitates Epicureanism as 'a practical ethics for living in a courtly or noble atmosphere' and that the tale provides no direct evidence that Chaucer wished to satirize the Franklin's values, one may still contend that Chaucer asks us to measure against Christian standards the manner in which the Franklin prosecutes his pleasures.
• Review by H.L. Spencer, *RES* 54 (2003), 518–19: Schildgen's arguments are sometimes compromised by lack of precision, as in her assertion that Chaucer overlooks the differences between ideologies by making the Christian word *grace* synonymous with *aventure*. In fact, he does apprehend the distinction ('aventure or grace,' line 1508), even casually calling attention to it (p 518).

1444 Battles, Paul. 'Magic and Metafiction in the *Franklin's Tale*: Chaucer's Clerk of Orléans as Double of the Franklin.' In *Marvels, Monsters, and Miracles: Studies in the Medieval and Early Modern Imaginations*. Ed. Timothy S. Jones and David A. Sprunger. Studies in Medieval Culture 42. Kalamazoo, MI: Medieval Institute Publications, 2002. Pp 243–66.
Although critics have drawn analogies between Chaucer and the clerk of Orléans, a stronger case can be made for pairing the clerk and the Franklin as makers of illusion. It is an error to rationalize away the tale's element of the supernatural as stagecraft. Real magic is involved, but it is the illusions themselves, not the process whereby they are produced, that are of key importance, in part because they are linked with the self-generated illusions generated by the 'over-active imaginations' (p 247) of Dorigen and Aurelius. The clerk bears some resemblance to minstrel figures (such as those in *HF*) who combine skill in conjuring with the arts of story-telling; he creates magical illusions that can be compared to poetic fictions and which, on a more literal level, are necessary to move the plot forward. The tale establishes multiple parallels between the clerk and the Franklin – both are associated with food, both have well-appointed households, and both display 'political acumen' (p 256) in their manipulation of their audiences' needs. In a further entangling of the tale and the frame of *CT*, Chaucer creates numerous similarities between Aurelius and the Squire. The Franklin hopes to educate the latter with his story. In a parallel fashion, the clerk acts as an agent of Aurelius's edification, both 'by showing him the images he wants to see' and also by creating 'the necessary conditions for his dis-illusioning' (p 261). Aurelius is specifically educated in the nature of true *gentilesse* – one of the Franklin's insistent preoccupations, connected in the tale, as it is in *Sq–FranL*, with the proper attitude toward money. Although Kittredge's argument for a corre-

spondence between teller and tale (**815**) is not appropriate for all of *CT*, it can profitably be applied to the Franklin's performance.

1445 Breeze, Andrew. 'The Name Kayrrud in the *Franklin's Tale.*' *ChauR* 37 (2002), 95–9.
Evidence from Old Breton, Cornish, and Welsh supports Kirby's claim (**1217**) that *Kayrudd* (line 808) was originally *Kairiud*, to be identified with Kérity, a small fishing village in Penmarch.

1446 Davis, Craig B. 'A Perfect Marriage on the Rocks: Geoffrey and Philippa Chaucer, and the *Franklin's Tale.*' *ChauR* 37 (2002), 129–44.
FranT depicts a fictional union between a lower-born knight and a higher-born lady that is structurally similar to the bourgeois Chaucer's own marriage to Philippa Roet, the daughter of a Flemish knight. In the poem, the pristine union between Dorigen and Arveragus is subjected to a variety of trials, and finally reestablished on a more mature and self-aware footing. The tale shows us that 'perfect marriages can be just as fraught emotionally as any other kind' (p 142). Although *FranT* should not be read as a naïve idealization the poet's own life, the 'joys and menaces' experienced by its protagonists may well reflect similar ups and downs in Chaucer's marriage to Philippa, both in their lives together and their many times apart (p 143).

1447 Davis, Steven. 'Guillaume de Machaut, Chaucer's *Book of the Duchess*, and the Chaucer Tradition.' *ChauR* 36 (2002), 391–405.
The Dreamer's apparent ignorance of the death of the Man in Black's lady in *BD* may reflect the stance of the sophisticated reader envisioned by Machaut, for whom the 'I' of a lyric utterance would not necessarily refer to its performer. This kind of reading is manifest in Dorigen's response to the love-complaints of Aurelius, himself a 'good Machauldian lover' (p 398). Dorigen is genuinely surprised by Aurelius's direct confession of desire because she never would have believed that his songs were anything but the generic sentiments of a 'lusty squier, servant to Venus' (line 937).

1448 Forste-Grupp, Sheryl L. 'A Woman Circumvents the Laws of Primogeniture in *The Weddynge of Sir Gawen and Dame Ragnell.*' *SP* (2002), 105–22.
Ragnell's erasure from *The Weddynge of Sir Gawen and Dame Ragnell* is similar to that of Dorigen in *FranT*. Once Dorigen has been released from her promise by Aurelius, she disappears, the remainder of the poem focusing on the male characters' negotiations among themselves to save their honors and reputations. Dorigen is omitted from the final question ('Which was the mooste fre?', line 1622) with the tacit assumption that her virtues are inconsequential to the men whose deeds and speeches occur in the public sphere (pp 118–19).

1449 Hirsh, John C. *Chaucer and the Canterbury Tales: A Short Introduction.* Malden, MA: Blackwell, 2002.
In Kittredge's influential interpretation (**805**), the Franklin preaches toler-

ance and forgiveness. But there is little tolerance in his tale, which seems 'calculated to outrage modern sentiment' and manifests 'studied insensitivity' in its reduction of everything to 'a conventional construction of chivalry' (p 71). The discomfort produced by the tale is usually traced to the Franklin's imperfect understanding of the courtly customs he attempts to reproduce. *FranT* is 'an odd duck, like its teller, and curiously at war with itself' (p 72).

1449a Jaroff, Leon. 'By Yonder Blessed Moon, Sleuths Decode Life and Art.' *NYT*, 16 July 2002, late edition: F.3.
Includes a brief summary of the evidence from *FranT* that leads Olson (**1421**) to believe that Chaucer was 'an advanced amateur astronomer.'

1450 Mann, Jill. *Feminizing Chaucer*. 2002. See **729**.
The marriage contract of Dorigen and Arveragus is based on a mutual surrender of *maistrye* (line 764) – not by establishing equality, but by embracing *pacience* (line 773), which for Chaucer is not a static virtue but an openness to change. The threats to the marriage posed by external and internal change are averted by accepting and absorbing change. The tale's commitment to movement rather than stasis and finality governs Dorigen's reluctance to kill herself, which in turn opens up space for Arveragus's questions and his insistence that she keep her promise to Aurelius. The narrative here replicates 'the doubling of roles intimated in the opening passage' (p 92): Arveragus's action allows Dorigen to take full responsibility for her promise, while his *suffrance* (line 788) – both bearing pain and giving up power – demonstrates his trust in his wife. Comparable surrenders govern the behavior of Aurelius and the clerk; the conclusion of the tale manifests not mere wishful thinking about the efficacy of patience, but rather demonstrates the authenticity of what does happen, by acknowledging, in 'alternative versions' of the story (p 95), that it does not always happen thus. (For an earlier version and reviews of this material, see **656**.)

In an 'Excursus: Wife-Swapping in Medieval Literature' (pp 152–73), Mann responds to Riddy's claim (**1337**) that *gentilesse* in *FranT* is class- and gender-based, and has to do with relations between men. In a variety of medieval literary texts, the renunciation of a wife, whether by a husband or a lover, enacts a man's regard for another man. In *FranT*, however, it 'testifies to Arveragus's regard for his wife, and to Aurelius's regard for Arveragus's regard for his wife' (p 172). The tale celebrates the power of a commitment to *trouthe*, and alone among the stories examined, it gives a woman's *trouthe* the same status as a man's.

1451 McCarthy, Conor. 'Love, Marriage, and Law: Three Canterbury Tales.' *ES* 83 (2002), 504–18.
See **1485**.

1451a Monz, Dominic. *Gentilesse und gentils. Der weltliche Adel und seine Werte in Geoffrey Chaucers Canterbury Tales*. 2002. See **729a**.

The central theme of *FranT* is the superior status of *trouthe*: without Arveragus's idealistic belief in *trouthe*, the tale's happy ending would not have been possible (p 155). None of the tale's characters are without flaws, but their essential virtuousness enables them to set into motion the chain of 'gentil dedes' that leads the story to a more ideal world. In a sense, it is chivalric *gentilesse* (manifested in Arveragus's quest for fame, in *fine amour*, and in the emphasis on the sacredness of oaths) that creates the tale's conflicts, but it is also *gentilesse* in the form of *trouthe* and integrity that brings about the resolution of what seems like a hopeless tangle of competing claims. The tale's acts of *gentilesse* form a social hierarchy, with Arveragus's renunciation of his exclusive claim on Dorigen producing, in turn, the renunciations made by Aurelius and the magician. But the tale also emphasizes the democratic availability of moral *gentilesse*, in which a squire as well as a knight can 'doon a gentil dede' (line 1543; p 157). The egalitarianism of the tale's conclusion suggests that, in addition to the chivalric and public aspects of *gentilesse*, a nobleman must also possess private virtue. Such a position may reflect the Franklin's lack of full chivalric status. Among the aristocratic classes, whose values he holds high, the Franklin must earn his place by exemplary behavior rather than inherited rank (p 162).

1452 Nelson, Marie. '"Biheste is dette": Marriage Promises in Chaucer's *Canterbury Tales.*' *PLL* 38 (2002), 167–99.
J.L. Austin's criteria for promising are employed to examine promises within marriage in six of the *CT*. Dorigen and Arveragus's marriage agreement meets all the requirements of promising, but Dorigen's promise to love Aurelius best if he removes the coastal rocks does not meet the sincerity requirement for promising, and hence is 'no promise at all' (p 191). Aurelius nevertheless takes Dorigen at her word, as does Arveragus, who – acting out of a concern for his wife's honor but disregarding his earlier vow not to exercise *maistrye* – treats her playful vow to Aurelius as a genuine promise. Although Aurelius ultimately frees Dorigen from her obligation, Chaucer's Parson, speaking in judgment, might have advised her simply to say 'no' to the lovesick squire rather than attempting a tactful answer.

1453 O'Brien, Timothy D. 'Glimpsing Medusa: *Astoned* in the *Troilus.*' *Quidditas* 23 (2002): 33–49.
Shoaf (**1205**) employs Medusa as a trope in *FranT* rather than discussing the tale's use of the figure. In fact, the tale 'depends upon images' – the rocks, the use of *graven* (line 830), and the allusion to Deucalion (lines 1613–15) – 'that develop an extended metaphor of petrification' and hence 'place the Medusa, however vaguely,' in *FranT* (pp 36–7).

1454 Osborn, Marijane. *Time and the Astrolabe in The Canterbury Tales.* 2002. See **730**.
The passage describing the clerk's astrological calculations is set up to make us believe that the submerging of the rocks is a trick. But the 'termes of as-

trologye' (line 1266) in fact refer to a real series of alignments of tidal forces that occurred in December 1340. Through his illusionist clerk, Chaucer 'creates the illusion of an illusion' (p 201).

1455 Pakkala-Weckström, Mari. 'Have her my trouthe—Til that myn herte breste: Dorigen and the Difficulty of Keeping Promises in the Franklin's Tale.' In *Variation Past and Present: VARIENG Studies on English for Terttu Nevalainen.* Ed. Helena Raumolin-Brunberg, Minna Nevala, Arja Nurmi, and Matti Rissanen. Mémoires de la Société Néophilogique de Helsinki 61. Helsinki: Société Néophilogique, 2002. Pp 287–300.

Examined in the light of speech act theory, the sequence of refusal-promise-refusal with which Dorigen answers Aurelius's lovelorn entreaty constitutes a simple refusal; her oath to love Aurelius best (line 998) is a performative, which depends on felicity conditions (i.e., on the speaker having the proper thoughts and intentions). But the characters in the tale (including Dorigen) do not see it that way; 'even though Dorigen's promise does not fulfill the felicity conditions necessary, she still has to live up to it, because she is a female character in a medieval romance' (p 298). Her deepest intentions become irrelevant when set against her husband's honor and the public value of *trouthe*.

1456 Pelen, Marc M. 'The Escape of Chaucer's Chauntecleeer: A Brief Revaluation.' *ChauR* 36 (2002), 329–35.

The concluding question in *FranT* (line 1622) exemplifies Chaucer's interest in ironic or contradictory endings. It can be argued that none of the characters is generous, because all have tried to deceive each other through deception and illusion (p 332).

1457 Rudd, Gillian. 'Making the Rocks Disappear: Refocusing Chaucer's Knight's and Franklin's Tales.' In *The Environmental Tradition in English Literature.* Ed. John Parham. Aldershot: Ashgate, 2002. Pp 118–29.

Dorigen views nature dualistically and egocentrically, seeing herself as of greater consequence than the rocks. By imposing her desires on the rocks, she implicitly asserts that nature may be manipulated by man, and thus lays herself open to being similarly manipulated via her gender and her association with the managed natural world (e.g., the garden arrayed 'by craft of mannes hand' [line 909]). In contrast to Dorigen, the clerk is able to control the natural world 'without actually risking tangling directly with its perils' (p 129).

1458 Salisbury, Eve. 'Chaucer's "Wife," the Law, and the Middle English Breton Lays.' In *Domestic Violence in Medieval Texts.* Ed. Eve Salisbury, Georgiana Donavin, and Merralls Llewelyn Price. Gainesville: UP of Florida, 2002. Pp 73–93. Repr. in *Recent Trends in Medieval Language and Literature in Honour of Young-Bae Park* (see **1500**). Pp 347–75.

In *FranT*, domestic violence takes the form of psychological abuse. Dorigen has been 'driven to contemplate suicide, virtually pimped, and threatened with homicide by her husband.' The question the Franklin asks at the end of his tale, however, is not 'why Dorigen was so mistreated,' but rather who among the men was most generous (p 89).

1459 Smith, Warren S. 'Dorigen's Lament and the Resolution of the *Franklin's Tale.*' *ChauR* 36 (2002), 374–90.
Dorigen's use of *Jov* in her lament corrects Jerome's artificial rhetoric and his rigid moral system, points up his inconsistencies, and directs his discourse in a more humane and emotionally persuasive direction, one that 'implies a strong insistence on the difference between right and wrong' (p 376). By deploring (rather than approving or praising) the suicides of the oppressed women and by stressing the wickedness of the men who drove them to it, Dorigen shifts the moral impact of Jerome's treatise, reorienting it through her compassion and *gentilesse*. One effect of Dorigen's transformation of Jerome is to anticipate the tale's 'gentle denouement' (p 389), hinting that the dilemmas posed by the narrative will be resolved ethically.

1460 Tajiri, Masaji. *Studies in the Middle English Didactic Tail-Rhyme Romances.* [Tokyo]: Eihosha, 2002.
Distinguishes between Middle English Breton *lais* in tail rhyme and those in couplets. The latter show more acquaintance with authentic Celtic elements – in the case of *FranT,* the rocky Breton coastline (p 65).

1461 Lucotti, Claudia. 'El tema del matrimonio en *The Canterbury Tales* de Geoffrey Chaucer.' *ALM* 11 (2002–3), 35–46.
Although it takes place in the idyllic world of romance, *FranT* revises the gender stereotypes of the romance form in its treatment of Dorigen, who assumes increasing responsibility for complex ethical issues, and in its problematizing of the traditional role of the husband as a rational guide who counsels and educates an inexperienced wife (p 43).

1462 Bodden, M.C. 'Disordered Grief and Fashionable Afflictions in Chaucer's Franklin's Tale and the Clerk's Tale.' In *Grief and Gender, 700–1700.* Ed. Jennifer C. Vaught and Lynne Dickson Bruckner. New York: Palgrave Macmillan, 2003. Pp 52–63.
By showing how prescribed roles of grieving subvert natural feelings, Chaucer reveals the way in which cultural contexts determine the expression of grief for both men and women in *FranT.* For men, the poles are the stoic suffering exhibited by Arveragus and Aurelius's ritualized courtly melancholia. Although neither code allows the men to participate in natural mourning, both are associated with nobility of character. In contrast to the men's suffering, Dorigen's grief is presented as excessive and disordered; it reduces her to a single dimension – 'grief personified' (p 58). For both men and women, however, suffering in *FranT* is non-transformative, and may be understood as a Chaucerian commentary on 'the fraudulence of those values that nearly

every cultural institution attributes to grief and loss' (p 63).

1463 Bourgne, Florence. *The Canterbury Tales, Geoffrey Chaucer*. Paris: Colin, 2003. *FranT* contains two kinds of space, pleasant and frightening. The rocks along the coast of Brittany, like the forest in medieval romance, are inimical to human life; the Christian coloring of Dorigen's complaint transforms them into an anti-Creation, the supposed work of the devil. The garden to which Dorigen's friends lead her as an alternative to the rocks derives from the classical tradition of the *locus amoenus*; decorated by 'craft of mannes hand' (line 237), it competes with the terrestrial paradise, the first garden of the Creation. The hunting park that the magician reveals to Aurelius is also a sort of paradise, reserved for masculine activities in contrast to the garden, which is accessible to women (pp 61–70).

1464 Burger, Glenn. *Chaucer's Queer Nation*. Medieval Cultures 34. Minneapolis: U of Minnesota P, 2003.
FranT 'reconfigures potentially destabilizing differences among characters ... as marginal to a deeper, integral "freedom" these subjects are capable of realizing' (p 114). The tale establishes 'a new disciplinary culture of the middle, modernizing elite'; rather than fulfilling the roles prescribed by their traditional estates (nobility by birth, by clerical schooling, and by courtly love schooling), the male characters are constituted as 'a new universal subject' in which *gentilesse* provides 'an empowering, "progressive" redefinition of "noble"' (p 115). Although differences of birth, education, and control of goods among the men are surmounted by the action of *fredom*, Dorigen is denied access to this new selfhood; she is rather traded among the male characters to secure for them the ideal of domestic stability that she represents.

1465 Di Rocco, Emilia. *Chaucer: Guida ai "Canterbury Tales."* 2003. See **734**.
In commanding Dorigen to fulfill her promise to Aurelius, Arveragus manifests a form of chivalry that is entirely self-centered and incapable of understanding the true significance of social ideals. Rather than demonstrating nobility of soul, the renunciations of both the husband and the squire show the two men as incapable of confronting a situation brought about by their own ideals. Initially associated with Aurelius, courtesy is ultimately located in the clerk, who gives up his payment in a gesture of disinterested generosity (pp 61–3). In Dorigen's Complaint, Chaucer abandons the dramatic verisimilitude that characterizes other moments in his tale. Although Dorigen compares her situation to that of classical heroines, the genre of *FranT* – romance rather than tragedy – calls for a less uncompromising denouement than do the earlier narratives. By placing the solution to her dilemma in her husband's hands, Dorigen gives him back the *maistrye* he had previously renounced and implicitly counters the Wife of Bath's claim that female sovereignty is necessary for a successful marriage (p 112). (Di Rocco also supplies

a summary of the tale's plot and a brief account of its sources, pp 38–9.)

1466 ———. *Letteratura e Legge nel Trecento Inglese: Chaucer, Gower e Langland.* Rome: Bulzoni, 2003.
Both civil and canon law may help us to interpret the promises in *FranT*. According to the former, the presence of an 'impossible condition' (the removal of the rocks) in Dorigen's playful vow to Aurelius would have rendered it null and void, while canon law might have justified Dorigen's tricking of the squire insofar as her ruse is intended to preserve her chastity (i.e., her faithfulness to her husband). Although the tale alludes to both Christian and chivalric moral codes, the latter dominates the crucial episode in which Arveragus, invoking the knightly virtue of *trouthe,* commands Dorigen to fulfill her promise to Aurelius. In an attempt to emulate what he understands as Arveragus's magnanimity, Aurelius frees Dorigen from her bond. He simultaneously acknowledges an aspect of promising central to the writings of the canonists – the element of 'intention,' the spirit behind the letter of Dorigen's promise that he was unable to recognize earlier in the tale (pp 238–46).

1467 Elliot, Dyan. 'Marriage.' In *The Cambridge Companion to Medieval Women's Writing.* Ed. Carolyn Dinshaw and David Wallace. Cambridge: Cambridge UP, 2003. Pp 40–57.
Arveragus's response to Dorigen's vow to Aurelius can be seen as prioritizing his wife's legal autonomy over her physical purity and his own marital rights. Yet the tale also demonstrates the downside of granting legal autonomy to women. Dorigen conforms to the stereotype enunciated by the canonist William Lyndwood (d. 1446), who cautioned clerics against women 'who are accustomed to emit vows more readily than men,' especially in situations of distress (p 46).

1468 Fein, Susanna. 'Boethian Boundaries: Compassion and Constraint in the *Franklin's Tale.*' In *Drama, Narrative and Poetry in the Canterbury Tales.* Ed. Wendy Harding. Toulouse: Presses Universitaires du Miral, 2003. Pp 195–212.
FranT raises essential questions about the value of constraint, especially as elaborated upon by Boethius in *Consol* 2.m8. The marriage agreement of Dorigen and Arveragus reflects a Boethian perspective on the binding of opposing forces into a harmonious whole. The events that follow the opening section of the tale, however, introduce multiple reversals, impossible contradictions, contrary impulses, and seemingly irreconcilable movements, many grounded in gender difference (e.g., Arveragus's physical quest away from home versus Dorigen's stationary, inward-looking monologues). The 'ultimate breaking point of imbalance' (p 211) between male and female – Arveragus's 'Is ther oght elles?' and Dorigen's answer 'This is to muche!' (lines 1469–71) – initiates a counter-movement in the form of Aurelius's

change of heart. 'Both gender systems merge in the transformed lover,' whose release of Dorigen from her vow is produced both by his admiration of and desire to imitate Arveragus's honorable action and by his newly awakened capacity for feminine compassion (p 211). Metaphorically, Aurelius is the 'legitimate progeny' of Dorigen and Arveragus, 'now whole in the Boethian sense' (p 212).

1469 Gray, Douglas. 'The Franklin's Tale.' In *The Oxford Companion to Chaucer*. 2003. See **735**. Pp 192–4.
As in *ClT*, Chaucer takes an extraordinary situation as a kind test case in *FranT*, delighting in 'making a folk tale with its strange absolutes into a moral tale with believable, dramatically conceived characters' (p 194).

1470 Hughes, Alan. *Signs and Circumstances: A Study of Allegory in Chaucer's Canterbury Tales*. 2003. See **737**.
Hughes reads *FranT* as an allegory of the relations of Richard II and Queen Anne, claiming, for example, that the 'inability of Aurelius to enforce the promise so fraudulently gained … indicates King Richard's inability to go against his … promise of granting sexual refusal to his young queen' (p 79).

1471 Lawler, Traugott. 'Delicacy vs. Truth: Defining Moral Heroism in the *Canterbury Tales*.' In *New Readings of Chaucer's Poetry*. Ed. Robert G. Benson and Susan J. Ridyard. Woodbridge, UK: Brewer, 2003. Pp 75–90.
Gentility in *FranT* is 'a middle ground' between decadence (represented by Aurelius's courtly dalliance) and 'stolid simplicity' (p 88). It is embodied in Arveragus's belief in keeping your word – present in lyrics like *Truth* and *Sted* – and associated in the tale with the rocks: 'they have always been there and are there still despite the slippery calculations of the clerk, [and] they stand for the old simple world of nature celebrated in the lyrics' (p 88).

1472 Lynch, Kathryn L. 'Team Teaching the Literature of the European and Islamic Middle Ages: The European Perspective.' 2003.
See **738**.

1473 Moon, Hi Kyung. 'Magic and the Containment of Desire: From Chaucer to Newton.' *JCERL* 12 (2003), 5–26.
The magic in *FranT* is problematic not because it deals in illusion, but because it is put to dubious ends – for Aurelius, the fulfillment of illicit desire, for the clerk, remuneration as Aurelius's accomplice. A potentially tragic outcome is averted not through magic but rather through the containment of desire, a human impulse that undoes magic's power.

1474 Nachtwey, Gerald R. 'Geoffroi de Charny's "Book of Chivalry" and Violence in *The Man of Law's Tale* and *The Franklin's Tale*.' *EMSt* 20 (2003), 308–12.
Aspects of the vertical hierarchies foundational in chivalric society appear in both *MLT* and *FranT*. A knight, according to Geoffroi de Charny, is judged by superior prowess in battle and tournament. Arveragus's departure to seek honor in arms is thus not a superfluous absence; as a knight, he 'had

to do what was expected of him' (p 115). The dilemma in which Dorigen finds herself is also created by her place in chivalric society; since the system of chivalry encouraged knights to have lovers, 'she could at least have power over one lover, even if it is not her husband' by playing a game of courtly love that is analogous to Arveragus's game of war-making (p 116). Arveragus is the best player of the game of *gentilesse;* he seems to know that Aurelius's consciousness of chivalric hierarchies will compel him either to relinquish his claim on Dorigen or have his reputation soiled. Indeed, it is arguably advancement up the ladder of chivalric worth that Aurelius has in mind when he imitates Arveragus's act of sacrifice in the tale's penultimate scene.

1474a Pakkala-Weckström, Mari. 'Genre, gender, and power: A study of address forms in seven *Canterbury Tales.*' In *Proceedings from the 8th Nordic Conference on English Studies.* Ed. Karind Aijmer and Britta Olinder. Göteborg, Sweden: Göteborg University, 2003. Pp 121–36.

An analysis of forms of address between Dorigen and Arveragus reveals 'a comfortable ease and mutual respect which does not need to be buttressed by formal behavior' (pp 128–9).

1475 Pitcher, John A. '"Word and Werk" in Chaucer's *Franklin's Tale.*' *L&P* 49 (2003), 77–109. Repr. in Pitcher, *Chaucer's Feminine Subjects: Figures of Desire in The Canterbury Tales.* The New Middle Ages. New York: Palgrave, 2012. Pp 59–80.

Attention to power relations in *FranT* must take into account structures of desire that are everywhere marked by division and ambivalence. Aurelius's quest for Dorigen is based on the anticipation of a satisfaction forbidden him under the law; at the moment the object of his desire becomes available, he chooses renunciation rather than fulfillment. Although Dorigen's promise to Aurelius is clearly intended as a rejection, 'the question of her desire exceeds the question of what she means to say' (p 90). Each time Dorigen confronts the consequence of honoring her promise, the moment 'carries the trace of desire under erasure' (p 90). The Complaint to Fortune, for example, reveals her investment in tableaux of sexual violence; by casting the courtly Aurelius as a rapist parallel to those in the classical tales she recounts, Dorigen creates 'both a fantasy of illicit satisfaction and the threat of punishment associated with it' (p 95), while her consultation with Arveragus contains both the supposition that he will save her from her desire and that he will order her to go through with her promise. In an analogous fashion, Arveragus's insistence that Dorigen keep her *trouthe* leaves open the question of which *trouthe* – her promise to Aurelius or her earlier promise to him – she should keep; the statement is a 'double exposure' (p 100) in which Arveragus at once orders and accommodates his wife.

• Review by Giselle Gos, *Arthuriana* 23 (2013), 119–22: Because Dorigen's alleged unconscious desires have no expression in the text, Pitcher must claim that their absence supports his point. 'The resulting logic is circular: her identification with the ideal of a faithful wife is exactly what provides the motivation for her repression' (p 120).

• Review by Susan Nakley, *TMR* (April 2013), n.p.: Pitcher's points about the relation of Arveragus to Aurelius, the rash promise, and the relationship between Arveragus's marriage vows and Dorigen's *trouthe* are more persuasive than his argument about Dorigen's conflicting desires, which is unfortunate since clarifying her desires is key to the project of revealing disjunctions between the narrative and performative aspects of the tale.

1476 Robertson, Elizabeth. 'Marriage, Mutual Consent, and the Affirmation of the Female Subject in the *Knight's Tale*, the *Wife of Bath's Tale*, and the *Franklin's Tale*.' In *Drama, Narrative and Poetry in the Canterbury Tales*. 2003. See **1468**. Pp 175–93.

In *FranT*, the model of marriage as a companionship of equal souls is compromised by the distinction between private and public. In both the initial marriage agreement (in which Arveragus retains 'the name of soverayntee ... for shame of his degree' [lines 752–3]) and in his response to Dorigen's promise to Aurelius (in which he invokes his wife's *trouthe* as paramount, but forbids her to reveal the circumstances under which she will keep that *trouthe*), Arveragus's concern with his honor compels him to present a front to the outside world. The tension between public and private manifested in Dorigen and Arveragus's marriage arrangement reflects contradictions in the medieval doctrines of wedlock, in which the notion of companionate marriage conflicts with the model of subordinate marriage that permeates theological commentary on the subject.

1477 Schutz, Andrea. 'Negotiating the Present: Language and Trouthe in the *Franklin's Tale*.' In *Speaking in the Medieval World*. Ed. Jean E. Godsall-Myers. Leiden: Brill, 2003. Pp 105–24.

Dorigen's speech shows her to be a literalist; she has 'one meaning for every sign and one nuance for every meaning' (p 110). In contrast, Aurelius manipulates language, first through courtly discourse in which meanings are occluded or hidden, later in his legalistic misreadings of Dorigen's clear intent in her rejection of his advances. Arveragus's speech is 'a sort of bridge between Dorigen's straightforward and Aurelius' manipulative language' (p 120). Dorigen's literalism, which makes no distinction between the letter and the spirit, is depicted by Chaucer as honorable; the misuse of eloquence and the self-interested interpretation practiced by Aurelius are condemned by the poet, both here and elsewhere in *CT*.

1478 Shibata, Takeo. '"Illusioun" in Chaucer's *The Franklin's Tale*.' *Kobe Shinwa Studies in English Linguistics and Literature* (Kobe Shinwa Women's College) 23 (2003), 36–53.

Full text at http://ci.nii.ac.jp/naid/110006159263/en. In Japanese.

1479 Smith, D. Vance. *Arts of Possession: The Middle English Household Imaginary.* 2003. See **792**.

The Franklin enjoys spectacle and possession while evading its consequences. In his prologue, he uses the humility topos both to flaunt his literacy and to identify himself as an unlearned man. The social world of the tale is an almost literal machinery of illusions, notably in the magician's evocation of chivalric spectacle. The tale's 'most seductive diversionary tactic' is its final question (line 1622), which enacts a fantasy of aristocratic behavior by asking who is the most free from dependence on wealth even as it extends an invitation to calculate (p 43).

1480 Stévanovitch, Colette. 'Polysyllabic words in End-of-Line Position in the *Franklin's Tale.*' In *Drama, Narrative and Poetry in the Canterbury Tales*. 2003. See **1468**. Pp 113–24.

In *FranT*, polysyllabic words at the end of lines may slow the line down, produce mimetic effects, or introduce an element of surprise. Frequently abstract and of French origin, they are often associated with intellectual operations and sometimes contrasted with monosyllables that suggest concretion and irreducible fact (e.g., lines 865–8, 889–92). As technical terms in the astrological passages, they may be intended to impress the reader or to poke fun at the clerk's learning. A few polysyllables in rhyming position are central to our construction of the tale's meaning: *soveraynetee* (line 751), *worthynesse* (line 738), *obeysaunce* (line 739), and, especially, *gentilesse* (lines 754, 1524, 1527, 1574, 1595).

1481 Wilcockson, Colin. 'Thou and Tears: The Advice of Arveragus to Dorigen in Chaucer's *Franklin's Tale.*' *RES* 54 (2003), 308–12.

Arveragus's choice of pronouns in lines 1479–86 supports a sympathetic interpretation of his character when he commands Dorigen to keep her promise to Aurelius. In switching from the formal *yow* to the intimate *thee* and *thou* as he bursts into tears, Arveragus implicitly assures Dorigen that he still loves her despite her misguided commitment to Aurelius. This reading of Arveragus's emotions gains support from a parallel moment in *ClT* (IV.890–3), and by contrast with *Fil,* in which there is no variation in pronouns of address from husband to wife in the corresponding scene.

1482 Cooper, Helen. *The English Romance in Time: Transforming Motifs from Geoffrey of Monmouth to the Death of Shakespeare*. 2004. See **370**.

The black rocks are significant because they represent Dorigen's fears for her husband. As physical objects, they are unimportant, as is the matter of whether they have actually disappeared. 'The question … is not how or whether the magic has worked, but how this will make everyone behave' (p 158).

1483 Ganze, Alison L. 'Seeking Trouthe in Chaucer's Canterbury Tales.' PhD diss.,

University of Oregon, 2004. Dir. Warren Ginsberg. ProQuest (53819395). See also *DAI*–A 65/11 (2005): 4189.
Ch. 4, '"The Hyeste Thyng": *Trouthe*, Honor and Reputation in The Franklin's Tale' (pp 122–69), argues that the dramatic tension in *FranT* arises from an apparent conflict of *trouthe*: two vows that contradict each other. Confronted with this apparent conflict, the tale's three main characters – and the Franklin himself – mistakenly privilege *trouthe* as honor, specifically in the context of public reputation. It is this misunderstanding of the significance of *trouthe* that leads to the central dilemma of the tale and leaves us uneasy with its resolution.

1484 Lee, Dongchoon. '*The Franklin's Tale*: A Moral Tale or a Fiction?' *Medieval and Modern English Studies* 14 (2004), 265–300.
FranT reveals its teller's pretensions and hypocrisies by exposing the inappropriateness of Dorigen and Arveragus's marriage when viewed in the light of Christian doctrine and the tenets of late-medieval common law. The Franklin is not Chaucer's mouthpiece, nor can the tale be read as the poet's portrait of an ideal marriage. (Not seen. Summary from http://hompi.sogang.ac.kr/anthony/mesak/Chbiblio.htm.)

1485 McCarthy, Conor. *Marriage in Medieval England: Law, Literature, and Practice.* Woodbridge, UK: Boydell, 2004.
FranT engages with the discussion of wedlock set out in the preceding Marriage Group tales, but rather than resolving the difficulties posed by these tales, it amplifies them. As in *ClT*, a problematic marriage agreement at the tale's outset contributes to the subsequent difficulties of the narrative; Arveragus's relinquishing of sovereignty at the tale's beginning can be seen as contributing to the later dilemma when there are two promises of *trouthe* to consider. In addition, *FranT*, like that of the Merchant, explores the problems of marital love by showing that the sorts of love more often found outside of marriage (e.g., Dorigen's lovesickness when her husband is absent) can be potentially disastrous within it (pp 102–6).

1486 Pakkala-Weckström, Mari. 'Discourse Strategies in the Marriage Dialogue of Chaucer's *Canterbury Tales*.' *NM* 105 (2004), 154–75.
An examination of male/female dialogue – primarily politeness strategies – in seven tales depicting marriage or close male-female relations. Of the women in the seven tales, Dorigen uses the fewest discourse strategies. Her only experiment with linguistic devices – her jokingly conditional promise to Aurelius – 'bitterly backfires' (p 173).

1486a Richmond, Velma Bourgeois. *Chaucer as Children's Literature: Retellings from the Victorian and Edwardian Eras*. Jefferson, NC: McFarland, 2004.
Includes comments on **20**, **27a**, and **44**. Kelman's adaptation 'stresses [Dorigen's] wifely dependence' (p 85), whereas Bailey's Dorigen 'behaves in ways that are sexually ambiguous, or at least provocative' (p 91). In Stead's

version, Arveragus agrees to give Dorigen up rather than allowing her to break her word to Aurelius; 'the implication is that divorce is preferable to adultery' (p 80).

1487 Ronquist, Eyvind. 'Chaucer's Provisions for Future Contingencies.' *Florilegium* 21 (2004), 94–118.
In solitude, Chaucer's characters sometimes employ induction from example to provide a basis for choosing the next step into the future. In her survey of examples of women responding to rape, Dorigen uses the dialectic procedure of a review of opinions, just as Aristotle and later the scholastic theologians began with a survey of opinions before making their own formulations (p 105).

1488 Saunders, Corinne. 'Chaucer's Romances.' In *A Companion to Romance from Classical to Contemporary*. 2004. See **743**. Pp 85–103.
Like *SqT, FranT* concerns magic and marvel, betrayal and deception, pity and *gentilesse,* and the question of romance idealism. In *FranT,* however, Chaucer pushes the romance form to its limits; Dorigen, for example, is not the object of chivalric combat, but the victim of deceit and illusion. False perception is set in opposition to the absolute value of *trouthe.* But the tale's uncompromising idealism finally feels constrictive; the 'neat' ending, 'so apparently positive in its upholding of *trouthe,* [is also] disturbing in its unnaturalness' (p 93).

1489 ———. 'Magic, Science and Romance: Chaucer and the Supernatural.' *SELIM XV.* 2004. See **744**.
In making transient what seemed to be permanent, the clerk's command of illusion creates a false perception – the rocks' apparent disappearance – that 'call[s] into question the solid foundation of the *trouthe* Dorigen has sworn' (p 137).

1489a Spearing, A.C. 'Textual Performance: Chaucerian Prologues and the French *Dit*.' In *Text and Voice: The Rhetoric of Authority in the Middle Ages*. Ed. Marianne Børch. Odense: UP of Southern Denmark, 2004. Pp 21–45.
FranP is the only one of the Canterbury prologues that defines itself in the same terms as does the French *dit* – as a poem that is not intended to be sung. It distinguishes itself from what the Bretons did by proposing to *say* the sort of poem – a lay – that they composed and sang to instrumental accompaniment (pp 40–1).

1490 Tovey, Barbara. 'Chaucer's Dialectic: How the Establishment Theology is Subjected to Scrutiny in Five *Canterbury Tales*.' *Interpretation* 31 (2004), 235–99.
The problem of evil, the guiding theme of *FranT,* is made explicit in Dorigen's address to the Deity, in which the black rocks represent the pain and injustice puzzlingly present in a universe ruled by a benevolent providence. Dorigen's central weakness is her inability to face up to the world's darker aspects. The clerk's magic represents the Christian theodicy that

makes these dark elements disappear by denying their existence, a solution that Chaucer rejects as unsound. The clerk's association with Orléans ('geographically close to Paris ... a center of theological debate') allows us to understand the tale as 'in part a large and magnificent satire on the sophistries of the schools' (p 287). In employing the clerk, Aurelius uses illusion – 'a sophistical solution to the problem of evil' – to seduce Dorigen from her marriage, which symbolizes her devotion to truth (p 293). Her subsequent dilemma – will she choose 'infidelity to the truth' or martyrdom? – 'may signify the choice faced by every holder of heterodox views in an age of religious persecution' (p 294). The tale – Chaucer's 'most devastating attack upon the established creed' (p 295) – is too dangerous to be given to a character who might seem to speak directly for the poet, hence its assignment to the duplicitous Franklin.

1491 Brewer, Derek S. 'Understanding Chivalry in Earlier English Literature.' *Rethinking Middle English: Linguistic and Literary Approaches*. Ed. Nikolaus Ritt and Herbert Schendl. Frankfurt am Main: Lang, 2005. Pp 2–16.
Chaucer addresses the problem of retaining the romantic excitement of chivalric love within marriage at the beginning of *FranT.* Married lovers must become 'friends,' with the 'special but not necessarily sexual warmth' that was attached to the idea of friendship in Cicero's *De amicitia* (p 7).

1491a ———. 'Some Notes on "Ennobling Love" and its Successor in Medieval Romance.' In *Cultural Encounters in the Romance of Medieval England*. Ed. Corinne Saunders. Studies in Medieval Romance. Woodbridge, UK: Brewer, 2005. Pp 117–33.
The *pacience* (line 773) that Dorigen and Arveragus practice in their marriage goes beyond the courtly 'feudalisation' of love. It involves the 'suppression of the feelings not *of* love, but *by* love,' the keyword being *freendes* (line 762) (p 130).

1492 Fernández Rodriguez, Carmen María. 'New Contexts for the Classics: Wanderers and Revolutionaries in the Tales of the Franklin and the Clerk.' *SELIM* 13 (2005), 225–47.
Dorigen and Griselda both denounce the constraints imposed on women by the patriarchy. A comparison of Chaucer's tales with Fanny Burney's *The Wanderer* (1814) and Maria Edgeworth's *The Modern Griselda* (1805) demonstrates that Chaucer's female characters lived in a world as debilitating for women as early nineteenth-century English society.

1493 Ginsberg, Warren. '"Gli scogli neri e il niente che c'è": Dorigen's Black Rocks and Chaucer's Translation of Italy.' In *Reading Medieval Culture: Essays in Honor of Robert W. Hanning*. Ed. Robert M. Stein and Sandra Pierson Prior. Notre Dame, IN: U of Notre Dame P, 2005. Pp 387–408.
Whether or not Chaucer actually knew Menedon's *questione* in *Fil, FranT* may be read as a 'cross-cultural translation' of Boccaccio's story, the two

works reflecting (in Walter Benjamin's phrase) different 'modes of meaning' (pp 387–8). In Boccaccio, 'gender ironically destabilizes sexual identity'; Chaucer is rather concerned with the 'precariousness of identity based on rank' (p 404). The debate that concludes Menedon's *questione* shows Boccaccio's aristocrats as concerned with making and maintaining distinctions; for Menedon, the issue is specifically the subtle tricks played by women that induce men to lose their name to love. The Franklin's unanswered *demande* at the end of his tale 'exposes the give and take of seemingly disinterested debate as an agent of Menedon's unexpressed desires' (p 401). In blurring the boundaries of social distinction, the Franklin translates Menedon's desire to thrive in a world where gender hierarchies are clear; Menedon's *questione* in turn 'exposes how class subsumes gender' in *FranT* (p 402).

1494 Hanks, D. Thomas, Jr. "Chaucer, Auctoritas, and the Problem of Pain." In *'Seyd in forme and reverence': Essays on Chaucer and Chaucerians in Memory of Emerson Brown, Jr.* Ed. T.L. Burton and John F. Plummer. Provo, UT: Chaucer Studio Press, 2005. Pp 219–36.
The explicit allusions to Job and the problem of human pain in *ClT* are implicit in Dorigen's musings on the black rocks, which also recall Arcite and Palamon's questioning of divine *purveiaunce* in *KnT*; 'the problem is the same in each tale' (p 234).

1495 Lochrie, Karma. *Heterosyncrasies: Female Sexuality When Normal Wasn't.* Minneapolis: U of Minnesota P, 2005.
FranT enacts a 'benign reduplication' of the feminine deference to male sovereignty in *ClT* (p 100). Although the Franklin ostensibly endorses mutual liberty in marriage, Dorigen is never free to shape her own fate. Moreover, marital companionship is displaced by the competition for honor among men. 'Masculinity is restored under the bogus sign of companionate marriage and a sovereignty that is secured in masculine, homosocial competition' (p 101).

1496 Lucas, Angela M. '"But if a man be vertuous withal"': Has Aurelius in Chaucer's *Franklin's Tale* "lerned gentillesse aright"?' In *Studies in Late Medieval and Early Renaissance Texts in Honour of John Scattergood.* Ed. Anne Marie D'Arcy and Alan J. Fletcher. Dublin: Four Courts, 2005. Pp 181–200.
The Franklin, concerned with his own son's behavior in contrast to that of the pilgrim Squire, tells his tale as an exemplum of a young man's education in *gentilesse* by way of an apprenticeship in love. The squire Aurelius seems ripe for amorous adventure. Although he exhibits some of the traits outlined in treatises like Andreas Capellanus's *De arte honeste amandi,* Aurelius is hardly an ideal courtly lover: he is egotistical, 'calculatedly duplicitous' (p 189), and imbues the lover's traditional attentiveness to his lady with a hint of menace. Arveragus's seemingly improbable insistence that Dorigen keep her promise to Aurelius may be intended to teach the young man a lesson

in honorable behavior: even a well-born squire may need to learn true *gentilesse*. Aurelius's foregoing of his claim to Dorigen may not be wholly selfless – his 'right to the lady is an illusory one' and he seems more 'the recipient of generous and noble actions than the doer of them' (p 198). But he appears at the end of the tale to be following the proper trajectory, and his progress holds out hope for an analogous education in *gentilesse* on the part of the Franklin's son.

1497 Mann, Jill, ed. *Geoffrey Chaucer: The Canterbury Tales*. 2005. See **128**.
Aventure (lines 1501, 1508) plays a benign role in *FranT*. The meeting of Dorigen and Aurelius on the way to the garden that brings about the latter's change of heart shows that chance does not always lead to disaster, but may create new beginnings as well (xxviii–xxix). Dorigen is held to the strict letter of her promise; the meaning behind her words is disregarded. In *FrT*, the devil refuses to take the literal sense of the carter's words as decisive, but rather focuses on his *entente*. 'In the world of *FrT*, Dorigen would have had no problems' (xxxviii). The changes Chaucer made in his Boccaccian sources transform the story into 'an exploration of patience in action' (p 950).

1498 McClellan, William. '"Ful Pale Face": Agamben's Biopolitical Theory and the Sovereign Subject in Chaucer's Clerk's Tale.' *Exemplaria* 17 (2005), 103–34.
In Chaucer's repertoire of conventionalized gestures, 'pale face' designates a state of extreme crisis, especially for women, and is often associated with death. The physical process described in lines 1339–53, culminating in Dorigen's 'face pale' (line 1353), indicates the degree of her despair and prepares us for her subsequent contemplation of suicide.

1499 Minnis, Alastair. '"I speke of folk in seculer estaat": Vernacularity and Secularity in the Age of Chaucer.' *SAC* 27 (2005), 25–58.
In three renegotiations of Boethian matter – Palamon's lament in *KnT* (I.1303–24), Troilus's disputation with himself about the workings of 'necessitee' (*TC* IV.956–66), and Dorigen's questioning of God's Providence (lines 865–80) – Chaucer explores the strengths and limitations of secular culture. Whereas the Boethius persona is led by Dame Philosophy to a right understanding of the relation between God's infallible knowledge and man's free will, in Chaucer 'we are simply, painfully, left with the problems' (p 48).

1500 Nakao, Yoshiyuki. 'Chaucer's *Gentil* with a Focus on its Modal Implications.' In *Recent Trends in Medieval Language and Literature in Honour of Young-Bae Park*. Vol. 1. Ed. Jacek Fisiak and Hye-Kyung Kang. Seoul: Thaehaksa, 2005. Pp 321–45.
In the narrator's final question about *gentilesse* ('Which was the mooste fre, as thynketh yow?', line 1619), the characters' conflict in choosing *gentil* actions becomes the audience's dilemma. The right answer may be found extratextually: 'the noblest, the most generous, and the kindest person is … the poet, creator and integrator of the characters of the story' (p 338).

1501 Pakkala-Weckström, Mari. *The Dialogue of Love, Marriage and Maistrie in Chaucer's Canterbury Tales*. Mémoires de la Société Néophilogique de Helsinki 67. Helsinki: Société Néophilogique, 2005.
Although *FranT* begins with the mutual surrender of *maistrye,* it seems to turn against its ideals when Arveragus later orders Dorigen to fulfill her promise to Aurelius. Arveragus is acting against his own deepest feelings, but he is nevertheless exercising the very power he had surrendered, and thus causing pain both to himself and to Dorigen (pp 139–40).

1502 Scase, Wendy. 'The English Background.' In *Chaucer: An Oxford Guide*. Oxford: Oxford UP, 2005. Pp 272–91.
FranT engages with the 'desires and frustrations of attempting to categorize romance' (p 288). The 'conflicted story' of the Breton *lai* in English finds a parallel in the journey of the Breton hero to England and the dangers and adventures precipitated by his journey (p 288).

1503 Sherman, Mark. 'Chivalry.' In *Chaucer: An Oxford Guide*. 2005. See **1502**. Pp 97–112.
Given the Franklin's own ambivalent social position, it is appropriate that his tale manifests 'class tensions over the status of knighthood and its claims to *gentilesse*' (p 107). *FranT* appears to take place in a 'theatrical otherworld' (p 110) where inverted strategies are required to win the game – as in Arveragus's private submission to Dorigen, the first step in making her an item of exchange in the chivalric economy. However much emphasis the knightly class puts on *gentilesse*, the source of its power resides 'just over the horizon' (p 110) – here, in the 'Briteyne' (line 810) that 'haunts the tale's courtly Brittany like an allegorical spectre' (p 108) – where knights seek worship and honor in arms.

1504 Smith, Warren S. 'The Wife of Bath and Dorigen Debate Jerome.' In *Satiric Advice on Women and Marriage: From Plautus to Chaucer*. Ed. Warren S. Smith. Ann Arbor: U of Michigan P, 2005. Pp 243–69.
See **1459**.

1505 Staley, Lynn. *Languages of Power in the Age of Richard II*. University Park: Pennsylvania State UP, 2005.
In *FranT,* Chaucer plays upon the perceived links between eloquence, deep feeling, and worthiness to illustrate the limitations and confusions of courtly talk practiced outside of the court. The 'charged terms' (p 72) employed in the tale for Dorigen and Arveragus's courtship and marriage – accord, lordship, *servage,* and *trouthe* – would have had for Chaucer's audience a political valence as well (*FranT* is probably a product of the 1390s). But Chaucer 'muffles this resonance in courtesy and sentiment, which, from his perspective, are indices of nobility' (p 72).

1506 Van Dyke, Carolynn. *Chaucer's Agents: Cause and Representation in Chaucerian Narrative*. 2005. See **746**.

In remaking his Boccaccian source, Chaucer enlarges and deepens Dorigen's role; she enlists 'not only admiration but subjective identification' (p 157). But the failure of some readers to recognize Dorigen as a genuine protagonist suggests the instability of Chaucer's representation of women's moral and narrative agency; Dorigen is alternately a fully realized subject and a narrative object ineligible for the reader's empathy. The equivocal presentation of female agency threatens to fracture the tale's formal coherence, challenging the scope of the tale's *sentence* and rendering questionable its moral basis.

1507 Wicher, Andrzej. 'Chaucer's "Franklin's Tale" Seen in the Context of the Tales About Calumniated Women.' In *Naked Wordes in Englissh*. Ed. Marcin Krygier and Liliana Sikorska. Medieval English Mirror 2. Frankfurt am Main: Lang, 2005. Pp 159–68.

FranT contains several motifs associated with folk tradition, albeit in rationalized and atypical form. Aurelius's attempt to fulfill Dorigen's impossible task, for example, adheres to the pattern of the 'presumption' or 'misguided certainty' taboo. The theme of a daughter falling victim to an unconventional suitor through her father's fault may lie behind Dorigen's rash promise, with the father and daughter figures here telescoped into one; Dorigen is responsible for her own plight but refuses to admit responsibility, styling herself a persecuted innocent. In the Cupid and Psyche tale, the heroine breaks a prohibition and stirs the anger of her supernatural husband; in *FranT*, the crisis is averted by Arveragus's forgiveness. If the female triad of *WBT* (the girl, the queen, and the hag) represents three aspects of the supernatural wife, the three male characters in *FranT* correspond to three avatars of the supernatural husband; the trio of men looks like a devilish conspiracy bent on Dorigen's undoing, although engineered by fate rather than personal malice. In readapting folk motifs, Chaucer achieves a critical analysis of received dogma, showing how unreliable the conventional model of marital faithfulness can be.

1508 Wright, Edmond. 'Faith and Narrative: A Reading of *The Franklin's Tale*.' *ParAns* 3 (2005), 19–45.

Any promise includes the possibility of the pain involved in being true to another. The marriage of Dorigen and Arveragus is ideal because it 'confronts its own imperfections' and exemplifies 'a "trouthe" that has to be continually and lovingly reimagined in the face of unexpected discord' (p 37).

ꙮ *The Physician's Tale*: Introduction

For much of the period during which *The Canterbury Tales* has been the subject of written commentary, critical opinion of *The Physician's Tale* has been 'expressed most eloquently in silence' (**1560**, p 902). The standard compendium of early responses to Chaucer's poetry, Caroline Spurgeon's *Five Hundred Years of Chaucer Criticism and Allusion, 1357–1900* (**1575**), contains a single (and unindexed) reference to *The Physician's Tale*. In her survey of criticism for the Variorum edition (**1559**), Helen Corsa turns up a handful of observations about the tale's literary qualities from the late nineteenth century; the first five decades of the twentieth century produced a dozen or so additional interpretive commentaries, most of them extremely brief. Three midcentury books that did much to shape the course of modern Chaucer criticism – Charles Muscatine's *Chaucer and the French Tradition* (1957), D.W. Robertson, Jr.'s *A Preface to Chaucer* (1962; **918**), and Robert O. Payne's *The Key of Remembrance* (1963; **477**) – refer to the tale only in passing, or omit mention of it entirely. And, as Emerson Brown (**1117**) noted, when E.T. Donaldson failed to include *The Physician's Tale* in his 1958 edition (**71**) of the poet's works, 'the outcry of offended Chaucerians was imperceptible' (p 129).

The past twenty-five years have witnessed a resurgence of interest in the tale. To some observers of the academic scene, this renewed attention after almost six centuries of critical indifference might seem stronger evidence of the need of scholars to find new fields to plow than of the work's intrinsic merits. Modern readings of *The Physician's Tale,* however, make no claims for it as a neglected masterpiece. Rather, the uncertainties of tone, structure, and moral vision that were viewed by earlier commentators as signs of Chaucer nodding or explained away by the presumed circumstances of the work's composition have come to seem precisely those aspects of the tale that call for careful investigation and that, suitably contextualized, enable us to place this problematic performance within the larger body of Chaucer's writings. In what follows, I will examine some of the ways in which recent criticism has responded to the challenge of *The Physician's Tale*. First, however, I want to look at several early studies of the tale's date, text, and sources, a body of scholarship that is in part an attempt to account for the presence of a weak link in the chain of Canterbury narratives.

The theory, firmly established early in the century (see **1630**, pp 294–5), that Chaucer wrote *The Physician's Tale* either before or at the very beginning of the period when he was actively engaged with *The Canterbury Tales* was based on several pieces of highly conjectural evidence: the apparent lack of a connection between teller and tale; the poem's supposed similarities to *The Legend of Good Women* (**1629**); and a possible allusion to a court scandal of the mid-1380s in the warning to parents and governesses (**1625**). Behind these arguments lay judgments about literary quality. In his introduction to the *Globe Chaucer* (**1512**), Pollard asserts that 'we need not hesitate to relegate such poor work as the story of Appius and Virginia ... to a less happy period of Chaucer's career than when he was writing the Prologue and others of his finest works' (xxvii). Adopting a similar logic, Tatlock (**1629**) writes that 'as in [*The Legend of Good Women*], Chaucer is singularly bald in his account and slavish toward his source. There is none of the warmth and expansiveness that characterizes most of the *Canterbury Tales*' (p 151). Although wholly unsubstantiated, the hypothesis that *The Physician's Tale* antedated the conception of *The Canterbury Tales* proved remarkably durable (see, e.g., **1697**, **1812**). One striking example of its influence is Manly's argument for authorial revision of the tale (**1539**; 2:498; 4:489), which is based as much on his belief in the tale's early date of composition as on the persuasiveness of the textual evidence. As Severs (**1685**) has demonstrated, the manuscript variants that in Manly's view show signs of the poet's correcting hand are for the most part explicable as instances of scribal editing.

Much of the early scholarship on *The Physician's Tale* was devoted to determining whether Chaucer knew Livy's account of the Appius and Virginia story (**1559**, pp 4–5; **1619,** pp 535–6). These debates have been characterized as 'quibbling, because it is certain that even if [Chaucer] did know [Livy] it made a negligible difference to his own version' (**1559r**, p 152). But the discussions of the tale's sources, like the arguments surrounding its date, are worth attending to because they show how ostensibly disinterested scholarly inquiries reflect time- and culture-bound assumptions about aesthetic value. Ten Brink, for example, notes that Chaucer, although he cites Livy, makes the 'fundamental mistake' of following the 'mutilated and vulgar tradition' of the story found in Jean de Meun's *Roman de la Rose* (Bernhard ten Brink, *The History of English Literature* [London: Bell, 1893], 2:120–1). Lounsbury takes a comparable view of the medieval retellings of Livy's anecdote, but is at pains to clear Chaucer of the charge of having deliberately chosen an inferior model: 'it is practically inconceivable that if Chaucer had known the original story he would have followed the debased version of it that had gathered additional and disgusting horrors on its way to the Middle Ages' (Thomas R. Lounsbury, *Studies in Chaucer* [London: Osgood, McIlvaine, 1893], 2:283). The defects of *The Physician's Tale,* Lounsbury maintains, are not only virtually conclusive proof that Chaucer was unacquainted with Livy's version of the story, but also a testimony to the poet's literary conscience: 'he was too great an artist ever to have adopted of his own accord clumsy devices and unnatural details, had he not felt himself bound by the requirements of historic fact' (2:283). What was for Lounsbury evidence of Chaucer's artistic integrity would be for Tatlock the 'slavish' dependence on sources typical of the poet's practice in *The Legend of Good Women*. Despite the differences in their assessments of the poet's relation to his source material, however, the two critics display a similar uneasiness with the idea of Chaucer freely making the compositional choices that resulted in the tale as we now have it.

A quite different response to the problems posed by *The Physician's Tale* was hinted at by Kittredge (**1622**), who in 1893 observed that the 'prosiness' of Nature's speech should be attributed to the Physician's 'formal' personality: 'it was Chaucer's artistic duty ... to make the method of delivery correspond to the character of the teller.' Kittredge's belief that it was the poet's task to establish clear links between teller and tale, briefly enunciated here, is developed more fully in his reading of the *Tales* as dramatic monologues in the 1914 lectures subsequently published as *Chaucer and His Poetry* (1915), with its famous statement about Chaucer's 'intention': 'the Pilgrims do not exist for the sake of the stories, but *vice versa*' (**759**, p 154). These lectures, however, contain no discussion of *The Physician's Tale*. It was not until the appearance, almost a half century later, of Robert Lumiansky's *Of Sondry Folk: The Dramatic Principle in the Canterbury Tales* (**1540**) that Chaucer's treatment of the Appius and Virginia narrative received a full-scale dramatic interpretation. Working from the premise, derived from Kittredge, that 'the proper context for a given story consists primarily of the individual traits and the dramatic purposes of the Pilgrim telling that story' (**1540**, p 4), Lumiansky describes a greedy Physician who tells a moralistic tale of chastity to cover up his real motives – only to have his hypocrisy exposed by Harry Bailly at the conclusion of his performance. Lumiansky gives more attention to the portrait of the Physician in *The General Prologue* and Harry Bailly's reaction than to the tale proper, a tacit acknowledgement that the tale signifies only insofar as it is about its teller.

Lumiansky's chapter set the tone for much subsequent writing on the poem. Although a few dissenting voices were raised, interpretations of the tale as an expression of its teller's character dominated criticism from the 1960s through the 1980s. For some commentators, the tale is congruent with the portrait of the Physician in *The General Prologue*; others find an ironic relation between the suggestions of corruption in the portrait and the moralistic tale; still others focus on the story itself as Chaucer's primary means of characterizing his narrator. What these interpretations have in common is the assumption that the tale's perceived weaknesses are evidence not of any lapse on Chaucer's part, but of the Physician's personal and professional limitations. Thus the oddly inappropriate allusion to Jephthah's daughter is said to confirm the observation in *The General Prologue* about the Physician's scant biblical knowledge and to reveal his inability to grasp the spiritual implications of his story (**1719, 1730, 1765, 1785, 1789, 1817, 1970**); the tale's intrusive moralizing is variously attributed to the Physician's puritanical nature (**1724**), to his desire to project a proper public image (**1800, 1815**), or to mask his avarice (**1686**), or to give ethical authority to a weak story (**1748, 1774, 1877**); the digressions – Nature's description of Virginia's beauty, the warning to parents and governesses – betray the preoccupation of a man of science with the body rather than the soul (**1744, 1788, 1789, 1819, 1830, 1977**); the brutality of Virginia's beheading displays the Physician's cold-bloodedness, seen either as a temperamental deficiency (**1724**) or as a vocational deformation (**1760**).

Explanations of structural, stylistic, or doctrinal elements as 'purposely bad art' (**1766**) intended to mirror the teller's flawed character are by no means an exclusive feature of commentary on *The Physician's Tale*. Several of the less-valued tales – those of the Man of Law and the Monk, for example – have been especially open to readings of this kind. But *The Physician's Tale*'s critical history – its reputation as the least satisfactory of the tales in verse, the possibility that it was written without a specific narrator in mind – makes it a test case for debates about the usefulness of the dramatic theory as a strategy for interpreting a Canterbury fiction. Once a critic commits to reading a tale as the performance of a highly individualized speaking subject, almost anything that seems excrescent, tonally awry, or difficult to account for can be 'explained' by invoking some aspect of the narrator's selfhood – usually a professional quirk or an ethical or intellectual shortcoming. Of the more ingenious analyses that follow this line of reasoning, one might say of *The Physician's Tale* what A.C. Spearing says of *The Man of Law's Tale*: that to read it 'as spoken in the voice of a fictional narrator is usually to avoid reading it at all' (**1976**, p 136).

Scholars unpersuaded by attempts to use the tale as means of reconstructing the occupational profile or the putative psychology of its teller (**1791, 1847, 1855, 1861, 1899, 1959r**) ground their case for the opposition not only on the methodogical flaws evident in dramatic readings, but also on the absence of basic textual support for such readings: for Derek Brewer, 'no pilgrim voice is even hinted at' (**1814**), Derek Pearsall asserts that 'nothing in the tale relates to any possible physician' (**1828**), while Brian Lee maintains that the tale 'bear[s] no relation at all to [the Physician's] character' (**1218**).

Although Chaucerians will continue to differ about the degree to which individual pilgrims are present in the tales they tell, dissenting opinions of the sort just cited have to some extent (but not entirely) moved *The Physician's Tale* down the list of likely candidates for impersonated interpretations, clearing some space for attention to the work's historical, formal, and generic features as carriers of meaning.

These new (or, in some cases, renewed) forms of attention employ a representative variety of approaches to Chaucer's poetry, and include the following:

- source and analogue study that contrasts the unambiguous political and moral anecdotes of Livy, Jean de Meun, Boccaccio, Gower, and Lydgate with Chaucer's less straightforward – and far more unsettling – treatment of the same story (**1737**, **1746**, **1773**, **1808**, **1828**, **1835**, **1879**, **1924**, **1926**, **1967**);
- rhetorical analyses that locate the Physician's 'barebones narrative' (**1760**) within the 'series of poetic experiments in various styles' (**1774**, p 375) that has been proposed as an alternative to the Kittredgean model of the *Tales* as a Human Comedy (**1700**, **1743**, **1861**, **1867**);
- historical contextualization that situates the tale in relation to the social forces and events of the late fourteenth century (**1791**, **1833**, **1834**, **1893**, **1971**);
- readings of the tale as an allegory or quasi allegory (**1712**, **1729**, **1735**, **1787**, **1847**, **1884**, **1960**);
- explorations of the poem's metatextual dimension, in which the narrator's treatment of his *matere* reproduces the narrative's handling of Virginia and makes the teller complicit in the violation of the maiden (**1860**, **1879**, **1923**, **1937**, **1967**);
- examinations of the tale as a saint's life *manqué* that exposes the hermeneutic limits of traditional virgin-martyr narratives (**1849**, **1873**, **1900**, **1912**, **1949**, **1974**, **1962**);
- investigations of the tale's problematic status as an exemplary fiction, a subject first treated in detail by Anne Middleton (**1746**) in an essay that remains one of the best commentaries on the poem (**1808**, **1924**, **1939**, **1942**, **1967**);
- studies of the tale in relation to late-medieval understandings of childhood, fatherhood, and the family (**1903**, **1907**, **1912**, **1925**, **1961**, **1969**);
- interpretations that locate the tale's *sentence* not in any paraphrasable meaning but in the 'actions of its readers' (**1746**) and in the response of Harry Bailly as a reader-surrogate (**1855**, **1910**, **1942**, **1953**, **1967**);
- patristic and medieval discourses of virginity (and conceptualizations of women's bodies and female sexuality more generally) as a context for the tale's representation of Virginia (**1860**, **1890**, **1893**, **1906**, **1908**,

1923, 1932, 1936, 1941, 1943, 1956, 1958);
- correctives to the view of the tale as a 'straightforward' story that 'reduces the complexities of life to the simple contest between alternate abstractions' (**1659, 1703**), proposing instead that the narrative's characteristic feature is a disorienting randomness that (among its other effects) 'dismantles the conceptual architecture of genre' (**1963**) and thereby frustrates our desire for unambiguous *sentence* (**1737, 1835, 1891, 1924, 1938, 1947, 1948**).

Comparing *The Physician's Tale* with Shakespeare's *Measure for Measure* (another 'problem' work that combines the plot elements of a corrupt judge, sex, and death) Cooper (**1861**) expresses doubt that 'future generations of readers will accord *The Physician's Tale* as high a ranking among Chaucer's works as the play has recently been accorded among Shakespeare's' (p 255). This prognostication is surely accurate. The willingness of recent critics to examine the tale with fresh eyes, however, ensures that at least some of these future readers will regard it neither as an embarrassment nor an anomaly, but rather as a poem 'utterly and modestly Chaucerian' (**1746**, p 9), a mirror of themes and concerns given more extended representation elsewhere in the poet's writings.

℘ *The Physician's Tale*: Editions and Modernizations

Four important nineteenth-century editions are followed by a selective listing of twentieth- and twenty-first-century editions and modernizations through 2005. The earliest editions, beginning with that of Caxton (ca 1478), are described by Hammond (**382**, pp 114–49, 202–19). Hammond also lists selections from and modernizations and translations of *PhyT* published before 1900 (p 294).

1509 *A Six-Text Print of Chaucer's Canterbury Tales. Part IV. The Tale of Melibeus; The Monk's Tale; The Nun's Priest's Tale; The Doctor's Tale; The Pardoner's Tale; The Wife of Bath's Tale; The Friar's Tale; The Summoner's Tale*. Ed. Frederick J. Furnivall. Chaucer Society Publications, First Series, 25. London: Trübner, 1868. Repr. New York: Johnson, 1967. [*The Six-Text Edition*.] Pp 303–13.
The text is printed in parallel columns as it appears in the following MSS: El, Hg, Cambridge Gg.4.27, Corpus, Petworth, and Lansdowne. The tales are given in the following order: I (A) II VII (B^1+ B^2) VI (C) III (D) IV (E) V (F) VIII (G) IX (H) X (I). See **1510, 1512, 1513, 1515, 1517, 1536, 1541, 1547, 1554, 1556.**

1510 *The Complete Works of Geoffrey Chaucer, Edited from Numerous Manuscripts*. Ed. Walter W. Skeat. 1894–7. [*The Oxford Chaucer*.] See **4**. Text: 4:290–300, explanatory notes: 5:260–9.
Skeat's text of *CT* is based on El, collated with Harley 7334 and the five MSS that, along with El, had been published by the Chaucer Society as the *Six-Text* print of *CT* (**1**). Selected variants are recorded below the text. As Corsa (**1559**) observes, 'El[lesmere] alone has sufficient authority to impose otherwise unsupported readings, but it is no tyrant, often being voted out by a majority rule of the other collated manuscripts' (p 84). Although he follows the Chaucer Society order, Skeat notes that Fragment VI (C) properly belongs after Fragment V (F), its position in 'the best MSS' (3:434; see **590**, pp 179–81 and **1559**, pp 54–5). In his brief discussion of sources, Skeat prints Jean de Meun's version of the Appius and Virginia story (3:434–7). He also prints the three spurious headlinks to *PhyT* (3:434–5; 4:289). Vol. 6 contains essays on Chaucer's pronunciation, grammar, and versification, a glossary of more than 300 pages, an index of proper names, and a list of authors and

biblical passages cited by Chaucer. For a detailed account of Skeat's edition, see **590**. For references to or editions based on Skeat, see **1511, 1517, 1519, 1523, 1524, 1526, 1527, 1532, 1533, 1534, 1541, 1545, 1574, 1818, 1865**.

1511 *The Works of Geoffrey Chaucer*. Ed. F.S. Ellis. 1896. [*The Kelmscott Chaucer*.] See **5**. Pp 96–8.
Ellis's text is based on the *Oxford Chaucer* (**1510**), with additional corrections approved by Skeat. The illustrations by Burne-Jones include none for *PhyT*. For facsimile editions, see **1545, 1551**.

1512 *The Works of Geoffrey Chaucer*. Ed. Alfred W. Pollard. 1898. [*The Globe Chaucer*.] See **6**. Pp 141–4.
The text of *CT* (prepared by Pollard) is based on El, emended by collation with the other *Six-Text* MSS (**1509**) and the Chaucer Society's edition of Harley 7334. Explanatory and textual notes appear at the bottom of the page. Lines 178–89 (Claudius's 'cursed bille') are printed in italics. Pollard adopts the Chaucer Society order (**1509**), but notes that this placement of Fragment VI (C) 'is not a matter of certainty' (p 141n). As an instance of the process of manuscript contamination, Pollard notes that in *PhyT*, Cambridge Gg.4.27 deserts El and Hg and joins the other three *Six-Text* MSS and Harley 7334 in a number of readings, 'a few of which are possible, while many are absurd' (xxix). See **1516, 1531, 1865**.

1513 *The Complete Works of Geoffrey Chaucer.* With an Introduction by Thomas R. Lounsbury. 1900. See **10**. Pp 605–11/2:605–11.
Comments on Chaucer's life, works, and language introduce the text (the basis of which is not stated), printed in double columns without notes; a full glossary with line references concludes the volume. The text of *CT* follows the Chaucer Society order (**1509**). See **1518**.

1514 *The Story of the Canterbury Pilgrims. Retold from Chaucer and Others*. Trans. F.J. Harvey Darton. 1900/1914. See **11**. Pp 113–16.
A free prose modernization. Nature's speech and the description of Virginia are abridged; the address to guardians and parents, the allusion to Jephthah, and the final *moralitas* are omitted.

1515 *The Cambridge Ms. Dd.4.24 of Chaucer's Canterbury Tales. Completed by the Egerton MS. 2726 (The Haistwell MS)*. Parts I and II. Ed. Frederick J. Furnivall. 2 vols. 1902. See **13**. 2:359–68.
Vol. 2 supplies page references to the *Six-Text* edition (**1509**) and reproduces woodcuts of the pilgrims based on the Ellesmere miniatures and on the six pilgrim portraits in Cambridge MS Gg.4.27, 'being all that were not cut out of the MS. by some scoundrel' (2: Appendix 3, n.p.).

1516 *Chaucer's Canterbury Tales. Reprinted from the Globe Edition*. Ed. Alfred W. Pollard. 1902. See **14**. Pp 141–4.
The *Globe* text of *CT* (**1512**), reprinted without introduction or glossary.

1517 *The Select Chaucer.* Ed. J. Logie Robertson. 1902. See **16**. Pp 146–9.

Comments on Chaucer's life and times, language, and meter introduce selections from *CT*; the text is based on El and Harley 7334, collated with the *Six-Text* (**1509**) and Skeat (**1510**). *PhyT* is represented by the portrait of Virginia (lines 1–70) and the address to parents (lines 93–104). Includes brief explanatory notes and a glossary.

1518 *The Canterbury Tales by Geoffrey Chaucer*. With an Introduction by Thomas R. Lounsbury. [1903.] See **17**. Pp 141–5.
Reprints the introduction, *CT* text, and glossary of **1513**.

1519 *The Canterbury Tales of Geoffrey Chaucer. A Modern Rendering into Prose of the Prologue and Ten Tales*. Trans. Percy MacKaye. 1904. See **22**. Pp 92–8.
A prose modernization of *GP, KnT, PrT, NPT, PhyT, PardT, WBT, ClT, SqT, FranT*, and *CYT*, based on Skeat (**1510**). 'The method followed has been to present, so far as possible, Chaucer's *ipsissima verba*' (viii).

1520 *The Canterbury Tales of Geoffrey Chaucer*. Trans. Percy MacKaye. 1904. See **21**. Pp 92–8.
This edition of **1519** omits *PrT*.

1521 *Tales of the Canterbury Pilgrims. Retold from Chaucer and Others*. Trans. F.J. Harvey Darton. 1904. See **25**. Pp 128–31.
Includes two line drawings: Appius eyeing Virginia in the street, and Virginius embracing Virginia and weeping.

1522 *The Works of Geoffrey Chaucer and Others, Being a Reproduction in Facsimile of the First Collected Edition 1532, From the Copy in the British Museum*. Introduction by Walter W. Skeat. 1904. See **26**. Pp 167–70.
The introduction to this facsimile of William Thynne's black-letter edition surveys earlier editions of Chaucer's works, the contents and foliation of 1532 and the contents of the 1542, ca 1550, and 1561 editions, Sir Brian Tuke's preface, Thynne's text, the arrangement of *CT*, the woodcuts (all but those of the Squire and the Knight are from Caxton's second edition), and other Chaucerian and spurious works in the volume. The spurious prologue to *PhyT* appears on p 167. For a later facsimile, see **1548**.

1523 *The Poetical Works of Geoffrey Chaucer, from the Text of Professor Skeat*. 1906. See **19**. 3:265–72.
The text of the *Oxford Chaucer* (**1510**) is followed by a note on language and meter and a glossary.

1524 *Chaucer's Canterbury Tales for the Modern Reader*. Ed. Arthur Burrell. 1908. See **30**. Pp 229–36.
Prints all of *CT* except *CkP* and *CkT*. *GP, PhyT*, and fifteen other tales are presented in spelling 'modernised just enough to leave its quaintness and take away some of its difficulty' (viii). Seven others (*MilT, RvT, ShT, Thop, FrT, SumT, MerT*), 'so broad, so plain-spoken, that no amount of editing or alteration will make them suitable for the twentieth century' (vii–viii), are printed in ME. The basis of the text is not stated, but Skeat's edition (**1510**) is

mentioned. For the later Everyman's Library edition, see **1544**.

1525 *The Ellesmere Chaucer, Reproduced in Facsimile*. 1911. See **34**.
The Ellesmere MS (El), owned by the Huntington Library, San Marino, California, has been used as the basis for many editions. The most elaborately decorated of the extant *CT* MSS, it contains celebrated miniatures of the individual pilgrims. In the 1911 facsimile, *PhyT* and the portrait of the Physician appear in vol. 2 (folios unnumbered in the reproduction). According to Hanna, the photographer of the facsimile (W. Griggs and Son) used multiple photographs of the same page to adjust the placement of the pilgrim portraits; the portrait of the Physician on 133r was moved 'about 8 mm to the left – a case in which Griggs enhanced the illuminator's intent, to echo in the lines of the portrait the line created by the ragged right-hand end of the text' (p 8). For a later facsimile, see **1563**.

1526 *The Complete Poetical Works of Geoffrey Chaucer*. Trans. John Strong Perry Tatlock and Percy MacKaye. 1912. See **37**. Pp 140–5.
A prose modernization, based on Skeat (**1510**), followed by an appendix on Chaucer's life and works, and a brief glossary. Includes a line drawing of Virginius, in Roman dress, holding a large sword and embracing Virginia, robed as a vestal.

1527 *The Canterbury Tales of Geoffrey Chaucer*. 1913. See **39**. 2:49–57.
The text of this artistic edition is based on Skeat (**1510**). There are no illustrations for *PhyT*.

1528 *The College Chaucer*. Ed. Henry Noble MacCracken. 1913. See **40**. Pp 207–17.
A school edition. The text of *CT* is based on El, with textual notes at the foot of the page. *MilT, RvT, CkT, ShT, FrT, SumT, MerT, CYT, Mel*, and *ParsT* are omitted. An appendix includes notes on Chaucer's language and meter, life, writings, dates, sources, a discussion of *CT* as a human comedy, and a full glossary.

1529 *Facsimiles of Twelve Early English Manuscripts in the Library of Trinity College, Cambridge*. Ed. W.W. Greg. Oxford: Oxford UP, 1913.
Plate 12 reproduces (with an accompanying transcription) the upper portion of Trinity College MS R.3.3, 76r, lines 1–20 and 42–63 of *PhyT*.

1530 *Geoffrey Chaucer's Canterbury Tales: Nach dem Ellesmere Manuscript mit Lesarten, Anmerkungen, und einem Glossar*. Ed. John Koch. 1915. See **42**. Pp 229–33.
A school edition, based on El. A general introduction treats the MSS, development, sources, and previous editions of *CT*. Textual and explanatory notes, Latin marginal glosses from selected MSS, and a full glossary.

1531 *The Works of Geoffrey Chaucer*. 8 vols. 1928–9. See **48**. 2:106–16.
The text of this artistic edition is that of the revised *Globe* edition (**1512**). Portraits of the pilgrims, modeled on the Ellesmere miniatures, appear with the *GP* descriptions and again at the heads of the individual tales. Limited to 375 copies, and eleven on vellum.

1532 *Geoffrey Chaucer: The Canterbury Tales*. Ed. Walter W. Skeat. 1929. See **50**. Pp 279–87.

The text of the *Oxford Chaucer* (**1510**) is presented with a brief introduction, notes on Chaucer's language and meter, and a glossary.

1533 *The Canterbury Tales by Geoffrey Chaucer*. With Wood Engravings by Eric Gill. 4 vols. 1929–31. 3:1–11. See **51**.

The text of this artistic edition is based on Skeat (**1510**). Accompanying *PhyT* are two elegantly stylized engravings: Virginius about to decapitate a kneeling Virginia, and Appius in conversation with Claudius (?).

1534 *The Canterbury Tales of Geoffrey Chaucer, Together with a Version in Modern English by William van Wyck*. 1930. See **52**. 2:238–44.

An artistic edition, with Skeat's text (**1510**) and van Wyck's modernization presented in parallel columns. Includes a full-length portrait of the Physician.

1535 *Tales from Chaucer: The Canterbury Tales Done into Prose*. Trans. Eleanor Farjeon. 1930/1959. See **53**. Pp 169–72/pp 165–8.

Condenses or omits much of the tale's rhetorical *amplificatio*: Nature's speech, the description of Virginia and her virtues, and the address to parents and governesses.

1536 *The Complete Works of Geoffrey Chaucer*. Ed. F.N. Robinson. 1933/1957. See **55**. Text pp 175–8/pp 145–7, explanatory notes pp 831–3/pp 726–8, textual notes pp 1010–11/p 894.

The text of *CT*, 'corrected for grammatical accuracy and for the adjustment of rimes' (xxxv/xxix), is based on El, collated with the Chaucer Society prints of Hg, Cambridge Dd.4.24, Cambridge Gg.4.27, Corpus, Petworth, Lansdowne, and Harley 7334, with Thynne's 1532 edition, and with the unpublished Cardigan and Morgan MSS. Robinson follows El in placing Fragment VI (C) after Fragment V (F). The general introduction to *CT* (pp 10–11/p 10) and the introduction to the explanatory notes (p 832/p 727) treat the tale's sources, its date, its suitability to the Physician, and its relation to *LGW* (see **1659**). In the revised edition, the text of *PhyT* is unchanged, as are the introductory material (p 10) and the textual notes. The explanatory notes have been slightly expanded. On Robinson's edition, see **1818**, **1865**. *The Riverside Chaucer* (**1560**) is based on Robinson's second edition. See also **1541, 1544, 1547, 1550, 1554, 1562, 1669**.

1537 *The Canterbury Tales*. Trans. Frank E. Hill. 1934 (2 vols)/1946 (1 vol.) See **56**. 1:301–10/pp 244–51.

A modernization, in rhymed couplets. The 1946 edition includes a color plate of the Physician.

1538 *Geoffrey Chaucer: Canterbury Tales*. Trans. J.U. Nicolson. 1934. See **57**. Pp 283–90.

A modernizations in rhymed couplets. Includes a full-length portrait of the Physician.

1539 *The Text of The Canterbury Tales, Studied on the Basis of All Known Manuscripts*. Ed. John Matthews Manly and Edith Rickert. 1940. See **61**. Classification of manuscripts, 2:317–24; text and textual notes, 4:64–76; critical notes, 4:488–90; glosses, 3:515–16; corpus of variants, 7:3–32.

Manly and Rickert sought to establish the archetype of the extant *CT* texts by collating all existing manuscripts against Skeat's 'Student's Edition' (2:5). The result, for *PhyT*, is a text similar to that of Hg (see **1559**, p 85). Manly and Rickert print their text without punctuation, in a spelling based on that of Hg and El (1:x). While noting that Fragment VI (C) contains no information that would allow us to determine its proper position in the sequence of tales (2:492), they accept the early scribes' placement of C before B^2 (VII), printing the tales in the El order (A B^1 D E–F C B^2 G H I). In their Classification of Manuscripts, the editors propose seven lines of descent for *PhyT*. Most MSS (the 'Large Group') were derived from the same ultimate ancestor; MSS of independent descent include Hg and El. Manly finds evidence in the readings of some of the Large Group MSS for an early, unrevised version of *PhyT*, support for the conjecture that *PhyT* 'was written for a particular occasion antedating the *CT* period' (2:498; but cf. **1559**, **1685**). The Critical Notes treat sources of error in the archetype; the Corpus of Variants records all the variants of all the MSS with the exception of spelling variants of nonclassificatory value. For a detailed critique of Manly and Rickert's edition, see **590**. See also **1668**, **1550**.

1540 *The Canterbury Tales of Geoffrey Chaucer*. Trans. Robert M. Lumiansky. 1948. See **63**. Pp 220–4.

A prose modernization. A color plate shows a stylized Virginius carrying Virginia's head to the judge.

1541 *The Canterbury Tales, Translated into Modern English*. Trans. Nevill Coghill. 1951/1958. 2 vols, 1956. See **65**. Pp 256–63 [1951]/2:7–15 [1956].

This widely used verse modernization (with synopses of *Mel* and *ParsT*) is based on Skeat (**1510**) and Robinson (**1536**). Coghill follows the Chaucer Society order (**1509**), placing Fragment VI (C) after Fragment II–VII [B^1+B^2].

1542 Item cancelled.

1543 *Chaucer's Poetry: An Anthology for the Modern Reader*. Ed. E. Talbot Donaldson. 1958/1975. See **71**.

Donaldson omits *PhyT* from the first edition of his anthology, observing that it 'shows Chaucer working rather routinely, without his characteristic originality' (p 927). The tale is reinstated in the 1975 edition (pp 396–405), with a fuller commentary (see **1693**). Donaldson's text of *CT* is based on Hg, with regularized spelling.

1544 *Geoffrey Chaucer: Canterbury Tales*. Ed. A.C. Cawley. 1958/1960, 1990, 1996. See **72**. Pp 335–42.

The text is that of Robinson's second edition (**1536**), with glosses in the margins and at the foot of the page. An introduction treats Chaucer's life, and the text, language, and themes of *CT*. An appendix includes brief notes on Chaucer's pronunciation, grammar, and versification. The 1990 and 1996 revisions incorporate readings from **1560**. For the earlier Everyman's Library edition, see **1524**.

1545 *The Works of Geoffrey Chaucer. A Facsimile of the William Morris Chaucer, with the Original 87 Illustrations by Edward Burne-Jones*. 1958. See **73**. Pp 96–8.
A brief discussion of Chaucer's life, works, language, Morris's career and the printing of the *Kelmscott Chaucer* (**1511**) introduces this reduced-type facsimile. A glossary based on the *Oxford Chaucer* (**1510**) concludes the volume. For a later facsimile, see **1551**.

1546 *Chaucer's Major Poetry*. Ed. Albert C. Baugh. 1963. See **78**. Pp 485–9.
After an introduction to Chaucer's life, language, and versification, a brief bibliography, and an introduction to *CT*, the text (based on El and complete except for *Mel* and *ParsT*) is presented. Explanatory notes and glosses are printed at the bottom of the page. A full glossary with line numbers and a list of common words conclude the volume. Baugh follows El in placing Fragment VI (C) after Fragment V (F) (see p 232).

1547 *Geoffrey Chaucer: The Canterbury Tales*. Trans. David Wright. 1964. See **80**. Pp 156–60.
A prose modernization, based on Robinson's second edition (**1536**); the tales are printed in the Chaucer Society order (**1509**).

1548 *Geoffrey Chaucer, The Works, 1532, with supplementary material from the Editions of 1542, 1561, 1598, and 1602*. 1969. Ed. Derek S. Brewer. 1969. See **91**.
Brewer's description of the sixteenth-century editions of Chaucer's works introduces a facsimile of Thynne's black-letter edition of 1532, supplemented by material from the 1542 reprint of Thynne, Stow's 1561 edition, and Speght's editions of 1598 and 1602. *PhyT*, illustrated with the woodcut of the Physician from Caxton's second edition, appears on lxxiii^{r}–lxxv^{v}. For an earlier facsimile of Thynne 1532, see **1522**.

1549 *The Canterbury Tales. A Facsimile Edition of Caxton's Second Edition*. 1972. See **93**.
A reprint of Pepys's copy of Caxton's second (1484) edition of *CT*. Woodcuts of the pilgrims introduce their respective tales. *PhyT* appears on fols 2F2r–2F5r.

1550 *The Tales of Canterbury, Complete*. Ed. Robert Armstrong Pratt. 1974. See **94a**. Pp 412–18.
The text is based on Robinson's second edition (**1536**), with frequent recourse to Manly and Rickert (**1539**), in an attempt 'to recreate the text as Chaucer wrote it' (p 561). The four readings in *PhyT* that differ from those in Robinson are listed on pp 573–4. Pratt places Fragment VII (B^{2}) after Fragment II (B^{1}), but adopts the Ellesmere tale order in placing Fragment VI (C)

after Fragment V (F). Includes a reproduction of the decapitation of Virginia from a fourteenth-century MS of *Les livres des estoires dou commencement dou monde.*

1551 *The Kelmscott Chaucer*, a facsimile edition, with *A Companion Volume to the Kelmscott Chaucer* by Duncan Robinson. 1975. See **95**.
A full-size facsimile of the 1896 edition (**1511**).The facsimile and the *Companion* were produced in 515 copies on paper. For an earlier facsimile, see **1545**.

1552 *The Complete Poetry and Prose of Geoffrey Chaucer*. Ed. John H. Fisher. 1977/1989/2006. See **96**. Pp 216–20/pp 216–20/pp 219–23.
Fisher's text of *CT* is based on El, occasionally corrected with Hg and other MSS. The textual notes, printed with glosses and explanatory notes on the page, list substantive variants from Hg and the 'more interesting' variants from other MSS (p 967). Fisher follows the Ellesmere order of the tales; 'aesthetically,' the placement of Fragment VI (C) after *FranT* is 'quite satisfactory,' *PhyT* being an appropriate sequel to Dorigen's lament about unfortunate women (p 214). End matter includes discussions of Chaucer's literary place, time, language, and versification, and (from the 3rd printing onwards) a short glossary. A notable feature of Fisher's edition is the substantial bibliography (revised in the 1989 and 2006 editions) of recent and important older studies; for *PhyT*, see p 1004/pp 1001–2/pp 432–3.

1553 *The Canterbury Tales: A Facsimile and Transcription of the Hengwrt Manuscript, with Variants from the Ellesmere Manuscript*. Ed. Paul G. Ruggiers. 1979. See **98**.
Hg, reproduced here with a paleographical introduction, is the base text for the Variorum Edition of *CT* (in progress). *PhyT* (fols 191v–5r) appears on pp 761–74, with facing-page plates and transcription.

1554 *Chaucer's Canterbury Tales Complete in Present-Day English*. Trans. James J. Donohue. 1979. See **99**. Pp 277–84.
A modernization, in rhymed couplets. Based on Robinson (**1536**); the tales are given in the Chaucer Society order (**1509**).

1555 *The Poetical Works of Geoffrey Chaucer. A Facsimile of Cambridge University Library MS GG.4.27*. 1979. See **100**.
A facsimile edition of 'the only surviving example of a fifteenth-century attempt to collect Chaucer's major poetical works in one volume' (3:1). The text of *PhyT*, which here follows *SqT–FranT* (2: fol. 302), is incomplete, beginning at line 167 and ending at line 242.

1556 *The Canterbury Tales by Geoffrey Chaucer, Edited from the Hengwrt Manuscript*. Ed. N.F. Blake. 1980. See **102**. Pp 427–35.
Alone among editors of *CT*, Blake follows the tale order as well as the text of Hg, which is printed with textual and explanatory notes at the foot of the page. Hg's text 'makes good sense with a minimum of emendation' (p 12); in *PhyT*, it is emended only in line 188. Hg's spellings are retained as well. As an alternative to the Chaucer Society division of the tales into nine

fragments (**1509**), Blake proposes a scheme of twelve sections. *PhyT PardT* is section 9; it occurs in Hg after *ClT* (section 8) and before *ShT PrT Thop Mel MkT NPT* (section 10). In his Introduction, Blake reconstructs the history of Hg's compilation, and explains his editorial decisions (e.g., the omission of *CYT*) in the light of that history.

1557 *Geoffrey Chaucer: The Canterbury Tales.* Trans. David Wright. 1985. See **105**. Pp 386–93.

A modernization in rhymed couplets, with a brief introduction and notes.

1558 *Geoffrey Chaucer: The Canterbury Tales.* Trans. David Wright. 3 vols. 1986. See **106**. 3:1–21.

A wood engraving by Robert Kettell shows Appius eyeing Virginia in a market place.

1559 Chaucer, Geoffrey. *The Physician's Tale.* Ed. Helen Storm Corsa. *A Variorum Edition of the Works of Geoffrey Chaucer,* Volume 2, Part 17. Gen. eds Paul G. Ruggiers, Donald C. Baker, and Daniel J. Ransom. Norman: U of Oklahoma P, 1987.

The only separate edition of *PhyT,* the Variorum contains, in addition to the text, a Critical Commentary, a Textual Commentary, bibliographical and general indexes, and reproductions (one in color) of Hg, 191v (lines 1–36) and 195r (lines 277–310). The Critical Commentary treats Sources and Analogues, Date, the Question of Revision, the Appropriateness of Tale to Teller, the Relation to Other Tales, *PhyT* and the Host. It concludes with a survey of criticism through 1984. The Textual Commentary examines the Textual Tradition, the Evidence of the Glosses, Spurious Lines, Spurious Headlinks, the *Phy–PardL, PhyT* and the Order of *CT.* It includes as well a description of the MSS collated for the Variorum (Hg, El, Additional 35286, Corpus, Cambridge Dd.4.24, Cambridge Gg.4.27, Harley 7334, Helmingham, Lansdowne, and Petworth), a description of the printed editions from Caxton (1478) to Fisher (1977; **96**), and a Table of Correspondences (a comparative tabulation of three categories of variants for the ten collated manuscripts and Caxton's 1478 edition). In accordance with the principles of the Variorum, the text is based on Hg; it is emended in two places (lines 71, 188) from El. Collations from the base ten MSS and the printed editions are given below the text, followed by textual and explanatory notes. See **1510, 1539, 1571, 1594**.

• Review by N.F. Blake, *ES* 69 (1988), 571–2: 'The most controversial point relates to whether [*PhyT*] has been subjected to authorial revision or not. Here the editor appears to adopt a non-committal stance … but in her notes she clearly accepts that Chaucer did make some revisions in his text … She follows Hg, but she never makes it clear whether this manuscript represents Chaucer's first or his revised version' (p 572).

• Review by R.T. Lenaghan, *SAC* 10 (1988), 141–3: Corsa's text and commentary are admirable, but her circumspection limits the usefulness of this edition; 'frequently she leaves the field to the disputants with no judgment on her part … The result is too often a series of disembodied glosses, a sort of deconstruction by default' (p 143).

• Review by Lorrayne Y. Baird-Lange, *Speculum* 64 (1989), 931–3: Although 'Corsa is always mindful of her role as objective editor,' the edition is 'flawed by many minor inaccuracies … few of the errors are serious enough to impede effective use of the book, but some are' (p 932).

• Review by J.D. Burnley, *RES* n.s. 40 (1989), 401–2: 'Corsa is rather reticent in pressing her own views, so that the Introduction often resembles an annotated bibliography … benefits could be gained in future editions if editors were more willing to overlook their duties as scholarly reporters to assert their individual authority' (p 402).

• Review by Helen Cooper, *MÆ* 58 (1989), 152–3: In her survey of criticism and scholarship, Corsa is 'a model of editorial dispassionateness … but one occasionally wishes … for some expression of skepticism, or for more guidance between opposing arguments' (pp 152–3). The edition is informative on all details of text and commentary, 'but the Tale itself remains as opaque as ever' (p 153).

• Review of *The Squire's Tale* (see **112r**) by Kenneth Bleeth, *Speculum* 69 (1993), 731–3: 'the extent of error in the Physician's Tale edition … has hardly been hinted at in published reviews' (p 733).

1560 *The Riverside Chaucer*. Gen. ed. Larry D. Benson. 1987. See **108**. Text pp 190–3, explanatory notes pp 901–4, textual notes pp 1129–30.

Based on Robinson's second edition (**1536**). Departs from Robinson's text at lines 97 and 252, in the capitalization of *Doctour* (line 117), and in minor matters of punctuation. Glosses appear at the foot of the page. The explanatory notes (by C. David Benson) have been thoroughly revised, as have the selective textual notes (by Ralph Hanna III). The latter indicate all changes from Robinson, and 'attempt to provide some notice of all those major readings about which editors in the past century have offered conflicting opinions' (p 1121). The volume also includes introductory essays on Chaucer's life, the canon and chronology of his works, his language and versification, and the treatment of his texts in this edition, a detailed bibliography, and a full glossary with line references. For Benson's comments on *PhyT*, see **1839**. See also **1544**, **1564**, **1565**.

1561 Partridge, Stephen Bradford. *Glosses in the Manuscripts of Chaucer's Canterbury Tales: An Edition and Commentary*. 1992. Dir. Larry D. Benson. See **114**.

An edition of the manuscript glosses to all of *CT* except *Mel* and *MkT*. Variant readings are recorded, and the sources of the glosses, where known, are identified. For *PhyT*, glosses occur at lines 14, 16, 58, 72, 91, 93, 101, 115, 154, 173, 174, 177, 200, 213, 240, and 272. 'The glosses at 14, 16, and 240 are essentially footnotes, naming a source where a reader can find more information about the figures briefly alluded to in the text' (VI–1).

1562 *The Canterbury Tales by Geoffrey Chaucer*. Trans. Ronald L. Ecker and Eugene Crook. 1993. See **115**. Pp 327–34.
A modernization of the tales in verse (by Ecker), and the prose tales (by Crook), based on Robinson's second edition (**1536**).

1563 *The New Ellesmere Chaucer Facsimile (of Huntington Library MS EL26 C9)*. Ed. Daniel Woodward and Martin Stevens. 1995. See **118**. Fols 133r–36r.
Limited to 250 copies, in three formats. For an account of the production of the facsimile, see Daniel Woodward, "The New Ellesmere Chaucer Facsimile," in *The Ellesmere Chaucer: Essays in Interpretation* (San Marino, CA and Tokyo: Huntington Library Press and Yushudo, 1995), pp 1–13.

1563a *The New Ellesmere Chaucer monochromatic facsimile (of Huntington Library MS EL26 C9)*. 1997. See **120**.
A full-size monochromatic facsimile of **118** (**1563**), made using the transparencies of the color facsimile. Limited to one thousand copies.

1564 *Geoffrey Chaucer: The Canterbury Tales, Complete*. Ed. Larry D. Benson. 2000. See **124**. Text pp 172–5, explanatory notes pp 427–9.
The text is that of *The Riverside Chaucer* (**1560**), as are the glosses at the foot of the page. The *Riverside* textual notes have been omitted. The explanatory notes have been extensively revised and provided with an index to the principal matters treated in the notes.

1565 *The Canterbury Tales in Modern Verse.* Trans. Joseph Glaser. 2005. See **127**. Pp 241–8.
A translation in couplets. An introduction surveys Chaucer's life, times, and works, 'The Religious Establishment in the *Canterbury Tales*,' and contains notes on the text, based on *The Riverside Chaucer* (**1560**), and the translation. There is a select bibliography.

1566 *Geoffrey Chaucer: The Canterbury Tales.* Ed. Jill Mann. 2005. See **128**. Text: pp 439–48; explanatory notes: pp 966–8.
A chronology, critical introduction, discussion of Chaucer's language, and a note on the text are followed by the text of *CT*, which is 'squarely based on' both El and Hg, with occasional emendations from other MSS and on metrical grounds (lxii–lxiii). The spelling follows that of Manly and Rickert (**1539**). Lexical glosses appear at the foot of each page. The text is followed by detailed interpretive notes (pp 795–1111) and a glossary.

ꝏ *The Physician's Tale*: Sources, Analogues, and Later Influence

The earliest scholarship on the sources of *PhyT* is summarized by Corsa (**1559**). For additional comments on sources and analogues, see **1510**, **1617**, **1628**, **1629**, **1637**, **1638**, **1640**, **1649**, **1652**, **1684**, **1687**, **1704**, **1713**, **1715**, **1737**, **1745**, **1761**, **1763**, **1781**, **1782**, **1789**, **1791**, **1792**, **1793**, **1795**, **1796**, **1801**, **1808**, **1828**, **1838**, **1847**, **1858**, **1861**, **1862**, **1875**, **1879**, **1896**, **1902**, **1915**, **1924**, **1926**, **1931a**, **1964**, **1967**, **1969**, **1970**, **1973**, **1975**.

For a guide to the literature on the sources and analogues of Chaucer's writings, see **1605a**.

1567 Bersuire, Pierre, trans. [Titus Livius, *Decades*.] 3 vols. Paris: [Jean Dupré], 1486–8.
The story of Appius and Virginia and its attendant circumstances appears in vol. 1, fols 117v–28r, of the 1486–8 printing of Bersuire's Livy (Yale University Library copy). For Chaucer's possible knowledge of Bersuire's translation of Livy, see **1610**.

1568 Ambrose, St. *De Virginibus*. In *Patrologiae Cursus Completus ... Series Latina*. Ed. J.-P. Migne. Vol. 16. Paris: Garnier, 1880.
The parallels to the description of Virginia cited by Tupper (**1576**) appear in cols 197–244. For an English translation, see **1570**.

1569 Rumbaur, Otto. *Die Geschichte von Appius und Virginia in der englischen Literatur*. Breslau: Brehmer & Minuth, 1890.
Surveys the treatment of Livy's anecdote in *RR*, *PhyT*, *CA*, and in plays by R.B. (1564), John Webster (1654), John Dennis (ca 1715), John Moncrieff (1755), Frances Brooke (1756), and James Sheridan Knowles (ca 1825). Of these dramatic versions, only R.B.'s *Apius and Virginia* makes use of *PhyT*.

1570 Ambrose, St. *Three Books of St. Ambrose, Bishop of Milan, Concerning Virgins, to Marcellina, His Sister*. In *St. Ambrose: Select Works and Letters*. Trans. H. de Romestin, with the assistance of E. de Romestin and H.T.F. Duckworth. Vol. 10 of *A Select Library of Nicene and Post-Nicene Fathers of the Christian Church*. Second Series. New York: Christian Literature Co.; Oxford: Parker, 1896.
An English translation of *DV* appears on pp 363–87.

1571 Gower, John. *The Complete Works of John Gower*. Ed. G.C. Macaulay. 4 vols.

Oxford: Clarendon, 1899–1902. Repr. Grosse Pointe, MI: Scholarly Press, 1968.

Gower's version of the Appius and Virginia story appears at the end of Book 7 of *CA* (lines 5131–5306; 3:377–82). It illustrates the fifth of the five points of policy for rulers (Truth, Liberality, Justice, Pity, and Chastity) by demonstrating the incompatibility of 'rihtwisnesse and lecherie' in governors. Scholars generally agree that *PhyT* does not reflect the influence of Gower's retelling of the story (see **1559**, **1585**). For an argument that Chaucer could have known *CA* (at least by hearsay) when he wrote *PhyT*, see **1610**.

1572 Ballmann, Otto. 'Chaucers Einfluss auf das englische Drama im Zeitalter der Königen Elisabeth und der beiden ersten Stuart-Könige.' 1902. See **247**.

A brief note on *PhyT* as the source of R.B.'s *Apius and Virginia* (p 4).

1573 Hertwig, Doris. *Der Einfluss von Chaucers "Canterbury Tales" auf die englische Literatur*. 1908. See **137**.

Of the dramatic and poetic treatments of the Appius and Virginia story in English through the mid-nineteenth century, only R.B.'s *Apius and Virginia* is directly indebted to *PhyT*.

1574 Fansler, Dean Spruill. *Chaucer and the Roman de la Rose*. 1914. See **148**.

Disputes Skeat's view (**4**) that Chaucer relied more heavily on *RR* than on Livy in composing *PhyT*; not more than a dozen lines can confidently be traced to the influence of the French poem. For much of the tale, Chaucer 'was evidently drawing upon his imagination or some unknown source' (p 34). Chaucer's version of the story is superior to those of Gower, Boccaccio, and Jean de Meun. Chaucer is 'greatest in his original scenes and situations'; *PhyT* is the 'finest English retelling' (p 35) of the Appius and Virginia tale. For a list of passages possibly indebted to *RR*, see p 258.

1575 Spurgeon, Caroline F.E. *Five Hundred Years of Chaucer Criticism and Allusion (1357–1900)*. 1914–24. See **149**.

The single (unindexed) reference to *PhyT* is from Milton's manuscript *Common Place Book* (ca 1674); commenting on the education of children, the poet cites lines 67–9 (1:249).

1576 Tupper, Frederick. 'Chaucer's Bed's Head.' *MLN* 30 (1915), 5–12.

Cites parallels between the description of Virginia in *PhyT* and the type of the 'consecrated virgin' in *DV*. These include Virginia's discretion in speech, her abstemiousness and avoidance of public festivities, her walk to the temple with her mother, and her citation of the Jephthah story. Lowes (**1638**) observes that Chaucer's 'omnivorous reading may well have led him to Ambrose's treatise, but the fact (if it be such) that he draws from it for Virginia has no real bearing on Tupper's case' for *PhyT* as an exemplum of Lechery (p 309n). See **1585**, **1586**, **1619**.

1577 *Livy, in Fourteen Volumes*. Ed. and trans. B.O. Foster, F.G. Moore, E.T. Sage, and A.C. Schlesinger. 14 vols. Loeb Classical Library. Cambridge, MA: Har-

vard UP; London: Heinemann; New York: Putnam, 1919–59.
The episode of Appius, Virginius, and Virginia and its attendant circumstances (Book 3, chs 44–58) is printed with a facing English translation in vol. 2, pp 142–99.

1578 Landrum, Grace W. 'Chaucer's Use of the Vulgate.' 2 vols. PhD diss., Radcliffe, 1921. Dir. John Livingston Lowes and F.N. Robinson.
In Livy, Jean de Meun, and Gower, Virginia is Virginius's only daughter; Chaucer echoes the Vulgate (Judges 11:34) in making her his only child (2:21).

1579 Koch, J. 'Chaucers Belesenheit in den römischen Klassikern.' *ESt* 57 (1923), 8–84.
If Chaucer had read Livy, he would have included in *PhyT* such dramatic details as the downfall of the *decemviri* and the presence of Icilius, Virginia's fiancé. He might also have noted the striking differences between the manner of Virginia's death in Livy and in *RR*. The evidence suggests that Chaucer knew no more of Livy's version of the Appius and Virginia story than was available to him from *RR* (pp 58–9). Despite marginal glosses in several MSS citing Ovid and Cicero, *RR* also seems to have been Chaucer's source for the allusions to Pygmalion, Apelles, and Zanzis (pp 24, 55–6).

1580 Magoun, Francis P., Jr. 'The Chaucer of Spenser and Milton.' *MP* 25 (1927), 129–36.
The folio number in Milton's reference to *PhyT* in his *Common Place Book* ('doctor of Phis. tale fol. 58') identifies the text Milton was using as Speght's second edition (1602) of Chaucer's works.

1581 Shannon, Edgar Finley. *Chaucer and the Roman Poets*. 1929. See **162**.
Cites Ovidian sources for lines 14 (Pygmalion), 59, and 65–6 (pp 317–18).

1582 Farnham, Willard. *The Medieval Heritage of Elizabethan Tragedy*. Berkeley: U of California P, 1936.
In making his story into a morality and a tragic drama, the author of *Apius and Virginia* develops a number of details in *PhyT*: the Vice figure may have been suggested by the *feend* who prompts Appius (line 130); the dialogue between Virginius and Virginia and the concluding moral lie behind the playwright's handling of his subject.

1583 Vincent of Beauvais. *De Eruditione Filiorum Nobilium*. Ed. Arpad Steiner. Medieval Academy of America Publications 32. Cambridge, MA: Medieval Academy of America, 1938.
The passages cited by Young (**1586**) as parallels to the description of Virginia's maidenly virtues appear in Ch. 42, *De puellarum custodia et absconsione*; Ch. 43, *De litterali et morali earum instruccione et I° de castitate*; Ch. 44, *De uitanda ornatus superfluitate*; Ch. 45, *De pudice societatis et famulatus eleccione*; and Ch. 46, *De humilitate puellari et taciturnitate atque maturitate*.

1584 Coffman, George R. 'Chaucer's Library and Literary Heritage for the *Canter-*

bury Tales.' SP 38 (1941), 571–83.

Agrees with Shannon (**1585**) that Chaucer knew Livy and used details from his account selectively. This procedure 'accords with what we know otherwise of Chaucer's methods of selection; and the results here create a more artistically human and poignant situation than would be possible through employing either Livy or Jean de Meun alone' (p 580).

1585 Shannon, Edgar Finley. 'The Physician's Tale.' In *Sources and Analogues of Chaucer's Canterbury Tales.* 1941. See **174.**

Summarizes the relations of *PhyT* and those versions of the Appius and Virginia story 'theoretically accessible' (p 398) to Chaucer. The poet clearly made use of Jean de Meun's *RR*; the presence in *PhyT* of several details found only in the ultimate source of the anecdote (Livy's *Ab urbe condita*) suggests that he had access to the Latin original as well. There is nothing in the versions of the tale in Boccaccio's *De mulieribus claris* or Pierre Bersuire's translation of Livy that Chaucer could not have found in *RR* or in Livy's Latin. *CA,* which also contains the story, probably postdates *PhyT*; the two treatments are, in any event, 'entirely independent of each other' (p 398). The relevant passages from *RR* and Livy are given, with Chaucerian parallels in footnotes for the latter. Also appended is a selection of the passages from *DV* cited by Tupper (**1576**) as analogues to the account of Virginia's maidenly virtues. See **1584, 1619.**

1586 Young, Karl. 'The Maidenly Virtues of Chaucer's Virginia.' *Speculum* 16 (1941), 340–9.

Proposes the *De eruditione filiorum nobilium* of Vincent of Beauvais as a source for the description of Virginia's virtues. The treatise was more accessible than *DV*; the parallels between *PhyT* and Ambrose cited by Tupper (**1576**) can largely be matched with passages from *De eruditione.* The latter text, moreover, offers several parallels to Chaucer's description of Virginia not present in Ambrose. Chaucer knew Vincent's *Speculum majus,* and he may also have known *De eruditione.* See **1583, 1619.**

1587 Cottle, A. Basil, review of Haldeen Braddy, *Chaucer and the French Poet Graunson* (see **179**). *RES* 24 (1948), 150–1.

An allusion to Pygmalion in Graunson seems to recall lines 14–15 of *PhyT,* but both poets may be echoing *RR.*

1588 Makarewicz, Sister Mary Raynelda. *The Patristic Influence on Chaucer.* 1953. See **289.**

Lists parallels between lines 39–155 and *DV* (pp 21–30).

1589 Zanco, Aurelio. *Chaucer e il suo mondo.* 1955/1965. See **293.**

A brief discussion of sources and analogues, with parallel passages from *RR* (pp 200–6).

• Review by Howard Rollin Patch, *Speculum* 34 (1959), 149–52: The story of Virginia could hardly have found a place in *LGW,* which concerns women who were always faithful in love.

1590 Boccaccio, Giovanni. *Concerning Famous Women*. Trans. Guido A. Guarino. New Brunswick, NJ: Rutgers UP, 1963.
An English translation of *De mulieribus claris* (see **1594**). Ch. 56, 'The Virgin Verginia,' appears on pp 128–30.

1591 Dickens, Louis George. *The Story of Appius and Virginia in English Literature.* PhD diss., University of Rochester, 1963. Dir. Robert B. Hinman. Ann Arbor, MI: University Microfilms, 1975. See also *DAI* 24–05 (1963): 0188.
A survey of the Appius and Virginia story from Livy through the nineteenth century. Virginius's 'self-centered moral folly' (p 61) in beheading his innocent daughter is paralleled by the Physician's 'refusal to scrutinize his own motives' (p 67).

1592 Happé, P. 'Tragic Themes in Three Tudor Moralities.' *SEL* 5 (1965), 209–27.
R.B.'s handling of his Chaucerian source in *Apius and Virginia* clarifies his conception of tragedy. In contrast to Chaucer, R.B. deals with Apius's mental state, showing him as frustrated and tormented. In *PhyT*, Virginius says he must kill his daughter. In the play, Virginia begs her father to kill her and even suggests that he take her head to Apius. The changes in Virginia's character make her a more dynamic personality, increasing the pathetic effect of her death and our sense of her virtue.

1593 Guillaume de Lorris and Jean de Meun. *Le Roman de la Rose*. Ed. Félix Lecoy. 3 vols. Classiques français du moyen âge. Paris: Champion, 1965–70.
The story of Appius and Virginia, part of Raison's argument for the superiority of Love to Justice, appears in vol. 1, pp 171–3 (lines 5559–5628) of the standard modern edition of *RR*. For an English translation, see **1596**.

1594 Boccaccio, Giovanni. *De Mulieribus Claris*. Ed. Vittorio Zaccaria. In *Tutte le Opere di Giovanni Boccaccio*. Vol. 10. Gen. ed. Vittore Branca. Milan: Mondadori, 1967.
Ch. 58, 'De Virginea virgine Virginii filia,' is printed on pp 236–42, with a facing Italian translation. (For an English translation, see **1590**.) Although most scholars agree that Boccaccio's version of Livy's anecdote contributed nothing to *PhyT*, see **1559**, pp 7–8.

1595 Branca, Geraldine Sesak. *Experience versus Authority: Chaucer's Physician and Fourteenth-Century Science.* PhD diss., University of Illinois (Urbana-Champaign), 1971. Dir. Richard H. Green. Ann Arbor, MI: University Microfilms International, 1972. See also *DAI*–A 33/10 (1972): 5731.
Notes parallels between the Physician's description of Virginia and the depiction of Natura in Alanus de Insulis's *De planctu naturae*. 'It might be argued that the Physician has simply employed a common rhetorical topos of medieval literature in having Nature, the maker of beautiful beings, pay special attention to Virginia … But [he] goes beyond this topos … when he has Nature draw Virginia … into an identical copy of Alain's familiar pic-

ture of Nature herself' (p 92).

1596 Guillaume de Lorris and Jean de Meun. *The Romance of the Rose.* Trans. Charles Dahlberg. Princeton, NJ: Princeton UP, 1971.
A prose modernization, with extensive notes, a bibliography, and reproductions of illustrations from several MSS. The episode of Appius and Virginia appears on p 114. Plate 29, from MS Douce 195 (Bodleian Library, Oxford), depicts the trial and death of Virginia.

1597 Sasamoto, Hisayuki. 'On the Source of Geoffrey Chaucer's "Physician's Tale."' *Senrizan Collected Papers on Literature* 8 (1972), 1–17.
Not seen. Listed in *BPMELLJ* (1983), p 150. In Japanese.

1598 Woolf, Rosemary. 'The Influence of the Mystery Plays upon the Popular Tragedies of the 1560's.' *RenD* n.s. 6 (1973), 89–105.
The changes that Jean de Meun made in Livy's anecdote prepared the way for Chaucer's version of the Virginia–Virginius story, in which the interest lies in the relationship between father and daughter. The dialogue in lines 213–50 is strikingly similar to that in the Abraham and Isaac mystery plays. Although he would not have required a model for this scene of pathos, 'it would not be uncharacteristic of Chaucer to draw attention to one analogue while in fact drawing substantially upon another' (p 91).

1599 Harbert, Bruce. 'Chaucer and the Latin Classics.' In *Geoffrey Chaucer*. Ed. Derek S. Brewer. London: Bell, 1974; Athens: Ohio State UP, 1975; pbk ed., 1982. Pp 137–53.
Although Chaucer names Livy as an authority in *PhyT,* the one detail in which the poem agrees with Livy against *RR* – the absence of Virginia's father when she is brought to trial – is not enough to establish that Chaucer was borrowing directly from the Roman author (p 143).

1600 Harty, Kevin J. 'Chaucer and the Fair Field of Anglo-Norman.' *Bonnes Feuilles* 5 (1975), 3–17.
In composing *PhyT,* Chaucer may have consulted the Anglo-Norman Life of St Margaret. He may also have known Nicholas Trevet's Latin commentary on Livy.

1601 Lancashire, Anne. 'Chaucer and the Sacrifice of Isaac.' *ChauR* 9 (1975), 320–6.
The dialogue between Virginius and his daughter, not paralleled in Livy or *RR,* is strikingly similar to the treatment of Abraham's sacrifice of Isaac in the English mystery cycles. Chaucer's model for this passage may have been the Abraham and Isaac dramatic tradition generally, or a lost Abraham and Isaac play.

1602 Waller, Martha S. 'The Physician's Tale: Geoffrey Chaucer and Fray Juan García de Castrojeriz.' *Speculum* 51 (1976), 292–306.
For the portrait of Virginia and some of *PhyT*'s narrative details, Chaucer may have relied on a Castilian version of Aegidius Romanus's *De regimine principum* composed by Fray Juan García de Castrojeriz for the heir apparent

to the throne of Castile, the Infante Pedro, who became Peter I in 1350. Castrojeriz's treatise accounts for 'nearly every phrase of *PhyT* not suggested by the *RR*' (p 296), including some material not paralleled in Ambrose (see **1570**) or Vincent of Beauvais (see **1583**). Chaucer could have encountered the Castrojeriz translation when he was in Spain in 1366. Alternatively, he could have seen it in England, during the period when his wife was in personal attendance on Constance of Castile, Peter's daughter and John of Gaunt's second wife; the volume might have been among Constance's household effects. See **1612**.

1603 Thompson, Ann. *Shakespeare's Chaucer: A Study in Literary Origins*. 1978. See **324**. Lists parallels between *PhyT* and R.B.'s *Apius and Virginia*. The play and Chaucer's poem share several details not found in Livy, suggesting that the playwright drew on *PhyT*. John Webster's *Apius and Virginia* (1624), on the other hand, owes little or nothing to Chaucer (pp 27–9).

1604 McCall, John P. *Chaucer Among the Gods: The Poetics of Classical Myth*. 1979. See **1088**.
For his acquaintance with Livy's account of the Virginia story, Chaucer may be indebted to Simon de Hesdin's translation into French of Valerius Maximus's *Memorabilia* (ca 1376) (p 178n35).

1605 Kanno, Masahiko. 'Chaucer no *The Physician's Tale* – Ruiwa tono Hikaku' ['*The Physician's Tale* – comparison with its analogue']. *SFLL* 21 (1985), 47–58. A comparison of *PhyT* and Gower's *Tale of Virginia*. Chaucer's narrator tries to make explicit the reversal or inversion of *right* (line 166) or justice in the trial. (Not seen. Annotation from *BPMELLJ* [1994], p 91. In Japanese.)

1605a Morris, Lynn King. *Chaucer Sources and Analogue Criticism: A Cross-Referenced Guide*. 1985. See **218a**.
A guide to the literature (through 1981) on the sources and analogues of Chaucer's writings, indexed by title of Chaucerian work, author of source or analogue, genre or origin of source, and title of source or analogue. The entry for *PhyT*, pp 167–8, lists fifty-eight sources or analogues, with accompanying bibliographical references. A dozen of these items are medical authorities mentioned in the *GP* portrait of the Physician. Single works are sometimes listed under separate titles (e.g., Livy: Book 3; Livy: Exemplum; Livy: Founding of the City; Livy: History; Livy: History of Rome) and occasionally misattributed (e.g., John Gower: Roman de la Rose).

1606 Spearing, A.C. *Medieval to Renaissance in English Poetry*. Cambridge: Cambridge UP, 1985.
Chaucer rarely refers to a specific *auctour* as the authority for a complete work. He does so at the beginning of *PhyT*, but although Livy is the ultimate source of the story, it is unclear whether Chaucer used Livy or the version of the anecdote in *RR* (p 100).

1607 Kupersmith, William. 'Chaucer's Physician's Tale and the Tenth Satire of

Juvenal.' *ELN* 34 (1986), 20–3.
Chaucer may have found the germ for his three additions to Jean de Meun's version of the story of Virginia – the digression on Nature, the excursus on Virginia's chastity, the admonition to governesses and parents – in Juvenal's tenth satire, lines 289–306.

1608 Mitchell, Jerome. *Scott, Chaucer, and Medieval Romance: A Study of Sir Walter Scott's Indebtedness to the Literature of the Middle Ages*. Lexington: UP of Kentucky, 1987.
Finds possible echoes of *PhyT* in *Kenilworth* and *Quentin Durward* (pp 147, 164).

1609 Oka, Saburo. 'An Introduction to Comparative-Narratological Approach to Chaucer, with Special Reference to the Killing Scene in "The Physician's Tale."' *BFL* 29 (1987), 69–85.
Compares Virginia's death in *PhyT* with treatments in ancient narratives (Diodorus, Livy), medieval narratives (Jean de Meun, Gower, etc), and modern dramatic narratives ('R.B.,' Webster, Dennis, etc). (Not seen. Annotation from *BPMELLJ* [1994], pp 93–4. See also http://ci.nii.ac.jp/naid/110006230777. In Japanese.)

1610 Brown, William H., Jr. 'Chaucer, Livy, and Bersuire: The Roman Materials of The Physician's Tale.' In *On Language: Rhetorica, Phonologica, Syntactica. A Festschrift for Robert P. Stockwell from his Friends and Colleagues*. 1988. See **1232**.
The emphasis on chastity and chastity's violation in *PhyT* strengthens Shannon's argument (**1585**) for Chaucer's debt to Livy. But Chaucer need not have read Livy in the original; the details Shannon attributes to Chaucer's knowledge of the Latin text can be found in Pierre Bersuire's French translation (ca 1355; see **1567**).

1611 Hedley, Judith, ed. *An Edition of R.B.'s Appius and Virginia*. New York: Garland, 1988.
This edition, based on the 1575 quarto, includes a bibliographical introduction, discussions of the play's authorship (the traditional attribution to Richard Bower is highly conjectural) and date, surveys of the history of the story and the play's performance history, and a critical assessment. *PhyT* is the play's sole source. Although the play lacks the 'subtle skepticism' (xlviii) generated by *PhyT*, R.B. follows Chaucer closely in the general organization of his plot and in many specific details.

1612 Olson, Glending. 'Juan García de Castrojeriz and John of Wales: A Note on Chaucer's Reading.' *Speculum* 64 (1989), 106–10.
The details of Virginia's portrait that Waller (**1602**) attributes to Chaucer's reading of the commentary on Aegidius Romanus's *De regimine principum* by Juan García de Castrojeriz can be found as well in the *Communiloquium* of John of Wales. Chaucer demonstrates his familiarity with John's compendium in other works; it seems likely that the similarities between *PhyT* and

Castrojeriz's treatise exist 'not because Chaucer read the Spanish commentary but because both Chaucer and the Spanish friar took their commonplaces from the *Communiloquium*' (p 107). See **1616**.

1613 Gonda, Caroline. 'Sarah Scott and "The Sweet Excess of Paternal Love."' *SEL* 32 (1992), 511–35.
Of the eighteenth-century treatments of the Appius and Virginia story, Samuel Crisp's *Virginia* (1754) and Frances Brooke's *Virginia* (1756) are closer to Chaucer than to Livy or *RR* in allowing Virginia to play an active part in her own fate (p 522).

1614 Pearsall, Derek. *The Life of Geoffrey Chaucer: A Critical Biography*. 1992. See **665**.
RR is the direct and probably the sole source for *PhyT*. Livy is cited as a Latin *auctoritas*, but is not used (p 241; see also pp 33, 81).

1615 Phillips, Helen. 'Chaucer and Jean Le Fèvre.' *Archiv* 232 (1995), 23–36.
Notes the possible influence of Jean Le Fèvre's *Livre de Leësce* on the Physician's distinction between history and fable (lines 155–7), and on the juxtaposition of the story of Jephthah's daughter with that of Virginia.

1616 Lázaro, Luis Alberto. 'Some Speculations about Chaucer's Spanish Literary Sources.' *SELIM* 5 (1996), 18–28.
Agrees with Olson (**1612**) that Chaucer is more likely to have used John of Wales's Latin text than the Castilian book by Castrojeriz. We do not know if Chaucer studied Spanish before he came to Spain, and it is unlikely that he would have learned enough Spanish in a few weeks to enable him to translate Castrojeriz. He would not have needed Spanish to conduct diplomatic negotiations in Castile. French was the language used both by Spaniards and Englishmen to communicate orally (p 24).

1617 Lee, Brian S. '"Well done of rash Virginius": Renaissance Transformations of Livy's Account of the Fall of the Decemvirs.' *ELR* 27 (1997), 331–60.
PhyT is mentioned (pp 332–3, 341, 350–1, 354) in this survey of the Renaissance fortunes of Livy's anecdote.

1618 Bullón-Fernández, María. *Fathers and Daughters in Gower's Confessio Amantis: Authority, Family, State, and Writing*. Woodbridge, UK: Brewer, 2000.
In his version of the Virginia/Virginius story in *CA*, Gower – in contrast to Jean de Meun and Chaucer – echoes Livy's political lesson (p 146). None of the three authors, however, shows much interest in Virginia's fiancé Icilius, who plays a central role in Livy's narrative (pp 149–50).

1619 Bleeth, Kenneth. 'The Physician's Tale.' In *Sources and Analogues of The Canterbury Tales*. Vol. 2. Ed. Robert M. Correale and Mary Hamel. Woodbridge, UK: Brewer, 2005. Pp 535–63.
This two-volume work (volume 1 was published in 2002) incorporates scholarship on the sources and analogues of *CT* produced since Bryan and Dempster's compilation (**174**, **1585**). Like Shannon, Bleeth reprints Livy's

account of the Appius and Virginia story, but departs from Shannon's view that Chaucer may have known the Latin version; the sole source for the narrative portion of *PhyT* is Jean de Meun's *RR*. In addition to the relevant passage from the latter, the chapter includes excerpts from Vincent of Beauvais' *De eruditione filiorum nobilium* (see **1586**) and John of Wales's *Communiloquium* (see **1612**). Modern English translations are provided for all sources and analogues in foreign languages.

• Review by A.S.G. Edwards, *Archiv* 244 (2007), 376–9: Bleeth does not explain why he cites John of Wales from an Italian incunable rather than from (say) a fourteenth-century English manuscript.

• Review by Warren Ginsberg, *SAC* 29 (2007), 476–9: Bleeth's arguments for Livy's story of Virginia as an analogue rather than as a direct source and for John of Wales as the most likely source of the Physician's comments on the education of children are 'all carefully considered and fully persuasive' (p 478).

1620 Crafton, John Micheal. '"The cause of everiche maladye": A New Source of the *Physician's Tale.*' *PQ* 84 (2005), 259–85.

The final chapter – the treatise on virginity – of the *Summa virtutem remediis anime* (a significant source for *ParsT*) provides several analogues to *PhyT*: descriptions of the 'chaste maid' that parallel that of Virginia; advice on guardianship, particularly of virgins; a reference to Jephthah's daughter and an exegesis of it; and an allegorical comparison of wise and foolish virginity. See **1970**.

1621 Culhane, Peter. 'Livy in Early Jacobean Drama.' *T&L* 14 (2005), 21–44.

Although Chaucer enlists Livy's authority in *PhyT*, he does not appear to have consulted Livy's works. But Livy's reputation was so great that Chaucer felt it worthwhile to cite him. In lines 154–7, he uses the trope of asserting the historical truth of his tale, but he saw no reason to look deeply into his ultimate source for verification (pp 22–3).

ꟹ *The Physician's Tale*, 1893–2005

In addition to interpretive commentaries, this section includes bibliographies and other research tools, studies of the manuscripts and early editions, and discussions of the tale's language, date, and possible references to contemporary events. For the earliest scholarship on *PhyT*, see Corsa (**1559**). Additional comments on the manuscripts are included in the annotations for some of the editions (see Index, under 'manuscripts').

The Physician's Tale, 1893–1949

1622 Kittredge, G.L. 'Chaucer's Pardoner.' *Atlantic* 72 (1893), 829–33. Repr. in Wagenknecht (see **381**). Pp 117–25.
Critics who cite Nature's address as an example of intrusive moralizing on Chaucer's part forget that it is spoken by the Physician, 'a very formal person, from whom a degree of prosiness is to be expected. It was Chaucer's artistic duty … to make the method of delivery correspond to the character of the teller' (p 829). See **1976**.

1623 Snell, F.J. *The Age of Chaucer*. 1901. See **376**.
'What strikes one as strange is the [Physician's] selection of the story of Virginia in preference to a "shoppy" tale. It may be that the praise of chastity – this being, as it were, a bodily virtue – was regarded as particularly apt in a person whose character and accomplishments made him, in an unusual degree, sensible of its value' (p 217).

1624 Herford, C.H., ed. *English Tales in Verse*. 1902. See **15**.
MLT, *SNT*, and *PhyT* share a common focus – 'the gracious but somewhat anæmic sisterhood of saintly martyrs' – and were all 'clearly composed long before Chaucer had planned *CT*' (xxvi and n).

1625 Kittredge, G.L. 'Chaucer and Some of His Friends.' *MP* 1 (1903), 1–18.
In composing the digression on the responsibilities of parents and guardians, Chaucer was probably thinking of his sister-in-law, Katherine Swynford, who was governess of the daughters of John of Gaunt, his mistress, and subsequently his third wife (p 5n). See **1629**.

1626 Jenks, Tudor. *In the Days of Chaucer*. New York: Barnes; London: Author's Syndicate, 1904.
The portrait of Virginia is 'especially notable, but the telling of the tragic deed should be enough to convince any doubter of Chaucer's power to write in the highest style' (p 196).

1627 Ker, William Paton. 'Chaucer.' In *Essays on Medieval Literature*. 1905. See **796**.
Lists *PhyT*, along with *WBT* and *PardT*, as among those tales 'planned without weakness or hesitation in the design' (p 96).

1628 Root, Robert Kilburn. *The Poetry of Chaucer: A Guide to its Study and Appreciation*. 1906/1922. See **378**.
PhyT is not particularly appropriate to its teller. Chaucer may have written it for another purpose (perhaps for *LGW*) and 'finding it in his desk drawer, determined, with his customary literary thrift' (p 219), to incorporate it into *CT*. The tale differs in several particulars from Livy's version, but there is no evidence that Chaucer made the changes himself; despite his ascription of the story to Livy, Chaucer clearly used *RR* as his source. (A prose translation of the relevant passage in *RR* is included.) Chaucer's two additions to the French version – the description of Virginia's beauty and the 'infinitely pathetic' (p 222) scene between father and daughter – change the focus of the tale. In *RR*, the main emphasis is on the unjust judge and his punishment; in Chaucer, Virginia's personality is the dominant feature. See **1721**.

1629 Tatlock, John Strong Perry. *The Development and Chronology of Chaucer's Works*. Chaucer Society Publications, Second Series, 37. London: Kegan Paul, Trench, Trübner, 1907. Repr. Gloucester, MA: Peter Smith, 1963.
Dates *PhyT* between 1386 and 1390, probably around 1388. In support of his dating, Tatlock invokes the general similarity of *PhyT* to the stories in *LGW*, the absence of any influence from Gower's version of the tale in *CA* (1390), and – developing a suggestion of Kittredge (**1625**) – the apparent allusion in the address to governesses in charge of 'lordes doghtres' (line 73) to the elopement in 1386 of John of Gaunt's daughter, then married to the Earl of Pembroke, with John Holland. See **1665**.

1630 Hammond, Eleanor Prescott. *Chaucer: A Bibliographical Manual*. 1908. See **382**.
Ch. 3, 'The *Canterbury Tales*' (pp 150–324), surveys manuscripts, chronology, printed editions, modernizations and translations, sources, and analogues. The section on *PhyT* provides, in addition, information on the position of Fragment VI in the manuscripts and the three spurious prologues.

1631 Koellreutter, Maria. *Das Privatleben in England nach den Dichtungen von Chaucer, Gower, und Langland*. 1908. See **800**.
Lines 213–15 and 249–50 are cited as illustrations of the use of the familiar *thou* (parents to children) and of the respectful *you* (children to parents or elders) (pp 96–7).

1632 Corson, Hiram. *Index of Proper Names and Subjects to Chaucer's Canterbury Tales together with Comparisons and Similes, Metaphors and Proverbs, Maxims, etc., in the Same*. 1911. See **389**.
The index of names and subjects (including scriptural quotations and allusions) is followed by separate listings of comparisons and similes (none in *PhyT*); metaphors (one in *PhyT*); proverbs, maxims, and sententious expressions (three in *PhyT*); prayers, entreaties, and imprecations (none in *PhyT*).

1633 Koch, J. 'Textkritische Bemerkungen zu Chaucers *Canterbury Tales*.' 1913. See **393**.
Textual notes on lines 49, 70, 103–4, and 313 (pp 382–3).

1634 Meyer, Emil. *Die Charakterzeichnung bei Chaucer*. 1913. See **809**.
PhyT seems to a modern reader so improbable that even the detailed description of Virginia's bodily and spiritual beauty cannot bring her to life for us (p 145).

1635 Tupper, Frederick. 'Saint Venus and the Canterbury Pilgrims.' 1913. See **811**. See **1637**.

1636 Hadow, Grace E. *Chaucer and His Times*. 1914. See **394**.
PhyT is 'curiously cold and lifeless. There is a touch of nature at the end where the child, forgetting her piety, flings her arms round her father's neck, and asks him if there is no remedy, and again where she begs him to smite softly, but these are not enough to atone for the perfunctoriness of the rest' (p 135).

1637 Tupper, Frederick. 'Chaucer and the Seven Deadly Sins.' 1914. See **813**.
As part of his argument that *CT* embodies a systematic treatment of the Seven Deadly Sins, Tupper reads *PhyT* as an exemplum of Lechery and its antitype, Chastity. The tale's didactic intent is evident in the warnings to governesses and parents, in the parallels between the portrait of Virginia and the description of the 'consecrated maiden' in *DV*, and in the concluding *moralitas* (pp 103–4). Gower, moreover, uses the same story to develop the theme of Lechery in *CA*. Chaucer may have intended satire in assigning a tale exalting maidenly purity to a member of a profession notorious for prescribing love philters of the sort 'described in the wicked book of our Doctor's master, "Dan Constantyn"' (p 110). The Physician's story of 'oppressed virginity courting death rather than disgrace' (p 97n) follows naturally upon the Franklin's treatment of this subject in Dorigen's monologue, thus supporting El's placement of Fragment VI directly after *FranT*.
• Review by J. Koch, 'Neuere beiträge zur Chaucerliteratur aus Amerika.' *AB* 25 (1914), 327–42: Chaucer's matching of teller and tale is not intended as satire; nowhere in his works does the poet depict physicians as abettors of Lechery (p 330).

1637a Vockrodt, Gustav. *Reimtechnik bei Chaucer als Mittel zur chronologischen Bestimmung seiner im Reimpaar geschriebenen Werke*. Halle: Hohmann, 1914.

An attempt to establish the relative chronology of Chaucer's works using a statistical analysis of the occurrence of various sorts of rhyme: rhyming by suffix, rhyming of simple and composite words, 'grammatical' or identical rhyme (the 'same' word but with a different grammatical function), and 'broken' rhyme (e.g., *tyme:by me*). The rhyming patterns in *PhyT,* like those of *KnT,* place it at an early period in the composition of *CT* (pp 68, 70).

1638 Lowes, John Livingston. 'Chaucer and the Seven Deadly Sins.' *PMLA* 30 (1915), 237–371.
A detailed critique of Tupper's argument that *CT* embodies an extended treatment of the Seven Deadly Sins (**1637**). Neither Gower nor Jean de Meun employs the story of Appius and Virginia as an exemplum of Lechery, nor does the concluding moral of *PhyT* make any mention of this sin. 'Tupper's remark about another interpretation of the Appius and Virginia story applies, I fear, *mutatis mutandis,* to his own: his "unhappy comment upon the moral of the story ignores utterly its traditional function"' (p 309). See **1640**.

1639 Tupper, Frederick. 'The Quarrels of the Canterbury Pilgrims.' *JEGP* 14 (1915), 256–70.
'Nowhere is Chaucer's irony more amusingly illustrated than in the Doctor–Pardoner link. The Physician, upon completing his glorification of purity … is commended by the Host for those very drinks and lectuaries that stimulate lust in the *MerT* … Too daring is the mockery which invokes the blessings of the Virgin upon pills and potions fatal to virginity' (pp 257–8n). See **1651**.

1640 ———. 'Chaucer's Sinners and Sins.' *JEGP* 15 (1916), 56–106.
Responding to Lowes (**1638**), Tupper defends his view of *PhyT* as an exemplum of Lechery. Gower employs the Appius and Virginia story 'to teach Chastity as a point of royal policy by exemplifying the ruler's "lust of lechery"' (pp 59–60). In adapting *RR,* Chaucer deliberately altered the emphasis of the story from the iniquity of judges to Virginia's spotless purity. The sin that 'hath his merite' (line 277) in the concluding moral is clearly Lechery; Chaucer's purpose, like Gower's, is '"the chastisement of the unchaste"' (p 61). The tale's focus on virginity is further established by the similar emphasis of R.B.'s *Apius and Virginia,* modeled on *PhyT,* and by Harry Bailly's expressions of pity for Virginia. Finally, the theme of *PhyT* sets up an ironical relation between tale and teller; 'the medieval reader must have been tickled by the praise of purity' (p 63) from the Physician, whose dispensing of aphrodisiacs establishes him as a 'professional stimulator of lust' (p 66).

1641 Wells, John Edwin. *A Manual of the Writings in Middle English, 1050–1400.* 1916. See **398**.
A brief summary of scholarship on the position of Fragment VI in the MSS, the tale's sources, date, and possible contemporary allusions (pp 714–15), with accompanying bibliographical notes (p 879). Nine supplements (1919–52) take the survey through 1945; supplements 1–4 and 6–9 contain addition-

al material on *PhyT*. The passage on the proper education of children is 'an instance of [Chaucer's] readiness to thrust doctrine into narrative' (p 714).

1642 Jack, Adolphus Alfred. *A Commentary on the Poetry of Chaucer and Spenser*. 1920. See **402**.
Virginius's address to his daughter is a passage 'of a gentle and heartstirring pity,' and the description of Virginia 'has a faint perfume to it' (p 110), but elsewhere the tragedy of Virginia proves unsuitable to Chaucer's temperament; in the address to parents, the poet indulges in a sort of moralizing almost unique in his writings.

1643 Cox, Sidney Hayes. 'Chaucer's Cheerful Cynicism.' *MLN* 36 (1921), 475–81.
Virginia's feigning of sickness to avoid unseemly social gatherings is cited as an example of the 'mawkishly other-worldly' nature of Chaucer's virtuous characters (p 479).

1644 Brusendorff, Aage. *The Chaucer Tradition*. 1925. See **824**.
In line 117 ('The Doctour maketh this descripcioun'), Chaucer puns on the narrator's profession and the 'honorary title of the bishop of Hippo.' The gloss *Augustinus* that appears in several manuscripts at this point must have been introduced by someone who prepared Chaucer's draft for publication after his death (p 129).

1645 Curry, Walter Clyde. 'Chaucer's Doctor of Phisyk.' *PQ* 4 (1925), 1–24. Repr. with revisions in *Chaucer and the Mediaeval Sciences*. New York: Oxford UP, 1926. 2nd ed. (with bibliography), New York: Barnes and Noble, 1960. Pp 3–36.
Although Curry doesn't comment on *PhyT*, his characterization of the Physician is echoed in numerous discussions (**1724, 1729, 1788, 1789, 1819, 1846**) that link the teller and his tale: 'he is a cold-blooded rationalist, a strictly scientific man who doubtless boasts that his study is but little on the Bible … the Doctor belongs to that class of physicians who find rational causes only at the root of all maladies and who depend exclusively on their own skill in the manipulation of natural laws for the working of cures' (p 19).

1646 Woolf, Virginia. 'The Pastons and Chaucer.' In *The Common Reader*. New York: Harcourt, Brace, 1925. Pp 13–38. Repr. in *Chaucer: The Critical Heritage* (see **390**). 2:377–84.
Cites the description of Virginia, a passage from the *GP* portrait of the Prioress, and a fragment of Emelye's prayer to Diana (I.2307–10) as 'parts … of the same personage, whom [Chaucer] had in mind, perhaps unconsciously, when he thought of a young girl' (pp 27–8).

1647 Manly, John Matthews. 'Chaucer and the Rhetoricians.' See **406**.
In *PhyT* and *MLT*, rhetorical devices are used almost exclusively by the narrators. Chaucer's failure to incorporate rhetoric as part of the dramatic action of the poems accounts in part for their crudeness as artistic compositions (p 110).

1648 Raleigh, Walter. 'On Chaucer.' In *On Writing and Writers*. Ed. George Stuart Gordon. New York: Longmans, Green; London: Edward Arnold, 1926. Pp 103–19. Repr. Freeport, NY: Books for Libraries Press, 1968. Repr. in *Geoffrey Chaucer: A Critical Anthology* (see **411**). Pp 131–4.
Chaucer's courtly style resembles the English spoken by cultivated women in society. 'His "facound," like Virginia's, is "ful wommanly and pleyn." He avoids all "counterfeted termes," all subtleties of rhetoric, and addresses himself to the "commune intente"' (p 116).

1649 Tupper, Frederick. *Types of Society in Medieval Literature*. New York: Holt, 1926. Several reprs, including Norwood, PA: Norwood, 1976.
The husband's advice to his young wife in *Le Ménagier de Paris* – she must avoid the feasts and dances of the highborn – recalls Virginia's shunning of similar entertainments. In the *CT*'s treatment of celibacy, the Wife of Bath's 'heretical views of maidenhood are offset by the chastity of Virginia and Cecilia (the old contrast of Venus and the Virgin)' (p 157).

1650 Cowling, George H. *Chaucer*. 1927. See **408**.
Chaucer saw only the story's pathos and hence made little effort at characterization. Lines 72–100 suggest that the poet's interest in the story was stimulated 'firstly by the scandal which attached to Katherine Roet's ward Elizabeth of Lancaster in 1386, and secondly by the inquiry into the abduction of Isabella atte Halle in 1387, which he was commissioned to attend' (pp 165–6).

1651 Manly, John Matthews, ed. *Canterbury Tales by Geoffrey Chaucer*. 1928. See **47**.
Manly omits *PhyT* (along with *ManT* and most of *Mel* and *ParsT*) from his edition, but supplies a brief note on the tale's sources and literary quality. He also takes issue with Tupper's view (**1639**) that the tale is ironically appropriate to the Physician (pp 611–12).

1652 French, Robert Dudley. *A Chaucer Handbook*. 1927/1947. See **272**.
Comments on the position of Fragment VI in the manuscripts; the sources of the tale (Chaucer may have read Livy, but in its general outline, the tale follows *RR*); Chaucer's additions to his source, which shift the emphasis from the false judge to the character of Virginia; and the connection of lines 72–92 with the court scandal of the late 1380s, evidence for dating *PhyT* as one of the earliest of *CT*.

1653 Naunin, Traugott. *Der Einfluss der mittelalterlichen Rhetorik auf Chaucers Dichtung*. 1929. See **413**.
Virginia's reference to Jephthah in her plea to be given time to bemoan her death reveals Chaucer ostentatiously parading his own learning (p 34).

1654 Engel, Hildegard. *Structure and Plot in Chaucer's Canterbury Tales*. Bonn: Neuendorff, 1931.
Chaucer's interest lies in the ideal portrayal of his heroine. The action is carried out almost mechanically; digressions and moral statements are nu-

merous. The poem's various elements fail to cohere into a united whole (pp 79–80).

1655 Chesterton, G.K. *Chaucer*. 1932. See **760**.
'What could be more apt than making the dignified anti-clerical Doctor careful to narrate, not a Christian or even romantic story, but a story of the stoic virtue of heathen Rome; the story of Virginius, precisely the sort of hero whom such secularists have always preferred to the saint' (p 171).

1656 Dempster, Germaine. *Dramatic Irony in Chaucer*. 1932. See **276**.
Except for Appius's 'premature exultation' (lines 146–8), *PhyT* contains no instances of dramatic irony (p 92n/p 336n).

1657 Harrison, Benjamin Samuel. *The Colors of Rhetoric in Chaucer*. 1932. See **418**.
PhyT contains more than thirty rhetorical figures of twenty-two different kinds; Harrison quotes an example of each. Given its brevity, *PhyT* 'is probably the most rhetorical of all the *CT*' (p 282). See **1706**.

1658 McCormick, William, with the assistance of Janet Heseltine. *The Manuscripts of Chaucer's Canterbury Tales, a Critical Description of Their Contents*. 1933. See **419**.
Describes the contents of fifty-seven complete or virtually complete copies of *CT* (including Caxton's first and second printed editions) and twenty-eight defective MSS. For *PhyT*, the details noted include omitted, repeated, transposed, and canceled lines, missing leaves, scribal rubrics, alternative versions of line 82, and the presence of three spurious headlinks. The rubrics include the following descriptions of the tale: *fabula Phisici sine prologg* (p 4), *the Maister of Phisikes tale* (p 16), *the Doctour tale of Phisik* (p 26), *Phisiciens tale* (p 43 et passim), *the tale of the Doctour of Phisik* (p 71 et passim), *fabula de le Fisician de Virginius Apius et Claudius sine prologo* (p 122), *narracio Phisici de quaedam virgine que erat filia eiusdem militis sine prologo* (p 141), and *fabula Magistri Phisicorum* (p 278).

1659 Robinson, F.N., ed. *The Complete Works of Geoffrey Chaucer*. 1933/1957. See **1536**.
PhyT 'is by no means without art, but it is certainly not in what we have come to recognize as Chaucer's latest manner … The narrative, in general simple and straightforward, is interrupted by a long digression on the character and education of young girls … The remarks are … not inappropriate to the Doctor, and were perhaps introduced by way of adapting the tale to the teller' (pp 10–11/p 10).

1660 Lowes, John Livingston. *Geoffrey Chaucer and the Development of His Genius*. 1934. See **421**.
The Host's response to *PhyT* is 'the most engaging embodiment I know of the attitude of a typical audience at melodrama' (p 206).

1661 Whiting, B.J. *Chaucer's Use of Proverbs*. 1934. See **423**.
PhyT contains four sententious remarks (lines 59–60, 101–2, 277, 286) and one proverb (lines 83–5). If the latter, part of the address to governesses, re-

fers to John of Gaunt's household and in particular to Katherine Swynford, it 'does not suggest too friendly a family spirit on Chaucer's part' (p 110).

1662 Goffin, R.C. 'Chaucer and Elocution.' 1935. See **843**.
Nature's speech exemplifies Chaucer's habit of differentiating between figures of poetry and colors of rhetoric; the passage maintains a clear distinction between 'forming,' 'figuring' on the one hand, and 'painting,' 'coloring' on the other (p 136).

1663 Tatlock, John Strong Perry. 'The *Canterbury Tales* in 1400.' 1935. See **424**.
The note of the scribe of MS Additional 5140 – 'incipit fabula Phisici sine prologg' – informs the reader that the lack was neither his fault nor that of his exemplar, but was due to Chaucer himself.

1664 Mersand, Joseph. *Chaucer's Romance Vocabulary*. 1937. See **430**.
PhyT contains only five instances of Romance-derived words used for the first time in English; the low number suggests an early date of composition, since Chaucer's later works contain a higher percentage of new Romance words (p 72). The total use of Romance words in *PhyT* is, however, proportionately greater than that in *Rom*; in his renderings of *RR* after 1387, Chaucer used a larger proportion of Romance words than in his earlier translation (p 117).

1665 Lossing, M.L.S. 'The Order of the Canterbury Tales: A Fresh Relation between A and B Types of MSS.' *JEGP* 37 (1938), 153–63.
Reviews critical opinion on the date of *PhyT*; agrees with Tatlock (**1629**) that *PhyT* may have been the first story written specifically for *CT* (p 155).

1666 Héraucourt, Will. *Die Wertwelt Chaucers, die Wertwelt einer Zeitwende*. 1939. See **434**.
Cites some thirty lines from *PhyT* in this study of Chaucer's value system, organized around four cardinal virtues: wisdom, justice, valor, and moderation. Chaucer's use of terms in *PhyT* (e.g., *worthinesse, chastitee, attempraunce, pacience, shamefastnesse, honestee, pitee*) is compared with his use of these terms elsewhere in his writings.

1667 Patch, Howard Rollin. *On Rereading Chaucer*. 1939. See **852**.
In conduct, Virginia 'might have been the Parson, in speech the Clerk, in morality and abstinence a veritable Sir Thopas.' The one 'potentially individualizing touch' is her feigning of sickness to avoid revels and dances; but even this 'point of diplomacy' is attributed to Virginia's upright character (p 180).

1668 Manly, John Matthews, and Edith Rickert, eds. *The Text of the Canterbury Tales, Studied on the Basis of All Known Manuscripts*. 1940. See **1539**.
Rickert speculates that the MSS of *CT* include 'extant copies of unrevised as well as revised versions of some tales ... it is clear that lines 1–104 [of *PhyT*] were originally addressed to persons concerned with the upbringing of children ... it is most unsuited to the worldly-minded, avaricious physician. Chaucer has thrust the tale almost unchanged into the *CT* framework'

(2:502).

1669 Tupper, Frederick. 'Chaucer and the Cambridge Edition.' *JEGP* 39 (1940), 503–26.
Responding to Robinson's criticism (**1536**) of his argument that *CT* embodies a systematic treatment of the Seven Deadly Sins, Tupper reiterates his view of *PhyT* as an exemplum of Lechery and of the ironic presentation of the Physician in *Phy–PardL* as himself tainted by the vice he assails.

1670 Vallese, Tarquinio. *La Poesia di Chaucer*. 1941/1946. See **439**.
The narrative of *PhyT* is pedestrian, the characterization thin, the tone lugubrious. Virginia's words to her father express some fleeting emotion, but the tale soon lapses into empty and vulgar tragic gestures (p 121/pp 129–30).

1671 Long, E. Hudson. 'Chaucer as a Master of the Short Story.' 1943. See **857**.
PhyT is anecdotal in nature and the characters are types rather than individuals. Although narrated with economy of style, it cannot be considered a good example of the short story.

1672 Schlauch, Margaret. 'Chaucer's Doctrine of Kings and Tyrants.' *Speculum* 20 (1945), 133–56.
The mob's execution of summary justice on Appius is an instance of the fall of a tyrant in which the people are sources of authority. 'The political implications are subordinate, however, to the moral' (p 154).

1673 Praz, Mario. *Geoffrey Chaucer e i racconti di Canterbury*. 1947. See **862**.
PhyT was perhaps originally intended for *LGW*; it clearly does not date from Chaucer's final years as a poet. The digression on the education of young persons may have been inserted into the narrative at a later point in an attempt to adapt it to the character of the Physician (p 137).

1674 Hulbert, J.R. 'The *Canterbury Tales* and their Narrators.' 1948. See **864**.
The subject matter of *PhyT* is inappropriate to its teller. Passages such as that giving advice to governesses and parents 'point rather to an ecclesiastic than to a medical man interested chiefly in success in his profession and the accumulation of money' (p 575).

The Physician's Tale, 1950–1959

1675 Lawrence, William Witherle. *Chaucer and the Canterbury Tales*. 1950. See **450**.
As retellings of classical stories, *PhyT* and *ManT* 'do not seem done with enthusiasm; they are among the weakest in the collection' (p 68).

1676 Malone, Kemp. *Chapters on Chaucer*. 1951. See **451**.
PhyT and *ManT* are only vaguely appropriate to their tellers: 'the cunning manciple tells a story dealing with duplicity, and the learned physician draws from learned sources. But if the manciple had told the physician's tale one could still say that he told a story dealing with duplicity, and if the

physician had told the manciple's tale one could still speak of his tale as more or less learned in character' (p 232). See **1732**.

1677 Pratt, Robert Armstrong. 'The Order of the *Canterbury Tales*.' *PMLA* 66 (1951), 1141–67.
Defends the placement of Fragment VI between IV–V and VIII on the grounds that this is the only position that does not produce an awkward effect. This placement 'offers no positive advantages of which I am aware … No theme attracts VI [C] toward either of its neighbors' (p 1159).

1678 Speirs, John. *Chaucer the Maker*. 1951. See **454**.
PhyT reads like one of the *LGW*. The tale is left relatively undeveloped, and is less interesting in itself than in the Host's reaction to it (p 168).

1679 Gerould, Gordon Hall. *Chaucerian Essays*. 1952. See **825**.
Virginius's dialogue with Virginia exemplifies Chaucerian pathos, the effectiveness of which rests on the 'exactitude with which emotional tensions are imagined and recorded … The simplicity and the very lack of stress in the brief exchange between father and daughter move us as only tragedy can do' (p 85).

1680 Preston, Raymond. *Chaucer*. 1952. See **456**.
The best thing in the tale is the 'shrewd aside' to governesses, in which Chaucer's voice is 'unmistakably heard … there is even a very distant rumour of the tone of the witty letter to Bukton' (p 228). 'The only thing I find … that obviously fits the reputation of a physician is the professionally brisk manner of piling the corpses. This would have been appreciated at least by the medieval preacher John of Mirfield, who gave as one of the most coveted medical qualifications of his time "boldness in killing." And from this point of view the justice of the *PhyT* is surgical rather than poetic' (pp 228–9).

1681 Brewer, Derek S. *Chaucer*. 1953/1960/1973. See **457**.
'There is one fine scene, of the death of Virginia. But the formula fails. It is easy to see why. The rhetorical dressing is not sufficiently related to the body of the subject; characters, motives, actions, are not sufficiently interwoven, and the style is often drab. There are good passages, but they do not add up to a poem' (1953/1960, p 158; 1973, p 136).

1682 Dempster, Germaine. 'A Period in the Development of the *Canterbury Tales* Marriage Group and of Blocks B^2 and C.' 1953. See **458**.
The story of Virginia (not necessarily assigned to a particular pilgrim) antedates the period in which Chaucer was working on the Marriage Group tales, as do the Host's comments on it. The second half of *Phy–PardL* is of a later date.

1683 Kökeritz, Helge. 'Rhetorical Word-Play in Chaucer.' 1954. See **460**.
Cites 'peynte … peynture … peynted' (lines 32–4) as an instance of *traductio* or *adnominatio* and 'shamefast … shamefastnesse' (line 55) as an example of 'the balancing of a simplex and its derivative' (p 950).

1684 Schaar, Claes. *Some Types of Narrative in Chaucer's Poetry*. 1954. See **461**.
Chaucer's use of 'close chronological narrative' (a detailed account of a chain of events falling within a brief period) in lines 251–9 closely resembles the treatment of the episode in *RR* (pp 154–5).

1685 Severs, J. Burke. 'Author's Revision in Block C of the *Canterbury Tales*.' *Speculum* 29 (1954), 512–30.
Questions Manly's contention (**1668**; 2:498; 4:488–90) that the manuscript tradition of *PhyT* contains evidence of substantial authorial revision. In the twenty-two lines that offer the possibility of such revision, authorial alteration is strongly suggested in only one (line 6), probable in two others (lines 97, 99), and either uncertain, unlikely, or highly unlikely in the rest. *Phy–PardL*, on the other hand, shows clear evidence of Chaucer's revisions.

1686 Lumiansky, R.M. *Of Sondry Folk: The Dramatic Principle in the Canterbury Tales*. 1955. See **462**.
PhyT is appropriate to the hypocritical character of its teller. The focus on Virginia's chastity, the plea to governesses and parents, and the concluding moral are part of the venal Physician's attempt to tell a moral tale to cover his real motives. But Harry Bailly sees through the Physician's scheme, and 'shrewdly explodes the bubble of his pomposity by pointed reference to the Physician's activities toward corrupting chastity' (p 195).

1687 Schaar, Claes. *The Golden Mirror: Studies in Chaucer's Descriptive Technique and its Literary Background*. 1955. See **463**.
Depictions of emotion in *PhyT* are a mixture of 'emotive' and 'behaviouristic' descriptions, the former focusing on inner feelings, the latter involving bodily or facial expressions of emotion. Livy primarily employs behavioristic description; Jean de Meun uses no behavioristic description at all (p 83). Except for the portrait of Blanche in *BD*, the description of Virginia is 'the most circumstantial piece of ... idealizing characterization' (p 231) in Chaucer's works. Machaut and Froissart offer the closest parallels to the technique of generalizing idealization in *PhyT* (pp 350–1).

1688 Mroczkowski, Przemysław. *Opowieści Kanterberyjskie na tle Epoki*. 1956. See **468**.
Includes chapters on the historical and cultural background of *CT*, on pilgrimages and the frame story, and on individual tales, with an English summary. The Physician is said to 'keep vestiges of primitive notions according to which science was the skill of marshaling the powers of the universe,' while remaining at the same time 'a man who knows how to take care of himself' (p 439).

1689 Owen, Charles A., Jr. 'Relationship between the *Physician's Tale* and the *Parson's Tale*.' *MLN* 62 (1956), 84–7.
The subdivision on sloth in *ParsT* contains a passage on *lachesse* (X.722) in which Chaucer departs from his Latin sources. The interpolation parallels the digression on negligent governesses in *PhyT*, which has been thought to

refer to the court scandal involving John of Gaunt's daughter Elizabeth and John Holland. Chaucer first took up the subject in *PhyT* 'under the immediate impact of the scandal, and later, when the meaning and language of the section on sloth brought the experience again to mind,' treated the subject more calmly and in more generalized terms (p 86).

1690 Schlauch, Margaret. *English Medieval Literature and its Social Foundations.* 1956. See **469**.

Although it deals with pagans, the story of *PhyT* 'was readily adapted to serve as an *exemplum* ... for Christian moralists' (p 265).

1691 Slaughter, Eugene Edward. *Virtue According to Love—in Chaucer*. 1957. See **470**.

Analyzes medieval ideas of love and virtue, both earthly and spiritual. Love is an axis with charity and cupidity as its two poles; the goodness or badness of a desire depends on the system of virtues being invoked. The virtues present in *PhyT*, a 'religio-philosophical' work, include chastity, humility, abstinence, and pity; the vices include falseness, sloth, drunkenness, lechery, and injustice (p 209).

1692 Baum, Paull F. 'Chaucer's Puns: A Supplementary List.' *PMLA* 73 (1958), 167–70.

Given the Physician's profession, Nature's *cure* (line 22) – her supervision or spiritual cure – suggests as well the medical sense of the word.

1693 Donaldson, E. Talbot, ed. *Chaucer's Poetry: An Anthology for the Modern Reader*. 1958/1975. See **1543**.

In the first edition of his anthology (which omits *PhyT*), Donaldson sees 'no connection between the Physician's character and his tale' and suggests that Chaucer may have arbitrarily assigned him a poem written before he had planned *CT* (1958, p 927). In 1975, he modifies this view somewhat; *PhyT* is 'a pious story assigned to a person of no real piety whose respect for propriety rather than sincere moral earnestness seems to lead him to speak as he does' (1975, pp 1090–1). Although the tale has 'little coherent interest,' nothing in the fabric of the story suggests that its intent is not wholly serious; 'stories of damsels in dreadful distress appeal to people who generally consider literature a poor substitute for the reality of everyday life' (1975, p 1091).

1694 Mroczkowski, Przemysław. 'Medieval Art and Aesthetics in *The Canterbury Tales*.' 1958. See **902**.

Nature's monologue incorporates arguments familiar from medieval aesthetic theory, in particular the analogy between the artist's creation of a painted statue and the development of human virtues.

1695 Owen, Charles A., Jr. 'The Development of the *Canterbury Tales*.' 1958. See **473**.

PhyT should be placed in the earliest period of composition of *CT* (1387–90?)

because of its reference to the court scandal of 1386–8 and its close relationship in sources and style to *LGW*.

The Physician's Tale, 1960–1969

1696 Howard, Donald R. 'The Conclusion of the Marriage Group: Chaucer and the Human Condition.' 1960. See **910**.
If, as the manuscript evidence suggests, Chaucer intended to follow *FranT* with either *PhyT* or *SNT*, the Franklin's view of marriage is unlikely to represent Chaucer's own opinion, as Kittredge maintained (**390**). Although *SNT* provides a more effective contrast to the Franklin's treatment of domestic felicity, Chaucer may at some point have thought of the *PhyT* as a foil to the worldly *FranT* and a reminder of Christian counsels of perfection.

1697 Baugh, Albert C., ed. *Chaucer's Major Poetry*. 1963. See **1546**.
PhyT was not originally composed for *CT*; the address to parents and governesses suggests that Chaucer wrote the tale in response to some specific external circumstances. The tale's assignment to the Physician, moreover, 'is not especially appropriate' (p 485).

1698 Beck, Richard J. 'Educational Expectations and Rhetorical Result in *The Canterbury Tales*.' 1963. See **476**.
Compares the use of rhetoric in *PhyT* and *NPT*. *PhyT* ineffectively alternates blocks of narrative with rhetorical set pieces, rather than integrating rhetoric into the whole poem, as in *NPT*.

1699 Kim, Sun Sook. '*The Physician's Tale* Among Chaucer's *Canterbury Tales*.' *ELL* 13 (1963), 1–10.
Not seen. Listed in Google Scholar (scholar.google.com). In Korean.

1700 Payne, Robert O. *The Key of Remembrance: A Study of Chaucer's Poetics*. 1963. See **477**.
In *MLT, ClT, PhyT, SNT,* and *PrT,* Chaucer seems to be working toward 'a medieval version of *poésie pure* – a moral statement which will be immediately comprehensible emotionally and nearly incomprehensible by any rational or intellectual faculty' (p 164).

1701 Bowden, Muriel. *A Reader's Guide to Geoffrey Chaucer*. 1964. See **478**.
If *PhyT* is considered as part of the Matter of Rome, it may be classified as a romance (p 136).

1702 Brewer, Derek S. 'Children in Chaucer.' *REL* 5:3 (July 1964), 52–60. Repr. in Brewer, *Tradition and Innovation in Chaucer* (see **523**). Pp 46–53.
Chaucer's ideal of behavior for children is made explicit in the description of the fourteen-year-old Virginia. Virginius's announcement to Virginia that he must behead her and her response is 'the tenderest scene between father and child in Chaucer's work' (p 58). But the poem as a whole is not up to Chau-

cer's standard, in part because the father, who should be the true center of the tale, is not brought sufficiently to life.

1703 Corsa, Helen Storm. *Chaucer: Poet of Mirth and Morality*. 1964. See **479**.
PhyT is comic insofar as it emphasizes divine justice; the tale 'illustrates not so much that virtue is its own reward, but that vice will be punished' (p 122). The Physician is 'as likely a narrator as not' for the tale; the narrative voice discloses a man who is something of a preacher and a puritan, who 'reduces the complexities of life to the simple contest between alternate abstractions' (p 123).

1704 Enkvist, Nils Erik. *Geoffrey Chaucer*. Stockholm: Natur och Kultur, 1964.
Offers a brief discussion of the tale's sources in Livy and *RR*, the possible reference to Katherine Swynford in the address to governesses and parents, and the tale's date (parallels to *LGW* suggest the late 1380s) (pp 74–5).

1705 Lewis, C.S. *The Discarded Image: An Introduction to Medieval and Renaissance Literature*. Cambridge: Cambridge UP, 1964; pbk ed., 1967.
With 'about ten lines of Amplification to every sixteen of narrative,' *PhyT* shows the precepts of medieval rhetoric 'working at full blast' (p 196).

1706 Murphy, James J. 'A New Look at Chaucer and the Rhetoricians.' 1964. See **482**.
Harrison's identification of no fewer than twenty-one rhetorical *figurae* in *PhyT* (**1657**) exemplifies his 'gratuitous assumptions' (p 16) concerning the influence of Geoffrey of Vinsauf on Chaucer; almost all of the figures he cites are typical of narrative writing from the time of Homer on.

1707 Walter, Gertrud. *Grundtypen der Erzähl- und Darstellungstechnik bei Chaucer*. 1964. See **484**.
The interchange between Virginius and Virginia exemplifies Chaucer's handling of the 'Kleinszene,' in which dialogue is employed to heighten a brief, dramatic encounter. In a tale generally uncharacteristic of Chaucer's narrative technique, this scene, with its deeply piteous tone, stands out as a self-contained narrative unit (p 86).

1708 Baltzell, Jane Lucile. *An Exploration of Medieval Poetic with Special Reference to Chaucer*. PhD diss., University of California, 1965. Dir. Arthur Hutson, Charles Muscatine, and Janette Richardson. Ann Arbor, MI: University Microfilms, 1965. See also *DAI*–A 26/08 (1966): 4622–3.
Ch. 9, 'The *Physician's Tale*' (pp 376–87), argues that the tale is better constructed than is usually supposed. An analysis of its figures of amplification (*prosopopeia, oppositio, digressio*) shows its central theme to be 'the preciousness of the spiritual and bodily chastity of the young and the duty of their guardians to respect and defend it' (p 376).

1709 Ruggiers, Paul G. *The Art of The Canterbury Tales*. 1965. See **942**.
In comparing the Physician to a prelate, Harry Bailly is responding to *PhyT*'s learned and moral cast. The tale's historical and pagan justification of Vir-

ginius's action, however, is not what one would expect of a churchman. The Physician is rather an educated layman for whom 'the line between moral law and expedience is not clearly drawn' (p 122). Harry's comment on the dangerous gifts of Fortune and Nature provides a link with *PardT*, in which these gifts also lead to death, albeit in a very different manner.

1710 Ussery, Huling E. 'The Appropriateness of *The Physician's Tale* to Its Teller.' *PMASAL* 50 (1965), 545–56.
See **1732**.

1711 Williams, George. *A New View of Chaucer*. 1965. See **489**.
Rejects the argument that lines 72–92 are addressed to Katherine Swynford. If the passage refers to any specific person, it might be to Chaucer's wife Philippa, who served in Gaunt's household longer than Katherine, and may possibly have been the mother of a 'lordes [i.e., Gaunt's] doghtre' (line 73) (pp 161–2).

1712 Bartholomew, Barbara. *Fortuna and Natura: A Reading of Three Chaucer Narratives*. The Hague: Mouton, 1966.
PhyT is a quasi allegory in which Natura's sovereignty is tested by 'earthly forces of evil resembling Fortuna' (p 47). In lusting after Virginia, Natura's paragon, Appius challenges the goddess's authority. Natura hates lust; the forces of unnatural desire are defeated in Virginia's death. Natura also hates death; in killing his daughter, Virginius transcends Natura's mandates and acts according to a higher principle. Virginia's death is an 'act of triumph'; her severed head 'points up the irony that Natura's children should reach moral and spiritual victory in a welter of blood' (p 56).
• Review by A.G. Rigg, *RES* 18 (1967), 448–50: 'This book illustrates the dangers of elevating a single idea into a critical theory.' There are occasional illuminating insights (e.g., 'the demonstration of the way in which both of Virginius's alternatives conflict with the dictates of Natura'). But 'these are feeble straws with which to build a house' (p 450).
• Review by P.M. Vermeer, *LT* 240 (1967), 405–7: Appius is said to be a representative of Fortuna, but this is nowhere stated or even implied in *PhyT*.

1713 Coghill, Nevill. 'Chaucer's Narrative Art in *The Canterbury Tales*.' In *Chaucer and the Chaucerians: Critical Studies in Middle English Literature*. 1966. See **491**. Pp 114–39.
PhyT is the 'faultiest' of *CT*, 'a horrifying piece of sentimental savagery … Whatever allowances be made for the mystical values of virginity, now or then,' they cannot compensate for the tale's 'crushing demerits' (p 126). If Virginius's murder of his daughter had been carried out in the heat of the moment (as it is in Livy, *RR*, and *CA*) it might have been endurable; but it is 'carefully and poetically premeditated' (p 127). The frequent brilliance of Chaucer's writing does not redeem the tale's 'false values and improbable circumstances' (p 128). See **1761**.

1714 Hackethal, Marietta. *Aufbau und Erzählstruktur der Erzählungen Chaucers.* 1966. See **947**.

In *PhyT*, an initial destined event shapes the course of the narrative. Appius's desire for Virginia and his command that Virginius deliver his daughter to him puts the plot in motion and determines its outcome, although the father delivers the maiden in a manner that Appius could not have anticipated. Between these two events, the plot takes several subsidiary turns, usually prompted by speech, as in Virginius's announcement to his daughter of her beheading (p 68).

1715 Hoffman, Richard L. *Ovid and the Canterbury Tales*. 1966. See **192**.

Nature's reference to Pygmalion in the description of Virginia recalls the common medieval gloss on Ovid's version of the story, in which the sculptor's love for his ivory statue is an example of *cupiditas*. Like Pygmalion, Appius transforms Virginia into an idol created by his own lustful imagination; both men experience 'the deadly fire of concupiscence' (p 181) in contemplating the possession of their respective idols. Marginal glosses in ten MSS attribute the *doctour*'s description of Envy (lines 113–17) to St Augustine. A similar definition also appears in *Metamorphoses*, 2.778–82.

1716 Lumiansky, R.M. 'Two Notes on the "Canterbury Tales."' In *Studies in Language and Literature in Honour of Margaret Schlauch*. 1966. See **954**. Pp 227–32.

The contrasting attitudes of the Franklin and the Physician toward diet, money, and astrology lend support to the placement of Fragment VI after Fragment V in the sequence of tales.

1717 Muscatine, Charles. '*The Canterbury Tales*: Style of the Man and Style of the Work.' 1966. See **953**.

In Virginia's reference to Jephthah's daughter, 'sententiousness jostles art a little harder than we should like' (p 94 and n/p 6 and n). Elsewhere in *PhyT*, 'we can hear Chaucer squeezing [the pathetic note] a bit hard, and falling into sentimentality' (p 107/p 19).

1718 Coghill, Nevill. *The Poet Chaucer*. 2nd ed., 1967. See **447**.

In the lecture to governesses we hear Chaucer's voice breaking through that of the Physician, addressing an actual court audience rather than the fictional audience of Canterbury pilgrims. The poet, who for many years must have had to endure Katherine Swynford's reputation as John of Gaunt's mistress, now speaks out, delivering a strong rebuke to his errant sister-in-law (pp 128–9).

1719 Hoffman, Richard L. 'Jephthah's Daughter and Chaucer's Virginia.' 1967. See **962**.

In his allusion to Jephthah and his daughter, the Physician misconstrues the original intent of the biblical story (Judges 11). Jephthah's daughter bewails the fact that she will die without issue, whereas Virginia dies so that her virginity might be preserved. The skewed reference clarifies several interpretive problems: it provides evidence for the observation that the Physician's 'studie was but litel on the Bible' (I.438); it supports the Ellesmere order of *CT*, in which *PhyT* directly follows *FranT* (like Jephthah, Dorigen makes a foolish vow, and in her Complaint recalls women who, like Virginia, chose death over defilement); in the light of patristic allegorizations of the biblical episode, in which Jephthah typically represents Christ and his daughter Christ's flesh, it reveals the Physician's inability to grasp the spiritual implications of his story.

1720 ———. 'Pygmalion in the *Physician's Tale*.' *ANQ* 5 (1967), 83–4.
See **1715**.

1721 Overbeck, Pat Trefzger. 'Chaucer's Good Woman.' *ChauR* 2 (1967), 75–94.
Questions Root's assertion (**1628**) that *PhyT* was first written for *LGW* and later transferred to *CT*. Virginia's chastity at her death sets her apart from all of the Good Women (except Thisbe), as does her docility in submitting to her father's authority (p 93).

1722 Brewer, Derek S. 'Class Distinction in Chaucer.' 1968. See **968**.
It is a commendation of Virginia that she speaks according to her degree (lines 50–4).

1722a Rodax, Yvonne. *The Real and the Ideal in the Novella of Italy, France, and England. Four Centuries of Change in the Boccaccian Tale*. 1968. See **498a**.
Virginia never comes to life. 'We do not know, as we do in the case of Griselda, how she prepares her green vegetables, her preference in mattresses or the state of her everyday coiffure' (p 14). Her virtue remains abstract.

1723 Wagenknecht, Edward C. *The Personality of Chaucer*. 1968. See **501**.
Chaucer must have been impressed by Mark 9:42, which contains Jesus' observation about adults' responsibility for children. Chaucer's interruption of *PhyT* with a warning to parents and guardians reflects his belief that all decent people must set a good example for their offspring (p 104).

1724 Whittock, Trevor. *A Reading of the Canterbury Tales*. 1968. See **502**.
FranT, which seems to 'put truth above chastity,' prompts the Physician to assert 'the cardinal importance of chastity' in his tale (p 179). *PhyT* reflects the puritanical temperament of its teller, who interrupts his narrative to warn against occasions of sin; the address to governesses is better explained as a reflection of the Physician's fanaticism than as Chaucer's own sentiments. Virginia's 'inhuman resignation' to her fate makes us uneasy, especially in light of the 'glib and callous' moralizing that follows it (p 183). Chaucer hasn't botched his tale; he is dramatizing the limitations of the Physician's 'cold-blooded' (p 183) conception of virtue, all the more evident when contrasted with the Host's warmly human response to Virginia's death.

1725 Beidler, Peter. 'The Pairing of the *Franklin's Tale* and the *Physician's Tale*.' 1969. See **976**.
See **976**.

The Physician's Tale, 1970–1979

1726 Galewski, Barbro. *Simplicity and Directness in Chaucer's Canterbury Tales.* University of Uppsala diss. 1970. See **982**.
Initially presented as the triumph of Nature, Virginia ends as 'the price of her father's moral triumph' (p 108). His ritualistic sacrifice of his daughter recalls less Abraham's sacrifice of Isaac than the martyrdom of the *clergeoun* in *PrT,* a 'New Testament child' who takes over Christ's suffering (p 110). The admonition to parents and governesses to protect their young charges, sometimes read as an allusion to scandal in the house of John of Gaunt, is more likely to reflect Chaucer's musings on his part in the *raptus* of Cecily Chaumpaigne. 'It is ... easier to imagine this as Chaucer's gruesome settlement with his own conscience than with anybody else's' (p 114).

1727 Pearsall, Derek. '*The Canterbury Tales.*' In *History of Literature in the English Language.* 1970. See **505**. Pp 237–66.
In *PhyT,* 'the moral imperative to one kind of virtuous action deliberately defies all other kinds of "natural" expectation ... Chaucer exploits the predictable pathos, but no more, and the allocation of the tale to the Physician is oddly arbitrary' (p 177).

1728 Woo, Constance, and William Matthews. 'The Spiritual Purpose of the *Canterbury Tales.*' 1970. See **987**.
PhyT may be taken as an exemplum of 'the ruthlessness of people in high places ... there is good reason to think that Chaucer had his eye in this instance on John of Gaunt' (p 104).

1729 Branca, Geraldine Sesak. *Experience versus Authority: Chaucer's Physician and Fourteenth-Century Science.* 1971. See **1595**.
PhyT is an allegorical presentation of the 'dilemma of nature versus faith, experience versus authority' (p 105). Representing nature in the figure of Virginia and faith in the figure of Virginius, the Physician raises the question of the role of authority, or faith, in situations involving physical realities. The Physician's emphasis on conscience at the end of the tale is more appropriate to himself than to any of his characters. Torn between 'what he knows and studies in the mundane world, and what he must believe about this same world in order to be "saved" by the faith' (p 105), the materialistic Physician makes his pilgrimage to correct his troubled spiritual vision.

1730 Longsworth, Robert. 'The Doctor's Dilemma: A Comic View of the "Physician's Tale."' *Crit* 13 (1971), 223–33.
PhyT is fitted 'not merely to the interests, but much more subtly, to the imaginative capacities' of its teller (pp 224–5). The Physician's 'morally disarranged imagination' (p 228), hinted at in *GP,* is clearly revealed in the tale's aesthetic failures. Among these weaknesses are the 'absurd digression' (p 226) on the duties of parents and governesses, the 'comically maladroit'

(p 228) allusion to Jephthah's daughter, the misunderstanding of virginity as a purely physical state, the breathless wrapping up of the narrative action, and the final pious moral, which focuses inappropriately on the tale's villains and leaves its heroine stranded. *PhyT* falls apart because it lacks a firm ethical center; 'throughout the story, the Physician claims a moral consciousness that he simply does not possess' (p 232).

1731 Rowland, Beryl. *Blind Beasts: Chaucer's Animal World*. 1971. See **511**.
Chaucer generally represents the wolf as rapacious, a threat to the sheep flock. His use of this image in the digression on the responsibilities of parents and guardians draws an analogy between the wolf and Appius, establishing sympathy for the innocent victim and emphasizing the immediacy of the danger (pp 104–5).

1732 Ussery, Huling E. *Chaucer's Physician: Medicine and Literature in Fourteenth-Century England*. Tulane Studies in English 19. New Orleans, LA: Tulane University Department of English, 1971.
Ch. 5, 'The Appropriateness of the Physician's Tale to its Teller: More Art than Error' (pp 119–72), argues for the suitability of *PhyT* to its narrator, who was 'almost certainly in orders' (p 120), and was probably a Master of Arts as well. The tale's sermon-like qualities reflect the Physician's clerical status; his training in the liberal arts is revealed in the poem's learned allusions and rhetorical embellishments; specific expressions (e.g., *abstinence*, *attempraunce*, 'sovereyn pestilence') and the concern with the proper rearing of the young reflect the Physician's professional training. The parts of the tale especially appropriate to the Physician are Chaucer's additions to his sources, suggesting that the poet adapted tale to teller. Ussery disagrees with Malone's view (**1676**) that the Physician and the Manciple could have exchanged tales, pointing out differences of tone and style. He argues as well against reading the warning to governesses as Chaucer's allusion to a contemporary court scandal; the passage rather reflects the concerns of a household physician. *PhyT* is skillfully integrated with the Canterbury roadside drama by means of parallels with *FranT*, and it succeeds as well as a moral treatise. Its 'improbabilities of narrative, motivation, and characterization' should not be attributed to the Physician's shortcomings as a storyteller, but arise rather 'from generic demands, which subordinate other factors to didactic moralization' (p 139).
• Review by R. Balfour Daniels, *SCB* 33:3 (October 1973), 158: The final chapter contains an 'excellent analysis' of the tale's appropriateness to its teller. If *PhyT* was originally written for *LGW*, however, such speculations may be unnecessary, unless Chaucer later revised the tale for the Physician.
• Review by Edward D. Kennedy, *SAB* 38 (1973), 108–9: The discussion of *PhyT* shows that 'Chaucer has done a better job adapting his source to the character of the Physician than critics have realized' (p 109).

• Review by C.H. Talbot, *RES* n.s. 24 (1973), 201–3: Ussery has been led astray by earlier critics who see *PhyT* as an encomium on chastity; the tale is equally a condemnation of unjust judges, a theme relevant to the contemporary controversy between physicians and lawyers about the relative dignity of their professions (p 203).

• Review by Joseph Grennen, *Speculum* 49 (1974), 158–9: 'This book ... is solidly based on the fallacy that the path to literary criticism leads through the Public Record Office' (p 158). 'The final two chapters, based on vastly over-simplified notions of literary realism and conventionalism ... betray a tin ear for the music of Chaucer's irony' (p 159).

• Review by Jill Mann, *MÆ* 43 (1974), 195–7: 'The awareness that most fourteenth-century physicians were clerics ... throws new light on the appropriateness of the learned, moralizing tale of Virginia and Appius for the Physician ... Mr. Ussery has made an honest and careful attempt to link the social history of the fourteenth century with Chaucer's work ... However, we are still waiting for a study that will work from the age to the poem *and back again*' (p 197).

• Review by Malcolm Andrew, *ES* 56 (1975), 154–6: 'As medical history, this book has some virtues and some uses; as literary criticism, virtually none' (p 155).

• Review by Wolfgang Weiss, *Anglia* 94 (1976), 505–7: Ussery's monograph is distinguished by a clearly formulated thesis and precise argumentation; it convinces both in its detailed documentation and in its careful application of historical materials to literary texts.

1733 Economou, George D. *The Goddess Natura in Medieval Literature*. Cambridge, MA: Harvard UP, 1972.

Nature's speech illustrates the traditional concept of the goddess as *vicaria Dei*, and reveals as well the hierarchy of creativity in which Nature, the representative of divine creative power in the sublunary world, is challenged in vain by the most famous of human artists (pp 26–7).

1734 Fisher, John H. 'Chaucer's Last Revision of the "Canterbury Tales."' *MLR* 67 (1972), 241–51.

PhyT 'is as bare of dramatic interplay as *ShT*. It has no headlink and the Host's comment at the end is the same sort of naïve reaction that he had shown at the end of *PrT* and *Thop*' (p 246).

1734a Hanson, Thomas B. 'Chaucer's Physician as Storyteller and Moralizer.' *ChauR* 7 (1972), 132–9.

Although the Physician endows Virginia with Christian virtues, he denies her the possibility of salvation. His handling of the story suggests 'not that virtue will be rewarded in Heaven but that virtue leads inexorably to death' (p 138), thus making Virginia into a victim rather than a martyr. The tale reveals more about the Physician than he intends; its amorality extends the implications of the 'gently ridiculing' (p 132) observation that 'his studie was but litel on the Bible' (I.438).

1735 Kean, P.M. *Chaucer and the Making of English Poetry*. 2 vols. Vol. 2: *The Art of Narrative*. 1972. See **515**.

PhyT can be understood as 'an *exemplum*, in human terms, of the war of the vices against the virtues' (p 183). Chaucer's additions to his sources define Virginia as the embodiment of human nobility; her threatened chastity, 'comparable to that of the Lady in *Comus*, but not to the dedicated bride of Christ' (p 181), is presented as part of a larger, traditional set of virtues. The tradition of the *psychomachia* also helps to explain the otherwise puzzling reference in the concluding moral to the 'worm of conscience' (line 280). But Chaucer does not treat his material schematically; he seems poised between medieval allegories of the vices and virtues and the later sort of allegory, exemplified by *FQ*, in which content and story are imaginatively fused.

• Review by Dieter Mehl, *Anglia* 92 (1974), 444–51: The connection between *gentilesse* and chastity in *PhyT* becomes more comprehensible when placed by Kean in the context of the Canterbury collection as a whole (p 450).

• Review by Elizabeth R. Hatcher, *Speculum* 50 (1975), 323–7: Kean is unable to explain why 'a poem whose villain never gives his sin a second thought should end with a warning to beware the inner pain of conscience's worm.' Her invocation of the *psychomachia* tradition 'does not account for what the text says' (p 325).

1736 Muscatine, Charles. *Poetry and Crisis in the Age of Chaucer*. 1972. See **516**.

PhyT 'lacks adequate underpinnings for the extremes of pathos that it attempts to engage us in. We know nothing of the Physician that would attract us to joining his feelings, and the tale generates neither the characterization nor the sense of a cosmos that in *TC* or *KnT* make the pathos acceptable. It is the gratuitousness of it that finally palls' (p 138/p 158).

• Review by Nicholas Jacobs, *EC* 24 (1974), 71–4: 'the morbidity associated by Huizinga with the decline of the Middle Ages goes a long way to account for the gross sensationalism of *PhyT*' (p 75).

1737 Ramsey, Lee C. '"The Sentence of It Sooth Is": Chaucer's *Physician's Tale*.' *ChauR* 6 (1972), 185–97.

Chaucer's emphasis on Virginia's personal tragedy turns what was in Livy, *RR*, and Gower a simple moral tale into 'a nightmare of contradictions' (p 194). In *RR*, the lesson about the world's injustice applies to Appius's actions; in *PhyT*, the world, 'even when it goes under the most virtuous guise' (p 196), is unjust to Virginia herself, rewarding her goodness in the same way it punishes Appius's sinfulness – with death. The tale's concluding words are an extreme example of the 'apparently mistaken or irrelevant moral' (p 189) found elsewhere in Chaucer; the innocent Virginia falls victim first to the judge's lechery, then to her father's harsh judgment, and finally to the narrator's 'pious but meaningless moralizing' (p 196).

1738 Robinson, Ian. *Chaucer and the English Tradition*. 1972. See **1005**.
PhyT is 'perfectly uncritical: everything is clear and decent and there is no irony and no exploration at all. All the values are given, and the tale refers to them rather than creating them or exploring them' (p 153).

1739 Ross, Thomas W. *Chaucer's Bawdy*. 1972. See **518**.
The Physician's 'shocked tone' in speaking of feasts, revels, and dances makes him sound like a 'latter-day fundamentalist' (p 66).

1740 Barney, Stephen A. 'An Evaluation of the *Pardoner's Tale.*' In *Twentieth-Century Interpretations of the Pardoner's Tale*. 1973. See **1010**.
PhyT is an 'anti-tale' (p 84), a foil to the adjacent *PardT*, which implicitly comments on its inadequacies. *PardT* highlights by contrast two major flaws in *PhyT*: the narrative imbalance that relegates Virginius, the operation of the legal system, and the role of the people to the periphery of the poem; and the conclusion, which fails to mention Virginia and focuses its conspicuously irrelevant moral on the villains and their punishment. Several motifs in *PhyT* and the Host's response to it are handled with greater skill and complexity by the Pardoner: the *feend* as the motivator of vice; the effects of bad company; the intertwined themes of grace and death; the gifts of Fortune and Nature as causes of death; the moral – that no one knows whom God will smite; the relation between Nature and rhetorical accomplishment.

1741 Faulkner, Dewey R. 'Introduction.' In *Twentieth-Century Interpretations of the Pardoner's Tale*. 1973. See **1010**.
The Physician includes in his tale several deliberate parallels to *FranT*, and responds to the Franklin's optimistic view that evil can be wished away by depicting man as 'a pawn in a cosmic battle between good and evil' (p 7) who has little control over his fate.

1742 Klafehn, Muriel F.J. 'Diagnosing the Doctor: A Summary of Criticism and Descriptive Bibliography of Chaucer's Physician and "The Physician's Tale" from 1910 to 1970.' MA thesis, University of Akron. 1973. Dir. Sally Slocum.
Surveys criticism of the Physician's portrait in the *GP*, *PhyT*, and *Phy–PardL*. The section on *PhyT* summarizes commentary on the tale's genre, position in the *CT*, text, date, sources, suitability to its teller, themes, literary artistry, and digressions. A selective annotated bibliography is also included.

1743 Knight, Stephen. *The Poetry of the Canterbury Tales*. 1973. See **521**.
A brief stylistic analysis, focusing on the tale's moral digressions, the compression of the narrative, and the contrast of levels of diction. *PhyT* seems 'pallid' when set beside Chaucer's other tales, but nevertheless manifests 'a sense of carefully controlled poetic power' put specifically to moral use (p 122).

1744 Kohl, Stephan. *Wissenschaft und Dichtung bei Chaucer: Dargestellt hauptsächlich am Beispiel der Medezin*. 1973. See **1015**.

The Physician's focus on the punishment of sin rather than on the rewards of virtue and his presentation of chastity as physical integrity rather than inner rectitude are in keeping with the *GP* portrait of a man for whom religion is secondary to science. Knowledgeable about Christian doctrine, the Physician is nevertheless unable to understand true virtue. He is a well-educated cleric who lacks a genuine connection with religion, a skillful doctor who fails to grasp the medieval Christian attitude toward sickness and healing (pp 134–8).

1745 Mathewson, Jeanne T. 'For Love and Not for Hate: The Value of Virginity in Chaucer's *Physician's Tale*.' *AnM* 14 (1973), 35–42.

A comparison of *PhyT* with Livy and Jean de Meun and with the biblical story of Jephthah's daughter reveals the young girl as a 'pawn' in all versions, but 'nowhere so pitifully and helplessly' as in Chaucer (p 40). Virginia is misjudged by Appius and Virginius as well as by the Physician and by Harry Bailly in his response to the tale. 'All of these judges fail to see Virginia's value as a person, while exalting and valuing beauty, youth, and state of virginity, exhibiting standard masculine unawareness of her humanity' (p 42).

1746 Middleton, Anne. 'The *Physician's Tale* and Love's Martyrs: "Ensamples Mo than Ten" as a Method in the *Canterbury Tales*.' *ChauR* 8 (1973), 9–32. Repr. in Middleton, *Chaucer, Langland, and Fourteenth-Century Literary History*. See **1078**. Pp 61–84.

PhyT stands midway between *LGW* and the tales of love's martyrs (*MLT, ClT, FranT, PrT, SNT*) in the development of Chaucer's conception of exemplary narrative. In shifting the tale's emphasis away from the punishment of injustice to Virginia's undeserved wrongs, Chaucer creates ethical complexities not present in other versions of the story; *PhyT* is 'less neat, less economical, and far less palatable' as a moral example than its sources are (p 15). By raising questions about the governance of human life, Chaucer's additions to the tale – Nature's speech, the discourse on the rearing of children, the allusion to Jephthah – encourage us to examine the moral problems of sacrifice. Assuming godlike power in disposing of his daughter's life, Virginius detaches himself from the human implications of his deed; Virginia is as much her father's victim as she is Appius's. The blurring of clear-cut ethical distinctions is reinforced by the play of disparate voices and generic perspectives, which creates multiple contexts for originally unambiguous story material and thus holds up for our inspection the nature and limits of the exemplum. The *sentence* of *PhyT* lies not in the deeds of its protagonists but in the actions of its readers, who willingly participate in 'the process of determining the end for which "this tale is seyd"' (p 31). See **1791**.

1747 Rowland, Beryl. 'The Physician's "Historial Thyng Notable" and the Man of Law.' *ELH* 40 (1973), 165–78.

Situates *PhyT* in the context of the ancient and medieval quarrel between law and medicine. The Physician's narrative is at once an indirect attack on his professional rival, the Man of Law, and a rebuttal of the traditional claim that law is nobler than medicine. *PhyT* concerns 'the very crime ... responsible for the institution of Roman law' (p 172) and exposes an official who, like the Man of Law, is charged with the administration of justice. For humanists like Petrarch and Salutati, law expressed the perfection of the reason and the will, while medicine was merely a mechanical art assisted by Nature. In response to this view, the Physician shows how the corruption of the will in a judge results in acts that are against Nature. The Physician, moreover, 'is no mechanic but a master of moral philosophy' who 'tries to exhibit all the skills the detractors would deny him' (p 178).

1748 Weissman, Hope Phyllis. *Chaucer's Bad Tales: The Aesthetic Forms of Late Medieval Pathos and the Tradition of Sermo Humilis.* PhD diss., Columbia University, 1973. Dir. Robert Hanning. Ann Arbor, MI: University Microfilms, 1984. See also *DAI*–A 34/06 (1973): 3362.

Ch. 7, 'Doctoring Up Virginia' (pp 434–502), examines the 'deliberate exploitation,' by both narrator and characters, 'of religious materials for personal glorification' (p 3). By means of his worldly, grand-bourgeois narrator, Chaucer tests the assumption that 'the bequests of pagan antiquity have continued to maintain their Christian validity in the increasingly greedy form of their late medieval appropriation' (p 437). 'Exploiting Christian form to invest pagan content with the robe of spiritual authority,' the Physician 'drapes his pagan vestal in a robe full of holes' (p 491). The elements of the tale that have provoked the greatest criticism from its modern readers – its digressions, its rhetorical flamboyance, its brutality and sentimentality – are in fact essential to its purpose as a piece of 'late medieval *haute vulgarisation*' in which Chaucer poses questions 'about the proper disposition of the natural world within the spiritual' (p 499).

1749 Amoils, E.R. 'Fruitfulness and Sterility in the "Physician's" and "Pardoner's Tales."' *ESA* 17 (1974), 17–37.

Fragment VI juxtaposes the Pardoner's essential falsity and spiritual sterility with Virginia's integrity and spiritual fertility. Virginia's virtues – her decorous speech, her humility, her eschewing of idleness, her avoidance of wine and riotous company – are contrasted with the Pardoner's sinful habits. The heroine of *PhyT* 'flour[s] in virginitee' (line 44), conquering death through the fruitfulness of her chastity. The Pardoner's theoretical goal is the defeat of Death, but his actual goal – the multiplication of money – leads not to salvation but to the death of both body and soul.

1750 Crampton, Georgia Ronan. *The Condition of Creatures: Suffering and Action in Chaucer and Spenser*. New Haven, CT: Yale UP, 1974.

PhyT and *SNT* are 'fundamentally passions, not actions ... But the protagonists are full of initiative' (p 194). Unlike the 'litel clergeoun' in *PrT*, Virginia 'faces her fate and chooses' (p 195).

1751 Dillon, Bert. *A Chaucer Dictionary: Proper Names and Allusions (Excluding Place Names)*. 1974. See **525**.

Entries for the proper names in *PhyT*, arranged alphabetically, give variant spellings, identification, references to other literary works and scholarly studies, and a list of occurrences in Chaucer's works. Also included are authors and texts used by Chaucer, with a list of specific indebtednesses (e.g., the entry for *DV* cites eight passages in *PhyT*).

1752 Engelhardt, George J. 'The Lay Pilgrims of the *Canterbury Tales*: A Study in Ethology.' 1974. See **1027**.

PhyT subverts rather than secures the teller's title of Doctor. St Augustine, for one, does not unequivocally endorse suicide for virgins threatened with physical defilement. But the Physician's 'interest in exploiting the union of body and soul blinds him to the principle that purity of spirit can survive defilement of flesh so long as there is no consent of will' (p 329).

1753 Scott, A.F. *Who's Who in Chaucer*. 1974. See **535**.

The names of characters and historical, biblical, and mythological personages in *PhyT* are briefly glossed, along with other names of people and animals in Chaucer's writings.

1754 Hieatt, A. Kent. *Chaucer, Spenser, Milton: Mythopoeic Continuities and Transformations*. 1975. See **200**.

PhyT is connected with several other *CT* in its concern with the overturning of the natural, and consequently of the just, in the service of seduction, and in its representation of innocence betrayed. Attempting to write an exemplary tale with mythic overtones of justification and redemption, Chaucer primarily creates pathos (pp 16–17).

1755 Joseph, Gerhard. 'The Gifts of Nature, Fortune, and Grace in the *Physician's*, *Pardoner's*, and *Parson's Tales*.' *ChauR* 9 (1975), 237–45.

The Host's remark about the fatal effects of the gifts of Fortune and Nature (line 295) links *PhyT* and *PardT*. In the former, Virginia is destroyed by the gifts of Nature – her beauty and the 'perverse intellectual gifts' (p 239) of Appius and his henchman. In the latter, the treasure that leads the rioters to their death is Fortune's gift. The gifts of Grace (the Parson's third category of human goods) sustain Virginia at her death, permitting her to triumph over the baleful effects of Nature; despite its classical setting, *PhyT* 'has all the allegorical trappings of a saint's legend' (p 240). In the 'anti-saint's life' (p 244) of *PardT*, the gifts of Grace are notable for their absence.

1756 Miskimin, Alice S. *The Renaissance Chaucer*. 1975. See **1046**.

The pattern of authority figure vs. subordinate in *PhyT* (father/child, master/slave, governess/youth, judge/accused) is ironically undermined by the uprising of the people, 'who seize authority and try to kill their judge' (p 119). The tale is further complicated by the ironies of the *GP* portrait, where fifteen medical and scientific authorities are set against one book – the Bible – that the Physician is said not to have read.

1757 Scheps, Walter. '"Up roos oure Hoost, and was oure aller cok": Harry Bailly's Tale-Telling Competition.' *ChauR* 10 (1975), 113–28.
Harry Bailly's claim that he has been deeply moved by *PhyT* is undercut by his need for a drink. The warning at the end of *PhyT* to forsake sin 'seems to have had no more effect on Harry than it has on the Physician,' whose faults are enumerated in *GP* (p 122).

1758 Weiger, John G. 'The Practicality of Chaucer, the English Department, and a Liberal Arts Curriculum.' *ADE Bulletin* 45 (May 1975), 21–4.
Sin is not punished in *PhyT.* The murderer is spared the death to which he was sentenced, while punishment falls on the innocent virgin. Public opinion, unable to defend Virginius when Appius deprives him of his daughter, condones that same father's act of murder. The tale is a parody that 'tells us how lacking in logic and justice were the customs of the day' (p 23).

1759 Haines, R. Michael. 'Fortune, Nature, and Grace in Fragment C.' *ChauR* 10 (1976), 220–35.
In addition to possessing the gifts of Fortune and Nature, Virginia is also endowed with the gifts of Grace, as evidenced by the parallels between the account of the maiden's virtues and the Parson's enumeration of the 'goodes of grace' (*ParsT* X.454). Virginius, acting as 'a somewhat benighted agent of Grace,' preserves these gifts by slaying his daughter; in dying without sinning, Virginia 'is assured of immortality' (p 224). The allusion to Jephthah's daughter is ironic; although Virginia contrasts her situation with that of the biblical character, Virginius does, in fact, '[yive] his doghter grace' (line 240) by allowing her to die a virgin.

Brown (**1789**) comments: 'that "Virginia has 'merited' eternal life through Christ's Grace" ... over five hundred years before the redemption should come as a pleasant surprise to the inhabitants of Limbo, among them Lucretia (*Inferno* 4.128), whose story is also told by Livy and who is often paired with Virginia in medieval accounts' (p 146n).

1760 Howard, Donald R. *The Idea of the Canterbury Tales.* 1976. See **545**.
PhyT is an example of 'misguided moralism'; virtue is praised in a tale that is 'morally revolting' (p 334). The Physician's 'barebones narrative' (p 334n) depicts 'a coldly rational world in which a father can save his daughter's virtue by killing her ... Underneath it all is a tacit feeling that life is cheap. And who more than an avaricious physician would be likely to harbor this callous estimate of human life?' (p 337).

1761 Itô, Masayoshi. *John Gower, The Medieval Poet.* Tokyo: Shinozaki Shorin, 1976.
In contrast to Gower, who neglects the mutual affection between Virginius and Virginia in his version of the tale, Chaucer focuses on the pathos of a father who must kill his own daughter. Although Coghill (**491**) condemns the

tale's 'sentimental savagery,' a Japanese reader can comprehend the conflict between love and duty; Virginius's beheading of his daughter is not a crime but an act of justice (pp 46–7).

1762 Mandel, Jerome H. 'Governance in the *Physician's Tale*.' *ChauR* 10 (1976), 316–25.
The relationships in *PhyT* are between those who govern and those who are governed. At the cosmic level, God governs Nature; Appius is governor of his *regioun* (line 122); Virginius governs his daughter at the familial level; at the level of the individual, Virginia governs herself. Appius corrupts the proper relation of governor and governed through hypocrisy and fraud. Virginius attempts to subvert Appius's misgovernance by slaying his daughter, but his sacrifice is unnecessary; a man 'strong of freendes' (line 4) might have deposed the wicked judge. The tale's bleakness is mitigated by Virginius's pardoning of Claudius, an act of charity that 'affirms God's governance of a frail and fallible world' (p 324).

1763 Weiher, Carol. 'Chaucer's and Gower's Stories of Lucretia and Virginia.' *ELN* 14 (1976), 7–9.
Both Gower and Chaucer tell tales of the classical heroines Lucretia and Virginia. Gower's stories (*CA*, Book 7) emphasize not the chastity or saintliness of the heroines, but the lustfulness of Aruns and Appius Claudius. Chaucer, on the other hand, puts the virtue of his heroines at the center of the Legend of Lucrece and *PhyT*. 'Chaucer's tale is predominately the legend of Virginia, the virgin counterpart of Lucrece' (p 9).

1764 Burlin, Robert B. *Chaucerian Fiction*. 1977. See **1056**.
PhyT begins with 'authoritative sententiousness,' followed by 'experiential exemplification, which proves to be dubiously pertinent' (p 241).

1765 Gardner, John. *The Life and Times of Chaucer*. 1977. See **1059**.
PhyT is 'a catastrophe' – stylistically inept, confusingly plotted, weakly motivated. When Chaucer performed the tale, 'presumably in the priggish Physician's voice and manner,' his audience 'must have been left in stitches' (p 293).

1766 ———. *The Poetry of Chaucer*. 1977. See **546**.
PhyT is 'purposely bad art' (p 295) that reveals the narrator's imaginative and moral deficiencies. The Physician is unable to decide whether his tale is allegory or history, he misuses the allusions to Pygmalion and Jephthah, and his concluding moral undermines the ostensible purpose of the story. *PhyT* satirizes its teller, but it also suggests the limitations of art itself.

1767 Owen, Charles A., Jr. *Pilgrimage and Storytelling in the Canterbury Tales: The Dialectic of "Ernest" and "Game."* 1977. See **551**.
PhyT has no special relevance to the character of its narrator; its main interest lies in its effect on the Host (p 169). The reference, in the address to governesses, to the court scandal involving John Holland and John of Gaunt's

daughter Elizabeth places *PhyT* in the early period of Chaucer's work on *CT,* 1387–91 (p 235n).

1768 Pichaske, David R. *The Movement of the Canterbury Tales: Chaucer's Literary Pilgrimage.* 1977. See **552**.
Aesthetic issues lie behind the digressions in *PhyT.* Nature's speech warns artists to conform their will to the divine will; the address to *maistresses* and parents suggests parallels between governance in the family and the artist's responsibility for his art. *PhyT* anticipates *Ret;* like Virginius, Chaucer 'kills his child to save it' (p 122).

1769 ———, and Laura Sweetland. 'Chaucer on the Medieval Monarchy: Harry Bailly in the *Canterbury Tales.*' *ChauR* 11 (1977), 179–200.
PhyT contains a lesson for the overbearing Harry Bailly. Despite his strong response to the tale's depiction of injustice, however, it is unlikely that he recognizes the applicability of one of its subjects – the rewards of tyranny – to his own case.

1770 Tripp, Raymond P., Jr. *Beyond Canterbury: Chaucer, Humanism, and Literature.* [Church Stretton]: Onny, 1977.
Virginius's lament before he beheads Virginia displays 'an intricate interpenetration of fatherly and erotic concerns, of selfishness and concern, and of religious and erotic language' (p 104).

1771 Breslin, Carol Ann. *Justice and Law in Chaucer's Canterbury Tales.* PhD diss., Temple University, 1978. Dir. Maxwell Luria, Dennis Lebofsky, and Robert Llewellyn. Ann Arbor, MI: University Microfilms International, 1981. See also *DAI*–A 39/04 (1978): 2246.
PhyT reflects the limited vision of its pilgrim narrator. The 'spiritually underdeveloped' (p 157) Physician recognizes and condemns Appius's corruption of his calling, but nowhere questions the justice of the sentence Virginius pronounces on his daughter (pp 151–72).

1772 Kinney, Thomas L. 'The Popular Meaning of Chaucer's "Physician's Tale."' *L&P* 28 (1978), 76–84.
Applies dream analysis technique to *PhyT,* reading it as an exploration of the conflict within Virginia between the claims of sexuality (represented by Appius) and the claims of parental love. The conflict is resolved with a denial of sexuality, figured as erotic death at the hands of the father. The tale presents 'the hesitation, perhaps refusal, of a young woman to accept her sexual maturation' (p 80).

1773 Mehl, Dieter. 'Chaucer's Audience.' *LeedsSE* n.s. 10 (1978), 58–73.
Chaucer recognized and may even have exaggerated the weaknesses of *PhyT* to make it an example of the sort of simple-minded didactic story that impresses the naïve listener. Harry Bailly reacts more strongly to *PhyT* than to any of the more sophisticated tales; 'Aristotle's theory of the almost physical impact of tragedy is taken literally' (p 69) in Harry's fear of a *cardynacle*

(line 313).

1774 Patterson, Lee W. 'The "Parson's Tale" and the Quitting of the "Canterbury Tales."' *Traditio* 34 (1978), 331–80.
The Physician, 'morally pretentious but spiritually negligent, tries to ennoble his flaccid tale with a collection of worn homiletic truisms (101–102, 114–116, 286)' (p 359).

1775 Trower, Katherine B. 'Spiritual Sickness in the Physician's and Pardoner's Tales: Thematic Unity in Fragment VI of the *Canterbury Tales*.' *ABR* 29 (1978), 67–86.
The Physician and the Pardoner are false healers who amass wealth by capitalizing on human sickness – physical disease in the case of the Physician, spiritual sickness in the case of the Pardoner. Their tales are linked by a common focus on dying as a terminal event and by 'an implicit repudiation of the life of the spirit' (p 67). Grace is absent from *PhyT*; Virginius can find no *remedye* (line 236) except death for his daughter's dilemma. The Physician's epilogue, moreover, emphasizes sin and death rather than the rewards of sanctity. In the light of the Physician's celebration of virginity, Harry Bailly's praise of his remedies is ironic; they are 'cure-alls for sexual impotence' (p 71) and hence spiritual poisons. The Pardoner's 'cures' are also poisonous. Harry asks for *triacle* (line 314) to counteract the effects of the Physician's sad story, but the Pardoner's self-revelations 'fail to provide ... an antidote to the negative implications raised by *PhyT*' (p 73).

1776 Baron, F. Xavier. 'Children and Violence in Chaucer's *Canterbury Tales*.' *JPsy* 7 (1979), 77–103.
Of the tales that depict children as victims, *PhyT* stands out in its unrelieved brutality; it offers no acceptable model of human love to contrast the inhuman violence presented. In making Virginius, the potential model of compassion, into an agent of violence, Chaucer compels us to conclude that wickedness is 'even more pervasive than we had thought' (p 91).

1777 Burnley, J.D. *Chaucer's Language and the Philosophers' Tradition*. 1979. See **559**.
The suffering of innocent women and children in *PhyT* and *PrT* 'evokes pathos unchecked' (p 86) in the pilgrim audience. But the protagonists' spiritual strength offsets their physical weakness and sweetens the moral teachings of the tales.

1778 McCall, John P. *Chaucer Among the Gods: The Poetics of Classical Myth*. 1979. See **1088**.
PhyT dramatizes an old Roman assumption that virtue is physical and material. Virginius's decision to kill his daughter arises from his incapacity to see beyond physical, temporal, natural virtue. The poem forces us to question human governance and that of the goddess Nature as well; the pagan setting reinforces the story's commentary on the 'uncertainties of the whole human natural condition ... everyone and everything in *PhyT* conspire in a failure

to govern reality and to judge it aright' (p 108).

1779 Satow, Tsutomu. *Sentence and Solaas: Thematic Development and Narrative Technique in the Canterbury Tales*. 1979. See **563**.
Discusses the treatment of male sovereignty and the problem of evil in *PhyT* and *FranT*; the '*kabuki*-like' (p 220) dialogue between Virginia and Virginius (like a Japanese samurai, Virginius cannot accept shame); and the inadequacy of Harry Bailly's response to *PhyT*.

1780 Stevens, Martin. 'The Royal Stanza in Early English Literature.' *PMLA* 94 (1979), 62–76.
Chaucer's use of the royal stanza in *MLT, ClT, PrT,* and *SNT* might suggest that he saw it as 'a medium to convey a particular subject matter, the travails of the martyr' (p 67). But *PhyT* makes such an explanation unlikely; although it shares this subject matter, it is written in rhymed couplets. See **1824**.

1781 Strohm, Paul. 'Social Form and Social Statement in *Confessio Amantis* and *The Canterbury Tales*.' *SAC* 1 (1979), 17–40.
In contrast to Gower's Genius, who draws from the story of Appius and Virginia a moral about good kingship, Harry Bailly responds personally to *PhyT*, 'half commending and half criticizing' its pathos (p 31).

1782 Windeatt, Barry. 'Gesture in Chaucer.' 1979. See **1095**.
In his retelling of Livy, Chaucer adds Appius's act of looking at Virginia to 'explain' the development of the judge's lust. Also added to Livy's account are the maiden's two faints before her father beheads her. Chaucer 'contrasts the fearfulness of Virginia's inner emotions with her voiced determination, and in the extremes of both Virginia acquires an awful dignity' (p 155).

The Physician's Tale, 1980–1989

1783 Aers, David. *Chaucer, Langland, and the Creative Imagination*. 1980. See **1097**.
PhyT exemplifies Chaucer's critical stance toward patriarchal power in its exposure of the cruelty and self-righteousness of Virginius's *pitee* (p 220n).

1784 Haas, Renate. *Die mittelenglische Totenklage: Realitätsbezug, abendländische Tradition und individuelle Gestaltung*. Regensburger Arbeiten zur Anglistik und Amerikanstik 16. Frankfurt: Lang, 1980.
PhyT treats the conventional lament for the dead ironically. Almost uniquely among classical and medieval instances of this topos, Virginius's speech (lines 213–30) is delivered by the person who himself brings about the lamented death. The speech is, in addition, rhetorically and emotionally excessive, and demonstrates Virginius's patriarchal inflexibility. Although some critics see the tale's ironies as artfully devised by the Physician, they are more likely to be unconscious, the result of his naïveté and ineptness as a narrator (pp 283–7).

1785 Leicester, H. Marshall. 'The Art of Impersonation: A General Prologue to the *Canterbury Tales.' PMLA* 95 (1980), 213–24. Repr. in *The Canterbury Tales: Nine Tales and the General Prologue* (see **111**). Pp 503–18.
When read in the light of the Physician's 'singularly inept' (p 218) use of the exemplum of Jephthah's daughter in his tale, I.438 ('His studie was but litel on the Bible') characterizes a man who employs his scant biblical knowledge for pathos at the expense of narrative consistency. 'It is the tale that specifies the portrait, not the other way around' (p 218).

1786 Stugrin, Michael. 'Ricardian Poetics and Late Medieval Cultural Pluriformity: The Significance of Pathos in the *Canterbury Tales.' ChauR* 15 (1980–1), 155–67.
The prominence of the 'pathetic voice' in *PhyT* (evident especially in the final scene between father and daughter) goes beyond the immediate needs of the plot (p 157). As in the other tales of pathos (*ClT, MLT, PrT*, the episode of Hugelino in *MkT*), this voice validates and celebrates a common sensibility shared by Chaucer and his audience.

1787 Allen, Judson Boyce, and Theresa Anne Moritz. *A Distinction of Stories: The Medieval Unity of Chaucer's Fair Chain of Narratives for Canterbury*. 1981. See **567**.
The real subject of *PhyT* is 'not chastity but judgment' (p 173n). Virginia is misjudged not only by Appius, but also by Virginius and Harry Bailly, all three of whom overmagnify the importance of the flesh and hence misinterpret the nature and value of the maiden's beauty. The references to Pygmalion and Jephthah's daughter underscore the tale's central emphasis; read in the context of their allegorical glosses, both allusions concern the duty of right judgment and the dangers of judging falsely (pp 158–63).
• Review by Thomas H. Bestul, *Speculum* 57 (1982), 850–2: 'I know of no other criticism which makes so much sense of such minor tales as the Manciple's, Second Nun's, and Physician's, leading us to see that their significance lies in their relationship to other tales' (p 851).
• Review by Theodore A. Stroud, *MP* (1982), 177–80: The authors' 'most remarkable excursion into exegetical wonderland' is the contention that *PhyT* is a tale of magic because the unjust judge has turned upside down the proper relation between his own flesh and spiritual wisdom (p 180).

1788 Arnold, Richard A. 'Chaucer's Physician: The Teller and the Tale.' *RUO* 51 (1981), 172–9.
The Physician is an 'avaricious atheist' (p 176) who preaches virtue to others. His worldly character emerges in the description of Virginia, which is more eloquent about her physical beauty than about her inner qualities. The tale's 'bewildering' (p 177) moral, focused on the story's villains rather than on Virginia's fate, demonstrates the Physician's inability to comprehend the spiritual dimension of the girl's martyrdom. The Host's joking praise of the

Physician's profession reflects Chaucer's view that this practitioner, like other doctors of his time, 'will never get beyond ... the world of urine samples' (p 178).

1789 Brown, Emerson. 'What is Chaucer Doing with the Physician and His Tale?' 1981. See **1117**.
Although the Physician's diagnostic skill is praised by the pilgrim Chaucer in *GP*, his tale reveals his inability to establish the cause of Virginia's death. Livy and Jean de Meun attribute the maiden's death to Appius's abuse of his power. The Physician loses sight of this essential issue; Nature's speech and the digression on the responsibility of governesses and parents blur the focus on Appius's wickedness, as do Virginius's premeditated killing of his daughter and his failure to seek the help of the people, the 'grossly irrelevant' (p 136) final moral, and the confused response of Harry Bailly. Our evaluation of the tale's morality is further complicated by Chaucer's downplaying of the circumstances which in his sources tend to excuse Virginius's act, by the allusion to Jephthah (whose sacrifice of his daughter was frequently condemned by medieval commentators), and by the Christian belief that true virginity is a spiritual rather than a physical condition. Often regarded as a 'floating fragment,' Fragment VI is 'firmly fixed in the linear structure of the pilgrimage' (p 141); the Ellesmere order links *PhyT* in a 'triad of variations on the theme of causality' (p 142) with *FranT*, which glosses over the question of the origin of evil, and *PardT*, which locates evil within the hearts of men. By joining and enriching two of Chaucer's masterpieces, 'a mediocre story told rather poorly by an incompetent narrator' (p 143) 'works' in the larger context of *CT*.

1790 Collins, Marie. 'Love, Nature and Law in the Poetry of Gower and Chaucer.' In *Court and Poet: Selected Proceedings of the Third Congress of the International Courtly Literature Society, Liverpool 1980*. 1981. See **1102**. Pp 113–28.
PhyT depicts the perversion of the law by the lawgiver, operating under the influence of irrational passion. The fate of the unjust judge is grimly appropriate: suicide is the ultimate offense against Nature, Reason, and God.

1791 Delany, Sheila. 'Politics and the Paralysis of Poetic Imagination in *The Physician's Tale*.' *SAC* 3 (1981), 47–60. Repr. in Delany, *Medieval Literary Politics: Shapes of Ideology* (see **1262**). Pp 130–40.
Livy and, to a lesser extent, Jean de Meun, Boccaccio, and Gower, employ the Appius and Virginia story as a vehicle for social criticism. In *PhyT*, the anecdote is almost wholly depoliticized. In reducing the role of the rebellious populace to insignificance, Chaucer mutes the commentary on social injustice present in the other versions of the story, and removes as well the justification for Virginia's death, which becomes a 'free-floating *acte gratuite*' (p 53). The tale's shortcomings cannot be attributed to the Physician, nor are they, as Middleton (**1746**) argues, an intentional part of Chaucer's artfully

ironic vision. They rather manifest the conservative poet's 'creative impasse' (p 56) when confronted with the political implications of his material. The subject of insurrection 'was simply too dangerous to write about for a courtier with everything to lose' (p 60).

1792 Diekstra, F.N.M. 'Chaucer's Way with his Sources: Accident into Substance and Substance into Accident.' *ES* 62 (1981), 215–36.
In his handling of source material with simple narrative and moral structure, Chaucer at once exaggerates the starkness of moral dilemmas and offsets the 'monolithic singlemindedness' (p 219) of his sources by pursuing certain complications that the material suggests. Virginia's choice is between life and death. But the father's fatal love 'gains perspective from a digression on the duties of parents and guardians' (p 219), while the pathos of the girl is clarified by the addition of a catalogue of maidenly virtues drawn from *DV*.

1793 Gardner, John. 'Signs, Symbols, and Cancellations.' In *Signs and Symbols in Chaucer's Poetry*. 1981. See **571**. Pp 195–207.
PhyT 'was conceived and wrought as a tale told by an idiot signifying nothing' (p 200). The heroine is described in 'pseudo-poetic' terms, the motivation for the story in Livy and Gower's versions is stripped away, and the Physician's moral is 'pure nonsense' (p 200), as Harry Bailly recognizes. 'Either Chaucer did not write *PhyT*, which obviously he did, or he was kidding' (p 200).

1794 Kelly, Henry Ansgar. 'Chaucer's Arts and Our Arts.' In *New Perspectives in Chaucer Criticism*. 1981. See **573**.
The famous artists of antiquity alluded to by Nature are to be regarded with respect; 'yet even here we notice a certain poverty of vocabulary in [Chaucer's] repetitious characterization of the artistic processes' (p 110).

1794a Kolve, V.A. 'From Cleopatra to Alceste: An Iconographic Study of *The Legend of Good Women*.' In *Signs and Symbols in Chaucer's Poetry*. 1981. See **571**. Pp 130–78.
Visual representations of the deaths of Lucrece and Anthony are compared to Virginia's martyrdom in *PhyT*. 'Such suffering is without purpose, and without redemptive potential: tragedy in a pagan world' (p 152).

1795 Lee, Brian S. '"This is no fable": Historical Residues in Two Medieval *Exempla*.' *Speculum* 56 (1981), 728–60.
In using moral anecdotes, medieval writers often sacrificed historical accuracy to rhetorical effectiveness. Although Chaucer reminds his audience that *PhyT* is 'no fable' (line 155), he uses the version of his story found in *RR* rather than Livy's historically more reliable account.

1796 Lundberg, Marlene Cooreman. *The Chaucer–Gower Analogues: A Study in Literary Technique*. PhD diss., Indiana University, 1981. Dir. Alfred David. Ann Arbor, MI: University Microfilms International, 1985. See also *DAI*–A 42/09 (1982): 3993.

Compares Gower's version of the story, which enforces the traditional notion that death is better than loss of chastity, with Chaucer's more problematic treatment of the same material. Chaucer's additions to his sources, the conflicting attitudes toward Virginius's deed, incongruous juxtapositions such as the Physician's cold-blooded moral and the Host's compassion for Virginia, our knowledge of the Physician's charlatanism, and the perspectives supplied by *FranT* and *PardT* all raise questions about the relation between the traditional *moralitas* and the real lesson of the tale. Chaucer points to a conflict between experience and the teachings of *auctoritee*; Gower, writing to instruct a king on the dangers of lust, is more concerned with maintaining the conventional ethos (pp 199–252).

1797 Orme, Nicholas. 'Chaucer and Education.' 1981/1989. See **574**.
The address to parents accords with the precepts of contemporary moralists on the need for household education. The admonition to *maistresses* demonstrates Chaucer's familiarity with the tradition of using mature women of good families to educate noble girls. Virginia could be a well-educated aristocratic girl of Chaucer's day; a Roman pagan, she nevertheless displays most of the essential Christian virtues.

1798 Owen, Charles A., Jr. 'A Certein Nombre of Conclusiouns: The Nature and Nurture of Children in Chaucer.' 1981. See **774**.
In giving Virginia's age as 'twelve yeer … and tweye' (line 30), Chaucer is perhaps indicating the time she has been free from the absolute restrictions imposed on children, since she is allowed to make decisions about important aspects of her life. Although he acknowledges Nature's role in creating Virginia, Chaucer also recognizes the importance of nurture, reminding parents and governesses of their responsibility for their young charges.

1799 Sola Buil, Ricardo. *Dinámica Social en los "Canterbury Tales."* 1981. See **1123**.
PhyT sets Appius's illicit desire for Virginia against Virginius's paternal dominion; had Appius sought Virginia in a socially acceptable way, he would not have encountered her father's opposition. The conflict of Appius's abuse of judicial power and Virginius's fatherly authority creates an outcome – the murder of Virginia – that is inadmissible from the point of view of natural behavior, the sort of behavior that Chaucer always defends (pp 82–4).

1800 Bookis, Judith May. *Chaucer's Creation of Universal Professional Stereotypes in Five of the "Canterbury Tales."* PhD diss., Drew University, 1982. Ann Arbor, MI: University Microfilms International, 1982. See also *DAI*–A 43/04 (1982): 1140.
The Physician is unaware of the spiritual implications of his narrative, which functions effectively as a saint's life. The teller's 'professional stereotype' – evident in his fondness for moralizing, his 'clinical approach' to his subject, and his physical view of reality (p 196) – overshadows the allegorical truths that his tale contains (pp 180–209).

1801 Crowther, J.D.W. 'Chaucer's *Physician's Tale* and Its "Saint."' *ESC* 8 (1982), 125–37.
Virginia shares with the saints in *Bokenham's Legendys of Hooly Wommen* youth and beauty, virginity, '(implied) faith' (p 126), and martyrdom. In contrast to these holy women, however, she is not allowed to confront directly and reject the man who lusts after her. Additionally, she does not choose willingly to die for her faith, but is a victim of her father's 'justice.' Her regret at leaving the world introduces a note of pathos not present in the saint's legends; the *pitous* (line 226) nature of her death derives as well from the fact that her executioner is not (as in the legends) her lustful tormentor, but her father, who claims to love her. Virginius himself lacks faith; rather than entrusting his daughter's life to God, he sees his own action as the only possible alternative to Appius's false judgment. Virginius's action reflects the Physician's sense that justice is manifested in this world only. Unlike the authors of the saint's lives, he seems unaware of the existence of 'another, eternal judgment' (p 135).

1802 Rowland, Beryl. '*Pronuntiatio* and its Effect on Chaucer's Audience.' *SAC* 4 (1982), 33–51.
PhyT is among those tales appropriate to their tellers; 'the Physician settles the traditional score between the medical and legal professions by citing the notorious case of judicial corruption that initiated the Roman legal system' (p 49).

1803 Burnley, J.D. *A Guide to Chaucer's Language*. 1983. See **580**.
Lines 5, 105, and 118 are analyzed as examples of the anaphoric use of the demonstrative *this*: 'the phrase *this mayde* is used to keep the theme clearly before our eyes and hold the text together through a series of digressive topics' (p 23). Four additional lines from *PhyT* are cited in this introduction to Chaucer's language.

1804 Burrow, J.A. '*Sir Thopas* in the Sixteenth Century.' In *Middle English Studies Presented to Norman Davis in Honour of his Seventieth Birthday*. Ed. Douglas Gray and E.G. Stanley. Oxford: Clarendon, 1983. Pp 69–91.
Outside of *Thop*, 'sir' occurs prefixed to a true proper name only five times in Chaucer's works. Four of these occurrences refer to priests; the fifth, 'sire Apius' in Claudius's bill of complaint (line 178), suggests the latter's respect for the corrupt judge's legal learning.

1805 Cooper, Helen. *The Structure of the Canterbury Tales*. 1983. See **581**.
Although *PhyT* and *PardT* are in some respects antitypes of each other – the one gives an exemplary portrayal of virtue, the other of vice – they share several plot motifs (concern with the things that corrupt the young, violent death), and the handling of both stories is indebted to the allegorical mode of the morality play (pp 154–7).

1806 Costigan, Edward. '"Privetee" in *The Canterbury Tales*.' *SELit* 60 (1983), 217–

30.

PhyT exemplifies the notion, expressed elsewhere in *CT,* that nothing, ultimately, is private; Appius's *secree* (line 143) iniquity is known to God and is also recognized by the community and appropriately punished.

1807 Delany, Sheila. 'Slaying Python: marriage and misogyny in a Chaucerian text.' In Delany, *Writing Woman: Women Writers and Women in Literature, Medieval to Modern.* New York: Schocken, 1983. Pp 47–75. Repr. in *Chaucer: Contemporary Critical Essays* (see **1200**). Pp 77–107.

In *PhyT* and *ManT* a woman is murdered by a man who loves her. Reduced to their skeletal form, the tales are 'two versions of the same story: It is as if the poet returns to the scene of the crime, the better to repeat it' (p 47).

1807a Diekstra, F.N.M. 'Chaucer's Digressive Mode and the Moral of *The Manciple's Tale.*' *Neophil* 67 (1983), 131–47.

In both *ManT* and *PhyT,* Chaucer juxtaposes different points of view. *PhyT* is about both the perversion of justice and 'the fatal love of parents' (p 139). The digression on governesses turns what seems like a piece of good advice into an implicit condemnation of governesses as old whores, by way of La Vieille in *RR.* Here, the narrator plays the role of 'the court jester who constantly emphasizes the "wrong" truths' (p 139).

1808 Fichte, Joerg O. 'Incident—History—Exemplum—Novella: The Transformation of History in Chaucer's *Physician's Tale.*' *Florilegium* 5 (1983), 189–207.

Noting that interpretations of *PhyT* have often been based on 'erroneous generic identification' (p 204), Fichte classifies the versions of the Virginia story according to genre. Before Livy, the story, dominated by the idea of class conflict, formed part of Roman historiography. Livy's treatment focuses on the ethical content of the historical episode. Jean de Meun, Boccaccio, and Gower removed the tale from its historical setting and used it as a self-contained exemplum. Although the Physician emphasizes the exemplary significance of his tale, it cannot be considered an exemplum. In its openness to individual interpretations, its stylistic variety, and its analysis of motive, it shows 'all the characteristic features of the novella' (p 203). Since Chaucer is unlikely to have known *Dec, PhyT* represents 'the independent creation of a new narrative form in Middle English literature' (p 203).

1809 Mann, Jill. 'Parents and Children in the "Canterbury Tales."' In *Literature in Fourteenth-Century England: The J.A.W. Bennett Memorial Lectures, Perugia, 1981–1982.* Ed. Piero Boitani and Anna Torti. 1983. Pp 165–83.

Examines 'the mystery of the relation between power and love' (p 165) as manifested in Chaucer's depictions of parents and children in *CT.* Virginius's seeming cruelty is complicated by the fact that he is an 'enthralled lord' (p 175), compelled to kill his daughter against his will; his cruelty is in reality an expression of his *pitee* (line 211). For revised versions of this argument, see **1880, 1953**. See **1903**.

1810 Mathewson, Effie Jean. 'The Illusion of Morality in *The Franklin's Tale*.' 1983. See **1149**.
Although Virginia's invocation of Jephthah's daughter has been seen as increasing the pathos of her own plight, some medieval commentators (including Aquinas) argue that Jephthah's vow was 'stupid, and its fulfillment impious' (p 29).

1811 Ridge, George Ross, and Benedict Chiaka Njoku. *The Christian Tragic Hero in French and English Literature*. Atlantic Highlands, NJ: Humanities Press, 1983.
Virginia embodies Noble Man, both physically and in her moral qualities. Her tragedy is that she dies when she is only twelve; as a 'Christian Tragic Hero' unable to 'relate to the World, the Flesh, and the Devil, as separate from the Kingdom, the Power, and the Glory,' she 'cannot survive her encounter with lechery' (p 83).

1812 Traversi, Derek. *The Canterbury Tales: A Reading*. Newark: U of Delaware P, 1983.
PhyT is 'as unsatisfactory a tale as Chaucer ever wrote.' It was probably written prior to the conception of *CT*; Chaucer's inclusion of this 'poorly told and morally repugnant' tale 'suggests a self-critical attitude toward his own past performances which is not out of line with the concern which he shows elsewhere for the implications of his art' (pp 164–5). Nature's discourse and the advice to parents on the bringing up of children neither advance the story nor offer any valid insight into it.

1813 Amoils, E.R. 'The Lady, the "Lemman" and the Saint: Some Images of Womanhood in Chaucer's "Canterbury Tales."' In *Middeleeuse Studies/Medieval Studies 1984*. 1984. See **1154**.
The Pardoner is a travesty of the ideal of femininity embodied in Virginia: in juxtaposing the tales, Chaucer contrasts his sterile effeminacy with her fruitful virginity.

1814 Brewer, Derek S. *An Introduction to Chaucer*. 1984. 2nd ed., *A New Introduction to Chaucer*. 1998. See **586**.
PhyT is similar to the folktale best known from the biblical story of Jephthah's daughter (Judges 11); the wide distribution of the tale attests to the appeal of the subject – the need to preserve personal integrity even at the cost of one's life – to traditional societies. Chaucer wasn't entirely comfortable with the mythic psychological structure of the story. The *Gawain* poet might have made more of it (pp 200–1). *PhyT* is 'quintessential connoisseur's Chaucer of his own time' (1998, p 341). It embodies both the paradox that individual members of a society must sometimes be sacrificed for the good of the society as a whole and the conflicting compulsions of Virginius's love for his daughter and his honor-driven need to preserve her from a fate 'literally … worse than death' (1998, p 343). Virginius's position is analogous to that of

Jephthah, also under compulsion through his vow to God to sacrifice his beloved daughter. In traditional societies, a daughter's honor was part of the father's honor; the central character of *PhyT* is not Virginia but Virginius, and his conflict is an extreme example of the dilemma that affects all fathers in patriarchal communities. Modern distaste for the theme of *PhyT* has produced readings that judge the tale by 'totally alien assumptions' (1998, p 349) and attribute its failures to the character of the Physician. But 'no pilgrim-voice is even hinted at' (p 342).

• Review of 2nd ed. by Matthew Woodcock, *MÆ* 68 (1999), 323–4: The 'personal immediacy' of many of Brewer's observations is illustrated most poignantly in his commentary on *PhyT* (p 324).

• Review of 2nd ed. by Matthew Giancarlo, *Speculum* 76 (2001), 138–40: Brewer's interpretation of *PhyT* is 'alarmingly off base' (p 140).

1815 Kempton, Daniel. 'The *Physician's Tale*: The Doctor of Physic's Diplomatic "Cure."' *ChauR* 19 (1984), 24–38.

PhyT is '*about* nothing other than the Physician' (p 26). The medieval doctor, generally unsuccessful in healing his patients, 'necessarily became an expert with placebos: his theory, drugs, and manner' (p 28). The Physician's handling of his story reflects these professional preoccupations: Virginia is 'a hygienic ideal illustrating the perfection of medical theory' (p 28), while Nature's *cure* (line 22) is seen as authorizing this theory. But the realities of medieval medicine, which 'treated disease with further injury' (p 31), surface in the depiction of guardians who harm their charges; 'the victim is smitten with the same mortal blow regardless of whether it is delivered by Appius or Virginius, the wolf or the shepherd, disease or a Doctor of Physic' (p 32). Having failed to save Virginia, the Physician turns to the needs of his listeners, attempting to distract them from the fact of mortality 'with a rhetorical placebo in the form of a happy ending' (p 34). Harry Bailly, for one, refuses his ministrations; he has fallen in love with Virginia, and 'feels forsaken when the care of her suddenly, unaccountably fails' (p 35).

1816 Orme, Nicholas. *From Childhood to Chivalry: The Education of the English Kings and Aristocracy, 1066–1530*. London: Methuen, 1984.

Mistresses – noble ladies charged with bringing up girls in later childhood and adolescence – were common enough in aristocratic households by the end of the fourteenth century to be addressed by Chaucer in lines 72–92. 'If Chaucer's wife were the sister of Katherine Swynford, as is possible, his encounters with a mistress well known for frailty were close ones' (p 27).

1817 Reiss, Edmund. 'Biblical Parody: Chaucer's "Distortions" of Scripture.' In *Chaucer and Scriptural Tradition*. Ed. David Lyle Jeffrey. Ottawa: U of Ottawa P, 1984. Pp 47–61.

The Physician's reference to Jephthah's sacrifice of his only child would have recalled the more familiar episode of Abraham and Isaac; despite the importance of grace in the medieval Christian view of the latter story, there is no grace for Virginia. 'Along with suggesting the folly of Virginius and reflecting the Physician's lack of understanding of Scripture,' the allusion 'serves to complicate the implicit questions of the tale concerning the relationship between intentions and actions and between judgment and mercy' (pp 53–4).

1818 Ruggiers, Paul G., ed. *Editing Chaucer: The Great Tradition*. 1984. See **590**.
A survey of editions of Chaucer's works from Caxton to Robinson. Includes essays on Skeat (**4**, **1510**) by A.S.G. Edwards, Manly and Rickert (**61**, **1536**) by George Kane, and Robinson (**55**, **1539**) by George F. Reinecke.

1819 Skerpan, Elizabeth Penley. 'Chaucer's Physicians: Their Texts, Contexts, and the *Canterbury Tales*.' *JRMMRA* 5 (1984), 41–56.
Locates *PhyT* in the context of the medieval debate on the physical and spiritual aspects of healing. The additions to the tale's sources – Nature's speech, the account of Virginia's behavior, the address to governesses – focus on the 'outward appearance of virtue' (p 48), while the transcendent implications of the story remain inadequately developed. Despite his attempt to give his tale a spiritual dimension, the Physician – a *medicus corporalis* 'who cannot look beyond the body into the soul' (p 49) – is rooted in the physical world of cause and effect.

1820 Sklute, Larry. *Virtue of Necessity: Inconclusiveness and Narrative Form in Chaucer's Poetry*. 1984. See **591**.
PhyT and *PardT* share a common assumption 'about how language means' (p 123). The Pardoner's humiliation is brought about by his confusion of the spiritual with the material. In *PhyT*, Virginius confuses Virginia's spiritual chastity with her physical virginity; 'he deprives his daughter of her maiden's head in order to save her maidenhead' (p 124). Like *PardT*, *PhyT* exemplifies 'the devastating effect of taking accident for substance' (p 124).

1821 Smith, Eric. *A Dictionary of Classical Reference in English Poetry*. 1984. See **592**.
Lists classical references in some eighty English poets, with paragraphs of background material at the beginning of each entry and an index of poems, poets, and references. Ten classical references are cited from *PhyT*.

1822 Wildermuth, M. Catherine Turman. *Innocence, Suffering, and Sensibility: The Narrative Function of the Pathetic in Chaucer's Tales of the Clerk, Prioress, and Physician*. PhD diss., Rice University, 1984. Dir. Jane Chance. Ann Arbor, MI: University Microfilms International, 1984. See also *DAI*–A 45/04 (1984): 1112.
The purpose of *PhyT* is not to teach a moral lesson but to move its audience to 'emotional introspection and spiritual reevaluation' (p 132). Nature's speech, the courtroom scene, the dialogue between Virginius and Virginia, and the final exhortation move us to participate in the tale's action and to examine our personal stake in the issues it raises. By dramatizing 'the dan-

gers of the world, the ideal human nature against which each is judged, the uncertainty of mortal life, and the certainty of death for just and unjust alike,' the Physician 'stimulates each of his listeners to get his own spiritual house in order' (p 160).

1823 Blake, N.F. *The Textual Tradition of the Canterbury Tales*. 1985. See **594**.
The omission by the Ellesmere scribe of lines 103–4, in which the Physician says that one example is sufficient, may have been deliberate rather than an instance of eyeskip; this scribe 'seems to have appreciated exempla' (p 142).

1824 Brody, Saul Nathaniel. 'Chaucer's Rhyme Royal and the Secularization of the Saint.' *ChauR* 20 (1985), 113–31.
Commenting on Stevens's suggestion (**1780**) that Chaucer didn't use the rhyme royal stanza in *PhyT* because he didn't associate the stanza with tales of martyrs, Brody proposes that the idea of a group of royal stanza Canterbury tales about martyrs may have occurred to Chaucer after he had written *PhyT*, and that he chose not to rewrite the tale for inclusion in the set.

1825 Guerin, Dorothy. 'Chaucerian Pathos: Three Variations.' *ChauR* 20 (1985), 90–112.
Compares Virginia and Hypermnestra (*LGW*) as 'pathetic victims of temporal injustice' (p 91) who (in contrast to the stereotyped victims of *PrT* and *MLT*) experience genuine psychological conflict. The two heroines are subjected to the authority of fathers whose fitness to rule their daughters is open to question. Chaucer alters his sources to focus on the confrontation of father and child, juxtaposing Virginia's candor with Virginius's insincerity. In both the Legend of Hypermnestra and *PhyT*, the narrators miss the meaning of their own stories. The Physician, who believes his tale to be about the punishment of false judges like Appius, is himself a false judge, 'made of the same inferior material' (p 109) as Appius and Virginius. The pathos of Virginia's death is heightened by this alliance of the narrator and his male characters.

1826 Keiser, George R. 'The Middle English *Planctus Mariae* and the Rhetoric of Pathos.' In *The Popular Literature of Medieval England*. Ed. Thomas J. Heffernan. Tennessee Studies in Literature 28. Knoxville: U of Tennessee P, 1985. Pp 167–93.
Like the Virgin in the *planctus*, Griselda (*ClT*), Custance (*MLT*), and Virginia are 'women of extreme virtue whose sufferings are intensified by their isolation' (p 184).

1827 Item cancelled.

1828 Pearsall, Derek. *The Canterbury Tales*. 1985. See **601**.
PhyT fails in part because Chaucer 'cannot find it in his heart to extol the virtue of Virginia, which is so much an enactment of her father's will, nor the virtue of her father, whose act is bound to seem brutal in the absence of any explicit role for him … as the instrument of destiny, or of divine providence'

(p 278). Chaucer omits from the story the political and social elements that made it intelligible in Livy, and to some extent in the versions of Jean de Meun, Boccaccio, and Gower. The tale cannot be salvaged by attributing its faults to the limitations of its teller; 'nothing in the tale relates to any possible physician' (p 278).

1829 Smallwood, T.M. 'Chaucer's Distinctive Digressions.' 1985. See **1181**.
The address to fathers, mothers, and governesses conforms to a pattern evident in *WBT, MerT, FranT, PardT,* and *ManT,* in which Chaucer breaks off the narrative shortly after it begins to insert a substantial digression. These digressions present generalized wisdom; they rarely advance the story line, and contribute little to our sense of an individualized narrator.

1830 Ellis, Roger. *Patterns of Religious Narrative in the Canterbury Tales.* 1986. See **782**.
PhyT invites comparison not only with the Canterbury religious narratives, but also with the Monk's tragedies, the romances, and even with certain aspects of the fabliaux. This mixture of generic features reflects the narrator's artistic uncertainties. The Physician presents Virginia as a saintly creature, but he sees her innocence as 'under siege and open to misunderstanding – like that of Fanny Price in *Mansfield Park*' (p 208). In contrast to the heroines of *MLT* and *ClT,* Virginia fails to inspire disinterested spiritual love in others; 'Nature falls in love with her physical beauty, and this, rather than her virtue,' catches Appius's eye (p 208). Her father's love also proves destructive; Virginius takes literally the narrator's injunction to parents not to spare the rod. The tale's 'moral and thematic incoherence' (p 211) emerges in the mingling of pagan setting and biblical allusions, and in the moralizing conclusion, which focuses on Appius and retrospectively makes the hymn to Virginia's virtues seem no more than 'holy window dressing' (p 216). Chaucer is notably independent of his sources in creating a heroine who heroically accepts her lot and who inspires active love in others (including the narrator and Harry Bailly). *PhyT* is also distinguished by its verse form; its couplets promote 'purely narrative values like speed, suspense and irony' (p 222), in contrast to the more meditative effect of the rhyme-royal stanza in the other tales of oppressed virtue.
• Review by Bernard O'Donoghue, *TLS,* 29 May 1987: Ellis's reading of *PhyT* contains a 'brilliant' suggestion: 'far from rhyme-royal being Chaucer's most exalted form, as the stories increase in complexity and seriousness they approximate to the condition of the *Tales* as a whole, reflecting this by their use of the "home" form, the rhyming couplet.'

1831 Frank, Robert Worth, Jr. 'The *Canterbury Tales* III: Pathos.' In *The Cambridge Chaucer Companion.* 1986/2003. See **606**. Pp 143–58/pp 178–94.
In *PhyT,* Chaucer gives weight to an abstract issue – 'the responsibilities of parental power and governance in relation to the priceless quality of youth-

ful beauty and goodness, innocence and chastity' (p 153/p 188) – by means of rhetorical elaboration: *effictio* (the description of Virginia's beauty), *notatio* (the description of her virtues), and *digressio* (the disquisition on parental responsibility).

1832 Haas, Renate. 'Chaucer's Use of the Lament for the Dead.' In *Chaucer in the Eighties*. 1986. See **607**. Pp 23–37.
Virginius's lament for his daughter – Chaucer's addition to his sources and the longest uninterrupted speech in the tale – creates compassion for the victim but runs the risk of subverting the tale's didactic purpose as a warning against sin.

1833 Knight, Stephen. 'Chaucer's Religious *Canterbury Tales*.' In *Medieval Religious and Ethical Literature: Essays in Honour of G.H. Russell*. 1986. See **609**.
PhyT pits the forces of social disruption – legal trickery and churlish pressure – against 'an increasingly feeble secular conservatism' (p 161) as embodied in the knight Virginius. When he beheads his daughter with the concurrence of the 'people,' the tale offers 'an incredible and desperate remedy to the impingement on feudal stasis of new forces which were increasingly powerful in the contemporary world' (p 162).

1834 ———. *Geoffrey Chaucer*. 1986. See **610**.
PhyT 'deals conservatively with medieval social and familial tension' (p 124). The description of Virginia and the address to governesses expresses anxiety about the growth of a powerful person and heiress who may in time lose her 'malleability to the parental will' (p 125). There are other threats to daughters and property as well: Appius attempts to consummate his lust for Virginia by sending a churl to frame a case against Virginius. *PhyT* deals with these threats by means of a 'scorched-earth policy towards the in-class disturbers and the associated social invaders' (p 125). The tale is a 'grimly despairing' expression of the 'feudal fear of legalistic and churlish incursion against an allegedly natural aristocratic power' (pp 125–6).

For Brian Lee (**1218**), Knight's 'astonishing interpretation puts Chaucer's primary audience squarely on the side of Apius' (p 158n6).

1835 Mehl, Dieter. *Geoffrey Chaucer: An Introduction to his Narrative Poetry*. 1986. See **611**.
The 'slightly provocative emphasis' given to 'the more puzzling or even repulsive aspects of the tale' (p 190) – the parting dialogue between father and daughter, the admonition to parents and teachers – produces a disturbing complexity in our response to *PhyT*. The Host's reaction strengthens our sense that the tale is intended as a contrast to the genuine homiletic narratives contributed by pilgrims more learned or spiritual than the Physician.

1836 Morgan, Gerald. 'Boccaccio's *Filocolo* and the Moral Argument of the *Franklin's Tale*.' 1986. See **1200**.
Virginius and Arveragus in *FranT* are noble characters caught in ethically

problematic situations. Although Virginius chooses 'the unyielding Roman way' (p 304), at odds with Christian mercy, his painful decision engages our sympathies no less than Arveragus's choice of moral over physical integrity.

1837 Rogers, William E. *Upon the Ways: The Structure of* The *Canterbury Tales*. 1986. See **615**.
PhyT and *PardT* both deal with the problem of evil. In contrast to *FranT*, which precedes it in the Ellesmere order, *PhyT* suggests that evil is not a matter of faulty perception (as in Dorigen's response to the rocks) but a historical reality. The tale's offensiveness lies less in the insensitivity and misplaced sententiousness of its teller than in its depiction of an intolerable world in which 'the innocent die at the hands of the moral' (p 82).

1838 Windeatt, Barry. 'Literary Structures in Chaucer.' In *The Cambridge Chaucer Companion*. 1986/2003. See **606**. Pp 195–212/pp 214–32.
The opening discourse on nature and nurture and the upbringing of children 'gives more substance to what is only a brief brutal incident in Livy and a passing exemplum in the *Roman de la Rose*' (p 197/p 216). Whatever ironic incongruities exist between this prologue, the character of the Physician, and the tale itself, the preface to the narrative proper creates the possibility of additional layers of meaning.

1839 Benson, Larry D., gen. ed. *The Riverside Chaucer*. 1987. See **108**.
Chaucer reshaped his sources to emphasize the story's pathetic possibilities, thus linking *PhyT* with his other explorations of domestic pathos. But the tale is not a success: the digression on governesses is intrusive, the final moral inappropriate. The moral does, however, serve to introduce *PardT*, in which 'sin secretly punishes itself' (p 15).

1840 Bishop, Ian. *The Narrative Art of the Canterbury Tales: A Critical Study of the Major Poems*. 1987. See **617**. Repr. in *Chaucer* (see **1355**). Pp 273–8.
Comments on Virginia's virtue (although old enough to have taken deliberate steps to maintain her chastity, Virginia is no less an innocent than the child in *Pearl* or the 'litel clergeon' in *PrT*); on the use of *amplificatio*; on the possible relation of the *maistresses* addressed in lines 72–92 and the duenna in *RR*; on the incongruities of the narrative and the teller's misplaced and tactless sententiousness, which blurs the tale's moral focus (pp 151–5).
• Review by Dieter Mehl, *Anglia* 108 (1990), 505–8: Middleton's distinguished interpretation (**1746**) should be read as a corrective to Bishop's old-fashioned view of *PhyT* as one of Chaucer's failures.

1841 Blamires, Alcuin. *The Canterbury Tales*. 1987. See **618**.
Virginia embodies a 'total accord between the private thought and its public projection ... she is a model of exterior-interior integrity' (p 58).

1842 Buffoni, Franco. 'L'elemento "magico" nei *Canterbury Tales* di Geoffrey Chaucer.' 1987. See **1211**.
No miracle, no superhuman intervention takes place in *PhyT*, a narrative

that depicts the amoral fragmentation of a teleological conception of existence. The Physician believes only in his astrological natural magic (p 44).

1843 De Weever, Jacqueline. *Chaucer Name Dictionary: A Guide to Astrological, Biblical, Historical, Literary, and Mythological Names in the Works of Geoffrey Chaucer*. 1987. See **619**.
Names in *PhyT* that fall under the categories listed in the title are explicated. Entries include biographical, historical, and mythological information; references to Chaucer's use of the name; etymologies and variant spellings; and bibliographical references.

1844 Gray, Douglas. 'Chaucer and Gentilesse.' In *One Hundred Years of English Studies in Dutch Universities*. 1987. See **620**.
Lines 51–4 are cited as exemplifying one extreme in the semantic range of *gentilesse* which foregrounds the word's ethical – and even religious – overtones (p 8).

1845 Harwood, Britton J. 'Chaucer and the Silence of History: Situating the *Canon's Yeoman's Tale*.' *PMLA* 102 (1987), 338–50.
Labor trouble, left out of Chaucer's topical reference to the events of 1381 in *NPT*, is also absent from the self-description of 'that ideal worker, Nature' (p 341), in *PhyT* (lines 24–5).

1846 Howard, Donald R. *Chaucer: His Life, His Works, His World*. 1987. See **621**.
PhyT is distinguished from *ClT*, *MLT*, and *SNT* – tales of heroic women written in stanzas. *PhyT* is in couplets, Virginia is not heroic but obedient, and her father's notion of virtue is misguided (p 419n).

1847 Lee, Brian S. 'The Position and Purpose of the *Physician's Tale*.' 1987. See **1218**.
Critics troubled by *PhyT*'s implausibilities of plot and characterization demand a verisimilitude not warranted by the tale's homiletic nature. For readers conversant with the medieval virtues tradition, Virginia is 'as vivid to the moral consciousness as the Miller's Alison is real to the erotic imagination' (p 153). Chaucer highlights, without exaggerating, the pathos of Virginia's death; the horror of Virginius's act foregrounds the 'intolerable dilemma' (p 157) of a father forced to demonstrate his love for his daughter by killing her. Since there is almost nothing in the tale to link it with the character of the Physician, its presumed deficiencies cannot be attributed to the limitations of the narrator. *PhyT* may be favorably compared to Gower's Tale of Virginia and to the Legend of Lucrece in *LGW*: the former is a mere anecdote; Lucrece's faithfulness is 'slightly suspect' (p 147) and the Legend lacks the proto-Christian overtones that deepen *PhyT*. The tale is further enriched by its connections and contrasts with *PardT* and *FranT* (which follows it in the Ellesmere order). Chaucer deliberately 'juxtaposed two tales of sudden death ... and placed them after one in which sudden death is narrowly and comically averted' (p 140).

1848 Pellegrini, Giuliano. 'Ancora in margine al "Doctour of Phisik."' *RLMC* 40 (1987), 301–15.

The *GP* portrait of the Physician is realistic rather than ironic. The moral tale of Appius and Virginia is appropriate to the serious professionalism of its teller.

1849 Stone, Brian. *Chaucer*. 1987. See **626**.

By eliminating almost entirely the political overtones of his sources and focusing on Virginia's maidenly virtues, Chaucer brings *PhyT* into line with the genre of the saint's life. The poet injects his 'characteristic pathos' (p 78) into the dialogue between father and daughter. 'For love, and nat for hate, thou most be deed' (line 225) reveals Virginius's wish that his daughter 'die into everlasting bliss [rather] than live besmirched this side eternity' (p 78).

1850 Way, Karen Grose. 'Keeping Trouthe: Fidelity and Speech in Chaucer.' PhD diss., Rutgers University, 1987. Dir. Andrew Welsh. See also *DAI*–A 47/11 (1987): 4082.

'Troilus's painful keeping of troth, admirable but helpless, offers a pattern to be found in other Chaucerian characters: saints and victims whose absolute integrity seems to attract the punishments that define it. For those whose trouthe is not part of God's integrity – Griselda, for example, or Virginia – the fixed relationship of word and deed can reduce to mere fixity, a kind of death, an expression of true self that is necessarily silence.' (Abstract from *DAI*; diss. not seen.)

1851 Baker, Denise. 'Chaucer's Experiments with the "Thrifty Tale": The Narratives of the Man of Law, the Clerk, and the Physician.' *Mediaevalia* 14 (1988), 115–26.

By reshaping the sources of *MLT*, *ClT*, and *PhyT* to increase both the virtue of his heroines and the pathos of their suffering, Chaucer highlights the 'ethical dilemma of evil' (p 116). In *MLT* and *ClT*, Chaucer augments the existing evidence for Constance's and Griselda's exemplary behavior; in *PhyT*, he reshifts the focus of his sources from Virginius's integrity and Appius's injustice to Virginia's pathetic innocence. Our response to Virginia's plight is complicated by the tale's status as history (we are 'denied the consolation of fiction,' p 121), and by inadequate interpretations offered by the Physician (who provides no satisfactory explanation of his heroine's suffering) and Harry Bailly (who blames Virginia's beauty for her fate). The allusion to Jephthah encapsulates *PhyT*'s 'moral murkiness' (p 123): in contrast to the echoes of the story of Abraham and Isaac in *ClT*, the Physician's scriptural reference 'complicates rather than clarifies' (p 123) the morality of Virginius's decision to murder his daughter.

1852 Besserman, Lawrence. *Chaucer and the Bible: A Critical Review of Research, Indexes, and Bibliography*. 1988. See **627**.

Lists eight biblical allusions in *PhyT* (lines 5–6, 93–100, 101–2, 107–9, 154,

215, 221–6, 231–55), with references to scholarly discussions (pp 128–9).

1853 Bloch, R. Howard. 'Chaucer's Maiden's Head: *The Physician's Tale* and the Poetics of Virginity.' *QPar* 2 (1988), 22–45.
See **1860** for this essay in an expanded form.

1854 Davenport, W.A. *Chaucer: Complaint and Narrative*. 1988. See **631**.
Despite his ironic allusion in *NPT* to Geoffrey of Vinsauf's lament for the death of King Richard, Chaucer accepted the poetic propriety of such laments – both elegies for someone dead (as in *BD*) or laments 'against' one's death, as in Virginia's request that she be allowed time to *compleyne* (line 241) before she dies (p 5).

1855 Hasenfratz, Robert Joseph. *"To Ears of Flesh and Blood": Some Uses of the Sensational in Medieval English Literature*. PhD diss., Pennsylvania State University, 1988. Dir. Ronald E. Buckalew. Ann Arbor, MI: University Microfilms International, 1989. See also *DAI*-A 50/02 (1988): 439–40.
The horror and pathos of Virginia's death, emphasized in Chaucer's additions to his sources, demand response rather than interpretation: 'the tale seeks to move its readers and it is in that movement that the meaning of the story resides' (p 290). *PhyT*'s grotesque elements are less a reflection of the teller's character than an inherited feature of the pathetic style, which calls for strong emotional reactions of the sort we see in Harry Bailly's response to the tale.

1856 Hornsby, Joseph Allen. *Chaucer and the Law*. 1988. See **1233**.
Claudius's *bille* (lines 178–90) follows closely the late-medieval formulas for such petitions, which were presented by the plaintiff directly to the court of the chancellor. Virginius's trial demonstrates how the law can be abused by fraudulent judges; 'a model of procedural propriety' (p 157), Appius's handling of the bill nonetheless perverts right and justice.

1857 Koff, Leonard Michael. *Chaucer and the Art of Storytelling*. 1988. See **785**.
'For Harry Bailly, *PhyT* is a comment on the treachery of good looks, as if Virginia's beauty, her gift from Dame Fortune ... was her fault – both the cause of Appius's lecherous passion and her own decapitation ... It is only partly true here that Harry Bailly is a misogynist; he sees Virginia's fortunate beauty as the occasion to indict fortune and nature as the cause of harm for man in general. Virginia's is only an especially pitiful case' (p 82).
• Review by Peggy A. Knapp, *MP* 88 (1990), 180–2: Koff aptly uses Harry Bailly's response to *PhyT* to introduce the subject of self-interested readings. But there is 'some dissonance between Gadamerian openness to each reader's prejudice and Koff's rhetorical invitation to take his own reading of *PhyT* as superior to the Host's' (p 182).

1858 Robertson, D.W., Jr. 'The Physician's Comic Tale.' *ChauR* 23 (1988), 129–39.
Chaucer's audience is not likely to have read Livy, but would have known Jean de Meun's version of the Appius and Virginia story and hence appre-

ciated Chaucer's deliberate distortions of it. Raison's exemplum in *RR* concerns 'the corruption of justice through unreasonable love' (p 132). In Chaucer, this lesson applies not only to Appius, but also to the Physician, whose avarice blinds him to his duty of charity towards his patients. Both Appius's conspiracy with Claudius and the Physician's friendship with apothecaries reflect the legal abuse known as 'champarty,' in which a 'maintainer' supports a second party's false claims to a piece of land in exchange for fees or gifts. The Physician is unaware of this parallel; without recognizing his similarities to Appius, he devises for the false judge the fate that he himself merits.

1859 Ruud, Jay. 'Natural Law and Chaucer's *Physician's Tale*.' *JRMMRA* 9 (1988), 29–45.

Introduced in Nature's remarks on her relationship to the Creator, the concept of Natural Law provides an ideal against which we measure *PhyT*'s narrator and its three main characters and find them wanting. The Physician's presentation of governance makes no mention of the love that is the foundation of Natural Law in both the cosmos and in personal relationships. Appius flouts Natural Law by allowing passion to overcome reason, and by corrupting justice, the Positive Law that should reflect Natural Law. Virginius violates the aspect of Natural Law that pertains to love within the family; the charity he should feel for his daughter is perverted into pride and self-love. Although she is treated with sympathy by the Physician, Virginia is also in violation of Natural Law in her 'negative approach to virtue' (p 39) and her passivity in the face of her father's 'unnatural' (p 40) command. 'Since preservation of life is Nature's first rule, she was under an obligation to resist ... her death is as much a sin against Nature as is Apius's suicide' (p 40).

1860 Bloch, R. Howard. 'Chaucer's Maiden's Head: "The Physician's Tale" and the Poetics of Virginity.' *Representations* 28 (1989), 113–34. Repr. in Bloch, *Medieval Misogyny and the Invention of Western Romantic Love*. Chicago: U of Chicago P, 1991. Pp 101–12. Excerpts repr. in *Chaucer: Contemporary Critical Essays* (see **1200**). Pp 145–56.

Medieval definitions of virginity provide a key to understanding motivation in *PhyT*. Patristic writers insisted that a virgin who has been looked at with desire is no longer a virgin. Thus Virginia has been deflowered from the moment Appius gazes at her. The virgin's desire to escape desire, to transcend the corporeal, is a kind of death wish. Virginia's death is therefore implicit in her virginity, rendering superfluous debates over her father's treatment of her. Since the very act of speaking about virginity entails its loss – the 'veiling' of the universal Idea of virginity by the 'defiling garment of words' (p 123) – Chaucer is complicit in the despoliation he narrates through the Physician. In his rhetoric of excessive praise, Chaucer excites the reader's desire even before Appius appears on the scene; by adorning and exposing perfect modesty in his opening encomium, the poet himself 'violates the virgin' (p 124).

1861 Cooper, Helen. *The Canterbury Tales*. 1989. See **635**.
Treats the tale's date and text, genre, sources and analogues, structure, themes, the tale in context, style, and the *Phy–PardL*. Although its ending suggests that *PhyT* is intended as a 'cautionary exemplum … it is very hard to see what it exemplifies' (pp 248–9). *PhyT* may also be read as history and as part of the group of 'pitous tale[s]' that includes *MLT, ClT,* and *PrT*. Chaucer changed his primary narrative source (*RR*) most notably in making Virginia's death a private rather than a public event. The parallels with Ambrose and Vincent of Beauvais in the exposition of Virginia's virtues may be evidence of the wide currency of these ideas rather than instances of direct borrowing. *PhyT* exhibits a structural disproportion between moralizing and descriptive elements, on the one hand, and the exposition of the plot, on the other. The tale is also problematic in its affinities with both a shame culture (which values outward honor and reputation) and a guilt culture (which focuses on inner conscience), and in the seeming irrelevance of its explicit moralizing to the plot. The tale's 'muddled morality' (p 253) cannot be explained away as a dramatic or ironic expression of its teller's inadequacies; among other things, there is no evidence that Chaucer wrote the story with the Physician in mind. Read in context, *PhyT* provides a contrast with *FranT*'s treatment of female sexuality, and stands as an 'antitype' (p 256) of *PardT*: the rioters embody sin as Virginia embodies virtue, yet in both stories violent death strikes when it is least expected. Stylistically, *PhyT* favors 'factual statement' (p 257), in keeping with its designation as an 'historial thyng' (line 156). But it exhibits considerable stylistic variety, especially in the rhetorical set pieces.

1862 Dinshaw, Carolyn. *Chaucer's Sexual Poetics*. Madison: U of Wisconsin P, 1989.
The tale of the Pardoner, who is preoccupied with the flesh, follows logically on that of the Physician, the pilgrim most concerned with – professionally dependent on – the body. In *RR*, Raison tells the story of Appius and Virginia directly after her account of Saturn's castration. 'The Pardoner follows the Physician's redaction of this tale as if to explain the sordid world of *PhyT*: it's an unjust world, a world cut off from natural justice, natural love – a castrated world' (p 161).

1863 Kim, Hyonjin. '"What is this world?": the Knight's Tale, the Man of Law's Tale, the Franklin's Tale, the Physician's Tale e natanan Chaucer eui yeoksakwan' ['"What is this world?": Chaucer's historical insight in the Knight's Tale, the Man of Law's Tale, the Franklin's Tale, and the Physician's Tale']. 1989. See **1250**.

1863a Oka, Saburo. 'A Comparative-Narratological Approach to Chaucer, with

Special Attention to the Introduction and Ending of *The Physician's Tale.' Eibungaku Kenkyuu* [The English Society of Japan] 65 (1989), 239.
Not seen. In Japanese. See **1609**.

1864 Patterson, Lee W. '"What Man Artow?": Authorial Self-Definition in *The Tale of Sir Thopas* and *The Tale of Melibee*.' 1989. See **1252**.
PhyT figures among Chaucer's stagings of 'the trope of the cruel parent' (p 161). Virginia's innocence is betrayed both by Appius and by her own father, who 'preempts Apius's legalized rape by himself taking from this "mayden" her "heed"' (p 161).

1865 Ramsey, Roy Vance. 'F.N. Robinson's Editing of the *Canterbury Tales*.' *SB* 42 (1989), 134–52.
Questions the assumption that Robinson (**55**) used El as his base text. Correspondences with Pollard (**6**) and, especially, Skeat (**4**) when these editors depart from El suggest that Robinson relied primarily on these early editions and not upon manuscript evidence. In *PhyT*, Robinson departs from El more frequently than either Pollard or Skeat (p 143).

1866 Item cancelled.

1867 Speed, Diane. 'Language and Perspective in the *Physician's Tale*.' In *Words and Wordsmiths: a volume for H.L. Rogers*. 1989. See **1254**.
PhyT's syntax, vocabulary, treatment of literary allusion, and handling of allegory invite us to consider the events of the story from different and sometimes contradictory points of view. The text as a whole explores 'the potential of multiple perspective in linear narrative' (p 136).

1868 Strohm, Paul. *Social Chaucer*. 1989. See **641**.
Although Chaucer has 'partially de-historicized' *PhyT*, Appius is nevertheless portrayed as 'an agent of social dislocation, setting a "cherl" against a worthy "knyght"' (p 159).

1869 Wetherbee, Winthrop. *Geoffrey Chaucer: The Canterbury Tales*. 1989. See **642**.
In *PhyT*, 'the appropriation of the feminine is carried to the point of virtual annihilation' (p 95). Virginia's lack of autonomy is most strikingly shown in her relationship to Virginius; beginning with her name, 'everything about her is her father's' (p 96). A saint without the power to convert, Virginia exists as 'a physical object to be possessed and violated, a vehicle for male self-assertion' (p 96). Invidiousness dominates both the tale's subject matter and its style, which neutralizes the value of Virginia's beauty and virtue. Like his professional role, the Physician's tale lacks a symbolic dimension, and is 'one of Chaucer's strongest comments on the failure of love in human life' (p 97).

1870 White, Hugh. 'Chaucer Compromising Nature.' 1989. See **643**.
See **1940**.

1871 Crafton, John Micheal. 'Chaucer's Treasure Text: The Influence of Brunetto Latini on Chaucer's Developing Narrative Technique.' *MedPers* 4–5 (1989–

90), 25–41.
Brunetto's account in chapter 25 of the *Tresor* of the ways in which a writer might win over an audience is 'virtually a *summa* of all the various appeals used by the prologues in *CT*' (p 33). The Physician's assertion of the historical truth of his tale, for example, recalls Brunetto's 'appeal to the quality of the text itself' (p 34).

The Physician's Tale, 1990–1999

1872 Bowers, John M. '"Dronkenesse is Ful of Stryvyng": Alcoholism and Ritual Violence in Chaucer's *Pardoner's Tale.*' *ELH* 57 (1990), 757–84.
The sick world of *PhyT* is diagnosed by a Physician who is himself sick, lusting for money rather than for virgins; he thus anticipates the Pardoner's own metaphoric substitution of the plague for the name of the more dreaded personal vice of alcoholism. Virginius's decapitation of his daughter takes on a sacrificial coloring, foreshadowing the ritual of scapegoating that runs deep in *PardT* as well as in the Pardoner's own psychology.

1873 Pearsall, Derek. 'Chaucer's Religious Tales: A Question of Genre.' In *Chaucer's Religious Tales*. Ed. C. David Benson and Elizabeth Robertson. Chaucer Studies 15. Cambridge: Brewer, 1990. Pp 11–19.
The absence of any explicit or allegorical Christian justification for Virginius's murder of his daughter makes it difficult to classify *PhyT* as a religious tale. At the same time, the narrative exhibits many of the stylistic and structural traits of a religious story, and Virginia 'has all the attributes of a Christian virgin-martyr except a good reason (in Christian faith) for dying' (p 16).

1874 Wallace, David. '"Whan She Translated Was": A Chaucerian Critique of the Petrarchan Academy.' In *Literary and Social Change in Britain, 1380–1530*. Ed. Lee Patterson. Berkeley: U of California P, 1990. Pp 156–215.
Chaucer's representation of 'the commons' in *PhyT* 'suggests that an aristocracy might save itself from tyranny (and from its own worst fatalistic and self-destructive tendencies) by counting upon the sound instincts of "the peple" at moments of crisis' (p 202).

1875 Baker, Denise. 'Chaucer and Moral Philosophy: The Virtuous Women of *The Canterbury Tales*.' *MÆ* 60 (1991), 241–56.
Chaucer associates the heroines of *MLT, ClT, PhyT,* and Prudence in *Mel* with the four cardinal virtues – fortitude, justice, temperance, and prudence, respectively. By presenting a static description that portrays her possession of the traditional parts of temperance, Chaucer avoids showing Virginia in the act of restraining her carnal desires. The passage praising Virginia's virtues includes most of those qualities associated with temperance in Cicero's

De Inventione and Macrobius's *Commentary on the Dream of Scipio*. Virginia also embodies virtues linked with temperance in Peraldus's *Summa de Virtutibus et Vitiis*.

1876 Dillon, Janette. 'Game in the *Pardoner's Tale*.' *EIC* 41 (1991), 208–21.
The heavy-handed moralizing that concludes *PhyT* is generalized so widely that it could fit any tale in which sin is punished. Despite the 'blandly conventional nature' (p 210) of the Physician's preaching, the Host becomes so involved in the story that he responds to the characters as if they were real people rather than fictional creations.

1877 Fyler, John M. 'Man, Men, and Women in Chaucer's Poetry.' In *The Olde Daunce: Love, Friendship, Sex, and Marriage in the Medieval World*. 1991. See **652**.
Chaucer often subjects male sympathy for women to an ironic critique by examining the motives of the men who praise them. The Man of Law and the Physician present Constance and Virginia as instances of female martyrdom, but their sentimental tales reveal the tellers' moral hypocrisy, their desire to establish their own piety.

1878 Kanno, Masahiko. 'The Physician's Tale: A Distorted Sense of Justice.' *HSELL* 36 (1991), 1–12. Repr. in Kanno, *Studies in Chaucer's Words: A Contexual and Semantic Approach* (see **1284**). Pp 85–97.
Through the repetition of key terms (*pitee, softe, right*), Chaucer calls attention to the ways in which justice is distorted in *PhyT*. The word *right*, for example, is associated with Appius and Claudius, while Virginius and Virginia, 'though they have a good reason to claim "right" never speak of "right"' (p 12).

1879 Kiser, Lisa J. *Truth and Textuality in Chaucer's Poetry*. Hanover, NH: UP of New England, 1991.
Although he identifies his source as Livy and reminds his audience of the story's historicity, the Physician falsifies his *matere* by eliminating its original political and historical content and by imposing Christian concepts and generic expectations on its pagan material. The Physician's manipulation of history parallels his treatment of Virginia, who – like the betrayed women of *LGW* – functions as 'a symbol of the victimized source' (p 134), an innocent pagan whose life story is altered by a later writer for some new purpose. Virginia is thus thrice betrayed: by Appius and Claudius, by her father, and by the narrator who tells her tale.

1880 Mann, Jill. *Geoffrey Chaucer*. 1991. See **656**.
See **1809, 1953**.
• Review by Helen Cooper, *TLS*, 19 July 1991: Mann's 'opposition to rape … is human rather than theological – though she is perhaps going a bit far in her acceptance of Virginius's killing of his daughter to save her from such misery: should he not at least have asked her first?'

1881 Patterson, Lee W. *Chaucer and the Subject of History*. 1991. See **659**.
PhyT is a 'fraudulent ... hagiography' (p 370) in which the betrayal of the saintlike heroine by masculine figures is mirrored in the narrator's betrayal of the tale's generic form. The purported celebration of Virginia's innocence is eclipsed by the Physician's preoccupation with the ways in which innocence can be destroyed; Virginia's 'only act of conversion is to transform Appius from a judge into a lecher ... while she fails to move her father' (pp 369–70). 'Like the pathetic figure it commemorates,' *PhyT* 'is unable to transcend its own fallen historicity' (p 370).
• Review by Derek S. Brewer, *Rev* 14 (1992), 87–100: 'It is true that traditional societies are not pluralist. They have a strong sense of absolutes that we think we have abandoned.' Yet the high moral tone of condemnation taken by Patterson against Virginius 'is in itself an absolute based upon modern standards' (p 90).

1882 Taylor, Paul Beekman. 'The Uncourteous Knights of *The Canterbury Tales*.' *ES* 72 (1991), 209–18.
Although he is presented as a noble knight, Virginius abuses his knightly duty to protect women by beheading his daughter in order to defend his and her public honor. Manifesting 'will untempered by mercy and uninstructed by reason,' Virginius 'kills what he cannot master' (p 213).

1883 Axton, Richard. 'Chaucer and "Tragedy."' In *Chaucer to Shakespeare: Essays in Honour of Shinsuke Ando*. Ed. Toshiyuki Takamiya and Richard Beadle. Cambridge: Brewer, 1992. Pp 33–43.
The Physician's observation that evildoers come to a bad end seems a perfunctory summation of the tragic nature of the story. But Harry Bailly sounds the genuine note of tragedy in his passionate and indignant response to Virginia's fate.

1884 Harley, Marta Powell. 'Last Things First in Chaucer's Physician's Tale: Final Judgment and the Worm of Conscience.' *JEGP* 91 (1992), 1–16.
PhyT is an allegory of the proper governance of the soul, specifically of the soul's rejection of sin. An allegorical reading clarifies the thematic relevance of five passages that have been deemed excrescent or artistically inept. The account of Nature's creation of Virginia and the catalogue of Virginia's physical and moral qualities recall contemporary representations of the soul as a beloved daughter, divinely beautiful and a compendium of virtues. The address to governesses and parents extends the notion of the governance of the soul 'to include ... parallel caretaker relationships that would be scrutinized at final judgment' (p 15). The dialogue preceding Virginia's death depicts Virginius's beheading of his daughter as a reasoned action, and, in merging the identities of father and daughter, suggests that Virginius 'may represent the dissenting will, an aspect of Virginia's rejection of sin' (p 14). Properly translated and glossed, the much-maligned epilogue reveals its subject as

the last judgment, in which Appius and Claudius, 'the tale's corrupt judge and false witness, are transcended in the vision of God and the worm of conscience, the incorruptible judge and the inveterately honest witness' (p 8).

1885 Leavy, Barbara Fass. *To Blight With Plague: Studies in a Literary Theme.* New York: New York UP, 1992.

The tales of Fragment VI contain striking parallels. Plague supplies the Physician with his gold and gold proves deadly in *PardT*. The moral diseases that the Pardoner is prey to and that he in turn exploits link him to Appius, who embodies the 'sovereyn pestilence' that betrays innocence (lines 91–2). *PhyT* contains images of disease, and when the Physician describes as under Nature's *cure* (line 22) all things that exist under the moon, he implies that he, too, possesses a remedy for earthly ills; both the Physician and the Pardoner 'offer material solutions to a spiritually diseased world' (p 48). Virginia's beauty leads to her death, but her willing submission to her father's decree shows that, unlike the rioters in *PardT*, she knows how to defeat death; the allusion to the story of Pygmalion and Galatea suggests that the physical body is 'no more … than an empty doll' unless completed by the soul (p 48).

1886 Mandel, Jerome H. *Geoffrey Chaucer: Building the Fragments of the Canterbury Tales*. 1992. See **664**.

Ch. 2, 'Fragment VI (Group C): The Physician's Tale and the Pardoner's Tale' (pp 50–70), examines the structural and thematic links between 'the most vilified and the most celebrated of *CT*' (p 50). An analysis of the sequence of narrative events reveals systematic parallels: the self-descriptions of Nature and the Pardoner (presented as opposites: the activities of the one authentic, of the other fraudulent); the contrasting portraits of Virginia (governed by her virtues) and the rioters (governed by their vices); the interruptions in the narratives (the Physician's address to parents and governesses; the Pardoner's sermon on gluttony); the impulse for action (Appius: 'This mayde shal be myn' [line 129]; the rioters: 'Deeth shal be deed' [line 710]); conspiracies (Appius and Claudius, the rioters); confrontation scenes (Virginius and Virginia; the Old Man and the rioters), followed by discussions and decisions (the deaths of Virginia and of the rioters, the one a sacrifice of love, echoing the Crucifixion, the other a 'blasphemous parody of the Crucifixion' [p 59]); pardon (Virginius of Claudius, 'the ultimate act of charity, the working out of Christ's pardon in the world of men' [p 60]; the Pardoner's invocation of Christ's pardon); Harry Bailly's 'playing' with the Physician and the Pardoner; the intervention of the *gentils*, who attempt to turn game into earnest, and of the Knight, who turns earnest into game. The Fragment VI tales are also unified thematically, in their shared concern with fraud (like her creator Nature, Virginia is defined by the absence of fraud; Appius and Claudius generate various kinds of fraud and hypocrisy; 'counterfeiting, misrepresentation, duplicity, and pretense' [p 65] are central to the Pardoner and his tale); governance (see **1762** on *PhyT*; the Pardoner and his characters 'are governed almost exclusively by their appetites' [p 67]); and death (the Old Man in *PardT* triumphs over Death by taking seriously God's governance of the world; in this respect, he parallels Virginia).

• Review by Catherine Batt, *MLR* 89 (1994), 965–7: Mandel's characterization of Virginia as a willing martyr 'obviates the need to confront ... complexities of judgment and the issue of audience complicity' (p 967).

• Review by Vincent DiMarco, *Speculum* 69 (1994), 831–4: 'Mandel's most important contribution is his discovery of the common narrative structure of the tales within the fragments. His analyses in this regard are eye-opening ... especially as regards the two-tale fragments' (p 832).

• Review by Dieter Mehl, *SAC* 16 (1994), 224–6: Mandel links the Fragment VI tales mainly through their contrasts. Readers may approach his interpretation skeptically, but may ultimately 'be swayed by the sum of supporting detail into at least partial acceptance' (p 225).

• Review by Richard Utz, *Anglia* 113 (1995), 251–4: In linking it with *PardT*, Mandel makes a persuasive case for the careful structure of *PhyT*.

1887 Pearsall, Derek. *The Life of Geoffrey Chaucer: A Critical Biography*. 1992. See **1614**, **1873**.

1888 Richmond, Velma Bourgeois. *Geoffrey Chaucer*. 1992. See **666**.
PhyT poses difficult questions about the relation of justice and mercy. Although Virginius assumes godlike power and does not show mercy to his daughter, he is forgiven. The two digressions, on governesses and fathers and mothers, provide a context for assessing Virginius's patriarchal severity (pp 102–4).

1889 Børch, Marianne Novrup. *Chaucer's Poetics: Seeing and Asking*. 1993. See **1313**.
PhyT is about 'failing to wait' (p 363). Virginia's 'Is ther no grace, is ther no remedye?' (line 236) suggests that there may be an alternative to the inflexible moral code that forces her to die, but her father is unable to postpone his action to see what might happen. 'The absence of grace in *PhyT* is ... linked with characters' trust in the infallibility of human judgment' (p 365).

1890 Hallissy, Margaret. *Clean Maids, True Wives, Steadfast Widows: Chaucer's Women and Medieval Codes of Conduct*. 1993. See **1318**.
Caught among conflicting medieval cultural assumptions about women's chastity, Virginius acts upon the wrong assumption and destroys his daughter. A daughter who forfeits her chastity disgraces her father; Virginius chooses loss of his daughter rather than loss of his honor. Since, for Virginia, neither suicide nor surrender is the clearly morally correct alternative, Virginius might be seen as sparing his daughter the risk of sin by killing her. But a third alternative – that Appius suffer death at the father's hands – is one he never considers. In patristic texts, virginity was presented as virtually impossible to preserve, subject to violation merely by the virgin's having

been seen with lustful eyes. *PhyT* thus demonstrates the 'moral confusion' produced by the anxiety about the 'liminal state of premarital virginity ... if even Virginia is somehow unchaste, who is chaste?' (p 54).

1891 Hirsh, John C. 'Modern Times: The Discourse of the *Physician's Tale*.' *ChauR* 27 (1993), 387–95.

The qualities that mark *PhyT* – 'fragmentation, not order; power, not empathy; emotion, not reason; surprise, not continuity' (p 389) – place us in the modern world. Nature and Justice are less transcendent figures than regulating norms; the implications of Virginia's plight are cast in social, not religious, terms; and it is the physical state of virginity, not its spiritual dimension, that is at issue. The narrative lacks any real sense of evil; the state it depicts 'seems not so much corrupted ... as broken' (p 390). *PhyT* may be viewed as a modern and secular version of *SNT*, in which the symbolic notation of the latter is present but emptied of authority; in *PhyT*, chastity serves the patriarchy rather than spiritual ends. The Physician, who in his professional life eschews principles and ideals but 'has an eye for what works' (p 391), concludes with an invocation of sin and divine justice that seems to reverse the secular ethic he has been developing. But these closing words only underscore the tale's pervasive 'sense of randomness and discontinuity' (p 392).

1892 Item cancelled.

1893 Lomperis, Linda. 'Unruly Bodies and Ruling Practices: Chaucer's *Physician's Tale* as Socially Symbolic Act.' In *Feminist Approaches to the Body in Medieval Literature*. Ed. Linda Lomperis and Sarah Stanbury. Philadelphia: U of Pennsylvania P, 1993. Pp 21–37.

The first part of *PhyT* records the Physician's failed attempt to erase the physical. Although he draws attention to Virginia's spiritual qualities, the sexual and the bodily exceed his strategies of control – in our recognition of the bodily forces that Nature represents, in the 'stubborn persistency of sexual, bodily acts' (p 25) in the Physician's addresses to governesses and parents. The Physician's failure to control Virginia's body is paralleled by contemporary instances of English aristocratic women (e.g., Joan of Kent) asserting the claims of their own sexuality over and against sociopolitical constraints designed to regulate them. In the second half of *PhyT*, however, the maid's body virtually disappears, transformed into a space across which male power relations move. This male-dominated power structure is marked by 'cracks, fissures, and internal tensions' (p 29). Virginius's judgmental behavior is tacitly linked with Appius's legalistic conduct; his beheading of Virginia reveals a sexual, even incestuous, basis that echoes hints of incestuous relations within English noble families in the fourteenth century. The beheading scene manifests as well a 'confusion of bodies' (p 32); Virginia's death is also the death of her father-ruler, and paves the way for 'a newfound alliance between Virginius and Claudius' (p 32). The Physician attempts to erase the 'newly organized social body' (p 33) of the people by focusing on metaphysical and moral issues at the end of his tale. But Harry Bailly's 'body-oriented' response to Virginia's fate reminds us that the Physician-narrator 'cannot make bodily concerns, or their political implications, simply go away' (p 33).

1894 Penninger, Frieda Elaine. *Chaucer's Troilus and Criseyde and the Knight's Tale: Fictions Used.* 1993. See **1323**.
Virginius, repeatedly designated as a knight, seems intended as a noble man and a caring father, but he loses our sympathy; he is a knight reduced from hero to victim (pp 78–9).

1895 Crafton, John Micheal. '*Paradoxicum Semiotica*: Signs, Comedy, and Mystery in Fragment VI of the *Canterbury Tales*.' In *Chaucer's Humor*. Ed. Jean E. Jost. New York: Garland, 1994. Pp 163–86.
In its avoidance of creativity and its adherence to perceived authority, *PhyT* embodies a theory of art that exemplifies an extreme version of philosophical Realism. In its exaggerations of these principles, however, the tale negates the appeal of the narrator's Realist *ars poetica*.

1896 Pelen, Marc M. 'Murder and Immortality in Fragment VI (C) of the *Canterbury Tales*: Chaucer's Transformation of Theme and Image from the *Roman de la Rose*.' *ChauR* 29 (1994), 1–25.
The clash of perspectives both within and between *PhyT* and *PardT* implies that a satisfying analysis of sin and its remission is beyond the powers of human discourse. 'Each tale seems to deny the other's apparent point, without, however, proposing an alternative' (p 9), as in the ridicule of the Physician's equation of physical purity with penance in the Pardoner's materialism. Chaucer's juxtaposition of unreconciled perspectives (which he may have learned from Jean de Meun) centers in Fragment VI on 'the opposition of murder and immortality to their sacramental analogues of contrition and the Redemption' (p 16); the inability of the Physician and the Pardoner to fathom the connections among these concepts generates an irony by means of which Chaucer silently transcends the 'discordant claims' (p 17) of his narrators, thus allowing us to apprehend the association between murder and immortality both within Fragment VI and in relation to the themes of *CT* as a whole.

1897 Pigg, Daniel. 'The Semiotics of Comedy in Chaucer's Religious Tales.' In *Chaucer's Humor*. 1994. See **1895**. Pp 321–48.
The Physician is 'subsumed under the discursive form' (p 336) of his tale; the tale itself points to 'a discursive and significative failure' in which 'earthly comedy ... is postponed and extended into the higher sphere of which it previously was a sign,' and Virginia becomes 'a part of the larger comic system' (p 337). The tale of which Virginia is the center is 'an anticipated

comedy of the future – a comedy of silence in a place where earthly signs are unnecessary' (p 337).

1898 Quinn, William A. *Chaucer's Rehersynges: The Performability of The Legend of Good Women.* Washington, DC: Catholic U of America P, 1994.
PhyT's explication of its own moral proves disorienting. The Physician invokes just punishment for sin, but the tale fails to demonstrate the workings of justice. Nature's pronouncements are undercut by her tone, which in Chaucer's oral performance could sound 'just plain ornery' (p 210). Virginia's integrity involves her in feigning and equivocation. In the tale's 'darkest irony' (p 212), Appius's lust merely reflects Virginius's paternal possessiveness. The concluding *moralitas* is invalidated by the tale's 'secular vacuity'; the final couplet reads like 'mere word juggling' (p 214).

1899 Spearing, A.C., ed. *The Franklin's Prologue and Tale from the Canterbury Tales by Geoffrey Chaucer*. 1966/1994. See **86**.
In the case of the Man of Law and the Physician, inter alia, 'an extremely fine-spun argument' is needed to establish a link between teller and tale (1994, p 69).

1900 Wogan-Browne, Jocelyn. 'The Virgin's Tale.' In *Feminist Readings in Middle English Literature: The Wife of Bath and All Her Sect*. 1994. Pp 165–94.
In *PhyT*, Chaucer adapts the traditional virgin martyr's hagiography to expose political and social issues. The absence of a Christian spiritual rationale for the killing of Virginia raises the question of how the virgin martyr's suffering can be licensed and problematizes the motives for the sacrifice of the patriarchy's virgin daughters.

1901 Chance, Jane. *The Mythographic Chaucer: The Fabulation of Sexual Politics*. 1995. See **675**.
The Physician employs two strands of the Pygmalion myth – the virginity of the statue and the artistry of the sculptor – to comment on his characters. Virginia's perfect virginity allies her with the ivory statue; like the *artifex* Pygmalion (who, in medieval commentaries on Ovid, is glossed as an exemplum of illicit desire), Virginius and Appius fall in love with their own creations. The 'increasingly pejorative' (p 269) appearances of the image of counterfeiting in *PhyT* convey an idea of falsity and deceit alien to Virginia but not to Claudius or Appius, who, along with the Physician, who 'profits from the plague, that is, turns dying flesh into gold' (p 270), Virginius, and perhaps Chaucer himself, are 'types of Pygmalion – those fraudulent and counterfeiting "fathers" who reify others, exchanging life for imagery and abstraction' (p 270). The Physician's relation to counterfeiting links him with the Pardoner, who also employs deception to help him achieve his 'worldly and selfish ends' (p 264).

1902 Collette, Carolyn P. '"Peyntyng with Greet Cost": Virginia as Image in the *Physician's Tale*.' *CY* 2 (1995), 49–62.

The description of Virginia may be understood not only in the context of the written, high culture of the time, but also within the vernacular tradition. The passage's language of painting and counterfeiting and its contrast of human and divine art are paralleled in contemporary Wycliffite writings, which emphasize the physical attractiveness of images and their potential misuse by the viewer. The action of the tale follows from the physical perfection of Virginia-as-image and the intellectual and affective disruptions wrought in Appius by the sight of this image. He becomes a 'false juge' (line 161) when his vision of Virginia distorts his judgment, his sense of basic right and wrong.

1903 Cowgill, Jane. 'Chaucer's Missing Children.' *EMSt* 12 (1995), n.p.
Virginia's virginity, humility, and modesty make her a prototype of the Christian martyr. Her death and her father's sufferings are presented against alternative backdrops: her father's unyielding world of vengeance and justice and the world of Christian sacrifice that Virginia represents. To be understood, the griefs of father and child must be extracted from the political, patriarchal worlds which produce them and set against the Christian and more feminine world of mercy and redemptive sacrifice.

Responding to Mann (**1809**), Cowgill argues that Mann puts too heavy a philosophical burden on the images of suffering fathers in these tales. 'Unlike the actions of God, the Father who may allow suffering for his own good, though shadowy purposes,' the actions of earthly fathers in *MkT* and *PhyT* 'are left morally ambiguous' or are presented as morally inadequate (*Mel*).

1904 Crafton, John Micheal. 'Emptying the Vessel: Chaucer's Humanistic Critique of Nominalism.' In *Literary Nominalism and the Theory of Rereading Late Medieval Texts: A New Research Paradigm*. Ed. Richard J. Utz. Lewiston, NY: Mellen, 1995. Pp 117–34.
See **1895**.

1905 Gray, Douglas. '"Pite for to here – pite for to se": Some Scenes of Pathos in Late Medieval English Literature.' *PBA* 87 for 1994 (1995), 67–99.
In *PhyT* 'we are directly confronted with violent and unjust *pathe* and with the extreme demands of … absolute ideals of honour' (p 88).

1906 Hallissy, Margaret. *A Companion to Chaucer's Canterbury Tales*. 1995. See **1345**.
In medieval culture, the father had a special duty to protect his daughter's virginity until she was married. Virginius's identity is wrapped up in that of his daughter Virginia, as suggested by their names. Virginius's decision to kill Virginia arises from the cultural assumption that 'a dead woman is preferable to a dishonored woman' (p 210). Although Virginius might have taken up arms against the false judge Appius, the victim rather than the perpetrator is blamed and punished. 'The illogic of Virginius's reaction – indeed the moral confusion of the whole tale – is a consequence of the over-

whelming importance attached to women's purity in medieval culture' (p 211).

1907 Kline, Daniel T. 'Textuality, Subjectivity, and Violence: Theorizing the Figure of the Child in Middle English Literature.' 1995. See **1903**.

Virginia exists at the crossroads of contending discourses – e.g., Nature's imprinting her with 'excellent … beautee' (line 39), the advice to governesses to discipline the natural proclivities of the young, Appius's counterfeit claim of paternity, the biblical narrative of Jephthah's daughter – that attempt to fix her into a particular subject position. In killing his daughter, Virginius turns against parental and natural affection and instead privileges his commitment to a patriarchal, honor-based culture. Thus the claims of Appius's counterfeit *bille* (line 166) efface the natural prerogatives of paternity, and Virginia is subjugated at the hands of her father.

1908 Laskaya, Anne. *Chaucer's Approach to Gender in the Canterbury Tales*. 1995. See **790**.

Although the tellers of *MLT*, *ClT*, and *PhyT* acknowledge the disenfranchised status of women in medieval society, these male narrators also praise women for their obedience; 'the more extreme the suffering and the more absolute the obedience, the better the women' (p 147). The praise for women's silence in these tales suggests that feminine heroism occurs 'in the inward realm of the will' – not by shaping events, but by conforming to events' (p 149). Watching Custance, Griselda, and Virginia reacting to other people's designs, we wonder whether they will assert themselves – but they do not; 'Virginia's struggle to accept death is contained in only nineteen lines' (p 153).

1909 León Sendra, Antonio R., and F. Javier García de Quesada. 'The Physician's Tale.' In *Proceedings of the VIth International Conference of the Spanish Society for Medieval English Language and Literature.* Ed. Purificación Fernández Nistal and José María Bravo Gozalo. Valladolid: Universidad de Valladolid, 1995. Pp 207–16.

PhyT includes three narratives, those of Appius (about the abuse of authority), Virginius (concerning shame and honor), and Virginia (a story of victimization). The Appius and Virginius narratives are parallel in that Virginia is smitten with the same mortal blow, whether it is delivered by judge or father. Unlike the child martyrs to whom she is sometimes compared, Virginia never faces her accuser, is not supported by the gift of grace, and is allowed no free choice; her death seems 'unnecessary and gratuitous' (p 214).

1910 Lynch, Kathryn L. 'East Meets West in Chaucer's Squire's and Franklin's Tales.' 1995. See **679**.

At first glance, *PhyT* (which follows *FranT* in the Ellesmere order) seems to continue *SqT* and *FranT*'s 'assault on the feminine pleasures of the text' (p 550). But the tale does not manage to erase Virginia; 'her claims on our sympathy and sense of justice continue to rise up' (p 551) in the populace's response, in Harry Bailly's tears, and in the outrage of modern critics at the maiden's fate.

1911 Minnis, A.J. *The Shorter Poems*. 1995. See **1351**.
As elsewhere in his writings, Chaucer makes us aware of the limits of exemplification in *PhyT*, which raises more issues than are covered in its 'imposed and artificial "conclusioun"' (p 340).

1912 Newman, Barbara. *From Virile Woman to WomanChrist: Studies in Medieval Religion and Literature*. Philadelphia: U of Pennsylvania P, 1995.
Although the Physician mentions Virginia's 'mooder deere' (line 119), the mother is nowhere to be found at the moment of the girl's death. Virginius, like Jephthah, makes a self-pitying speech in which he projects his unacknowledged guilt onto the victim. Chaucer's warning to parents to guard their children may be covertly disapproving of Virginius. 'The more his daughter is assimilated to a virgin martyr, the more the father falls into the stereotypical role of torturer' (p 80).

1913 Pelling, Margaret. 'The Women of the Family? Speculations around Early Modern British Physicians.' *Social History of Medicine* 8 (1995), 383–401.
PhyT, in which a father kills his only offspring who is both a worthy descendent and a daughter, is cited as possible early evidence for the elite male physician's ambivalence about the family and the female world.

1914 Whitaker, Elaine E. 'John of Arderne and Chaucer's Physician.' *ANQ* 8 (1995), 3–5.
John of Arderne's requirements for the ideal physician in *Fistula in Ano* include the ability to tell tales that will cheer his patients. In continuously frustrating the expectations of his audience, Chaucer's Physician fails in this aspect of the healer's art.

1915 Astell, Ann W. *Chaucer and the Universe of Learning*. 1996. See **682**.
Fragment VI of *CT* is best understood as a response to Dantean lunarity as represented in *Paradiso* 3–5. Nature's appearance at the beginning of *PhyT* locates the tale in the sphere of the Moon and sounds the theme of ordered love that prevails in Dante's lunar cantos; Virginia's and Virginius's names evoke the virginity that is the peculiar province of the Moon. Responding to the question of 'ingiusta ... giustizia' raised by Beatrice (*Paradiso* 4.67), Chaucer shifts attention away from God's seemingly 'unjust justice' to the indisputably false justice of Appius, a corrupt earthly judge. In condemning an innocent person to death, Virginius also becomes a false judge, whereas Virginia's response parallels the sacrifice of Christ, innocent Lamb of God, on the cross. Medieval medical practitioners looked to the Moon to determine methods of treatment; *PhyT* suggests 'the terrible limits of medicine ... in dealing with disease and preserving life' (p 206) – the Physician's narrative fails to save Virginia's life, casts doubt on the efficacy of his cure, and

succeeds in making Harry Bailly ill.

• Review by Karla Taylor, *MP* 97 (2000), 445–51: Astell's notion of planetary structure 'sometimes actively thwarts intertextual interpretation' (p 447). Although her treatment of Fragment VI 'is full of surprising lunar associations ... the detailed structure ... works against a clear reading of *CT* as an answer to the *Paradiso*' (p 448).

1916 Hirsh, John C. 'Chaucer's Roman Tales.' *ChauR* 31 (1996), 45–57.
The depiction of arbitrary and corrupt civil power in *SNT* and *PhyT* shows Chaucer 'thinking theoretically about secular politics' (p 47). The climax of each tale centers on the unjust actions of unscrupulous, but also duly established, judges, and on the reactions of the people to a system that has lost its authority. In *PhyT*, the people display unerring insight into the determination of right and wrong in the matter; in both tales, we can see Chaucer 'turning away from the confidence in philosophical authority' (p 55) privileged in (for example) *KnT*, and offering instead a 'reading of the requirements of social justice and popular authority ... predicated more on actual than on intended effects' (p 55).

1917 Ireland, Richard W. '"He Hanged Rumbold ...": The Iconology of Judicial Partiality in the Middle Ages.' *Law and Critique* 7 (1996), 3–33.
Ireland juxtaposes *PhyT* with *The Judgment of Cambyses*, a late fifteenth-century panel painting by Gerard David. *PhyT* brings together two themes depicted separately in the paintings – 'the grave wickedness of one who uses judicial office for his own ends and the impossibility of deceiving God as to the truth of the matter' (p 11).

1918 McIlhaney, Anne E. 'Sentence and Judgment: The Role of the Fiend in Chaucer's *Canterbury Tales*.' *ChauR* 31 (1996), 173–83.
In *PhyT*, as in the other Canterbury narratives in which the Devil appears, the character (Appius) whom the fiend tempts is a poor reader who falsely reads the book of Virginia's virtue, is thus open to the Devil's enticements to further misread and misapply the law which he has been entrusted to administer, and, having corrupted his own faculty of judgment and delivered a false *sentence* (line 190), is appropriately judged by God's 'sentence.'

1919 Robson, Margaret. 'Cloaking Desire: Re-reading *Emaré*.' In *Romance Reading on the Book: Essays on Medieval Narrative Presented to Maldwyn Mills*. Ed. Jennifer Fellows, Rosalind Field, Gillian Rogers, and Judith Weiss. Cardiff: U of Wales P, 1996. Pp 64–76.
Virginius's rhetoric in line 224 suggests that the figure of the father and the figure of the judge are interchangeable. Virginia asks her father, not the persecuting judge, for mercy, which he denies (p 76n).

1920 Shibata, Takeo. 'On the Narrative of Chaucer's *Physician's Tale*.' *Review of Kobe Shinwa Women's University* 29 (1996), 1–25.
Full text at http://ci.nii.ac.jp/els/110006606886.pdf?id=ART0008574150&-

type=pdf&lang=en&host=cinii&order_no=&ppv_type=0&lang_sw=&-no=1392572610&=. In Japanese.

1921 Taylor, Paul Beekman. *Chaucer's Chain of Love*. 1996. See **1371**.
Nature's 'as me list' (line 22) may sound like 'blasphemous willfulness' (p 23), but it can be explained as a joining of Nature's will and God's providence.

1922 Blamires, Alcuin. *The Case for Women in Medieval Culture*. Oxford: Clarendon, 1997.
As an example of sobriety as a feminine ideal, Virginia voluntarily eschews excess; 'the encompassing constraint which Virginia unconstrainedly serves is patriarchy, which wants to police the sexuality of wives and daughters by inculcating such respect for feminine *mesure* that women like Virginia will constrain themselves' (p 151).

1923 Cox, Catherine S. *Gender and Language in Chaucer*. Gainesville: UP of Florida, 1997.
PhyT's linking of sexual chastity with chaste speech points to a cultural unease with the female body; the transfer of masculine responsibility and shame to the woman is exacerbated by the expectation of the virgin's silence. Virginius murders his daughter to preserve his own sense of feminine value. Virginia is marked as Virginius's property, with the disquieting hints of his incestuous desire 'transferred into an economic and political arena that deflects sexual overtones' (p 61); Virginia exists as a sign of the power struggle between Virginius and Appius, his political superior. Virginity as a trope of masculine domination is underscored by the Physician's abundant commentary, which dominates the poem and thus erases Virginia's subjectivity, and by the Host's 'outrageous blame-the-victim interpretation' (p 63). *PhyT*'s perceived aesthetic weaknesses reproduce on a metatextual level the narrative's suppression of the feminine; 'in straining to impose patriarchal limitations, the Physician strips the text of its fecundity and depth' (p 63).
Commenting on Cox's interpretation, Mann (**729**) observes that 'the notion that Virginius acts solely out of a rigid adherence to a 'masculine-feminine ideal of virginity (Cox, p 63) finds no support in the text' (p 113).

1924 Fichte, Jörg O. 'Konkurriende und Konstrastierende Zeitmuster in Chaucers *Canterbury Tales*.' In *Zeitkonzeptionen, Zeiterfahrung, Zeitmessung: Stationen ihres Wandels vom Mittelalter bis zur Moderne*. Ed. Trude Ehlert. Paderborn: Schöningh, 1997. Pp 223–41.
In contrast to the earlier versions of the Virginia story, *PhyT* does not serve a straightforward exemplary function. Its complex and problematic worldview, exploration of human motivation, and openness to individual interpretation link it with the *novelle*, in which the universal time of the exemplum becomes personal and delimited.

1925 Kline, Daniel T. '"My sacrifice with thy blood": Violence, Discourse, and

Subjectivity in the Representation of Children in Middle English Literature.' PhD diss., Indiana University, 1997. Dir. Lawrence M. Clopper. See also *DAI*–A 58/08 (1998): 3125.

Ch. 3, '"Take thou thy death, for this is my sentence": The Discourses of Childhood and the Resistant Subject in the *Physician's Tale*' (pp 87–129), argues that *PhyT* rehearses a succession of contradictory discourses that reveal the conflicted nature of medieval childhood within the feudal family and define Virginia's identity as a child and daughter within an ever-narrowing range of personal possibilities. The first discourse, of Nature, finds Virginia to be a perfect artifact of creation; the second, a discourse of nurture, finds her to be a pious exemplar of courtesy; the third, the discourse of law, finds her to be a potential orphan and ward; the fourth, the discourse of paternity, finds her to be an obedient daughter; and finally, Virginia's self-articulation makes her a biblical interpreter, parental critic, and resistant victim. As daughter to her father, Virginia occupies the relatively stable subject position of a blood relation who accepts conventional family and gender roles. As a young woman moving from childhood to puberty, however – neither wholly a child nor fully an adult – Virginia also occupies a liminal and ultimately dangerous cultural position that allows her to challenge the efficacy of the cultural scripts that confine her to standard social roles. Though murdered by her father, Virginia ultimately resists the tale's violent ideology of family and parenthood through her brief but trenchant invocation of Jephthah's daughter and in her carefully modulated final speech.

1926 Lee, Brian S. 'Justice in the *Physician's Tale* and the *Pardoner's Tale*: A Dialogic Contrast.' *CY* 4 (1997), 21–31.

PhyT tends toward monologue, *PardT* toward dialogue. The historical and allegorical distancing in *PhyT* combines with monologue to silence inquiry or argument; 'the events in the tale abide no question' (p 23), its speakers 'pronounce rather than discuss' (p 24). In contrast to the treatment of Virginius's trial in Livy, the dialogue of defense is suppressed by Chaucer; Appius moves as quickly as possible to his judgment. Also suppressed in this monologic text are the voices and actions of Virginia's potential guardians. Unlike *PardT, PhyT* does not interrogate itself. But it is in dialogue with *PardT*; in Fragment VI, 'pagan injustice culminates in the mercy of Christian reconciliation' (p 30), dramatized in the epilogue to *PardT*.

1927 Wallace, David. *Chaucerian Polity: Absolutist Lineages and Associational Forms in England and Italy*. Stanford, CA: Stanford UP, 1997.

PhyT dramatizes the contrast between private female pain and public masculine suffering. Virginius converts Virginia's pain into a dramatic rendering of his own suffering, while Virginia's pain remains unknown, 'denied any hope of objectification through social expression' (p 232).

1928 Item cancelled.

1929 Burger, Glenn. 'Doing What Comes Naturally: The Physician's Tale and the Pardoner.' In *Masculinities in Chaucer: Approaches to Maleness in the Canterbury Tales and Troilus and Criseyde*. 1998. See **1390**. Pp 116–30.
See **1956**.

1930 Davenport, W.A. *Chaucer and His English Contemporaries: Prologue and Tale in The Canterbury Tales*. 1998. See **698**.
In the apparent irrelevance of its moralizing passages, the absence of social or political context to explain the actions in the story, and the 'mixture of exemplary narrative and over-insistent lecturing' (p 192), *PhyT* 'seems wayward, even perverse' (p 190). The Host's emotional response and implicit commendation of this badly told tale is in striking contrast to his refusal to be moved by the well-told tale of the Pardoner that follows it.

1931 Quinn, William A. 'The Rapes of Chaucer.' *CY* 5 (1998), 1–17.
PhyT is the 'worst treatment of rape' (p 14) in *CT*, even though the rape is aborted. The court of Roman law is itself abused by Appius's attempt to take Virginia.

1931a Riehle, Wolfgang. 'From Chaucer to Lessing: Some Intertextual Relations of the "Appius and Virginia" Story.' In *Zum Begriff der Imagination in Dichtung und Dichtungstheorie: Festschrift für Rainer Lengeler zum 65. Geburtstag*. Ed. Manfred Beyer. Trier: WVT, 1998. Pp 186–205.
Critics have overlooked similarities between Livy's version of the Appius and Virginia story and *PhyT*. One can read Livy's story as moving tale of a private family drama in which Virginius decides to kill his daughter out of an ideological commitment to avenging outraged honor. The affective and exemplary qualities shared by Livy's and Chaucer's narratives appear as well in later dramatic versions of the story, some of which were influenced by Chaucer's poem: R.B.'s interlude *Apius and Virginia,* Frances Brooke's *Virginia* (1756), and Lessing's *Emilia Galotti*. These retellings suggest that Chaucer did not simply admire Virginia and condemn Virginius, but rather expected his audience to feel pity for a father moved to a terrible deed by the compulsions of honor.

1932 Weisl, Angela Jane. '"Quiting" Eve: Violence Against Women in the *Canterbury Tales*.' In *Violence Against Women in Medieval Texts*. 1998. See **1393**.
Men's violence against women in *PhyT* is mediated: Satan is the actor, bringing evil into Appius's heart. Despite her perfection, Virginia is an Eve-like temptress, and Appius is her Adam. Praising God that she will die a maid, Virginia chooses to quit Eve with her own destruction. In delivering the tale's moral – 'Forsaketh synne, er synne yow forsake' (line 286) – the Physician forgets that Virginia is 'without sin, except the sin of her female body, which locks her into a terrible choice between secular and sacred violence' (p 126).

1933 Brewer, Derek S. 'The Compulsions of Honour.' In *From Arabye to Engelond*.

Medieval Studies in Honour of Mahmood Manzalaoui on His 75th Birthday. Ed. A.E. Christa Canitz and Gernot R. Wieland. Ottawa: U of Ottawa P, 1999. Pp 75–92.
See **1814**.

1934 Condren, Edward I. *Chaucer and the Energy of Creation: The Design and Organization of the Canterbury Tales*. 1999. See **704**.
Virginius, torn between the love of his daughter and his loathing of Appius's intentions, is the center of interest in *PhyT*. Like Arveragus in *FranT*, he is motivated by male pride; his beheading of Virginia secures her reputation for all time, and 'demonstrates that no judge ... will ever bring ignominy upon an extension of himself' (p 183). Virginius's act also links *PhyT* with *PardT*, in which both the rioters and the Pardoner himself 'pursue lesser ideals while sacrificing greater' (p 183).

1935 Foster, Edward E. *Understanding Chaucer's Intellectual and Interpretative World: Nominalist Fiction*. 1999. See **1398**.
In concentrating on the pathetic aspects of his story, the Physician misses the more significant aspect of the resolution of his narrative – the role of the people in purging the city and restoring civil order (pp 229–31).

1936 Prior, Sandra Pierson. 'Virginity and Sacrifice in Chaucer's "Physician's Tale."' In *Constructions of Widowhood and Virginity in the Middle Ages*. Ed. Cindy L. Carlson and Angela Jane Weisl. New York: St Martin's, 1999. Pp 165–80.
The clash between pagan and Christian views of virginity in *PhyT* is further complicated by the presence of 'the sacrificial/cultic tradition that values virginity for the sake of killing and/or offering up a perfect victim' (p 168). The allusion to the biblical story of Jephthah's daughter suggests that we are to regard Virginius's beheading of Virginia as an unholy sacrifice, a pagan ritual that foregrounds melodrama and violence rather than the Christian topos of sacrifice as a figure of the Crucifixion. Although sacrifice can be understood as a ritualized means of controlling violence in society, the Physician's concluding comments 'work against the traditional use of Virginia's story as a critique of social justice – or lack thereof' (p 175).

The Physician's Tale, 2000–2005

1937 Fletcher, Angus. 'The Sentencing of Virginia in the *Physician's Tale*.' *ChauR* 34 (2000), 300–8.
The tension between fixed frameworks for determining the meaning of a text and the variable interpretations of individual readers is especially evident in *PhyT*, 'where the Physician's notions of *sententia, auctoritas*, and *genus* are juxtaposed with a maiden who cannot be understood in terms of

these critical concepts' (p 300). The Physician's assertion that his tale will be history rather than a fable is undercut by the poem's mingling of historical details with elements of pagan fable; Nature claims both autonomy and divine sanction; like that of Nature and the tale's genre, Virginia's status is ambiguous – it is unclear whether her true author is Nature, her parents, or herself. Although Virginia's virtuousness seems to place her outside the traditional power structures, her autonomy is foreclosed by Virginius's arrival in court (which legitimizes Appius's authority) and by her father's naming of her when he declares his *sentence* (lines 213–14), an act that moves her definitively into the realm of history. The sentencing of Virginia fixes, and then extinguishes, her textual existence; the tale's final *sentence* makes no mention of her. But Harry Bailly's response to the tale, 'with its blatant disregard for the Physician's description of Nature's artistic efforts ... restores Virginia's agency' (p 307) and reminds us that texts are subject to continual reinterpretation.

1938 Phillips, Helen. *An Introduction to the Canterbury Tales: Reading, Fiction, Context.* 2000. See **714**.
PhyT combines the Roman concept of public family honor and the more personal, interior values of Christian literature; when these two cultural worlds come together in the scene of Virginia's beheading, 'style and content become discordant ... As in *ClT*, [Chaucer] seems to seek a deliberate conflict of values to construct a narrative enigma' (p 147).

1939 Welsh, Andrew. 'Story and Wisdom in Chaucer: The Physician's Tale and The Manciple's Tale.' In *Manuscript, Narrative, Lexicon: Essays on Literary and Cultural Transmission in Honor of Whitney F. Bolton.* 2000. See **709**. Pp 76–95.
PhyT and *ManT* illustrate in different ways the 'fundamental incompatibility' in *CT* of 'the voice of the story' and 'the voice of sentence, or wisdom' (p 90). *PhyT* is 'a story in search of a moral'; *ManT* is 'a collection of morals in search of a story' (p 85). Both the Physician and Harry Bailly draw morals from the tale, the former about the workings of Providence, the latter about the workings of Fortune. Yet neither of these moralizations bears a clear relation to the story of Virginia, the tale's heroine. Intended as an exemplum, *PhyT* nowhere moralizes its central action – Virginius's beheading of his daughter. Although this event is the heart of the story, it 'seems to be impossible to moralize ... what would the moral say?' (p 88).

1940 White, Hugh. *Nature, Sex, and Goodness in a Medieval Literary Tradition.* 2000. See **716**.
In her speech, Nature displays a self-satisfaction that is not justified by the events of the tale. Despite Nature's *cure* (line 22), the sublunary world fails to exhibit the harmony of the divine plan she sponsors. Nature would seem to be responsible for the depravity of Appius and Claudius as well as for Virginia's moral excellence. Virginia's beauty, moreover, has disastrous

consequences. 'Chaucer presents an apparently benign Nature ... only to compromise that presentation by implicating Nature in debility, disorder, depravity, and destruction' (p 246).

1941 Zangen, Britta. 'Frauen(körper) in der patriarchalen Welt des Mittelalters: Chaucers *Canterbury Tales*.' In *Sprachformen des Körpers in Kunst und Wissenschaft*. 2000. See **1427**. Pp 244–58.
Although Virginia naïvely asks her father if there is *grace* or *remedye* (line 236) for her plight, neither exists for her in a culture governed by patriarchal values. No one questions the perverse assumption that it is the girl's disgrace if a man takes her virginity from her.

1942 Allen, Elizabeth. 'The Pardoner in the "Dogges Boure": Early Reception of the *Canterbury Tales*.' *ChauR* 36 (2001), 91–127.
The Physician tells an ostensibly ideal exemplum that advocates 'moral virtue as rejection or forsaking of desires' (p 92). But Virginia's death suggests that making a figure exemplary has its costs. Moreover, the moral that ends the tale is 'strangely murky' (p 93). The Host's affective response to Virginia's victimization avoids the problem of forsaking sin, replacing exemplary stability with pathos. The Host's *pitee* 'salvages the tale by way of involvement ... But in his very effort to place the tale in a moral context of sympathy ... the Host also calls attention to its moral instability' (p 94).

1943 Bott, Robin L. '"O, Keep Me from Their Worse than Killing Lust": Ideologies of Rape and Mutilation in Chaucer's *Physician's Tale* and Shakespeare's *Titus Andronicus*." In *Representing Rape in Medieval and Early Modern Literature.* Ed. Elizabeth Robertson and Christine Rose. The New Middle Ages. New York: Palgrave, 2001. Pp 189–211.
The Virginia/Virginius story is employed in both *PhyT* and *Titus Andronicus* to point up the danger to social order represented by unauthorized sexual control of women's bodies. Lineage and inheritance depend upon who has access to a woman's womb; a crime against the female body thus '"became a crime against the male estate"' (p 191). The raped woman is more than simply damaged goods; she is also a polluted object that threatens to contaminate the patriarchal social body, a perception encoded in the metaphors of disease present in both texts. The Chaucerian narrator's figure of the betrayal of innocence as a 'sovereyn pestilence' (line 91), Virginia's plea for a *remedye* (line 235), and the Physician's occupation itself invite a 'medical reading' of Livy's political anecdote, in which Virginius's slaying of his daughter becomes a preventative gesture, 'separating the potentially diseased member from the social body *before* it is infected' (p 194). The real malady infecting the body social, however, is the homosocial power struggle between Virginius and Appius, in which Virginius takes the maiden's head to prevent Appius's access to her maidenhead. Female suffering is passed over as inconsequential in comparison to the reestablishment of

good government – 'an act that really boils down to one powerful male defeating another' (p 196).

1944 Collette, Carolyn P. *Species, Phantasms, and Images: Vision and Medieval Psychology in The Canterbury Tales*. 2001. See **1429**.
The discussion of *PhyT* in Ch. 4, 'Objects of Desire: Sight, Judgment, and the Unity of Fragment VI' (pp 99–127), contains material from **1902**.

1945 Ishino, Harumi. 'The Death of the Vergin [*sic*] in *The Physician's Tale.*' *Shuryu* 62 (2001), 1–24.
Attempts to unravel enigmatic aspects of *PhyT*, especially the death of Virginia. (Not seen. Annotation from *SAC* 25 [2003], pp 516–17. In Japanese.)

1946 Kanai, Noriko. 'Nature and Sexuality in Chaucer's *The Physician's Tale.*' *Seishin joshi daigaku daigakuin ronshu* [Seishin University of the Sacred Heart essays] 23 (2001), 228–60.
Virginia and Appius represent two aspects of Nature: Virginia is Nature's ideal creation, while Appius represents the corruption of Nature in mankind. Although Virginia is seemingly presented with a choice between 'deeth or shame' (line 214), the decision lies with her father, for whom virginity means as much as for Virginia herself. Virginia's sacrifice of her life puts an end to Appius's lust and hence to his transgression against Nature's law. As a judge, Appius should be to society what reason is to an individual, but Chaucer reminds us that sexuality cannot always be controlled by reason. Chaucer's view of sexuality is a progressive one that acknowledges the force of man's animal instincts.

1947 Mehl, Dieter. *English Literature in the Age of Chaucer*. 2001. See **1437**.
PhyT exhibits a 'jarring ... contrast' between the untroubled narration and the brutality of the story's actions (p 53). Although Chaucer may not have endorsed the tale's harsh moral, it is presented without comment; we are left to draw our own conclusions.

1948 Rudd, Gillian. *The Complete Critical Guide to Geoffrey Chaucer*. 2001. See **724**.
PhyT may seem straightforward enough, but its numerous unanswered questions – is Appius or Virginia the tale's central figure? why are guardians warned to keep a close eye on their charges? is the narrative primarily a form of history or a 'piteous tale'? – create a complexity that contradicts the view that it is among the weakest of *CT* (pp 132–3).

1949 Saunders, Corinne J. *Rape and Ravishment in the Literature of Medieval England*. 2001. See **1442**.
PhyT emphasizes the legal aspects of Appius's attempted abduction; 'the trumped-up case conceals the real legal crime of *raptus* that is to take place, and that no justice system exists to rectify' (p 280). Although the death of Virginia draws on the hagiographical tradition of the virgin martyr, the Christian structures of the tale are devoid of meaning. Virginia can have no recourse to miracle and salvation; divine authority is replaced by that of her

earthly father; and the temporal threat of rape leads not to heavenly reward, but only to death and silence.

• Review by Christopher Cannon, *Speculum* 72 (2003), 984–6: For Virginia, rape is a threat that transforms her virginity into power; 'the extreme measure of her sacrifice is itself the necessary injustice … that causes the necessary and general reformation' (p 985).

1950 Shoaf, R.A. *Chaucer's Body: The Anxiety of Circulation in the "Canterbury Tales."* Gainesville: UP of Florida, 2001.

PhyT is to *MkT* as *PardT* is to *NPT*; the former are instances of reductive unisemy, the latter of polysemy or 'disseminative impropriety' (p 47). The Physician attempts to co-opt the power of Nature by creating a counterfeit person, the perfectly obedient daughter. He seeks to close off the circulation of life in his definitive formulas or *sentences,* which admit of no error. But the language of his tale (e.g., the 'circulation of sound' in the frequent repetition of the final syllable of *sentence* in rhyme position) introduces a lability that 'denies the finality of sentences' (p 52).

• Review by Stephen Knight, *Speculum* 78 (2003), 1405–7: 'Do multiple rhymes on "–ence" really mean anything except a normal final use of a polysyllable?' (p 1406).

1951 Spearing, A.C. 'Narrative Voice: The Case of Chaucer's Man of Law's Tale.' *NLH* 32 (2001), 715–46.

See **1976**.

1952 Kamowski, William. 'Chaucer and Wyclif: God's Miracles Against the Clergy's Magic.' *ChauR* 37 (2002), 5–35.

Virginius's killing of Virginia is predicated on a Roman ethic that valued honor over one's life. The sacrifice of Virginia is a response to corruption in the legal system, a corruption purged when the populace invades the court and punishes the villains (p 15).

1953 Mann, Jill. *Feminizing Chaucer*. 2002. See **729**.

In *PhyT,* human suffering reflects divine suffering. Like Christ, Virginia does not deserve to die; like Christ, she is slain by her father, whose cruelty is an expression of his love. The tale contrasts two acts of male violence: Appius desires to 'enthral' (p 113) Virginia, to extinguish her selfhood; Virginius destroys his daughter's body to save her self. The tale both demonstrates Virginius's fatherly pity for his child and nurtures a corresponding pity in the reader. Although Virginia's Christlike acceptance of death 'in pacience' (line 223) may seem to us a dubious honor, 'a Christian society had no greater to bestow' (p 145). (For earlier versions and a review of this material, see **1809, 1880**).

1954 Sanok, Catherine. 'The Geography of Genre in the *Physician's Tale* and *Pearl*.' In *New Medieval Literatures* 5. Ed. Rita Copeland, David Lawton, and Wendy Scase. Oxford: Oxford UP, 2002. Pp 177–201.

In *PhyT,* Chaucer reframes the relation between his narrative and saints' lives as a question of hermeneutics. For the Physician, the death of Virginia 'lacks any meaning at all' (p 183); he acknowledges only the deaths of the conspirators, and the moral platitudes with which he closes his performance are 'so familiar that their irrelevance to the central event of the story is almost obscured' (p 184). Virginia's absence from the tale's moral underlines the hermeneutic limits of the saints' lives, which 'cannot accommodate meaningless death and which deny meaning to the death of an innocent, but pagan, girl' (p 185). In hagiographic representations, feminine virtue lacks social or political significance; in imitating virgin martyr legends, *PhyT* also critiques this popular narrative tradition.

1955 Uebel, Michael. 'Public Fantasy and the Logic of Sacrifice in *The Physician's Tale.*' *ANQ* 15 (2002), 30–3.
Virginius's beheading of his daughter is a social act, a sacrificial process where the sanctity of the group is at stake. It is also an act of transmutation that bestows symbolic value on Virginia's body. The crowd of people who distribute justice at the conclusion of the tale reminds us that virginity is void of meaning unless a social group has a role to play in it.

1956 Burger, Glenn. *Chaucer's Queer Nation*. 2003. See **1464**.
PhyT 'focuses on the care of masculinity needed to secure the proper reproduction of masculine identity and authority' (p 132). The tale is less concerned with the inscription of sex difference than 'with proving the natural ability of an active and essential masculine will to frame and control the perversity of a passive and accidental feminine carnality' (p 132). To achieve this end, the tale must excise the accidental altogether: Virginius maintains intact Virginia's essence (i.e., his own reputation) by cutting off her head, the Physician maintains the authority of his text by attempting to erase its materiality as fable, and the tale's audience (the Host and the *gentils*) announce their authoritative reception of the tale by recognizing and rejecting what they see as the Pardoner's threatening perversity.

1957 Di Rocco, Emilia. *Letteratura e Legge nel Trecento Inglese: Chaucer, Gower e Langland*. 2003. See **1466**.
The false *bille* (lines 166, 176, 190) presented by Claudius parallels contemporary legal prodecures in which a verbal or written denunciation is presented in court. If it succeeds, such a *bille* would mandate both restitution of goods and compensation for damages. In *PhyT,* this outcome would require the return of Virginia, said by the *bille* to be Claudius's servant stolen from him by Virginius, to her supposedly rightful owner, and, by an agreement between Claudius and Appius, Virginia's subsequent delivery to Appius. Initially condemned to death for his beheading of Virginia, Virginius is saved by the intervention of the populace, an outcome consonant with Roman law, which exempts from punishment someone who slays a family member to save that

person from rape. *PhyT* is an exemplum demonstrating the consequences of the sin of Luxuria. Appius is responsible for Virginia's death. His perversion of justice indirectly forces Virginius to kill his daughter and brings about his own suicide in prison (pp 182–5).

1958 Evans, Ruth. "Virginities.' In *The Cambridge Companion to Medieval Women's Writing*. 2003. See **1467**. Pp 21–39.
The two options presented to Virginia by Virginius – death or shame (line 214) – show to what extent her virginity is valued by her father as representative of patriarchal culture. Nor does Virginia authorize the meaning of her narrative, as virgin martyrs typically do by answering the male tyrant's lustful gaze with defiance (p 34).

1959 Gray, Douglas. 'The Physician's Tale.' In *The Oxford Companion to Chaucer*. 2003. See **735**. Pp 379–81.
Virginius acts from a sense of moral revulsion that blends an ancient Roman sense of justice with a hatred of lechery and an admiration of chastity that would have been recognized by an audience familiar with medieval Christian religious writing.
• Review by Derek S. Brewer, *SAC* 27 (2005), 309–12: The notion that the character of a tale's narrator can be deduced from the tale itself has led some (not Gray) to absurd judgments, 'as, for example, that when *PhyT* is regarded ... as bad poetry, the Physician himself must be a bad medical doctor' (p 311).

1960 Hughes, Alan. *Signs and Circumstances: A Study of Allegory in Chaucer's Canterbury Tales*. 2003. See **737**.
The description of Virginia's physical beauty and virtuous behavior recalls the 'identical qualities' of young Anne of Bohemia when she arrived in England (p 80). The condemnation of guardians of the young who fail in their duties is a 'veiled warning' to those in charge of Queen Isabel and a reminder of Queen Anne's absence from sensuous gatherings (p 81).

1961 Kline, Daniel T. 'Female childhoods.' In *The Cambridge Companion to Medieval Women's Writing*. 2003. See **1467**. Pp 13–20.
Virginia, portrayed at the moment of transition between childhood and marriageability, exemplifies the tensions of growing up female in medieval England. Chaucer's additions to his sources (the linking of Virginia with conduct literature, the addresses to parents and guardians, the dialogue between Virginia and Virginius just before her beheading) ground *PhyT* in contemporary issues concerning wardship, marriage, and child custody, and 'critique the forms of violence' required to perpetuate patriarchal control over young women's lives (p 18).

1961a Lewis, Celia. 'Framing Fictions with Death: Chaucer's *Canterbury Tales* and the Plague.' In *New Readings of Chaucer's Poetry*. 2003. See **1471**. Pp 139–64.
The tellers of the two tales in Fragment VI both make use of the plague's

threat: the Physician 'kepte that he wan in pestilence' (I.442) and the Pardoner places his tale of greed and unconfessed death in a plague setting. Both tales suggest human impotence in the face of death. Virginia meets her fate without knowledge of the meaning of her sacrifice and without the promise of the saint's reward in heaven (pp 154–5).

1962 Phillips, Kim M. *Medieval Maidens: Young Women and Gender in England, 1270–1540.* Manchester, UK: Manchester UP, 2003.

The 'uneasy combination' of a maiden's defiant will to preserve her virginity and her acquiescence to parental authority in the virgin martyr *vitae* is reproduced and exaggerated in *PhyT,* which calls attention to the genre's extreme violence (p 80).

1963 Pitcher, John A. 'Chaucer's Wolf: Exemplary Violence in "The Physician's Tale."' *Genre* 36 (2003), 1–28. Repr. in Pitcher, *Chaucer's Feminine Subjects: Figures of Desire in the Canterbury Tales* (see **1475**). Pp 109–29.

The 'characteristic operation' of *PhyT* involves 'dismantling the conceptual architecture of genre' (p 5). The text invokes historical narrative, allegory, typology, eschatology, and pathos, only to locate discontinuities within and among these registers. The play of genres produces analogous dislocations of clear-cut meaning in the tale. Appius and Virginius are shown to be morally equivalent, the rigidly virtuous father ultimately representing a greater threat to his daughter's well-being than the forces outside the family that seek to corrupt her. Virginius also functions as a double of the Physician, who cannot contemplate Virginia's innocent virtue without envisioning her debasement; she becomes a casualty of the very defensive regime that the Physician advocates. Virginia is deprived of the redemption that she might have attained within a Christian framework, while the possible typological implications of her death are introduced only to be blocked. The tale blurs the potential allegorical contrast between good and evil suggested by the narrative; it also makes problematic the notion of pity that is invoked to characterize Virginius's actions and our response to those actions. In frustrating our desire for unambiguous *sentence, PhyT* functions as a cultural critique, revealing the family itself as a locus of violence.

• Review by Giselle Gos (**1475r**): 'Pitcher's goal for the chapter is to demonstrate Chaucer's investment in cultural critique – "an indictment of an absolute commitment to chastity, as well as the ideology of feminine obedience that supports it" (p 117) – but that there is no discussion of Virginia as a subject seems a strange oversight' (p 123).

• Review by Susan Nakley (**1475r**): Pitcher's account of the politics of Christian theology shows how this telling of Livy's tale makes a unique rhetorical impact. Its only shortcoming is Pitcher's inattention to Chaucer's reordering of class politics.

1964 Farber, Lianna. 'The Creation of Consent in the *Physician's Tale.*' *ChauR* 39

(2004), 151–64. Repr. in Farber, *An Anatomy of Trade in Medieval Writing: Value, Consent, and Community*. Ithaca, NY: Cornell UP, 2006, pp 129–40, and in *Geoffrey Chaucer's Canterbury Tales.* New Edition. Ed. Harold Bloom. New York: Infobase, 2008, pp 203–16.

The additions and changes Chaucer makes to his source material – the discursus on Nature's formation of Virginia's character and beauty, the abstract discussion of the responsibility governesses and parents bear for the care of children, and the conversation between Virginius and Virginia that precedes her beheading – establish a frame for Virginia's agreement with her father's judgment that she must die. In demonstrating how and why Virginia accepts both her father's logic and his right to govern her, *PhyT* shows the shocking result of a parent's teaching gone wrong. Although not specifically political in the manner of Livy's original anecdote, Chaucer's tale 'posits a broader idea of what constitutes politics' (p 160) in its demonstration of the way consent can be created. Virginia exemplifies not only virginity but also the political subject; as a young woman with little control over her fate, she is 'the proper allegorical embodiment of men who … do not have as much power as they think they do' (p 161).

• Review by Kathy Lavezzo, *SAC* 29 (2007), 489–92: Farber convincingly responds to scholarly complaints that the Physician's emphasis on guardianship clashes with Virginia's moral independence and defends the role that the apparent digressions on Nature, parents, and governesses play in the tale.

• Review by Kellie Robertson, *TMR* (February 2009), n.p.: Farber's reading suggests that Virginia's 'consent' amounts to little more than ideological false consciousness. Although somewhat tangential to the book's stated purposes, the section on *PhyT* usefully identifies several domains where conversations about what constitutes 'consent' were taking place simultaneously.

1965 Stanbury, Sarah. 'Ecochaucer: Green Ethics and Medieval Nature.' *ChauR* 39 (2004), 1–16.

The description of Nature as a painter (lines 32–6) raises the question of whether Virginia's beauty is the product of nature or of art. In thus personifying the goddess, the poet makes problematic her accomplishments and even her very existence (pp 6–7).

1966 Zangen, Britta. 'Women in Chaucer's Male Universe: Literary Critics Coping with Misogynism.' In *Misogynism in Literature: Any Place, Any Time.* Ed. Britta Zangen. Frankfurt am Main: Lang, 2004. Pp 39–58.

See **1941**.

1967 Allen, Elizabeth. *False Fables and Exemplary Truth in Later Middle English Literature.* New York: Palgrave, 2005. Pp 83–109.

PhyT is 'a study in misalignment between narrative strategies and moral framework' (p 85). While asserting historical truth as a guarantee of Virginia's unchanging exemplary value, the Physician at the same time adjusts her meaning through a series of 'different, even incoherent discourses' (p 84) that call attention to the act of narration and to his own mediating presence. The effect of the Physician's rhetorical interventions is to evoke an analogy between his own role and that of the false judge Appius, both of whom want to appropriate Virginia, and to leave the reader without adequate tools for interpretation of the narrative. Although the Host's emotional response marks the tale as an 'affective success' (p 97), *PhyT* – in contrast to Gower's version of the Virginia anecdote in *CA*, which 'suggests the importance of poetic fictions in creating moral meanings' (p 96) and to Lydgate's retelling of the story in *The Fall of Princes*, which responds to Chaucer by offering a clear alignment of source text, authorial role, and narrative *sentence* – raises serious doubts about how authors use stories to shape readers' judgments.

• Review by Alison Ganze, *TMR* (July 2006), n.p.: Allen's examination of the audience reactions called forth by Gower's, Chaucer's, and Lydgate's reformulations of the story of Virginia's death demonstrates the ways in which exemplary narratives elicit certain affective responses and suppress others. Although Allen continually refers to Virginia's exemplarity, her analysis suggests that the exemplary force of the story lies rather in her father's conduct.

• Review by Edward Wheatley, *SAC* 28 (2006), 273–6: Allen's analysis of *PhyT* 'is basically another rehearsal of the topos of Chaucerian indeterminacy, here viewed through the lens of exemplarity' (p 275).

• Review by Judith Ferster, *Speculum* 82 (2007), 950–2: The parameters Allen establishes to discuss Livy and Gower help her to assess Chaucer's and Lydgate's versions of the Virginia story. By allowing Virginia to speak for herself, for example, Chaucer enhances her victimization and the scene's appeal to pity, thus preparing the way for Harry Bailly's outburst of sympathy for her.

1968 Allen, Valerie. 'Waxing Red: Shame and the Body, Shame and the Soul.' In *The Representation of Women's Emotions in Medieval and Early Modern Culture*. Ed. Lisa Perfetti. Gainesville: UP of Florida, 2005. Pp 190–210.

Virginia being '"eye-fucked"' by Appius is a paradigmatic example of the traditional depiction of woman as the passive, shamed object of the male gaze (p 198).

1969 Barefield, Laura. '"No children hadde he mo": Kinship in Livy's Account of Virginia and Chaucer's *Physician's Tale*.' *MedPers* 20 (2005), 1–19.

In Livy, Virginia exists as part of a kinship system that includes the father's power to marry his daughter to a suitor of his choosing. Appius's unsanctioned desire threatens to disrupt kinship, and thus the status quo between plebeians and patricians. Virginia's death at her father's hands becomes a political act that serves as a catalyst to social unrest and eventual reform.

Although *PhyT* omits the political dimension of Livy's anecdote, kinship remains an issue. Within a Christian society, Virginia's value to her family lies in her being kept a virgin. She dies as a kind of virgin martyr, and her father still exercises his right to determine her status, creating for himself 'the ultimate son-in-law: God himself' (p 15).

1970 Crafton, John Micheal. '"The cause of everiche maladye": A New Source of the *Physician's Tale*.' 2005. See **1620**.
Read in the light of the *Summa virtutem remediis anime*, Virginia represents the principles of true virginity, while Virginius – who interprets virginity only as integrity of the flesh – is a figure for foolish virginity. Chaucer's use of vices and virtues material underlines the Physician's mishandling of the hagiographical form; like Virginius, he 'betrays Virginia's innocence' (p 278) by substituting literality and physicality for figurative or spiritual understanding.

1971 Federico, Sylvia. 'New historicism.' In *Chaucer: An Oxford Guide*. 2005. See **1502**. Pp 416–31.
In *PhyT*, the issue of social class competes for significance with the plight of Virginia. In telling the story of the girl's abduction, Claudius revises her social status in calling her a *thral* (line 183). The hanging of the 'remenant ... moore and lesse' (line 275) who knew of the conspiracy of Appius and Claudius recalls, by way of Harry Bailly's condemnation of 'thise juges and hire advocatz' (*Phy–PardL* line 291), the indiscriminate slaughter of lawyers in the 1381 Peasant's Revolt, which 'asserts itself as symbolic presence in the story of Virginia' (p 425).

1972 Lee, Brian. 'The "Mayde Child" in *The Shipman's Tale*.' *SAJMRS* 15 (2005), 55–68.
PhyT forms part of a sequence of tales (*ShT*, *PardT*, *PrT*, and perhaps *Thop*) that concern themselves with the education of the young. The tale alludes to two types of education: that enjoyed by aristocrats' children at home, and that acquired at school. The tirade against governesses envisions the former group, while Virginia (like the clergeoun in *PrT*) attends a school.

1973 Mann, Jill, ed. *Geoffrey Chaucer: The Canterbury Tales*. 2005. See **1566**.
In contrast to Livy, Boccaccio, and Gower, who are interested in the political and social dimensions of the Virginia story, Chaucer foregrounds the tale's pathetic and exemplary character and gives it a religious dimension by adding Virginia's reference to the Old Testament story of Jephthah's daughter, which was read as a prefiguration of Christ's sacrifice (p 961).

1974 Orme, Nicholas. 'Education and Recreation.' In *Gentry Culture in Late Medieval England*. 2005. See **793**.
The portrait of Virginia, which concentrates on her virtues rather than on any practical accomplishments, may reflect some contemporaries' view of a perfect young gentlewoman. But it is misleading, since such women would

have possessed various skills (e.g., reading, sewing, singing, dancing) that Chaucer ignores in favor of more abstract virtues (pp 65–6).

1975 Owens, Margaret E. *Stages of Dismemberment: The Fragmented Body in Late Medieval and Early Modern Drama*. Newark: U of Delaware P, 2005.
In Livy, Virginia is silent, almost marginal to the action. By supplying her with dialogue and (following Jean de Meun) rendering her death as beheading rather than stabbing, Chaucer creates a more actively courageous martyr-like figure, and moves her in the direction of the Christian exemplarity that she will attain in R.B.'s mid-sixteenth-century *Apius and Virginia* (pp 91–2).

1976 Spearing, A.C. *Textual Subjectivity: The Encoding of Subjectivity in Medieval Narratives and Lyrics*. Oxford: Oxford UP, 2005.
Commenting on Kittredge's observation in his discussion of *PhyT* and *PardT* that 'it was Chaucer's artistic duty … to make the method of delivery correspond to the character of the teller' (**1622**), Spearing notes that Kittredge never clarifies the basis for that duty, 'presumably because he regards it as obvious' (p 102).

1977 Tasioulas, J.A. 'Science.' In *Chaucer: An Oxford Guide*. 2005. See **1502**. Pp 174–89.
It is not Virginia's soul but her body that matters to Appius, to Virginius, and to the Physician; concerned only with his daughter's physical intactness, Virginius is 'a fitting protagonist for the tale of a minimally religious physician' (p 185). Just as God is sidelined in Nature's account of her own role as creator, so bodies for the Physician are biological entities rather than divine mysteries.

ꝏ Index

Authors' names and titles of publications in the introductions or headnotes that do not appear in the annotations are identified by page numbers, preceded by 'p' or 'pp.' All other references are to individual item numbers. Numbers 1 through 1508 refer to *The Squire's Tale, The Squire–Franklin Link,* and *The Franklin's Tale*; numbers 1509 through 1977 refer to *The Physician's Tale*. Boldface indicates the author, editor, or translator of an item, regular typeface indicates that the person, work, or topic is discussed in that item, and a bold lower case '**r**' following an item number indicates that the person named is the author of a review of that item. The name of an author following an 'r' entry distinguishes that review from other reviews of the same item. Names, phrases, and titles that appear in the titles of publications but not in the accompanying annotations are not indexed.